MINORITY RIGHTS IN AMERICA

MINORITY RIGHTS IN AMERICA

ALAN AXELROD

A Division of Congressional Quarterly Inc.
Washington, D.C.

CQ Press
1255 22nd Street, N.W., Suite 400
Washington, D.C. 20037

202-729-1900; toll-free, 1-866-4CQ-PRESS (1-866-427-7737)

www.cqpress.com

♾ The paper used in this publication meets the minimum requirements of the American National Standard for Information Sciences—Permanence of Paper for Printed Library Materials, ANSI Z39.48-1992.

Cover design by Debra Naylor. Cover photo courtesy of Getty Images, Inc., © 1999–2002.

Printed and bound in the United States of America

06 05 04 03 02 5 4 3 2 1

Library of Congress Catologing-in-Publication Data
(In process)
ISBN 1-56802-685-4

CONTENTS

PREFACE

As the Old Testament and other ancient texts and histories attest, the struggle for the rights of the minority has long been a fixture of civilization. However, it is hardly necessary to delve into the ancient past to retrieve examples of minority persecution. In the early twentieth century, before and during World War I, hundreds of thousands of Armenians fell victim to their Ottoman overlords. Before and during World War II, Japanese conquerors raped and murdered untold numbers of Manchurian Chinese. Some twelve million members of European minorities, including six million Jews, were systematically persecuted and then murdered by Adolf Hitler's Third Reich. More recently, apartheid was the way of life in South Africa, and in the Balkans during the 1990s former Yugoslav president Slobodan Milosevic presided over the "ethnic cleansing" of thousands. Today the international human rights organization Human Rights Watch has identified ongoing acts and even full-scale policies of oppression against minorities in more than seventy nations and territories worldwide.

That the United States is among the nations Human Rights Watch monitors may shock and even offend some Americans. After all, we have fought wars to end genocide and other forms of oppression. Our Constitution and the laws based on it protect rather than persecute minorities. Equality is proclaimed within the first few words of the nation's founding document, the Declaration of Independence—a text drafted by Thomas Jefferson, who was enlightened, liberty loving, and, like many of the nation's other founders, an owner of slaves.

Perhaps Jefferson's ambivalence concerning minority rights was—and still is—emblematic of a collective cultural and national ambivalence. Throughout history, even before America's independence, the country has consistently defined itself as a haven of freedom and tolerance in a world mostly unfree and intolerant. This compelling self-perception has resisted the fact of some four hundred years of white warfare against Native Americans. It has resisted the fact of almost three centuries of slavery in colonial and independent America. It has resisted the fact of the disenfranchisement of American women until 1920. It has resisted the fact of "greaser laws" and other legislation restricting the rights of Hispanic Americans in the nineteenth century. It has resisted the fact of exclusionary laws restricting the rights of Asian Americans during the late nineteenth and early twentieth centuries. It has resisted the fact of state-mandated racial segregation during more than half of the twentieth century. And it has resisted much more.

Are Americans hypocrites? The contents of this book argue persuasively against that conclusion. Like Jefferson, most Americans have remarkably high ideals and equally high expectations for the realization of those ideals. And like Jefferson, Americans are imperfect, and the gaps between the ideals and the facts can be wide and ugly. Yet it is also true that in no other nation have so many voices spoken for the ideal; nowhere else have so many heads, hearts, and hands worked to realize the ideal.

Without exaggeration, we can conclude that no subject is more central to the American experience than minority rights. Although this might have been most apparent during the civil rights movement in the 1960s, the observation holds true from very nearly the first contact of Europe with America. The early sixteenth-century writings of the Spanish missionary Bartolomé de Las Casas (1474–1566) were devoted to exposing the oppression of Native Americans by the conquistadors and other colonizers. Needless to say, issues of minority rights figured prominently among the causes and justifications of the American Revolution in the eighteenth century, and such rights were the foundation on which the American republic was raised. Moreover, when conflicts surrounding minority rights remained unresolved, the country reached its point of greatest crisis in the Civil War.

It is no surprise, then, that the historical, social, political, and legal literature on minority rights in the United States is extensive. Yet within this literature there are few comprehensive, single-volume, readily accessible reference works. This book is an effort to provide just that. It is an alphabetically arranged reference to the major themes, concepts, laws, events, documents, and people bearing on the history and present state of minority rights in the United States.

I invite readers to adjust their expectations of this book in light of three issues that have influenced its composition. First, what or who constitutes a minority? Historically (perhaps the better word is *traditionally*) in the United States, white Protestant men have been considered the majority, and all others have been deemed minorities. More recently, the Equal Employment Opportunity Commission (EEOC), a federal agency, has defined as minorities certain groups whose members merit special legal protection in matters of employment. Included are nonwhites (blacks, Hispanics, Asians, Pacific Islanders, American Indians, and Alaskan natives), women, and all persons age forty and older. In addition, federal statutes classify as miniorities, subject to EEOC protection, religious groups, persons with disabilities, Vietnam veterans, and disabled veterans of all wars.

Most speakers of English would agree that the word *minority* necessarily implies a contrast with some *majority,* and that the minority is a smaller group than the majority. Viewed either historically, traditionally, or according to more recent legal opinions, however, this apparently self-evident definition of *minority* will not always stand. For example, although the white majority outnumbers the black minority in the United States, the female minority outnumbers the male majority. Furthermore, if all the minorities recognized as legally protected are added up, they greatly outnumber the remaining majority, which is not universally afforded special protection.

Indeed, in some contexts, the majority may become vanishingly small. As legally defined by the government, almost anyone may be classed as a member of a minority in certain situations. Ordinarily, for instance, a twenty-five-year-old white Baptist man would not be deemed a member of a protected minority. However, if he were denied employment because he was a Baptist, he could claim legal status as a member of a religious minority who has been discriminated against and then file a discrimination suit sanctioned by federal law.

One does not have to push very hard to wreck a definition of *minority* based on numbers, nor push much harder to knock down, at least in some contexts, almost any definition of the term. In this book, however, *minority* is defined in three pragmatic ways:

1. As the term has been applied today and most frequently in U.S. history to African Americans, Hispanic Americans, Native Americans, Asian Americans, and women.
2. As a term denoting any group perceived by the economically and politically dominant group or groups as significantly different from the dominant group or groups. In other words, a minority is any group defined as a minority by those who collectively define themselves as the majority. Examples may include groups encompassed by the first definition, in addition to gays and lesbians, disabled persons, Italian Americans, Polish Americans, Jews, Mormons, people with HIV or AIDS, Quakers, transsexuals, the mentally retarded, and so on.
3. As a term to denote any group persecuted or otherwise discriminated against by the group or groups who enjoy economic and political dominance. Examples may include any of the groups mentioned in the first two definitions, in addition to others.

The second issue that readers should understand is scope. This book aims to be comprehensive within the relatively brief compass of a single volume, but it is by no means exhaustive. Making a book useful is as much a process of leaving out as it is of putting in. The object here has been to include topics deemed by historical and current consensus to be most central to the subject of minority rights in the United States. Some readers may detect a paradox here: a book on minority rights that deliberately reflects what the majority deems of greatest interest and importance. If this is, in fact, a paradox, I earnestly hope it will be accepted as a paradox necessary in a book of limited size that aims to include the information most valuable to students and instructors in such disciplines as African American studies, U.S. history, American studies, public policy, political science, social work, law, education, and criminal justice, as well as social and political activists, social services professionals, and the general reader interested in minority rights.

The third issue concerns my own biases. I have endeavored to research and present the material here with the objectivity of a reference author. Doubtless this will disappoint some readers, who expect a book on this subject to be a work of outright advocacy. Doubtless, too, other readers may identify and object to a liberal bias in these pages, complaining that if I am not an outright advocate, I am a closet advocate nevertheless. I have tried to research and write with *objectivity*. But I do not believe that it is possible to assemble a book on this subject with *neutrality*. If a sense of right and wrong, of admiration and condemnation, and of compassion and contempt were wholly suppressed in the articles presented here, I would be far less than the human being I believe myself to be, and my words would be of little value or interest to any reader, regardless of his or her politics, heritage, or conviction.

I wish to thank CQ Press acquiring editor Christopher Anzalone and copy editors Sandy Chizinsky and Molly Lohman for their skilled dedication to this project.

Alan Axelrod
Atlanta, Georgia

MINORITY RIGHTS IN AMERICA

ABERNATHY, RALPH DAVID (1926–1990)

A close associate of MARTIN LUTHER KING JR., Ralph Abernathy was prominent in the civil rights movement during the 1950s and 1960s. He was a principal activist in the Montgomery Bus Boycott and in the Birmingham protests by the SOUTHERN CHRISTIAN LEADERSHIP CONFERENCE (SCLC). After King's assassination in 1968, Abernathy became the leader of the SCLC.

Abernathy was born in Linden, Alabama, on March 11, 1926, to a farming family. He was ordained as a Baptist minister in 1948, then went on to earn a B.A. from Alabama State University in 1950 and an M.A. (in sociology) from Atlanta University in 1951. That same year he was named dean of men at Alabama State and became pastor of the First Baptist Church in Montgomery. During the early 1950s Abernathy became closely associated with Rev. Vernon Johns of the Dexter Avenue Baptist Church; when Martin Luther King Jr. replaced Johns in 1955 Abernathy befriended him as well.

King and Abernathy jointly headed the MONTGOMERY IMPROVEMENT ASSOCIATION (MIA), which coordinated the Montgomery Bus Boycott in 1955–1956 and ultimately brought an end to segregation on the city's buses. In 1957 Abernathy worked with King to found the SCLC; King was the organization's president and Abernathy its secretary-treasurer. In 1960, at King's prompting, Abernathy accepted the position of pastor at West Hunter Street Baptist Church in Atlanta so that the two could continue working together when King became pastor of the nearby Atlanta's Ebenezer Baptist Church. The pair continued to direct the central struggles of the early civil rights movement—at Albany (Georgia), Birmingham (Alabama), St. Augustine (Florida), Selma (Alabama), and elsewhere.

With King, Abernathy planned the POOR PEOPLE'S CAMPAIGN, in which thousands of people moved to "Resurrection City" in Washington, D.C., to expose poverty to the world and to begin the long struggle to end hunger and poverty in America. Abernathy took over leadership of the campaign in 1968 after King's assassination; he also became president of the SCLC and continued as a civil rights leader, most notably organizing a highly effective strike of hospital workers in Charleston, South Carolina, in 1969.

Abernathy ran for Congress in 1977 but failed to win election. Although he stunned many members of the liberal community by throwing his support behind Ronald Reagan's 1980 run for the presidency, this was but one controversial event in Abernathy's history as a civil rights activist. Because the Poor People's Campaign failed to bring about any significant reforms, some compared Abernathy unfavorably to King. Others bitterly criticized Abernathy for discussing King's marital infidelities in his 1989 autobiography. Abernathy died on April 17, 1990.

Suggested Reading

Abernathy, Ralph David. *And the Walls Came Tumbling Down: An Autobiography.* New York: Harper and Row, 1989.

ABOLITION MOVEMENT

From early colonial times, many Americans opposed SLAVERY. The first organized opposition in America came from the QUAKERS, who issued a statement against the institution as early as 1724. Although it is true that during the colonial period slave markets were active in the North as well as the South, the agricultural economy of the northern colonies was built upon small farms rather than vast plantations. Thus the North lacked the economic motives for slavery; this circumstance, coupled with a moral aversion to the practice, strengthened abolitionism in the region. After the colonies achieved independence, various states outlawed slavery: Rhode Island, for example, traditionally a seat of tolerance, abolished the institution as early as 1774.

The American Colonization Society, founded in 1817, not only led antislavery protests but mounted a campaign to send freed slaves to what would become the African nation of Liberia, a territory which the society acquired in 1821. In 1819 in Jonesborough, Tennessee, Elihu Embree began publishing a weekly newspaper devoted to abolition; it was followed by the *Emancipator*, a monthly journal that debuted in 1820. It was not until 1831, however, when William Lloyd Garrison began the *Liberator*—a newspaper that called for immediate and universal emancipation—that the abolition movement became truly nationwide.

Garrison's demands were radical for the time. The *Liberator* called not only for emancipation but for giving blacks the same political and economic rights accorded whites. Inspired by the *Liberator*, the three most prominent antislavery interest groups—Philadelphia Quakers, New York reformers, and New England partisans of Garrison—met with freed blacks in December 1833 to form the American Anti-Slavery Society. Garrison took the helm, setting down as the society's goal the immediate emancipation of slaves without compensation to slave owners. Working primarily through white liberal clergy, Garrison and his followers focused on making an uncompromising moral appeal.

From the 1830s until the Civil War, the abolition movement was split between uncompromising radicals, such as Garrison, and those who believed that a more gradual approach to emancipation had a better chance of succeeding. (Regardless of their objections to slavery, many northerners continued to believe in black inferiority and were resistant to the idea of equal rights for all Americans.)

Resistance to abolition in the South, and even in the North, was strong and often violent. The risks faced by abolitionist activists ranged from harassment, ostracism, and economic boycott to beatings and murder. In some places the violence was directed against free blacks, many of whom were forced to flee to Canada. The American Anti-Slavery Society faced opposition from the American Colonization Society, which saw a back-to-Africa program as the only viable means of ending slavery.

Amid the tumult, Garrison and his followers realized that the abolition movement had to take steps to integrate blacks into white society rather than simply demand that whites accept them. Out of a belief that education would make blacks more acceptable to white society, abolitionists began to work with black churches on programs of education. However, such programs often backfired because some whites were afraid that educated blacks would take jobs away from whites and would intermarry with whites.

In the face of such sentiments, many abolitionists strove to change the attitudes of whites—an effort that inspired eloquent writing by the poets James Russell Lowell and John Greenleaf Whittier, by the reformer Wendell Phillips, and by a number of women activists, including Lucretia Mott and the Grimké sisters. Many in the women's suffrage movement saw the issue of women's rights as inextricably bound up with the cause of abolition. Free blacks were also in demand as speakers and writers. The most prominent were Frederick Douglass, a former fugitive slave from Maryland, and Sojourner Truth, a freed slave from New York.

In 1840 the abolition movement entered a new phase with the founding of the Liberty Party, which in 1840 and again in 1844 put up James G. Birney—a former slaveholder born in Kentucky—as its first candidate for president. The abolitionist platform was also essential to the formation of the Free Soil Party, which fielded candidates in the elections of 1848. When the Republican Party was founded in 1854 it absorbed the Free Soil Party and other reform and antislavery parties and attracted many abolitionists.

Although abolitionism became an important force in American party politics, most abolitionists failed (or chose not) to integrate this issue into a larger array of issues—which may explain why few strongly abolitionist candidates enjoyed broad political success. Most abolitionists were not politicians but activists who combined political protest with direct action. Many were instrumental in the Underground Railroad, a loose network of whites and free blacks who were committed to secretly transporting as many slaves as possible to free states. Abolitionist homes were often safe houses along the Underground Railroad route.

In the years leading up to the Civil War abolitionism spread throughout the North; in the South, however, because of a combination of social pressure, intimidation, and legislation (most state legislatures had banned antislavery publications), abolitionism all but disappeared.

The first fruits of the abolition movement were the Civil War and the Emancipation Proclamation, and the final flowering of the movement was the Thirteenth Amendment to the U.S. Constitution, ratified on December 18, 1866, which abolished slavery in the United States. After passage of the amendment many abolitionists turned to the fight for social and political equality for black people.

Suggested Reading

Blackburn, Robin. *The Overthrow of Colonial Slavery, 1776–1848.* 1988. Reprint, New York: Verso, 1989.

Lowance, Mason I. *Against Slavery: An Abolitionist Reader.* New York: Penguin, 2000.

Stewart, James Brewer. *The Holy Warriors: The Abolitionists and American Slavery.* New York: Hill and Wang, 1997.

ABORTION AND ABORTION RIGHTS

In colonial and post–Revolutionary America, abortion was generally legal if carried out before fetal movements could be perceived, effectively permitting abortion up to about the middle of pregnancy. In 1821, however, citing the fact that one-third of all abortions resulted in the death of the mother, Connecticut banned abortions entirely—and, in the course of the same decade, other states banned the procedure after the fourth month of pregnancy. Nevertheless, by 1840 only eight states regulated or restricted abortions in any way, and abortions before the fourth month continued to be common and were considered an acceptable method of BIRTH CONTROL. The services of abortionists were freely advertised in popular periodicals—and during the 1860s, physicians estimated that American women had one abortion for every four live births.

Just before the Civil War, Dr. Horatio Storer of the newly formed American Medical Association (AMA) began a campaign to outlaw abortion unless it was deemed medically necessary by qualified physicians. Although the AMA's campaign was undertaken on ethical, professional, and hygienic—rather than on moral or religious—grounds, many churches did view abortion as a sin. In 1869 the Catholic Church formally decreed that abortion was the taking of life, and many Protestant churches followed suit.

Lobbying chiefly by the AMA resulted in wave upon wave of state legislation mandating that the procedure be performed only by licensed physicians. Although the purpose of the legislation was not so much to ban abortion as to classify it as one of the many medical procedures that could legally be performed only by physicians, the result was that by 1900 most abortions had been effectively outlawed in the United States. Why? Because physicians were generally willing to perform the procedure only in cases they judged medically necessary.

Although no federal law banned abortion, the Comstock Law of 1873 (named after ANTHONY COMSTOCK, founder of the New York Society for the Suppression of Vice) made it a crime to send "obscene" or "immoral" matter through the U.S. mail, which effectively barred the inclusion of abortion-related advertisements, information, and even surgical instruments in mailed shipments. However, the explicit state bans and the Comstock Law hardly put an end to nonmedical procedures—so-called back-alley abortions. Alarmed by the dangers of often inept and unsanitary abortions and outraged that the government was attempting to seize control of women's bodies, nurse, feminist, and social reformer MARGARET SANGER promoted birth control as an alternative to unwanted pregnancy. In 1914 Sanger founded the National Birth Control League; in that same year, she was charged with obscenity (under the Comstock Law) for having distributed the *Woman Rebel*—a magazine that advocated (and explained) birth control—through the U.S. mail. When the case was dismissed in 1916, Sanger opened the first birth control clinic in the United States and was again arrested. Despite government and social harassment, Sanger and other activists continued to promote reproductive rights.

By the early twentieth century, legal, religious, and general social pressure was sufficient to drive nonmedical abortionists entirely underground; at the same time, however, views of birth control were gradually liberalizing. Until 1936 states permitted birth control only for the prevention of disease, but in that year a federal court ruled that birth control was legal for its own sake—a decision that made birth control devices more readily available and therefore decreased the demand for abortion. In 1960 the Food and Drug Administration approved the birth control pill, and the fight over reproductive rights then shifted from birth control—a fait accompli—to abortion.

The first major legal challenge to laws banning abortion came in 1939, when Connecticut officials shut down a birth control center under an 1879 antiabortion statute. The defendants claimed that the 1879 law was unconstitutional because married couples had a "natural right" that protects their decisions regarding procreation. The Connecticut Supreme Court upheld the lower court's decision, and by 1965, all fifty states had banned abortion (with various exceptions, including to save the life of the mother, in cases of rape or incest, or if the fetus was deformed). During the 1960s groups such as the NATIONAL ABORTION RIGHTS ACTION LEAGUE and the Clergy Consultation Service on Abortion responded to such legislation by working to liberalize antiabortion laws. In 1967 the NATIONAL ORGANIZATION OF WOMEN added the "right of women to control their reproductive lives" to its landmark Women's Bill of Rights.

Under pressure from various groups, New York and Hawaii repealed their antiabortion laws in 1970, prompting Dr. John C. Wilke to organize the nation's first antiabortion campaign in 1971, an effort that developed into the national Right to Life movement. At about the same time, the Catholic Church began a formal campaign against abortion. Both antiabortion movements were dealt a severe blow, however, when the U.S. SUPREME COURT ruled in *ROE V. WADE* (1973), and in the companion case *Doe v. Bolton,* that most state abortion laws were unconstitutional because they violated the "right of personal privacy." Guidelines issued with the decision barred any legislative interference in the first trimester of pregnancy and limited the restrictions that could be introduced in the later stages of pregnancy.

With *Roe v. Wade,* views on abortion were polarized as never before. Supporters of abortion rights called themselves *prochoice,* while opponents called themselves *prolife.* Opponents of abortion took legal action. In 1974, for example, Sen. Jesse Helms, R-N.C., and Sen. James Buckley, R-N.Y., both conservatives, attempted unsuccessfully to introduce a constitutional amendment banning abortion. Two years later the mainstream of the Republican Party bound itself to the party's prolife wing by including as a plank in the party platform a call for a constitutional amendment to "restore the protection of the right to life for unborn children."

As legal attempts to undo *Roe v. Wade* failed, some prolife proponents turned to intimidation, violence, and even murder. Operation Rescue, founded in 1984 and led by Randall Terry, began organizing physical blockades of abortion clinics. On Christmas Day 1984 three abortion clinics were bombed; those convicted of the crime called the bombings "a birthday gift for Jesus." Since the 1984 incident the harassment campaigns, blockades, assaults, bombings, and murders have continued. Although the principal prolife organizations have denounced such crimes, the violence and intimidation have probably been effective in discouraging many physicians and hospitals from performing abortion procedures.

Since the 1976 presidential campaign the abortion issue has figured prominently in national politics. In fact, many voters choose candidates primarily or solely on the basis of their stand on abortion. During the late 1990s antiabortion forces in Congress and in state legislatures began focusing on late-term abortions—referred to by opponents as "partial-birth abortions." Late-term abortions are performed well beyond the first trimester and are ordinarily undertaken in cases of medical necessity or advisability—that is, to save the life or health of the mother or when the fetus cannot survive birth or cannot survive long after birth. Opponents of the procedure regard it as an especially brutal form of infanticide. Those on both sides of the issue agree that any federal restriction on late-term abortion opens the door to federal restrictions on all abortions. The administration of President George W. Bush has clearly aligned itself with the prolife movement by blocking federal funding for international groups that perform or advocate abortion (as of this writing, the ban was being challenged in Congress) and by supporting state bans on late-term abortions. As of the beginning of the twenty-first century, the abortion issue remains extraordinarily divisive and far from resolution.

Other important abortion-related Supreme Court cases include *Planned Parenthood of Southeastern Pennsylvania v. Casey* (1992), *Harris v. McRae* (1980), and *Planned Parenthood of Central Missouri v. Danforth* (1976). For further discussion of birth control as a rights issue, see BIRTH CONTROL.

Suggested Reading

Hull, N. E. H., and Peter Charles Hoffer. *Roe v. Wade: The Abortion Rights Controversy in American History.* Lawrence: University of Kansas Press, 2000.

Reagan, Leslie J. *When Abortion Was a Crime: Women, Medicine, and Law in the United States, 1867–1973.* Berkeley: University of California Press, 1998.

Solinger, Rickie, ed. *Abortion Wars: A Half Century of Struggle, 1950–2000.* Berkeley: University of California Press, 2000.

ADARAND CONSTRUCTORS, INC. V. PEÑA (1995)

Adarand, a Colorado firm competing to be a subcontractor on a federal highway construction project, filed suit against the U.S. Secretary of Transportation after Adarand submitted the low bid but lost to another firm that had been certified as "disadvantaged" by the Small Business Administration—a certification clearly based on the fact that the winning firm was owned by AFRICAN AMERICANS. Adarand argued that the race-based presumptions used to select subcontractors violated the equal protection principle of the DUE PROCESS clause of the FIFTH AMENDMENT. After losing its case at both the district and circuit court levels, Adarand appealed to the SUPREME COURT. In *Adarand Constructors, Inc. v. Peña,* the high court ruled that an individual can and may challenge any agency's AFFIRMATIVE ACTION program simply by alleging that race has been used as a factor in a hiring decision or in the awarding of a contract. The Court ruled, further, that unless an agency can prove that it has discriminated against African Americans in the past, race cannot be invoked in hiring decisions or in contract awards. Thus the courts must permit a public or private employer or contracting agency to adopt an affirmative action program only if a case for a previous history of discrimination can be successfully made.

By providing non–African Americans with the right to challenge any affirmative action policy, Adarand, in effect, gave non–African Americans access to a legally sanctioned policy that was originally intended for African Americans. Cheryl J. Hopwood, for example, a white woman, successfully challenged the affirmative action program of the University of Texas Law School, alleging that the program discriminated against her; using a similar argument, a Hispanic student prevailed in a challenge to an African American scholarship program at the University of Maryland.

Suggested Reading

Curry, George E., and Cornel West, eds. *The Affirmative Action Debate.* New York: Perseus, 1996.

Jost, Kenneth. "Affirmative Action." *CQ Researcher,* September 11, 2001, 737–760.

ADDAMS, JANE (1860–1935)

Perhaps the best-known of nineteenth- and early twentieth-century antipoverty activists, Jane Addams became a principal founder of the settlement house movement in 1889 when she and her friend Ellen Starr founded Hull House in the slums of Chicago. Addams also holds the distinction of being the first American woman to receive the Nobel Peace Prize. Less well known, but equally important, was Addams's activism in labor reform, especially in the promotion of laws to regulate working conditions for women and children. An early activist in the African American civil rights movement, Addams was also a founding member of the National Association for the Advancement of Colored People (NAACP) and the American Civil Liberties Union (ACLU).

Addams was born and raised in Cedarville, Illinois, the daughter of a prominent and wealthy family that included five brothers and sisters. The death of Addams's mother (when Jane was two) and her father's subsequent remarriage brought two stepbrothers into the family. It was Jane Addams's father who first instilled in her the value of tolerance, philanthropy, and a strong work ethic.

After graduating from the all-female Rockford Seminary, a women's college, Addams decided to pursue a degree in medicine. To divert her from what they considered an inappropriate goal for a young lady, her father and stepmother sent Addams on a two-year "grand tour" of Europe. That experience, however, produced only emotional and physical stress, including symptoms of what would be diagnosed today as clinical depression. Her condition was aggravated by the death of her father, which occurred shortly after her return from Europe, and Addams became a virtual invalid, barely able to walk. After being diagnosed with curvature of the spine, she underwent surgery and was compelled to remain in a confining back harness for nearly a year. This period of enforced inactivity induced her to reflect on her life and goals. When she recovered she embarked on a second trip to Europe in 1887, but this time she and her traveling companion, Ellen Starr, went far beyond the conventional itinerary of the grand tour. They became fascinated by Toynbee Hall, a settlement house in the slums of London. Addams's life now had direction.

In 1889 Addams and Starr purchased Hull House, on Halsted Street, in an impoverished immigrant section of Chicago. They took up residence in the facility on September 8 of that year, offering hot meals, child care, tutoring in English, and classes in vocational and other subjects. Hull House also sponsored neighborhood clubs and cultural and recreational activities. The goal was to tend to the physical and intellectual needs of the community as well as to improve morale, creating a cooperative spirit in which residents would work together to improve the conditions in which they lived. Hull House became a center of community activism, successfully petitioning the city for street improvements and for the creation of public baths, parks, and playgrounds.

Within a few years Hull House was enjoying a steady flow of large donations from many philanthropic sources. Eventually, in addition to its various educational and social programs, the center offered medical care and legal aid. Addams herself began to focus as much on attacking the sources of poverty as on remedying its effects. She led successful campaigns to reform child labor laws, the laws governing the factory inspection system, and the juvenile justice system. Her efforts were instrumental in bringing about legislation to protect immigrants from exploitation, to limit the working hours of women, to enforce mandatory schooling for children, to afford legal recognition and protection for labor unions, and to provide for industrial safety. Addams was also active in the women's suffrage movement—first on the local level, working for Chicago municipal suffrage, and then as the first vice president of the National American Woman Suffrage Association, a post she held beginning in 1911. She was a vigorous campaigner for Theodore Roosevelt and the Progressive (Bull Moose) Party in 1912.

Addams's local success served as an example for the nation and spawned community centers and settlement houses across America. Moreover, Hull House became a kind of social laboratory, drawing educators, reformers, and social philosophers who explored a wide range of social and political issues.

Addams herself was a gifted lecturer and writer, and her best-known book, *Twenty Years at Hull-House,* is a classic of autobiography and a handbook of social activism. In 1911 Addams became the first president of the National Federation of Settlements and Neighborhood Centers.

Addams was never afraid of controversy. Her support of the demonstrators in the Haymarket Riot of 1886 brought her much criticism, and doubtless cost Hull House many donors. Fortunately, revenues from Addams's lecture tours—and, after 1910, from *Twenty Years at Hull-House*—enabled Hull House to operate more or less independently of donations.

Addams's advocacy of social justice included a belief in pacifism, and she was an outspoken opponent of American involvement in World War I. In 1915 she and other women pacifists formed the Women's Peace Party, which not only sought a peaceful end to World War I but worked to establish a permanent international peacekeeping organization. Despite pressure from organizations that supported the war, Addams persisted in her opposition and was instrumental in organizing the Women's International League for Peace and Freedom, serving as its president until her death in 1935. With fellow peace activist Nicholas Murray Butler, Addams was awarded the Nobel Peace Prize in 1931, but such recognition did not prevent her from being condemned as a socialist, an anarchist, and a Bolshevik, especially after she participated in the founding of both the NAACP and the ACLU.

Despite being stricken with cancer, Addams worked practically until the day of her death. She was buried in Cedarville, the town of her birth.

Suggested Reading

Addams, Jane. *Twenty Years at Hull-House.* 1910. Reprint, New York: Signet, 1999.

Elshtain, Jean Bethke. *Jane Addams and the Dream of American Democracy.* New York: Basic Books, 2001.

———. *The Jane Addams Reader.* New York: Basic Books, 2001.

"ADDRESS TO A MEETING IN NEW YORK" (MALCOLM X)

The 1964 speech of Malcolm X, which was delivered after his pilgrimage to Mecca and his break with Elijah Muhammad and the Black Muslims, illustrates what might be termed the mature thought of Malcolm X. (See Appendix A for the text of the speech. Also see Islam, Nation of.)

Suggested Reading

Breitman, George. *Malcolm X Speaks: Selected Speeches and Statements.* 1965. Reprint, New York: Grove, 1990.

ADOPTION PROMOTION AND STABILITY ACT

Enacted by Congress and signed into law by President Bill Clinton, the Adoption Promotion and Stability Act became effective on January 1, 1997, and is intended to promote adoption by providing a tax credit for adoption expenses incurred during the year that the adoption is formalized. Credits include $5,000 for expenses associated with finalized international adoptions, $5,000 for domestic adoption expenses, and $6,000 for special-needs expenses associated with domestic adoptions. Credits are reduced for higher-income adoptive families (with adjusted gross incomes between $75,000 and $115,000), and families whose adjusted gross income exceeds $115,000 are ineligible for credits.

Section 1808 of the act states that no adoption can be delayed or denied on the basis of the "race, color, or national origin" of the parent or child involved—a provision that was intended to reduce barriers to transracial placements. However, because some Native American groups expressed concern over possible conflict with the Indian Child Welfare Act, amendments have been proposed to ensure that tribes would be informed if a child with Native American heritage might be placed for adoption; an additional amendment would impose criminal sanctions if the child's heritage were willfully hidden. As of mid-2002 the amendments, which have proven controversial, were pending in the form of free-standing bills that might modify the Adoption Promotion and Stability Act as it was originally passed.

Suggested Reading

Lyons, Christina L. "Adoption Controversies." *CQ Researcher,* September 10, 1999.

Sifferman, Kelly Allen. *Adoption: A Legal Guide for Birth and Adoptive Parents.* New York: Chelsea House, 1997.

AFFIRMATIVE ACTION

Affirmative action was born in the same era—and grew out of the same impetus—that produced the Civil Rights Act of 1964 and the Voting Rights Act of 1965. Affirmative action, however, is a policy rather than a discrete item of legislation. The phrase originated with the administration of Lyndon B. Johnson, who urged both government agencies and leaders in the private sector to take "affirmative action"—that is, not merely to end racial discrimination but to compensate for the many years of past discrimination.

Affirmative action policies attempt to correct long-standing patterns of racial discrimination by introducing measures to provide or enhance equality of opportunity in employment and education. Affirmative action programs have included quotas, targets, or set-asides in hiring, promotion, admission to institutions of higher learning, and the award of scholarships. Some affirmative action comes in the form of economic aid packages, some in the form of adjusted or scaled standards for admission to particular colleges and universities (for example, test-score cutoff points may be lower for members of minorities than for others), and some in the form of adjusted criteria for employment or promotion.

Beginning in the mid-1960s affirmative action programs were implemented by the federal government and by state and local governments—often at the urging of the federal government, which sometimes tied economic assistance to compliance with affirmative action targets. In the private sector, affirmative action is primarily voluntary; however, it may be mandated in the case of certain federal contractors or vendors to government agencies, for example.

Affirmative action has always been controversial, but a pronounced backlash against it began in 1980 with the election of conservative Republican president Ronald Reagan. At that time many Americans felt strongly that affirmative action policies were inherently unfair and even unconstitutional. The 1978 Supreme Court decision in *Regents of the University of California v. Bakke* initiated a sharp decline in the federal, state, local, and private resolve to continue to pursue affirmative action policies, and since then various states and local jurisdictions have enacted legislation to limit or end such policies.

Other noteworthy Supreme Court cases associated with affirmative action include *Richmond v. J. A. Croson Co.* (1989), *Johnson v. Transportation Agency of Santa Clara County* (1987), and *Fullilove v. Klutznick* (1980).

Suggested Reading

Curry, George E., and Cornel West, eds. *The Affirmative Action Debate.* New York: Perseus, 1996.

Jost, Kenneth. "Affirmative Action." *CQ Researcher,* September 11, 2001, 737–760.

AFRICAN AMERICAN CIVIL RIGHTS MOVEMENT

The national legal breakthrough that may be said to have launched the African American civil rights movement came on May 17, 1954, when the U.S. Supreme Court ruled in *Brown v. Board of Education of Topeka, Kansas* that segregation in public schools is inherently unequal protection under the law, and therefore violates the Fourteenth Amendment. The ruling opened the door to desegregation not only in public education but, ultimately, throughout American society.

The next landmark came on December 1, 1955, when Rosa Parks refused to give up her seat near the front of a Montgomery, Alabama, city bus to a white passenger—a violation not only of southern segregationist custom but of a city ordinance. Parks's arrest for this violation triggered the Montgomery Bus Boycott, which lasted for more than a year—until the buses were desegregated, on December 21, 1956—and focused national attention on the daily injustices of racism, especially in the South. The boycott also occasioned the rise of Martin Luther King Jr. as the most important leader of the civil rights movement. With Charles K. Steele and Fred L. Shuttlesworth, King founded the Southern Christian Leadership Conference (SCLC) during January–February 1957 and became its first president. The SCLC was the major early force in organizing the civil rights movement throughout the South and the nation.

One of the first big tests following *Brown v. Board of Education* came in September 1957 when Arkansas governor Orval Faubus led the resistance to the federally mandated integration of Little Rock's Central High School. President Dwight D. Eisenhower dispatched U.S. Army troops and federalized the state National Guard to ensure that nine black students slated to enroll at the school would be able to do so. The confrontation demonstrated the difficulty of legislating social justice, but it also showed that to protect civil rights, the federal government was determined to override state resistance.

Segregation pervaded every aspect of southern life, not just the schools. On February 1, 1960, in Greensboro, North Carolina, four black college students staged a sit-in at a segregated lunch counter in Woolworth's. As the number of demonstrators grew from day to day—and attracted media attention—Woolworth's and other Greensboro establishments were peacefully integrated, setting the pattern for many other nonviolent protests throughout the South.

In April 1960, at Shaw University in Raleigh, North Carolina, black students founded the Student Nonviolent Coordinating Committee (SNCC) for the purpose of coordinating civil rights protests and other action. SNCC would eventually become radicalized and—under the leadership of Stokely Carmichael during 1966–1967—militant.

The most important of the early, large-scale student actions came on May 4, 1961, when the Congress of Racial Equality (CORE) began sending student volunteers on interstate bus trips in the South to test the implementation of federal laws prohibiting segregation in all interstate travel facilities. Despite outbreaks of violence—including the torching of a bus in Alabama—about one thousand Freedom Riders, black and white, continued their work through the summer.

The nonviolent approach of the mainstream civil rights movement did not prevent violent white retaliation, and on June 12, 1963, in Jackson, Mississippi, Medgar Evers, the field secretary of the Mississippi chapter of the National Association for the Advancement of Colored People, was assassinated outside his home. The gunman, white supremacist Byron De La Beckwith, was arrested, indicted, and tried twice in 1964. Both trials resulted in hung juries, and it was not until 1994 that Beckwith was convicted of the murder.

Despite violence and intimidation, the civil rights movement gained overwhelming momentum, culminating in the March on Washington. On August 28, 1963, a quarter of a million marchers gathered before the Lincoln Memorial, where Martin Luther King Jr. delivered his famous "I Have a Dream" speech. The event and the speech stirred the nation, and together represented one of the high points of the civil rights movement. Tragically, the following month the Sixteenth Street Baptist Church, in Birmingham, Alabama, was bombed, and four black girls were killed. Their deaths sparked riots in the city that led to the deaths of two more black youths.

During the summer of 1964 the Council of Federated Organizations, a newly formed coalition of civil rights groups that included CORE and SNCC, focused the civil rights movement on a major effort to register black voters. That same summer, on July 2, President Lyndon Johnson signed into law the momentous Civil Rights Act of 1964, which made segregation in all public facilities and discrimination in employment illegal.

The Civil Rights Act of 1964 was a major achievement of the movement, but it did not end discrimination, persecution, or violence. On August 5, 1964, three Mississippi civil rights volunteers, who had last been seen on June 21, were declared missing. The murdered bodies of James E. Chaney, Andrew Goodman, and Michael Schwerner, all CORE volunteers working on voter registration, were found after President Johnson dispatched troops to assist in the search. It was later revealed that police had apprehended the three, then released them to the Ku Klux Klan. Early the next year, on February 21, black nationalist Malcolm X was assassinated while giving a lecture in Harlem, apparently by Black Muslims, a group with which he had recently broken.

On March 7, 1965, in Selma, Alabama, demonstrators marching to Montgomery to support voting rights were first blocked, then assaulted, by police at the Pettus Bridge. Television and newsreel pictures of demonstrators being beaten, teargassed, and attacked by police dogs shocked the nation and made many Americans more fully aware of the issues at stake in the civil rights struggle. The year 1965 saw passage of the Voting Rights Act on August 10, which was, in significant measure, the fruition of the voter rights efforts of CORE and other organizations.

On April 4, 1968, the single most visible leader of the nonviolent civil rights movement, Martin Luther King Jr., was assassinated in Memphis by James Earl Ray. Seven days later President Johnson signed the Civil Rights Act of 1968, prohibiting discrimination in the sale, renting, and financing of housing.

The 1960s, a time of intense social ferment, was the high-water mark of the African American civil rights movement. Although the April 20, 1971, Supreme Court decision in *Swann v. Charlotte-Mecklenburg Board of Education,* which upheld busing as a legitimate means of integrating public schools, was an important step and an affirmation of the spirit of *Brown v. Board of Education,* as the 1970s gave way to the 1980s, the conservative mood that ushered Ronald Reagan's administration into the White House led to significant retrenchment in civil rights. The era of executive activism had ended. On March 22, 1988, Congress had to override President Reagan's veto to pass the Civil Rights Restoration Act, which expanded the application of nondiscrimination laws within private institutions that receive federal funds. Reagan's successor, George H.W. Bush, similarly opposed the Civil Rights Act of 1990—but after much resistance signed into law the Civil Rights Act of 1991 (November 22), which bolstered existing civil rights legislation and provided for civil damages in cases of intentional employment discrimination.

For an overview of the history of African Americans from the perspective of minority rights before 1954, see African Americans. (See also Birmingham church bombing, Bloody Sunday, Fair Housing Act, Freedom Summer, Greensboro sit-in, and Little Rock school crisis.)

Suggested Reading

Graham, Hugh Davis. *The Civil Rights Era: Origins and Development of National Policy, 1960–1972.* New York: Oxford University Press, 1990.

Levy, Peter B. *The Civil Rights Movement.* Westport, Conn.: Greenwood, 1998.

Sigler, Jay A. *Civil Rights in America: 1500 to the Present.* Detroit: Gale, 1998.

AFRICAN AMERICANS

Africans were the only group of immigrants brought to America involuntarily. The first arrived in 1517, brought by the Spanish to replace Indian workers, who often succumbed to disease and exposure as a result of the brutal working conditions on plantations. In 1619 the first twenty slaves brought to a British American colony arrived on a Dutch slave ship and were put to work at Jamestown, Virginia. Slavery would not be abolished on the entire North American continent until 1865, with the Union's victory in the Civil War. Because of the special demand for cheap labor created by the plantation system in the South, slavery flourished there—and not, for the most part, in the North, where the economy was based on smaller farms and, later, on industry. It is a painful irony that Crispus Attucks, an escaped slave, was the first man to die in the Boston Massacre of 1770 and is therefore often regarded as the first American casualty in the cause of American liberty and independence.

The Constitution (1788) protected slavery and included the Three-Fifths Compromise, whereby slaves—who had no rights—were to be counted as three-fifths of a person for the purpose of levying taxes and apportioning congressional representation. Moreover, in 1793, Congress passed the first Fugitive Slave Act, making it illegal for anyone to harbor escaped slaves or to interfere with their arrest and return.

Although southerners took legal and political steps to protect their property by ensuring the return of fugitive slaves, they worried constantly about slave rebellion. The first major rebellion took place in 1800, when a slave named Gabriel massed more than a thousand armed slaves near Richmond, Virginia. The revolt was put down before it got fully under way, and thirty-five slaves, including Gabriel, were hanged. Although other minor rebellions broke out from time to time, it was 1831 before another major action occurred. In a rebellion and rampage that left sixty whites dead, Nat Turner, a slave and a lay preacher, along with some seventy-five followers terrorized Virginia. The insurrection was put down, and Turner and others were executed; local whites also exacted revenge on whatever blacks happened to cross their paths.

In 1817 a group of freeborn blacks and freed slaves founded the American Colonization Society. One of the aims of the society was to transport blacks to a territory in Africa that the society had purchased from local tribes. For years the society controlled the colony, but in 1847 it became the independent Republic of Liberia.

In the meantime, as new states were admitted to the Union, Congress repeatedly wrestled with the problem of maintaining a balance between slave and free states in the Senate: any upset in this balance had the potential to lead to civil war. In 1820 efforts to maintain balance prompted the Missouri Compromise, under which Missouri was admitted to the Union as a slave state, and Maine, newly created from Massachusetts, was admitted as a free state. The territories north of the parallel that ran through Missouri's southern border were to be perpetually free soil, except for Missouri itself.

Organized white opposition to slavery had been present in America since the early eighteenth century, mostly among such religious groups as the Quakers; however, a more aggressive, even militant abolition movement began to develop in the 1820s. In 1829 the abolitionist David Walker published *Appeal . . . to the Colored Citizens of the World . . .*, which called for a universal slave revolt. Two years later, William Lloyd Garrison began publication of the *Liberator*, the most influential abolitionist newspaper in the nation. Although Garrison did not actively encourage violent rebellion, he did advocate immediate and unconditional emancipation. In 1833 Garrison founded the American Anti-Slavery Society, the most active and influential organization of the abolitionist movement, which formed the nucleus of the Liberty Party. In 1840, however, when that party held its first national convention in Albany, New York, party members opposed Garrison's advocacy of immediate, unconditional emancipation and voted in favor of more measured and gradual political action to achieve eventual abolition.

In 1847 Frederick Douglass, a fugitive slave, began to publish the *North Star*, the first black-edited antislavery newspaper. The following year, in yet another political approach to the slavery question, the Free Soil Party began calling not for abolition but for a ban on the extension of slavery into any of the western territories.

Another impressive black voice in the abolitionist movement belonged to Sojourner Truth, who began lecturing throughout the Midwest in 1850, and quickly developed a reputation for personal magnetism and for the ability to draw large crowds. That same year, Harriet Tubman, a fugitive slave, risked her freedom by returning to Maryland to lead members of her family out of bondage via what was being called the Underground Railroad—an informal but extensive network of abolitionists who offered assistance and protection for fugitives bound for free states. Tubman, who eventually helped more than three hundred slaves to escape, became a leading figure in the Underground Railroad and was referred to as "the Moses of her people."

In the aftermath of the United States–Mexican War of 1846–1848, through which the United States had acquired territory encompassing the states of California, Utah, and New Mexico, yet another set of compromises was made to maintain the balance of slave and free states. As part of the Compromise of 1850, the slave trade was discontinued in the District of Columbia, thereby ending what most American diplomats considered a profound embarrassment in the capital of the "land of liberty." In 1854 both the Compromise of 1850 and the earlier Missouri Compromise were superceded by the Kansas-Nebraska Act, under which the inhabitants of the western territories were given "popular sovereignty"—that is, the right to decide whether to be free soil or slaveholding. The option of exercising local choice triggered a violent guerrilla war between proslavery and antislavery forces in Kansas—where in 1856 the radically militant abolitionist John Brown led a bloody retaliation against proslavery forces at Pottawatomie Creek.

If the situation in "Bleeding Kansas" presaged a coming civil war, the Supreme Court's *Dred Scott decision* (1857) made it all but inevitable. By affirming that the federal government had a constitutional obligation to protect slavery, and declaring that no slave could become free by virtue of escaping to, or living in, a free state, the decision ended any possibility of compromise on the issue of slavery. After *Dred Scott,* the only means available for abolishing slavery was a constitutional amendment—and because any amendment required ratification by three-quarters of the states, this was an impossibility, at least for the foreseeable future.

During this period of great political ferment and headlong drift toward war, a novel by Harriet Beecher Stowe, *Uncle Tom's Cabin* (1852), did much to dramatize the plight of the southern slave and to crystallize northern abolitionist sentiment. (Far less popular was Harriet E. Wilson's 1859 autobiographical novel *Our Nig,* which portrayed northern racism in the antebellum years.)

Long looming, the Civil War began on April 12, 1861, with an attack by forces of the Confederate States (states that had seceded from the Union) against Fort Sumter, in Charleston Harbor. President Abraham Lincoln portrayed the war not as a crusade to free the slaves but as a campaign to enforce federal authority—and thereby save the Union from dissolution. Despite continual pressure for emancipation from Radical Republicans in the federal government, the president believed that he lacked the constitutional authority to free the slaves; moreover, he had no desire to alienate the so-called border states—slaveholding states that had remained, however tenuously, loyal to the Union. In the absence of presidential action, Congress passed two Confiscation Acts; although the second, passed in 1862, proclaimed that slaves of both civilian and military Confederate officials "shall be forever free," it was enforceable only in the parts of the South occupied by the Union army.

By 1863 President Lincoln had come to believe that emancipation had become both morally and politically desirable. After a narrow Union victory at the Battle of Antietam (September 17, 1862), Lincoln issued the Preliminary Emancipation Proclamation (September 22, 1862), which was followed by the Final Emancipation Proclamation (January 1, 1863). These documents, however, liberated slaves only in areas still "in rebellion"; slaves in the border states and in parts of the Confederacy that were under Union military occupation were not freed.

Although many blacks were eager to serve in the Union army, they were, for the most part, barred from service. Nevertheless, in 1861–1862, a company of black volunteers, the Corps d'Afrique, was raised in New Orleans. On August 25, 1862, the War Department authorized the military governor of the Union-occupied South Carolina Sea Islands to raise five regiments of black troops. After the Final Emancipation Proclamation was issued, President Lincoln personally called for four black regiments, and, by the end of the war, nearly 180,000 blacks were serving in 166 regiments. At war's end, black soldiers constituted about 10 percent of the Union army, serving in segregated regiments led almost exclusively by white officers. Most of the black troops were relegated to labor and fatigue duties, but a few were committed to combat, in which they universally distinguished themselves. To southerners, the North's use of black troops was an outrage, and when Confederate forces captured Fort Pillow, Tennessee (April 12, 1864), the rebel soldiers massacred most of the black garrison.

The Civil War ended on April 26, 1865. President Lincoln, perhaps the only leader on either side capable of crafting a just peace, had been assassinated on April 14. Andrew Johnson, the new president, favored extending great leniency to the South and permitting a significant degree of self-government. Johnson was perpetually at odds with Congress, which was controlled by Radical Republicans intent on imposing a punitive, highly restrictive, and ultimately humiliating Reconstruction policy.

Much of Reconstruction was instituted with the best of intentions, largely to ensure that some four million liberated slaves would be assisted in their transition to freedom and would be safe from persecution by southern whites. Congress created the U.S. Bureau of Refugees, Freedmen, and Abandoned Lands to aid in the transition and to provide financial and other assistance. Additionally, the Thirteenth Amendment (1865) and the Fourteenth Amendment (1866) were intended to ensure that abolition would have a constitutional basis and that freed slaves would enjoy the rights and "equal protection of law" guaranteed to all citizens.

Despite the amendments and the creation of the Freedmen's Bureau, however, the states of the former Confederacy began to enact "black codes," legislation intended to circumvent the amendments—and Reconstruction itself—by severely curtailing black enfranchisement and other legal rights. In response the national government instituted federal military governments for the southern states, a move that provided some protection to blacks but created long-lasting animosity between black and white southerners. Worse, in many places local federal officials put illiterate and ill-prepared former slaves into important government and administrative positions, exacerbating racial tensions and leading to inefficiency and corruption.

In 1870 Joseph Hayne Rainey of South Carolina became the first black elected to the U.S. House of Representatives, and another black man, Hiram R. Revels, of Mississippi, assumed the seat of Jefferson Davis (former president of the Confederate States of America) in the U.S. Senate. But because of a political deal that resolved the contested presidential election of 1876 (Republican Rutherford B. Hayes versus Democrat Samuel J. Tilden), the federal government abruptly ended Reconstruction in 1877, withdrawing the last of the federal troops from the southern states. Southern conservatives quickly regained control of the state governments, initiating a long era of official government repression of blacks in the South.

In the remaining years of the nineteenth century, relatively few voices were raised in protest against the marginalization of black America. In Alabama in 1881 Booker T. Washington founded the Tuskegee Normal and Industrial Institute, a center of practical higher education for blacks. Washington advocated black economic self-determination as a means of improving the lives of black people. Washington believed that legal equality was less important than economic improvement—and that, in exchange for white cooperation in black economic advancement, blacks should be willing to accept, at least for the present, segregation and other forms of racial discrimination.

Although Washington was popular with blacks and with many whites, other figures, such as black journalist T. Thomas Fortune, editor of the *New York Age,* defended the civil rights of blacks and condemned racial discrimination. When Ida B. Wells, in the *Memphis Free Speech,* denounced the lynching of three of her friends in 1892, a white mob burned down the offices of the paper.

During the post–Civil War years black churches emerged as centers for social change. Three major black Baptist conventions merged in 1895, creating the National Baptist Convention, U.S.A., Inc., in Atlanta, which would become a powerful black religious and political organization. In this very year, however, at the Atlanta Exposition, Booker T. Washington delivered his celebrated "Atlanta Compromise" speech, in which he articulated the idea that black vocational education to achieve economic competence should take precedence over issues of social equality or access to political office.

In 1896 Mary Church Terrell was elected the first president of the National Association of Colored Women—an organization that, in opposition to Washington's approach, was dedicated not only to educational and social reform but to an end to racial discrimination. It was Washington, however, who continued to get the nod from the white establishment. In 1901 the black educator was invited to the White House to dine with President Theodore Roosevelt—an invitation many whites criticized as a breach of racial propriety.

In 1903 W. E. B. Du Bois published *The Souls of Black Folk,* which dramatically defined "the problem of the Twentieth Century [as] the problem of the color-line." Du Bois became the most articulate and influential opponent of Washington's accommodationist ideology, proposing instead that black society strive to develop a "Talented Tenth," an elite cadre of college-educated blacks who would bear the burden of elevating the race economically, culturally, and socially. Du Bois was also instrumental in the Niagara Movement, which was founded at a 1905 meeting (near Niagara Falls, Ontario) of black intellectuals; the movement adopted resolutions demanding full equality in American life.

Interest in the Niagara Movement was catalyzed by a 1908 race riot in Springfield, Illinois, in which the black community was stormed by several thousand whites, and two elderly black men were lynched. The following year a group of whites, horrified by the Springfield riot, joined the black Niagara Movement to create the National Association for the Advancement of Colored People (NAACP), which became the nation's most progressive and influential black social and political organization. In 1910 Du Bois began editing the NAACP's monthly magazine, the *Crisis,* a vehicle for black social as well as literary expression.

In New York City in 1911 another important organization came into being. The National League on Urban Conditions Among Negroes (later known as the National Urban League) was founded to help blacks—who had begun migrating from the South in substantial numbers—find jobs and housing and adjust to northern urban life.

Yet another important black movement had its origin in the years before World War I. In 1913 Timothy Drew—also known as Prophet Noble Drew Ali—founded the Moorish Science Temple of America in Newark, New Jersey. Drew taught that blacks were of Muslim origin, and his temple offered a wholly black alternative to the Christian church. The Universal Negro Improvement Association, founded by Marcus Garvey in 1914, created yet another movement toward black identity, pride and, ultimately, separatism. The following year the black historian Carter G. Woodson founded the Association for the Study of Negro Life and History, which was dedicated to conducting research in African American history.

In 1917 America's entry into World War I brought large numbers of African American men into the armed forces (in segregated units) and also into northern war industries, fueling the Great Migration of rural southern blacks to the industrial cities of the North. White resentment of the influx of blacks often led to race riots, including the East Saint Louis riot of 1917, in which forty blacks and eight whites were killed; and the Chicago riots of 1919, in which twenty-three blacks and fifteen whites died, 537 people were injured, and more than a thousand black families were left homeless.

A phenomenon that contrasted with the escalating racial violence was the Harlem Renaissance a decade-long flowering of the arts—especially literature—within the black community, which created unprecedented (if short-lived) solidarity between black and white intellectuals. While the black cultural elite was evolving a sense of pride and achievement, in 1920 Marcus Garvey addressed 25,000 blacks at New York's Madison Square Garden and led a parade of more than 50,000 through the streets of Harlem. It was the greatest and boldest American demonstration of black pride and solidarity to that time. Five years later, in 1925, the black labor movement began in earnest when A. Philip Randolph founded the Brotherhood of Sleeping Car Porters. In 1930, as blacks were making strides on the cultural and labor fronts, Benjamin Oliver Davis Sr. became the first black colonel in the U.S. Army. Promoted to general in 1940, Davis would oversee race relations and the morale of black soldiers during World War II.

The onset of the Great Depression exacerbated racial tensions. As hard hit as white labor was during this period, blacks generally suffered even more. The arrest and trial in 1931 of nine young black men accused of raping two white women on a freight train in Scottsboro, Alabama, became the focus of a crusade by northern liberal and radical groups, who saw the proceedings as a judicial lynching. (The case was decided in 1932 by the Supreme Court in *Powell v. Alabama.* See also Scottsboro Boys.) At this time, too, the NAACP turned its attention to a largely successful campaign to combat violence against blacks, especially lynchings.

Black America found a much-needed occasion for pride in the triumph of track-and-fielder Jesse Owens, who won four gold medals in the 1936 Olympic Games at Berlin—thereby embarrassing (and outraging) Adolf Hitler, who claimed the intellectual and physical superiority of the "Aryan race." Two years later, the great black heavyweight champion Joe Louis defeated the German champion Max Schmeling.

In 1939, after the Daughters of the American Revolution (DAR) refused to allow her to perform at Constitution Hall, singer Marian Anderson performed at the Lincoln Memorial before an audience of 75,000. The DAR's action prompted first lady Eleanor Roosevelt and other prominent liberal women to resign from the organization in protest. The year 1939 also saw the establishment of the NAACP Legal Defense and Education Fund. The NAACP had resolved to mount concerted attacks against all legally sanctioned bias—an approach that would bear fruit in such momentous Supreme Court decisions as *Brown v. Board of Education of Topeka, Kansas,* in 1954.

The outbreak of World War II raised familiar issues concerning the role of blacks in the military. Were they fit to serve in combat roles rather than as menial laborers? But the war also accelerated progress in race relations. In 1941 the War Department formed the all-black 99th Pursuit Squadron of the U.S. Army Air Corps, the first unit of African American fighter pilots, which was commanded by Benjamin Oliver Davis Jr., son of the army's only black general. This step forward was somewhat overshadowed, however, by the armed forces' decision to accept blood donations from blacks only if the supply was strictly segregated.

In 1942 the Congress of Racial Equality was founded in New York City by Bayard Rustin, who in 1963 would become a key organizer of the momentous March on Washington. In Chicago in 1945 John H. Johnson started *Ebony* magazine. In contrast to most other black periodicals, *Ebony* was directed at the rising black middle class, and it became an immediate hit. Further evidence of the integration of blacks into the American social mainstream was the 1947 induction of Jackie Robinson into the Brooklyn Dodgers as the major leagues' first black baseball player. Blacks as well as whites saw this crossing of the color line as a singularly momentous step. Other black achievers during the postwar period include Ralph Bunche, who received the Nobel Peace Prize for his work as United Nations mediator in the Arab-Israeli dispute in Palestine, and Gwendolyn Brooks, who was awarded the 1950 Pulitzer Prize for poetry.

For most white Americans the 1950s was a prosperous era when attention was directed less toward domestic issues than toward the international threat of communism, the Korean War, and the Cold War. But the 1950s also saw the birth of the civil rights movement, including such momentous events such as the 1954 Supreme Court ruling in *Brown v. Board of Education of Topeka, Kansas;* the defiance of Rosa Parks, whose refusal to relinquish her seat to a white passenger on a Montgomery, Alabama, city bus sparked the Montgomery Bus Boycott of 1955–1956; and the emergence of Martin Luther King Jr. as the overall leader of the civil rights movement.

According to the 2000 national census, 36,419,434 Americans identify themselves as "Black or African American alone or in combination with one or more other races"—that is, nearly 13 percent of the total U.S. population of 281,421,906. More than 53 percent of African Americans still live in the South (18 percent live in the Northeast, 18.8 percent in the Midwest, and 9.6 percent in the West). In 2000 the overall U.S. poverty rate dropped to 11.3 percent, down half a percentage point from 1999. Among whites the 2000 poverty rate was 9.4 percent—7.5 percent among non-Hispanic whites. For blacks, however, the 2000 poverty rate was 22.1 percent, down from a 1999 rate of 23.6 percent. Even after years of economic development and a sustained campaign for the full attainment of civil rights, black Americans, as a group, remain economically disadvantaged when compared with whites.

For a concise chronological outline of the civil rights movement—and an outline of the history of African Americans from the perspective of minority rights through the end of the twentieth century—see AFRICAN AMERICAN CIVIL RIGHTS MOVEMENT. (See also FREEDMEN'S BUREAU, SLAVERY, and TUSKEGEE AIRMEN.)

Suggested Reading

Bennett, Lerone, Jr. *Before the Mayflower: A History of Black America*. New York: Penguin, 1993.

Franklin, John Hope. *From Slavery to Freedom: A History of African Americans*. New York: McGraw-Hill, 1994.

AGE DISCRIMINATION

Age discrimination is deemed to have occurred when any term, condition, or privilege of employment—including (but not limited to) hiring, firing, promotion, layoff, compensation, benefits, job assignments, and training—is based on age. Because people over age forty have historically been the most likely targets of age discrimination, they are defined as the "protected group" in both the AGE DISCRIMINATION IN EMPLOYMENT ACT OF 1967 and the AGE DISCRIMINATION ACT OF 1975.

Suggested Reading

Gregory, Raymond F. *Age Discrimination in the American Workplace: Old at a Young Age*. New Brunswick: Rutgers University Press, 2001.

Worsnop, Richard L. "Age Discrimination." *CQ Researcher.* August 1, 1997.

AGE DISCRIMINATION ACT OF 1975

The purpose of the Age Discrimination Act of 1975 is stated as follows in the statute: "to prohibit discrimination on the basis of age in programs or activities receiving Federal financial assistance." More specifically (section 6102, "Prohibition of Discrimination"): "No person in the United States shall, on the basis of age, be excluded from participation in, be denied the benefits of, or be subjected to discrimination under, any program or activity receiving Federal financial assistance." The Age Discrimination Act of 1975 does not cover employment discrimination, which is addressed by the much more comprehensive AGE DISCRIMINATION IN EMPLOYMENT ACT OF 1967.

Suggested Reading

Worsnop, Richard L. "Age Discrimination." *CQ Researcher,* August 1, 1997.

AGE DISCRIMINATION IN EMPLOYMENT ACT OF 1967

The Age Discrimination in Employment Act of 1967, which became Public Law 90-202 on December 15, 1967, prohibits employment discrimination against persons forty years of age or older. (See Appendix A for excerpts from the text of the Age Discrimination in Employment Act of 1967.)

Suggested Reading

Gregory, Raymond F. *Age Discrimination in the American Workplace: Old at a Young Age*. New Brunswick: Rutgers University Press, 2001.

AIDS

AIDS—Acquired Immune Deficiency Syndrome—is a disease caused by the Human Immunodeficiency Virus (HIV) and transmitted through contact with infected blood or semen. Because AIDS is both greatly dreaded and widely misunderstood, people who are HIV-positive (carry the virus but show no signs of active disease), as well as those who are ill with AIDS are sometimes subject to discrimination in the workplace, in educational settings, in housing, and in public accommodations. Such discrimination is prohibited by federal law because people at any stage of HIV disease are classified as disabled and are therefore protected under the AMERICANS WITH DISABILITIES ACT and the 1988 Amendment to the Fair Housing Act, as well as under two other federal statutes, the Rehabilitation Act of 1973 and the Air Carriers Access Act. Some state antidiscrimination statutes provide further protection.

Under these federal protections, people with HIV or AIDS may not legally be denied access to any public accommodation. Children with HIV or AIDS may not legally be segregated from other children at school. Employers may not require employees or job applicants to take an HIV test, and employees who are HIV-positive or who have AIDS may not be dismissed on that account, nor can they be discriminated against by employers in any other way. People with HIV or AIDS may not be discriminated against in buying or renting a dwelling, nor can they be evicted because of their health status.

In the area of insurance, special rules apply regarding HIV and AIDS. Life and health insurance carriers may legally require an HIV or AIDS test as a precondition for obtaining a policy, and carriers may decline to issue a policy to a person who is HIV–positive or has AIDS. Unless an existing insurance policy specifically excludes HIV and AIDS coverage, however, the carrier may not arbitrarily refuse to pay claims related to the condition.

Suggested Reading

Rubenstein, William B., Ruth Eisenberg, and Lawrence O. Gostin. *The Rights of People Who Are HIV Positive: The Authoritative ACLU Guide to the Rights of People Living with HIV Disease and AIDS.* Carbondale: Southern Illinois University Press, 1996.

ALABAMA CHRISTIAN MOVEMENT FOR HUMAN RIGHTS

Reverend Fred Shuttlesworth, an African American Baptist minister in Birmingham, Alabama, founded the Alabama Christian Movement for Human Rights (ACMHR) to initiate and coordinate protests against the policies of the municipality MARTIN LUTHER KING JR. called "the most thoroughly segregated city in America." The ACMHR sponsored boycotts and other antiracism activities in Birmingham. But when Shuttlesworth became dissatisfied with the progress his local group was making, he and other ACMHR activists called for assistance from the SOUTHERN CHRISTIAN LEADERSHIP CONFERENCE (SCLC).This request brought King, the leader of the SCLC, to Birmingham and focused national attention on the racial injustice in the city.

The ACMHR and the SCLC collaborated on Project C (for "confrontation"), a thirty-two-day protest that targeted segregated facilities in downtown Birmingham and employers who discriminated in hiring. Launched from the Sixteenth Street Baptist Church, Project C drew the participation of thousands of African American residents of Birmingham. From April 3 to 6, small groups of demonstrators attempted to march to downtown department stores and to city hall, but they were intercepted and arrested by public safety commissioner EUGENE "BULL" CONNOR. While the protesters were detained, a local judge issued an injunction barring further protest. This action triggered the second phase of protest, from April 6 to 20, when several hundred blacks, in defiance of the court order, marched from the Sixteenth Street Baptist Church toward downtown. This time, Bull Connor's police force used dogs and high-powered water hoses against the protestors, creating scenes that were televised nationally. (See also BIRMINGHAM SCLC PROTESTS.)

Suggested Reading

Manis, Andrew Michael. *A Fire You Can't Put Out: The Civil Rights Life of Birmingham's Reverend Fred Shuttlesworth.* Tuscaloosa: University of Alabama Press, 1999.

White, Marjorie L., and Andrew M. Manis, eds. *Birmingham's Revolutionary: The Reverend Fred Shuttlesworth and the Alabama Christian Movement for Human Rights.* Macon and Atlanta: Mercer University Press, 2000.

ALBANY MOVEMENT

During the summer of 1959 a group of classmates from the segregated Monroe High School, in Albany, Georgia, formed the NATIONAL ASSOCIATION FOR THE ADVANCEMENT OF COLORED PEOPLE Youth Council. Among the council's first initiatives was an effort to persuade local white businesses to hire blacks. When the group achieved limited success on its own, however, it invited assistance from the national STUDENT NONVIOLENT COORDINATING COMMITTEE (SNCC). In September 1961 SNCC field officers Charles Sherrod and Cordell Reagon arrived in Terrell County to begin voter registration drives and, on September 12, initiated workshops on nonviolent protest for the youth of Albany.

Albany young people launched their first nonviolent protest on November 1, 1961, the day that the Interstate Commerce Commission (ICC) mandated the DESEGREGATION of interstate transportation facilities. Students staged a SIT-IN at a Trailways bus station to test the new ICC ruling.

In the activist climate created by SNCC and the Albany students, the Albany Movement, a coalition of black civic improvement organizations, was formed on November 17, 1961, in the home of Dr. E.D. Hamilton, with Dr. William G. Anderson as president. Just five days later five black students were arrested for sitting in at the Trailways bus station and, on November 25, the Albany Movement held its first mass meeting at Mount Zion Baptist Church. Two days later—the day the sit-in students were put on trial—a march was held in protest.

Despite official harassment the test of the ICC ruling continued. On December 10, 1961, at the invitation of the Albany Movement, an integrated group of nine FREEDOM RIDERS arrived in Albany by train from Atlanta and was promptly arrested outside the railroad station on charges of disturbing the peace. On December 12 college and high school students mounted a mass march to protest the Freedom Riders' trial. Police arrested 267 marchers and, on the next day, arrested over two hundred more for marching at city hall without a permit.

The cycle of protests and arrests at Albany would become the pattern for many civil rights protests. National attention was focused on Albany on December 15, 1961, when Martin Luther King Jr. spoke at Shiloh Baptist Church and at Mount Zion Baptist Church. The next day King, with fellow activist Ralph David Abernathy, led 264 black residents of Albany in a march to pray in front of city hall. All were arrested then released on December 18 after securing an oral agreement from city officials to listen to the concerns of the Albany Movement at the first city commission meeting in January.

On January 9, 1962, before that meeting took place, U.S. district judge W. A. Bootle declared that racial segregation in voting procedures in Albany and in Dougherty County was unconstitutional. Just three days later, Ola Mae Quarterman was arrested for refusing to give up her seat to a white person on a segregated city bus. Her arrest triggered an Albany Movement–sponsored boycott of the white-run city bus system and other white-owned businesses. Although the Albany City Commission voted 5–2 on January 31 to deny the Albany Movement's request for an integrated committee and negotiations, the bus boycott forced the city's bus station to close on February 1, 1962.

With national attention still focused on Albany, King returned to the city on February 27 for trial and was found guilty of disorderly conduct and parading without a permit. His sentencing was delayed until July 10 when he and Abernathy returned to Albany. Sentenced to pay a fine of $178 or be imprisoned for forty-five days of hard labor, they chose the jail sentence as the more powerful indictment of the system they confronted. Their sentencing provoked demonstrations on July 11, 1962. After some demonstrators began throwing rocks at police, Albany police chief Laurie Pritchett asked the Albany Movement to cooperate in enforcing nonviolence rules. On July 13, the fine levied against King and Abernathy was anonymously paid, and the pair was released. Only later was it revealed that B. C. Gardner, a local white attorney, had donated the cash for the fine.

On July 20, seeking to bring an end to "disturbances" in Albany, federal judge Robert Elliot issued an injunction against further demonstrations in the city, stipulating that King and others were specifically barred from marching. Two days later Rev. Samuel Wells led a march without King that prompted the arrest of 160 people and triggered widespread violence throughout the city. In an effort to quell the violence, King called for a "day of penance." Although on July 25 federal judge Elbert Tuttle vacated the earlier injunction against demonstrations, a group of 217 demonstrators were subsequently arrested for conducting a prayer meeting in front of city hall.

Following Tuttle's decision Albany police chief Pritchett sought a new injunction on July 31, stating that his department had arrested 1,100 demonstrators since December. On August 4 city officials claimed victory in the struggle, declaring that by "firm and fair law enforcement" the police had "broken the back" of the Albany Movement. City officials also claimed that the "disturbances" had been caused by outsiders and by professional agitators, in this case numbering no more than thirty. In response King remarked that "segregation is on its deathbed in Albany, and the only thing uncertain about it is how costly the City Commission will make the funeral."

The city commission persisted in attempting to enforce segregation. On August 11, 1962, the Carnegie Library, Tift Park, and Tallulah Massey Park were all closed in response to desegregation attempts. Shortly afterward Thomas Chatmon Sr., the adviser who had helped the Monroe High School students form the NAACP Youth Council, declared his candidacy for Ward 2 of the city commission, and Albany Movement attorney C. B. King declared himself a candidate for U.S. representative from the Second District. In a direct attempt to intimidate voter registration workers, black churches in Terrell and Lee Counties were burned during August and September; and on September 1 the homes of four black families near Leesburg were sprayed with gunfire.

Despite violence and intimidation the momentum of the Albany Movement led to an attempt to integrate Albany High School on September 2, 1962—an effort that provoked a Ku Klux Klan rally, attended by more than a thousand, the next day. But the tide could not be stemmed. On March 6, 1963, in compliance with federal law, segregation ordinances were removed from the city statute book. Carnegie Library reopened on March 11, and blacks were admitted for the first time. On April 7 sixteen black students filed a civil suit seeking integration of all the schools in Dougherty County. The enrollment of the first black students at Albany High School in September marked the culmination of the work of the Albany Movement.

Suggested Reading

Carson, Clayborne. *In Struggle: SNCC and the Black Awakening of the 1960s.* 1981. Reprint, Cambridge: Harvard University Press, 1995.

ALEXANDER V. HOLMES COUNTY

Along with COLUMBUS BOARD OF EDUCATION V. PENICK (1979), the 1969 SUPREME COURT decision in *Alexander v. Holmes County* further amplified the landmark school DESEGREGATION decision handed down in 1954, in BROWN V. BOARD OF EDUCATION OF TOPEKA, KANSAS. Although *Brown* had specified the creation of "unitary" school systems, the Court did not make clear whether this requirement referred to a deliberate reapportionment on the basis of race or merely to some mixing of students and an end to all legal efforts to create or enforce segregation. *Alexander* provided a definition of a unitary system as one "within which no person is to be effectively excluded from any school because of race or color."

Suggested Reading

Kluger, Richard. *Simple Justice: The History of Brown v. Board of Education and Black America's Struggle for Equality.* New York: Random House, 1977.

Patterson, James T. *Brown v. Board of Education: A Civil Rights Milestone and Its Troubled Legacy.* New York: Oxford University Press, 2001.

ALGEBRA PROJECT

Civil rights activist, teacher, and mathematician ROBERT PARRIS MOSES started the Algebra Project in 1982 when Mary Lou Mehrling, his daughter's eighth-grade teacher in a Cambridge, Massachusetts, public school, asked him to help several of her students with the study of algebra. Moses, who had taught high school math in New York City and Tanzania, decided to give this class of inner-city students not merely help in basic algebra but sufficient skills to qualify for honors math and science courses in high school. Moses's tutelage produced the first students from the minority-oriented Open Program of the Martin Luther King School to pass a citywide algebra examination and qualify for ninth-grade honors geometry.

Moses was gratified by this success, but he also realized that it underscored a profound problem: the success was remarkable precisely because inner-city students were not expected to do well in mathematics. When Moses asked himself what algebra is for, and why we want children to study it, he concluded that the level of mathematical literacy necessary to master algebra was also necessary for full participation in the economic life of American society. Without it, students would be excluded from many opportunities offered by higher education, and adults would be segregated into lower-paying jobs and less satisfying lives. In Moses's words, "The main goal of the Algebra Project is to impact the struggle for citizenship and equality by assisting students in inner city and rural areas to achieve mathematics literacy. Higher order thinking and problem solving skills are necessary for entry into the economic mainstream. . . . Without these skills children will be tracked into an economic underclass" ("The Algebra Project Online," www.algebra.org).

The methods that Moses used in the Algebra Project were developed into a standardized curriculum for achieving mathematical literacy that is now a part of programs in many schools throughout the nation.

ALIANZA HISPANO-AMERICANA

The Alianza Hispano-Americana (AHA) was founded on January 14, 1894, in Tucson, Arizona, by Carlos I. Velasco, Pedro C. Pellón, and Mariano G. Samaniego, as a fraternal benefit society. Over the next sixteen years, branches were opened across much of the Southwest, and the AHA became the largest and best known Mexican American special interest group in the nation. Originally the AHA was a men-only organization, but women were admitted in 1913.

Although the AHA's ostensible purpose was to offer affordable life insurance and to provide social activities for Mexican Americans, its founding was also a response to long-standing hostility against Mexican Americans. In that sense the AHA was similar to any number of late-nineteenth-century fraternal aid organizations formed by ethnic immigrant groups in the United States. Besides performing many of the functions of today's labor unions and federal social security programs, the AHA undertook efforts to promote and preserve the culture of its members. At the same time the AHA promoted "Americanism" and assimilation by teaching its members about democratic traditions.

By the mid-1950s the AHA had become intensely active in the civil rights movement, especially in the fight against segregation. Although AHA membership was limited to Mexican Americans, in 1954 the AHA joined forces with the NATIONAL ASSOCIATION FOR THE ADVANCEMENT OF COLORED PEOPLE to assist in the fight against racial and ethnic discrimination; in 1957, it offered musician Louis Armstrong an honorary membership.

AHA membership reached its height in 1939 with 17,366 members. By the mid-1960s, however, membership had greatly diminished, and most of the organization's operations had ended. In the early 1970s a bankrupt AHA was forced into receivership, and its last president was convicted of embezzlement (the convictions were subsequently dismissed).

Suggested Reading

Gonzales, Sylvia Alicia. *Hispanic Voluntary Organizations.* Westport, Conn.: Greenwood, 1985.

Meier, Matt S., and Margo Gutierrez. *Encyclopedia of the Mexican American Civil Rights Movement.* Westport, Conn.: Greenwood, 2000.

ALIEN LAND LAW OF 1913

Under California's Alien Land Law of 1913—also known as the Webb-Heney Bill—"aliens ineligible for citizenship" and corporations in which the majority of the stock was owned by ineligible aliens had to "comply with the land ownership provisions of any treaty existing between the countries involved." The 1913 law also allowed the state to seize any land owned in violation of the law. Although the law did not specifically refer to Japanese residents or to members of other Asian groups, it was, in effect, directed against Asians, who were at that time ineligible for naturalization under U.S. immigration law. The ALIEN LAND LAW OF 1920 extended and strengthened the 1913 legislation.

Suggested Reading

McCain, Charles. *Japanese Immigrants and American Law: The Alien Land Laws and Other Issues.* New York: Garland Publishing, 1994.

ALIEN LAND LAW OF 1920

The California Alien Land Law of 1920, which was intended to eliminate loopholes in the ALIEN LAND LAW OF 1913, enacted further restrictions by barring immigrants from owning and leasing their own land. (The 1913 law had merely prevented those ineligible for citizenship from owning land.) The 1920 law also prohibited the transfer of land to noncitizens by sale or lease, and barred aliens who were not eligible for citizenship (that is, Asians, who were by federal law ineligible for naturalization) from holding land in guardianship for their children who were citizens. Moreover, if it was determined that land had been purchased in a citizen's name, but with money from an alien, the land would be subject to state seizure. In response to the law the Japanese government declared that it would bar immigration to the United States as of January 1, 1921.

Although the intent of the 1920 law was to drive the Japanese out of California agriculture, neither the 1913 nor the 1920 laws were vigorously enforced. Between 1912 and 1946 only seventy-six escheat (seizure) proceedings were filed in California under the Alien Land Laws.

Suggested Reading

McCain, Charles. *Japanese Immigrants and American Law: The Alien Land Laws and Other Issues.* New York: Garland Publishing, 1994.

ALIEN AND SEDITION ACTS

Soon after the end of the American Revolution, the Franco-American alliance that had been so important in the struggle for independence began to unravel as the Federalist government—first under George Washington, then under John Adams—recoiled at the excesses of the French Revolution. The Jay Treaty, signed by Britain and the United States in 1794, resolved disputes about frontier boundaries and other matters and improved relations with Britain but greatly alarmed the French, who feared that the United States was about to join forces with their greatest rival. Such fears were understandable—just a year before the Jay Treaty was concluded, President Washington had rebuffed the overtures of Edmond Charles Edouard Genêt, a French diplomat sent to secure U.S. aid for France in its war with England.

Despite Washington's rebuff, Citizen Genêt (as French revolutionary etiquette styled him) was warmly greeted by some of the American public, which he interpreted as a show of popular support. In defiance of the president he schemed with American privateers (mercenary mariners) to prey on British vessels in U.S. coastal waters. When the president warned him that he was in violation of U.S. sovereignty, Genêt threatened to make a direct appeal to the American people. At this, Washington asked the French government to recall Genêt. By this time, however, a new French revolutionary party, the Jacobins, had replaced the Girondists, the party to which Genêt belonged. The Jacobin government sent a new foreign minister to the United States and asked Washington to send Genêt back—under arrest. Observing strict neutrality, Washington refused to compel Genêt to return to a Jacobin guillotine, and Genêt ultimately chose to become a U.S. citizen—and even married the daughter of New York governor George Clinton.

Although the ending was happy for Genêt, this episode, along with the Jay Treaty, brought France and the United States to the brink of war, and President Washington quickly sent a new foreign minister, Charles Cotesworth Pinckney, to France, hoping to repair the breach. The French Directory refused to receive him, however, and Washington's successor, John Adams, dispatched a commission—consisting of Pinckney, John Marshall, and Elbridge Gerry—to Paris in a last-ditch effort to avert war by concluding a new Franco-American treaty of commerce. This time, in October 1797,

French prime minister Charles Maurice de Talleyrand-Perigord sent three agents to greet the American commissioners in Paris. The agents told them that before a treaty could even be discussed the United States would have to loan France $12 million and pay Talleyrand a personal bribe of $250,000. On April 3, 1798, an indignant Adams submitted to Congress the correspondence from Pinckney, Marshall, and Gerry, which designated the French agents as "X," "Y," and "Z." Congress, in turn, published the entire portfolio, and in this way the public learned of the "XYZ Affair."

On the heels of the XYZ Affair a small-scale, undeclared naval war—often called the Franco-American Quasi-War—broke out between the United States and France. During the summer of 1798, while the Quasi-War was being fought, a Federalist-dominated Congress passed the ALIEN AND SEDITION ACTS—the most repressive set of legislation ever enacted by an American legislature. The Alien and Sedition Acts consisted of the Naturalization Act (June 18, 1798), which required immigrants seeking U.S. citizenship to have been resident in the country for fourteen years instead of the originally mandated five; the Alien Act (June 25), which authorized the president to deport any alien he deemed dangerous; the Alien Enemies Act (July 6), which authorized the president, in time of war, to arrest, imprison, or deport nationals of any enemy power; and, most infamous of all, the Sedition Act (July 14), which banned any assembly convened "with intent to oppose any measure . . . of the government" and outlawed printing, uttering, or publishing anything "false, scandalous, and malicious" concerning the government.

The Sedition Act was an infringement of the constitutional rights to peaceable assembly and FREE SPEECH, and the legislation governing naturalization and the status of aliens was an effort to target many of the leading Democratic-Republicans—the liberal party that was opposed to the conservative Federalists. Many of these men were relatively recent refugees from turbulent Europe and had not been resident in the United States for anything approaching fourteen years; postponing citizenship for them would greatly erode the power base of the party to which they belonged.

Leading the Democratic-Republican opposition to the Alien and Sedition Acts was THOMAS JEFFERSON, who declared that if the acts were permitted to stand, "We shall immediately see attempted another act of Congress, declaring the President shall continue in office during life, reserving to another occasion the transfer of the succession to his heirs, and the establishment of the Senate for life." Jefferson drew up a set of resolutions attacking centralized governmental authority and promoting the sovereignty of the states. Because he was serving as vice president at the time, he thought it unseemly to make the resolutions public himself, so he persuaded the legislature of Kentucky (which had become a state in 1792) to publish them on November 22, 1799. James Madison, Jefferson's friend and protégé, had drafted a similar set of resolutions, which were published by the Virginia legislature on December 24, 1798.

Both the Kentucky and the Virginia resolutions argued that the Alien and Sedition Acts were unconstitutional and, therefore, not binding on the states. Jefferson's original draft explicitly maintained that a state not only had the right to judge the constitutionality of acts of Congress but also to "nullify" any acts it determined to be unconstitutional. The outright statement of nullification authority was too radical for the Kentucky legislature to accept, so the passage was suppressed in the final draft of the resolutions. Nevertheless, nullification was unmistakably implied in both the Kentucky and the Virginia documents.

While Jefferson did not contest the powers specifically given to the federal government by the Constitution, he did hold that federal acts outside of the constitutionally enumerated powers were inherently unconstitutional and, therefore, had no binding force on the states. In this respect, Jefferson was a "strict constructionist" on constitutional matters.

The Virginia and Kentucky resolutions galvanized opposition to repressive Federalism in the United States. Although the resolutions did not secure the immediate repeal of the Alien and Sedition Acts, they did ensure that, for the most part, the laws would be short-lived. Moreover, the electorate repudiated Federalism by electing Jefferson over Adams in 1800. In 1801, shortly after taking office, Jefferson sponsored the repeal of the Sedition Act. The Alien and Naturalization Acts expired without renewal in 1802. The Alien Enemies Act remained in force and has resurfaced on occasion, most notably during World Wars I and II.

Suggested Reading

Miller, John Chester. *Crisis in Freedom: The Alien and Sedition Acts.* Boston: Little, Brown, 1951.

Smith, James Morton. *Freedom's Fetters: The Alien and Sedition Laws and American Civil Liberties.* Ithaca: Cornell University Press, 1966.

ALI, MUHAMMAD (1942–)

Muhammad Ali was one of the greatest athletes in history. The three-time world heavyweight boxing champion was also an articulate, compelling, and controversial champion of civil rights, a protester against the VIETNAM WAR, and a dedicated member of the Black Muslims.

Ali was born Cassius Marcellus Clay Jr. on January 17, 1942, in Louisville, Kentucky. It was a white Louisville police officer, Joe Martin, who encouraged the teenaged Clay to box and train at Louisville's Columbia Gym, but Clay's early education in the "sweet science" was at the hands of an African American trainer, Fred Stoner. Clay won an Olympic gold medal at age eighteen, which he later renounced in protest against RACISM in the United States. At the time he won the medal, however, Clay had created such a sensation that he was signed to the most lucrative contract—a 50–50 split—ever negotiated by a neophyte professional boxer.

Clay's rapid rise came through a combination of dazzling ability and disarming wit. Just as Clay danced in the ring, he danced verbally, with seemingly improvised rhymes and elegant boasts that often grabbed headlines. In March 1964 Clay fought the much-feared heavyweight champion Sonny Liston. Before the match, Clay had described his style to reporters: "Float like a butterfly, sting like a bee." Using brains more than brawn, he went on to defeat the powerful Liston. At twenty-two, Clay was heavyweight champion of the world.

The year before his championship bout, after meeting the controversial activist and Black Muslim minister MALCOLM X, Clay had converted to Islam, a move that Malcolm X saw as a great inspiration to African Americans. Clay, Malcolm X told *Sports Illustrated,* "will mean more to his people than any athlete before him. JACKIE ROBINSON was . . . the white man's hero. But Cassius is the black man's hero" ("Muhammad Ali," in *Contemporary Black Biography,* vol. 16, Detroit: Gale Research, 1997). Shortly after his conversion, Clay was given the name Muhammad Ali ("Beloved of Allah") by Black Muslim leader Elijah Muhammad, and Clay stirred great public controversy by fully adopting his new name. In 1965 Ali retained his world heavyweight champion title with a stunning knockout of Liston.

In 1966 Ali announced that, if drafted, he would refuse to serve in the U.S. Army on the grounds of conscientious objection and in protest against the Vietnam War. His stance stirred public and official outrage, and in May 1967— immediately after Ali was drafted and announced that he would not submit to induction—the New York State Athletic Commission and the World Boxing Association suspended his boxing license and stripped him of his heavyweight title. In an interview with *Sports Illustrated* contributor Edwin Shrake, Ali commented: "I'm giving up my title, my wealth, maybe my future. Many great men have been tested for their religious beliefs. If I pass this test, I'll come out stronger than ever" ("Muhammad Ali," in *Contemporary Black Biography,* vol. 16, Detroit: Gale Research, 1997). Tried for violating the selective service laws, Ali was convicted and sentenced to five years in prison. Released on appeal, he managed to get his conviction overturned three years later. When Ali was victorious against Jerry Quarry in 1970, the fight signified to Ali's supporters in both the white and black communities a triumph of civil disobedience. Four months after the Quarry bout Ali lost the heavyweight crown to Joe Frazier in Manila. In a 1974 rematch Ali regained the championship. The following year he wrote a best-selling autobiography, *The Greatest: My Own Story.*

In 1980, when he lost a title bout to Larry Holmes, it was clear that Ali was not fighting up to his usual ability. Physicians initially diagnosed a thyroid deficiency, but it was eventually determined that his symptoms were those of Parkinson's disease, which had been brought on by head injuries suffered during his career. He was treated with L-dopa, which temporarily improved his condition but did not arrest the progress of the disease.

Ali's boxing career was over, but he became increasingly active in politics. In 1980, even before retiring from the ring, he had supported Democratic presidential candidate JIMMY CARTER. In February 1985 he worked (unsuccessfully) to secure the release of four Americans kidnapped in Lebanon.

Since his retirement from boxing in 1981 Ali has suffered increasingly from the symptoms of the Parkinson's syndrome, but he has remained active in civil rights, human rights, and social causes through the Muhammad Ali Foundation. He is also active as a missionary for the NATION OF ISLAM. Most of all, he continues to stand as a symbol of achievement, especially for black Americans. (See also, ISLAM, NATION OF.)

Suggested Reading

Early, Gerald Lyn, ed. *The Muhammad Ali Reader.* New York: Ecco Press, 1998.

AMERICAN-ARAB DISCRIMINATION COMMITTEE

The American-Arab Discrimination Committee (ADC) was founded in 1980 by former U.S. senator James G. Abourezk, D-S.D., and is currently the largest Arab-American grassroots organization in the United States, with chapters throughout the country. Nonsectarian and nonpartisan, the ADC is "committed to defending the rights of people of Arab descent and promoting their rich cultural heritage." Through its department of legal services, the ADC carries out selected immigration litigation and offers counseling in cases of discrimination and defamation. The organization also identifies and combats defamation and negative stereotyping of Arab Americans in the media and elsewhere. According to the organization's website (at www.adc.org), the ADC promotes what it calls "a more balanced" U.S. Middle East policy, and it offers itself as a reliable source of information for the news media and educators.

The ADC publishes a bimonthly newsletter, *ADC Times,* in addition to "Issue Papers" and "Special Reports," series that study important aspects of defamation and discrimination. The ADC also, from time to time, issues community studies; legal, media, and educational guides; and "action alerts," which call on members to act on issues necessitating grassroots response.

The ADC's department of educational programs maintains a research institute, known as ADCRI, which publishes information on issues of concern to Arab Americans and sponsors ADC's Reaching the Teachers campaign, which focuses on ensuring an accurate, objective, and fair portrayal of Arab history and culture in schools. In addition, ADCRI administers a year-round college internship program for Arab American students and others.

Suggested Reading

Abourezk, James. *Advise and Dissent: Memoirs of South Dakota and the U.S. Senate.* Chicago: Lawrence Hill Books, 1989.

Said, Edward, and Christopher Hitchens. *Blaming the Victims: Spurious Scholarship and the Palestinian Question.* New York: Norton, 2001.

AMERICAN ASYLUM FOR THE EDUCATION OF THE DEAF AND DUMB

Now known as the American School for the Deaf, the American Asylum for the Education of the Deaf and Dumb is the oldest existing school for the deaf in America. Founded on April 15, 1817, by Thomas Gallaudet and Laurent Clerc, in 1819 it became the first recipient of state aid to education in America when the Connecticut General Assembly awarded its first annual grant to the school. The following year, in the first instance of federal aid to elementary and secondary special education in the United States, Congress awarded the school a land grant in the Alabama Territory. State and federal aid to the American Asylum for the Education of the Deaf and Dumb set a precedent for government funding of programs for people with special needs.

Suggested Reading

Van Cleve, John. "American Asylum for the Education of the Deaf and Dumb." In *Gallaudet Encyclopedia of Deaf People and Deafness,* ed. John Van Cleve. New York: McGraw-Hill, 1987.

AMERICAN CIVIL LIBERTIES UNION

The stated mission of the American Civil Liberties Union (ACLU), the largest public interest law firm in the United States, is to fight civil liberties violations wherever and whenever they occur. With autonomous affiliated offices in all fifty states, a policy-setting national board of directors, and a New York–based national office to coordinate operations, the ACLU is able to maintain various national projects that address specific civil liberties issues, including AIDS discrimination, capital punishment, reproductive freedom, voting rights, workplace rights, and the rights of gay men and lesbians, immigrants, prisoners, and women. The national organization is staffed by more than sixty attorneys who collaborate with some two thousand volunteer attorneys in handling nearly six thousand cases annually.

In 1920, when Roger Nash Baldwin, Crystal Eastman, Albert DeSilver, and others founded the ACLU, the world had just emerged from World War I, and the United States was gripped by what was known as the Red Scare. Antiwar activists were still in prison, immigrants and others suspected of "red sympathies" or political radicalism were subject to imprisonment or summary deportation, racial segregation was supported in many places by law, and gender discrimination was routine. As of 1920 the U.S. Supreme Court had yet to uphold a single free speech claim under the First Amendment.

The first public interest law firm of its kind, the ACLU entered the fray by initiating a legal fight against the Palmer Raids, a campaign of harassment and deportation—led by U.S. Attorney General A. Mitchell Palmer—against trade unionists, including the members of the Industrial Workers of the World, and politically radical immigrants. During its first years of operation the ACLU secured the release of hundreds of imprisoned political activists.

The ACLU first captured widespread national attention in 1925 when it obtained the services of Clarence Darrow, the most famous defense attorney in America, to defend John T. Scopes, a Tennessee biology teacher charged with having violated a state ban on the teaching of evolution. Although the Scopes trial ended in Scopes's conviction (and the imposition of a trivial fine), the ACLU financed an appeal to the Tennessee Supreme Court, which upheld the statute but reversed the conviction.

In 1933 the ACLU supported the defense in a landmark anticensorship case, when the U.S. Customs Service declared James Joyce's novel *Ulysses* "obscene material" and banned its importation into the United States. Partly as the result of the ACLU's advocacy, a New York federal court that year lifted the ban.

In 1939 ACLU lawyers successfully argued before the U.S. Supreme Court in *Hague v. CIO* that a ban on union organizers' political meetings, imposed by the mayor of Jersey City, Frank Hague, was unconstitutional. The victory was a reaffirmation of the First Amendment right to freedom of assembly.

During World War II the ACLU was virtually alone in its condemnation of the internment of Japanese Americans and was unsuccessful in its efforts to challenge the constitutionality of internment. After the war, beginning in 1950, the ACLU once again confronted anticommunist hysteria by challenging the loyalty oaths that the federal government—and many state governments—demanded from employees. (Even public schoolteachers were often required to swear that they did not belong to the Communist Party or to any other "subversive organization.")

In 1954 the ACLU joined forces with the NATIONAL ASSOCIATION FOR THE ADVANCEMENT OF COLORED PEOPLE to challenge school segregation. ACLU backing was essential to the landmark decision in *BROWN V. BOARD OF EDUCATION OF TOPEKA, KANSAS,* which forever overturned the doctrine of "separate but equal" public schools. The 1954 action was among the first in a long line of civil rights legal struggles in which the ACLU participated.

ACLU attorneys were instrumental in arguing before the Supreme Court the 1973 cases of *ROE V. WADE* and *Doe v. Bolton,* securing a decision that held that the constitutional right to privacy encompassed a woman's right to ABORTION. The ruling decriminalized abortion and struck down all criminal abortion laws in the states.

In 1981, more than a half-century after the Scopes trial in Tennessee, the ACLU challenged a state statute requiring that the biblical story of creation be taught as a "scientific alternative" to the theory of evolution. Supporters of the statute, most of whom were fundamentalist or conservative Christians, viewed the law as a model for other states to emulate, but a federal court found the statute in violation of the constitutionally mandated separation of church and state because "creation science" was, in fact, religion, and state law could not require the teaching of religious doctrine.

Another high-profile free speech issue arose in 1989 when, after hearing ACLU arguments in *Texas v. Johnson,* the U.S. Supreme Court invalidated a Texas statute punishing "flag desecration" (chiefly, flag burning). The high court concurred with the ACLU that such "desecration" was an exercise of political speech protected by the First Amendment. In response, the U.S. House of Representatives passed an amendment to the Constitution to "protect" the flag against acts of desecration. The ACLU responded by arguing before Congress that such an amendment would be an assault on the very principles for which the flag stands, and the Senate voted down the proposed amendment.

The ACLU achieved a significant human rights milestone in 1996 when it successfully argued *Romer v. Evans* before the U.S. Supreme Court. For the first time in its history, the high court recognized the civil rights of lesbians and gay men by overturning a state constitutional amendment, passed by public referendum in Colorado, that prohibited the state and its municipalities from enacting any GAY RIGHTS laws.

In 1996 Congress passed the Communications Decency Act, which effectively censored the Internet by banning "indecent" speech. The following year, in *ACLU v. Reno,* the Supreme Court struck down the law.

According to the ACLU's website, it "played a major role, either as direct counsel or as a friend-of-the-court" in several other landmark Supreme Court cases, including *Chicago v. Morales* (1999), *LOVING V. VIRGINIA* (1967), *Gideon v. Wainwright* (1963), *West Virginia v. Barnette* (1943), *Powell v. Alabama* (1932), and *Gitlow v. New York* (1925). (See also JAPANESE INTERNMENT.)

Suggested Reading

Cottrell, Robert C. *Roger Nash Baldwin and the American Civil Liberties Union.* New York: Columbia University Press, 2001.

Walker, Samuel. *In Defense of American Liberties: A History of the ACLU.* 2d ed. Carbondale: Southern Illinois University Press, 1999.

AMERICAN COORDINATING COUNCIL OF POLITICAL EDUCATION

The American Coordinating Council of Political Education (ACCPE) was founded in Phoenix, Arizona, during the 1960s as a Mexican American political action group. It enjoyed local success during the decade, electing Mexican American candidates to city councils and school boards. At its peak, in the mid-1960s, the ACCPE had some 2,500 members in Phoenix and in nine other chapters throughout Arizona.

Suggested Reading

Meier, Matt S., and Margo Gutierrez. *Encyclopedia of the Mexican American Civil Rights Movement.* Westport, Conn.: Greenwood, 2000.

Rosales, Francisco A. *Chicano! The History of the Mexican American Civil Rights Movement.* Houston: Arte Publico Press, 1997.

AMERICAN COUNCIL OF THE BLIND

Founded in 1961, the American Council of the Blind (ACB) is the nation's largest membership organization for blind and visually impaired people; including both ACB members and those who are members of one or more of the seventy-one affiliated organizations, ACB's membership numbers in the tens of thousands. Although membership is not limited to blind or visually impaired people, legal blindness is a requirement to serve on the ACB board of directors (with the exception of the secretary and treasurer positions).

The purpose of the ACB is to improve the well-being of all blind or visually impaired people by serving as their representative national organization; by elevating their social, economic, and cultural levels; by improving their educational and rehabilitation facilities and opportunities; by cooperating with public and private institutions and organizations that provide services to blind and visually impaired people; by encouraging and assisting all blind or visually impaired people to develop their abilities; and by promoting greater understanding of visual impairment and the capabilities of blind or visually impaired people.

The ACB publishes the *Braille Forum,* a free monthly national magazine that contains articles on employment, legislation, and sports and leisure activities as well as information on new products and services and other topics of interest to blind or visually impaired people. The ACB also produces a monthly half-hour radio information program, *ACB Reports,* for radio reading information services (which provide spoken text of books and other printed material) and distributes public service announcements to television and radio broadcasters.

The ACB offers many service programs, including toll-free information and referral on all aspects of visual impairment, scholarship assistance to blind or visually impaired postsecondary students, public education and awareness training, support to consumer advocates and legal assistance on matters relating to visual impairment, leadership and legislative training, consultation with industry regarding the employment of blind or visually impaired people, and general advocacy of the rights of blind and visually impaired people. ACB's "Washington Connection" is a national hotline that reports on legislative regulations and initiatives affecting the visually impaired.

The issues of greatest concern to the ACB include improved education and rehabilitation services; the implementation and enforcement of the Americans with Disabilities Act of 1990; improved health care; the accreditation of agencies serving blind and visually impaired people; improved services to older blind or visually impaired Americans; the preservation and expansion, through litigation related to the Randolph-Sheppard Act, of the employment of blind or visually impaired people as fast-food service operators; publication in accessible media, such as Braille, audio recording, and large-print books; reauthorization and expansion of the Targeted Jobs Tax Credit legislation, which grants tax benefits to employers who hire people with disabilities; training to assist airline personnel in serving blind or visually impaired passengers; and implementation of the Air Carriers Access Act, which is designed to expand access to airline travel for blind and visually impaired travelers.

Suggested Reading

Braille Forum, American Council of the Blind, Washington, D.C.

AMERICAN COUNCIL OF SPANISH-SPEAKING PEOPLE

The American Council of Spanish-Speaking People (ACSSP) was a national Mexican American civil rights organization founded in Austin, Texas, in 1951, with funding from the Robert C. Marshall Trust in New York. The Marshall trust granted $53,000 over four years, but the ACSSP never became self-supporting. During its brief existence, before it closed in 1956, the ACSSP furnished grants-in-aid, legal assistance, and research services to Mexican American civil rights groups across the nation. Its principal focus was on litigating test cases to challenge discriminatory practices, including a segregation case in Glendale, Arizona; *Hernández v. Texas* (1954); the Anthony Ríos police brutality case in Los Angeles (1954); a California deportation case involving an alleged communist alien (1954); and a Winslow, Arizona, swimming pool desegregation case (1954). The ACSSP funded various school desegregation cases and was instrumental in the desegregation of Austin and Houston public housing and two Texas public schools.

Suggested Reading

Rosales, Francisco A. *Chicano! The History of the Mexican American Civil Rights Movement.* Houston: Arte Publico Press, 1997.

AMERICAN FEDERATION OF LABOR

An outgrowth of the Federation of Organized Trades and Labor Unions, which had been established in 1881, the American Federation of Labor (AFL), an association of skilled trade unions, was founded in 1886 by the controversial labor activist Samuel Gompers. Under Gompers's leadership the AFL worked to extract from the capitalist system the best possible deal for the skilled workers who made up its membership. The AFL did not ally itself with radical political parties and movements, nor did it permanently attach itself to the political mainstream; rather, its policy (in Gompers's words) was to reward "its friends and punish its enemies." Most consistently, however, its "friend" proved to be the Democratic Party: it was largely thanks to the AFL—which, by 1907, had grown to a membership of 1.7 million—that the party, badly crippled after the Civil War, grew into a formidable political presence.

In its pragmatic way the AFL advocated the rights of all labor, although its membership was restricted to skilled craftspeople and excluded unskilled industrial laborers. The AFL went through hard times during 1904–1914 when management pushed, often successfully, for "open" (non-unionized) shops. But the AFL enjoyed the benefits of government protection during World War I, so that by 1920 its ranks had swelled to some four million members. During the 1920s, however, the AFL lost ground to union-busting business practices, and with the onset of the Great Depression in the 1930s it was torn by internal dissent. Craft unions, the organizational constituency of the AFL, were ineffective in organizing mass industries such as auto and steel producers. Working within the AFL, John L. Lewis founded the Committee for Industrial Organization, which then became the Congress of Industrial Organizations (CIO). Eventually, the CIO grew so powerful that the AFL effectively broke with it in 1937. The AFL and CIO were reunited in 1955 and became the dominant labor organization in the United States.

Suggested Reading

Foner, Philip S. *History of the Labor Movement in the United States: From Colonial Times to the Founding of the American Federation of Labor.* New York: International Publishers Company, 1979.

Gompers, Samuel. *The Samuel Gompers Papers,* 8 vols. Champaign: University of Illinois Press, 1986–2000.

Greene, Julie. *Pure and Simple Politics: The American Federation of Labor and Political Activism, 1881–1917.* New York: Cambridge University Press, 1998.

AMERICAN FOUNDATION FOR THE BLIND

The American Foundation for the Blind (AFB) was founded in 1921 by Helen Keller, the remarkable deaf and blind author who devoted her life to advocacy of the rights and potential of disabled people. Keller was closely associated with the foundation for more than forty years.

The purpose of the AFB is to work in social, technological, and political ways to overcome or eliminate the barriers that prevent blind and visually impaired people from reaching their potential. The foundation's programs address such issues as literacy, independent living, and employment for the ten million Americans who are blind or visually impaired. Headquartered in New York City, the AFB has offices in Atlanta, Chicago, Dallas, and San Francisco, as well as a governmental relations office in Washington, D.C.

In addition to serving as an advocacy organization, the AFB is the leading publisher of professional materials on blindness and low vision and is a pioneer in the development of "talking books." The organization also maintains the Helen Keller Archives, which contains Keller's correspondence, documents, photographs, and memorabilia.

Suggested Reading

Herrmann, Dorothy. *Helen Keller: A Life.* Chicago: University of Chicago Press, 1999.

AMERICAN GI FORUM OF THE UNITED STATES

The American GI Forum of the United States, the nation's first organization of Hispanic veterans, was founded on March 26, 1948, in Corpus Christi, Texas, by Dr. Hector Perez-Garcia, a World War II veteran of the Army Medical Corps. At its founding, the focus of the organization was on fighting discrimination in housing, employment, and education. Within a single year, the American GI Forum had spread throughout the Southwest, with one hundred chapters springing up in Texas alone. New Mexico and Colorado followed suit, then Arizona and California. Today, there are five hundred American GI Forum chapters in thirty states.

The organization achieved national attention in 1949 when the widow of Private Felix Longoria attempted to make funeral arrangements for her husband. Longoria was a Mexican American soldier whose remains had just been returned from overseas, four years after he had been killed in action in the Philippines. The owner of the Rice Funeral Home in Three Rivers, Texas, agreed to arrange burial in the town's "Mexican" cemetery, but would not allow use of his chapel for the wake because local "whites" would object. With the help of Rep. Lloyd M. Bentsen Jr., D-Texas, and Sen. Lyndon B. Johnson, D-Texas, Garcia and the American GI Forum were able to arrange the burial of Longoria—with honors—in Arlington National Cemetery.

Suggested Reading

Meier, Matt S., and Margo Gutierrez. *Encyclopedia of the Mexican American Civil Rights Movement.* Westport, Conn.: Greenwood, 2000.

Rosales, Francisco A. *Chicano! The History of the Mexican American Civil Rights Movement.* Houston: Arte Publico Press, 1997.

AMERICAN INDIAN RELIGIOUS FREEDOM ACT OF 1978

Commonly known as the American Indian Freedom of Religion Act, AIRFA is a clarification of U.S. government policy regarding the protection of the religious freedom of Native Americans. The act was deemed necessary because of conflicts between some federal laws, including those protecting wilderness areas or endangered species, and Native American religions. For example, under federal law, Native Americans had been denied access to sacred sites and had been prohibited from possessing sacred objects, such as those made from eagle feathers, derived from endangered and protected animals. The act was amended in 1994 to provide some protection for the "traditional Indian ceremonial use of peyote," a substance otherwise defined by federal law as an illegal narcotic. (See also religion, freedom of. See Appendix A for the text of the American Indian Religious Freedom Act.)

Suggested Reading

Grinde, Donald A. Jr., ed. *Native Americans.* American Political History Series. Washington, D.C.: CQ Press, 2002.

Wunder, John R. *Native American Cultural and Religious Freedoms.* New York: Garland Publishing, 1999.

"AMERICAN PROMISE, THE" (LYNDON B. JOHNSON'S "SPECIAL MESSAGE TO THE CONGRESS, 1965")

After the successful passage of the Civil Rights Act of 1964, President Lyndon B. Johnson continued to advocate sweeping civil rights legislation. "The American Promise" speech, perhaps the strongest pronouncement any president has ever made on the subject of civil rights, was delivered to Congress on March 15, 1965, in support of the Voting Rights Act of 1965. (See Appendix A for the text of "The American Promise" speech.)

Suggested Reading

Davidson, Chandler. *Controversies in Minority Voting: The Voting Rights Act in Perspective.* Washington, D.C.: Brookings Institution Press, 1992.

Davidson, Chandler, and Bernard Grofman. *Quiet Revolution in the South: The Impact of the Voting Rights Act, 1965–1990.* Princeton: Princeton University Press, 1994.

Langston, Thomas S. *Lyndon Baines Johnson.* American Presidents Reference Series. Washington, D.C.: CQ Press, 2002.

AMERICAN PROTECTIVE LEAGUE

In April 1917, following the entry of the United States into World War I, the U.S. Department of Justice embarked on an extensive program to detect and root out "disloyalty" in the nation. The targets were chiefly pacifists and German sympathizers, but anyone who criticized the war or the war effort was at risk. As part of this initiative, the Department of Justice sponsored the American Protective League, a citizen auxiliary charged with reporting instances of suspected disloyalty. At best the creation of the APL amounted to an effort, on the part of an agency of the government, to set citizen against citizen. At worst, individual units of the American Protective League sanctioned vigilantism on the part of league members, including breaking and entering and searches and seizures.

By June 1917 there were American Protective League units in some six hundred American towns and cities, with membership totaling perhaps 100,000. Most members were prominent local merchants and business leaders—people active in such mainstream community organizations as the Masons, the Elks, the Moose, and the Odd Fellows. By the time the war ended in November 1918 the League claimed to have found three million individual cases of disloyalty.

Suggested Reading

Feuerlicht, Roberta Strauss. *America's Reign of Terror: World War I, the Red Scare, and the Palmer Raids.* New York: Random House, 1971.

Kennedy, Kathleen. *Disloyal Mothers and Scurrilous Citizens: Women and Subversion during World War I.* Bloomington: Indiana University Press, 1999.

Kornweibel, Theodore Jr. *"Investigate Everything": Federal Efforts to Compel Black Loyalty During World War I.* Bloomington: Indiana University Press, 2002.

AMERICANS FOR DEMOCRATIC ACTION

Americans for Democratic Action (ADA), an independent political organization, was founded in 1947 by liberal leaders including social activist and former first lady Eleanor Roosevelt, labor leader Walter Reuther, economist John Kenneth Galbraith, historian Arthur Schlesinger Jr., theologian Ronald Niebuhr, and liberal Democratic politician Hubert H. Humphrey. The organization is "dedicated to promoting individual liberty and economic justice" and currently enrolls some 30,000 members. Headquartered in Washington, D.C., the ADA has some twenty chapters across the country.

The ADA is not affiliated with any political party, but it works in coalition with civil rights groups, civil liberties groups, labor unions, and other organizations to promote social progress and economic justice. The ADA's first major action came in 1948 when it led the fight for the addition of a strong civil rights plank to the Democratic Party platform. In subsequent years the ADA organized opposition to the Vietnam War and to South African apartheid. The organization has advocated such causes as workers' rights, WOMEN'S RIGHTS, and increases in the minimum wage.

Currently, the ADA leads organized support for universal health care coverage and organized opposition to proposals to privatize public services such as Social Security, Medicare, and national parks. ADA supports equitable foreign trade agreements, meaning those that include safeguards for labor as well as the environment. In addition, the ADA is pro-choice, advocates drug education and rehabilitation over incarceration, and is committed to public education and to the protection and promotion of human and civil rights, including the preservation of affirmative action principles and programs.

Suggested Reading

Brock, Clifton. *Americans for Democratic Action: Its Role in National Politics.* Westport, Conn.: Greenwood, 1985.

AMERICANS WITH DISABILITIES ACT

The Americans with Disabilities Act (ADA), which was passed on July 26, 1990, is a long and complex piece of legislation intended to "establish a clear and comprehensive prohibition of discrimination on the basis of disability." The act prohibits discrimination in the following areas: employment; public services, including public transportation; public accommodations and services operated by private entities; and telecommunications (including telecommunications relay services for people with hearing or speech impairments and closed captioning of public service announcements). The ADA also provided for the creation of the Office of Technology Assessment, whose purpose is to study and determine the access needs of people with disabilities and to formulate means of meeting those needs.

Important SUPREME COURT cases related to the ADA include *PGA Tour, Inc. v. Martin* (2001), *Board of Trustees of the University of Alabama v. Garrett* (2001), and *Bragdon v. Abbott* (1998). (See Appendix A for representative excerpts of the ADA.)

Suggested Reading

National Council on Disability. *Equality of Opportunity: The Making of the Americans with Disabilities Act.* Washington, D.C.: U.S. Government Printing Office, 1999.

AMERICANS UNITED FOR THE SEPARATION OF CHURCH AND STATE

Founded in 1947, Americans United for the Separation of Church and State is an advocacy organization that works "to protect the [First Amendment] constitutional principle of church-state separation, a vital cornerstone of religious liberty." Headquartered in Washington, D.C., with a membership of sixty thousand representing all fifty states, the organization funds legal challenges to legislation and other measures that threaten church-state separation. Issues the organization addresses, and has addressed, include mandatory prayer in public schools, tax dollars for parochial schools, government intrusion into religious affairs, and "meddling in partisan politics" by religious groups. In addition to sponsoring litigation, Americans United publishes *Church & State,* a magazine devoted to church-state issues and directed especially at lawmakers, clergy, attorneys, scholars, journalists, and concerned citizens. The organization also produces issue papers, legislative alerts, reference materials, and books.

Suggested Reading

Curry, Thomas J. *Farewell to Christendom: The Future of Church and State in America.* New York: Oxford University Press, 2001.

Gaustad, Edwin S. *Church and State in America.* New York: Oxford University Press, 1999.

Wilson, John F., and Donald L. Drakeman, eds. *Church and State in American History.* 3d ed. Boston: Beacon Press, forthcoming.

AMISTAD MUTINY

On July 2, 1839, when the Spanish slaver *Amistad* was en route from a market in Havana to Puerto Príncipe, Cuba, fifty-three African slaves on board revolted. Under the leadership of one Joseph Cinqué, the slaves killed the captain and the cook but spared the Spanish navigator, intending to force him to sail back to Sierra Leone, their home. Instead, the navigator guided the vessel northward. After two months at sea, the *Amistad* was seized by U.S. Navy warships off Long Island, New York. The vessel and its human cargo were towed to port at New London, Connecticut, and the mutineers were incarcerated at New Haven. At the time, SLAVERY was legal in Connecticut.

The Spanish embassy demanded the return of the slaves to Cuba, and the U.S. government was inclined to comply: President Martin Van Buren, facing reelection, was eager to court proslavery southern votes. But New England abolitionists, led by Lewis Tappan, generated public sympathy for the slaves and financed a suit against the government to prevent their return.

At the trial, held in 1840 in a Hartford, Connecticut, federal court, the government argued that as slaves the mutineers were subject to nothing more or less than the laws governing conduct between slaves and their masters. Abolitionist attorneys argued that although slavery was indeed legal in Cuba, the importation of slaves from Africa was not, and provided evidence that the slaves had not merely been transported from one Cuban port to another but had originally been transported from Africa. In light of this evidence the judge ruled that the Africans were not property but kidnap victims who had the common-law right to escape their captors by any means necessary.

When the U.S. government appealed the case before the SUPREME COURT in 1841, the aged John Quincy Adams, Massachusetts congressman and former president, argued on behalf of the mutineers. The Supreme Court upheld the lower court's decision, and private and institutional donations financed passage home for the thirty-five surviving mutineers. They arrived in Sierra Leone in January 1842 along with five missionaries and teachers who intended to found a Christian mission.

The *Amistad* case did much to sharpen the focus on the slavery issue in the United States and revealed that abolitionists would find little support from the government. Spain, meanwhile, continued to demand indemnification for the Cuban vessel and its cargo. Over the next twenty years Congress debated the final disposition of the *Amistad* case in a sporadic and desultory manner. The commencement of the Civil War in 1861 rendered such debate moot.

Suggested Reading

Jones, Howard. *Mutiny on the Amistad*. 1987. Reprint, New York: Oxford University Press, 1997.

AMNESTY INTERNATIONAL

Perhaps the best-known international human rights organization, Amnesty International (AI) was launched in 1961, when British lawyer Peter Benenson published "The Forgotten Prisoners" in the *Observer,* a London newspaper. The article was an appeal for amnesty for two Portuguese students who had been imprisoned by their government for having raised their wineglasses in a toast to freedom. The appeal was widely reprinted—and led, in July 1961, to an international meeting attended by delegates from Belgium, France, Germany, Ireland, Switzerland, the United Kingdom, and the United States. The delegates resolved to establish "a permanent international movement in defense of freedom of opinion and religion." A small headquarters was opened at Mitre Court, London, and other AI groups were founded in France, Holland, Italy, Switzerland, and the former West Germany. From this beginning AI has grown into an organization with more than one million members, subscribers, and donors in more than 140 countries and territories. The principal headquarters, the International Secretariat, remains in London and coordinates the activities of more than 7,500 local, youth and student, and professional AI groups.

The stated mandate of AI, detailed in an "international statute," is to "free all prisoners of conscience"—that is, people who have been detained anywhere for their beliefs or because of their color, sex, language, or ethnic, national, or social origin. The one caveat is that such prisoners must not have used or advocated violence in pursuit of their cause or beliefs. In addition, AI works to ensure fair and prompt trials for political prisoners; to abolish the death penalty, torture, and cruel, inhuman, or degrading treatment of prisoners; and to bring an end to extrajudicial executions and so-called disappearances. Although AI's work has focused largely on government abuses, the organization also opposes abuses by opposition groups, including the taking of hostages and the torture or killing of prisoners and others. AI also assists asylum seekers who risk being returned to a country where they may be subject to violations of their basic human rights. AI cooperates with other nongovernmental organizations, with the UNITED NATIONS, and with regional intergovernmental organizations.

AI engages in regular fact-finding missions, sending delegates to locations worldwide to meet victims of human rights violations, to observe trials, and to interview local human rights activists and officials. The information thus obtained is then publicized to mobilize public pressure on governments—and on others who have influence—to stop human rights abuses. In addition to undertaking fact finding, AI organizes and sponsors public demonstrations, letter-writing campaigns, human rights education programs, fund-raising programs and concerts, lobbying efforts, and, in certain cases, targeted appeals on behalf of individuals. The AI website (www.amnesty.org) includes AI contact information for many nations.

Suggested Reading

Amnesty International, *Annual Report* London: Amnesty International, published annually.

Power, Jonathan. *Like Water on Stone: The Story of Amnesty International*. Boston: Northeastern University Press, 2001.

AMSTERDAM NEWS

The *Amsterdam News,* founded on December 4, 1909, by James H. Anderson, to serve New York City's African American community, grew into one of the most influential black newspapers of the twentieth century. Based in Harlem, the weekly paper always had a local emphasis—but because Harlem was regarded as the nation's premier black community throughout much of the century, the impact of the *Amsterdam News* was often national. At its peak, circulation was over 100,000, and by the mid 1940s it was one of four leading black newspapers, alongside the *Pittsburgh Courier,* the *Afro-American,* and the *CHICAGO DAILY DEFENDER*.

Anderson began the paper with a capital investment of $10 and published it out of his home at 132 West 65th Street, near Amsterdam Avenue, which was at the time part of a middle-class black neighborhood known as San Juan Hill. The paper was moved to Harlem in 1910, and from about 1910 through the 1920s it was edited by prominent African American journalists, including T. Thomas Fortune.

In 1926 the *Amsterdam News* was purchased by Sadie Warren, the wife of Edward Warren, one of the paper's first publishers. Ten years later she sold it to two West Indian physicians, Clelan Bethan Powell and Phillip M. H. Savory. It was under their leadership that the paper actively enlarged its focus to include national events, and a host of African American activists and politicians, including W.E.B. DU BOIS, ROY WILKINS, and ADAM CLAYTON POWELL JR., contributed regular columns and occasional articles.

Beginning during World War II, the *Amsterdam News* was in the forefront of the civil rights struggle. During the 1950s and 1960s the paper chronicled such events as the MONTGOMERY BUS BOYCOTT and the FREEDOM RIDES. It was the first newspaper to draw attention to MALCOLM X, and in 1958 it began publishing his by-line column, "God's Angry Man."

In 1971 the paper was purchased for $2.3 million by a group of investors that included Percy E. Sutton, a former Manhattan borough president; in 1983, it was sold to Wilbert A. Tatum and several Harlem business associates. In December 1997 Tatum's daughter, Eleanor Tatum, became publisher and editor in chief of the newspaper.

Suggested Reading

Pride, Armistead S., and Clint C. Wilson II. *A History of the Black Press.* Washington, D.C.: Howard University Press, 1997.

ANDERSON, MARIAN (1897–1993)

A contralto of compelling power, Marian Anderson would have made her mark on the basis of musicality alone. That she was an African American who achieved fame in the esoteric—and traditionally white—world of classical music performance made her life and career that much more extraordinary. For many African Americans Anderson became both an example and a symbol of the possibility of achievement. She also became the target of prejudice and a cause célèbre in the struggle to overcome racial discrimination.

Although Anderson's talent was recognized when she was a child, her family was too poor to afford formal training. Beginning at age six, she sang in the choir of Philadelphia's Union Baptist Church, taking bass, alto, tenor, and soprano parts. Congregation members raised enough money to send her to a music school for a year, and at nineteen she became a student of Giuseppe Boghetti, who appreciated her talent so deeply that he donated his lessons for a year. In 1925 Anderson won a contest that entitled her to a recital at Lewisohn Stadium in New York City with the New York Philharmonic Orchestra. Her appearance in August 1925 created a sensation.

Had Anderson been a young white woman, concert offers would no doubt have poured in, but the combination of audience expectations and rigid color barriers limited her opportunities. Nevertheless, she appeared with the Philadelphia Symphony and she toured African American college campuses in the South. Europe at that time was a much more hospitable environment for black artists than the United States, and in 1930 Anderson made her European debut in Berlin, then embarked on very successful European tours in 1930–1932, 1933–1934, and 1934–1935. Though she earned wide acceptance abroad—receiving scholarships and appearing before the monarchs of Denmark, England, Norway, and Sweden—Anderson remained little known in the United States. By the time of Anderson's New York concert debut—at Town Hall in December 1935—many Europeans regarded her as the greatest contralto of the age. Astonished New York audiences were similarly impressed.

After a triumphal tour of South America and, during 1938–1939, another European tour, Anderson returned to the United States. When her management attempted to book Constitution Hall, in Washington, D.C.—a facility owned by the Daughters of the American Revolution (DAR)—the DAR refused to allow a black woman to perform there. It was a heartbreaking development, but one that stirred widespread sympathy—and protest—over the injustice of denying a great American artist access to a hall that had been named for the Constitution, that was owned by those who traced their lineage to the fight for liberty, and that was located in the heart of the nation's capital. Among the many who raised their voices in protest was the first lady, ELEANOR ROOSEVELT—who, along with other prominent women, publicly resigned from the DAR. On the heels of Anderson's rejection, a recital was arranged for Easter Sunday at the Lincoln Memorial. Anderson drew a massive audience of 75,000.

To many, Anderson was best known for her stirring performances of African American spirituals; however, on January 7, 1955, she crossed an important color barrier when she became the first black singer to perform as a member of the Metropolitan Opera in New York City.

In 1957 Anderson—by then a national figure of long standing—published an autobiography, *My Lord, What a Morning.* That same year the U.S. Department of State sponsored a twelve-nation international goodwill performance tour, and in 1958 Anderson was named a delegate to the UNITED NATIONS. President LYNDON B. JOHNSON presented Anderson with the Presidential Medal of Freedom in 1963, and during 1964–1965, she made a grand international and national farewell tour.

Suggested Reading

Anderson, Marian. *My Lord, What a Morning: An Autobiography.* 1957. Reprint, Champaign–Urbana: University of Illinois Press, 2002.

ANGELOU, MAYA (1928–)

Born Marguerite Johnson in St. Louis, Missouri, Maya Angelou turned her harrowing early life into the stuff of autobiography, including prose and poetry rife with themes of racial, economic, and sexual oppression. Her first volume of autobiography, the 1970 memoir *I Know Why the Caged Bird Sings,* recounts her early life in the care of her paternal grandmother in rural Arkansas. Later memoirs—*Gather Together in My Name* (1974), *Singin' and Swingin' and Gettin' Merry Like Christmas* (1976), *The Heart of a Woman* (1981), and *All God's Children Need Traveling Shoes* (1986)—advance the story of her life.

At age eight, Angelou was raped by her mother's boyfriend. In 1940 she moved with her mother to San Francisco, where she worked as a cocktail waitress, a prostitute, a madam, a cook, and a dancer. It was while she was working as a dancer that she assumed the name Maya Angelou. Toward the end of the 1950s Angelou moved to New York City and joined the Harlem Writers' Guild, which nurtured her talent as a writer. Meanwhile she was appearing on stage in a production of George Gershwin's *Porgy and Bess* sponsored by the U.S. Department of State. As a member of this production Angelou toured twenty-two countries in Europe and Africa. After returning to the United States she began to study dance with Martha Graham and Pearl Primus, then made her nonmusical dramatic debut in a 1961 performance of Jean Genet's *The Blacks.* In 1961 she married a South African dissident and moved to Cairo, Egypt, where she worked as a correspondent for the *Arab Observer.* After divorcing her husband she moved to Ghana, where she worked on the *African Review.* In 1966 Angelou returned to the United States and settled in California, where she wrote a ten-part television documentary, *Black, Blues, Black,* about the role of African culture in American life. The series was aired two years later. In 1972, she adapted one of her short stories, "Georgia," into a screenplay for a feature film. In addition to writing for the screen, Angelou also acted on it—in *Poetic Justice* (1993), *How to Make an American Quilt* (1995), and other films. She directed *Down in the Delta* in 1998.

Although Angelou has been active in all the arts, she is best known for her poetry. Her collected works include *Just Give Me a Cool Drink of Water 'fore I Die* (1971), *And Still I Rise* (1978), *Now Sheba Sings the Song* (1987), and *I Shall Not Be Moved* (1990). In 1993 President-elect BILL CLINTON invited Angelou to compose and deliver a poem for his inauguration. Since 1981 Angelou has been a professor of American studies at Wake Forest University in Winston-Salem, North Carolina.

Suggested Reading

Angelou, Maya. *I Know Why the Caged Bird Sings.* New York: Random House, 1970.

———. *Even the Stars Look Lonesome.* New York: Random House, 1997.

ANTHONY, SUSAN B. (1820–1906)

Susan B. Anthony was one of the foremost American figures in the women's suffrage movement and served as president of the NATIONAL AMERICAN WOMAN SUFFRAGE ASSOCIATION from 1892 to 1900. She was instrumental in laying the groundwork that ultimately resulted in passage of the Nineteenth Amendment (1920) to the Constitution, which gave women the vote.

Born in Adams, Massachusetts, into a politically progressive Quaker family, Anthony was raised in Battensville, New York, where her family had moved in 1826. She was educated at the local public school and then at a boarding school outside Philadelphia. Trained as a teacher, she took a position in a Quaker seminary in New Rochelle, New York, in 1839, then taught in upstate New York at a "female academy" from 1846 to 1849. She then moved to her family's new home near Rochester, New York, where she became deeply involved in the abolition movement. At the same time, she became active in the temperance movement and, after becoming acquainted with Amelia Bloomer and ELIZABETH CADY STANTON, in the cause of women's suffrage as well.

The event that focused Anthony's energies on the rights of women was a rebuff she received in 1852 when she attempted to speak at a temperance meeting dominated by men. In response, she immediately organized the Woman's New York State Temperance Society (with Stanton as president), a move that gave her a platform to further not only the cause of temperance but that of WOMEN'S RIGHTS. Anthony earned a reputation as a tireless activist, and her high profile attracted publicity—as well as ridicule.

Anthony had a keen understanding of power and politics, and she relentlessly lobbied New York state legislators to revise New York's statutes regarding the property rights of married women. Thanks to her, new state laws passed in 1860 gave married women the right to own property in their own name, to earn a wage, and to keep that wage. The New York law became a model soon emulated by other states.

As the Civil War approached, Anthony became increasingly dedicated to the cause of radical abolition. In 1856 she was appointed chief New York agent for the American Anti-Slavery Society, which had been founded by WILLIAM LLOYD GARRISON. After the war broke out Anthony was a principal organizer of the Women's National Loyal League, which pushed for an emancipation proclamation.

The end of the Civil War brought the FOURTEENTH AMENDMENT, which was intended to guarantee all blacks the right to vote. Anthony campaigned to include women's suffrage in the amendment as well, and in 1866 she became corresponding secretary of the newly founded American Equal Rights Association. Despite her efforts and those of others, the Fourteenth Amendment did not extend suffrage to women. Undaunted, Anthony embarked on an organizing and speaking tour of Kansas, in 1867, in an effort to coax passage of a state enfranchisement law for women. The effort failed.

In 1868 Anthony (as publisher) and Stanton (as editor) joined forces to create *Revolution,* a periodical advocating women's rights. Anthony also represented the Working Women's Association of New York at the National Labor Union convention, and in 1869 she organized a women's suffrage convention in Washington, D.C. Later that year, with Stanton, she founded the National Woman Suffrage Association (NWSA). For its time, NWSA was a radically uncompromising group—so much so that a faction splintered off to join Lucy Stone's more conservative American Woman Suffrage Association. Nevertheless, Stone's group never commanded the attention the NWSA enjoyed.

By 1870 *Revolution* was crippled by debt, which Anthony sought to relieve by embarking on a whirlwind series of lecture tours. In 1872, determined to force a SUPREME COURT test of the Fourteenth Amendment—which, she argued, was constitutionally flawed in discriminating against women while enfranchising black men—Anthony voted in the general election at a Rochester, New York, polling place. She was arrested, tried, convicted, and fined. She refused to pay the fine, but officials, apparently unwilling to make a martyr of her, declined to press the case.

During the rest of the 1870s and through the end of the century, Anthony (often in company with Stanton) conducted campaigns in many states to secure the franchise for women. In 1890 the NWSA merged with the rival American Woman Suffrage Association to become the National American Woman Suffrage Association. In 1892, when Stanton stepped down as president of the newly created organization, Anthony replaced her. No longer derided by opponents, she was a figure of great national prominence and had become an icon of the women's movement and the cause of women's suffrage. Anthony retired as president of the National American Woman Suffrage Association in 1900. Four years later, at age eighty-four, she headed the U.S. delegation to the international Council of Women, an organization she had helped to found in 1888. Her hectic lifelong schedule as an activist did not prevent Anthony from writing extensively, including collaborating on the monumental six-volume *History of Woman Suffrage.*

Suggested Reading

DuBois, Ellen Carol. *Feminism and Suffrage: The Emergence of an Independent Women's Movement in America, 1848–1869.* Ithaca: Cornell University Press, 1999.

Harper, Judith E. *Susan B. Anthony: A Biographical Companion.* New York: ABC-CLIO, 1998.

ANTI-DEFAMATION LEAGUE

The Anti-Defamation League (ADL) was founded in 1913 by Sigmund Livingston, a Jewish attorney in Chicago, with the sponsorship of the Independent Order of B'NAI B'RITH. The goals of the league were, in Livingston's words, "to stop, by appeals to reason and conscience, and if necessary, by appeals to law, the defamation of the Jewish people . . . to secure justice and fair treatment to all citizens alike . . . to put an end forever to unjust and unfair discrimination against and ridicule of any sect or body of citizens."

Much of the ADL's early work focused on eliminating the many negative images and stereotypes of Jews that appeared in print, on stage, and in the movies. In this effort the ADL proved extraordinarily successful. As the organization grew, expanded, and matured, its mandate was enlarged to encompass all anti-Semitism and all forms of bigotry in the United States and abroad. According to the organization's recent literature, "ADL combats international terrorism, probes the roots of hatred, advocates before Congress, comes to the aid of victims of bigotry, develops educational programs, and serves as a public resource for government, media, law enforcement and the public, all toward the goals of countering and reducing hatred."

Today the ADL serves as a clearinghouse for information on organized bigotry, particularly anti-Semitism. The organization also researches and monitors extremists, from obscure domestic militia groups to international terrorists. Two organizations within the ADL—the William and Naomi Gorowitz Institute on Terrorism and Extremism and the Leon and Marilyn Klinghoffer Memorial Foundation—work to combat terrorism in the United States, the Middle East, and elsewhere by promoting counterterrorism legislative initiatives and other programs.

The ADL has also addressed the problem of hate crimes by creating a model statute that has been used as the basis for legislation in approximately four-fifths of the states. Through its *Law Enforcement Bulletin,* the organization advises some 5,000 law enforcement professionals on developments in the fight against hate crimes and what it calls "extremism."

On the international scene, the ADL maintains several programs in support of Israel and "combats efforts to delegitimize Israel by the Arab world, the international community and the media."

Suggested Reading

Anti-Defamation League. *Annual Report.* New York: ADL, published annually.

ANTI-SALOON LEAGUE

Founded in 1893 by Howard Hyde Russell, an Ohio Congregationalist minister and temperance advocate, the Anti-Saloon League became one of the major forces in bringing about passage of the Eighteenth Amendment, Prohibition, in 1919. Under the leadership of Wayne Wheeler, whom Russell recruited out of Oberlin College, the league merged with a similar Washington, D.C.–based group to become a national political force. Rather than back the small and ineffective Prohibition Party, the league worked with the two major parties (Republicans and Democrats) to support candidates who favored Prohibition.

When the United States entered World War I, league propaganda shaped Prohibition into a patriotic cause by vilifying Germans and German Americans—who had, according to the league, introduced beer into American life and were among the chief purveyors of the beverage. The Anti-Saloon League published a newspaper, the *American Issue,* in which the anti-German theme was prominent. The league's influence diminished rapidly after the Eighteenth Amendment was repealed in 1933.

Suggested Reading

Hamm, Richard F. *Shaping the Eighteenth Amendment: Temperance Reform, Legal Culture, and the Polity, 1880–1920.* Chapel Hill: University of North Carolina Press, 1995.

Kerr, K. Austin. *Organized for Prohibition: A New History of the Anti-Saloon League.* New Haven: Yale University Press, 1985.

ARRESTS, LAWS GOVERNING

Police powers of arrest are restricted by the Fourth Amendment to the Constitution, which forbids unreasonable searches or seizures, including arrests without probable cause. Within this framework, state laws define what constitutes an arrest, who may make an arrest, and when an arrest may be made.

Although there is variation from state to state, most state laws define arrest as taking a person into custody for the purpose of presenting that person before a magistrate to answer for the commission of a crime. Arrests may be made by police or other peace officers or by private individuals ("citizen's arrest"). Provided that a crime is committed in the presence of the arresting officer, or the arresting officer has probable cause to believe that a person has committed a felony, no warrant is required to make an arrest. Whenever possible, however, police officers will secure a warrant because possession of a warrant places upon the defense the burden of proving that the arrest was illegal. Arrests for non-felony offenses (misdemeanors) generally require that the offense be committed in the presence of the arresting officer. In some states important exceptions to this rule exist; in Florida, for example, the arresting officer need not have witnessed a retail theft or a "gas skip" (driving off from the gas pump without paying) to make an arrest. In many, but not all, states a private citizen who witnesses a misdemeanor may make an arrest and then turn the suspect over to the police.

Most warrant arrests are restricted to daytime hours unless a magistrate specifically allows a nighttime arrest (through what is called a *nightcap provision*). Officers may use "reasonable force" to make an arrest—that is, the amount of force any reasonable, prudent person would use in similar circumstances. This limitation prohibits gratuitous or excessive brutality, such as striking a suspect who does not resist. After identifying himself as a police officer, stating the purpose for entry, and demanding admittance, an officer is permitted to break an inner or outer door, if necessary, to make an arrest. However, a "no-knock" entry may be legal in cases where evidence would probably be immediately destroyed if the police announced their presence and intention to enter. Doors or windows may be broken to arrest a suspect who attempts an escape. If a suspect takes refuge in a locked vehicle, the officer may break the window.

The use of deadly force is permitted in an arrest if the suspect is threatening the officer or another person with a weapon; if the officer has probable cause to believe that the suspect has committed a crime involving the infliction or earnest threat of serious bodily harm; or if the suspect is fleeing after committing an inherently violent crime and the officer has given a clear warning. The use of deadly force is usually further governed by state statutes and departmental policies.

Suggested Reading

Klein, Irving J. *Principles of the Law of Arrest, Search, Seizure, and Liability Issues.* Coral Gables, Fla.: Coral Gables Publishing, 1994.

ARTICLES OF CONFEDERATION

Drafted in 1777 and ratified in 1781, the Articles of Confederation were the first constitution of the United States. The principal author of the document was John Dickinson, a Pennsylvania delegate to the Continental Congress. As Dickinson originally conceived them, the Articles framed a powerful federal government. In debate over the Articles, however, the states laid claim to more rights, especially the exclusive authority to levy taxes. What finally emerged under the Articles as they were ratified was not so much a single nation but a "firm league of friendship" among thirteen sovereign states. While the Articles provided for a permanent national Congress consisting of two to seven delegates from each state (though each state was given one vote, regardless of population), they created neither an executive nor a judicial branch.

Although charged with conducting foreign policy, declaring war, making peace, and maintaining an army and navy, Congress was essentially powerless under the Articles and entirely at the mercy of the states. Congress could issue directives and even enact laws, but it had no means of enforcing them. Indeed, the states were explicitly free to comply or not. Nor, as mentioned, did Congress have authority to levy or collect taxes.

The deficiencies of government under the Articles of Confederation became apparent after a very few years, and in 1789 the document was replaced by the current (repeatedly amended) Constitution.

Suggested Reading

Jensen, Merrill. *The Articles of Confederation: An Interpretation of the Social-Constitutional History of the American Revolution, 1774–1781.* Madison: University of Wisconsin Press, 1970.

ARYAN NATIONS

Also known as the Church of Jesus Christ Christian, Aryan Nations is perhaps the most widely known paramilitary white-supremacist and anti-Semitic organization now active in the United States. In its current configuration, Aryan Nations was founded in the mid-1970s by Rev. Richard Butler, and, until recently, was headquartered near Hayden Lake, Idaho. Butler built his organization on the basis of an earlier group that had probably been founded in the 1940s in opposition to the creation of the state of Israel.

Butler's Church of Jesus Christ Christian is one of several hundred churches affiliated with the Identity, a quasi-theological movement that holds that Anglo-Saxons, not Jews, are the "chosen people" of the Old Testament. Identity doctrine also holds that nonwhites are subhuman "mud people," and are "children of Satan" (see www.christian-aryannations.com). Butler has claimed some 400 members in the United States and 6,000 worldwide, but most outside observers believe that membership is between 150 and 200.

As its name suggests, Aryan Nations is a neo-Nazi organization that openly advocates anti-Semitism and the establishment of a white supremacist state. Aryan Nations is linked to the National Alliance, a neo-Nazi group, and to a secret society known as the Silent Brotherhood, which is sometimes referred to simply as the Order. The Order, which includes some members of Aryan Nations, the National Alliance, and the Ku Klux Klan, has reportedly plotted a coup to overthrow the federal government and has been implicated in crimes ranging from counterfeiting, bank robbery, and armored-car holdups to murder—all aimed at raising money for its revolutionary efforts.

The Order seems to have been silenced with the death of its leader, Robert J. Matthews, in a shootout with federal agents in December 1984. A number of its members were convicted of felonies and imprisoned following this confrontation. Aryan Nations, however, continues to be active, and in 1996 published a "Declaration of Independence" for the Aryan race on its website, www.christian-aryannations.com.

Aryan Nations has periodically convened the World Congress of Aryan Nations at Hayden Lake. Typically, the congresses have offered courses in urban terrorism and guerilla warfare. Aryan Nations is loosely associated with various militia movements (paramilitary vigilante organizations, typically with a white supremacist slant) and actively recruits prison inmates through the Aryan Brotherhood prison outreach program.

In September 2000 an Idaho jury ordered Richard Butler to pay a $6.3 million civil judgment to Victoria Keenan and her son Jason, who, in 1998, were chased, beaten, and then shot at by Aryan Nations guards. The Keenans were awarded the Hayden Lake property in a bankruptcy sale, and the Carr Foundation—established by businessman Gregory Carr—bought it for $250,000, then donated it to Northern Idaho College, which planned to turn it into a "peace park." Although Aryan Nations chapters remained active elsewhere in the United States after the closure of the Idaho headquarters, Butler himself fell victim to a coup early in 2002 and was ousted as leader of Aryan Nations by Pastor Ray Redfeairn.

Suggested Reading

Quarles, Chester L. *The Ku Klux Klan and Related American Racialist and Antisemitic Organizations: A History and Analysis.* Jefferson, N.C.: McFarland & Co., 1999.

Walters, Jerome. *One Aryan Nation under God: How Religious Extremists Use the Bible to Justify Their Actions.* Naperville, Ill.: Sourcebooks, 2001.

ASIAN-AMERICAN LEGAL DEFENSE AND EDUCATION FUND

The Asian-American Legal Defense and Education Fund (AALDEF) was founded in 1974 by a group of lawyers, law students, and community activists who "believed that the law should be used as a tool to achieve social and economic justice for Asian Americans and all Americans."

Currently the AALDEF addresses issues in a number of areas. In 1985 it reached an agreement with the New York City Board of Elections to provide, for the first time, bilingual materials and assistance for Chinese-speaking voters. In 1992, through its Voting Rights Project, the organization led the nation's first successful campaign, under the federal Voting Rights Act, to secure fully translated ballots for Chinese American voters in New York City.

The AALDEF programs also target anti-Asian violence and police brutality. The organization regularly provides legal assistance and representation to Asian American victims of hate crimes and police brutality. During the 1990s AALDEF legal advocacy resulted in the passage of model state legislation that increased penalties for bias crimes in New Jersey.

From its founding the AALDEF has been active in efforts to obtain redress for the 120,000 Japanese Americans who were unjustly interned during World War II. The organization has provided legal representation to former internees in their redress claims and has submitted amicus briefs and provided testimony in support of redress to Congress and to the U.S. Commission on the Wartime Relocation and Internment of Civilians.

On the labor front, the AALDEF works toward the elimination of sweatshops in immigrant communities and maintains workers' rights clinics to provide legal assistance in labor matters. Low-income tenants also receive legal assistance from the AALDEF, which in 1986 won a landmark ruling from the New York Court of Appeals requiring that the impacts of new development on low-income tenants and small businesses be considered under state environmental laws.

Since its founding the AALDEF has defended equal opportunity for Asian Americans by filing numerous amicus briefs in the Supreme Court supporting affirmative action programs. The organization is also vigorously active in the area of immigration law reform and in the defense of the rights of individual immigrants.

In 1992 the AALDEF, with the Asian Law Caucus in San Francisco and the Asian Pacific American Legal Center in Los Angeles, founded the National Asian Pacific American Legal Consortium (NAPALC), which is headquartered in Washington, D.C.

Suggested Reading

Avakian, Monique. *Atlas of Asian-American History.* New York: Facts on File, 2002.

ASIAN LAW CAUCUS

The nation's oldest legal and civil rights organization serving low-income Asian-Pacific American communities, the Asian Law Caucus—founded in 1972 in San Francisco—undertakes community education and organizing, provides direct legal services, and engages in litigation calculated to achieve strategic impact.

Since its founding the Asian Law Caucus has litigated cases related to sweatshops, wage violations by subcontractors, compensation for World II–era internment of Japanese Americans, discriminatory arrests of youths in San Francisco's Chinatown, discrimination based on accent, and naturalization for immigrants with disabilities. (See also Japanese internment.)

Suggested Reading

Avakian, Monique. *Atlas of Asian-American History.* New York: Facts on File, 2002.

ASIATIC EXCLUSION LEAGUE

The Asiatic Exclusion League developed in San Francisco in 1907 from the Japanese Exclusion League. Although it was founded chiefly by California farmers, the Asiatic Exclusion League was not an agricultural organization. Its principal purpose was to make common cause with other groups that were fearful of competition from Asian immigrants, principally Japanese. Thus, among those who attended the first meeting of the organization were labor leaders Patrick Henry McCarthy and Olaf Tveitmoe of the Building Trades Council of San Francisco and Andrew Furuseth and Walter McCarthy of the Sailors' Union. All four of these men were themselves immigrants, albeit from Europe. Tveitmoe was named the first president of the organization.

Most historians see the founding of the league as the commencement of the anti-Japanese movement in California. Largely because of pressure from the league, the San Francisco school board segregated Japanese schoolchildren from whites in 1906; and, in response to growing anti-Japanese prejudice, President Theodore Roosevelt negotiated the Gentleman's Agreement in 1907, under which the Japanese government agreed to restrict the immigration of laborers to the United States.

Suggested Reading

Avakian, Monique. *Atlas of Asian-American History.* New York: Facts on File, 2002.

Daniels, Roger. *The Politics of Prejudice: The Anti-Japanese Movement in California and the Struggle for Japanese Exclusion.* Berkeley: University of California Press, 1978.

ASSOCIATION FOR PERSONS WITH SEVERE HANDICAPS

The Association for Persons with Severe Handicaps, known as TASH, is an international association of people with disabilities and their family members, other advocates, and professionals. A civil rights organization for, and of, people with mental retardation, autism, cerebral palsy, physical disabilities, and other conditions that make full social integration a challenge, TASH advocates the inclusion of all people in all aspects of society.

Headquartered in Baltimore, TASH has more than thirty chapters and members in thirty-four countries and territories. The organization works to eliminate physical and social obstacles that prevent, interfere with, or diminish equity, diversity, and quality of life, and it focuses its efforts on those who are most likely to have their rights abridged, are perceived by traditional service systems as being most challenging, and are most at risk of being excluded from the mainstream of society or of living, working, playing, or learning in segregated environments. The organization creates opportunities for collaboration among families, professionals, policy makers, and other advocates; provides advocacy for equity, opportunities, social justice, and rights; publishes and distributes information; and works toward the elimination of segregated institutions, segregated schools and classrooms, and sheltered work environments, advocating instead systems and services within the mainstream that supply high-quality, individualized, and inclusive support. TASH supports legislation, litigation, and public policy that are consistent with its goals.

TASH was founded in 1974 as the American Association for the Education of the Severely/Profoundly Handicapped (AAESPH). In 1980, it became the Association for the Severely Handicapped. Although its name was changed in 1983 to the Association for Persons with Severe Handicaps, the TASH acronym persisted.

Suggested Reading

TASH Connections, published monthly by TASH.

ASSOCIATION ON AMERICAN INDIAN AFFAIRS

The Association on American Indian Affairs (AIAA) was founded in 1922 to promote the welfare of the American Indians, Aleuts, and Inuits of the United States. The organization's missions include protecting the constitutional rights of American Indians, Aleuts, and Inuits; improving their health and economic and educational conditions; and supporting the perpetuation of their cultures. Membership in AIAA is open to any person who wishes to help the AIAA's constituent groups.

To increase public awareness and to help create a constructive national policy, the AIAA gathers and disseminates facts about the welfare of American Indians, Aleuts, and Inuits. Specific AIAA initiatives include efforts to preserve sacred sites and to repatriate human remains (through the provisions of the Native American Graves Protection and Repatriation Act), and scholarship and health-related programs for Native Americans, Aleuts, and Inuits.

Suggested Reading

Echo-Hawk, C. Roger, and Walter R. Echo-Hawk. *Battlefields and Burial Grounds: The Indian Struggle to Protect Ancestral Graves in the United States.* Minneapolis: Lerner Publications Co., 1994.

Mihesuah, Devon, ed. *Repatriation Reader: Who Owns American Indian Remains?* Lincoln: University of Nebraska Press, 2000.

"ATLANTA COMPROMISE" SPEECH (BOOKER T. WASHINGTON)

On September 18, 1885, in an address made at the Atlanta Cotton States and International Exposition, Booker T. Washington articulated what came to be known as the "accommodationist" or "compromise" position in race relations. Washington expressed a willingness to accept segregation and social and political disfranchisement in exchange for white encouragement of black economic and educational progress. It was a position that the National Association for the Advancement of Colored People was formed, in 1909, explicitly to oppose. (See Appendix A for the text of the "Atlanta Compromise" speech.)

Suggested Reading

Hawkins, Hugh, ed. *Booker T. Washington and His Critics: Black Leadership in Crisis.* Boston: D. C. Heath, 1975.

Washington, Booker T. *Booker T. Washington Papers.* 14 vols. Champaign: University of Illinois Press, 1972–1989.

ATTAINDER

Attainder was a provision in English law that extinguished the civil and political rights of anyone convicted of treason or a felony. In the case of treason, the traitor's lands were permanently forfeited to the king. The person "attainted" was also barred from inheriting or transmitting property—and, by virtue of the doctrine of "corruption of blood," lost the rights of inheritance and bequest: that is, the traitor's descendants were barred from inheriting any rights to title that had belonged to the attainted. In the case of felony the felon's lands were forfeited to the king for a year and a day, then permanently forfeited (in medieval parlance, *escheated*) to the lord from whom the attainted held his tenure.

Attainder in the case of felony was eliminated under the Magna Carta (1215), and all forms of attainder—except in the case of treason— disappeared during the nineteenth century. In the United States, attainder is specifically barred by the Constitution, Article III, section 3: "The Congress shall have Power to declare the Punishment of Treason, but no Attainder of Treason shall work Corruption of Blood, or Forfeiture except during the Life of the Person attainted."

In English law a person could be attainted by legislative act, without judicial trial. In the case of a capital sentence (that is, the death penalty) such an act was called a bill of attainder; if a lesser punishment was decreed, the act was called a bill of pains and penalties. From late medieval times through the end of the eighteenth century, the English Parliament commonly enacted bills of attainder. The last time a bill of pains and penalties was issued was in 1820, against Queen Caroline, the wife of George IV, on charges of adultery. The bill was not passed.

In colonial America some legislatures occasionally enacted bills of attainder and bills of pains and penalties. These were specifically barred by the U.S. Constitution in Article I, section 8. Subsequently, the U.S. Supreme Court used the concept of attainder, and the prohibition against it, in a number of important decisions. For example, in *Cummings v. Missouri* and *Ex parte Garland,* (both 1867), the high court struck down "test oaths," which were intended to disqualify Confederate sympathizers from practicing certain professions. In *United States v. Lovett* (1946), the Court ruled that a section of an appropriation bill that barred payment of salaries to named government officials who had been accused of being subversive was a bill of attainder and therefore invalid.

Suggested Reading

Hudson, John. *The Formation of the English Common Law: Law and Society in England from the Norman Conquest to Magna Carta.* London and New York: Longmans, 1996.

ATTICA PRISON RIOT

On September 9, 1971, in a carefully planned uprising, the prisoners in the D Block of the Attica Correctional Facility in upstate New York took over the prison. During the initial onslaught, fifty correctional officers and civilian employees were beaten and taken hostage—including one, correctional officer William Quinn, who was so badly injured that the inmates soon freed him. The inmates, who numbered between 1,200 and 1,500, presented a list of demands that included safe passage out of the country and amnesty for the takeover. When officials learned, however, that Officer Quinn had died of his injuries, amnesty was ruled out of the question.

After state officials had negotiated with the inmates for four days, New York governor Nelson A. Rockefeller ordered a full-scale assault to retake the prison and rescue the hostages. On September 13, supported by National Guard helicopters deploying chemical agents (mainly tear gas and nausea-inducing gas), a rescue force of some two hundred New York State police and two corrections officers stormed the prison. The operation was disastrously bloody: ten of the hostages were killed, along with thirty-two inmates.

The worst prison riot in American history, the Attica uprising took place at a time of national upheaval over racial injustice and minority rights. Because the U.S. prison population was disproportionately African American and Latino, some commentators have argued that that many inmates were in fact political prisoners. Certainly, the Attica rebels' demands were built on this argument. The fact that Governor Nelson Rockefeller, scion of one of the wealthiest families in America, directed the response further heightened the political drama and led many contemporary commentators to see the Attica riot as a classic confrontation between the oppressed and the ruling class. Even those who did not take this view, however, regarded Attica as the symbol of a penal system that degraded inmates. Horrific as Attica was, it succeeded in raising national awareness of the rights of prisoners.

Suggested Reading

Wicker, Tom. *A Time to Die.* New York: Times Books, 1975.

ATTUCKS, CRISPUS (CA. 1723–1770)

Crispus Attucks was one of five Americans killed in the Boston Massacre of March 5, 1770. Attucks, the first to fall, is generally identified as the first patriot casualty in the American struggle for independence.

Little is known about the life of Crispus Attucks; although most historians believe that he was a black man, some scholars hold that his ancestry was a mixture of African and Natick Indian. What is known, however, is that in 1750 a resident of Framingham, Massachusetts, advertised a reward for the recovery of a runaway slave named Crispus; most historians believe that the slave was Crispus Attucks. Historians also believe that Attucks made his living as a hand aboard whaling vessels.

The Boston Massacre began when a British soldier attempted to secure part-time employment at Grey's Rope-walk, a wharf-side business. What began as an expression of local outrage in the form of heated words had grown into a riot by late evening, and when a British redcoat was struck by a colonist, other troops opened fire, killing three Americans and fatally wounding two others.

Those who favored American independence and hoped to fan the incident at Boston into a cause for immediate revolution had Attucks's body carried to Faneuil Hall, where it lay in state until March 8. On that day, all five victims were interred in a common grave. A monument to Attucks was unveiled on the Boston Common in 1888.

Suggested Reading

Neyland, James. *Crispus Attucks: Patriot.* New York: Holloway House, 1995.

B

BAKER V. CARR

The Supreme Court decision in *Baker v. Carr* (1962), a legal landmark in the area of legislative reapportionment, laid the doctrinal foundation for federal courts to exercise jurisdiction enforcing the equal protection clause of the Fourteenth Amendment, even in matters traditionally deemed political rather than judicial. The reapportionments that have resulted from this case have helped to ensure that representation in state and federal legislatures more accurately reflects the sentiments of voters.

Prior to *Baker v. Carr,* malapportionment was common: in many places, even though the urban population was greater, voting districts favored rural areas, an arrangement that was intended to keep certain groups—primarily urban minorities—from having their votes counted equally in the electoral process. As a result, political influence in some areas was largely in the hands of a minority of voters.

In 1960 Charles Baker, an African American voter, brought suit in federal district court against the state of Tennessee, arguing that the state's failure to reapportion in response to actual population diluted his vote, and therefore violated the equal protection clause (Joe Carr, named as defendant, was a state elections official). The court dismissed the complaint, claiming that it had no authority to decide a political question. Baker appealed to the U.S. Supreme Court, which ruled that a case that raised a political issue could and would be heard. This decision opened the way for a host of suits on legislative apportionment throughout the country, many of which resulted in districts being redrawn, thereby reducing disparities in voting power.

Suggested Reading

Grofman, Bernard N. *Voting Rights, Voting Wrongs: The Legacy of Baker v. Carr.* Washington, D. C.: Priority Press Publications, 1990.

Keyssar, Alexander. *The Right to Vote: The Contested History of Democracy in the United States.* New York: Basic Books, 2001.

BAKER, ELLA JO (1903–1986)

An activist with the National Association for the Advancement of Colored People (NAACP) and the Southern Christian Leadership Conference (SCLC), Ella Jo Baker was also an adviser to the Student Nonviolent Coordinating Committee (SNCC).

The daughter of a waiter and a teacher, Baker was born in Norfolk, Virginia, on December 13, 1903. She graduated from Shaw University, in Raleigh, North Carolina, and moved to New York City—where she launched her career as an activist during the 1920s. Baker first became head of the Young Negroes Cooperative League, then, during the 1930s, worked as a labor and consumer educator for the Works Progress Administration. In 1940 she became a field secretary for the NAACP, recruiting new members throughout the South. By 1946 she had risen to become the NAACP's director of branches, but she broke with the organization because it took a top-down rather than a grassroots approach to activism.

After leaving the NAACP, Baker worked for the National Urban League and In Friendship, as well as other organizations. In the 1950s she returned to the NAACP's New York branch, and in 1957 she joined the SCLC, organizing its Crusade for Citizenship, a voter registration campaign. Baker served as acting director of the SCLC for a number of years.

In 1960 Baker helped found SNCC, organizing the Raleigh, North Carolina, conference at which it was formed and delivering the keynote address. At her urging SNCC remained independent of the more established civil rights organizations, principally the SCLC and the NAACP. Throughout the early sixties Baker served in the unofficial capacity of chief adviser to SNCC. Baker died on December 13, 1986, in New York City. Many consider her the single most influential woman in the civil rights movement.

Suggested Reading

Grant, Joanne. *Ella Jo Baker: Freedom Bound.* New York: Wiley, 1998.

BALCH INSTITUTE FOR ETHNIC STUDIES

The Balch Institute for Ethnic Studies was established in 1976, pursuant to a bequest from Philadelphia's Emily Swift Balch and her two sons, Thomas Willing Balch and Edwin Swift Balch. The institute's purpose is to document and interpret the ethnic and immigrant experience in the nineteenth- and twentieth-century United States. The institute's library and archives contain books, personal papers, organizational records, photographs, audio recordings, and newspapers and pamphlets, and its largest collections pertain to Chinese, German, Greek, Italian, Irish, Japanese, Jewish, Polish, Latino, Carpatho-Rusyn, Scottish, Slovak, and Ukrainian communities. Specific collections include the Leonard Covello Papers, the *Atlantis National Daily* Greek Newspapers, the Nelson Diaz Papers, the Shigezo and Sonoko Iwata Papers, the Scots Thistle Society papers, and the Fiorani Radio Production Records.

In 2002 the Balch Institute merged with the Historical Society of Pennsylvania and is now known as the Balch Institute for Ethnic Studies of the Historical Society of Pennsylvania.

Suggested Reading

Balch Institute for Ethnic Studies, www.balchinstitute.org.

BARNETT, ROSS (1898–1987)

Ross Barnett entered the national spotlight as one of the South's most adamantly segregationist governors when, in defiance of a Supreme Court decision and a U.S. Department of Justice order, he personally blocked the admission of James Meredith, an African American, to the University of Mississippi. (Barnett was already notorious for having remarked that "the Negro is different because God made him different to punish him.") On October 1, 1962, attorney general Robert F. Kennedy sent federal marshals to escort Meredith to classes, and federal troops had to be called in to quell the campus disturbances that followed.

Barnett was born in Leake County, Mississippi, and was a veteran of World War I. He was elected governor of Mississippi in 1960 and served until 1964.

Suggested Reading

Meredith, James. *Three Years in Mississippi*. Bloomington: Indiana University Press, 1966.

BARRON V. BALTIMORE

In the landmark Supreme Court decision in *Barron v. Baltimore* (1833), chief justice John Marshall defined the Bill of Rights as having application only to the national government and not to the states. Marshall's opinion was based on the fact that neither the First Amendment nor the Bill of Rights mentions the states (although the First Amendment does refer to Congress).

The case in question was that of John Barron, co-owner of a wharf in Baltimore's harbor. As the city expanded, streams were diverted to aid development. The massive quantities of sand that accumulated in the harbor effectively wiped out Barron's access to deep water, and he sued the city to recover a portion of his financial losses, arguing that his Fifth Amendment right to protection from unlawful seizure of property had been violated.

The legal question Marshall had to decide was this: Does the Fifth Amendment deny the states, as well as the national government, the right to take private property for public use without just compensation? The Court's unanimous decision, which it handed down without even hearing the Baltimore attorneys' arguments, was that the Fifth Amendment, like the rest of the Bill of Rights, was intended to limit only the powers of the national government; therefore, the Supreme Court had no jurisdiction in the case. Thus, in matters relating to the state, citizens had recourse only to the state constitution.

Barron v. Baltimore stood until it was superseded by the Fourteenth Amendment (1868), which explicitly asserted the primacy of the rights of national citizenship: "No State shall make or enforce any law which shall abridge the privileges or immunities of citizens of the United States; nor shall any State deprive any person of life, liberty, or property, without due process of law; nor deny to any person within its jurisdiction the equal protection of the laws."

Suggested Reading

Nelson, William E. *The Fourteenth Amendment: From Political Principle to Judicial Doctrine*. Cambridge: Harvard University Press, 1988.

BARTON, CLARA (1821–1912)

Clara Barton is best remembered as a valiant Civil War nurse and as the founder of the American Red Cross. The focus of her efforts was not only practical—the immediate aid of the battlefield wounded and the relief of civilians during times of disaster—but moral: Barton's was a strong humanitarian voice.

Born in 1821 in North Oxford, Massachusetts, Barton discovered her vocation when, beginning at age eleven, she nursed her brother through a two-year convalescence from a bad fall. During the Civil War she volunteered as a battlefield nurse, delivering medical supplies and food and caring for the wounded, usually in the field. She was known as "the Angel of the battlefield."

In 1870, while touring Europe, Barton became involved in the International Red Cross movement. In Paris and in other cities she worked energetically for the relief of refugees from the Franco-Prussian War, and when she returned to the United States in 1873 she began working toward the creation of an American Red Cross, which she formally founded in 1877. Over the succeeding twenty-three years Barton built and led the organization, personally leading relief campaigns for fires, floods, hurricanes, and other disasters.

The eighty-two-year-old Barton retired from the presidency of the Red Cross in 1904 and lived in active retirement at her home, in Glen Echo, Maryland, near Washington, D. C.

Suggested Reading

Oates, Stephen B. *A Woman of Valor: Clara Barton and the Civil War.* New York: Free Press, 1994.

BECKWITH, BYRON DE LA (1921–2001)

On June 12, 1963, Medgar Evers, field secretary of the National Association for the Advancement of Colored People, was murdered in Mississippi. In 1964 Byron de la Beckwith, a white supremacist, was twice tried for the murder; both trials, with juries made up entirely of whites, ended in hung juries. In 1989, as the result of the tireless work of Evers's widow, Myrlie, Bobby DeLaughter, the assistant district attorney of Hinds County, Mississippi, reopened the case. An aged and defiant Beckwith was tried for a third time—and, in 1994, was convicted (by an integrated jury) and sentenced to life in prison. On appeal, Beckwith's conviction was upheld by the Mississippi Supreme Court in 1997. Beckwith died in prison of heart failure at age eighty.

Suggested Reading

DeLaughter, Bobby. *Never Too Late: A Prosecutor's Story of Justice in the Medgar Evers Case.* New York: Scribner, 2001.

Vollers, Maryanne. *Ghosts of Mississippi: The Murder of Medgar Evers, the Trials of Byron De La Beckwith, and the Haunting of the New South.* Boston: Little, Brown, 1995.

BETHUNE, MARY MCLEOD (1875–1955)

Born on July 10, 1875, in Maysville, South Carolina, Mary McLeod was one of seventeen children of former slaves. She labored in the cotton fields with her family and married Albertus Bethune, with whom she had a son.

Bethune was educated at the Maysville Presbyterian Mission School, the Scotia Seminary, and the Moody Bible Institute (Dwight Moody's Institute for Home and Foreign Missions). In 1904 she founded the Daytona Normal and Industrial Institute for Negro Girls, which subsequently became Bethune-Cookman College. She served as the institute's president from 1904 to 1942, and again during 1946–1947.

Bethune was a leader in the black women's club movement, which organized programs for the advancement of African Americans. She also served as president of the National Association of Colored Women and served as a delegate and adviser to various national conferences on African American education, child welfare, and homeownership.

During the administration of President Franklin D. Roosevelt, Bethune was appointed Director of Negro Affairs in the National Youth Administration and served in this capacity from 1936 to 1944. During World War II she was appointed special consultant to the U.S. Secretary of War to assist with the selection of the first female officer candidates. Bethune was also asked to serve as a consultant on interracial affairs and understanding at the United Nations charter conference. Bethune founded the National Council of Negro Women and was elected vice president of the National Association for the Advancement of Colored People.

Among the many honors Bethune received for her life's work was the Haitian Medal of Honor and Merit, that country's highest award, and the title of Commander of the Order of the Star of Africa, presented by the government of Liberia.

Suggested Reading

Poole, Bernice Anderson. *Mary McLeod Bethune.* New York: Holloway House, 1994.

BILL OF RIGHTS

As originally adopted in 1789, the U.S. Constitution did not contain a bill of rights. James Madison subsequently drafted the amendments that became the Bill of Rights, which were largely based on the Virginia Declaration of Rights that had been written earlier by George Mason.

On September 25, 1789, Congress proposed twelve amendments for ratification by the state legislatures. The first was never ratified:

> After the first enumeration required by the first Article of the Constitution, there shall be one Representative for every thirty thousand, until the number shall amount to one hundred, after which the proportion shall be so regulated by Congress, that there shall be not less than one hundred Representatives, nor less than one Representative for every forty thousand persons, until the number of Representatives amount to two hundred, after which the proportion shall be so regulated by Congress, that there shall not be less than two hundred Representatives, nor more than one Representative for every fifty thousand persons.

The second was not ratified until 1992, when it became the Twenty-Seventh Amendment: "No law[,] varying the compensation for the services of Senators or Representatives[,] shall take effect[,] until an election of Representatives shall have intervened."

The other ten amendments, collectively known as the Bill of Rights, were ratified by 1791. The fundamental source of individual rights in the United States, the Bill of Rights has been the subject of important debate and deliberation in American legislatures and courts—and, above all, in the Supreme Court.

Suggested Reading

Alderman, Elaine, and Caroline Kennedy. *In Our Defense: The Bill of Rights in Action.* 1991. Reprint, New York: Avon, 1992.

Cogan, Neil H., ed. *The Complete Bill of Rights: The Drafts, Debates, Sources, and Origins.* New York: Oxford University Press, 1997.

Levy, Leonard Williams. *Origins of the Bill of Rights.* New Haven: Yale University Press, 1999.

BIRMINGHAM CHURCH BOMBING

On September 15, 1963, a dynamite bomb exploded at the Sixteenth Street Baptist Church, an African American church in Birmingham, Alabama. Killed in the blast were eleven-year-old Carol Denise McNair and three fourteen-year-old girls, Cynthia Wesley, Addie Mae Collins, and Carole Robertson. The girls had been preparing for a youth church service.

After a two-year investigation, agents from the Birmingham office of the Federal Bureau of Investigation (FBI) recommended that four suspects be charged, but FBI director J. Edgar Hoover blocked the prosecution, arguing that the chance of winning a conviction was "remote." Three years later federal authorities officially pulled out of the investigation. No charges had been filed.

In 1971 Alabama's attorney general, Bill Baxley, acting on his own authority, reopened the case, and in 1977 Robert Edward Chambliss was brought to trial and convicted of one count of murder in the death of Carol Denise McNair. Nine years later, following the release of a U.S. Department of Justice report that concluded that Hoover had not only blocked prosecution of the case but had concealed evidence that prosecutors could have used, the district attorney of Jefferson County, Alabama, reopened the federal case, but no additional charges were filed.

On October 29, 1985, eighty-one-year-old Robert Edward Chambliss, who had never publicly admitted to having played any role in the bombing, died in prison of natural causes. Three years later Gary A. Tucker, a former bus driver terminally ill with cancer, declared that he had helped plant the bomb, and federal and state prosecutors reopened the investigation of the bombing in October 1988. Again, however, no new charges were filed.

On July 10, 1997, the case was reopened yet again, this time by the FBI, pursuant to its own year-long secret review of the bombing. As a result of the new work on the case, a grand jury, in the spring of 2000, returned first-degree murder indictments against two former Ku Klux Klan members, Thomas Blanton Jr. and Bobby Frank Cherry.

In 2001 a Birmingham jury of eight whites and four blacks convicted the sixty-two-year-old Blanton on all four counts of first-degree murder, and he was sentenced to life in prison. His attorney promised to appeal. In April an Alabama judge ruled that the other man indicted, Bobby Frank Cherry, age seventy-one, was not mentally competent to assist his attorneys. Prosecutors appealed the ruling, and Cherry was subjected to further psychological testing. In December 2001 psychiatrists who had studied Cherry for ten weeks in a mental hospital reported to the court their conclusion that he had been faking mental illness. In January 2002 Cherry was declared competent to stand trial. On May 21, 2002, he was found guilty of first-degree murder. He was subsequently sentenced to life imprisonment.

Suggested Reading

Sikora, Frank. *Until Justice Rolls Down: The Birmingham Church Bombing Case.* Tuscaloosa: University of Alabama Press, 1991.

BIRMINGHAM SCLC PROTESTS

Early in 1963 Rev. Fred Shuttlesworth, a civil rights activist in Birmingham, Alabama, invited Martin Luther King Jr. and the Southern Christian Leadership Conference (SCLC) to the strife-torn city. Because of the eighteen unsolved bombings in black neighborhoods that had occurred over a half-dozen years, Birmingham was by then known as "Bombingham"; in addition, on Mother's Day, 1961, a white mob had viciously attacked a group of Freedom Riders.

By 1963 Birmingham voters had decided to replace the three-man city commission with an elected mayor—a step that was aimed primarily at forcing from office Eugene "Bull" Connor, the commissioner of public safety who was held largely responsible for the attack on the Freedom Riders. When Connor lost the mayoral race to moderate Albert Boutwell, the city commission refused to step down, and it was left to the courts to decide which city government was legitimate.

In the midst of this melee, on April 3, 1963—a day designated as B (Birmingham) Day—the SCLC launched Project C (for "confrontation"). Led by Dr. King, the organization staged sit-ins and promulgated the "Birmingham Manifesto," a document that received little national notice. On April 6, city police arrested forty-five protesters marching from the Sixteenth Street Baptist Church to city hall. The next day, Palm Sunday, more were arrested. Then, as a crowd looked on, two police dogs viciously mauled a protester, nineteen-year-old Leroy Allen. At the behest of city officials, Judge W. A. Jenkins Jr. issued an order barring 133 civil rights leaders—including Shuttlesworth, King, and the SCLC's Ralph David Abernathy—from organizing further demonstrations. King refused to obey the order and was arrested, with some of the other leaders, on April 12, Good Friday.

While in solitary confinement, King read an ad, taken out by local white ministers in the *Birmingham News,* that labeled him a troublemaker. Writing in the margins of the newspaper and on toilet paper, King responded with the widely published "Letter from Birmingham Jail."

King was released on April 20. In the meantime SCLC organizers planned D Day, a protest to be staged by children. On May 2 children ages six to eighteen assembled in Kelly Ingram Park, across the street from the Sixteenth Street Baptist Church. At about one in the afternoon fifty teenagers marched downtown singing "We Shall Overcome" and were arrested by police. When another group followed, they, too, were arrested. More and more followed until, within three hours, the Birmingham police had jailed 959 children.

On May 3 more than a thousand children stayed out of school and assembled in Kelly Ingram Park. Commissioner Connor knew he had no more space left in the city jail. Determined to prevent the children from marching downtown, he ordered city firefighters to turn high-pressure hoses on the demonstrators. Most of the youngsters scattered, but one group stubbornly resisted. The pressure was turned up, and the force of the water literally rolled young protesters down the street. At this point, Connor also brought in police dogs, who were encouraged to attack demonstrators.

Still photographs and television images depicting black children and teens being attacked by high-pressure hoses and snarling police dogs instantly became visual icons of the civil rights struggle. Unwittingly, Connor had elevated the Birmingham SCLC protests to national prominence—shocking the nation and, ultimately, startling many white Americans out of their complacency.

Locally the demonstrations broadened and intensified. With the jails filled the police could do little—and, at long last, the merchants of Birmingham, fearing for their property and their livelihood, agreed to hire more blacks and to integrate hitherto segregated lunch counters. For the civil rights movement, the protests achieved both local and national victory.

Suggested Reading

Nunnelly, William A. *Bull Connor.* Tuscaloosa: University of Alabama Press, 1991.

BIRTH CONTROL

Birth control rose to prominence as a rights issue in 1921 when, at the First American Birth Control Conference in New York City on November 10, Margaret Sanger founded the American Birth Control League (ABCL).

The purpose of the ABCL was to educate men and women about birth control and to initiate and sponsor a program of research and legislative reform. (Although it was not the first, the ABCL was the most political of early birth control organizations; the National Birth Control League and the Voluntary Parenthood League had both been founded earlier.) In 1923 the ABCL took over the *Birth Control Review,* a monthly journal Sanger had launched independently in 1917.

The ABCL was supported by a national council consisting of prominent physicians, scientists, and progressive, socially influential women. Membership peaked in 1926 at 37,000 nationwide. Under ABCL auspices the first legal birth control clinic in the United States, the Clinical Research Bureau (CRB), was opened in 1923. The clinic was the medical research arm of the ABCL and became a model for clinics nationwide.

Sanger resigned from the ABCL in 1928 but retained direction of the CRB, which she renamed the Birth Control Clinical Research Bureau (BCCRB). In 1939 the ABCL merged with the BCCRB to form the Birth Control Federation of America, an organization that in 1942 changed its name to the PLANNED PARENTHOOD FEDERATION OF AMERICA. (See also ABORTION.)

Suggested Reading

Chesler, Ellen. *Woman of Valor: Margaret Sanger and the Birth Control Movement in America*. New York: Summit, 1992.

Sanger, Margaret. *Margaret Sanger: Pioneering Advocate for Birth Control: An Autobiography*. New York: Cooper Square Press, 1999.

"Margaret Sanger Papers Project," www.nyu.edu/projects/sanger/.

BIRTH OF A NATION, THE

Produced and directed by the pioneering American film genius D. W. Griffith, *The Birth of a Nation,* released in 1915, has been hailed as a groundbreaking cinematic masterpiece and condemned as racist propaganda.

Based on *The Clansman,* a blatantly antiblack novel and play by Rev. Thomas Dixon Jr., Griffith's film portrays, in epic fashion, the story of friendship between a southern family and a northern family that is tested during the Civil War and the RECONSTRUCTION period. Griffith's depiction of Reconstruction focuses on the depredations of blacks who, put in charge of government in the South, prey upon their former masters and rape white women. The KU KLUX KLAN (KKK), portrayed as the sole defender of the white South in general and of the honor of Southern white women in particular, is cast in a heroic light. Reportedly, the film is still used today to recruit members for the Klan.

From the perspective of the evolution of the film medium, *The Birth of a Nation* introduced a host of cinematic firsts, including sophisticated technical effects and various artistic advancements that would become conventions of modern cinema. At nearly three hours in length it was also the longest commercial film produced up to the time of its release. A sensational box office success, it had made $18 million by the beginning of the talkie era (when movies began to use sound). President Woodrow Wilson, who saw the film in a private screening at the White House, reportedly remarked that it was "like writing history with lightning. And my only regret is that it is all terribly true."

Tremendously popular among white audiences, the film was immediately denounced by the NATIONAL ASSOCIATION FOR THE ADVANCEMENT OF COLORED PEOPLE as "the meanest vilification of the Negro race." This response was mild, however, compared to the RACE RIOTS the film's release touched off in several major cities. For years after its premiere, showings of the film drew demonstrators, picketers, lawsuits, and injunctions.

The film remains interesting not only for its technical excellence but because it offers a portrait of RACISM in the United States early in the twentieth century. It exploited the romantic, quasi-mythic view of the gallant Old South, and it explored two social taboos: interracial sex and the social and political empowerment of African Americans. While playing upon white fears, the film ultimately reassured white audiences by portraying the suppression of the black menace by white society.

In response to criticism, Griffith subsequently released a shortened version without reference to the KKK. Many scholars of film also believe that his next masterpiece, the four-part 1916 epic *Intolerance,* which chronicles the history of human intolerance, was an effort to make amends for the racist excesses of *The Birth of a Nation.*

Suggested Reading

Lang, Robert, ed. *The Birth of a Nation*. New Brunswick: Rutgers University Press, 1994.

Schickel, Richard. *D. W. Griffith: An American Life*. New York: Simon and Schuster, 1984.

BLACK CODES

In 1865, immediately following the Civil War and the emancipation of the slaves, the states of the former Confederacy enacted laws intended to limit the rights of the newly freed blacks. These so-called black codes varied from state to state, but generally included similar restrictions.

Most codes compelled freedmen to work; unemployed blacks were typically subject to arrest for vagrancy. The codes also regulated hours of labor, permissible duties, and even the behavior required of agricultural workers. Most of the codes restricted blacks to agricultural labor or to domestic work and categorically barred them from other employment, except in cases where a special license and certificate (issued by a local judge) were obtained.

Black codes were generally designed to inhibit or discourage self-sufficiency; for example, codes barred blacks from raising their own crops and typically restricted property ownership. In Mississippi the codes prohibited blacks from renting or leasing any land outside of cities or towns, thereby effectively preventing them from owning farms. Within cities and towns, black ownership of property was left to the discretion of local authorities.

The black codes touched almost every aspect of daily life. Usually, blacks were prohibited from entering towns without written permission, and residency within many towns and cities was made all but impossible unless a white employer agreed to assume responsibility for the conduct of a black employee. In 1866 federal officials intervened to suspend black codes throughout the South. (See Appendix A for an 1865 act of the Louisiana state legislature, a typical example of southern black codes.)

Suggested Reading

Wilson, Theodore Brantner. *The Black Codes of the South*. Tuscaloosa: University of Alabama Press, 1965.

BLACK, HUGO L. (1886–1971)

One of the most influential associate justices in the history of the U.S. SUPREME COURT (he served from 1937 to 1971), Hugo Black was a staunch advocate of the BILL OF RIGHTS as an absolute guarantee of civil liberties. Until Black articulated the view that the FOURTEENTH AMENDMENT rendered the Bill of Rights applicable to state as well as federal authority, prevailing judicial opinion held that the Bill of Rights did not restrict the power of the states to pass laws that might infringe on individual freedom.

A native of Alabama, Black graduated from the University of Alabama School of Law and began practicing in Birmingham in 1906. In 1926 he was elected to the U.S. Senate, in which he served until 1937. A vigorous supporter of the NEW DEAL, Black earned the attention of President FRANKLIN D. ROOSEVELT, who appointed him to the high court in 1937. To Roosevelt's great satisfaction, Black voted—along with a developing majority—to reverse previous Supreme Court objections to much of the New Deal legislation. Black thus began to combine a willingness to give the federal government wide latitude in certain matters with an equally strong advocacy of individual civil liberties. During the 1940s and 1950s, as he dissented from any high court decisions that infringed freedom of speech or individual liberties, his stand often put him at odds with his fellow justices.

During the increasingly liberal 1960s Black emerged as a prominent voice of what had become the liberal majority. He wrote major opinions striking down mandatory SCHOOL PRAYER and ensuring the availability of legal counsel to accused criminals. His last momentous opinion was *New York Times v. United States,* written in 1971 in support of the *New York Times,* to enable publication of the Pentagon Papers, which detailed decades of deceit and constitutional violations in the government's conduct of policy regarding Vietnam and the Vietnam War. The 1971 decision is considered a triumph of the First Amendment guarantee of FREE SPEECH. (See also *BAKER V. CARR*.)

Suggested Reading

Newman, Roger K. *Hugo Black: A Biography.* New York: Fordham University Press, 1997.

BLACK LEGEND

The Black Legend, according to which Spain was the gratuitously cruel and brutal exploiter of New World natives, originated in 1542, when an account written by Father BARTOLOMÉ DE LAS CASAS, *The Destruction of the Indies,* detailed the abusive policies of the Spanish conquistadors.

The Black Legend persisted well into the nineteenth century, however, influencing mainstream American views of Hispanics in the United States. The social and religious conflicts that helped to foster the Texas War of Independence, in 1836; the UNITED STATES–MEXICAN WAR of 1846–1848; and the Spanish-American War of 1898 were largely outgrowths of the Black Legend. Not until the twentieth century did historians seriously reevaluate the Spanish experience in the New World, question the accuracy of the Black Legend, and point out how it has shaped—and, often, deformed—other Americans' perceptions of Hispanic heritage, culture, and attitudes.

Suggested Reading

Powell, Philip Wayne. *Tree of Hate: Propaganda and Prejudices Affecting United States Relations with the Hispanic World.* New York: Basic Books, 1971.
Weber, David J. *The Spanish Frontier in North America.* New Haven: Yale University Press, 1992.

BLACK LEGIONNAIRES

Its name notwithstanding, the Black Legion, or Black Legionnaires, was a secret white supremacist society briefly active during the 1930s. Its origins are obscure. Some authorities believe it was a self-help social club organized by unskilled factory laborers in Detroit, while others believe that it was founded in Ohio in 1931 by Virgil Effinger, a former KU KLUX KLAN (KKK) member. Whatever its origin, the Black Legion was headquartered in Detroit, and its members consisted chiefly of white men who had moved from Kentucky, Mississippi, and Tennessee. Although some members were unquestionably former Klansmen, some authorities hold that *only* former Klansmen were accepted for membership. From Detroit, Black Legion lodges spread to industrial areas in Ohio and Indiana. At its height in the mid-1930s, the Black Legion had a membership of perhaps 40,000.

Black Legionnaires were antiblack, anti-Semitic, anti-Catholic, and generally anti-immigrant. They came under intense public scrutiny in 1936 when a Works Progress Administration worker named Charles Poole was found murdered, execution-style, near Detroit, on May 13. In the fall of that year, eleven Black Legionnaires were convicted of the killing, and nearly one hundred public employees of Oakland County, Michigan, were dismissed from their positions after having been exposed as Black Legionnaires.

Following the murder, the trial, and the dismissals, the Black Legion essentially ceased to exist, but it continued to figure in the popular imagination as the archetypal hate organization. Even the KKK called for prosecution of Black Legionnaires, and, when the Klan discovered that a 1937 Humphrey Bogart movie, *The Black Legion* (which was loosely based on the activities of the organization), included scenes that featured the Klan's trademarked insignia on Black Legion robes, the KKK sued Warner Bros. for trademark infringement and libel.

Suggested Reading

Axelrod, Alan. *The International Encyclopedia of Secret Societies and Fraternal Orders.* New York: Facts on File, 1997.

BLACKMUN, HARRY A. (1908–1999)

Harry Andrew Blackmun was an associate justice of the U.S. SUPREME COURT from 1970 to 1994 and wrote the majority opinion in the landmark ABORTION RIGHTS case *ROE V. WADE*.

Born in Nashville, Illinois, Blackmun received an undergraduate degree in mathematics from Harvard in 1929 but went on to study law, receiving his Harvard law degree in 1932. Two years later he joined a law firm in Minneapolis, and from 1935 to 1941 he also taught at the St. Paul College of Law. From 1950 to 1959 he served as resident counsel for the famed Mayo Clinic in Rochester, Minnesota, then accepted an appointment to the U.S. Court of Appeals. President RICHARD M. NIXON nominated Blackmun to the Supreme Court in 1970. Although Nixon had appointed Blackmun in the expectation that he would toe the conservative line, in 1973 Blackmun stunned conservatives by writing the court's majority decision in *Roe v. Wade,* which held that the constitutional right to privacy protected a woman's right to terminate pregnancy.

Although Blackmun was enduringly identified with abortion rights, it is really with the right to privacy that he should be more closely associated. Blackmun wrote the dissenting opinion in *Bowers v. Hardwick* (1986), for example, in which he argued in favor of the right-to-privacy claim of a gay man who had been convicted under a state sodomy law. Blackmun's dissent in this case has framed subsequent legal debate about both privacy issues and about a citizen's right, in general, "to be left alone" by the government.

In addition to his eloquent efforts in support of privacy, Blackmun upheld the primacy of the FIRST AMENDMENT and the separation of church and state. He was also an advocate of AFFIRMATIVE ACTION. In contrast to many liberal jurists, however, Blackmun believed in the constitutionality of the death penalty—until late in his career, when what he deemed the arbitrary and even random application of the death penalty made CAPITAL PUNISHMENT appear to him inherently unconstitutional (*Callins v. Collins,* 1994). Blackmun retired from the bench in 1994 and died in 1999.

Suggested Reading

Cushman, Clare. *The Supreme Court Justices: Illustrated Biographies, 1789–1995.* 2d ed. Washington, D. C.: CQ Press, 1996.

BLACK MUSLIMS

See ISLAM, NATION OF.

BLACK PANTHER PARTY FOR SELF-DEFENSE

The Black Panther Party for Self-Defense (usually shortened to the Black Panther Party, or BPP) was founded in 1966, in Oakland, California. Its principal organizers were HUEY NEWTON and BOBBY SEALE.

As originally conceived, the purpose of the Black Panther Party was self-defense: party members would patrol black ghettos—in part to protect residents from crime, but mainly to counter acts of police brutality. Within a relatively short time, however, the Black Panthers became increasingly political in orientation and, before the end of the decade, had become a Marxist revolutionary group that called for the arming of all African Americans, for their exemption from the military draft, and for their immunity from virtually all legal sanctions imposed by "white America." The Black Panthers also demanded the release of all blacks from jail on the grounds that, in white America, they were political prisoners. Some Black Panthers called for the payment of reparations to all African Americans in compensation for SLAVERY and for subsequent exploitation, discrimination, and persecution.

The Black Panthers had reached the height of their power and popularity by 1968, when Black Panther groups were active in several major American cities and total membership was greater than 2,000. During their early years, Black Panthers frequently came into conflict with the police, and there were highly publicized gun battles between Panthers and law enforcement officials in California, Chicago, and New York. Newton was convicted of having murdered a police officer during one shootout. While some Black Panthers did indeed commit crimes, the group as a whole appears to have been subjected to excessive surveillance and to police harassment.

The harassment sometimes exploded into police-initiated violence, which became so blatant that from March 4, 1970, to November 17, 1970, Congress conducted investigations of police policy toward the Black Panthers.

By the early to mid-1970s, the Panthers' reputation for violence and their uncompromising adherence to Marxism led many African American leaders to distance themselves from the group. As membership declined precipitously, the Black Panther Party turned from revolutionary rhetoric and violent protest to community activism (providing day care, for example), and even made some forays into mainstream politics. Although the Black Panther Party never officially dissolved, it was effectively inoperative by the early 1980s.

Suggested Reading

Foner, Philip S., ed. *The Black Panthers Speak.* 1970. Reprint, New York: Da Capo Press, 1995.

BLACK POWER MOVEMENT

Although some scholars of African American history and the black power movement point out that the phrase *black power* was first used by Robert Williams, a National Association for the Advancement of Colored People (NAACP) activist, in the late 1950s Stokely Carmichael is generally credited with having coined the phrase—or at least with having given it popular currency—in a speech he made on June 16, 1966, in Greenwood, Mississippi.

"This is the twenty-seventh time," Carmichael told some three thousand listeners, referring to his most recent arrest, incarceration, and release for protest activities. "We been saying 'Freedom' for six years." ("Freedom" was a slave-era chant that protesters had been using against police officers as well as politicians.) "What we are going to start saying *now* is 'Black Power!' "

Not only was the phrase instantly taken up by the crowd at Greenwood, it made national headlines and quickly became the rallying cry for a political movement that arose to rival the nonviolent approach of Martin Luther King Jr. and others. For many both within and outside the movement, black power connoted militancy, even violence. For others it referred to economic enfranchisement and the effective application of political pressure. For others still, its deeper meaning was connected to racial dignity and self-reliance—complete cultural autonomy from white authority.

If Carmichael catalyzed the black power movement by giving it a label, it was Malcolm X who supplied the principal rhetoric, style, and attitude of the black power movement, and who directed its focus to improving African American communities rather than attempting to achieve integration into white society. And, apart from Malcolm X, it was the Black Panther Party that most vividly embodied the idea of vigorous, uncompromising, and formidable black political and economic enfranchisement. Simultaneously with the rise of the Black Panther Party, Carmichael's reorganization of the Student Nonviolent Coordinating Committee, which excluded whites from leadership, underlined the separatist aspect of the black power movement.

The black power movement was also associated with, and helped to drive, what might be called the black pride movement, a renewed interest in the African roots of African American identity and in the development of a "black consciousness." This aspect of the movement reached broadly into popular culture and the mass media, touching whites as well as blacks.

At its most extreme, black power called for a revolutionary political struggle that would wholly reject and overcome white racism and what the movement's leaders called "white imperialism" in the United States. This inherently antiwhite stance drew criticism from whites as well as from mainstream black civil rights leaders, including King and the NAACP.

After reaching the peak of its influence and appeal in the late 1960s, the black power movement rapidly receded in the 1970s, coinciding with the decline (or destruction) of the Black Panther Party and the general perception that the implications of black power were both separatist and antiwhite. Although the slogan "Black Power!" slipped into history, the concept behind it continued to influence both black leaders and the black community in their efforts to achieve greater cultural autonomy and to strengthen black identity and self-esteem.

Suggested Reading

Collier-Thomas, Bettye, and V. P. Franklin, eds. *Sisters in the Struggle: African-American Women in the Civil Rights-Black Power Movement.* New York: New York University Press, 2001.

Kwame Toure and Charles V. Hamilton. *Black Power: The Politics of Liberation.* 1967. Reprint, New York: Vintage, 1992.

Van Deburg, William L. *New Day in Babylon: The Black Power Movement and American Culture, 1965–1975.* Chicago: University of Chicago Press, 1993.

BLOODY SUNDAY

To protest the killing of a civil rights demonstrator by an Alabama state trooper in Marion, Alabama, the Marion black community resolved to conduct a march from Selma, Alabama, to the state capital in Montgomery. There they planned to make a direct appeal to Governor George Wallace to call a halt to police brutality. Martin Luther King

Jr. agreed to lead the march, which was to be held on Sunday, March 7, 1965.

When Wallace refused to allow the march, King went to Washington to speak with President Lyndon Johnson—a trip that would have delayed the march by one day. Believing that to postpone the march would be to admit defeat, the people of Selma, without King to lead them, began the march on Sunday as planned.

When the marchers reached the Selma city limits, at the Edmund Pettus Bridge, they were confronted by a contingent of state troopers and ordered to disperse. Without waiting to see if their order would be obeyed, the troopers attacked the marchers, who had halted and bowed their heads in prayer. When the troopers began to use tear gas and to wade into the crowd with batons, many of the demonstrators fled, but the troopers pursued them into a black housing project. Here they continued to wield their batons, not only against the demonstrators but against housing project residents as well. The March 7 police action was dubbed Bloody Sunday by the civil rights movement and by the national press.

On Tuesday, March 9, to protest Bloody Sunday, King led a march to the Selma bridge. Once again, state troopers attacked, this time killing one marcher. It was only with the intercession of President Johnson that King was able to complete a successful march from Selma to Montgomery on March 25, 1965.

Bloody Sunday and the Selma marches that followed prompted many demonstrations nationwide. It was in the wake of Bloody Sunday and the subsequent demonstrations that President Johnson delivered to Congress "The American Promise," his most important speech on civil rights, which was in support of passage of the Voting Rights Act of 1965. (See also Selma SNCC–SCLC demonstration.)

Suggested Reading

Boynton, Ameila Platts. *Bridge across Jordan: The Story of the Struggle for Civil Rights in Selma, Alabama.* New York: Carlton Press, 1979.

Leonard, Richard D. *Call to Selma: Eighteen Days of Witness.* Boston: Unitarian Universalist Association, 2001.

B'NAI B'RITH

B'nai B'rith—the name means "children of the covenant"—is a venerable Jewish service organization founded in October 1843 by twelve German-Jewish immigrants living on New York's Lower East Side. The purpose of the organization, like that of many other immigrant service groups, was to find, in unity, the strength to combat prejudice and discrimination.

During the Civil War, B'nai B'rith opposed General Ulysses S. Grant's attempt, under martial law, to expel Jews from several states and succeeded in securing from President Abraham Lincoln a revocation of Grant's order. In the next decade none other than President Grant chose former B'nai B'rith president Benjamin Peixotto as honorary U.S. consul to Romania, which was reeling under a pogrom (a massacre of Jews). This was the first instance in which B'nai B'rith advocacy reached beyond the borders of the United States.

B'nai B'rith has a long tradition of promoting secular Jewish learning, beginning in 1851 with the construction of Covenant Hall in New York City, the first Jewish community center in the nation. Informal education programs continue to be a major part of B'nai B'rith activity.

As a service organization B'nai B'rith also sponsors emergency and other relief programs. Its first disaster relief campaign was conducted in 1868 in response to flooding in Baltimore. The organization supports various medical and welfare programs, such as the National Jewish Medical and Research Center, which specializes in allergies and in lung and immune diseases.

In recent years major B'nai B'rith projects have focused on human rights issues, including the pursuit and prosecution of Nazi-era war criminals. On the international level the organization works with diplomats, heads of state, and the Vatican to address issues affecting world Jewry.

B'nai B'rith has chapters throughout the United States and in several other countries. It is also the parent organization of the Anti-Defamation League.

Suggested Reading

Moore, Deborah Dash. *B'nai B'rith and the Challenge of Ethnic Leadership.* Binghamton: State University of New York Press, 1981.

BOLLING V. SHARPE

At issue in *Bolling v. Sharpe,* a companion case to *Brown v. Board of Education of Topeka, Kansas,* was a challenge to the segregated schools of the District of Columbia. Chief justice Earl Warren wrote the unanimous opinion for the high court on May 17, 1954. (See Appendix A for the text of the opinion.)

Suggested Reading

Kluger, Richard. *Simple Justice: The History of Brown v. Board of Education and Black America's Struggle for Equality.* New York: Random House, 1977.

Patterson, James T. *Brown v. Board of Education: A Civil Rights Milestone and Its Troubled Legacy.* New York: Oxford University Press, 2001.

BOND, JULIAN (1940–)

Julian Bond was a central figure in the civil rights movement of the 1960s and continues to be an activist in civil rights and economic justice.

Horace Julian Bond was born in Nashville, Tennessee, the son of Dr. Horace Mann Bond—a distinguished educator, the first president of Fort Valley State College, and later the first black president of the country's oldest black private college, Pennsylvania's Lincoln University. In 1957 the family moved to Atlanta, where Bond's father became dean of the School of Education at Atlanta University. In that same year Julian Bond graduated from the George School, a Quaker preparatory school in Pennsylvania, then entered Atlanta's Morehouse College.

While attending Morehouse Bond helped found, in 1960, the Committee on Appeal for Human Rights (COAHR), the student civil rights organization that coordinated three years of nonviolent antisegregation protests that ultimately succeeded in integrating Atlanta's movie theaters, lunch counters, and parks. (Bond was arrested for participating in a SIT-IN at the then-segregated cafeteria at Atlanta City Hall.) Also in 1960 Bond became a charter member of the STUDENT NONVIOLENT COORDINATING COMMITTEE (SNCC). He was soon named communications director of SNCC, heading the publicity department and editing the SNCC newsletter, the *Student Voice.* Bond participated in voter registration drives throughout rural Alabama, Arkansas, Georgia, and Mississippi.

Bond left Morehouse in 1961, one semester short of graduation, to join the staff of a new civil rights newspaper, the *Atlanta Inquirer,* of which he later became managing editor. It was not until ten years later that Bond returned to Morehouse to complete his bachelor's degree in English. By then, however, Bond had entered politics. In 1965, following a special election pursuant to a court-ordered reapportionment of the legislature, he was elected to a one-year term in the Georgia House of Representatives. House members voted not to seat him, however, because of his opposition to the war in Vietnam.

In 1966 Bond won a second election, to fill his own vacant seat, but was again barred from membership. In November 1966, he won a third election—this time for a two-year term—and in December the SUPREME COURT ruled unanimously in *Bond v. Floyd* (1966) that the Georgia House had violated his rights in refusing him his seat. After serving in the Georgia House, Bond was elected to the Georgia Senate in 1974. In all Bond served four terms in the House and would serve six terms in the Senate, ending his tenure only after an unsuccessful 1986 congressional race prevented him from seeking reelection to the Senate. By this time, Julian Bond had been elected to public office more times than any other black Georgian in history.

In the Georgia Senate Bond served as the first black chairman of the Fulton County Senate Delegation, chaired the Committee on Consumer Affairs, and served as a member of the Human Resources, Governmental Operations, and Children and Youth Committees. During his tenure in the Georgia General Assembly, Bond sponsored or cosponsored more than sixty bills that passed into law, including a testing program for sickle-cell anemia, a minority set-aside program for Fulton County, and a program providing low-interest home loans to low-income Georgians. He led a successful effort to create a majority black congressional district in Atlanta, and he gained his greatest national exposure as the organizer of the Georgia Legislative Black Caucus, at the time the largest black political caucus in the country.

In 1968 Bond cochaired the Georgia Loyal National Delegation to the Democratic Convention, an insurgent group that successfully fought to unseat handpicked party regulars. The tumultuous 1968 convention nominated Bond for vice president of the United States, but he withdrew his name because he was, by law, too young to serve.

Bond has been active on the boards of many organizations dedicated to civil rights and social change. He founded and served as president of the Southern Elections Fund, which provided financial aid for the campaigns of rural southern black candidates. Bond has served several terms on the national board of the NATIONAL ASSOCIATION FOR THE ADVANCEMENT OF COLORED PEOPLE (NAACP) and was elected NAACP chairman in 1998.

Bond has appeared often on television and radio (his credits include the narration of *Eyes on the Prize*—PBS, 1987 and 1990—and of the Academy Award–winning documentary *A Time for Justice,* 1994). His essays have been collected in *A Time to Speak. A Time to Act,* and his writing has appeared in national magazines and newspapers. Bond has been a Papas Fellow at the University of Pennsylvania and a visiting professor in history and politics at Drexel University. He was also a visiting professor at Harvard University (1989–1990, 1991–1992) and at Williams College (1992–1993).

Suggested Reading

Bond, Julian. *A Time to Speak. A Time to Act.* New York: Simon and Schuster, 1972.

BONUS ARMY

World War I veterans of the U.S. armed forces were entitled by law to a cash payment, called a bonus, payable in 1945. In 1932, however, amid the desperate economic conditions of the Great Depression, many veterans (and others) were out of work, and a movement developed to demand immediate payment of the bonuses. In May of that year between 15,000 and 20,000 unemployed veterans marched on Washington in a demonstration that they hoped would shame Congress into releasing the bonus money. This group, which was known as the Bonus Army (and which also called itself the B. E. F., Bonus Expeditionary Force) camped within the city and just outside of it, at Anacostia Flats, Maryland.

On June 15, 1932, when the House of Representatives passed a bonus bill, it seemed that the Bonus Army's march would have its desired effect, but the substantially more conservative Senate voted down the bill. By the time of the Senate action the marchers' camp at Anacostia Flats had grown into a sprawling array of crates, shacks, and shanties. Here in the shadow of the Capitol was a Hooverville—as the Depression-era shantytowns that had appeared across the country were called. This particular Hooverville, however, was ready to explode.

On July 28, after the Senate's rejection of the bonus bill, rioting broke out at Anacostia Flats. Fearing a major insurrection, President Herbert Hoover ordered General Douglas MacArthur to march against the camp and break up the riot. MacArthur went about this mission with resolute zeal. Using cavalry, infantry, and armor (tanks and armored cars), he advanced against the unarmed Bonus Army, which included women and children from the veterans' families. MacArthur made extensive use of tear gas, and he ordered his cavalrymen to wade into the crowds and strike out with the flats of their sabers.

The highly publicized assault on the Bonus Army was generally perceived as a profound national disgrace. Seeking to defend his action, President Hoover called the demonstrators a "pack of criminals." An angry public and an avalanche of newspaper editorials demanded to know of what the Bonus Army was guilty. Poverty? Joblessness? Despair? If so, more than a quarter of the nation shared in the crime.

Although, from the perspective of history, the assault on the Bonus Army stands as a symbol of government insensitivity to poverty and an example of the elevation of public order over public welfare, when Hoover recalled the episode in his *Memoirs* (1952–1953), it was as an imminent threat to national security:

> The bonus march was in considerable part organized and promoted by the Communists and included a large number of hoodlums and ex-convicts determined to raise a public disturbance. They were frequently addressed by Democratic congressmen seeking to inflame them against me for my opposition to the bonus legislation. They were given financial support by some of the publishers of the sensational press. It was of interest to learn in after years from the Communist confessions that they also had put on a special battery of speakers to help [future president Franklin Delano] Roosevelt in his campaign, by use of the incident.
>
> When it was evident that no legislation on the bonus would be passed by the Congress, I asked the chairmen of the Congressional committees to appropriate funds to buy tickets home for the legitimate veterans. This was done and some 6,000 availed themselves of its aid, leaving about 5,000 mixed hoodlums, ex-convicts, Communists, and a minority of veterans in Washington.

Suggested Reading

Fausold, Martin L. *The Presidency of Herbert C. Hoover.* Lawrence: University Press of Kansas, 1985.

Waters, Walter W. *B. E. F.: The Whole Story of the Bonus Army.* New York: AMS, 1933.

BORK, ROBERT H. (1927–)

Robert H. Bork is best known for having been rejected by the U.S. Senate when President Ronald Reagan nominated him, in 1987, to the Supreme Court.

The outspokenly conservative jurist received his law degree from the University of Chicago in 1953, was a professor of law at Yale University from 1962 to 1973 and from 1977 to 1981, served as United States solicitor general from 1973 to 1977, and was a judge for the federal Circuit Court of Appeals for the District of Columbia from 1982 to 1988.

Bork brought an unapologetically conservative ideology to the bench, taking positions against abortion and affirmative action and against the doctrine that the First Amendment protects nonpolitical speech. His stance on such issues put Bork at odds with judicial and political liberals, including those in the forefront of the civil rights movement. However, Bork's role in the Watergate scandal blackened his reputation even among those who did not espouse a liberal agenda. In the fall of 1973, when it was discovered that President Richard M. Nixon had made covert recordings of White House conversations, the congressional committee investigating Watergate subpoenaed the tapes. In an attempt to sidestep the subpoena the president asserted executive privilege, then ordered attorney general Elliot L. Richardson to dismiss Archibald Cox, the special Watergate prosecutor. Indignant, Richardson refused, and resigned in protest. President Nixon then called on Richardson's deputy, William Ruckelshaus, who also refused to fire Cox and was therefore dismissed. Bork, however, the U.S. solicitor general at the time, did not scruple to discharge Cox. The press referred to the entire episode—the resignation of Richardson, the firing of Ruckelshaus, and Bork's dismissal of Cox at the behest of the president—as the Saturday Night Massacre. Bork's action haunted him for the rest of his career and returned again when President Reagan nominated him to the Supreme Court.

Liberals met the 1987 Bork nomination with vehement opposition. In particular, his apparent opposition to advancement in civil liberties was widely criticized. Bork's rejection by the Senate followed a singularly acrimonious confirmation hearing and was the result of a 58–42 vote, mainly along party lines.

In 1988 Bork resigned from the federal bench to become a resident scholar at the American Enterprise Institute for Public Policy Research, a conservative think tank.

Suggested Reading

Vieira, Norman, and Leonard Gross, eds. *Supreme Court Appointments: Judge Bork and the Politicization of Senate Confirmations.* Carbondale: Southern Illinois University Press, 1999.

BRANDEIS, LOUIS DEMBITZ (1856–1941)

Associate justice of the Supreme Court from 1916 to 1939, Louis Brandeis earned a reputation as one of the high court's most eloquent champions of judicial liberalism and of social and economic reform.

Born in Louisville, Kentucky, Brandeis graduated from Harvard law school in 1877 and practiced as a prominent Boston attorney from 1879 to 1916. During his practice, Brandeis distinguished himself with investigations of insurance practices and by establishing Massachusetts savings-bank insurance in 1907. Such efforts, in addition to his advocacy of the public interest in Boston utility cases during 1900–1907, established him as an advocate of progressive economic and political reform.

During 1907–1914, Brandeis served as counsel for the people in proceedings involving the constitutionality of wages and hours laws in California, Illinois, Ohio, and Oregon. In the landmark case of *Muller v. Oregon* (1908), Brandeis successfully argued before the Supreme Court that minimum-hours legislation for women was both constitutional and reasonable. In what became known as the Brandeis brief, he based his argument on what was, at the time, an unprecedented presentation of statistical, sociological, economic, and physiological data. The use of such material has had a profound impact on the practice of law.

Brandeis opposed New England transit monopolies during 1907–1913, and during 1910–1914 he successfully argued before the Massachusetts Interstate Commerce Commission the case against increases in railroad rates. His reputation as a reformer, however, went beyond economic issues. In 1910, acting as counsel in the congressional investigation of secretary of the interior Richard A. Ballinger, Brandeis was instrumental in bringing to light Ballinger's decidedly anticonservationist views. In the same year Brandeis successfully arbitrated a strike of predominantly Jewish garment workers in New York, an experience that transformed him into a Zionist activist.

Brandeis played a major role in the 1912 presidential campaign of Woodrow Wilson by creating the economic doctrine known as the New Freedom, which was aimed at ending industrial and financial monopoly. It was Wilson who braved the opposition of both big business and anti-Semites when he appointed Brandeis to the Supreme Court in 1916. For years Brandeis was the high court's leading (and sometimes sole) liberal voice, offering eloquent opinions that often dissented from those of the majority. Brandeis retired from the bench in 1939 and died in 1941.

A distinguished author, Brandeis wrote *Other People's Money* (1914), and *Business, a Profession* (1914). Brandeis University, founded in 1948, in Waltham, Massachusetts, is named in his honor.

Suggested Reading

Brandeis, Louis Dembitz. *Brandeis on Democracy.* Edited by Philippa Strum. Lawrence: University Press of Kansas, 1995.

Strum, Philippa. *Brandeis: Beyond Progressivism.* Lawrence: University Press of Kansas, 1995.

Key cases: *American Column and Lumber v. United States* (1921), *Whitney v. California* (1927), *Olmstead v. United States* (1928).

BROTHERHOOD OF SLEEPING CAR PORTERS

The Brotherhood of Sleeping Car Porters (BSCP) was organized on August 25, 1925, when about five hundred black Pullman Car porters met at the Imperial Lodge of Elks in New York City's Harlem neighborhood. The meeting, described by the *Amsterdam News* as "the greatest labor mass meeting ever held of, for and by Negro working men," was organized by A. PHILIP RANDOLPH, a black radical labor activist.

Pullman porters, all of whom were black, were a notoriously exploited class of laborers. A typical porter worked four hundred hours a month for less than $100. Randolph proposed that the only way to improve compensation and working conditions was to organize into a union.

As it turned out the 1925 meeting was only the beginning of a very difficult, and often dangerous, twelve-year struggle to secure a union contract with the Pullman Sleeping Car Company. In its efforts to intimidate union organizers and would-be union members and to undermine unionization, the company hired thugs to physically assault organizers, maintained a network of spies who reported on union activities, and donated money to black churches to win over black ministers and others who were influential in the black community, who were then induced to speak out against the BSCP.

Despite all obstacles, the BSCP became the first successful black-led trade union in this country—and, most important, through the success of the BSCP, blacks began to gain access to various other labor unions that were either segregated or entirely closed to African Americans, which spelled the beginning of the end of organized labor's discriminatory and exclusionary policies.

Suggested Reading

Harris, William H. *Keeping the Faith: A. Philip Randolph, Milton P. Webster, and the Brotherhood of Sleeping Car Porters, 1925–1937.* Champaign–Urbana: University of Illinois Press, 1991.

BROWN II

Formally known as *Brown v. Board of Education* (1955), *Brown II* is the enforcement decree pursuant to *BROWN V. BOARD OF EDUCATION OF TOPEKA, KANSAS* (1954), which details the high court's orders concerning school DESEGREGATION. These specifics were not included in the 1954 decision. (See Appendix A for the text of the *Brown II* opinion, delivered by Chief Justice Earl Warren on May 31, 1955.

Suggested Reading

Kluger, Richard. *Simple Justice: The History of Brown v. Board of Education and Black America's Struggle for Equality.* New York: Random House, 1977.

Patterson, James T. *Brown v. Board of Education: A Civil Rights Milestone and Its Troubled Legacy.* New York: Oxford University Press, 2001.

BROWN BERETS

Regarded by its founders as a Chicano version of the BLACK PANTHER PARTY (BPP), the Brown Berets was founded in 1967 in Los Angeles not long after the BPP had been founded in Oakland. The organization's primary goal was to mobilize and unify Chicanos to defend themselves against police brutality. From the beginning, however, the Brown Berets also focused on the needs of youth in the local neighborhoods and were particularly concerned with education issues.

To show a strong and unified presence in the face of police intimidation, the Brown Berets initially employed militant, confrontational tactics. They organized and encouraged such high-profile events as school walkouts in East Los Angeles (1969) and the Chicano Moratorium Against the Vietnam War (1970). During April 22–23, 1970, the Brown Berets occupied a public park in San Diego's Logan neighborhood, reclaiming it as Aztlán, the ancestral land of the Aztecs, which the Brown Berets also called La Tierra Mia ("our land").

Soon after the occupation of the park the police began to crack down on Brown Beret demonstrations and events, and the organization all but ceased to exist. In September 1992 David Sanchez, often identified as the founder of the Brown Berets, resurrected the organization but restyled it as the Brown Beret National Organization, a nonviolent group working to create jobs and to "promote real political representatives" for the Chicano community.

Suggested Reading

Navarro, Armando. *La Raza Unida Party: A Chicano Challenge to the U.S. Two-Party Dictatorship.* Philadelphia: Temple University Press, 2000.

BROWN V. BOARD OF EDUCATION OF TOPEKA, KANSAS

Brown v. Board of Education of Topeka, Kansas, the landmark SUPREME COURT decision declaring the segregation of public schools unconstitutional, was handed down on May 17, 1954. Throughout the early 1950s, racial segregation in public schools was universal in the South, and prevalent in other regions as well. The legality of this segregation rested largely on the "SEPARATE BUT EQUAL" DOCTRINE articulated in *PLESSY V. FERGUSON,* a late-nineteenth-century Supreme Court decision. According to this doctrine, separate schools for blacks and whites were legal, provided that, in a given district, the schools were equal in quality and in the resources they offered. Although the doctrine rested on the theory that schools that were separate could, in fact, be equal, the reality was that most black schools were far inferior to their white counterparts.

It was against this background that *Brown v. Board of Education* was litigated. In Topeka, Kansas, a black third grader named Linda Brown had to walk one mile through a railroad switchyard to get to her all-black elementary school, even though a white school was a safe, seven-block walk away. When the principal of the white school refused to enroll Brown, her father, Oliver Brown, requested the help of the Topeka branch of the National Association for the Advancement of Colored People (NAACP). Other black parents joined Brown, and, in 1951, the NAACP requested an injunction to forbid the segregation of Topeka's public schools.

The U.S. District Court for the District of Kansas heard the case on June 25–26, 1951. The NAACP argued that segregated schools sent a message to black children that they were inferior to whites; therefore, the schools were inherently unequal. As an expert witness for the NAACP, Dr. Hugh W. Speer, testified: "If the colored children are denied the experience in school of associating with white children, who represent 90 percent of our national society in which these colored children must live, then the colored child's curriculum is being greatly curtailed. The Topeka curriculum or any school curriculum cannot be equal under segregation." As a defense, the Topeka Board of Education claimed that because segregation was pervasive in Topeka and elsewhere, segregated schools prepared black children for the segregation they would experience as adults, and therefore represented sound and appropriate education for black children coming of age in a predominantly white society.

Although the district court agreed with the NAACP's argument that segregation "has a detrimental effect upon the colored children," instilling in them a "sense of inferiority" that negatively "affects the motivation of a child to learn," the court decided that the precedent of *Plessy v. Ferguson* allowed separate but equal school systems for blacks and whites. Without a Supreme Court ruling overturning *Plessy,* the district court believed itself "compelled" to rule in favor of the board of education. This decision left the door wide open to a Supreme Court appeal, which Brown and the NAACP undertook on October 1, 1951. Their case was combined with other cases that challenged school segregation in Delaware, South Carolina, and Virginia.

The high court first heard the case on December 9, 1952, but failed to reach a decision. In the reargument, heard on December 7–8, 1953, the Court requested that both sides discuss "the circumstances surrounding the adoption of the Fourteenth Amendment in 1868." When this discussion failed to shed light on the issue, the Supreme Court based its decision solely on whether or not segregated schools deprived black children of equal protection under the law. On May 17, 1954, chief justice Earl Warren read the decision of the unanimous Court.

Because Warren believed that it was important to deliver a unanimous opinion, he decided not to include a remedy in the 1954 ruling. A year later, the Supreme Court issued an enforcement decree, which put lower federal courts in charge of implementing the *Brown* decision "with all deliberate speed." The 1954 decision is often referred to as *Brown I* and the 1955 enforcement decree as *Brown II.* (See Appendix A for the text of the 1954 and 1955 Supreme Court decisions.)

Suggested Reading

Kluger, Richard. *Simple Justice: The History of Brown v. Board of Education and Black America's Struggle for Equality.* New York: Random House, 1977.

Patterson, James T. *Brown v. Board of Education: A Civil Rights Milestone and Its Troubled Legacy.* New York: Oxford University Press, 2001.

BROWN, JOHN (1800–1859)

John Brown took up arms in the cause of abolition, brutally avenged the free-soilers of Bleeding Kansas, and, in 1859, raided the federal arsenal at Harpers Ferry, Virginia (present-day West Virginia). To some, he was a fanatic. To others, he was a powerful martyr in the fight against slavery.

Born in Torrington, Connecticut, Brown drifted, settling briefly in Ohio, Pennsylvania, Massachusetts, and New York and finding work, catch-as-catch-can, as a sheep drover, tanner, wool trader, farmer, and land speculator. In 1849, Brown, a white man, settled his family in a black community founded at North Elba, New York, on land donated by an abolitionist philanthropist named Gerrit Smith. While living in North Elba, Brown, who was himself vehemently opposed to slavery, decided to plan some bold action to free blacks. In 1855, with half-formed intentions, he and five of his sons moved to the Kansas Territory to throw in their lot with the antislavery forces then vying for control of the territory, in hopes that when it was admitted to the Union, it would be as a free state.

Settling at Osawatomie, Brown became the leader of the local free-soil guerrillas. On May 21, 1856, a proslavery mob raided, sacked, and burned the free-soil stronghold of Lawrence, Kansas—an act that moved Brown to action. On the night of May 24, believing that he had been called by God to avenge the attack on Lawrence, Brown and his raiders attacked a proslavery camp at Pottawatomie Creek, hacking to death five men.

Two years later, in the spring of 1858, Brown held a meeting of blacks and whites in Chatham, Ontario, Canada, where he outlined a plan to create a stronghold for fugitive slaves—not merely a safe haven, but a headquarters for slave rebellion—in the hills of Maryland and Virginia. The meeting also produced a new provisional government for the United States—one that outlawed slavery. Elected commander in chief of the provisional government, Brown secured the financial backing of Gerrit Smith and other Boston abolitionists to finance a military action. In the summer of 1859, leading an "army" of sixteen whites and five blacks, Brown established a headquarters in a rented farmhouse in Maryland, across the Potomac River from Harpers Ferry. After spending the summer in preparation, he and his band raided the Harpers Ferry arsenal on the night of October 16, 1859. The arsenal fell, and Brown took about sixty town residents hostage.

Brown planned to use the arsenal to arm a spontaneous "army of emancipation"—a force of runaway slaves who would fight to liberate their fellows. In fact, the slaves did not rally around Brown, and the rebellion failed to materialize. Brown and his small band held off the local militia through the next day and night, but surrendered on October 18 to a force of U.S. Marines led by Robert E. Lee. When the marines stormed the arsenal, they wounded Brown and killed ten of his followers, including two of his sons.

Brown was tried in a Virginia court for murder, slave insurrection, and treason against the state, found guilty, and hanged, on December 2, 1859. His detractors painted Brown as a dangerous fanatic, but his dignified and fearless behavior during his trial and at his execution greatly impressed the public and gave the abolitionist cause a compelling martyr. Although the raid on Harpers Ferry failed to create a slave rebellion, it intensified the efforts of the abolition movement and hastened the onset of the Civil War. (See also KANSAS-NEBRASKA ACT.)

Suggested Reading

Rossbach, Jeffrey S. *Ambivalent Conspirators: John Brown, the Secret Six, and a Theory of Slave Violence*. Philadelphia: University of Pennsylvania Press, 1983.

BUNCHE, RALPH (1904–1971)

Ralph Johnson Bunche, a distinguished African American diplomat, was instrumental in planning the UNITED NATIONS (UN) and for more than twenty years was a leading member of that organization. His efforts to negotiate an Arab-Israeli truce in Palestine in 1949 earned him the Nobel Peace Prize in 1950. Many American blacks looked to Bunche as a role model and as an example of achievement.

Bunche received graduate degrees in government and international relations from Harvard University in 1928 and 1934, then joined the faculty of Howard University in Washington, D. C., where he founded the political science department. During his early years in academia Bunche studied the French-mandate government of French Togoland and the colonial government of Dahomey. He then completed advanced research at Northwestern University and the London School of Economics, after which he resumed his study of colonialism in Africa.

During 1938–1940 Bunche turned his focus to the United States, collaborating with the sociologist Gunnar Myrdal on *An American Dilemma* (1944), a massive pioneering study of American race relations. With the outbreak of World War II Bunche worked for the Department of War, the Office of Strategic Services (the precursor of the Central Intelligence Agency), and the Department of State. As the war wound down he became a key planner for the UN and participated in the 1945 San Francisco Conference, at which that organization was formally founded. In 1947 Bunche joined the permanent UN Secretariat in New York as director of the Trusteeship Department.

In 1948 he headed a special UN committee to negotiate a settlement between Arabs and Israelis in Palestine. When the principal mediator, Count Folke Bernadotte, was assassinated, Bunche replaced him and successfully negotiated a series of armistices, culminating in a final cease-fire in May 1949. The following year Bunche became the first African American to receive the Nobel Peace Prize.

Bunche was appointed UN undersecretary in 1955 and, in 1957, undersecretary for special political affairs. In this capacity he was effectively the organization's principal troubleshooter. Reporting directly to Secretary-General Dag Hammarskjöld, Bunche played important roles in addressing many of the world crises of the 1950s and early 1960s.

Bunche's absorption in the work of the UN and in the world of international diplomacy drew criticism from some African American leaders, who accused him of turning his back on the U.S. civil rights movement. By the mid-1960s, however, perhaps in response to such criticism, Bunche had begun to speak out against segregation and discrimination. In 1965, although ailing, he marched in Selma and in Montgomery, Alabama. For twenty-two years Bunche served on the board of the NATIONAL ASSOCIATION FOR THE ADVANCEMENT OF COLORED PEOPLE. (See also BLOODY SUNDAY, and SELMA SNCC–SCLC DEMONSTRATION.)

Suggested Reading

Henry, Charles P., ed. *Ralph Bunche: Model Negro or American Other?* New York: New York University Press, 1999.

Urquhart, Brian. *Ralph Bunche: An American Odyssey.* New York: Norton, 1998.

BURGER, WARREN (1907–1995)

Warren Earl Burger was the fifteenth chief justice of the United States, serving from 1969 to 1986. A lifelong Republican appointed by President RICHARD M. NIXON to succeed the liberal EARL WARREN, Burger stunned many with his political independence and by his refusal, for the most part, to reverse the liberal trend of the high court.

Burger graduated from St. Paul (now William Mitchell) College of Law in 1931, practiced law, and became active in Republican politics. He was appointed an assistant U.S. attorney general in 1953 and two years later was nominated by President DWIGHT D. EISENHOWER to the U.S. Court of Appeals for the District of Columbia. It was Burger's predominantly conservative record during his tenure on this court, from 1956 to 1969, that prompted President Nixon to nominate him to succeed Warren on the SUPREME COURT.

At the time that he appointed Burger, President Nixon had also elevated three associate justices to the Supreme Court, and most Americans assumed that these appointments would be the undoing of the era of judicial activism and liberal reform that Earl Warren had spearheaded. But nothing of the kind occurred: in the realm of general civil rights and in that of civil rights in criminal law, the Burger court generally supported and perpetuated the Warren legacy—upholding, for example, the *MIRANDA V. ARIZONA* decision, busing as a means of achieving racial integration of public schools, and AFFIRMATIVE ACTION in the distribution of federal grants and contracts to minorities. Most stunning of all was Burger's vote with the majority in the 1973 *ROE V. WADE* decision.

Burger retired from the Supreme Court in 1986 and served as chairman of the commission that planned the bicentennial celebration of the U.S. constitution (1987). He was awarded the Presidential Medal of Freedom in 1988. Burger died on June 25, 1995. (See also BUSING, SCHOOL.)

Suggested Reading

Lamb, Charles M., and Stephen C. Halpern, eds. *The Burger Court: Political and Judicial Profiles.* Champaign–Urbana: University of Illinois Press, 1991.

Maltz, Earl M. *The Chief Justiceship of Warren Burger, 1969–1986.* Columbia: University of South Carolina Press, 2000.

Key cases: *Miranda v. Arizona* (1966), *Roe v. Wade* (1973), *Adams v. Williams* (1973), *Moore v. East Cleveland* (1976), *Lewis v. United States* (1980).

BURLINGTON INDUSTRIES, INC. V. ELLERTH

In *Burlington Industries, Inc. v. Ellerth* (1998), the SUPREME COURT ruled that employers are subject to vicarious liability for unlawful SEXUAL HARASSMENT committed by supervisors in their employ. That is, a supervisor's sexually harassing conduct in the workplace will be imputed to the employer. The high court's ruling was stringent: an employer is "strictly liable" (a legal term of art meaning that no defense is possible) for any sexual harassment by a supervisor that results in a "tangible employment action." The court decision defined *tangible employment action* as any "significant change in employment status, such as hiring, firing, failing to promote, reassignment with significantly different responsibilities, or a decision causing a significant change in benefits." However, even if the harassment does not result in such a tangible action, an employer may still be vicariously liable if the actions and behavior of managers and supervisors create a HOSTILE WORK ENVIRONMENT. In such cases, however, the high court defined grounds for possible defense.

Suggested Reading

Lemoncheck, Linda, and James P. Sterba, eds. *Sexual Harassment: Issues and Answers.* New York: Oxford University Press, 2001.

Related cases: *Meritor Savings Bank, FSB v. Vinson* (1986) and *Community for Creative Non-Violence v. Reid* (1989).

BUSING, SCHOOL

The 1954 SUPREME COURT decision in *BROWN V. BOARD OF EDUCATION OF TOPEKA, KANSAS* held racial segregation in public education unconstitutional. However, both in the South, where segregated schools had been mandated by law, and in the North, where no laws mandated the racial segregation that nevertheless existed, many school districts redrew their maps so that certain schools would remain white and others black—apparently for reasons of geography. The resulting segregation was de facto (by fact) rather than de jure (by law). The Supreme Court decision in *ALEXANDER V. HOLMES COUNTY* (1969) indirectly attacked de facto segregation by mandating "unitary" school systems; subsequent decisions called for school systems to act "affirmatively" to remove all racial discrimination. In 1979 the Supreme Court decision in *COLUMBUS BOARD OF EDUCATION V. PENICK* supported a controversial but common affirmative DESEGREGATION program that was already in place in numerous school districts: busing.

Busing was intended to better balance white and black school populations by transporting black children to white schools and white children to black schools. The hope was not merely to end de facto segregation but to improve the educational experience of black students by giving them opportunities to associate with white students.

In some jurisdictions busing was voluntary; that is, parents could choose to have their children bused or not. Typically, some black parents would choose to have their children bused to a school in a white neighborhood because, presumably, it would be better staffed and more adequately supplied. By the early 1970s, however, involuntary busing programs were introduced, under which parents—black and white—could be compelled to put their children on buses for transportation to relatively distant schools.

Busing was seen as a kind of social catalyst, a way of bringing blacks and whites together earlier in their development in the hope that by the time they reached adulthood they would have fewer racial biases—and that the nation, ultimately, would be more effectively integrated. However, busing was never very popular, even among black parents and liberal white parents—largely because of parents' emotional need to send their children to a *neighborhood* school. Wave upon wave of lawsuits resulted—appealing, in various ways, for the overturn of federally mandated local busing plans.

By the early 1970s antibusing protests had become strident—and sometimes militant. In cities across the nation, including northern cities (most notoriously, Boston), acts ranging from civil disobedience to outright violence and intimidation, including violence directed against students, were common. The 1972 Democratic presidential campaign of GEORGE WALLACE, Alabama's segregationist governor, was largely based on an antibusing platform. Considering Wallace's status as a political outsider, his strong showing among primary voters was surprising. Two years later, in 1974, Judge W. Arthur Garrity overrode the involuntary busing plan passed by the Boston School Committee, a move that added fuel to what had become a nationwide debate—a debate between an activist minority that favored busing and a general majority that opposed it. While polls taken during the 1970s showed that about three-quarters of the population favored racially mixed schools, those same polls also revealed that busing was opposed by almost precisely this same three-to-one margin. ("*Globe* Poll: Views on Race in America," June 22, 1998, www.boston.com/globe/nation/packages/rethinking_integration/views_on_race_poll.htm).

Resolution of the busing dilemma seemed impossible until the early 1980s, when sociological data called into question the assumption that mixing black and white students would necessarily improve black academic performance. During the 1980s and the early 1990s, school districts dismantled their involuntary busing programs. While voluntary busing is still in place in most jurisdictions, only a small fraction of black parents take deliberate steps to send their children to schools in predominantly white neighborhoods.

Suggested Reading

Formisano, Ronald P. *Boston against Busing: Race, Class, and Ethnicity in the 1960s and 1970s.* Chapel Hill: University of North Carolina Press, 1991.

Pride, Richard A. *The Burden of Busing: The Politics of Desegregation in Nashville, Tennessee.* Knoxville: University of Tennessee Press, 1985.

Schwartz, Bernard. *Swann's Way: The School Busing Case and the Supreme Court.* New York: Oxford University Press, 1986.

CALHOUN, JOHN C. (1782–1850)

Republican congressional representative and senator from South Carolina, secretary of war under President James Monroe, and seventh vice president of the United States (1825–1832), John C. Calhoun achieved his greatest fame—and notoriety—as a champion of the ways of the Old South, as an apologist for SLAVERY, and as a theorist and advocate of the twin doctrines of states' rights and nullification.

Early in his political career Calhoun was an intense nationalist, favoring policies that promoted national rather than regional identity and interests. He was elected vice president in 1824 (under John Quincy Adams) and reelected in 1828 (under ANDREW JACKSON). During his service with Jackson Calhoun performed an about-face and became a "strict constructionist"; that is, he held that only those powers explicitly enumerated in the Constitution resided with the federal government and that all other authority resided with the states. Along with this strict constructionist view, Calhoun embraced regionalism—specifically, advocacy of the interests and needs of the South—over nationalism. This position brought Calhoun into conflict with Congress, which passed a strongly protective tariff law in 1828 that levied a heavy duty on all imported manufactured goods. Southerners called this the Tariff of Abominations because it threatened to cripple southern trade in cotton exports.

In response to the tariff Calhoun anonymously published a pamphlet entitled the *South Carolina Exposition and Protest,* which argued that any state that deemed the federal tariff unconstitutional could pronounce it "null and void." At first, the doctrine of nullification found little support even among southern states, and in any case the crisis was defused by the election of Andrew Jackson, who had campaigned in part on a platform of tariff reform. But when the Tariff Act of 1832, passed during the Jackson administration, offered little improvement on the earlier tariff, Calhoun angrily resigned as Jackson's vice president and stood for election to the Senate. He won, and at his urging and instigation the state of South Carolina called a convention that, on November 24, 1832, enacted an "ordinance of nullification" forbidding collection of tariff duties in the state. This action prompted Robert Y. Hayne, Calhoun's fellow senator from South Carolina, to declare that a state could not only nullify an unconstitutional law, but could, if need be, withdraw from the Union itself.

Nullification and its tie to secession threw the nation into crisis—not a crisis brought about by the abstract advocacy of states' rights but by a deliberate attempt to perpetuate an economy based on slavery. Calhoun and his southern colleagues understood that slavery would eventually be abolished by a northern majority in Congress. Nullification was a means of circumventing the democratic principle of majority rule and thereby preserving, as long as possible, slavery and the old southern way of life. On December 10, 1833, to Calhoun's surprise, President Jackson responded to nullification by threatening to use federal troops to compel the collection of tariff duties in any state that refused to enforce the tariff. Although a compromise tariff was enacted later in the year that mollified the South, the doctrines of states' rights and nullification would eventually provide the foundation for the Civil War. And even after the war these doctrines would be used in the South in an effort to evade the force of federal civil rights legislation.

Calhoun's last two decades were spent in the Senate, where he worked to unite the South against the forces of abolition and where he defended slavery as a "positive good."

Suggested Reading

Calhoun, John C. *The Papers of John C. Calhoun.* Vols. 4–25. Edited by Clyde N. Wilson, Shirley B. Cook, and Alexander Moore. Columbia: University of South Carolina Press, 1981–1990.

Lence, Ross M., ed. *Union and Liberty: The Political Philosophy of John C. Calhoun.* Indianapolis, Ind.: Liberty Fund, 1992.

Niven, John. *John C. Calhoun and the Price of Union: A Biography.* Baton Rouge: Louisiana State University Press, 1993.

CAPITAL PUNISHMENT

With several notable exceptions, including the United States, capital punishment—the execution of a person who has been convicted of committing a crime—is no longer practiced among Western nations. At one time, however, capital punishment was virtually universal and was applied to a wide variety of offenses, including not only crimes against people but against property. Today in the United States only murder and high treason are punishable by death. Moreover, while the death penalty applies in federal capital crimes, not all states have death penalty statutes.

There has long been an anti–death penalty movement in the United States, and in 1972 the Supreme Court ruled in *Furman v. Georgia* that capital punishment laws, as enforced at the time, were unconstitutional because they were not applied equitably. Subsequently, however, in *Gregg v. Georgia* (1976), the high court ruled that capital punishment per se *was* constitutional. In response to these two rulings, many states enacted capital punishment statutes that were very specific as to the crimes, and the circumstances surrounding the crimes, for which the death penalty may be invoked—thus preserving the practice of capital punishment while satisfying the requirements of the 1972 ruling.

Proponents of the death penalty maintain that it is a powerful deterrent to the most serious of crimes, is a punishment eminently suited to such crimes, and is the only means of delivering justice to the relatives of murder victims. In addition, proponents argue that some criminals are clearly beyond any hope of redemption and that their crimes render them unfit to live in civilized society.

Opponents of the death penalty counter that life imprisonment without parole is an equally effective deterrent to capital crimes—and, moreover, that because the death penalty is the one punishment that cannot be reversed in case of judicial error, innocent people are sometimes executed. Finally, opponents argue that the death penalty is still applied unequally: defendants who can afford costly lawyers and multiple appeals frequently escape capital punishment, whereas the poor and members of minority groups are most likely to be executed. For example, from 1995 to 2000 federal prosecutors sought the death penalty for 183 defendants, 74 percent of whom were members of minority groups. Of the twenty-one convicts on federal death row as of June 2001, 81 percent were black or Latino. In 2001, however, a study of racial and ethnic bias conducted by the U.S. Department of Justice concluded that no bias exists.

Suggested Reading

Banner, Stuart. *The Death Penalty: An American History.* Cambridge: Harvard University Press, 2002.

Goldman, Raphael. *Capital Punishment.* Washington, D.C.: CQ Press, 2002.

Jost, Kenneth. "Rethinking the Death Penalty." *CQ Researcher,* November 16, 2001, 945–967.

CARMICHAEL, STOKELY (1941–1998)

Stokely Carmichael was prominent in the black power movement and is credited with having coined the phrase *black power* in 1966. At that time Carmichael was serving as chairman of the Student Nonviolent Coordinating Committee (SNCC), and it was under his leadership that the organization moved in a radical direction, advocating militancy and rejecting integration.

Born in Port of Spain, Trinidad, Carmichael came to live in Manhattan's Harlem neighborhood in 1952 when he was twelve. He had become politically active before he was out of his teens, and in 1961, while he was a freshman at Howard University in Washington, D.C., he joined the Freedom Riders and the Nonviolent Action Group, a SNCC affiliate. Carmichael was arrested repeatedly and, after one Freedom Ride, was arrested, tried, and sentenced to forty-nine days in Mississippi's notorious Parchman Penitentiary.

Carmichael became a SNCC organizer in 1964 and was elected chairman in 1966, succeeding John Lewis. The new chairman immediately made headlines with a speech in Greenwood, Mississippi, in which he declared his support for "black power." Through the work of Carmichael and others this slogan evolved into an economic and social agenda focused on increasing blacks' political and economic clout as well as their pride in their African and African American heritage. In Carmichael's 1967 book *Black Power,* which explained the concept most fully, he was careful to distinguish between militancy and simple violence: black power was intended as a call to social consciousness, not to arms. Nevertheless, many who identified themselves as Carmichael's followers believed in black separatism and, if necessary, the use of violence, both of which Carmichael himself increasingly embraced.

Carmichael left SNCC in 1967 and established ties with the Black Panther Party, where he served briefly as "prime minister" before breaking with the Panthers, largely because he disagreed with the party's effort to create links with groups of white student radicals such as Students for a Democratic Society. In a widely publicized letter to the

Black Panther Party, Carmichael declared, "The alliances being formed by the party are alliances which I cannot politically agree with because the history of Africans living in the United States has shown that any premature alliance with white radicals has led to complete submission of the blacks by the whites."

Carmichael's black separatism and pan-Africanism (a conviction of cultural and political solidarity with all persons of African origin) also moved him to deny common cause with poor whites. In a speech on February 17, 1968, at a Black Panther Party rally in Oakland, California, Carmichael explained:

> Poor white people are not fighting for their humanity, they're fighting for more money. There are a lot of poor white people in this country. You ain't seen none of them rebel yet, have you? Why is it that black people are rebelling? Don't think it's because of poor jobs. Don't believe that junk that honky is running down. It's not poor jobs. It's a question of a people fighting for their culture, for their nature, for their humanity.

Shortly after leaving the Panthers Carmichael moved to Guinea, West Africa. With Kwame Nkrumah, the ousted revolutionary leader of Ghana, he founded the All-African Peoples Revolutionary Party, which acquired a small following in Africa and the United States. Carmichael adopted the names of Kwame Nkrumah and Guinea's leader, Sekou Toure, as his own: Kwame Toure. Until his death at age fifty-seven from prostate cancer (November 17, 1998), Toure frequently left his home in Conakry, the capital of Guinea, to lecture in the United States.

Suggested Reading

Ture, Kwame, and Charles V. Hamilton. *Black Power: The Politics of Liberation.* 1968. Reprint, New York: Vintage, 1992.

CARTER, JIMMY (1924–)

James Earl Carter Jr. was the thirty-ninth president of the United States, serving from 1977 to 1981. A liberal Democrat, he was widely blamed for a host of national economic problems and for the Iran hostage crisis of 1980–1981. Yet he was also recognized as a distinguished champion of human rights.

Carter was born in the small town of Plains, Georgia, the son of Earl Carter, a peanut warehouser and local politician, and Lillian Gordy Carter—"Miss Lillian"—a registered nurse. Carter was educated at Georgia Southwestern College, Georgia Tech, and the U.S. Naval Academy at Annapolis, from which he graduated in 1946. He served in the navy for seven years, five of them under Admiral Hyman Rickover, the father of the nuclear submarine fleet. Carter resigned his commission in 1953 to take over the family peanut business after the death of his father.

Carter was elected to the Georgia Senate in 1962 and was reelected in 1964. He made an unsuccessful run for governor in 1966, but won a second bid in 1970. Carter had announced in his inaugural address that "the time for racial discrimination is over," and, true to his word, he opened Georgia government to African Americans and to women—groups that had been excluded or grossly underrepresented. Carter earned national recognition for extensively reforming the Georgia state bureaucracy and was widely identified with the emergence of the "New South" as a region of liberalized thinking and economic growth.

Carter's two-year campaign for the Democratic presidential nomination was based, in large measure, on his reformist reputation. He captured the nomination in July 1976, and, with Minnesota Democrat Sen. Walter F. Mondale as his running mate, he defeated Gerald R. Ford.

Carter presented himself as a man of the people and, like Lyndon B. Johnson before him, introduced an ambitious program of social, administrative, and economic reform. Unlike Johnson, however, he had little success in promoting his proposals, many of which put him at odds with Congress even though his own party enjoyed a majority there. Carter did move aggressively and productively, however, to include women and minorities in his cabinet, including Juanita Morris Kreps (secretary of commerce), Patricia Roberts Harris (first as secretary of the Department of Housing and Urban Development and later as secretary of the Department of Health and Human Services), and Andrew Young (U.S. representative to the United Nations).

Carter's idealism fared better in the international arena: he distinguished himself, and the office of chief executive, by advancing human rights initiatives. On a more pragmatic plane, he concluded, in 1977, two treaties that gave Panama eventual control over the Panama Canal while guaranteeing the canal's neutrality in perpetuity. In 1978 he brokered peace talks between Egyptian president Anwar el-Sadat and Israeli prime minister Menachem Begin; the result was the Camp David Accords, which ended the war between Egypt and Israel that had been ongoing since 1948. In 1979 Carter opened full diplomatic relations with China and severed official ties with Taiwan. With Soviet premier Leonid Brezhnev he concluded a new and sweeping strategic arms limitation treaty (SALT II), but boldly withdrew the treaty from the Senate advice and consent process in January 1980 after the Soviet Union invaded Afghanistan. Carter applied additional pressure to the Soviets by placing an embargo on American grain shipments to the Soviet Union and calling for an American boycott of the 1980 Moscow Summer Olympics.

Despite Carter's many international successes, the taking of American hostages by Iranian extremists at the U.S. embassy in Teheran (November 4, 1979) overshadowed the rest of the Carter presidency. The administration's inability to negotiate the release of the hostages, and the subsequent failure of a secret military mission to rescue them, cost Carter credibility. These woes were compounded by economic "stagflation"—simultaneous recession and inflation—and an acute energy crisis that resulted from U.S. overdependence on foreign oil.

Carter was soundly defeated by Republican candidate RONALD W. REAGAN in 1980. The Iranians released the U.S. hostages on the day of Reagan's inauguration—although, to the new president's credit, Reagan asked Carter to serve as his special envoy and to officially greet the hostages as they landed in Germany.

After leaving the White House Carter embarked on a distinguished career. He established the Carter Center in Atlanta, a presidential library and center for the peaceful resolution of conflict, and he has often served in an informal capacity as a diplomat, especially in Central America and Africa, where he monitored elections to ensure their legitimacy. In 1994 he negotiated with North Korea to end nuclear weapons development. In the same year he provided assistance in turbulent Haiti, helping to ensure the peaceful end to a coup and the restoration of exiled president Jean-Bertrand Aristide. And he entered the fray in Bosnia, where he succeeded in mediating a short-lived cease-fire. Carter has also been deeply involved in the Habitat for Humanity program, working hands-on to build homes for the poor.

Suggested Reading

Brinkley, Douglas. *The Unfinished Presidency: Jimmy Carter's Journey Beyond the White House.* New York: Viking, 1998.

Kaufman, Burton I. *The Presidency of James Earl Carter, Jr.* Lawrence: University Press of Kansas, 1993.

CATHOLIC BISHOPS' COMMITTEE FOR THE SPANISH-SPEAKING

Catholic bishops in the United States established the Committee for the Spanish-Speaking in 1945. The committee was headquartered in San Antonio, Texas, and was intended to provide for the religious, social, economic, educational, and cultural advancement of Mexican Americans, including migrant workers. In 1964 the committee merged with the Bishops' Committee for Migrant Workers to become Catholic Bishops' Committee for the Spanish-Speaking.

CATHOLIC WORKER MOVEMENT

The Catholic Worker movement was founded in 1933, during the Great Depression, by radical social and political activist, Catholic convert, and lay worker DOROTHY DAY at the urging of the like-minded Peter Maurin. The movement is best known for the "houses of hospitality" maintained in the run-down sections of many cities, and in a few rural areas, by independent Catholic Worker "communities." Essentially privately run shelters, the houses of hospitality offer food and clothing to those in need. There are currently more than 130 Catholic Worker communities located throughout the United States.

From 1933 until Day's death in 1980 the movement published a newspaper, the *Catholic Worker.* Under Day's editorial guidance the newspaper published work by Catholic activists, literary notables, and spiritual philosophers including Daniel Berrigan, Jacques Maritain, and Thomas Merton. Nonviolence and pacifism are central to the Catholic Worker movement, and, during times of war and conscription, Catholic Workers have been in the forefront of the CONSCIENTIOUS OBJECTOR movement. In addition to promoting nonviolence, both the *Catholic Worker* and activists within the various Catholic Worker communities have supported labor and human rights causes, the work of labor unions, and the creation of cooperatives.

Although it is a lay organization (a body of the unordained faithful), the members of the Catholic Worker movement embrace voluntary poverty, which links the movement to the ideals of the early Franciscans; at the same time, the movement's emphasis on community, prayer, and hospitality partakes of Benedictine traditions. Each Catholic Worker community is autonomous, and the movement is without central governance of any kind. Dorothy Day was the last figure whose function approached that of a central leader.

Suggested Reading

Cornell, Tom, Robert Ellsberg, and Jim Forest, eds. *A Penny a Copy: Writings from The Catholic Worker.* Maryknoll, N.Y.: Orbis, 1995.

CENSUS, U.S.

Census data is crucial to apportioning legislative representation; to federal funding of social, educational, and other programs; and to monitoring for compliance with various civil rights and nondiscrimination measures. To obtain census counts the U.S. Bureau of the Census relies primarily on citizens to return the census forms that are mailed to them. However, between 1970 and 1990, the percentage of forms returned dropped from 78 percent to 65 percent. It was estimated that, as a consequence, the 1990 census failed to count some five million persons, most of whom were living below the poverty line, were members of ethnic or racial minority groups, or both. The 1990 census was less accurate than any previous census, and census officials, as well as advocates for minorities and the poor, believe that the hard-to-reach segments of the population were the most severely undercounted.

Along with various advocacy groups, liberal politicians (mostly Democrats) proposed augmenting the 2000 census with sophisticated statistical sampling, arguing that this method would provide a more accurate picture than an actual count alone. In response, the census bureau proposed sending out the questionnaires as usual, then performing random sampling in areas that had a low response rate. On the basis of this sampling, statistical estimates could be made to augment the actual count.

Most congressional Republicans opposed sampling, arguing that the Constitution unambiguously calls for an "actual enumeration" of the population, language that the Republicans interpreted as barring any attempt at estimate. Proponents of sampling countered that Republicans and other conservatives were insisting on an actual enumeration precisely because it tended to exclude those who might be recipients of social welfare programs, and would therefore reduce the cost of such programs. The Republican-controlled Congress rejected the census bureau's sampling plan for the 2000 census.

Nevertheless, in 2000 the Census Bureau attempted to ensure—even without sampling—that minority groups were counted. For the first time, census questionnaires were made available in six different languages: English, Chinese, Korean, Spanish, Tagalog, and Vietnamese. (Although the bureau also worked with community and minority organizations to reach out to individuals, such efforts were complicated by the reluctance of illegal aliens to respond to any government questionnaire, even though census information cannot be used to identify or target illegal aliens.)

In addition to being challenged because of issues related to the undercounting of minorities and the poor, the 1990 census was challenged by minority advocates for the limitations it imposed on how respondents might identify their ethnic and racial origin. The 2000 census was the first that permitted respondents to indicate mixed racial or ethnic origin and to choose from among racial categories, including white, African American, American Indian, and nine Asian categories. Native Americans could choose their specific tribe and, in some cases, their specific band of that tribe. Finally, because American Latinos come from various backgrounds, a census question about family origin—Mexican, Puerto Rican, Cuban, or other—also appeared on the 2000 census form.

Suggested Reading

Anderson, Margo J., ed. *Encyclopedia of the U.S. Census.* Washington, D.C.: CQ Press, 2000.

Frey, William H., et al. *America by the Numbers: A Field Guide to the U.S. Population.* New York: New Press, 2001.

CENTER FOR CIVIL AND HUMAN RIGHTS

The Center for Civil and Human Rights was founded in 1973 at the University of Notre Dame as an institute for advanced research and teaching. Although initially focused on civil rights in the United States, the center eventually expanded its work to include international human rights. Funded by a Ford Foundation grant, the center provides lawyers with opportunities to gain practical experience in international human rights law and conducts research and advocacy intended to improve international mechanisms of accountability. The center is part of the University of Notre Dame Law School and is the only institution at an American law school with observer status at the African Commission on Human and Peoples' Rights.

Suggested Reading

Notre Dame Human Rights Advocate, published periodically by the Center for Civil and Human Rights, www.nd.edu/~cchr/publications/advocate/advocate.html.

CENTER FOR LAW AND SOCIAL POLICY

Founded in 1968 by Charles Halpern and three other lawyers, with the aid of SUPREME COURT justice Arthur Goldberg, the Center for Law and Social Policy (CLASP) is a national public policy and law organization that undertakes policy advocacy before state and federal government agencies and conducts policy research on family poverty and on civil legal assistance to the poor. The organization also provides technical guidance and training to legal professionals and others who provide civil legal assistance to the poor. Before 1982 the organization helped to develop new areas of legal advocacy in WOMEN'S RIGHTS, mental health, environmental protection, international human rights, health care for the poor, international trade, employment rights, and mine health and safety. Since 1982 the organization has focused primarily on increasing the economic security of poor families with children and on securing full access to the civil justice system for such families.

Suggested Reading

Center for Civil and Human Rights, www.clasp.org.

CENTER FOR WOMEN'S POLICY STUDIES

The Center for Women's Policy Studies was founded in 1972 as the first feminist policy research organization in the United States. Its purpose is "to promote justice and equality for women," and its earliest work consisted of groundbreaking research demonstrating that banks engaged in sex discrimination when granting credit. On the basis of this research the organization participated in drafting the Equal Credit Opportunity Act (15 USC. 1691 et seq.), passed in 1997. Other early research conducted by the center contributed to the Violence Against Women Act (108 Stat.1902 et seq.), passed in 1994 and amended in 1998 and 2000, and led to the creation of model programs to respond to rape. The center also sponsored the establishment of the first National Resource Center on Family Violence.

In the 1980s the center produced pioneering research on gender bias in the Standard Achievement Test, which is a prerequisite for most college admissions, and sponsored Feminist Futures, the first national conference by, for, and about young women. In 1996 the center published a landmark report that defined violence against women as a bias-motivated hate crime; this definition laid the foundation for the 1998 amended Violence against Women Act, which, if approved by the Senate, would provide legal relief under federal civil rights law for violence against women. The center has focused on issues relating to HIV, AIDS, and women since the late 1980s; most recently, it has also focused intensively on programs and policies for low-income women.

Suggested Reading

Center for Women's Policy Studies, www.centerwomenpolicy.org.

CHANEY, JAMES EARL (1943–1964)

James Earl Chaney was a Congress of Racial Equality (CORE) activist, who, with fellow CORE members Andrew Goodman and Michael Schwerner, was murdered in Mississippi; he is recognized as one of the martyrs of the civil rights movement of the 1960s.

Born in Meridian, Mississippi, Chaney was the son of a plasterer. As a high school student he became an early civil rights supporter and was suspended from school for wearing a National Association for the Advancement of Colored People badge. He attended Harris Junior College, in Mississippi, then apprenticed to his father.

Chaney became a CORE volunteer in October 1963; he soon impressed Michael Schwerner, the director of the Meridian office, who recommended him for a full-time position with CORE. Chaney was working on the Freedom Summer campaign when, on June 21, 1964, he, Goodman, and Schwerner traveled to Longdale to visit the Mt. Zion Methodist Church, which had been firebombed by the Ku Klux Klan (KKK) because it was going to be used as a CORE-sponsored "freedom school." On their return to Meridian the three men were arrested by Deputy Sheriff Cecil Price and detained at the Neshoba County Jail. Released later in the evening, the three were intercepted on a rural road, shot dead, and buried in an earthen dam.

In response to the news that the three activists were missing, U.S. attorney general Robert Kennedy dispatched the Federal Bureau of Investigation (FBI) to investigate. Agents found the bodies on August 4, 1964. Some weeks later, on October 13, KKK member James Jordan confessed to FBI agents that he had witnessed the murders and agreed to cooperate with the investigation. As a result, nineteen men—including Sheriff Lawrence Rainey and Deputy Sheriff Cecil Price—were arrested and indicted on federal charges of having violated the civil rights of Chaney, Schwerner, and Goodman.

On February 24, 1967, Judge William Cox dismissed seventeen of the nineteen indictments, but the Supreme Court overruled his action, and what came to be known as the Mississippi Burning Trial began on October 11, 1967. According to Jordan's testimony, Price had released Chaney, Goodman, and Schwerner at 10:25, then re-arrested them before they crossed into neighboring Lauderdale County. Price then took them to Rock Cut Road, a secluded area, and delivered them to the KKK.

In the seven convictions that were handed down on October 21, 1967, defendants were given prison sentences of from three to ten years. Price was convicted and sentenced to a six-year term, but Rainey was acquitted.

Suggested Reading

Norst, Joel. *Mississippi Burning.* New York: New American Library, 1989.

CHAVEZ, CESAR (1927–1993)

An agrarian labor organizer, Cesar Chavez is best known for organizing grape pickers in California and founding the NATIONAL FARM WORKERS ASSOCIATION (NFWA). His work gave migrant agricultural workers the first effective labor organization they had ever known.

Born near Yuma, Arizona, Chavez was the son of a Mexican American rancher and store owner. Hard hit by the Great Depression of the 1930s, the family was ultimately forced to give up both the store and the ranch. Like many other Depression-era farm families, the Chavezes headed to California in search of work and became migrant laborers. Cesar Chavez attended more than thirty elementary schools before dropping out after the eighth grade to work in the vineyards. In 1944 Chavez enlisted in the U.S. Navy; he completed his tour in 1946 and returned to California, where he married Helen Fabela in 1948. The young couple moved into a one-room shack in Delano.

Chavez returned to the fields, but he also became involved in the labor movement. In 1952, discouraged because vineyard and ranch owners easily broke up strikes, Chavez joined forces with Fred Ross, a member of the Community Service Organization (CSO), an independent group dedicated to the empowerment of minorities. After joining the CSO Chavez became active in registering Mexican Americans to vote. Then in 1958 he was appointed general director of the CSO. He left the organization in 1962 to found the NFWA, which in 1966 became the United Farm Workers (UFW).

Through the NFWA Chavez created a means of uniting migrant workers, and in 1965 he led the organization in organizing a strike of California grape pickers to demand higher wages. The strike gained national attention and was remarkably successful in persuading Americans to boycott table grapes as a show of support. The strike was the beginning of a five-year struggle highlighted in 1968 by Chavez's dramatic fast to call attention to the plight of migrant workers.

Chavez found that he had to struggle not only against vineyard owners and agribusinesses but also against the Teamsters Union, which attempted to seize power from the UFW. It was not until 1977, after nearly a decade of battle, that the two groups came to terms, and the Teamsters conceded to the UFW the sole right to organize field workers.

In 1973 the UFW organized a highly effective strike against lettuce growers to secure higher wages. By the 1980s, however, Chavez had turned his attention to another problem: the use of toxic pesticides on grapes, which posed a threat not only to consumers but to the health of vineyard workers. A new boycott was undertaken, Chavez again publicly fasted, and, as with previous work actions, new, more favorable work agreements resulted.

Chavez died on April 23, 1993. A little more than a year later, President BILL CLINTON awarded him, posthumously, the Presidential Medal of Freedom. In 1994 California governor Pete Wilson signed the Cesar Chavez holiday bill, designating March 21 as a state holiday. (Chavez was born in March.)

Suggested Reading

Etulain, Richard W., ed. *Cesar Chavez: A Brief Biography with Documents.* New York: Palgrave, 2002.

Ferriss, Susan, and Ricardo Sandoval. *The Fight in the Fields: Cesar Chavez and the Farmworkers Movement.* New York: Harcourt Brace, 1997.

CHICAGO DAILY DEFENDER

Founded by Robert S. Abbott on May 5, 1905, as the *Chicago Defender,* the newspaper had become America's most influential black weekly by 1917. The first black newspaper to reach a circulation of over 100,000, the *Defender* was truly national in scope: more than two-thirds of the readership lived outside Chicago.

The *Defender* was started with an initial investment of twenty-five cents, a first press run of three hundred copies, and "offices" in the kitchen of Abbott's landlord's apartment. In 1910, however, Abbott hired a professional journalist, J. Hockley Smiley, who did not hesitate to dramatize such issues as racial injustice through stories covering horrific lynchings and assaults.

The *Defender* had great influence in the South—although, to evade white efforts to block its distribution in the region, it had to be smuggled in by African American entertainers and Pullman porters. During World War I, by actively promoting life in the North to southern blacks (even including job listings and train schedules in its pages), the *Chicago Defender* became the champion of the GREAT MIGRATION, by which some 500,000 southern blacks moved to the North during 1915–1925. The *Defender* also provided black coverage of a rash of RACE RIOTS across the country (known as the Red Summer Riots of 1919), and it campaigned actively in support of antilynching laws and in support of the integration of professional sports.

In 1940 John H. Sengstacke, Abbott's nephew and heir, became the paper's most distinguished editor. He founded the National Negro Publishers Association (later the National

Newspaper Publishers Association) and served as its first president, bringing unity to the publishers of African American newspapers across the country. Under Sengstacke's direction, the *Chicago Daily Defender,* became the largest black-owned daily in the world. In 1965 he also bought the *Pittsburgh Courier,* which joined the *Michigan Chronicle* (Detroit), the *Tri-State Defender* (Memphis), and the Chicago paper in what became informally known as the "Sengstacke newspaper chain." Sengstacke died in 1997, but the *Chicago Daily Defender* continues as a major voice in African American journalism.

Suggested Reading

Ottley, Roi. *The Lonely Warrior: The Life and Times of Robert S. Abbott.* Chicago: Regnery, 1955.

CHICANO STUDIES

Beginning about 1970, a number of American colleges and universities introduced Chicano (later called Chicana and Chicano to avoid SEXISM) studies programs. In 1972 the National Association for Chicana and Chicano Studies (NACCS) was founded to foster a movement to develop academic programs and research "to further the political actualization of the Chicana and Chicano community." The NACCS gave Chicana and Chicano studies a political direction. Academic research, the association contended, should not merely generate new knowledge about the Chicana and Chicano community but "should also help solve problems in the community."

As articulated by the NACCS, the object of Chicana and Chicano studies is to "facilitate dialogue about Chicana and Chicano experiences among scholars, students, and community members," to "encourage, promote, and assist the development of Chicana and Chicano studies centers, programs, and departments," to "facilitate the recruitment of Chicanas and Chicanos at all levels of education," to "promote and develop curriculum and the integration of Chicana and Chicano Studies from kindergarten to college," and to "provide mentorship for undergraduate and graduate students and faculty to facilitate their entrance and success in the academy and the community."

Suggested Reading

Noriega, Chon A., and Eric R. Avila, eds. *The Chicano Studies Reader: An Anthology of Aztlán 1970–2000.* Los Angeles: UCLA Chicano Studies Research Center Publications, 2001.

CHILD ABUSE

The protection of children from abuse has long been a driving force in American social reform. Many of the reform movements that developed in the United States toward the end of the nineteenth century and the beginning of the twentieth focused on "child welfare"—in particular, on the reform of child labor laws. More recently, the focus has shifted to child abuse in domestic settings. In 1996 the National Center on Child Abuse and Neglect of the U.S. DEPARTMENT OF HEALTH AND HUMAN SERVICES issued its *Third National Incidence Study of Child Abuse and Neglect.* The study found that the total number of abused and neglected children was two-thirds higher in 1996 than it had been in 1986, the year of the previous study. "Physical abuse nearly doubled, sexual abuse more than doubled, and emotional abuse, physical neglect, and emotional neglect were all more than two and one-half times their [1986] levels. The total number of children seriously injured and the total number endangered both quadrupled during this time."

The 1996 study found that girls were sexually abused three times more often than boys, but that boys were at greater risk of emotional neglect and serious injury than girls. Children of both sexes were seen as "consistently vulnerable to sexual abuse from age three on." The 1996 study found "no significant race differences in the incidence of maltreatment or maltreatment-related injuries." According to the 1996 study, "children of single parents had a 77-percent greater risk of being harmed by physical abuse, an 87-percent greater risk of being harmed by physical neglect, and an 80-percent greater risk of suffering serious injury or harm from abuse or neglect than children living with both parents." Additionally, "children from families with annual incomes below $15,000 as compared to children from families with annual incomes above $30,000 per year were over 22 times more likely to experience some form of maltreatment." Children from the lowest-income families were found to be eighteen times more likely to suffer sexual abuse, almost fifty-six times more likely to be educationally neglected, and over twenty-two times more likely to be seriously injured from maltreatment than children from the higher-income families. (See also CHILDREN'S RIGHTS.)

Suggested Reading

Clark, Robin E., et al. *The Encyclopedia of Child Abuse.* 2d edition. New York: Facts on File, 2000.

CHILD ABUSE PREVENTION AND TREATMENT ACT

Originally enacted in 1974, the Child Abuse Prevention and Treatment Act (CAPTA) is the most important piece of federal legislation addressing CHILD ABUSE and neglect. The act has been amended on several occasions.

CAPTA provides federal funding to states to support prevention, assessment, investigation, prosecution, and treatment of child abuse. The legislation also provides grants to public agencies and nonprofit organizations for demonstration programs and projects. In addition, CAPTA set out the federal government's role in supporting research, evaluation, technical assistance, and data collection; it established the Office on Child Abuse and Neglect; and it mandated the creation of the National Clearinghouse on Child Abuse and Neglect Information. Not the least important of CAPTA's provisions is a minimum definition of child abuse and neglect, which serves as a model for state legislation.

Suggested Reading

Kluger, Miriam P., Gina Alexander, and Patrick A. Curtis, eds. *What Works in Child Welfare.* Washington, D.C.: Child Welfare League of America, 2001.

CHILD WELFARE LEAGUE OF AMERICA

The idea behind the Child Welfare League of America (CWLA) came into being at the 1909 White House Conference on the Care of Dependent Children, which made recommendations to establish the United States Children's Bureau and a national organization of agencies and institutions whose mission was to help children. The CWLA was founded in 1920 and began operations in New York City on January 2, 1921.

Today, the CWLA is an association of more than 1,100 public and not-for-profit agencies dedicated to improving life for more than 3.5 million at-risk children and youths and their families. In addition to working to prevent and to treat CHILD ABUSE and neglect, CWLA member agencies provide services such as kinship care, family foster care, adoption, youth development programs, residential group care, child care, family-centered medical practice, and programs for pregnant and parenting teenagers.

Suggested Reading

Child Welfare League of America, www.cwla.org.

CHILDREN'S DEFENSE FUND

Founded in 1973 by Marian Wright Edelman, the Children's Defense Fund (CDF) is a private nonprofit organization supported by foundations, corporate grants, and individual donations. Its mission is "to ensure every child a Healthy Start, a Head Start, a Fair Start, a Safe Start, and a Moral Start in life." The CDF functions as a political advocacy organization for the rights and welfare of America's children, with special emphasis on the needs of poor and minority children and those with disabilities.

Suggested Reading

Children's Defense Fund. *The State of America's Children Yearbook.* Washington, D.C.: Children's Defense Fund, published annually.

Children's Defense Fund, www.cdf.org.

CHILDREN'S RIGHTS

In the United States the issue of children's rights was historically tied to that of child labor. By the mid-nineteenth century American reformers believed that all children required an adequate primary education, and they succeeded in pressuring many states to enact both minimum schooling requirements and minimum wage requirements—which, in combination, somewhat discouraged child labor. However, with the explosion in labor needs created by the Industrial Revolution, and with the influx of immigrants into the United States, child labor actually rose during the late nineteenth and early twentieth century. In 1900, 18 percent of American children between the ages of ten and fifteen were employed in industry, and one-fourth of the workers in southern cotton mills were under fifteen years of age—and of this number half were younger than twelve.

The National Child Labor Committee, organized in 1904 by concerned citizens and Progressive activists, including the brilliant documentary photographer Louis Hine, worked with a host of state committees to advance the cause of child labor reform. Although by 1915 most states had enacted strict child labor statutes, the SUPREME COURT struck down federal child labor statutes passed in 1916 and 1918. In response to the high court's decision, Congress passed a constitutional amendment authorizing federal child labor legislation, but the states failed to ratify the amendment. It was not until the Great Depression of the 1930s, when increasing adult employment was paramount, that popular support for strict child labor laws resulted in regulations under the

National Industrial Recovery Act of 1933 and the Fair Labor Standards Act of 1938.

More recently, children's rights have been defined as freedom from abuse and have become a focus of federal attention. Americans have also shown great concern in recent years for the welfare of children internationally. Organizations such as Human Rights Watch, for example, monitor human rights abuses against children around the world and campaign to end them. The United States is also a signatory to the Convention on the Rights of the Child, adopted by the United Nations General Assembly on November 20, 1989. The convention seeks to ensure that children around the world enjoy the right to life, liberty, education, and health care.

Suggested Reading

Andrews, Arlene Bowers, and Natalie Hevener Kaufman, eds. *Implementing the UN Convention on the Rights of the Child.* New York: Praeger, 1999.

Hempelman, Kathleen A. *Teen Legal Rights.* Westport, Conn.: Greenwood Publishing, 2000.

Raskin, Jamin B. *We the Students: Supreme Court Cases for and about Students.* Washington, D.C.: CQ Press, 2000.

CHINESE FOR AFFIRMATIVE ACTION

Chinese for Affirmative Action (CAA) was founded in 1969 in San Francisco by a small group of community activists who recognized the need for an advocacy group for Chinese Americans who, like other minorities, were systematically denied equal opportunity in many sectors of society. The CAA's goal was to obtain equal access to employment and to create job opportunities for Chinese Americans. Targets identified for immediate action were the building trades, service industries, the mass media, the finance and insurance industries, and civil service at local, state, and federal levels.

After achieving significant success in opening job opportunities in the target industries in the San Francisco area, the CAA steadily expanded in scope during the 1970s and redefined its objectives:

> To promote equal employment opportunity for Chinese Americans and to support and assist Chinese Americans in pursuing complaints against employment discrimination.
>
> To promote equal participation of Chinese Americans in appointed commissions and boards in both private and public sectors.
>
> To promote the availability of a fair share of public resources and programs for the Chinese American community in such areas as health care, housing, welfare, education, recreation, and small business development.

Suggested Reading

Chinese for Affirmative Action annual reports, www.caasf.org.

Jost, Kenneth. "Affirmative Action." *CQ Researcher,* September 21, 2001, 737–759.

CHINESE EXCLUSION REPEAL ACT

On December 17, 1943, the Seventy-Eighth Congress approved "An Act to repeal the Chinese Exclusion Acts, to establish quotas, and for other purposes," thus ending the permanent ban on Chinese immigration into the United States that had begun in 1882 with the Chinese Exclusion Treaty and Act. A series of Supreme Court cases, collectively known as the Chinese Exclusion Cases, had progressively undermined the 1882 act: these were *Chew Heong v. United States* (1884), *United States v. Jung Ah Lung* (1888), *Chae Chan Ping v. United States* (1889), and *Fong Yue Ting v. United States* (1893). (See Appendix A for the text of the Chinese Exclusion Treaty and the Chinese Exclusion Act.)

Suggested Reading

Gyory, Andrew. *Closing the Gate: Race, Politics, and the Chinese Exclusion Act.* Chapel Hill: University of North Carolina Press, 1998.

CHINESE EXCLUSION TREATY AND ACT

The Chinese Exclusion Treaty and Act were the first significant efforts to restrict immigration to the United States. Chinese immigrants constituted only 0.002 percent of the American population in the 1880s—but white workers, primarily on the West Coast, were concerned about Chinese laborers usurping jobs, and others touted theories of racial purity, which was deemed to be under threat from the Chinese.

A treaty between the United States and China concluded November 17, 1880, and ratified and proclaimed in 1881 gave the United States leave to regulate Chinese immigration. The legislation that resulted from the treaty was the Chinese Exclusion Act of 1882, which suspended Chinese immigration for ten years and declared Chinese people ineligible for naturalization. The act was renewed for another ten years in 1892; in 1902 Chinese immigration was made permanently illegal. (See Appendix A for excerpts from both the treaty and the 1882 act.)

Suggested Reading

Gyory, Andrew. *Closing the Gate: Race, Politics, and the Chinese Exclusion Act.* Chapel Hill: University of North Carolina Press, 1998.

CHISHOLM, SHIRLEY (1924–)

Shirley Anita St. Hill Chisholm was the first African American woman to be elected to the U.S. Congress.

The daughter of immigrants—her father was from British Guiana (now Guyana) and her mother from Barbados—Chisholm was born in Brooklyn and grew up in Barbados. She graduated from Brooklyn College in 1946 and became director of Brooklyn's Friends Day Nursery while studying elementary education at Columbia University, from which she received a master's degree in 1952. She married Conrad Q. Chisholm in 1949 (and was divorced in 1977).

Chisholm served as an education consultant to New York City's Department of Social Services on matters relating to day care and, during the 1960s, became increasingly active in community and political groups as well as in the civil rights movement. She was elected to the state legislature in 1964 and represented her Brooklyn district through 1968, when she was elected to the U.S. House of Representatives, defeating civil rights leader JAMES FARMER. In 1972 she stood for the Democratic nomination for U.S. president, winning 152 delegates before withdrawing.

A leading House liberal until she retired from Congress in 1983, Chisholm was a founding member of the National Women's Political Caucus, a strong supporter of the Equal Rights Amendment, and a proponent of ABORTION RIGHTS. After leaving Congress Chisholm lectured widely and served as Purington Professor at Mount Holyoke College (1983–1987) and as a visiting scholar at Spelman College (1985).

Suggested Reading

Chisholm, Shirley. *Unbought and Unbossed.* Boston: Houghton Mifflin, 1970.

CHURCH OF JESUS CHRIST OF LATTER-DAY SAINTS

See MORMON CHURCH.

CHURCH WOMEN UNITED

Church Women United (CWU) was founded in 1941 as an ecumenical movement of Protestant, Roman Catholic, Orthodox, and other Christian women for the purpose of "spiritual nourishment and faith-based advocacy." Over 1,400 local units in the United States and Puerto Rico sponsor or participate in community ministries, including prison ministries, food pantries, tutoring and child care, and job skills training. On a national level the organization works in coalition with other advocacy groups to achieve social goals.

As of 2002 the top priorities of the CWU included programs on diversity and antiracism; health and health care; education (good schools for all children, parental education, literacy, and preschool education); violence ("making the world safe for women and children") and economic justice (living wage, work with dignity and safety, availability of jobs and adequate job training, support services for those seeking work, gender equity, child care). In the areas of media and technology, the CWU works to promote positive images of women, children, and families.

Suggested Reading

Church Women United, www.churchwomen.org/newcwu/.

CITADEL CASE

In 1994 a young woman named Shannon Faulkner sought enrollment as a cadet at the South Carolina Military Academy, a prestigious, state-run, publicly funded educational institution familiarly known as the Citadel. At the time, the 150-year-old Citadel enrolled men only. Faulkner challenged this enrollment policy in the courts and gained admission for herself, and for a handful of young women after her.

Faulkner's challenge was upheld by a federal judge, who ordered the Citadel to admit Faulkner to day classes during the spring semester of 1994 (previously, women had attended only nighttime extension classes); later in the year, a U.S. District Court ruled that the Citadel must also admit Faulkner to the Corps of Cadets. Faulkner enrolled in the corps but was harassed unremittingly by her classmates and withdrew after a week.

In the 2000–2001 academic year, 1,327 young men were accepted out of 1,639 applicants, and 126 young women were accepted out of 165 applicants. Freshman men numbered 528, freshman women 25.

Suggested Reading

Mace, Nancy. *In the Company of Men: A Woman at the Citadel.* New York: Simon and Schuster, 2001.

Manegold, Catherine S. *In Glory's Shadow: Shannon Faulkner, the Citadel, and a Changing America.* New York: Knopf, 2000.

Strum, Philippa. *Women in the Barracks: The VMI Case and Equal Rights.* Lawrence: University Press of Kansas, 2002.

CITIZEN'S COMMISSION ON CIVIL RIGHTS

The Citizen's Commission on Civil Rights (CCCR) was founded in 1982 in response to action by the conservative Republican administration of President RONALD REAGAN and Congress—which, in the view of the CCCR's founders, seemed to "put into question the basic foundations of civil rights policy as it had operated since the enactment in the 1960s of laws providing basic protections." Specifically, the members of the CCCR believed that the U.S. Commission on Civil Rights, the public agency responsible for monitoring civil rights enforcement, fostering public understanding of civil rights issues, and recommending effective policies, had abandoned its role.

The commission's founders had all served during the 1950s, 1960s, and 1970s in positions of major responsibility in the federal government. The CCCR was established on a strict bipartisan basis, with equal numbers of Democrats and Republicans.

Under the chairmanship of the late Arthur Flemming the CCCR began to monitor civil rights enforcement, to examine important policy issues affecting equality of opportunity, to publish reports, and to alert decision makers to major issues of concern. The CCCR continues today, chaired by attorney William Taylor. (See also CIVIL RIGHTS COMMISSION.)

Suggested Reading

Reports issued by the Citizen's Commission on Civil Rights, www.cccr.org/reports.html.

CITY OF RICHMOND V. J.R. CROSON CO.

The 1989 SUPREME COURT ruling in *City of Richmond v. J. R. Croson Co.* declared unconstitutional the Minority Business Utilization Plan of Richmond, Virginia, "requiring prime contractors awarded city construction contracts to subcontract at least 30% of the dollar amount of each contract to one or more 'Minority Business Enterprises' (MBE's), which the Plan defined to include a business from anywhere in the country at least 51% of which is owned and controlled by black, Spanish-speaking, Oriental, Indian, Eskimo, or Aleut citizens." As the high court summarized the circumstances of the case, "although the Plan declared that it was 'remedial' in nature, it was adopted after a public hearing at which no direct evidence was presented that the city had discriminated on the basis of race in letting contracts or that its prime contractors had discriminated against minority subcontractors." The Supreme Court held that because there was an absence of proof of prior discriminatory action, such an AFFIRMATIVE ACTION policy violated the FOURTEENTH AMENDMENT guarantee of equal protection of the law. In this, the high court upheld the earlier decision of a court of appeals, which had "held that the city's Plan violated both prongs of strict scrutiny, in that (1) the Plan was not justified by a compelling governmental interest, since the record revealed no prior discrimination by the city itself in awarding contracts, and (2) the 30% set-aside was not narrowly tailored to accomplish a remedial purpose."

As a result of *City of Richmond v. J. R. Croson Co.,* affirmative action programs are now required to be based on strong proof of prior discriminatory action.

Suggested Reading

Curry, George E., and Cornel West, eds. *The Affirmative Action Debate.* New York: Perseus, 1996.

Jost, Kenneth. "Affirmative Action." *CQ Researcher,* September 21, 2001, 737–759.

CIVIL DISOBEDIENCE

Civil disobedience is the nonviolent refusal to obey the orders or demands of a government or other power. The object of this refusal is to prompt or compel the authority in question to make certain defined concessions.

An act of civil disobedience is both practical and symbolic. Because it is practical, it is focused on a particular policy or set of policies. And because civil disobedience is by definition a crime—typically punishable by arrest, trial, and imprisonment—being subject to the legal process becomes part of the symbolic gesture. Prosecution of civil disobedience lends the act moral weight and publicizes the conditions that motivated the disobedient act in the first place.

Notable practitioners of civil disobedience include the nineteenth-century essayist, naturalist, ethicist, and philosopher HENRY DAVID THOREAU; the Indian nationalist leader MOHANDAS GANDHI; and American civil rights leader MARTIN LUTHER KING JR.

Suggested Reading

Bedau, Hugo Adam, ed. *Civil Disobedience in Focus.* New York: Routledge, 1991.

CIVIL RIGHTS ACT OF 1866

The first civil rights statute ever passed by a nation, the Civil Rights Act of 1866 was intended to enforce the provisions of the Thirteenth Amendment, abolishing slavery and involuntary servitude in the United States. (See Appendix A for the text of the act.)

Suggested Reading

Vorenberg, Michael. *Final Freedom: The Civil War, the Abolition of Slavery, and the Thirteenth Amendment.* New York: Cambridge University Press, 2001.

CIVIL RIGHTS ACT OF 1875

The objective of the Civil Rights Act of 1875 was to guarantee freedom of access, regardless of race, to the "full and equal enjoyment" of inns, public conveyances, and public places of amusement. The act entitled citizens deprived of such access to sue in federal court. The act also prohibited any qualified person from being barred from service as a grand or petit juror (however, violation of this prohibition was defined as a misdemeanor only).

The Civil Rights Act of 1875 was overturned by the Supreme Court in *Civil Rights Cases* (1883) and was the last civil rights legislation until 1957. The Supreme Court held that the 1875 act violated states' rights, although Justice John Marshall Harlan dissented, holding that

> such discrimination [denial of access to public facilities] is a badge of servitude, the imposition of which congress may prevent under its power, through appropriate legislation, to enforce the thirteenth Amendment; and consequently, without reference to its enlarged power under the fourteenth Amendment, the act of March 1, 1875, is not, in my judgment, repugnant to the constitution.

(See Appendix A for the substantive text of the Civil Rights Act of 1875.)

Suggested Reading

Vorenberg, Michael. *Final Freedom: The Civil War, the Abolition of Slavery, and the Thirteenth Amendment.* New York: Cambridge University Press, 2001.

CIVIL RIGHTS ACT OF 1957

The Civil Rights Act of 1957 created the Commission on Civil Rights to study race relations in the United States. The act also created the Civil Rights Division of the Department of Justice and gave the attorney general authority to sue on behalf of African Americans who were discriminated against in federal elections. The act was the first civil rights legislation since the Civil Rights Act of 1875. (See Appendix A for selected text from the Civil Rights Act of 1957. See also Civil Rights Commission.)

Suggested Reading

Sigler, Jay A. *Civil Rights in America: 1500 to the Present.* Detroit: Gale Research, 1998.

Smolla, Rodney A., and Chester James Antieau. *Federal Civil Rights Acts.* 3d ed. New York: Clark Boardman Callaghan, 1994.

CIVIL RIGHTS ACT OF 1964

The Civil Rights Act of 1964 was the most sweeping and significant civil rights legislation of the twentieth century. The impetus for the act came during the administration of John F. Kennedy, but the legislation was passed during the administration of Lyndon B. Johnson, who, to marshal support for passage, invoked the memory of the man the nation regarded as his martyred predecessor.

The Civil Rights Act of 1964 was aimed at eliminating voter discrimination; among other things, it also funded school desegregation, renewed the Commission on Civil Rights for another four years, banned the use of federal funds for schools or programs that practiced racial or other discrimination, banned discrimination in employment and unions, and barred federal courts from remanding civil rights cases back to state or local courts. (See Appendix A for the text of the Civil Rights Act of 1964.)

Suggested Reading

Grofman, Bernard, ed. *Legacies of the 1964 Civil Rights Act.* Charlottesville: University Press of Virginia, 2000.

Loevy, Robert D., ed. *The Civil Rights Act of 1964: The Passage of the Law That Ended Racial Segregation.* Albany: State University of New York Press, 1997.

CIVIL RIGHTS ACT OF 1990, VETO OF

The Civil Rights Act of 1990 was intended to reaffirm and strengthen affirmative action by placing the burden of proof on employers to prove that they were not discriminating. In vetoing the measure, President George H.W. Bush called it a "quota bill," a phrase that reflected the fears, on the part of many employers, that the new legislation would compel them to hire in strict accordance with federally mandated formulas.

A modestly revised version of the bill was resubmitted and signed by President Bush in 1991. (See also CIVIL RIGHTS ACT OF 1991.)

Suggested Reading

Babkina, A. M., ed. *Affirmative Action: An Annotated Bibliography.* Commack, N.Y.: Nova Science Publishers, 1998.

Landsberg, Brian K. *Enforcing Civil Rights: Race Discrimination and the Department of Justice.* Lawrence: University Press of Kansas, 1997.

CIVIL RIGHTS ACT OF 1991

After vetoing the CIVIL RIGHTS ACT OF 1990 President GEORGE H.W. BUSH signed the 1991 act into law. The purpose of the 1991 act was "to amend the Civil Rights Act of 1964 to restore and strengthen civil rights laws that ban discrimination in employment, and for other purposes." Principally, the 1991 legislation enabled victims of intentional discrimination based on religion, gender, or disability to recover both compensatory and punitive damages through civil litigation. Earlier legislation had allowed this relief only to victims of race-based discrimination. (See Appendix A for excerpts from the Civil Rights Act of 1991.)

Suggested Reading

Cathcart, David A., et al. *The Civil Rights Act of 1991.* Philadelphia: American Law Institute, 1993.

"CIVIL RIGHTS, ADDRESS ON" (JOHN F. KENNEDY)

On June 11, 1963, President JOHN F. KENNEDY delivered a televised speech—known as the "Address on Civil Rights"—to the nation calling for profound and sweeping civil rights legislation. The speech ended the equivocal position Kennedy had taken on race since his inauguration in 1961 and stands as one of the most important pronouncements any president has ever made on civil rights. (See Appendix A for the text of the "Address on Civil Rights.")

Suggested Reading

Giglio, James N. *The Presidency of John F. Kennedy.* Lawrence: University Press of Kansas, 1992.

Stern, Mark. *Calculating Visions: Kennedy, Johnson, and Civil Rights.* New Brunswick: Rutgers University Press, 1992.

CIVIL RIGHTS COMMISSION

Created by the CIVIL RIGHTS ACT OF 1957 as an independent, bipartisan, fact-finding agency of the executive branch, the U.S. Commission on Civil Rights was given the following mandate:

> To investigate complaints alleging that citizens are being deprived of their right to vote by reason of their race, color, religion, sex, age, disability, or national origin, or by reason of fraudulent practices;
>
> To study and collect information relating to discrimination or a denial of equal protection of the laws under the Constitution because of race, color, religion, sex, age, disability, or national origin, or in the administration of justice;
>
> To appraise federal laws and policies with respect to discrimination or denial of equal protection of the laws because of race, color, religion, sex, age, disability, or national origin, or in the administration of justice;
>
> To serve as a national clearinghouse for information in respect to discrimination or denial of equal protection of the laws because of race, color, religion, sex, age, disability, or national origin;
>
> To submit reports, findings, and recommendations to the president and Congress;
>
> To issue public service announcements to discourage discrimination or denial of equal protection of the laws.

Suggested Reading

Babkina, A. M., ed. *Affirmative Action: An Annotated Bibliography.* Commack, N.Y.: Nova Science Publishers, 1998.

Landsberg, Brian K. *Enforcing Civil Rights: Race Discrimination and the Department of Justice.* Lawrence: University Press of Kansas, 1997.

CIVIL RIGHTS DIVISION, U.S. DEPARTMENT OF JUSTICE

According to the official statement, "Civil Rights Division Activities and Programs," the Civil Rights Division of the U.S. Department of Justice is "the primary institution within the federal government responsible for enforcing federal statutes prohibiting discrimination on the basis of race, sex, handicap, religion, and national origin."

The division, established by the CIVIL RIGHTS ACT OF 1957, enforces all federal civil rights acts as well as civil rights provisions within other laws and regulations. Such laws prohibit discrimination in education, employment, credit, housing, public accommodations and facilities, voting, and certain federally funded and conducted programs. The division also prosecutes actions under criminal civil rights statutes designed to preserve personal liberties and safety. The division has responsibility for coordinating the civil rights enforcement efforts of federal agencies whose programs are covered by Title VI of the Civil Rights Act of 1964 and certain other civil rights laws. In addition, the division assists federal agencies in identifying and removing discriminatory provisions within their policies and programs.

Suggested Reading

Babkina, A. M., ed. *Affirmative Action: An Annotated Bibliography.* Commack, N.Y.: Nova Science Publishers, 1998.

Landsberg, Brian K. *Enforcing Civil Rights: Race Discrimination and the Department of Justice.* Lawrence: University Press of Kansas, 1997.

CIVIL UNIONS

For legal, political, social, or spiritual reasons, many gay men and women would like their long-term relationships to be recognized as equivalent to a heterosexual marriage. As of late 2002 Vermont is the only state that recognizes a legal relationship—known as a civil union—that affords the members of such unions the same legal rights that are accorded to men and women in heterosexual marriages. Gay rights organizations are pressing for such recognition in other states.

Although Vermont is the only state that has enacted civil union legislation, some other states have enacted "domestic partner" legislation, which gives same-sex partners some of the legal rights enjoyed by the parties in a heterosexual marriage. Still other states are explicitly hostile to legal recognition of same-sex unions and expressly refuse to recognize any same-sex marriage contracts. (See also Defense of Marriage Act.)

Suggested Reading

Eskridge, William N., Jr. *Equality Practice: Civil Unions and the Future of Gay Rights.* New York: Routledge, 2001.

Sullivan, Andrew, and Joseph Landau, eds. *Same-Sex Marriage: Pro and Con.* New York: Vintage, 1997.

CLAYTON ACT

Formally titled the Clayton Antitrust Act of 1914, the Clayton Act regulates practices that may be detrimental to fair competition. The provision that sometimes bears on minority rights is the prohibition against price discrimination: "It shall be unlawful for any person engaged in commerce, in the course of such commerce, either directly or indirectly, to discriminate in price between different purchasers of commodities of like grade and quality." It is thus forbidden to discriminate—for whatever reason—between one customer and another.

The law also limits the use of injunctions in labor disputes—which, at the time of its passage, represented an important gain in the area of labor rights.

Suggested Reading

Posner, Richard A. *Antitrust Law.* Chicago: University of Chicago Press, 2001.

Wells, Wyatt C. *Antitrust and the Formation of the Postwar World.* New York: Columbia University Press, 2002.

CLEAVER, ELDRIDGE (1935–1998)

Leroy Eldridge Cleaver personified the militant wing of the African American civil rights movement in the 1960s, and his memoir, *Soul on Ice,* remains a quintessential expression of African American disenfranchisement and alienation.

Born in rural Arkansas (in Wabbaseka, near Little Rock), Cleaver became a career criminal and spent much of his early life in prison for convictions ranging from drug possession to assault with intent to murder. It was in prison that he began reading intensively and became a follower of Malcolm X. It was also while incarcerated that Cleaver wrote the essays that make up *Soul on Ice.* First published in the radical *Ramparts* magazine, the essays were instrumental in helping Cleaver achieve parole, in 1966, and were published in book form in 1967. Shortly after his release from prison, Cleaver became acquainted with Huey Newton and Bobby Seale, the founders of the Black Panther Party. Cleaver joined that organization as its "minister of information."

Although the publication of *Soul on Ice* elevated Cleaver to the status of spokesman for militant black America, his involvement in an April 1968 shoot-out between Black Panthers and police in Oakland, California, threatened to put him back behind bars. While awaiting trial Cleaver jumped bail in November 1968. By this time he had become a Marxist and secured refuge in Cuba, but he subsequently moved on to Algeria, which had no extradition treaty with the United States.

Cleaver broke with the Black Panthers in 1971, and he also became disenchanted with Marxism. In 1975 he returned to the United States voluntarily and cut a deal with prosecutors. Four years later, in exchange for a plea of guilty to assault charges in connection with the 1968 shoot-out, all other charges were dropped, and Cleaver was sentenced to five years' probation. He became increasingly conservative during his later years, proclaiming himself a born-again Christian and even joining the Republican Party.

Cleaver lectured widely on religion and politics during the 1980s and in 1984 ran unsuccessfully as an independent candidate for Ron Dellums's seat in the House of Representatives. Later, he ran for a seat on the Berkeley, California, city council. His 1994 arrest for drug possession made his longtime struggle with cocaine addiction public knowledge.

In addition to *Soul on Ice* and numerous articles and essays, Cleaver wrote *Eldridge Cleaver: Post-Prison Writings and Speeches* and *Eldridge Cleaver's Black Papers* (both 1969).

Suggested Reading

Cleaver, Eldridge. *Soul on Ice*. New York: McGraw-Hill, 1967.

CLINTON, BILL (1946–)

William Jefferson Clinton, forty-second president of the United States, was born William Jefferson Blythe III on August 19, 1946, in Hope, Arkansas. His father, William Jefferson Blythe II, was killed in an automobile accident three months before his son was born; Clinton's mother, Virginia Dell Blythe, subsequently married Roger Clinton.

Young Bill Clinton was inspired to enter politics by the example of John F. Kennedy, and he enrolled in Georgetown University in Washington, D. C., with a political career in mind. Clinton was a Rhodes Scholar at Oxford University, and graduated from Yale University Law School in 1973. He taught law at the University of Arkansas School of Law from 1973 to 1976 and worked on the presidential campaigns of Democrats George McGovern (1972) and Jimmy Carter (1976). He was defeated in his bid for the U.S. House of Representatives in 1974, married attorney Hillary Rodham in 1975, and was elected attorney general of Arkansas in 1976. Two years later he was elected governor of Arkansas. He failed to win reelection in 1980 but returned to the statehouse in 1982 and was reelected to three more two-year gubernatorial terms.

Although inspired by the idealist Kennedy, Clinton was essentially a pragmatist who devoted much effort to improving Arkansas's abysmal public education system and to engineering tax breaks for industry to attract investment to the state. Clinton helped lead the Democratic Party away from McGovern-era liberalism and toward the more pragmatic center. However, he always projected an air of inclusiveness, which proved highly effective in attracting the support of women and African Americans.

Despite a sex scandal (an allegation of a twelve-year extramarital affair), Clinton captured the Democratic presidential nomination in 1992 and went on to defeat incumbent George H. W. Bush, who was widely perceived as weak and inept on domestic and economic issues.

Liberals expected Clinton to usher in an administration with a strong emphasis on minority rights. And indeed, early in his first term Clinton attempted to fulfill a campaign promise to end discrimination against gay men and lesbians in the American military. However, in the face of harsh criticism from the military, he backed off and endorsed a "don't ask, don't tell" policy—which, in effect, skirted the issue. Under this policy the military was barred from inquiring into the sexual orientation of any personnel, but gay men and women troops were expected to avoid giving any indication of their sexual orientation.

Another major Clinton campaign issue was the creation of a universal health insurance system. Clinton appointed his wife to chair the Task Force on National Health Care Reform, a move that alienated conservative Republicans, who, inclined in any case to oppose major health care reform, now dug in their heels with even greater determination. The Health Security Act failed to pass.

Clinton did fulfill his promise to create a more inclusive federal government, appointing women and minorities to key administration posts: Janet Reno as attorney general, Donna Shalala as secretary of the Department of Health and Human Services, Joycelyn Elders as surgeon general, Madeleine Albright as the first woman secretary of state, and Ruth Bader Ginsburg as the second woman justice on the Supreme Court (Sandra Day O'Connor, nominated by President Ronald Reagan, was the first). Clinton's first term also saw passage of thirty important bills related to families and to women's issues, including the Family and Medical Leave Act and the Brady Handgun Violence Prevention Act.

In midterm elections the Republicans gained a majority in both houses of Congress, and Speaker Newt Gingrich led what was widely billed as a "conservative revolution," in opposition to much of the Clinton program. Partly in response to this opposition Clinton compromised on a number of issues, including policy governing the federal welfare system. Under the Clinton administration various measures were enacted that generally reduced the availability of certain welfare programs.

Clinton's moderate approach was generally viewed favorably, and the most strident of the conservative Republicans lost ground. Clinton also gained prestige internationally for efforts to restore peace in Bosnia and Herzegovina and to broker a permanent peace between the Palestinians and the Israelis. With the U.S. economy rapidly improving, Clinton was reelected by a wide margin in 1996, and, during his second term, oversaw the first balanced federal budget and budget surpluses since 1969.

Clinton's second term, however, was dogged by scandals: the first concerned the president's role in an Arkansas real estate development known as Whitewater, the second a possible sexual impropriety—specifically, an affair between Clinton and a White House intern, Monica Lewinsky. The scandal and the associated litigation—for example, *Clinton v. Jones* (1997)—led to a highly partisan movement to impeach the president. In 1998 the House of Representatives approved two articles of impeachment, for perjury and obstruction of justice, but Clinton was acquitted by the Senate in 1999.

Despite personal scandals, President Clinton enjoyed a high public approval rating. And despite compromise with conservative forces, he was perceived as generally progressive in minority rights. Nevertheless, many blamed him for tarnishing the image of the presidency, and some accused him of having torpedoed the presidential aspirations of his vice president, Al Gore Jr., who lost to Republican George W. Bush in the exceedingly close election of 2000.

Suggested Reading

Klein, Joe. *The Natural: The Misunderstood Presidency of Bill Clinton.* New York: Doubleday, 2002.

Metz, Allan. *Bill Clinton: A Bibliography.* Westport, Conn.: Greenwood Publishing, 2002.

Wickham, Dewayne. *Bill Clinton and Black America.* New York: Ballantine Books, 2002.

COCA-COLA COMPANY, CLASS ACTION SUIT AGAINST

On April 22, 1999, Motisola Malikha Abdallah, Gregory Allen Clark, Linda Ingram, and Kimberly Gray Orton, African American employees of the Coca-Cola Company, filed a class-action suit against the company claiming widespread discrimination. This widely publicized suit against a high-profile corporate giant came to be regarded as a model of antidiscrimination litigation against an employer.

In 2000 Coca-Cola agreed to pay a settlement of $192.5 million, including $113 million in cash, $43.5 million to adjust salaries, and $36 million for oversight of the company's employment practices. Oversight included the appointment of a seven-member watchdog group charged with ensuring that Coca-Cola was fair in pay, promotions, and performance evaluations. Modeled on a similar task force established in the settlement of a discrimination suit against Texaco, Coca-Cola's watchdog group included professors, lawyers, "diversity consultants," and former government officials who had positions related to labor and civil rights. (See Appendix A for section 1 of the civil complaint, which summarizes the allegations of this landmark suit.)

Suggested Reading

Pendergrast, Mark. *For God, Country, and Coca-Cola: The Definitive History of the Great American Soft Drink and the Company That Makes It.* 2nd Edition. New York: Basic Books, 2000.

Player, Mack A. *Federal Law of Employment Discrimination in a Nutshell.* Los Angeles: West Information Publishing Group, 1999.

COINTELPRO

An acronym for COunter INTELligence PROgram, COINTELPRO was a Federal Bureau of Investigation (FBI) program intended to undermine dissident political organizations in the United States.

The program came to light in 1971 when a self-appointed "Citizens Committee to Investigate the FBI" removed secret files from an FBI office in Media, Pennsylvania, and released them to the press and to certain members of Congress. Before the end of the year FBI director J. Edgar Hoover had announced that COINTELPRO had been terminated and that future counterintelligence operations would be handled on a case-by-case basis. Lawsuits filed by NBC correspondent Carl Stern and others yielded more information on COINTELPRO. In 1976 the Select Committee to Study Governmental Operations with Respect to Intelligence Activities of the United States Senate (better known as the Church Committee, after its chairman, Sen. Frank Church, D-Idaho) also filed suit to obtain the release of documents. Although much remained—and remains—unreleased, the Church Committee was able to document a history of FBI operations that had been conducted explicitly for purposes of political repression; these operations had begun during World War I (when the FBI was known as the Bureau of Investigation) and continued through the Palmer raids and Red Scare of the 1920s. In 1936 FBI operations against communists as well as "anarchists and revolutionaries" were stepped up and continued through 1976.

The primary target in the early days of COINTELPRO operations was the Communist Party, USA, but operations expanded to encompass many other leftist and liberal groups—including, during the Vietnam War, individuals and organizations involved in the antiwar movement. Also periodically targeted were black activist groups (including the Black Panther Party), Puerto Rican independence groups, and Native American groups. The Ku Klux Klan was both investigated and, apparently, sometimes co-opted as a source of information.

According to the Church Committee investigation, COINTELPRO's methods ranged from infiltration, intimidation, and the dissemination of disinformation and propaganda to assault and assassination. The organization even framed activists for a variety of crimes, including some committed by FBI personnel—and, when all else failed, FBI officials unleashed lawsuits and IRS audits against targeted organizations and individuals.

Suggested Reading

Churchill, Ward, and Jim Vander Wall. *The COINTELPRO Papers: Documents from the FBI's Secret Wars against Dissent in the United States.* Cambridge, Mass.: South End Press, 1990.

COLLECTIVE BARGAINING

Collective bargaining is negotiation between the representatives of workers (usually a union) and management. At issue, typically, are conditions of employment—including wages and hours, hiring practices, promotions, and benefits. In the United States, the right to collective bargaining is protected by federal and state statutes.

Suggested Reading

Sloane, Arthur A., and Fred Witney. *Labor Relations.* 10th ed. Paramus, N.J.: Prentice Hall, 2000.

COLOR LINE

Color line was long the informal term for racial segregation as it was practiced in any number of areas of American life, especially in housing and employment. The term received widespread currency in 1947, when JACKIE ROBINSON "crossed the color line" to become the first black baseball player in the major leagues.

Suggested Reading

Dorinson, Joseph, and Joram Warmund, eds. *Jackie Robinson: Race, Sports, and the American Dream.* Tarrytown, N.Y.: M. E. Sharpe, 1998.

Simon, Scott. *Jackie Robinson and the Integration of Baseball.* New York: Wiley, forthcoming.

COLUMBUS BOARD OF EDUCATION V. PENICK

Along with the 1969 SUPREME COURT decision in *ALEXANDER V. HOLMES COUNTY,* the 1979 decision in *Columbus Board of Education v. Penick* amplified the landmark school DESEGREGATION decision handed down in 1954, in *BROWN V. BOARD OF EDUCATION OF TOPEKA, KANSAS,* by defining the concept of a "unitary" school system. In the 1979 decision the Court stated that the term *unitary* denotes the status a school system achieves "when it no longer discriminates between school children on the basis of race." The Court suggested, further, that this status is achieved when a school system "affirmatively" removes all vestiges of racial discrimination that remain from the formerly dual (segregated) system. The implication of *Columbus Board of Education v. Penick* was that integration could not be left to chance, but was to be fostered—"affirmatively"—by programs such as school busing. (See BUSING, SCHOOL.)

Suggested Reading

Jacobs, Gregory S. *Getting around Brown: Desegregation, Development, and the Columbus Public Schools.* Columbus: Ohio State University Press, 1997.

Kluger, Richard. *Simple Justice: The History of Brown v. Board of Education and Black America's Struggle for Equality.* New York: Random House, 1977.

Patterson, James T. *Brown v. Board of Education: A Civil Rights Milestone and Its Troubled Legacy.* New York: Oxford University Press, 2001.

COMMISSION ON THE STATUS OF WOMEN

The Commission on the Status of Women (CSW) is a UNITED NATIONS commission that was established, on June 21, 1946, as a functional commission of the Economic and Social Council. The CSW's mandate is to work in support of the principle that men and women shall have equal rights. In furtherance of that mandate, the CSW prepares recommendations and reports to the Economic and Social Council addressing women's political, economic, civil, social, and educational rights. The CSW also calls the council's attention to WOMEN'S RIGHTS issues requiring immediate attention.

The commission consists of forty-five members elected by the Economic and Social Council for a period of four years. There are thirteen members from African states; eleven from Asian states; four from Eastern European states; nine from Latin American and Caribbean states; and eight from Western European and other states.

Suggested Reading

The website of the United Nations Division for the Advancement of Women (www.un.org/womenwatch/daw/public/) includes a bibliography of current publications from the Commission on the Status of Women.

COMMITTEE ON THE ELIMINATION OF DISCRIMINATION AGAINST WOMEN

In November 1967, the United Nations (UN) General Assembly adopted the Declaration on the Elimination of Discrimination against Women, and in 1974 the Commission on the Status of Women began drafting a convention on the elimination of discrimination against women. The Convention on the Elimination of All Forms of Discrimination against Women was adopted by the UN General Assembly in 1979. Article 17 of the convention created the Committee on the Elimination of Discrimination against Women. That committee oversees implementation of the convention by the signatory states.

The twenty-three experts on the committee—people "of high moral standing and competence in the field covered by the Convention"—are elected by secret ballot from a list of nominees created by the parties to the convention. With only one exception, the committee has consisted entirely of women since its inception. The committee monitors implementation of the convention principally by examining reports submitted by those states that are parties to the convention, and by making suggestions and recommendation on the basis of those reports. The committee reports annually to the General Assembly through the Economic and Social Council.

Suggested Reading

United Nations. "UN Fact Sheet No. 22, Discrimination against Women: The Convention and the Committee." www.unhchr.ch/html/menu6/2/fs22.htm.

COMMON LAW

Common law, or customary law, is the basis of present-day Anglo-American law and traces its origins to the common-law courts of medieval England after the Norman Conquest of 1066. What distinguishes common law is that it was created by judges ruling in individual cases and is therefore guided more by precedent and custom than by recourse to statutes. The common-law tradition was refined, preserved, and promoted in the seventeenth century by Sir Edward Coke and in the eighteenth century by Sir William Blackstone. It was Blackstone's *Commentaries on the Laws of England* (1765–1769) that most significantly influenced law in colonial America.

Although the influence of common law remains strong in the United States, which continues to emphasize case law and precedent, it is waning in England, which increasingly emphasizes statute law.

Suggested Reading

Van Caenegem, R. C. *The Birth of English Common Law.* Cambridge, U.K.: Cambridge University Press, 1989.

COMMUNITY REINVESTMENT ACT

The Community Reinvestment Act, familiarly known as the CRA, was passed in 1977 to combat redlining—the refusal, on the part of some banks, to make loans in low- and moderate-income communities. The CRA was intended to ensure that "regulated financial institutions have a continuing and affirmative obligation to help meet the credit needs of the local communities in which they are chartered."

Federal regulatory agencies periodically evaluate banks for compliance with the CRA and assign them one of four ratings: outstanding, satisfactory, needs to improve, or substantial noncompliance. Enforcement of the CRA, however, occurs only when a bank applies to federal regulators for permission to merge with another institution or to expand its operations.

Some activists believe that federal ratings under the CRA are habitually inflated; in 1998, for example, more than 98 percent of banks were rated as either outstanding or satisfactory. Moreover, the Gramm-Leach-Bliley Act of 1999 blunted the effect of the CRA by reducing the examination cycle for banks with assets below $250 million to once every four or five years. The 1999 act also imposed new reporting requirements on community groups that seek to enforce the CRA. (See Appendix A for the opening of the statute, which explains its purpose and scope.)

Suggested Reading

Squires, Gregory D., and Sally O'Connor. *Color and Money: Politics and Prospects for Community Reinvestment in Urban America.* Albany: State University of New York Press, 2001.

COMPREHENSIVE EMPLOYMENT AND TRAINING ACT

The Comprehensive Employment and Training Act (CETA), enacted by Congress in 1973, was designed to assist both the unemployed and the economically disadvantaged by providing funding for vocational training programs (including stipends for trainees) and for public service employment. To receive funding public service employment programs were required to provide participants with opportunities to learn skills that would be useful in the private sector. Although federally funded, CETA programs were locally administered. CETA was replaced in 1982 by the Job Training Partnership Act.

Suggested Reading

Bullock, Paul. *CETA at the Crossroads: Employment Policy and Politics.* Los Angeles: Regents of UCLA, 1981.

COMPROMISE OF 1850

Like the MISSOURI COMPROMISE (1820) before it, the Compromise of 1850 was an attempt to stave off civil war by maintaining a balance in the Senate between slaveholding and free states. Although the 1850 compromise ended the slave trade in the District of Columbia, it also included provisions to make it easier for slave owners to recover fugitive slaves escaped to the North.

In 1846, seeking a means of bringing the UNITED STATES–MEXICAN WAR to a quick end, Congress had debated a bill to appropriate $2 million to compensate Mexico for "territorial adjustments." Pennsylvania congressional representative David Wilmot proposed an amendment to this bill, known as the Wilmot Proviso, to prohibit the introduction of SLAVERY into any territory acquired as a result of the war. The proposed amendment provoked South Carolina's JOHN C. CALHOUN to introduce four resolutions embodying the position of the slaveholding South:

1. All territories are the common and joint property of the states.
2. With respect to territories, Congress acts as agent for the states and, therefore, can make no law discriminating among the states or depriving any state of its rights with regard to any territory.
3. Any federal law governing slavery violates the Constitution and the doctrine of states' rights.
4. The people of a state may form their state government as they wish, provided that government is republican in form.

After introducing these resolutions Calhoun warned that failure to maintain a balance between the conflicting demands of the North and the South would mean civil war. The Wilmot Proviso failed, and the Compromise of 1850 was hammered out.

In an effort to respond to Calhoun's fourth resolution, the compromise embodied the principle of "popular sovereignty," under which the people of a territory could determine by popular vote whether to seek admission to the Union as a free state or a slave state. The territories of Arizona, Nevada, New Mexico, and Utah, created by the compromise, were to be organized without mention of slavery, and were therefore subject to popular sovereignty. California, however, would be admitted free, without a popular vote. In addition, the slave trade would be barred from Washington, D. C.; and Texas, which was in a dispute with New Mexico concerning certain land, would relinquish that land but would be compensated by the federal government in the amount of $10 million—money that would discharge part of Texas's debt to Mexico. One of the most important elements of the compromise was the passage of the FUGITIVE SLAVE ACT, which facilitated recovery of escaped slaves.

The Compromise of 1850 was presented on January 29, 1850, by the venerable Henry Clay of Kentucky, champion of the Missouri Compromise. Debate consumed eight months.

Suggested Reading

Ashworth, John. *Slavery, Capitalism, and Politics in the Antebellum Republic: Commerce and Compromise, 1820–1850.* New York: Cambridge University Press, 1996.

COMPROMISE OF 1877

The 1876 presidential election contest between Democrat Samuel J. Tilden and Republican Rutherford B. Hayes was both bitter and extremely close. The popular vote gave Tilden a 250,000-ballot lead over Hayes, but Republicans contested electoral votes in Florida, Louisiana, Oregon, and South Carolina in a legislative battle that seemed unlikely to be resolved before the March 4, 1877, inauguration date. Plans were even made to authorize the current secretary of state to serve as interim chief executive—and worse, some southerners had started talking about secession.

Unable to resolve the disputed election, Congress authorized a bipartisan electoral commission of ten congressmen and five SUPREME COURT justices. Even as the commission was being organized, however, legislators negotiated a behind-the-scenes deal—the Compromise of 1877—to settle the dispute. In essence, the compromise required the Democratic South to concede the election to Hayes, in return for which the Republicans would pledge to end RECONSTRUCTION by restoring full home rule to the southern states and withdrawing the military governments that had been installed in these states.

The sudden dismantling of Reconstruction allowed state governments to violate the rights of black citizens and fostered a social and political climate characterized by segregation, discrimination, oppression, and violence toward blacks. The end of Reconstruction also ushered in the era of the "Solid South," the near-absolute rule of the Democratic Party, determined to exclude blacks from the electoral process and to resist northern Republican attempts to protect the rights of black citizens or promote their social and political equality. Although the Compromise of 1877 resolved the disputed election and held the nation together, it created a new gulf between North and South as well as a vast chasm between white and black America. The race-based inequities born of the compromise would not be seriously addressed until the advent of the civil rights movement in the 1950s.

Suggested Reading

Robinson, Lloyd. *The Stolen Election: Hayes versus Tilden—1876*. Chicago: University of Chicago Press, 2001.

Woodward, C. Vann, *Reunion and Reaction: The Compromise of 1877 and the End of Reconstruction*. New York: Oxford University Press, 1991.

COMSTOCK, ANTHONY (1844–1915)

Over four decades the immensely influential Anthony Comstock led a crusade against what he deemed to be obscenity as it appeared in both high culture and popular culture.

Comstock was associated with the Young Men's Christian Association (YMCA) in New York City and lobbied successfully in 1873 for federal passage of what became known as the Comstock Law, which sought to curb obscenity by barring the transportation of "obscene matter" via the U.S. mail. From the year in which the Comstock Law was passed until his death in 1915, Comstock served—uncompensated until 1906—as a so-called special agent of the U.S. Post Office Department, investigating and rooting out obscenity wherever it appeared in the mail. Comstock also founded the New York Society for the Suppression of Vice in 1873.

For the most part, Comstock directed his efforts at what most people of his time and place would have considered frankly pornographic material, which could be readily classified as commercial and explicit pornography. On occasion, however, he attacked serious literature, including groundbreaking contemporary works as well as established classics. He declared that good morals were far more important than art or literature. Of perhaps greatest social consequence was the use of the Comstock Law to bar the dissemination of medical information on BIRTH CONTROL and ABORTION, as well as birth control devices, through the mail.

To American liberals and champions of the First Amendment right to FREE SPEECH, Comstock embodied the opposing cultural and political forces—and the prudery and self-righteousness—that eventually came to be summed up in the word *Comstockery.* Although the crusade against what he deemed to be pornography consumed most of Comstock's attention, he was, as a special postal agent, also instrumental in using postal regulations to combat fraudulent banking and financial schemes, various mail frauds and confidence schemes, and medical quackery.

Suggested Reading

Bates, Anna Louise. *Weeder in the Garden of the Lord: A Biography of Anthony Comstock*. Lanham, Md.: University Press of America, 1995.

Comstock, Anthony. *Traps for the Young*. 1884. Reprint, Campbell, Calif.: Universe, 1999.

CONFESSIONS, LAW GOVERNING

A confession is information supporting the elements of a crime that is given by a person involved in committing the crime. In this it differs from an *admission,* which includes information concerning the elements of a crime but is not a full confession or, necessarily, acknowledgment of substantive involvement in the crime.

In the United States laws governing the legal admissibility of confessions flow from the Constitution, especially the FIFTH and SIXTH AMENDMENTS, which guarantee protection against self-incrimination and the right to "assistance of counsel." In case law, the SUPREME COURT decision in *MIRANDA V. ARIZONA* is especially important in governing confessions. Because the admissibility of a confession requires that it be voluntary, a suspect must be fully aware of his or her rights at the time of the confession. Therefore, pursuant to the *Miranda* decision, police officers issue a "Miranda warning"—a "reading of rights"—to a suspect at the time of arrest. A voluntary confession also requires that a suspect be capable of understanding his or her rights and understanding the confession itself. No threat, torture, or other coercion may be used to obtain a confession.

In most states, oral confessions are admissible in court, but written confessions are always preferable. Officers generally put an oral confession into writing as soon as possible; they may also videotape an oral confession or ask the suspect to repeat an oral confession in front of witnesses. An oral confession that is on videotape or has been heard by witnesses is usually admissible in court, even if the suspect refuses to sign the written confession.

For prosecutors confessions are powerful evidence, but they are only evidence. Suspects or defendants may retract a confession or claim that it was involuntary or otherwise coerced. A confession alone is rarely sufficient to convict a defendant: it must be supplemented with corroborative evidence.

Suggested Reading

Hogrogian, John G. *Miranda v. Arizona: The Rights of the Accused.* San Diego: Lucent Books, 1999.

Wice, Paul B. *Miranda v. Arizona: "You Have the Right to Remain Silent."* New York: Franklin Watts, 1996.

CONFISCATION ACTS

During 1861–1864, while the Civil War was ongoing, the United States enacted a series of laws intended to liberate slaves in the seceded states. The most significant of these acts was the first, passed on August 6, 1861, which authorized Union seizure of rebel property and declared that all slaves who fought with or worked for the Confederate military establishment were summarily freed of further obligations to their masters.

Because he feared that it would push the border states (slaveholding states that remained loyal to the Union) into secession, President ABRAHAM LINCOLN opposed the act and subsequently persuaded Congress to pass a resolution providing compensation to states that initiated a system of gradual emancipation. However, the border states did not support this plan.

Although Lincoln repudiated and overruled generals John C. Frémont and David Hunter, who declared that the Confiscation Act of 1861 was in fact a proclamation of emancipation, the second Confiscation Act, passed July 17, 1862, was indeed tantamount to an emancipation law. It declared that slaves of civilian and military Confederate officials "shall be forever free." As before, Lincoln worried that the measure would alienate the border states.

The first and second acts were followed, on March 12, 1863, and July 2, 1864, by two "Captured and Abandoned Property Acts," which defined as subject to seizure any property owned by absent individuals who supported the Confederate cause. Cotton was the property most frequently confiscated under these acts. (See Appendix A for the text of the Confiscation Act of 1861.)

Suggested Reading

Klingman, William K. *Abraham Lincoln and the Road to Emancipation, 1861–1865.* New York: Penguin, 2001.

CONGRESS OF RACIAL EQUALITY

Founded in 1942 in Chicago by JAMES FARMER, the Congress of Racial Equality (CORE) is the third-oldest of the nation's major civil rights organizations. It is dedicated to the use of direct, nonviolent action to improve race relations and to end segregation and racial discrimination in the United States. In 1963 CORE was a leading force behind the MARCH ON WASHINGTON.

CORE began by working toward the DESEGREGATION of public accommodations in Chicago, then expanded to the South, where it led a series of SIT-INS to protest the segregation of restaurants, bus stations, and other public accommodations. In 1961 CORE came to national prominence as sponsor of the FREEDOM RIDES, in which interracial groups of CORE workers and supporters rode interstate buses in the South in defiance of segregated seating and station-facility policies. Despite threats and occasional assaults by angry whites, the Freedom Rides were instrumental in bringing about the end of segregation on interstate bus routes.

Farmer stepped down as leader of CORE in 1966, and the organization shifted its focus to registering southern blacks for the vote. More recently, CORE has directed its efforts to empowering African Americans both politically and economically, an emphasis that has sometimes led to alignment with mainstream politicians, including conservatives such as presidents RONALD REAGAN and GEORGE H. W. BUSH. In 1987, for example, CORE leader Roy Innis supported the confirmation of President Reagan's controversial SUPREME COURT nominee ROBERT BORK, whose judicial record hardly defined him as a friend to the civil rights movement. In 1991 Innis and CORE also supported President Bush's nomination of CLARENCE THOMAS to the high court bench, despite Thomas's conservatism and accusations that he had engaged in SEXUAL HARASSMENT.

At the opening of the twenty-first century, CORE had some 100,000 members in 5 regional groups, 39 state groups, and 116 local groups.

Suggested Reading

CORE, www.core-online.org.

Meier, August, and Elliott Rudwick. *CORE: A Study in the Civil Rights Movement, 1942–1968.* Champaign–Urbana: University of Illinois Press, 1975.

CONNOR, T. EUGENE "BULL" (1897–1973)

The 1963 protests led in Birmingham, Alabama, by the SOUTHERN CHRISTIAN LEADERSHIP CONFERENCE (SCLC) produced one of the catalytic images of the civil rights movement when, at the direction of Birmingham commissioner of public safety Eugene "Bull" Connor, police dogs and high-pressure fire hoses were turned against demonstrators. Connor's attempt to crush the Birmingham protest was nationally televised, making him unwittingly responsible for images of southern bigotry that moved the nation and its leaders. Connor's response to the SCLC demonstration spurred President JOHN F. KENNEDY'S efforts to secure passage of a civil rights bill, which, under President LYNDON JOHNSON, was passed as the CIVIL RIGHTS ACT OF 1964.

Connor was born in Selma, Alabama, the son of an itinerant railroad telegrapher. After the death of his mother, when he was eight years old, young Connor had to accompany his father from job to job and lived in more than thirty states. This unsettled life doubtless contributed to Connor's failure to complete high school. Nevertheless, having learned telegraphy from his father, Connor was able to read Morse Code telegraph news reports and secured a job as a sports announcer on Birmingham radio. This job made his name known in the city, and he entered politics, gaining election to the Alabama legislature in 1934 and to the position of commissioner of public safety in Birmingham in 1937.

An outspoken segregationist, Connor earned reelection (with the exception of one term) by a mostly white electorate through 1961. In 1962, however, Birmingham voters elected to change the form of government from city commission to mayor-council, mainly to rid the government of Connor and his two fellow (and equally conservative) commissioners, mayor Art Hanes and commissioner of public improvements J. T. Waggoner. The three men sued to retain their jobs, but on May 23, 1963, the Alabama Supreme Court ruled that the newly elected Birmingham City Council was the city's legal government, and Connor was compelled to leave office—but not before directing the infamous response to the Birmingham demonstrations.

In 1964 Connor was elected president of the Alabama Public Service Commission. He served two terms but was defeated for a third in 1972. He died the following year.

Suggested Reading

Nunnelly, William A. *Bull Connor.* Tuscaloosa: University of Alabama Press, 1991.

CONSCIENTIOUS OBJECTORS

On the basis of conscience, religion, philosophy, or political beliefs, conscientious objectors oppose taking up arms or in any way serving the military. Typically, a conscientious objector (CO) holds specific religious beliefs that bar service. In sixteenth-century Europe the Mennonites developed the first explicit and cogent policy of conscientious objection; during the following century the Society of Friends (QUAKERS) emerged with a similar doctrine.

Few governments have recognized the legitimacy of conscientious objection, and citizens who refused military conscription were generally punished by law. A notable exception was nineteenth-century Prussia, which exempted Mennonites from military service but levied a military tax on them instead. The United States has been more liberal than most other governments. The first U.S. conscription law, enacted during the Civil War, provided for alternative service in cases of conscientious objection. In 1940, when new selective service laws were passed in anticipation of U.S. entry into World War II, provision was made for "conscientious objector status," which was exclusively defined as membership in a recognized pacifistic religious sect. Philosophical, ethical, moral, or political beliefs were not accepted as a basis for securing CO status. During World War II COs were assigned various forms of national service that were neither related to the military nor controlled by it. Currently, in the absence of compulsory military service in the United States, conscientious objection is something of a moot issue.

Suggested Reading

Brock, Peter, ed. *Liberty and Conscience: A Documentary History of Conscientious Objectors in America throughout the Civil War.* New York: Oxford University Press, 2002.

Tollefson, James W. *The Strength Not to Fight: Conscientious Objectors of the Vietnam War—In Their Own Words.* New York: Brasseys, 2000.

CONTEMPT

In law, contempt encompasses insulting, interfering with, or otherwise violating the authority of a judicial court or legislative body. Contempt is a concept inherited from COMMON LAW and is intended to defend and preserve judicial or legislative authority. Because the authority to hold someone in contempt is vested primarily in a judge or whomever presides over a particular judicial or legislative proceeding, penalties for contempt are without most of the legal safeguards that constrain state power to punish alleged wrongdoing. Thus, one is not "charged" with contempt, but "found" in contempt: no presumption of innocence exists. The dangers of abuse (known as vindictive contempt) are apparent. (See also contempt of Congress.)

Suggested Reading

Goldfarb, Ronald L. *Contempt Power.* New York: Columbia University Press, 1963.

CONTEMPT OF CONGRESS

In the United States until 1927 the authority to hold individuals in contempt was generally reserved to the courts, and federal courts stringently limited both the investigative and the contempt powers of the legislative branch. Beginning in the late 1920s and continuing into the 1930s, however, Congress increasingly took on investigative tasks and, as it did so, its contempt powers were repeatedly upheld by the courts.

Congressional committees may compel the attendance of witnesses, but a witness who attends but refuses to testify, or who refuses to answer a question, cannot be held in contempt—except in cases where it has been made clear to the witness that such refusal will be treated as contumacious. Within this constraint, the instance of contempt must be both deliberate and intentional, and the question addressed to the witness must be demonstrably pertinent to the inquiry at hand, which must be authorized by Congress. Further, the pertinence of the inquiry must be made clear to the witness. A witness's recourse to the Fifth Amendment right to protection from compulsory self-incrimination applies to witnesses before congressional committees as it does to witnesses in courts of law.

The inherent danger in Congress's authority to find witnesses in contempt is that this authority may be used vindictively. The issue of vindictive contempt arose during the anti-communist "witch hunts" of the late 1940s and early 1950s, when contempt of Congress was used to intimidate and coerce witnesses. (See also House Un-American Activities Committee and McCarthy, Joseph.)

Suggested Reading

Goldfarb, Ronald L. *Contempt Power.* New York: Columbia University Press, 1963.

Mikva, Abner L., and Eric Lane. *Legislative Process.* 2d ed. New York: Aspen Publishers, 2002.

CONVENTION ON THE ELIMINATION OF ALL FORMS OF DISCRIMINATION AGAINST WOMEN

In November 1967 the United Nations (UN) General Assembly adopted the Declaration on the Elimination of Discrimination against Women, and in 1974 the Commission on the Status of Women began drafting a convention on the elimination of discrimination against women. The Convention on the Elimination of All Forms of Discrimination against Women was adopted by the UN General Assembly in 1979.

(See Appendix A for the substantive provisions of the Convention on the Elimination of All Forms of Discrimination against Women. See also Committee on the Elimination of Discrimination against Women.)

Suggested Reading

United Nations. "UN Fact Sheet No. 22, Discrimination against Women: The Convention and the Committee." www.unhchr.ch/html/menu6/2/fs22.htm.

CORPORAL PUNISHMENT

Corporal punishment—inflicting pain on a person's body (*corpus*) as judicial punishment—has historically included penalties such as beating, flogging, branding, blinding, and mutilation; the use of the stock and pillory, which exposes the subject to public humiliation (and emotional pain) is also generally classified as corporal punishment.

In judicial history, corporal punishment has been documented as far back as ancient Babylon, where it appears as the doctrine of *lex talionis* ("law of the claw"). A similar doctrine appears in the Old Testament as "an eye for an eye, a tooth for a tooth": that is, a criminal's punishment should replicate the wrong inflicted on the victim. Over time the effort to replicate the exact wrong inflicted by a criminal became cumbersome and impractical, but many societies still retained the practice of corporal punishment. In the United States and most other western countries, corporal punishment was common through the eighteenth century for criminal offenses that did not merit long prison terms, the death penalty, or (in Britain and some other countries) penal "transportation" or exile. With the Enlightenment—and, in the United States, the rise of an essentially liberal democracy—corporal punishment was generally abandoned as inhumane except as a form of military discipline. Under the U.S. Constitution most, if not all, forms of corporal punishment would be disallowed as "cruel" and, viewed in a contemporary social context, also as "unusual," because they are rarely used.

In the United States a flogging statute was on Delaware's books until 1972, and the punishment was last administered in 1952 to a prostitute. Britain did not formally abolish whipping until 1967. In some other parts of the world corporal punishment remains common despite international conventions, including a number of United Nations conventions that prohibit the use of corporal punishment as inconsistent with basic and universal human rights. (See also Cruel and Unusual Punishment.)

Suggested Reading

Scott, George Ryley. *History of Corporal Punishment*. Detroit: Gale Group, 1974.

COUNCIL OF FEDERATED ORGANIZATIONS

The Council of Federated Organizations (COFO) was a confederation of civil rights organizations including, in addition to smaller, local groups, the Student Nonviolent Coordinating Committee (SNCC), the Congress of Racial Equality (CORE), and the Southern Christian Leadership Conference (SCLC). COFO was founded in May 1961, then reorganized in February 1962 with the explicit purpose of coordinating the voter registration efforts of the member organizations. In 1963, under the leadership of Robert Moses, COFO conducted a "freedom vote"—a mock election to demonstrate to the federal government and others that African Americans wanted to vote but were often denied the opportunity. In 1964 COFO became the moving force behind Freedom Summer, the most ambitious voter registration and education project of the civil rights movement.

COFO staff was drawn primarily from the ranks of Moses's fellow SNCC workers. Despite its successes, COFO disbanded in 1965.

Suggested Reading

Belfrage, Sally. *Freedom Summer*. Charlottesville: University Press of Virginia, 1990.

COXEY, JACOB (1854–1951)

Jacob Coxey is best remembered as a social reformer who, on March 25, 1894, in a time of financial depression, led about a hundred unemployed men from Massillon, Ohio, to Washington, D. C., to persuade Congress to increase the amount of currency in circulation. The idea for "Coxey's Army" grew out of Coxey's belief that the government had an obligation to provide employment for its citizens—specifically, that to reduce the severe unemployment that had developed in the wake of the financial panic of 1893, the government was obligated to use its power to print and circulate money that would be used to finance public works projects.

Born in Selinsgrove, Pennsylvania, Coxey worked as an engineer, then as a scrap-iron dealer; he finally became the owner of a sandstone quarry in Massillon. At the time that he undertook the march on Washington, Coxey claimed a following of 100,000—so that when his "army" (augmented by others who had joined him along the way) reached Washington with only about five hundred men, the effect was anticlimactic and ineffectual.

After the Washington demonstration Coxey continued to enjoy success in business and served as Republican mayor of Massillon during 1931–1933. His bids for other offices, including the presidency (1932 and 1936), failed.

Suggested Reading

Schwantes, Carlos A. *Coxey's Army: An American Odyssey*. Lincoln: University of Nebraska Press, 1985.

CRAZY HORSE (CA. 1840–1877)

Crazy Horse was an Oglala Lakota (Sioux) war chief who earned renown among whites as well as Indians for defeating Brigadier General George Crook at the Battle of the Rosebud and, even more famously, Lt. Col. George Armstrong Custer at the Battle of Little Bighorn. In the 1970s Crazy Horse became one of the icons of the Native American civil rights movement.

Born near Butte, South Dakota, Crazy Horse was the son of an Oglala warrior and medicine man (also called Crazy Horse) and of Rattle Blanket Woman, a Minneconjou Lakota. Earning early fame as a warrior, he figured in many important actions against the U.S. Army. During the War for the Bozeman Trail, Crazy Horse led the assault against Captain William Fetterman at Fort Phil Kearny, Montana, in 1866, killing Fetterman and the eighty soldiers under his command.

Crazy Horse's success in combat earned him a large following among Lakotas who refused to endorse the Treaty of Fort Laramie, which ended the Bozeman conflict in April 1868. After this refusal Crazy Horse became perhaps the most important—and certainly the most visible—leader of the Lakota resistance. He was a leader in the fight to retain the Black Hills of South Dakota, which the Lakota held sacred, as well as the Lakota hunting grounds in the Yellowstone River basin.

In 1874, when gold was discovered in the Black Hills, the government broke treaty agreements that had reserved the hills to the Lakota and, in 1875, ordered the Indians to retire to reservations in Nebraska or along the Missouri River. Crazy Horse and his followers refused. After the U.S. Army conducted an offensive against a Northern Cheyenne village in March 1876, Crazy Horse and Sitting Bull emerged as the two central leaders of what was now a Lakota-Cheyenne alliance, and they organized an offensive in what the U.S. Army called the Sioux War. It was during this war that Crazy Horse successfully led some fifteen hundred warriors against thirteen hundred men under the command of General George Crook in the Battle of the Rosebud, on June 17, 1876. Eight days later, at the Battle of Little Bighorn, Crazy Horse defeated Lt. Col. George Armstrong Custer and his Seventh Cavalry. Custer and all 211 men directly under his command were killed.

Although the victories of Crazy Horse did not decide the outcome of the Sioux War, his prowess in battle created a strong and enduring symbol of Native American resistance. Crazy Horse himself yielded to the inevitable on May 7, 1877, when he led his people to surrender at Camp Robinson, Nebraska. On the reservation, he soon became a victim of his own legend. Government officials and army officers paid him inordinate attention and courtesy, arousing the jealousy of other war chiefs. They disseminated rumors that Crazy Horse was planning an uprising, leading the government to order his arrest. On September 5, 1877, during an arrest attempt, a trooper fatally bayoneted the chief. (See also Siege at Wounded Knee.)

Suggested Reading

Mari Sandoz, *Crazy Horse: The Strange Man of the Oglalas.* 1942. Reprint, Lincoln: University of Nebraska Press, 1992.

McMurty, Larry. *Crazy Horse.* New York: Viking Press, 1999.

CRISIS, THE

Published by the National Association for the Advancement of Colored People (NAACP), the *Crisis* was founded in 1910 by W.E.B. Du Bois, who edited the monthly magazine for twenty-four years. Within its first decade the magazine had achieved a high level of social influence and literary excellence, as well as a monthly circulation of 100,000.

During the Du Bois years—and especially during the 1920s, the time of the great movement in African American intellectual and artistic expression known as the Harlem Renaissance—the *Crisis* was the nation's premier vehicle for black writers, including Arna Bontemps, Countee Cullen, Langston Hughes, and Jean Toomer. The magazine also featured important discussions of racial justice and racial equality. Today the NAACP continues to publish the *Crisis* on a bimonthly basis; although the magazine continues to be important as an NAACP organ, it no longer carries the cultural and political weight of its Harlem Renaissance heyday.

Suggested Reading

Huggins, Nathan I., ed. *Writings of W. E. B. Du Bois: The Suppression of the African Slave-Trade; The Souls of Black Folk; Dusk of Dawn; Essays; Articles from The Crisis.* New York: Library of America, 1996.

CRUEL AND UNUSUAL PUNISHMENT

The text of the Eighth Amendment to the U.S. Constitution is brief: "Excessive bail shall not be required, nor excessive fines imposed, nor cruel and unusual punishments inflicted." Argument as to what constitutes "cruel and unusual punishments" continues to this day, however, in part because many opponents of capital punishment argue that it is inherently "cruel" and, in a world in which most developed nations have abandoned the death penalty, also "unusual."

In *Wilkerson v. Utah* (1878), the Supreme Court held:

> Difficulty would attend the effort to define with exactness the extent of the constitutional provision which provides that cruel and unusual punishments shall not be inflicted; but it is safe to affirm that punishments of torture, such as drawing and quartering, embowelling alive, beheading, public dissecting, and burning alive, and all others in the same line of unnecessary cruelty, are forbidden by that amendment to the Constitution.

This opinion was delivered in the context of a decision upholding capital punishment inflicted by a firing squad. Before rendering the decision the Supreme Court took traditional practices into consideration and also examined the history of executions in the territory concerned, military practice and policy regarding executions, and then-current writings on the death penalty.

In subsequent decisions—including *In re Kemmler* (1890), the high court approved death by electrocution, under the due process clause of the Fourteenth Amendment rather than under the Eighth Amendment, as a permissible method of administering punishment. In *Louisiana ex rel. Francis v. Resweber* (1947), a divided Court held that a second electrocution following a mechanical failure during the first (which injured but did not kill the prisoner) did not constitute cruel and unusual punishment.

Less common are high court decisions that hold a particular punishment cruel and unusual. In *Trop v. Dulles* (1958), a divided Court held that divesting a natural-born citizen of citizenship was a punishment more cruel and "more primitive than torture" because it created statelessness, "the total destruction of the individual's status in organized society," and was therefore in violation of the Eighth Amendment. Even so, four justices dissented on the grounds that denationalization was not a judicial punishment but a means by which Congress regulated discipline in the armed forces.

Trop v. Dulles concluded that the criterion for determining whether a punishment is cruel and unusual "is whether [a] penalty subjects the individual to a fate forbidden by the principle of civilized treatment guaranteed by the Eighth Amendment." The punishment must therefore be examined "in light of the basic prohibition against inhuman treatment," for the Eighth Amendment was intended to preserve the "basic concept . . . [of] the dignity of man" by regulating the power to impose punishment such that it is "exercised within the limits of civilized standards."

Suggested Reading

Buranelli, Vincent. *The Eighth Amendment.* The American Heritage: History of the Bill of Rights Series. Upper Saddle River, N.J.: Silver Burdett Press, 1991.

CUBAN REFUGEES

Following the communist coup d'état in Cuba in 1959 a massive group of refugees, mainly from the middle and professional classes, fled to the United States, settling mostly in Miami and Tampa, Florida, and in New York City and establishing major ethnic communities in all three places.

Like most communist countries, Cuba controlled emigration through coercion and force. But in 1965 Cuba and the United States signed the Agreement Concerning the Movement of Cuban Refugees to the United States, under which any Cubans who wished to leave for the United States would be permitted to do so. Families were given priority, as were Cubans who had immediate family members already living in the United States. The regime of Cuban dictator Fidel Castro insisted on certain restrictions, however. The departure of technicians, skilled workers, and others deemed vital to Cuba's interests might be postponed indefinitely; nor did young men between the ages of seventeen and twenty-six (who were subject to compulsory military service) or young men who were fifteen or sixteen years old (and therefore subject to military call-up within two years) have the right to leave Cuba.

In 1980 the Cuban government authorized a new wave of immigration, allowing 125,266 Cubans—including a significant number of criminals and people with mental illness—to leave Cuba in what was dubbed the "Mariel boat lift." As of 2000, 1,425 of the "Marielitos" had been sent back to Cuba, and 1,750 remained in the custody of the U.S. Immigration and Naturalization Service (INS). Although a significant number of Marielitos clearly experienced greater difficulty in establishing themselves socially and economically than the earlier generation of Cubans, many others have enjoyed success in the United States.

In 1994 the last major influx of Cuban refugees were permitted to enter the United States: some 30,000 "rafters"—refugees in small, hazardously overloaded vessels. On September 9, 1994, the United States and Cuba issued the *Joint Communiqué Concerning Normalizing Migration Procedures,* which specified that because unauthorized attempts to reach the United States in small craft were unsafe, immigrants rescued at sea would not be permitted to enter the United States. Since the agreement INS policy has called for all Cubans who are intercepted in the water to be sent back to Cuba. Those who manage to reach land, however, have been permitted to stay.

The 1994 agreement was put in jeopardy late in 1999 when controversy erupted over the fate of Elian Gonzalez, a six-year-old refugee rescued on Thanksgiving Day by American fishermen after the boat that carried him, his mother, his stepfather, and others sank. The boy was the only survivor, and while relatives in Florida petitioned for custody, Gonzalez's birth father, a Cuban citizen, called for his return to Cuba. Fidel Castro orchestrated mass demonstrations protesting the "kidnapping" of Gonzalez as a violation of the 1994 agreement, and, in 2000, federal officers forcibly removed the boy from the Miami home of his relatives and returned him to the custody of his father in Cuba.

Suggested Reading

Masud-Pilato, Felix Roberto. *From Welcomed Exiles to Illegal Immigrants: Cuban Migration to the U.S., 1959–1995.* New York: Rowman and Littlefield, 1996.

CUSTER, GEORGE ARMSTRONG (1839–1876)

A military leader of legendary fame and great controversy, George Armstrong Custer was first celebrated as the "Boy General" of the Civil War, then gained prominence as an Indian fighter and finally went to his death—and entered popular myth—when he led the Seventh Cavalry to defeat at the Battle of Little Bighorn on June 25, 1876.

Born in New Rumley, Ohio, Custer spent part of his childhood with a half-sister in Monroe, Michigan. He enrolled in the U.S. Military Academy (West Point) and, on the eve of the Civil War, graduated at the bottom of his class. He quickly proved himself a dashing field officer. At twenty-three he was promoted to brigadier general of volunteers, and from Gettysburg to Appomattox he became known for daring, if often reckless, cavalry charges. By the end of the war, he was a major general commanding a full division; however, he reverted to lieutenant colonel after the war and was given command of the newly authorized Seventh Cavalry.

During the Civil War Custer had affected gaudy uniforms, and he now adopted a new uniform better fitting the "Wild West": fringed buckskin. Custer's first engagement against Indians—in Kansas in 1867—not only resulted in failure to defeat the enemy but in a court-martial for harsh treatment of his men and for going absent without leave. He was sentenced to a year's suspension of rank and pay, but (in the eyes of the army) he redeemed himself in 1868 by making a surprise attack against Chief Black Kettle's Cheyenne village on the Washita River in present-day Oklahoma. Despite the fact that Black Kettle was no longer hostile, and that most of Custer's victims were women, children, and noncombatant men, the engagement was viewed as a victory and became the basis of Custer's popular image as a ruthless but gallant Indian fighter.

In 1874 Custer led the Seventh Cavalry out of Fort Abraham Lincoln to explore the Black Hills of the Dakota Territory. Part of the Great Sioux Reservation, the Black Hills region had been guaranteed to the Sioux by the Treaty of Fort Laramie (1868) but coveted by whites who thought its dark recesses held gold. Indeed, miners traveling with the Custer expedition found gold, prompting the federal government to offer to purchase the Black Hills and legalize the mining settlements that had sprung up. When the purchase effort failed, raids by Sioux bands—led by SITTING BULL and CRAZY HORSE against Indians friendly to the whites—gave officials a pretext to wage a war that would solve the problem of the Black Hills by depriving the Sioux of their independence and, of course, of their power to obstruct the sale. The result was the Sioux War of 1876.

Custer's Seventh Cavalry rode with one of the armies that converged on the Indian country. On June 25 Custer impetuously attacked, without preliminary reconnaissance, the village of Sitting Bull and Crazy Horse on Montana's Little Bighorn River. The Sioux wiped out Custer and the five companies of troopers he led.

"Custer's Last Stand" stunned and enraged white Americans; it tended to dispel liberal sympathy for the plight of the Indians and led Congress to support increasingly vigorous military action against the Plains Indians to quickly confine them to reservations. Since the battle the Sioux and other tribes have celebrated the defeat of Custer as a significant victory, and during the 1970s, at the height of the NATIVE AMERICAN CIVIL RIGHTS MOVEMENT, Custer became a symbol of white RACISM and of federal oppression of Native Americans. (See also SIEGE AT WOUNDED KNEE.)

Suggested Reading

Deloria, Vine, Jr. *Custer Died for Your Sins: An Indian Manifesto.* Norman: University of Oklahoma Press, 1988.

Utley, Robert M. *Custer: Cavalier in Buckskin.* Revised ed. Norman: University of Oklahoma Press, 2001.

DALEY, RICHARD J. (1902–1976)

The bigger-than-life mayor of Chicago from 1955 until his death, in 1976 Richard Daley was often called "the last of the big-city bosses" because he held absolute sway over Chicago politics, primarily through the skillful distribution of patronage jobs. Although he held only municipal office, Daley was a major power in national Democratic Party politics. During the 1968 Democratic National Convention in Chicago he drew the wrath and contempt of liberal Democrats, anti–Vietnam War Democrats, and the tens of thousands of young men and women who had established themselves in the city's lakefront parks to protest the convention and to attempt to move it to nominate antiwar candidate Eugene McCarthy. Daley, a resolute supporter of Hubert Humphrey, the mainstream candidate, authorized a police response against the demonstrators so brutal that it has been called by the press and eyewitnesses a "police riot," which spread from the area of the protest, Chicago's Grant Park, southward into the black ghetto. Here newspaper photographers recorded gratuitous police brutality against AFRICAN AMERICANS, principally in the form of clubbing and stomping.

Born and raised in a working-class Irish neighborhood in Chicago, Daley studied law in night school and was admitted to the bar in 1933. Before becoming mayor he served as a state representative and senator (1936–1946), as state director of revenue (1948–1950), and as clerk of Cook County (1950–1955). He brought unprecedented prosperity to the Chicago business community, promoted large-scale urban renewal and highway construction projects, and was enormously popular among most Chicagoans. Daley also undertook repeated reforms of the Chicago police department, although he never fully dispelled the scent of scandal that had surrounded the department since the 1920s and the mayoral administration of William Hale Thompson, when the department was typically in the pocket of Prohibition-era organized crime.

In some ways Daley's administration was highly progressive, yet in others it preserved the status quo—particularly in regard to the de facto segregation that prevailed in Chicago's housing and public schools. The fiasco of the 1968 Democratic National Convention brought sharp and embarrassing national attention to Chicago, which came to be viewed as an exemplar of northern RACISM, discrimination, and segregation. Nevertheless, Daley survived that scandal and subsequent scandals within his administration (none of which involved him personally). Most Chicagoans mourned his death of a heart attack suffered while in office. Thirteen years after Daley's passing his eldest son, Richard M. Daley, was elected mayor of Chicago.

Suggested Reading

Cohen, Adam, and Elizabeth Taylor. *American Pharaoh: Mayor Richard J. Daley—His Battle for Chicago and the Nation*. Boston: Little, Brown, 2000.

Grimshaw, William J. *Bitter Fruit: Black Politics and the Chicago Machine, 1931–1991*. Chicago: University of Chicago Press, 1992.

DARROW, CLARENCE (1857–1938)

Perhaps the most famous lawyer in American legal history, Clarence Darrow earned his chief reputation as a defender in the service of controversial causes, usually involving LABOR RIGHTS or individual rights.

Born and raised in Ohio, Darrow attended only one year of law school before gaining admission to the Ohio bar in 1878. In 1887 he moved to Chicago, where he was one of the attorneys for the defense in the HAYMARKET RIOT trials. In 1890 Darrow was appointed corporation counsel for the city of Chicago, then became the chief attorney for the Chicago and North Western Railway. He left this lucrative position to defend American Railway Union president EUGENE V. DEBS and other union leaders who had been found in CONTEMPT of court in the aftermath of the Pullman Strike of May–July 1894. Darrow did not prevail, but the case thrust him into the national spotlight, and in 1902–1903 his representation of striking Pennsylvania coal miners brought to light the unsafe and exploitative working conditions in the mines as well as the extensive use of child labor. In 1907 Darrow scored another major labor victory when he won the acquittal of radical labor leader William D. "Big Bill" Haywood, who stood accused of having assassinated former governor Frank R. Steunenberg of Idaho.

Darrow left labor law in 1911 after the McNamara brothers, two labor leaders he was defending against charges of detonating a bomb in the *Los Angeles Times* building, suddenly pleaded guilty in midtrial. Nevertheless, Darrow continued to represent the underdog—the persecuted, the unpopular, and those whose rights had been trampled or threatened. After World War I he took on the cases of war protesters who had been charged with violating state sedition laws.

In 1924 Darrow created a sensation, as well as legal history, with his defense of Richard Loeb and Nathan Leopold, two privileged Chicago youths who, in a "thrill murder," killed a fourteen-year-old neighbor. A vigorous opponent of capital punishment, Darrow successfully introduced a new concept at the trial—that of the psychopathic criminal, who is legally sane but nevertheless mentally ill by virtue of being unable to distinguish right from wrong. The young men were sentenced to prison rather than executed.

During July 10–21, 1925, Darrow, sponsored by the American Civil Liberties Union, took up another high-profile case, that of John T. Scopes, a high school biology teacher in Dayton, Tennessee, who was accusing of having violated a state law prohibiting the teaching of evolutionary theory. In a histrionic trial that pitted Darrow against perennial Populist presidential candidate William Jennings Bryan, Darrow failed to gain acquittal, but he succeeded in dramatically airing the two central issues of the case: the separation of church and state, and the First Amendment right to free speech.

Darrow also represented defendants in several race-related cases, most famously the *Sweet* case (1925–1926), in which he won acquittal for an African American family that had resisted when a white mob tried to force it from its home in an all-white Detroit neighborhood.

In addition to his forensic virtuosity, Darrow was a prolific speaker and author; a leading advocate for unions and for complete freedom of expression; and an opponent of capital punishment, Prohibition, protective tariffs, and the United States' entry into the League of Nations. His books include a novel, *An Eye for an Eye* (1905); a criminological treatise, *Crime: Its Cause and Treatment* (1922); an anti-Prohibition study, *The Prohibition Mania* (1927); and a memoir, *The Story of My Life* (1932). (See also International Workers of the World.)

Suggested Reading

Weinberg, Arthur, ed. *Attorney for the Damned: Clarence Darrow in the Courtroom*. Chicago: University of Chicago Press, 1989.

DAWES SEVERALTY ACT

Passed on February 8, 1887, and also known as the Dawes Act and the General Allotment Act, the Dawes Severalty Act (U.S. Statutes at Large, Vol. XXIV, p. 388 ff.) was the foundation of U.S. Indian policy until it was supplanted by the Indian Reorganization Act of 1934. The purpose of the Dawes Severalty Act was to assimilate Native Americans into mainstream American society by dissolving tribal land holdings and instead granting plots ("allotments") to Indians on an individual basis. In receiving allotments the Indians became United States citizens; those who had already separated from their tribes and lived in white communities were immediately declared citizens. Many Indians opposed the act, which they saw as a threat to their culture and traditions, and some tribes that protested sufficiently were excluded from its provisions.

The Dawes Severalty Act rested on the assumption that Indians could be assimilated as self-supporting citizens within the span of a single generation, and reformers believed that the only effective way to catalyze such an assimilation was to break up tribal lands. However, the Dawes Severalty Act was not entirely the work of reformers. Because the act called for the sale of any "surplus" tribal lands, perpetually land-hungry westerners enthusiastically supported the measure. Moreover, once an allotment had been distributed to an Indian, it could, in turn, be sold—with the result that, in addition to the surplus lands, even more land would potentially find its way onto the market. Subsequent amendments, made between 1891 and 1908, took even more land by easing or eliminating restrictions on the sale or lease of allotted lands. Impoverished Indians sold their land to survive. In 1887, when the act was passed, Indians owned some 138 million acres. By 1931 they owned 48 million, and about one-third of this was leased to non-Indians. In 1934 the Indian Reorganization Act put a halt to allotments under the Dawes Severalty Act, and unsold "surplus" lands were returned to tribal ownership.

Suggested Reading

Greenwald, Emily. *Reconfiguring the Reservation: The Nez Perces, Jicarilla Apaches, and the Dawes Act*. Albuquerque: University of New Mexico Press, 2002.

Hoxie, Frederick E. *A Final Promise: The Campaign to Assimilate the Indians, 1880–1920*. Lincoln: University of Nebraska Press, 1984.

McDonnell, Janet. *The Dispossession of the American Indian*. Bloomington: Indiana University Press, 1991.

DAY, DOROTHY (1897–1980)

Dorothy Day founded the Catholic Worker movement, a lay Catholic organization that espouses poverty and simplicity and is dedicated to providing for the urban poor.

Born in Brooklyn, New York, Day was raised without religion in San Francisco and Chicago. In early adulthood she was a Communist and atheist, but she gradually embraced Catholicism and decided to dedicate herself to improving the lot of working people and the urban poor. Although Day won a scholarship to the University of Illinois in 1914, she dropped out in 1916 and moved to New York, where she began to write for the *Call,* a socialist daily. She worked next for the *Masses,* and in November 1917 was imprisoned for her participation in a women's suffrage protest. After her release she returned to New York and decided that she could better serve the poor by training to become a nurse; however, she continued to work as a radical journalist and began to write fiction as well.

In 1924 Day began a four-year common-law marriage with Forster Batterham, a botanist and anarchist, whose atheism soon conflicted with Day's religious convictions. She had a daughter with Batterham, but when she insisted on baptizing the girl in the Catholic Church, Batterham broke with her.

In 1932 Peter Maurin, a French immigrant who had formerly been a Christian Brother, inspired Day to start a newspaper to promote Catholic (mainly Franciscan) social teaching and thereby foster the peaceful transformation of society from atomistic capitalism to a more holistic spiritual socialism. In cooperation with the Paulist Press, Day began to produce the *Catholic Worker,* which, with its combination of political radicalism and Catholic doctrine, proved an immediate success. Within a year the paper became the nucleus of a movement that created and ran "houses of hospitality" for the homeless. By 1936 there were thirty-three Catholic Worker houses nationwide.

Day was an early U.S. opponent of the rise of fascism and Nazism, and, fearing that the Jews of Europe would suffer under these regimes, she was among the founders of the Committee of Catholics to Fight Anti-Semitism. However, even when the United States entered World War II after the December 7, 1941, Japanese attack on Pearl Harbor, Day continued to espouse absolute pacifism. In 1955, during the cold war, Day was issued a warning for refusing to participate in mandatory civil defense drills in New York City. The following year she and others were briefly jailed for again refusing. In 1957 she and others were jailed for thirty days; in 1958, convicted of the same offense, she received a suspended sentence. Day was jailed in 1959 but not in 1960 or in 1961 (the last year of mandatory civil defense drills in New York).

During the civil rights movement, Day was an active advocate of desegregation and racial equality; however, the primary thrust of her activism (beyond continuing to foster the Catholic Worker movement) was in support of disarmament and peace. Day died on November 29, 1980.

Suggested Reading

Coles, Robert. *Dorothy Day: A Radical Devotion.* Reading, Mass.: Addison-Wesley, 1987.

Cornell, Tom, Robert Ellsberg, and Jim Forest, eds. *A Penny a Copy: Writings from The Catholic Worker.* Maryknoll, N.Y.: Orbis, 1995.

Miller, William. *Dorothy Day: A Biography.* New York: Harper and Row, 1982.

DEBS, EUGENE V. (1855–1926)

Eugene V. Debs was a radical labor organizer and advocate of the rights of labor. Between 1900 and 1920 he campaigned five times for the presidency of the United States on the Socialist Party ticket.

Born in Terre Haute, Indiana, Debs started working for the railroads at age fourteen, and in 1875 he was instrumental in organizing a local lodge of the Brotherhood of Locomotive Firemen. In addition to his work as a labor organizer Debs became a politician, serving as city clerk of Terre Haute (1879–1883) and as a member of the Indiana state legislature (1885).

Debs's goal in the labor arena was to organize workers by industry rather than by craft, because he believed this would create greater solidarity. In 1893 he became president of the newly created American Railway Union, which he brought to national prominence the following year by leading it through a successful strike against the Great Northern Railroad (April 1894). In 1895 Debs was jailed for refusing to yield to a federal injunction to stop the great strike against the Chicago Pullman Palace Car Company. While serving his six-month sentence, Debs read Karl Marx and, thereafter, increasingly embraced socialism and was the principal founder of the organization that, in 1901, became the Socialist Party of America. In 1905 he participated in the creation of the Industrial Workers of the World, but quickly found this group too radical in its views and withdrew.

During World War I Debs protested federal persecution of individuals under the Espionage Act of 1917 and, in 1918, was convicted for his protests and stripped of his citizenship. Despite his conviction, he enjoyed—while in prison—his most successful run at the presidency, polling more than

900,000 votes. He was released from prison in 1921 by order of the president, but his citizenship was not restored until 1976, long after his death.

A passionate advocate of the working man, Debs is still revered as a champion of dissent and individual liberty.

Suggested Reading

Pelz, William A., ed. *Eugene V. Debs Reader: Socialism and the Class Struggle.* Chicago: Institute of Working Class History, 2000.

Salvatore, Nick. *Eugene V. Debs: Citizen and Socialist.* Champaign–Urbana: University of Illinois Press, 1984.

DECLARATION OF INDEPENDENCE

In June 1776 the Continental Congress appointed a committee to draft a declaration of independence, naming to it John Adams, Benjamin Franklin, Robert Livingston, Roger Sherman, and Thomas Jefferson. The committee, in turn, chose Jefferson to draft the document. No one expected a particularly momentous moral or philosophical statement: all that was required was a legally defensible justification of the colonies' break with the mother country—one that would stand up to the scrutiny of the foreign powers, most notably France, to which the United States would have to appeal for aid in battling an empire that commanded the world's mightiest army and navy.

Years later, writing in 1825, Jefferson himself explained that his purpose had not been to "find out new principles, or new arguments, never before thought of . . . but to justify ourselves in the independent stand we are compelled to take" and to "appeal to the tribunal of the world . . . for our justification." He did add, most significantly, that the declaration was "intended to be an expression of the American mind." Jefferson went on to cite his sources: "All its authority rests on the harmonizing sentiments of the day, whether expressed in conversation, in letters, printed essays, or in the elementary books of public right, as Aristotle, Cicero, Locke, Sidney, etc" (Letter to Henry Lee, 1825, quoted in Alan Axelrod, *The Life and Work of Thomas Jefferson,* New York: Alpha, 2001, 27).

Of these authors, it was to the seventeenth-century British philosopher John Locke that the declaration owed its most direct debt. Locke had enumerated the basic rights of human beings as life, liberty, and property. Jefferson, of course, wrote of "inalienable rights" to life and liberty, but then changed Locke's "property" to the "pursuit of happiness." It is in this change, some later commentators have remarked, that Jefferson most keenly captured "the American mind" by suggesting that he believed that Americans were driven, first and foremost, by the pursuit of happiness.

Jefferson's original draft included a condemnation of King George III—specifically, for having "waged cruel war against human nature itself, violating its most sacred rights of life & liberty in the persons of a distant people who never offended him, captivating & carrying them into slavery in another hemisphere, or to incur miserable death in their transportation thither." Congress deleted this reference to slavery and also made other changes that softened the document. Although a slaveholder himself, Jefferson was most disappointed by the striking of the slavery clause, for it meant that the United States of America would fight for its liberty and for the "inalienable rights" of humankind, but would do so as a slave nation.

The Declaration of Independence was signed by the members of the Continental Congress on July 4, 1776. (See Appendix A for the text of the Declaration of Independence.)

Suggested Reading

Gerber, Scott Douglas, ed. *Declaration of Independence: Origins and Impact.* Landmark Events in U.S. History Series. Washington, D.C.: CQ Press, 2002.

Maier, Pauline. *American Scripture: The Making of the Declaration of Independence.* New York: Alfred A. Knopf, 1997.

DEFENSE OF MARRIAGE ACT

The Defense of Marriage Act (28 USC 1738C), passed by Congress and signed into law in 1996, provides that no state shall be required to give effect to a law of any other state with respect to a same-sex "marriage." In addition, the act defines, for the first time in U.S. history, the terms *marriage* and *spouse* for purposes of federal law. The law does not affect the right of individual states to grant legal status to same-sex unions within that state.

Critics of the law have questioned its constitutionality on the grounds that the "full faith and credit" clause of the Constitution requires states to recognize the "acts, records and proceedings" of all other states. Critics also charge that the federal definitions of *marriage* and *spouse* are unprecedented intrusions by the federal government into an area that is properly and traditionally the province of the states. Moreover, because the law defines marriage as "a legal union between one man and one woman as husband and wife" and spouse as "a person of the opposite sex who is a husband or a wife," critics fear that individuals in unions that do not fit this description automatically become ineligible for many of the benefits offered by the federal government to married couples and their families. (See Appendix A for the text of the Defense of Marriage Act.)

Suggested Reading

Eskridge, William N., Jr. *Equality Practice: Civil Unions and the Future of Gay Rights.* New York: Routledge, 2001.

Sullivan, Andrew, and Joseph Landau, eds. *Same-Sex Marriage: Pro and Con.* New York: Vintage, 1997.

DEPARTMENT OF HEALTH AND HUMAN SERVICES, U.S.

The U.S. Department of Health and Human Services (HHS) is a cabinet-level department and the principal federal agency for protecting the health of all Americans and for providing essential human services, especially for those who are least able to help themselves. The Department of Health, Education and Welfare was created on April 11, 1953. In 1979, the Department of Education Organization Act was signed, creating a separate Department of Education, and, on May 4, 1980, the Department of Health and Human Services was created.

The HHS administers more than three hundred programs, including medical and social science research; food and drug safety; Medicare (health insurance for elderly and disabled Americans) and Medicaid (health insurance for low-income people); financial assistance and services for low-income families; maternal and infant health; Head Start (preschool education and services); child abuse and domestic violence prevention; substance abuse treatment and prevention; services for older Americans; and comprehensive health services for Native Americans.

Until March 31, 1995, when it was made an independent agency, the Social Security Administration was part of the HHS. (See Appendix A for the organization of the Department of Health and Human Services.)

Suggested Reading

Department of Health and Human Services, www.hhs.gov.

DEPARTMENT OF HOUSING AND URBAN DEVELOPMENT, U.S.

The Department of Housing and Urban Development (HUD) was brought into being by the Department of Housing and Urban Development Act (42 USC 3532–3537), effective November 9, 1965. Created as part of President Lyndon B. Johnson's War on Poverty and Great Society initiatives, the new cabinet-level department brought together a number of independent federal agencies already in existence.

HUD's mission is to create and administer national policy and programs to address housing needs in the United States, to foster growth and development in the nation's communities, and to enforce fair-housing laws. HUD thus has immediate responsibility for enforcing an aspect of civil rights law; perhaps more importantly, however, the existence of the department is based on the proposition that decent housing is a human right.

HUD programs aid community development, spur economic growth in distressed neighborhoods, provide housing assistance for the poor, help rehabilitate and develop moderate- and low-cost housing, and ensure that fair-housing laws are enforced on the community level. A HUD mortgage-insurance program is specifically designed to aid low- and moderate-income families in buying a home.

Suggested Reading

Department of Housing and Urban Development, www.hud.gov.

DEPARTMENT OF THE INTERIOR, U.S.

The U.S. Department of the Interior (DOI) is a cabinet-level agency that manages public lands; mineral, timber and water resources; Indian affairs; the Patent Office; and the Census Bureau. Much of the department's focus is on land management and on its role as the "nation's principal conservation agency." However, the agency's oversight of Indian affairs and the census often mean that it is deeply involved in matters relating to minority rights and civil rights.

Suggested Reading

Department of the Interior, www.doi.gov.

DEPARTMENT OF JUSTICE, U.S.

The Department of Justice (DOJ) was established in 1870 (by 28 U.S.C. 501, 503), with the attorney general as its head. Before the DOJ was created the attorney general (whose office was created in 1789) was a member of the cabinet, but not the head of a department.

The DOJ is one of the most powerful agencies of the federal government, and its work is central to issues involving both minority rights and individual rights. The DOJ's mission is to represent "the citizens of the United States in enforcing the law in the public interest." In addition, the department protects the citizens of the United States against criminals; enforces laws to ensure healthy competition between businesses; safeguards the interests of consumers; enforces drug, immigration, and naturalization laws; promotes effective law enforcement; conducts all suits in the Supreme Court in which the United States is concerned; and represents the government in legal matters. (See Appendix A for the organization of Department of Justice.)

Suggested Reading

Belknap, Mical R., ed. *Administrative History of the Civil Rights Division of the Department of Justice during the Johnson Administration.* New York: Garland Publishing, 1992.

Landsberg, Brian K. *Enforcing Civil Rights: Race Discrimination and the Department of Justice.* Lawrence: University Press of Kansas, 1997.

DEPARTMENT OF LABOR, U.S.

The mission of the U.S. Department of Labor (DOL), a cabinet-level department of the federal government, is to prepare the American workforce for new and better jobs and to ensure the adequacy of America's workplaces. The more than 180 federal statutes administered and enforced by the DOL concern workers' wages, health and safety, and employment and pension rights; job training, unemployment insurance, and workers' compensation; equal employment opportunity; and collective bargaining. In addition, through its Bureau of Labor Statistics, the DOL analyzes and publishes labor and economic statistics.

The DOL was created by an act of Congress in 1913 "to foster, promote and develop the welfare of working people, to improve their working conditions, . . . to enhance their opportunities for profitable employment." Historically, the principal focus of DOL has been workers' wages, hours, working conditions, and employment opportunities; employment discrimination; cooperative labor-management relations; and labor's role in the nation's industrial productivity. Initially, the DOL consisted of four bureaus that had been transferred from the old Department of Commerce and Labor: the Bureau of Labor Statistics, the Bureau of Immigration, the Bureau of Naturalization, and the Children's Bureau. Added to this group was a conciliation service to mediate labor disputes. Two years later the DOL also created a small employment service, which quickly grew into a national network that placed millions of workers into jobs during World War I.

After World War I the DOL was charged with administering and enforcing the immigration laws of 1921 and 1924, which introduced a quota system into U.S. immigration policy. During the 1920s the DOL created the Women's Bureau to promote the status and employment opportunities of women. During the Great Depression of the 1930s the DOL's employment service was expanded, and in 1933 President Franklin Roosevelt appointed Frances Perkins to be secretary of labor; it was the first time a woman had been named to a cabinet post. Perkins administered many New Deal reform and relief programs whose influence is still felt today, including unemployment insurance and three components of the Fair Labor Standards Act: the minimum wage, overtime, and child labor standards. Perkins also chaired the committee that developed the Social Security program.

After World War II the DOL relinquished immigration responsibilities to the Department of Justice, and labor-management conciliation functions were transferred to the National Labor Relations Board. However, veterans' reemployment rights became a major DOL responsibility. During the 1950s, with passage of important worker safety legislation, employee safety became a major DOL focus. The landmark passage of the Occupational Safety and Health Act (OSHA) in 1970 made safety an even more extensive DOL concern. In 1978 mine safety and health were also transferred to the DOL.

Beginning in the 1950s the DOL took on added regulatory responsibilities pursuant to the Welfare and Pension Plans Disclosure Act of 1958 and the Labor-Management Reporting and Disclosure Act of 1959. The 1974 Employee Retirement Income Security Act gave the DOL significantly increased authority to protect the assets of workers and other beneficiaries participating in private pension and welfare plans.

The 1950s and 1960s also saw the beginning of increasing concern about ensuring an adequate supply of well-trained workers and eliminating employment discrimination against women, members of minority groups, and workers with disabilities. During this period the DOL took on many added responsibilities for administering and enforcing a number of laws, including the Manpower Development and Training Act of 1962, the Comprehensive Employment and Training Act of 1973, the Job Training Partnership Act of 1982, and equal employment opportunity measures such as the Equal Pay Act of 1963, the Age Discrimination in Employment Act of 1967, and the Rehabilitation Act.

Suggested Reading

Laughlin, Kathleen A. *Women's Work and Public Policy: A History of the Women's Bureau, U.S. Department of Labor, 1945–1970.* Boston: Northeastern University Press, 2000.

DESEGREGATION

Desegregation is the general name for the policy and process of racial integration of social institutions, including schools, housing, the armed forces, and the workplace. Desegregation was a principal objective of the civil rights movement of the 1950s and 1960s and the objective of important civil rights legislation, especially the CIVIL RIGHTS ACT OF 1964.

Suggested Reading

Raffel, Jeffrey A. *Historical Dictionary of School Segregation and Desegregation*. Westport, Conn.: Greenwood Publishing, 1998.

Thernstrom, Stephan, and Abigail M. Thernstrom. *America in Black and White: One Nation, Indivisible*. New York: Simon and Schuster, 1997.

DISABILITY RIGHTS EDUCATION AND DEFENSE FUND

The Disability Rights Education and Defense Fund (DREDF) was founded in 1979 by people with disabilities and the parents of children with disabilities. It is a national law and policy center dedicated to protecting and advancing the civil rights of people with disabilities through legislation, litigation, advocacy, and technical assistance, and through the education and training of attorneys, advocates, people with disabilities, and parents of children with disabilities.

In law and policy reform the DREDF has successfully lobbied for such legislation as the Handicapped Children's Protection Act, the Civil Rights Restoration Act, and the AMERICANS WITH DISABILITIES ACT. For individuals, the DREDF carries out advocacy efforts on behalf of adults and children with disabilities, sometimes taking on litigation in disability rights cases. The organization also maintains close ties with the disability community nationwide.

Suggested Reading

Disability Rights Education and Defense Fund, www.dredf.org.

DIX, DOROTHEA (1802–1887)

A champion of reform, Dorothea Lynde Dix led a pioneering international humanitarian crusade for prisoners' rights and the rights of the institutionalized mentally ill.

Dix was a New England schoolteacher born in Hampden, Maine, who, for health reasons, traveled in 1836 to England where she was inspired by the work of Henry Tuke, a British advocate of prison reform. After her return to the United States in 1841 she volunteered to teach a Sunday school class at the jail in East Cambridge, Massachusetts. In this decrepit prison, Dix found her calling. Appalled by the primitive conditions and by the brutal treatment of prisoners—especially those who were mentally ill—Dix set out on a mission of reform, writing eloquent letters to newspapers and legislatures throughout the country. Her 1844 "Memorial to the Legislature of Massachusetts," a comprehensive report on the treatment of the mentally ill in Massachusetts, resulted in legislation to enlarge the Worcester insane asylum and made Dix a national celebrity, enabling her to appeal successfully for reform in several states and in Canada during 1844–1852.

As a result of her efforts, facilities in Massachusetts and Rhode Island were expanded, new institutions were constructed in New Jersey, Pennsylvania, and Canada, and reform legislation was passed in ten other states. She was instrumental in founding thirty-two mental hospitals and drew up broad plans for other institutions in the United States, Canada, Russia, and Turkey. Among the most basic reforms Dix advocated were the separation of mentally ill prisoners from the general prison population and the substitution of humane treatment for the ropes, chains, and other primitive methods of restraint and control used in institutions for the mentally ill. In 1854 Dix successfully petitioned Congress to authorize $12 million for the care of the mentally ill, but the legislation was vetoed by President Franklin Pierce.

During the Civil War Dix served as superintendent of women nurses for the Union army and created the foundation for what would become the U.S. Army Nursing Corps. After the war she continued to campaign on behalf of penal inmates and the mentally ill. She spent her final days in retirement at Trenton Hospital, in New Jersey, one of the institutions she had founded. (See also MENTALLY ILL, RIGHTS OF THE; PRISONERS, RIGHTS OF.)

Suggested Reading

Gollaher, David L. *Voice for the Mad: The Life of Dorothea Dix*. New York: Free Press, 1995.

Lightner, David L., ed. *Asylum, Prison, and Poorhouse: The Writings and Reform Work of Dorothea Dix in Illinois*. Carbondale: Southern Illinois University Press, 1999.

DOMESTIC VIOLENCE

Domestic violence is any abuse of a family member or members by another family member or members. Elder abuse and CHILD ABUSE are prevalent forms of domestic violence; however, most commonly, domestic violence involves the battering of a woman by a man, often a wife by a husband or a female domestic partner by her male domestic partner. "Battering" may take physical or other forms; the most common categories of domestic violence include

- Physical battering, which ranges from inflicting bruising injuries to murder
- Sexual abuse, a type of physical attack in which the woman is forced to have unwanted sexual contact with her abuser
- Psychological battering, which may take the form of verbal abuse, harassment, or excessive possessiveness, or may involve isolating the victim from friends and family, depriving the victim of physical or economic resources, or destroying the victim's personal property.

Until recent years police and judicial authorities were reluctant to respond to complaints of domestic violence, particularly those involving husband against wife, in part because the marital relationship was considered private, and in part because the seriousness of domestic violence was largely unrecognized. By the mid-1970s, however, most police and judicial jurisdictions had begun to regard domestic violence as a grave concern, and today most states have enacted legislation designed specifically to combat domestic violence. In many jurisdictions, for example, arrest and prosecution for domestic violence no longer requires one party to "press charges" against the other: whenever police intervene in an incident of domestic violence, the abuser is arrested and, typically, arraigned. If cause is shown, he (and it is usually a man) is prosecuted without regard to the expressed sentiment or will of other family members.

Suggested Reading

Berry, Dawn Bradley. *Domestic Violence Sourcebook.* New York: McGraw-Hill/NTC, 2000.

Wilson, Karen. *When Violence Begins at Home: A Comprehensive Guide to Understanding and Ending Domestic Abuse.* Alameda, Calif.: Hunter House, 1997.

"DON'T ASK, DON'T TELL" POLICY

Bill Clinton campaigned for the presidency, in part, on a pledge to end discrimination against gay men and women in the United States military. Once in office, however, Clinton compromised with conservative forces to formulate a "Don't ask, don't tell" policy under which military officials were barred from inquiring into the sexual orientation of personnel, but gay men and women were also required to refrain from openly expressing their sexuality while in military service (a requirement that included a prohibition against all "homosexual conduct"). Formally known as the Policy Concerning Homosexuality in the Armed Forces, the legislation outlining the "Don't ask, don't tell" policy was passed by the Senate on September 9, 1993, and by the House on September 28, 1993. (See Appendix A for the text of An Act Concerning Homosexuality in the Armed Forces.)

Suggested Reading

Lindsey, Daryl. *Gays in the Military: Don't Ask, Don't Tell, Don't Fall in Love.* New York: Salon.com, 2001.

Rimmerman, Craig A., ed. *Gay Rights, Military Wrongs: Political Perspectives on Lesbians and Gays in the Military.* New York: Garland Publishing, 1996.

Shilts, Randy. *Conduct Unbecoming: Gays and Lesbians in the U.S. Military.* Orlando, Fla.: World Publications, 1998.

DOUGLAS, WILLIAM O. (1898–1980)

A champion of civil liberties, William O. Douglas served just over thirty-six years as an associate justice of the Supreme Court, the longest tenure in American history.

He was born in Maine, Minnesota, but settled in Yakima, Washington, with his mother and siblings after his father died. After graduating from Whitman College in 1920 he taught school, then moved to New York and enrolled at Columbia University Law School in 1922. He graduated in 1925, second in his class.

Douglas practiced with a prestigious Wall Street firm for one year, then taught at Columbia and a year later at Yale, where he served on the faculty until 1936 when he became a member of the Securities and Exchange Commission (SEC). He was appointed SEC chairman in 1937. During his tenure on the SEC Douglas spearheaded reorganization of the nation's stock exchanges, introducing measures to protect small investors and bringing a degree of government regulation to the sale of securities.

Upon the retirement of Justice Louis Brandeis in February 1939, President Franklin D. Roosevelt nominated Douglas to the high court. When he took his seat on April 17, 1939, at age forty he was the second-youngest Supreme Court justice in American history.

Douglas's background in finance law meant that he was chosen to write many of the court's opinions in complex financial cases; however, he quickly became best known to jurists, legislators, and the public as an uncompromising voice in defense of civil liberties. Along with Justice Hugo Black, Douglas was a staunch supporter of the Bill of Rights and an opponent of all government limitations on free speech, including censorship of the press. Douglas became a lightning rod for criticism from political conservatives and the religious right.

Douglas was also outspoken in his defense of the constitutional rights of those accused of criminal acts, and decisions that he wrote—curbing illegal police searches, preventing coerced confessions, and ensuring enforcement of the accused's FIFTH AMENDMENT right to avoid self-incrimination—reflected this commitment. Ill health forced Douglas's retirement in 1975.

In addition to his Supreme Court opinions, Douglas left a legacy of writing on ecology, history, and politics.

Suggested Reading

Douglas, William O. *The Court Years, 1939 to 1975*. New York: Random House, 1980.

DRAFT LAWS

The first U.S. conscription law was enacted in 1862 during the Civil War. Those drafted could avoid service either by presenting a substitute or by paying a $300 "commutation fee"—an arrangement that effectively discriminated against recent immigrants, the poor, and members of the working class, none of whom could afford to buy their way out of the draft. Largely as a result of the inequity of the Conscription Act, a spate of draft riots swept the North in 1863, with the worst riot occurring in New York City during July. Of the 2,128,948 men fielded by the Union army, the overwhelming majority were volunteers. Only 52,068 draftees served; 86,724 others paid the commutation fee to avoid service.

The next draft did not occur until the U.S. entry into World War I. The Selective Service Act, passed on May 18, 1917, authorized the president to temporarily increase the U.S. military establishment. Under the act the SELECTIVE SERVICE SYSTEM, administered by the office of the provost marshal general, was responsible for selecting men for induction into military service. The system itself was made up of 52 state or territorial boards and 4,648 local boards, which were responsible for registering and classifying men, taking into consideration the labor needs of agriculture and certain industries and the family situations of the registrants; handling any appeals of the classifications; determining registrants' medical fitness; determining the order in which registrants would be called; calling registrants; and placing inductees on trains bound for training centers.

Some 24,000,000 men registered for the draft during World War I. In 1917, 516,212 men were inducted; in 1918, 2,294,084. The draft ended with the close of World War I; however, as new war clouds gathered, President FRANKLIN ROOSEVELT signed into law the Selective Training and Service Act of 1940, which authorized the nation's first peacetime draft and formally created a permanent Selective Service System as an independent federal agency. In 1940, 18,633 men were inducted; in 1941, 923,842; in 1942, 3,033,361; in 1943, 3,323,970; in 1944, 1,591,942; and in 1945, the last year of the war, 945,862.

In contrast to what had occurred after World War I, the Selective Service System and the draft did not end with the cessation of hostilities. Soldiers continued to be drafted in modest numbers until the Korean War (1950–1953), during which 1,219,837 men were inducted. But it was the increasingly unpopular Vietnam War (1965–1975) that transformed the selective service system and the draft into despised icons of the "military-industrial complex."

During the Vietnam War selective service initially functioned much as it had in the past, but in December 1969 a lottery drawing—the first since 1942—was held at the national headquarters of the selective service, in Washington, D.C.: 366 blue plastic capsules, each containing a birth date, were placed in a large glass container and drawn by hand to determine the order of call for induction, during calendar year 1970, for registrants aged eighteen to twenty-six (that is, those who had been born between January 1, 1944, and December 31, 1950). The lottery replaced the "draft the oldest man first" method, which had historically governed the order of call.

In reality selective service during the Vietnam War was never as impartial as the lottery method would have led one to expect. Deferments were abundantly available; among these was a II-S deferment for full-time students in educational programs beyond high school, which tended to remove middle-class young men—especially middle-class young white men—from the draft pool, contributing to the perception that the Vietnam War was being fought disproportionately by minority—especially black—troops. Popular perceptions aside, however, two-thirds of U.S. soldiers who served in Vietnam were voluntary enlistees, eighty-six percent of the U.S. troops who were killed in Vietnam were white, 12.5 percent were black, and 1.2 percent were of other races.

The Vietnam War brought the end of the draft. In 1973 the United States converted to an all-volunteer military, and in April 1975 the requirement that all eighteen-year-old young men register with the Selective Service System was suspended. Mandatory registration—but not the draft itself—was resumed in 1980 in response to the Soviet invasion of Afghanistan, and registration continues today. See also CONSCIENTIOUS OBJECTORS.

Suggested Reading

Flynn, George Q. *The Draft, 1940–1973*. Lawrence: University Press of Kansas, 1993.

DRED SCOTT DECISION

Dred Scott was a fugitive Missouri slave who had belonged to John Emerson of St. Louis. An army surgeon, Emerson was transferred first to Illinois and then to the

Wisconsin Territory, and he took Scott with him to each of these posts. After Emerson's death in 1846, Scott returned to St. Louis, where he sued Emerson's widow for his freedom, arguing that he was now a citizen of Missouri, having been made free by virtue of his residence in Illinois, where SLAVERY was banned by the Northwest Ordinance, and in the Wisconsin Territory, where the provisions of the MISSOURI COMPROMISE made slavery illegal. After a Missouri state court ruled against Scott, his lawyers appealed to the U.S. SUPREME COURT, which handed down its decision in 1857.

The Supreme Court's antislavery northern justices, predictably, sided with Scott, while the proslavery southerners upheld the Missouri court's decision. Chief Justice Roger B. Taney, a native of the slaveholding state of Maryland, who had the final word, held that neither free nor enslaved blacks were citizens of the United States and, therefore, could not sue in federal court. This alone would have settled the case, but Taney ruled further that the Illinois law banning slavery had no force on Scott once he returned to Missouri, a slave state, and that the law obtaining in Wisconsin was likewise without force, because the Missouri Compromise was unconstitutional, a violation of the FIFTH AMENDMENT, which barred the government from depriving an individual of "life, liberty, or property" without DUE PROCESS of law.

The *Dred Scott* decision galvanized the ABOLITION MOVEMENT, which asked, "Had the nation come to this—that the highest court in the land could use the BILL OF RIGHTS to *deny* freedom to a human being?"

But the *Dred Scott* decision was more than a moral outrage. By defining slavery strictly as a property issue—that is, a Fifth Amendment issue—the decision mandated that slavery had to be *protected* in all the states, even where it was neither practiced nor permitted. The decision put slavery beyond any further compromise. As abolitionists saw it, if the rights of slave holders had to be universally upheld as long as slavery existed, then slavery had to be universally abolished. There was no middle course, and civil war became inevitable. (See Appendix A for excerpts from the opinion of Chief Justice Taney.)

Suggested Reading

Fehrenbacher, Don E. *The Dred Scott Case: Its Significance in American Law and Politics.* New York: Oxford University Press, 2001.

———. *Slavery, Law and Politics: The Dred Scott Case in Historical Perspective.* New York: Oxford University Press, 1981.

DRUG TESTING

Although many employers subject job applicants or current employees to drug screening tests, drug testing—especially random drug testing—is prohibited by law in some states, and, even where drug testing is permitted, the law typically limits how employers may respond. For instance, the AMERICANS WITH DISABILITIES ACT (ADA) protects employees who suffer from alcoholism, which is considered a medical disability under the law. Thus, an employer may not refuse to hire a qualified individual because of his or her alcoholism, and may not punish an alcoholic employee more severely than nonalcoholic employees for the same conduct.

Though the ADA does not similarly protect people with other chemical dependencies, federal and state law, as well as civil case law, have made drug testing legally complex. For example, when employees challenged a company policy that required them to disclose their prescription drug use at the time of a test for illegal drugs, a federal circuit court ruled in favor of the company, which had claimed that the disclosure was necessary to ensure the accuracy of the drug test. Rejecting the employees' claim that the policy constituted an invasion of privacy, the court ruled that since the information was not disclosed to others, it was an "insignificant" invasion of privacy, and therefore permissible. In another case in California, however, a federal court ruled that it was illegal for an employer to require disclosure of prescription drug use as part of a medical exam for applicants and for candidates for promotion; in this case the court viewed the employer's policy as a violation of the ADA and of an individual's right to privacy under the California constitution.

Drug testing in the workplace remains an area of concern to employers, to legislators, and to rights organizations such as the AMERICAN CIVIL LIBERTIES UNION.

Suggested Reading

Tulacz, Gary. *What You Need to Know about Workplace Drug Testing.* Englewood Cliffs, N.J.: Prentice Hall, 1989.

DU BOIS, W.E.B. (1868–1963)

Among the most influential leaders of the American black community in the first half of the twentieth century, William Edward Burghardt Du Bois was born in Great Barrington, Massachusetts. In 1896 he became the first African American to receive a Ph.D. from Harvard University, and between 1897 and 1914 he researched and wrote several landmark sociological studies of black America. His belief was that through the application of social science, racial inequality in America could be analyzed, understood, and, ultimately, eliminated. In the course of his career, however, he became convinced that RACISM was so virulent and deeply ingrained in American culture and institutions that only vigorous social activism—including agitation and protest—could begin to improve the condition of African Americans.

At the start of the twentieth century Du Bois embraced the notion that black capitalism and economic equality could be precursors to social equality. However, he soon broke with the leading advocate of this position, Booker T. Washington, because he believed that Washington's willingness to accept segregation—and to hold in abeyance broader questions of social equality—was destructive to the black cause. In 1905 Du Bois was a chief founder of the Niagara Movement, which organized in opposition to Washington's "accommodationism." The movement led to the founding of the National Association for the Advancement of Colored People (NAACP), in which Du Bois played a prominent part. Until 1934 Du Bois served as the NAACP's director of research and as editor of its magazine, The *Crisis,* and became one of the most influential voices among the middle-class blacks and progressive whites calling for complete social equality of the races.

Throughout his career Du Bois wrestled with the notion of black separatism versus black integration into the white mainstream. He became increasingly interested in black nationalism and was an early advocate of Pan-Africanism, the doctrine that all people of African descent have common interests and should therefore work together toward common goals. Du Bois led the first Pan-African Conference in London, in 1900, and was the motivating force behind four others held between 1919 and 1927.

In addition to supporting black political nationalism, Du Bois championed black cultural nationalism, especially in the *Crisis,* where he put forth an early version of "black pride," a philosophy that was later given voice during the civil rights movement. Finally, Du Bois also advocated the immediate development of black economic nationalism, through the creation of black-owned businesses and cooperatives. It was this position that, in 1934, precipitated Du Bois's break with the NAACP. Developing simultaneously with Du Bois's interest in black economic autonomy was a growing commitment to Marxism.

After he left the NAACP Du Bois taught at Atlanta University for a decade and founded the magazine *Phylon,* in 1940, a "review of race and culture." In 1945 Du Bois published the preparatory volume of what was intended as an encyclopedia of the black race, black history, and the black experience. He also wrote other major books, including *Black Reconstruction: An Essay toward a History of the Part Which Black Folk Played in the Attempt to Reconstruct Democracy in America, 1860–1880* (1935) and *Dusk of Dawn: An Essay Toward an Autobiography of a Race Concept* (1940). These joined his most popular volume, *The Souls of Black Folk* (1903), as major contributions to the sociology of the African American.

Du Bois returned to a research post at the NAACP from 1944 to 1948, but again broke with the organization and became increasingly dedicated to Marxism. In 1951 he was indicted as an "unregistered agent for a foreign power"; a federal judge ordered acquittal, but Du Bois, in disgust, drifted further from American society. He joined the International Communist Party in 1961 and moved to Ghana, where he renounced his American citizenship in 1962. He died in Africa.

Suggested Reading

Huggins, Nathan I., ed. *Writings of W.E.B. Du Bois: The Suppression of the African Slave-Trade; The Souls of Black Folk; Dusk of Dawn; Essays; Articles from The Crisis.* New York: Library of America, 1996.

DUE PROCESS

The phrase *due process* refers to legal proceedings that are carried out according to rules constitutionally established for the enforcement and protection of civil rights. In the United States due process refers specifically to the exercise of the powers of government, including sanctions, as regulated by the safeguards enumerated in the Constitution. However, the concept of due process is founded in English common law and is expressed in article 39 of the Magna Carta (1215): "No freeman shall be taken or (and) imprisoned or disseised or exiled or in any way destroyed . . . except by the legal judgment of his peers or by the law of the land." The language of the Fifth Amendment to the U.S. Constitution clearly echoes the language of the Magna Carta: "No person shall . . . be deprived of life, liberty, or property, without due process of law." Importantly, it was not until the ratification of the Fourteenth Amendment, in 1868, that the states became subject to due process restraints as enforced by the federal government.

Over the years, Supreme Court decisions have led to a "due process standard" by which the constitutionality of legislation may be evaluated. If a law promotes the public welfare and the means of its enforcement are consonant with the public interest, it meets the due process standard. If, however, a law regulates a fundamental right guaranteed by the Constitution, it must meet the "compelling interest test," a stricter standard by which public benefit resulting from the law is judged.

Suggested Reading

Keynes, Edward. *Liberty, Property, and Privacy: Toward a Jurisprudence of Substantive Due Process.* State College: Pennsylvania State University Press, 1996.

EBONICS

Ebonics is the study of black English, which is also sometimes called African American Vernacular English (AAVE). As defined by Ebonics, black English consists of a distinct set of vocabulary, pronunciations, syntax, and grammatical forms used by some African Americans. The simplicity of this definition, however, belies the social and linguistic complexity of black English itself—and the sometimes controversial cultural and political freight that burdens the field of Ebonics.

To begin with, black English varies widely among African American speakers and is significantly influenced by socioeconomic and regional factors. Further complicating the picture is the fact that black English has much in common with the speech of rural white southerners. Moreover, black English has been widely imitated by white entertainers (and even by black entertainers)—on film and television, and in music—which has certainly affected its use, as well as the way it is perceived by whites and blacks alike.

Politically, Ebonics has been a source of controversy. Some educators and others believe that black English should be treated, respected, and even promoted as a distinct dialect. Opponents argue that because black English is not a dialect but simply substandard English—and, as such, should be corrected (that is, eradicated)—Ebonics has no legitimate place in the academic curriculum. While students of Ebonics believe that black English enriches African Americans' sense of their cultural heritage, critics argue that it perpetuates negative cultural stereotypes and hinders educational and economic progress among its speakers.

To the casual listener, pronunciation is the most distinctive feature of black English. For example, the letter *r* is rarely pronounced after a vowel, or is pronounced "uh"; the *th* sound may be pronounced as the letter *d* ("dis" for "this"), the letter *v* ("bruvuh" for "brother"), or the letter *f* ("baf-room" for "bathroom"). Although other aspects of pronunciation, along with many features of syntax and grammar, are common to southern folk dialects, white and black alike, black English is unique in its suppression of final consonants and, especially, consonant combinations—so that, for example, "hold" becomes "ho." This characteristic is so pervasive that it affects inflection. Possessive endings are frequently dropped, so that "his father's friends" becomes "his father friend," and "she runs" becomes "she run."

Linguists have long been interested in the way black English treats verbs, especially the verb *to be*. *Is* and *are* are routinely eliminated, as in "he goin' home." And while black English eliminates some verb forms, it adds others: the "habitual *be*": "he be makin' the same mistake over and over"; the "perfective *done*": "she done tol' me already"; the "remote-time *been*": "he been finish the job"; and the "double modal": "I might could do that." Again, although some of these forms are found in white southern folk speech, they are most closely and consistently identified with black English.

Whatever one's political position on black English—and, therefore, on the role of Ebonics in formal education—there is no question that black English has had a great impact on American popular culture, slang, and general vocabulary, both within and outside the African American community.

Suggested Reading

Baugh, John. *Beyond Ebonics: Linguistic Pride and Racial Prejudice.* New York: Oxford University Press, 2000.

Perry, Theresa, and Lisa Delpit, eds. *The Real Ebonics Debate: Power, Language, and the Education of African-American Children.* Boston: Beacon, 1998.

EDUCATION LAW CENTER

The Education Law Center (ELC) was founded in 1973 to promote school reform by enforcing and expanding the rights of individual students to a thorough, efficient, and appropriate education under state and federal law. Specifically, the ELC is dedicated to the aggressive pursuit of equal educational opportunity on behalf of poor children, minority children, and children with disabilities, especially in New

Jersey's urban communities. The ELC conducts research, advocacy efforts, litigation, and education and training for parents and the community.

Suggested Reading

Education Law Center, www.edlawceter.org.

EDUCATION RIGHTS

Education rights constitute an aspect of minority rights that is both fundamental and complex—fundamental because democracy implies the universal right to education, and complex because education rights touch on, sometimes impinge upon, and encompass other rights.

Right to Education

Founders such as Thomas Jefferson held that education is not only a right essential to the individual but a prerequisite to genuine and effective self-government. Thus the right to education in a democracy is implied, but *only* implied. The U.S. Constitution makes no explicit mention of a right to education, unless one chooses to interpret the phrase "to promote the general welfare," which is included in the preamble, as encompassing a mandate to provide for public education. Nevertheless, even under the Articles of Confederation, before the Constitution was adopted, Congress, pursuant to the Land Ordinance of 1785 and the Northwest Ordinance of 1787, made provision for the financing of public education in the territories and in the new states created from the territories. In contrast to the federal Constitution, state constitutions do provide for free public education, and every state has compulsory attendance laws that specify a minimum age for beginning school and a minimum age or minimum number of years of schooling after which one may leave school. Most states require children between the ages of six and sixteen to attend school; some extend this to age seventeen or eighteen. All states permit students to remain in school, at state expense, until age twenty-one.

Compulsory Public Education

While all states provide free public education, most states do not require attendance at public schools. Parents are free to send their children to private or parochial schools, provided that the minimum attendance requirements are observed. However, during the early twentieth century, when an influx of immigrants was perceived by some to threaten American identity, certain states passed laws requiring attendance at public schools. The objective was to ensure that these state-controlled institutions would be given ample opportunity to "Americanize" all students.

These laws were challenged in the courts, most notably in the case of *Pierce v. Society of the Sisters of the Holy Names of Jesus and Mary,* a 1925 challenge to Oregon legislation mandating attendance at public schools. The parochial school argued that the state's Compulsory Education Act violated the school's Fourteenth Amendment rights by denying "valuable property interests" without due process; that is, the law would economically destroy parochial schools. While recognizing the state's power to require compulsory school attendance, the Supreme Court held that the Fourteenth Amendment rights of the parochial schools had, in fact, been violated—and furthermore, that parochial and private schools were (or could be made) competent to meet the state's compulsory attendance requirement without having to forfeit property interests.

Challenges to Compulsory Attendance

Challenges to compulsory attendance that are based on religious belief have been more difficult to decide. In 1972 the Supreme Court heard *Wisconsin v. Yoder,* in which an Amish family challenged compulsory attendance requirements on the grounds that education beyond the eighth grade conflicted with Amish religious values. On the basis of freedom of religion, the court granted the Amish an exception to the compulsory education requirement, prompting other states to define various exceptions on religious grounds while excluding others; for instance, the Iowa Supreme Court rejected the challenge brought by a fundamentalist Baptist group, holding that the Baptist group's religious practices were not as distinctive as those of the Amish and, therefore, that compulsory public education did not represent a basic threat to the practice of the group's religion.

Homeschooling has posed another challenge to the policy of compulsory attendance. By the mid-1990s thirty-five states had enacted home schooling statutes, which establish standards that enable home schooling to serve as an equivalent alternative to compulsory public education.(See also religion, freedom of.)

Racial Integration of Public Education

During the twentieth century public education became the first arena in which legally sanctioned segregation was successfully challenged. The integration of public schools is covered in the following articles: affirmative action; African American civil rights movement; Algebra Project; *Brown II; Brown v. Board of Education of Topeka, Kansas;* busing, school; Civil Rights Act of 1964; *Columbus Board of Education v. Penick;* Education

LAW CENTER; FAUBUS, ORVAL; FOURTEENTH AMENDMENT; LITTLE ROCK SCHOOL CRISIS; MARSHALL, THURGOOD; MEREDITH, JAMES HOWARD; "PHILADELPHIA PLAN, REMARKS ON THE"; *PLESSY V. FERGUSON;* "SEPARATE BUT EQUAL" DOCTRINE.

Economic Inequality

Economic inequality in education—the fact that some school districts are better funded, and therefore better staffed and better equipped than others—has been challenged periodically. The federal courts, including the SUPREME COURT, have consistently knocked down these challenges. Most significantly, in the case of *San Antonio Independent School District v. Rodriguez* (1973), the Supreme Court decided that education is not a fundamental constitutional right under the Fourteenth Amendment and, therefore, the efforts of state legislatures to "tackle the problems" of public education, including funding, "should be entitled to respect" without federal intervention.

Language Requirements

At various times states have enacted "English-only" legislation declaring English the official language in the state, a move that has affected public education. In 1974 in *Lau v. Nichols,* the parents of Chinese-speaking students sued the San Francisco Unified School District to obtain multilingual education. The Supreme Court decided that the state of California and the San Francisco public schools had violated the CIVIL RIGHTS ACT OF 1964 by requiring, as a prerequisite for education, that a child be fluent in English. Because such a prerequisite effectively denied the child an education, the schools were required to institute appropriate multilingual education. Following this landmark decision public school districts across the nation introduced multilingual education wherever the student population warranted it. Under Title VII of the Elementary and Secondary Education Act of 1968, known as the Bilingual Education Act, federal money was already available for bilingual education. However, that law was allowed to expire on January 8, 2002, and was replaced by the English Acquisition Act, which provides funding not for bilingual education but for English education for non-English-speaking students. (See also ENGLISH-ONLY LEGISLATION AND MOVEMENTS.)

Rights of Students with Special Needs

Most states have historically provided for the education or training of children with disabilities; however, such students were generally segregated from the general school population. In *State ex rel. Beattie v. Board of Education* (1919), a Wisconsin state court held that a child with disabilities could be excluded from regular public school, even if he or she was capable of meeting academic standards, because disability has a "depressing and nauseating effect on the teachers and school children."

The segregation of students with special needs was overturned by two landmark cases. In *Pennsylvania Association for Retarded Children v. Commonwealth* (1971), a federal court ruled that not only were retarded children entitled to a free public education, they were entitled to an education in regular classrooms where they would not be segregated from other students. The following year, in *Mills v. Board of Education of the District of Columbia* (1972), a federal court required the board of education to provide a free and appropriate education for all students with special needs. (See also INDIVIDUALS WITH DISABILITIES EDUCATION ACT.)

Suggested Reading

Alexander, Kern, and M. David Alexander. *The Law of Schools, Students and Teachers.* 2d ed. St. Paul, Minn.: West Publishing, 1995.

Fraser, James W. *Reading, Writing and Justice: School Reform As If Democracy Mattered.* Albany: State University of New York Press, 1997.

Rose, Mike. *Possible Lives: The Promise of Public Education in America.* Boston: Houghton Mifflin, 1995.

EISENHOWER, DWIGHT D. (1890–1969)

Dwight David Eisenhower, who served as supreme commander of the Allied forces in Europe during World War II, was elected the thirty-fourth president of the United States in 1952 and served until 1961.

"Ike" Eisenhower was born in Denison, Texas, and raised in Abilene, Kansas. After graduating from West Point in 1915 he was assigned to various training missions, then was quickly promoted and assigned to important staff and strategic posts. From 1933 to 1935 Eisenhower served as General Douglas MacArthur's chief of staff, then accompanied MacArthur to the Philippines, where he served until 1939. When the United States entered World War II, Eisenhower was assistant chief of the Army War Plans Division and, on June 25, 1942, was given command of the European Theater of Operations. In 1944 Eisenhower directed plans for the Normandy invasion (D day) and, in December was appointed supreme commander of the Allied Expeditionary Force and promoted to the rank of general.

Following Germany's surrender on May 7–8, 1945, Eisenhower assumed command of Allied occupation forces until November, when he returned to the United States and a hero's welcome. He served as army chief of staff from November 1945 through February 1948, retired, then became president of Columbia University from 1948 to December 1950. In December 1950 President HARRY S. TRUMAN recalled Eisenhower to active duty as supreme allied commander, Europe, and commander of North Atlantic Treaty Organization forces. Two years later Eisenhower again retired from the military, this time to run for president on the Republican ticket.

With his running mate, RICHARD M. NIXON, the enormously popular Eisenhower carried thirty-nine states, defeating Democrat Adlai Stevenson. Eisenhower's conservative views on domestic affairs led to a call for reduced taxes, a balanced federal budget, a general reduction in government control over the economy, and a "new federalism"—the return of certain federal responsibilities to the states. Yet Eisenhower generally avoided any sharp break with the liberal and even activist policies of the Roosevelt and Truman administrations. In a flush economy the minimum wage was raised to $1 an hour, the Social Security system was expanded, and, most importantly, a cabinet-level Department of Health, Education, and Welfare was created.

If anything, during his first term, Eisenhower had sharper differences with conservatives in his own party than with most Democrats. Nevertheless he was criticized by liberals for his support (albeit grudging and halfhearted) of the red-baiting Wisconsin senator JOSEPH R. MCCARTHY. Eisenhower also supported a "loyalty-security program," intended to root out communists in the federal bureaucracy, in which hundreds lost their jobs, and backed passage of controversial legislation designed to outlaw the American Communist Party. Despite a heart attack in September 1955 and surgery for ileitis in June 1956, Eisenhower once again ran against Stevenson and prevailed by a landslide—although he now faced a Democrat-controlled Congress.

The greatest minority rights challenge of Eisenhower's second term was the U.S. SUPREME COURT decision, on May 17, 1954, in the case of *BROWN V. BOARD OF EDUCATION OF TOPEKA, KANSAS*, which declared racial segregation in public schools unconstitutional. When attempts to enforce the decision met with violent resistance in the South, Eisenhower sent a thousand federal troops to Little Rock, Arkansas, to prevent Governor ORVAL E. FAUBUS from obstructing a federal court order requiring the integration of Little Rock's Central High School. It was also during Eisenhower's second term that the CIVIL RIGHTS ACT OF 1957—the first civil rights legislation since the CIVIL RIGHTS ACT OF 1875—was passed into law.

Despite Eisenhower's action to enforce public school integration and in support of the Civil Rights Act of 1957, liberals tended to perceive him as generally complacent in the area of minority rights—a view that was not entirely fair, although Eisenhower was hardly a social activist.

After his second term ended Eisenhower retired to his farm in Gettysburg, Pennsylvania, where he wrote his memoirs and other books. He died on March 28, 1969, in Washington, D.C. (See also LITTLE ROCK SCHOOL CRISIS.)

Suggested Reading

Burk, Robert Fredrick. *The Eisenhower Administration and Black Civil Rights, 1953–1961*. Knoxville: University of Tennessee Press, 1984.

Pach, Chester J., and Elmo Richardson. *The Presidency of Dwight D. Eisenhower*. Rev. ed. Lawrence: University Press of Kansas, 1991.

EMANCIPATION PROCLAMATION

For his authorship of the Emancipation Proclamation, ABRAHAM LINCOLN would go down in history as "the Great Emancipator." In truth, he was neither an enthusiastic abolitionist nor an advocate of emancipation. Although he personally abhorred SLAVERY, he believed himself bound by his oath of office to uphold the Constitution, which clearly protected slavery in the slave states. More immediately, in the midst of civil war, Lincoln feared that a declaration of universal emancipation would drive the four slave-holding border states into the Confederate camp—and might, moreover, incite renewed and intensified rebellion in those portions of the Confederacy then under Union military occupation.

Lincoln therefore moved cautiously. In August 1861 he prevailed on Congress to declare slaves in the rebellious states "contraband" property. As such, they could be seized by the federal government, which could then refuse to return them. In March 1862 Congress passed a law *forbidding* army officers from returning fugitive slaves, and in July of that year Congress passed legislation that freed any slaves confiscated from owners who were "engaged in rebellion." In addition, a militia act authorized the president to use freed slaves in the army; the intention was to assign them to labor details, but at the president's discretion they could also be used in combat.

Secretary of State William H. Seward warned, early in the war, that an outright proclamation of emancipation would ring hollow if it followed a series of Union defeats. It was not until the Battle of Antietam, a narrow and costly Union victory, that Lincoln felt sufficiently confident to issue a preliminary proclamation on September 23, 1862.

The preliminary Emancipation Proclamation did not free the slaves but instead warned slave owners living in states "still in rebellion on January 1, 1863," that their slaves would be declared "forever free." Only after that deadline had passed did Lincoln issue the final Emancipation Proclamation, which gave freedom only to those slaves who were living in parts of the Confederacy that were not under the control of the Union army. Slaves in the border states—which had not seceded from the Union—were not liberated.

Although timid when viewed from a twenty-first-century perspective, the Emancipation Proclamation galvanized the North by making slavery the central issue of the war, and thereby elevating the conflict to a higher moral plane. (See Appendix A for the text of the final Emancipation Proclamation.)

Suggested Reading

Franklin, John Hope. *The Emancipation Proclamation.* 1963. Reprint, Wheeling, Ill.: Harlan Davidson, 1995.

Pinsker, Matthew. *Abraham Lincoln.* American Presidents Reference Series. Washington, D.C.: CQ Press, 2002.

ENGLISH-ONLY LEGISLATION AND MOVEMENTS

On April 27, 1981, Sen. S.I. Hayakawa of California proposed an "English language amendment" to the Constitution that would ban most uses of languages other than English by federal, state, and local governments. As of late 2002 the measure had not come to a congressional vote. At the time of Hayakawa's proposal, four states already had active legislation on the books, and since 1981 twenty-two states have passed various forms of "official English" legislation. However, because the English-only laws of Alaska and Arizona were declared unconstitutional, only twenty-four states, as of mid-2002, had official English laws; other states were contemplating such measures.

As an alternative to a constitutional amendment, English-only advocates have also proposed legislation to make English the official language of government. A number of these "statutory English" bills have been introduced, which would apply to the federal government only. The best-known, H.R. 123, passed in the House of Representatives in 1996 but failed to gain passage in the Senate. As of late 2002 another language of government bill is pending in Congress. If passed, the bill would do the following:

- Designate English as the official language of the federal government and restrict federal employees and officials, including members of Congress, to the use of English for most government business
- Designate English as the only acceptable language for all federal "actions, documents, policies . . . publications, income tax forms, informational materials," and so on
- Allow civil lawsuits by people who believe that they have been injured by any violation of the English-only law
- Restrict naturalization ceremonies to English only
- Repeal the bilingual provisions of the VOTING RIGHTS ACT OF 1965.

English-Only Advocacy Groups

The leading advocacy groups for adoption of an official English or English-only policy are U.S. English, Inc., founded by Senator Hayakawa in 1983, and English First, founded in 1986, and which describes itself as a "grassroots organization." Both organizations believe that the adoption of English as an official language will strengthen American national identity and unity, will improve economic opportunities for immigrants and ethnic minorities, will "give every child a chance to learn English," and will eliminate "costly and ineffective multilingual policies" in government and education.

Historical Perspective

Throughout most of the history of the United States, governments at all levels have taken an essentially laissez-faire approach to language, offering little official interference in the matter of what language people choose to speak. From time to time, however, the English-only perspective has emerged.

In colonial America, even before independence, Benjamin Franklin was in the forefront of a movement to compel "Pennsylvania Germans"—who accounted for about one-third of the population of Pennsylvania—to learn English, lest Pennsylvania be plagued by "great disorders and inconveniences." Franklin further proposed suppressing the use of German in advertisements, newspapers, street signs, legal contracts, and other public contexts.

During the early years of the Republic, the Louisiana Purchase (1803) brought a substantial French-speaking minority into the United States. When the territorial governor appointed by President THOMAS JEFFERSON immediately decreed that all public and government business would be transacted in English, the response was a manifesto called *The Louisiana Remonstrance,* which, in turn, prompted Jefferson to order the governor to rescind the English-only policy. However, when Louisiana became a state in 1812 Congress required that the Louisiana constitution stipulate that all laws and official records be published in the language "in which the Constitution of the United States is written." This did not rule out bilingual publication, however, and the Louisiana constitution of 1845 guaranteed that the legislature would continue to operate bilingually; moreover, an 1847 law authorized bilingual instruction in public schools. During RECONSTRUCTION in 1868 the federal government abolished French language rights, but some of those rights were restored in 1879 after the end of Reconstruction.

After the United States acquired California as a result of the UNITED STATES–MEXICAN WAR (1846–1848), the state constitution of 1849 recognized Spanish language rights and stipulated the bilingual publication of state laws. However, as the Gold Rush brought an overwhelming influx of non-Spanish-speaking immigrants into the new state, a series of anti-*Californio* (a *Californio* was a Californian of Mexican heritage) laws—referred to collectively by the disparaging phrase "greaser laws"—was passed, including a law that ended Spanish-language schooling in 1855. Moreover, federal legislation, the California Land Act of 1851, required all landowners to prove title to their holdings in English-language courts, and when the California constitution was rewritten in 1878–1879 an English-only provision was adopted: "All laws of the State of California, and all official writings, and the executive, legislative, and judicial proceedings shall be conducted, preserved, and published in no other than the English language." The English-only provision was not discarded until 1966.

American Indians were long the targets of English-only laws. During the period of the so-called Indian Wars, from 1868 to 1891, federal officials acted on the belief that English-only schooling was an effective means of assimilating and pacifying the Indians, and in the 1880s the federal government hired the equivalent of private bounty hunters to "collect" Indian children, who were taken from their families and sent to boarding schools where they were compelled to speak English—and were subjected to CORPORAL PUNISHMENT if they were caught speaking their native tongue (or practicing tribal religions, ceremonies, or other customs). In one form or another, aggressive anglicization—what critics have described as "linguistic genocide"—was the policy of the U.S. Bureau of Indian Affairs until the 1960s.

Following the Spanish-American War of 1898 the federal government sponsored a program to anglicize the newly acquired territory of Puerto Rico through compulsory public education in English-only classrooms. The policy hardly succeeded in expunging the Spanish language from Puerto Rico, but it did drive many Puerto Rican youngsters away from school. Spanish was restored as the basic language of instruction in 1948 when Puerto Rico gained commonwealth status.

Also annexed in 1898 was Hawaii, which, though previously an independent nation, had long been under U.S. economic domination. Throughout the nineteenth century missionaries from the mainland educated Hawaiian children in English. In 1896 the Republic of Hawaii, a United States puppet government, passed a law ordering that all public education be conducted in English.

The English-Only Initiative

Within the contiguous United States, a strong English-only initiative came with U.S. entry into World War I, when much of the nation was swept up in anti-German sentiment. In some states (especially in the Midwest), even the speaking of German in public was prohibited, ostensibly for fear of espionage. German-language newspapers and other publications came under attack, and some were banned. The teaching of German was forbidden in many schools and institutions of higher learning. In some places German books were publicly burned, although no law sanctioned this.

Both during and after the war, anti-German sentiments expanded into general xenophobia, one aspect of which was the Red Scare, touched off by the Bolshevik Revolution in Russia. In 1919 fifteen states passed English-only instruction laws.

The founding of U.S. English, Inc., in 1983, did much to revive the flagging English-only movement. The organization currently claims a membership of 400,000. (See Appendix A for the text of the proposed "official English amendment." See also EDUCATION RIGHTS.)

Suggested Reading

Crawford, James. *Hold Your Tongue: Bilingualism and the Politics of English Only.* New York: Addison-Wesley, 1992.

Crawford, James, ed. *Language Loyalties: A Sourcebook on the Official English Controversy.* Chicago: University of Chicago Press, 1992.

English First, www.englishfirst.org.

U.S. English, Inc., www.us-english.org.

EQUAL ACCESS ACT

The Equal Access Act, signed into law on August 11, 1984, makes it "unlawful for any public secondary school which receives Federal financial assistance and which has a limited open forum to deny equal access or a fair opportunity to, or discriminate against, any students who wish to conduct a meeting within that limited open forum on the basis of the religious, political, philosophical, or other content of the speech at such meetings." The law defines "limited open forum" as existing "whenever [a public secondary] school grants an offering to or opportunity for one or more noncurriculum related student groups to meet on school premises during noninstructional time."

The law was sponsored chiefly by Christian organizations that wanted to ensure that school facilities could be used after hours for prayer meetings and the meetings of religion-based clubs; however, the legislation is also used to support the right of students to organize other types of meetings, ranging from support groups (for gay, lesbian, or bisexual students, for example), to interest-based groups (for students who want to explore heavy-metal music, for example), to affiliation-based groups (for students who are atheists; who are involved in "Goth" culture; or who are adherents of Satanism, Wicca, or other belief systems, for example). The only provisos are that attendance must be voluntary, groups must be student-initiated, and groups may not be sponsored by the school itself, by teachers or other school employees, or by the government. Groups and clubs that meet these criteria must be given equal access to facilities such as meeting space, the public address system, school periodicals, and bulletin board space.

While school officials may not restrict equal access, they do have the right to monitor meetings. School officials may also require all clubs to follow a set of rules, including nondiscrimination policies; however, a federal court has ruled that religious clubs can discriminate against persons of other faiths in the selection of officers. The only way in which school districts can opt out of the provisions of the act is by disallowing all extracurricular clubs.

Suggested Reading

Colby, Kimberies W. *A Guide to the Equal Access Act.* Annandale, Va.: Christian Legal Society, 1988.

EQUAL CREDIT OPPORTUNITY ACT

The Equal Credit Opportunity Act (ECOA) is designed to ensure that all consumers are given an equal chance to obtain credit, provided that they meet the creditor's customary requirements in areas such as income, expenses, debt, and credit history. (See Appendix A for the opening provision of the Equal Credit Opportunity Act.)

Suggested Reading

U.S. Department of Justice, www.usdoj.gov/crt/housing/housing_ecoa.htm.

EQUAL EMPLOYMENT OPPORTUNITY COMMISSION, U.S.

The Equal Employment Opportunity Commission (EEOC) was established by Title VII of the CIVIL RIGHTS ACT OF 1964 and began operating on July 2, 1965. Its responsibility is to enforce the following federal statutes:

Title VII of the Civil Rights Act of 1964, as amended, which prohibits employment discrimination on the basis of race, color, religion, sex, or national origin

The AGE DISCRIMINATION IN EMPLOYMENT ACT of 1967, as amended, which prohibits employment discrimination against workers forty years of age or older

The EQUAL PAY ACT OF 1963, which prohibits discrimination in compensation on the basis of gender for substantially similar work under similar conditions

Titles I and V of the AMERICANS WITH DISABILITIES ACT of 1990, which prohibits employment discrimination on the basis of disability in the private sector and state and local government

Sections 501 and 505 of the Rehabilitation Act of 1973, as amended, which prohibits employment discrimination against federal employees with disabilities

The CIVIL RIGHTS ACT OF 1991, which provides monetary damages in cases of intentional discrimination and includes clarifying provisions regarding so-called "disparate impact actions" (actions that have a disproportionate effect on a particular group).

Headquartered in Washington, D.C., the EEOC operates fifty field offices nationwide to coordinate all federal equal employment opportunity regulations, practices, and policies. The EEOC interprets employment discrimination laws, monitors discrimination within federal employment, provides funding and support for state and local fair employment practices agencies, and sponsors outreach and technical assistance programs.

Suggested Reading

Equal Employment Opportunity Commission, www.eeoc.gov.

EQUALITY LEAGUE OF SELF-SUPPORTING WOMEN

The Equality League of Self-Supporting Women was founded in 1907 by Harriet Stanton Blatch, the daughter of ELIZABETH CADY STANTON, because existing women's suffrage organizations tended to exclude the working class in general—and, in particular, the working (self-supporting) woman. The league made extensive use of the tactics of British suffragists, including parades, street speakers, and pickets. In 1910, the organization became the Women's Political Union. (See also WOMEN'S SUFFRAGE MOVEMENT.)

Suggested Reading

DuBois, Ellen Carol. *Feminism and Suffrage: The Emergence of an Independent Women's Movement in America, 1848–1869.* Ithaca: Cornell University Press, 1999.

Flexner, Eleanor. *Century of Struggle: The Women's Rights Movement in the United States.* 1973. Reprint, Cambridge, Mass.: Belknap Press, 1996.
Kraditor, Aileen S. *The Ideas of the Woman Suffrage Movement, 1890–1920.* New York: Norton, 1981.

EQUAL PAY ACT OF 1963

The purpose of the Equal Pay Act is "to prohibit discrimination on account of sex in the payment of wages by employers engaged in commerce or in the production of goods for commerce." (See Appendix A for the text of the Equal Pay Act.)

Suggested Reading

Fogel, Walter A. *Equal Pay Act.* New York: Praeger, 1984.

EQUAL RIGHTS AMENDMENT

The Equal Rights Amendment (ERA) was written and proposed in 1923 by Alice Paul, a radical suffragist who founded the NATIONAL WOMAN'S PARTY. Paul believed that the ERA was the next step necessary after ratification of the Nineteenth Amendment, which gave women the vote.

Beginning in 1923 the ERA was introduced at every session of Congress until 1972, when it achieved passage and was sent to the states for ratification. When the requisite three-fourths of the states failed to ratify the amendment before the seven-year time limit included in its proposing clause had expired, Congress extended the deadline to June 30, 1982. By that date thirty-five states had ratified, leaving the amendment three states short of ratification. The ERA has been reintroduced into every Congress since 1982. (See Appendix A for the text of the proposed amendment.)

Suggested Reading

Steiner, Gilbert. *Constitutional Inequality: The Political Fortunes of Equal Rights Amendment.* Washington, D.C.: Brookings Institution, 1985.

ESPIONAGE ACT

The Espionage Act was passed by Congress on June 15, 1917, after the United States entered World War I. Among other provisions the act prescribed a $10,000 fine and up to twenty years' imprisonment for such offenses as interfering with the recruiting of troops or disclosing information pertaining to the national defense. The act also prescribed penalties for refusing to perform military service.

Widely criticized as unconstitutional, the act resulted in the imprisonment of many antiwar protestors, including such prominent figures as labor leader EUGENE V. DEBS, who was sentenced to ten years in prison for attacking the Espionage Act in a 1918 speech. Some 450 conscientious objectors were imprisoned under the act, and the socialist journal the *Masses* was prosecuted and forced to cease publication.

After the war attorney general A. Mitchell Palmer and his right-hand man, J. EDGAR HOOVER, used the Espionage Act as well as the Sedition Act to justify a nationwide campaign against radicals and left-wing organizations. (See also ALIEN AND SEDITION ACTS and PALMER RAIDS.)

Suggested Reading

Feuerlicht, Roberta Strauss. *America's Reign of Terror: World War I, the Red Scare, and the Palmer Raids.* New York: Random House, 1971.

EUTHANASIA

See RIGHT TO DIE.

EVERS, MEDGAR (1925–1963)

In 1954 Medgar Evers became Mississippi's first field director of the NATIONAL ASSOCIATION FOR THE ADVANCEMENT OF COLORED PEOPLE (NAACP), and the following year gained national recognition for bringing to light the case of a fourteen-year-old Chicago boy named EMMETT TILL, who, while visiting Mississippi, had been lynched for allegedly "talking fresh" to a white woman. In the early 1960s Evers championed the cause of JAMES MEREDITH, who became the first African American to attend the traditionally segregated University of Mississippi.

Evers was born on July 25, 1925, in Decatur, Mississippi, served in the army during World War II, then returned to Mississippi, where he and other black veterans were prevented by white mobs from registering to vote. He earned a B.A. degree from Alcorn Agricultural and Mechanical College, then applied to the law school of the University of Mississippi but was rejected because of his race. Evers found employment as an insurance agent, which gave him the opportunity to travel all over Mississippi and gain firsthand knowledge of how AFRICAN AMERICANS lived in the state. His personal experience of discrimination and his observations as an insurance agent motivated his connection with the NAACP.

In 1963 Evers was working on a major campaign in Jackson, the capital of Mississippi, to integrate public accommodations, to register black voters, and to increase black employment. On June 11, 1963, he was gunned down outside of his home by a white supremacist named BYRON DE LA BECKWITH. In 1964 Beckwith was tried twice; both trials, with juries made up entirely of whites, ended in hung juries. Arrested again in December 1990, Beckwith was brought to trial for a third time in 1994, convicted of Evers's murder, and sentenced to life imprisonment. He died in prison at age eighty on January 21, 2001.

Suggested Reading

DeSlaughter, Bobby. *Never Too Late: A Prosecutor's Story of Justice in the Medgar Evers Case.* New York: Scribner's, 2001.

Evers, Myrlie B. *For Us, the Living.* Oxford: University of Mississippi Press, 1996.

EXCLUSIONARY ZONING

The term *exclusionary zoning* refers to zoning requirements that effectively exclude certain groups from living in the area subject to those requirements. The federal FAIR HOUSING ACT prohibits zoning that is intended to exclude on the basis of race, and states may have additional laws regulating zoning; for instance, zoning ordinances that permit only single-family homes on large lots have the effect of excluding low-income families and are therefore deemed discriminatory in some states.

Not all exclusionary zoning, however, is a violation of federal or state law. For example, although federal law generally prohibits age discrimination in housing, the Fair Housing Amendment Act of 1988 created an exception that permits "housing for older persons." In some states, housing discrimination laws have been written or amended to allow housing developments that are designed exclusively for older tenants and that exclude those under a certain age.

Suggested Reading

Babcock, Richard F. *Exclusionary Zoning: Land Use Regulation and Housing in the 1970s.* New York: Praeger, 1974.

EX PARTE VIRGINIA

In 1878, after he had barred black citizens from serving as grand jurors and petit jurors in Pittsylvania County, Virginia, Judge J. D. Coles was arrested by federal officers on a charge of having violated the CIVIL RIGHTS ACT OF 1875. Coles filed a petition with the U.S. SUPREME COURT asking that all charges be dropped on the grounds that his arrest and imprisonment were not warranted by the Constitution and the laws of the United States, and that his personal rights and his judicial rights as an officer of Virginia had also been violated.

In *Ex parte Virginia* (1879), the high court denied Coles's petition, holding that he had violated the Civil Rights Act of 1875 as well as the equal protection clause of the FOURTEENTH AMENDMENT. The greatest significance of the decision is the interpretation of the Fourteenth Amendment as barring any state, or its officers or agencies, from denying equal protection of the law to any person within its jurisdiction. Moreover, the decision demonstrated that the federal government had a limited but nevertheless potent power to protect the rights of American citizens when those rights were compromised or abridged by a state.

Suggested Reading

Curtis, Michael Kent. *No State Shall Abridge: The Fourteenth Amendment and the Bill of Rights.* Durham: Duke University Press, 1990.

FAIR EMPLOYMENT PRACTICES COMMITTEE

Established in 1941 within the Office of Production Management by executive order of President FRANKLIN D. ROOSEVELT (FDR), the Fair Employment Practices Committee (FEPC) was created to promote the fullest employment of all available Americans and to eliminate discriminatory employment practices. FDR's successor, HARRY S. TRUMAN, wanted to establish a permanent peacetime FEPC, but the Senate terminated the FEPC in 1946. The EQUAL EMPLOYMENT OPPORTUNITY COMMISSION, created in 1964, was the next federal agency charged with fighting discrimination in employment.

Suggested Reading

Burstein, Paul. *Discrimination, Jobs, and Politics: The Struggle for Equal Employment Opportunity in the United States Since the New Deal.* Chicago: University of Chicago Press, 1985.

McElvaine, Robert S. *Franklin Delano Roosevelt.* American Presidents Reference Series. Washington, D.C.: CQ Press, 2002.

FAIR HOUSING ACT

Title VIII of the Civil Rights Act of 1968 and the Fair Housing Act of 1988 together constitute the Fair Housing Act, federal legislation that makes fair housing a national policy.

Title VIII of the Civil Rights Act of 1968 was enacted after the assassination of MARTIN LUTHER KING JR. Much as the assassination of President JOHN F. KENNEDY had spurred passage of the CIVIL RIGHTS ACT OF 1964, so the murder of Dr. King undoubtedly aided passage of Title VIII. The act prohibits discrimination in the sale, lease, or rental of housing, and further prohibits making housing otherwise unavailable because of the race, color, religion, sex, disability, familial status, or national origin of the prospective tenant or purchaser. Exempted from the act are owner-occupants of multifamily dwellings (up to three rental units) and owners of three or fewer rental houses who rent without using a real estate agent and who do not indicate racial preference in advertising.

The 1968 act also outlaws redlining (lenders' refusal to approve mortgages in certain neighborhoods) and blockbusting (a practice in which realtors encourage property owners to sell hastily and often at a loss by appealing to fears of depressed values because of minority encroachment; the realtors then resell at inflated prices).

As originally passed, the Fair Housing Act mandated a minor role for federal enforcement and, as a consequence, never worked adequately. Amendments enacted in 1988 gave the DEPARTMENT OF JUSTICE and the DEPARTMENT OF HOUSING AND URBAN DEVELOPMENT (HUD) a much greater role in enforcing the law. Under the 1988 legislation the Department of Justice litigates fair housing cases in court, and HUD investigates and attempts to resolve complaints of housing discrimination. In addition to providing for federal enforcement, the 1988 amendment extended the protections of the 1968 act to people with disabilities and to families with children.

Suggested Reading

Spada, Marcia Darvin. *Fair Housing.* Mason, Ohio: South-Western Publishing, 2001.

FAIR LABOR STANDARDS ACT

Signed into law in 1938 and amended many times since, the Fair Labor Standards Act (FLSA) is published in sections 201–219 of Title 29, U.S. Code. The act's four basic provisions are

- Require employers to pay the minimum wage
- Require employers to pay overtime pay for time worked over forty hours within a work week
- Restrict the employment of children

Require employers to maintain adequate and accessible records on wages, hours, and other items.

As of late 2002 the minimum wage was $5.15 per hour, and overtime was required to be at least 1.5 times the regular rate of pay. The current minimum wage law makes exceptions in the case of disabled workers, full-time students, youths under age twenty in their first ninety days of employment, employees who receive tips, and certain trainees or interns.

The FLSA's child labor provisions are intended to protect the educational opportunities of young people and prohibit their employment in jobs or under conditions that are detrimental to their health or safety. The regulations restrict work hours for youths under sixteen and list occupations deemed too hazardous for young workers.

As specified under the FLSA, wages are due on the regular payday for the pay period covered. Items to be deducted from wages, such as repayment for cash or merchandise shortages, employer-required uniforms, and tools of the trade, are illegal if the resulting wage amount is below the minimum wage or if they reduce the amount of overtime pay due under the FLSA.

Suggested Reading

U.S. Department of Labor, "Employee/Employer Advisor." www.dol.gov/elaws/flsa.htm.

FAIRNESS DOCTRINE

In 1949 the U.S. Federal Communications Commission (FCC) established the Fairness Doctrine, an attempt to ensure that coverage of controversial issues by broadcast stations would be balanced and fair. The FCC based the doctrine on the premise that station licensees were, in effect, "public trustees," and therefore had an obligation to afford reasonable opportunity for the discussion of contrasting points of view on controversial issues of public importance. Later, in 1971, the FCC held that stations were also obligated to make a positive effort to seek out issues of importance to their community and to broadcast programming that addressed those issues. The Fairness Doctrine held sway until 1987, when it was swept up in the tide of deregulation that came with the administration of President RONALD REAGAN.

The Fairness Doctrine paralleled section 315 of the Communications Act of 1937, which required stations to offer "equal time" to all legally qualified political candidates for any office if a station had allowed any person running for that office to use the station. In contrast to section 315, however, the Fairness Doctrine was FCC policy, not federal law.

In 1969, in the case of *Red Lion Broadcasting Co., Inc. v. FCC,* the SUPREME COURT upheld the Fairness Doctrine. A station in Pennsylvania had aired a program called the "Christian Crusade," in which an author, Fred J. Cook, was verbally attacked. When Cook requested time to reply, the station refused, and the FCC ruled that the attack obligated the station to provide opportunity for a reply. The station filed a series of appeals, which led eventually to the Supreme Court. Despite the Court's ruling, however, some broadcast journalists and freedom of speech advocates have objected to the Fairness Doctrine as a violation of the First Amendment rights of FREE SPEECH and a free press. Moreover, to avoid being compelled to actively seek contrasting viewpoints on issues that are raised, some broadcast stations have refrained from covering certain controversial issues, creating a "chilling effect," which was hardly what the FCC had intended.

By the 1980s, in a political climate of deregulation and amid technological advances (cable and satellite) that had greatly increased the number of channels available on television, the view that broadcasters were stewards of a public trust lost its power, and in its *Fairness Report* of 1985 the FCC declared that the doctrine was no longer producing its intended effect and might be in violation of the First Amendment. In 1987, in *Meredith Corp. v. FCC,* the Federal Circuit Court for the District of Columbia declared that the doctrine was not, in fact, mandated by Congress, and the FCC was given leave to discontinue enforcement of the doctrine. Accordingly, the FCC dissolved the doctrine in August 1987—but not before Congress had enacted a statutory fairness doctrine. President Reagan vetoed the measure, however, and there were insufficient votes for an override. A new law, passed by Congress during the administration of GEORGE H.W. BUSH, was vetoed by that president, and debate on the desirability of a statutory fairness doctrine continues.

Suggested Reading

Brennan, Timothy A. "The Fairness Doctrine as Public Policy." *Journal of Broadcasting and Electronic Media* (fall 1989).

Hazlett, Thomas W. "The Fairness Doctrine and the First Amendment." *Public Interest* (summer 1989).

Simmons, Steven J. *The Fairness Doctrine and the Media.* Berkeley: University of California Press, 1978.

FAMILY AND MEDICAL LEAVE ACT

The federal Family and Medical Leave Act (FMLA), which became effective on August 5, 1993, entitles eligible employees to take up to twelve weeks of unpaid, job-protected leave in a twelve-month period for specified family and medical reasons. Among other protections, the law provides for entitlement to leave, maintenance of health benefits during leave, and job restoration after leave.

Unpaid leave, if requested, must be granted:

For the birth and care of a newborn child of the employee
For the care of an adoptive or foster child placed with the employee
To allow the employee to care for an immediate family member (spouse, child, or parent) with a serious health condition
To allow the employee to take medical leave if he or she is unable to work because of a serious health condition.

Suggested Reading

U.S. Department of Labor, "Family and Medical Leave Fact Sheet." www.dol.gov/dol/esa/fmla.htm.

FARMER, JAMES (1920–1999)

During the 1960s James Farmer directed the Congress of Racial Equality (CORE), organizing nonviolent protests that included the Freedom Rides.

Farmer was born in Marshall, Texas, on January 12, 1920. His father, a minister, was also a professor at Rust College. Farmer studied at Wiley College, in Marshall, then completed his bachelor of divinity degree at Howard University, in Washington, D.C., in 1941. A conscientious objector during World War II, Farmer identified himself as a follower of Mohandas Gandhi's international nonviolent movement. After working for the Fellowship of Reconciliation, an interfaith peace and justice organization, he founded CORE in 1942. CORE first came to broad national attention in 1947 when it sponsored the Journey of Reconciliation, a project dedicated to the desegregation of public transportation in the upper South.

Farmer left CORE in the 1950s to work as a labor organizer, but he rejoined the organization in 1960 as its national director. In 1961, under his direction, CORE began staging a series of Freedom Rides to desegregate public transportation in the deep South. Farmer was arrested during one Freedom Ride and sentenced to forty days in Mississippi's notorious Parchman Penitentiary.

Farmer was a highly visible advocate of nonviolence and racial integration (he was married to a white woman). A central promoter of the March on Washington in 1963, Farmer dedicated much of his energy to seeking greater employment opportunities for African Americans. He left CORE in 1966 after the organization became increasingly militant and renounced its commitment to integration and nonviolence. After a brief stint as a professor at Lincoln University, in Pennsylvania, Farmer ran for Congress in 1968 as a third-party candidate representing Brooklyn; he lost to Shirley Chisholm. When he accepted an appointment as assistant secretary of health, education, and welfare in the cabinet of Richard M. Nixon, Farmer was widely criticized by his former colleagues in the civil rights movement. He resigned from the cabinet in 1971 to found the Council on Minority Planning and Strategy, a short-lived social think tank. From the 1970s through the 1990s Farmer lectured widely. In 1985 he published his autobiography, an invaluable first-person account of the civil rights movement, *Lay Bare the Heart.* In 1998 President Bill Clinton presented Farmer with the Congressional Medal of Freedom. Farmer died on July 9 of the following year. (See also Poor People's Campaign.)

Suggested Reading

Farmer, James. *Lay Bare the Heart: An Autobiography of the Civil Rights Movement.* New York: New American Library, 1985.

FARM LABOR RIGHTS

See Chavez, Cesar; Hispanic Americans; Hispanic civil rights movement; migrant labor; Migrant Legal Action Program.

FARRAKHAN, LOUIS (1933–)

Since 1978 Louis Farrakhan has been head of the Nation of Islam, which advocates black separatism and adheres to some of the practices and beliefs of Islam. Farrakhan's supporters praise his leadership in the struggle for black economic self-sufficiency and his efforts to create and foster a sense of black identity and black pride. Farrakhan's critics denounce him as a racist and an anti-Semite. Some U.S. government officials, moreover, have criticized Farrakhan for his visits—during a "world friendship tour"—to countries run by dictators who are hostile to the United States.

Born Louis Eugene Wolcott in New York City, Farrakhan was raised in Boston and worked as a nightclub singer in his early twenties under the stage name of Calypso Gene. In 1955 he met Malcolm X, who encouraged him to join the Nation of Islam. In conformity with Black Muslim practice, Wolcott dropped his "slave name" and called himself Louis X, a name he later changed to Louis Farrakhan.

Farrakhan rose quickly in the leadership of the Nation of Islam, and in 1963, when Malcolm X split with Elijah Muhammad, the leader of the Nation of Islam, Farrakhan sided with Muhammad. Farrakhan later admitted to being among the Black Muslim leaders who created the divisive climate in which Malcolm X was assassinated in 1965. After the death of Malcolm X Farrakhan became head of the Harlem Mosque and leader of the American Muslim Mission.

In 1978 Farrakhan himself parted company with the original Nation of Islam after Elijah Muhammad's son and successor, Wallace Muhammad, altered the name and the purpose of the organization. In 1983 Farrakhan threw his support behind the presidential candidacy of the Reverend JESSE JACKSON, and, two years later founded POWER, a health and beauty products company that functioned as part of a Nation of Islam program to promote black economic self-determination.

During the 1980s and 1990s, because of his outspoken and often extreme views—particularly those concerning racial separatism and the role of the Jews as "oppressors" of blacks—many moderate white and black leaders accused Farrakhan of fomenting racial hatred. His reputation was probably improved, however, by the success of the Million Man March, a large-scale demonstration of black solidarity and black pride held in Washington, D.C., in 1995. However, his 1996 "world friendship tour," which included formal calls on a number of dictators openly hostile to the United States, drew much criticism, as did his 1997 visit to Palestinian leader Yasir Arafat. (See also ISLAM, NATION OF.)

Suggested Reading

Haskins, James. *Louis Farrakhan and the Nation of Islam.* New York: Walker and Company, 1996.

White, Vibert L. *Inside the Nation of Islam: A Historical and Personal Testimony by a Black Muslim.* Gainesville: University Press of Florida, 2001.

FAUBUS, ORVAL E. (1910–1994)

A native of Arkansas, Orval Faubus was a schoolteacher who, after serving in the military during World War II, became Arkansas highway commissioner and served as governor of Arkansas from 1955 to 1967. A liberal by inclination, Faubus was also highly responsive to what he perceived as the prevailing climate of his state during the early phases of the AFRICAN AMERICAN CIVIL RIGHTS MOVEMENT, and in 1957 he earned national notoriety after he called out the Arkansas National Guard to prevent the integration of Central High School in Little Rock. Faubus was forced by federal order to withdraw the Guard, but after rioting broke out President DWIGHT D. EISENHOWER sent in federal troops and federalized the National Guard to restore order and to enforce the integration of the school.

Faubus's defiance of the federal government was popular with the white majority in Arkansas, who repeatedly returned him to the statehouse, but it effectively barred him from running for national office. As the political mood changed, Faubus's politically expedient support for segregation became a liability, and he was defeated in gubernatorial races in 1970, 1974, and 1986. (See also LITTLE ROCK SCHOOL CRISIS.)

Suggested Reading

Reed, Roy. *Faubus: The Life and Times of an American Prodigal.* Little Rock: University of Arkansas Press, 1997.

FEDERAL BUREAU OF INVESTIGATION

The FBI, a division of the U.S. DEPARTMENT OF JUSTICE and perhaps the most famous law enforcement agency in the world, is the largest investigative agency of the federal government. Generally, any investigation in which there is a federal interest is within FBI jurisdiction.

For much of its history the FBI was headed by its first director, J. EDGAR HOOVER, who was frequently criticized for running the agency as a kind of private fiefdom and assuming powers and prerogatives not only beyond the FBI's charter but outside of the Constitution as well. Particularly during the Hoover years, the FBI engaged in a number of questionable, and sometimes extralegal, surveillance missions; the principal subjects of such missions were prominent political liberals, and, especially during the 1960s, civil rights leaders including MARTIN LUTHER KING JR.

Headquartered in Washington, D.C., the FBI has field offices in major cities throughout the United States and in Puerto Rico. Since the FBI is the U.S. law enforcement agency designated to address international crime and criminals, there are also FBI liaison posts in certain foreign cities.

Until 1968 the director of the FBI was appointed by the attorney general; since 1968 the director has been appointed by the president with the advice and consent of the Senate. The director is responsible for a small army of employees, including 6,000–7,000 special agents, the FBI's investigators and enforcement personnel. Special agents, who must first have a background in law or accounting, are trained at the FBI Academy at Quantico, Virginia.

The FBI was established in 1908 as the Bureau of Investigation by attorney general Charles J. Bonaparte. Because Congress feared that a federal police agency might abuse its authority, the bureau was given little power, and it quickly became a haven for political hacks seeking patronage jobs. During World War I, however, the Bureau of Investigation was assigned to pursue draft evaders, suspected spies, and radical aliens. In 1920 Hoover, at the time a young lawyer at the Department of Justice, became assistant director of the bureau and stepped up the surveillance and pursuit of individuals suspected of radical subversion. In 1924, however, Congress clamped down on such activities, director William J. Burns was removed, and Hoover replaced him. It was a post he would hold until his death in 1972.

Hoover transformed the feeble and corrupt agency into a successful and high-profile crime-fighting organization. He began by adopting the more impressive *Federal* Bureau of Investigation designation, then set about professionalizing the staff, creating a small, elite force of special agents. Although Prohibition had fostered the rapid development of organized crime in the United States, Hoover focused instead on apprehending notorious individual criminals who had become federal felons by robbing federally insured banks or fleeing across state lines. A brilliant publicist, Hoover created the "Ten Most Wanted" list and a roster of "public enemies"—headed by "Public Enemy Number One."

Hoover also raised the standard for law enforcement and criminal investigation. At its best the FBI conducted and coordinated effective nationwide police efforts; provided much-needed support, instruction, and assistance to local police agencies; developed sophisticated scientific methods of forensic analysis; compiled useful databases of crime and criminals; and advocated such proactive investigative approaches as criminal profiling, an attempt to "get into" the criminal mind to anticipate where a criminal would strike next. Despite the threats that the FBI often posed to basic American freedoms, it did bring police work to an unprecedented level of sophistication and efficiency.

Suggested Reading

Theoharis, Athan G., and Tony G. Poveda, eds. *The FBI: A Comprehensive Reference Guide.* New York: Checkmark, 2000.

FEDERALIST PAPERS, THE

The Federalist Papers, a series of eighty-five essays written by Alexander Hamilton, JAMES MADISON, and John Jay and published during 1787–1788 (under the collective pseudonym of "Publius"), were intended to promote ratification of the new U.S. Constitution, which had been drafted to replace the ineffectual ARTICLES OF CONFEDERATION. *The Federalist,* as it is often known, was published serially: seventy-seven essays appeared in book form on May 28, 1788; the remaining eight were published in New York newspapers between June 14 and August 16 of that year. Most historians agree that Hamilton wrote numbers 1, 6–9, 11–13, 15–17, 21–36, 59–61, and 65–85; Madison numbers 10, 14, 18–20, 37–58, and 62–63; and Jay numbers 2–5 and 64.

The principal argument of *The Federalist Papers* is that government under the new Constitution would, without compromising individual liberties, eliminate the weaknesses of the loose confederation established by the Articles of Confederation. To this day the essays are regarded as the definitive philosophical treatise on republican government.

At the heart of *The Federalist* is the popular eighteenth-century assumption that individuals are motivated chiefly by self-interest, which may even override rationality. Republican government does not, of itself, provide protection against excessive self-interest or against irrational or oppressive behavior; however, as regulated by a sound constitution, republican government can compensate for deficiencies of reason by establishing a self-correcting system of checks and balances, ensuring that no individual or group can gain disproportionate or absolute power.

In the often-cited tenth essay, countering the principal Anti-Federalist argument—namely, that the nation was too large and diverse to be regulated by a central government—Madison argued that precisely *because* the nation was so large, it would be most effectively governed by a strong central government, which would prevent any single special interest from taking control.

Suggested Reading

Hamilton, Alexander, James Madison, and John Jay. *The Federalist Papers.* 1788. Reprint, New York: Mentor, 1999.

FIFTEENTH AMENDMENT

This amendment, guaranteeing black enfranchisement, was ratified and adopted during RECONSTRUCTION in 1870 and was intended to thwart efforts in southern states to keep blacks from the polls.

Curiously, the SUPREME COURT initially interpreted the amendment in a negative and constraining sense, holding in *United States v. Reese* (1876) and *UNITED STATES V. CRUIKSHANK* (1876) that the amendment does not confer the vote on anyone, but guarantees exemption from discrimination in the exercise of the franchise on account of race, color, or previous condition of servitude. It was not until the high court struck down GRANDFATHER CLAUSES in southern states that the amendment was interpreted as conferring an affirmative right to vote, as in *Guinn v. United States* (1915).

The Supreme Court referred to the Fifteenth Amendment in decisions declaring unconstitutional white primaries (*Terry v. Adams* 1953), LITERACY TESTS (*Davis v. Schnell* 1949), and some aspects of racial GERRYMANDERING (*Whitcomb v. Chavis* 1971; *White v. Regester* 1973; and *City of Mobile v. Bolden* 1980). (See also VOTING RIGHTS ACT OF 1965. See Appendix A for the full text of the Fifteenth Amendment.)

Suggested Reading

Davidson, Chandler. *Controversies in Minority Voting: The Voting Rights Act in Perspective.* Washington, D.C.: Brookings Institution, 1992.

Goldman, Robert Michael. *Reconstruction and Black Suffrage: Losing the Vote in Reese and Cruikshank.* Lawrence: University Press of Kansas, 2001.

Mathews, John Mabry. *Legislative and Judicial History of the Fifteenth Amendment* (Johns Hopkins University Studies in Historical and Political Science). Union, N.J.: The Lawbook Exchange, 2001.

FIFTH AMENDMENT

As the BILL OF RIGHTS forms the core of individual liberties guaranteed under the Constitution, so the Fifth Amendment is the "core of the core," insofar as judicial proceedings are concerned. While all of the rights enumerated in the Fifth Amendment are of crucial importance, the most familiar is the freedom from compulsion to testify against oneself in a criminal case. (See Appendix A for the text of the Fifth Amendment.)

Suggested Reading

Alderman, Ellen, and Caroline Kennedy. *In Our Defense: The Bill of Rights in Action.* New York: Morrow, 1991.

Amar, Akhil Reed. *The Bill of Rights: Creation and Reconstruction.* New Haven: Yale University Press, 2000.

Levy, Leonard Williams. *Origins of the Bill of Rights.* New Haven: Yale University Press, 1999.

FIRST AMENDMENT FOUNDATION

The First Amendment Foundation was created in 1984 by the Florida Press Association, the Florida Society of Newspaper Editors, and the Florida Association of Broadcasters "to ensure that public commitment and progress in the areas of FREE SPEECH, free press, and open government do not become checked and diluted during Florida's changing times." The organization's mission is "to protect and advance the public's constitutional right to open government by providing education and training, legal aid and information services."

Suggested Reading

First Amendment Foundation, www.floridafaf.org.

Georgia First Amendment Foundation, www.gfaf.org.

FLAG LAWS

Rules and regulations for displaying the flag of the United States are codified in law under title 4, chapter 1, sections 1 and 2, U.S. Code, and by Executive Order 10834. In addition, various states have enacted laws addressing the proper display and treatment of the flag. In 1989 the U.S. SUPREME COURT overturned the conviction of Gregory Johnson, who had been prosecuted under Texas law for burning an American flag in a protest. The high court defined Johnson's act as "political speech," which is protected by the First Amendment. In response, a conservative-dominated Congress passed the Flag Protection Act of 1989.

When the Supreme Court ruled in *United States v. Haggerty* and *United States v. Eichman* (both 1990) that the Flag Protection Act was unconstitutional, Congress attempted to enact a constitutional amendment that would have given the states the right to pass flag laws regardless of previous Supreme Court decisions. The bill passed the House on June 28, 1995, but fell three votes short of the two-thirds Senate majority required for passage of proposed constitutional amendments. The amendment has been reintroduced in subsequent sessions of Congress. (See Appendix A for an excerpt from the Flag Protection Act of 1989.)

Suggested Reading

Goldstein, Robert Justin. *Flag Burning and Free Speech: The Case of Texas v. Johnson.* Lawrence: University Press of Kansas, 2000.

Welch, Michael. *Flag Burning: Moral Panic and the Criminalization of Protest.* Hawthorne, New York: Aldine De Gruyter, 2000.

FORD, GERALD R. (1913–)

At noon on August 9, 1974, following the resignation of RICHARD M. NIXON, Gerald Rudolph Ford became the thirty-eighth president of the United States. Not only was Ford the first vice president in American history to succeed to office because of the president's resignation, he was the first president to serve without having been elected as either president or vice president: Nixon appointed Ford to the vice presidency when the previous vice president, Spiro T. Agnew, resigned after pleading nolo contendere to a charge of federal income tax evasion.

Ford was born Leslie King Jr., in Omaha, Nebraska, on July 14, 1913, but took the name of his stepfather, Gerald R. Ford, after his mother's remarriage. Ford was raised in Grand Rapids, Michigan, and educated at the University of Michigan and at Yale University Law School, from which he graduated in 1941. He began practicing law in Grand Rapids but left to serve in the navy during World War II as an aviation operations officer. After the war he returned to law, then entered Congress in 1948. He rose steadily through the ranks to leadership of the Republican House minority and was minority leader when he accepted appointment as vice president in 1973.

Ford's quarter-century record in Congress was conservative. He opposed the expansion of the federal government, including federal aid to education. Ford frequently clashed with labor unions, and he sought more restrictive increases in the minimum wage. Although he voted in favor of the Civil Rights Act of 1964 and the Voting Rights Act of 1965, Ford typically voted to limit federal intervention for the purpose of protecting civil rights and was often criticized by civil rights organizations for seeking to dilute ancillary federal civil rights measures and for endorsing the Nixon administration's efforts to weaken the Voting Rights Act. And in 1970 Ford attempted unsuccessfully to initiate impeachment proceedings against leading liberal Supreme Court justice William O. Douglas on grounds of unseemly behavior, after Douglas made a fourth trip to the altar with a very young bride. Thus liberals and civil rights activists were disheartened when President Nixon nominated Ford as vice president after Agnew resigned. Nevertheless, Ford was confirmed by Congress and was sworn in as vice president on December 6, 1973.

When Ford assumed the presidency, however, even liberals were impressed by his warmth and openness, which were a welcome change from the remote and secretive Nixon White House. However, Ford's preemptive pardon of President Nixon—for any crimes committed or that "might have been committed"—was viewed by many Americans as unjust and as smacking of backroom politics of the worst kind.

Ford had inherited an economy plagued by stagflation (simultaneous recession and inflation), which prompted him to veto as too costly some fifty pieces of Democratic legislation, including much legislation that was related to welfare and education. Liberals were more pleased with Ford's initiatives to reform intelligence activities, especially those conducted by the Central Intelligence Agency (CIA) and the Federal Bureau of Investigation (FBI), agencies that had been tainted by the Nixon Watergate scandal. Ford sought limitations on the domestic activities of U.S. agencies engaged in foreign intelligence, but he also sought improved procedures to protect classified information on intelligence sources and methods; that is, he was concerned to stop the kinds of leaks that had exposed Watergate. Although most of these reforms were made by executive order rather than legislation, it was during Ford's administration that the Senate created the Select Intelligence Committee, which was given broad authority over the CIA, FBI, and other federal intelligence agencies.

President Ford also inherited the end of the Vietnam War, and it was he who ordered the evacuation of American citizens and pro-American Vietnamese from Saigon after the fall of the capital.

In 1976 Ford ran for election to the presidency in his own right but was defeated by Democrat Jimmy Carter.

Suggested Reading

Greene, John Robert. *The Presidency of Gerald R. Ford*. Lawrence: University Press of Kansas, 1995.

FORD MOTOR COMPANY, CLASS ACTION SUIT AGAINST

Title VII of the Civil Rights Act of 1964 prohibits employment discrimination on the basis of sex, race, religion, color, or national origin. Case law has defined discrimination to encompass sexual harassment, and in 1999 the U.S. Equal Employment Opportunity Commission reached a landmark settlement with the Ford Motor Company, which agreed to provide $7.5 million in damages to settle a class-action lawsuit in which female employees claimed to have been victims of a long-standing pattern of sexual harassment—including groping, name-calling, and other abuses.

Ford agreed to pay the damages, which were to be distributed among a class of up to six hundred eligible claimants who had been employed at two Ford plants in Chicago between 1996 and the date the settlement was signed. Ford also agreed to train all company employees on the prevention of sexual harassment and to increase to 30 percent, over a three-year period, the percentage of women appointed to entry-level supervisory positions at its Chicago stamping and assembly plants. Finally, the company agreed to the appointment of a three-member panel of independent monitors to oversee implementation of the settlement and to approve company policies for prevention and correction of employment discrimination and for the internal resolution of employee complaints.

The settlement is widely regarded as a model for the resolution of such grievances.

Suggested Reading

Petrocelli, William, and Barbara Kate Repa. *Sexual Harassment on the Job: What It Is and How to Stop It.* 4th ed. Berkeley, Calif.: Nolo Press, 2000.

FORTAS, ABE (1910–1982)

Abe Fortas served as associate justice of the U.S. SUPREME COURT from 1965 to 1969. President LYNDON B. JOHNSON nominated him as chief justice in 1968, but the nomination failed to receive Senate approval. In 1969, under threat of impeachment, Fortas resigned—the first Supreme Court justice to do so under such threat.

The son of a British immigrant, Fortas graduated from Yale Law School in 1933 at the head of his class and became a protégé of WILLIAM O. DOUGLAS. Fortas taught at Yale until 1937 when he went to work under Douglas at the federal Securities and Exchange Commission. Beginning in 1946 Fortas engaged in private law practice, and in 1963 successfully argued before the Supreme Court the case of *Gideon v. Wainwright,* a landmark case that established the right of the accused to counsel in criminal trials, regardless of ability to pay.

President Johnson nominated Fortas to the Supreme Court in 1965. When, three years later, his nomination as chief justice was opposed by the Senate, Fortas requested that his name be withdrawn. A year later, Fortas's one-time involvement with a financier who was subsequently imprisoned for securities violations seemed likely to bring about impeachment proceedings, and Fortas resigned. He spent the rest of his professional life in private practice.

Suggested Reading

Murphy, Allen Bruce. *Fortas: The Rise and Ruin of a Supreme Court Justice.* New York: Morrow, 1988.

FOURTEENTH AMENDMENT

The Fourteenth Amendment, which was ratified after the Civil War, reinforced several RECONSTRUCTION-era measures intended, in some degree, to punish the South for its rebellion; however, the most enduring provision of the amendment is section 1, which bars states from abridging rights guaranteed by the federal Constitution—effectively overturning the 1833 SUPREME COURT decision in *BARRON V. BALTIMORE,* which had defined the Bill of Rights as applying only to the national government and not to the states. Pursuant to the Fourteenth Amendment, any action of any state or local government may be challenged if it denies any person "equal protection of the laws." During the 1950s and 1960s the amendment's equal protection clause was frequently used as the basis for overturning segregationist state laws, especially those pertaining to equitable voting practices and to access to voter registration and the polls. (See Appendix A for the text of the Fourteenth Amendment.)

Suggested Reading

Hudson, David. *The Fourteenth Amendment: Equal Protection Under the Law.* Berkeley Heights, N.J.: Enslow Publishers, 2002.

FRANKFURTER, FELIX (1882–1965)

Felix Frankfurter, who served as associate justice of the U.S. SUPREME COURT from 1939 to 1962, was most closely associated with the doctrine of judicial self-restraint, which holds that judges should disregard their own opinions in deference to legal precedent and should base legal decisions exclusively on "whether legislators could in reason have enacted [the] law [at issue]" (*Standard Oil Co. of California v. United States*, 1949.)

Frankfurter immigrated to the United States from Vienna, Austria, as a young boy. He attended the City College of New York and Harvard Law School, where he later had a long and distinguished career as a professor from 1914 to 1939. Before beginning his academic career Frankfurter was assistant to Henry L. Stimson, at the time U.S. attorney for the Southern District of New York (1906–1909) and then secretary of war under President William Howard Taft (1911–1913). In 1919 President Woodrow Wilson called on Frankfurter to serve as his legal adviser at the Paris Peace Conference—where, in the wake of World War I, the Treaty of Versailles was forged and the League of Nations was created.

Frankfurter was Jewish, and early in his career became an active Zionist. He helped found the AMERICAN CIVIL LIBERTIES UNION (ACLU), and was perhaps the most eloquent critic of the conviction of Nicola Sacco and Bartolomeo Vanzetti, Italian immigrants and anarchists sentenced to death after a highly questionable and explosive 1921 trial for the murder of a paymaster and a guard during the robbery of a Massachusetts shoe factory.

Frankfurter's association with FRANKLIN D. ROOSEVELT (FDR) began when FDR was governor of New York and Frankfurter served as his legal adviser. After FDR entered the White House Frankfurter advised him on New Deal legislation and other controversial matters. Roosevelt appointed him to the Supreme Court on January 5, 1939.

Despite his earlier position on Sacco and Vanzetti, as a Supreme Court justice Frankfurter focused on the integrity of government rather than on the injustice suffered by individuals; nevertheless, his support for procedural safeguards in government and in the criminal justice system did have the effect of protecting the rights of the accused. Even in this focus, however, Frankfurter was sometimes circumspect. In the difficult opinion he rendered in the case of *Wolf v. Colorado* (1949), he condemned as unconstitutional the illegal seizure of evidence by police, but also ruled that the DUE PROCESS clause of the FOURTEENTH AMENDMENT does not require a state court to exclude evidence unlawfully obtained—a position that was overturned by a Supreme Court decision in *Mapp v. Ohio* (1961).

Frankfurter retired in 1962. (See also SACCO AND VANZETTI CASE.)

Suggested Reading

Frankfurter, Felix. *Law and Politics.* New York: Peter Smith, 1971.
Hirsch, H. N. *The Enigma of Felix Frankfurter.* New York: Basic Books, 1981.

FREEDMEN'S BUREAU

Officially known as the U.S. Bureau of Refugees, Freedmen, and Abandoned Lands, the Freedmen's Bureau was created by Congress in 1865 at the start of RECONSTRUCTION to render practical aid to some four million newly freed black Americans. Major General OLIVER O. HOWARD headed the bureau, which was in effect the first federal welfare agency.

The Freedmen's Bureau built hospitals and provided medical care for some one million former slaves and distributed emergency food rations not only to former slaves but to desperate southern whites as well. Under Howard (who went on to found Howard University, a college for AFRICAN AMERICANS located in Washington, D.C.), the Freedmen's Bureau devoted much effort and resources to educating former slaves, most of whom were illiterate. With aid from the bureau more than one thousand black schools and many black colleges were established.

The Freedmen's Bureau had little authority to carry out its mandate to safeguard the civil rights of freedmen and rarely succeeded in doing so in the courts. Under President Andrew Johnson, who resisted much of Congress's Reconstruction program, abandoned lands were summarily restored to pardoned southerners. The bureau appealed to Congress to override the president by enacting land redistribution legislation, but to no avail. The overwhelming majority of freedmen were thus forced to subsist as sharecroppers—tenants on white-owned lands.

The Freedmen's Bureau was terminated by Congress in July 1872.

Suggested Reading

Cimbala, Paul A., and Randall M. Miller, eds. *The Freedmen's Bureau and Reconstruction: Reconsiderations.* New York: Fordham University Press, 1999.

FREEDOM HOUSE

Freedom House was founded in the 1940s by ELEANOR ROOSEVELT, Wendell Wilkie, and others as an advocacy organization to represent democratic values and to counter dictatorships, whether on the far left or far right, and to promote human rights internationally. Today Freedom House is led by a board of trustees composed of leading Democrats, Republicans, and independents; business and labor leaders; former senior government officials; and scholars, writers, and journalists.

Freedom House supported the Marshall Plan and the North Atlantic Treaty Organization in the 1940s and the U.S. civil rights movement during the 1950s and 1960s. During the 1970s the organization worked to remedy the plight of the "boat people"—refugees from Vietnam—and in the 1980s was a strong supporter of Poland's Solidarity movement and the democratic opposition in the Philippines. The organization lends support to emerging democracies worldwide and has worked to oppose dictatorships in Central America and Chile, apartheid in South Africa, the suppression of the Prague Spring, the Soviet invasion of Afghanistan, genocide in Bosnia and Rwanda, and human rights violations in Burma, China, Cuba, and Iraq.

Suggested Reading

Freedom House, www.freedomhouse.org.

FREEDOM OF INFORMATION ACT

The original Freedom of Information Act was signed into law in 1966 by President LYNDON B. JOHNSON and extensively amended by the Electronic Freedom of

Information Act Amendments of 1996, signed into law on October 2, 1996, by President BILL CLINTON. The legislation is fundamental to issues of human rights, minority rights, and government accountability. (See Appendix A for the text of the Freedom of Information Act.)

Suggested Reading

Foerstel, Herbert N. *Freedom of Information and the Right to Know: The Origins and Applications of the Freedom of Information Act.* Westport, Conn.: Greenwood Publishing Group, 1999.

FREEDOM RIDES

The administration of JOHN F. KENNEDY received support from African Americans partly on the strength of Kennedy's campaign pledge to introduce civil rights reforms. When the administration proved slow to live up to that promise, the CONGRESS OF RACIAL EQUALITY (CORE) and other civil rights groups sought ways to pressure Kennedy individually and the federal government generally.

In *Boynton v. Virginia* (1960), the SUPREME COURT had declared segregation in interstate transit—including the maintenance of segregated waiting rooms and rest rooms in bus stations—unconstitutional. CORE decided to force a test of the federal ruling by sending thirteen men and women, some black, some white, on two separate buses through the South. The thirteen were to ride in a "desegregated manner"; that is, the blacks would use facilities reserved for whites, and the whites would use those reserved for blacks. CORE anticipated that southern authorities would refuse to abide by *Boynton,* and that the Kennedy administration would be forced to intervene to enforce the high court's decision.

The Freedom Riders left Washington, D.C., on May 4, 1961. At first the journey was free of incident, except when whites attacked JOHN LEWIS, a black Freedom Rider, at Rock Hill, South Carolina, as he entered a white waiting room a few days into the first Freedom Ride. Then on May 14, in Anniston, Alabama, whites slashed the tires of one of the Freedom Riders' buses, then set it on fire. Hours afterward in Birmingham Alabama, a white mob met the second Freedom Rider bus and attacked the Freedom Riders in the white waiting room.

Journalists recorded the burning of the bus in Anniston and the melee in Birmingham, providing coverage that not only rallied popular national support for the Freedom Rides but moved the Kennedy administration to demand that Alabama authorities protect the Freedom Riders. When another mob attack occurred, this time at the Montgomery bus terminal, and police failed to intervene, Kennedy dispatched more than five hundred federal marshals to Montgomery. The presence of the marshals, however, failed to quell the riot that developed outside Montgomery's First Baptist Church as MARTIN LUTHER KING JR. addressed a rally within the church.

Anticipating more violence when the Freedom Riders entered Mississippi, the Kennedy administration made a deal with Mississippi governor ROSS BARNETT, who agreed to protect the Freedom Riders in exchange for a pledge of federal noninterference in state and local plans to arrest them when they reached Jackson, the state capital. After what, from today's perspective, seems like a shocking willingness to bargain with a racist, attorney general ROBERT F. KENNEDY went on to pressure the Interstate Commerce Commission to issue a regulation explicitly barring segregated facilities in interstate commerce. The Freedom Rides were essential in securing this federal regulation; however, the Kennedy administration still held back from advocating truly sweeping civil rights legislation.

Suggested Reading

Levy, Peter B. *The Civil Rights Movement.* Westport, Conn.: Greenwood Press, 1998.

FREEDOM SUMMER

During the summer of 1964, while the CIVIL RIGHTS ACT OF 1964 was still under debate in Congress, the STUDENT NONVIOLENT COORDINATING COMMITTEE, principally at the urging of ROBERT MOSES, organized some one thousand volunteers to travel to Mississippi to participate in what was billed as "Freedom Summer," a drive to register black voters in the state and to organize "Freedom Schools."

While some volunteers registered the voters, others created almost fifty Freedom Schools throughout the state. Organized by Staughton Lynd, a white history professor at Spelman College (a black institution), the schools offered a wide variety of subjects (including topics in African American history, in addition to the traditional three R's) taught by both volunteers and professional instructors.

Freedom Summer also saw the founding of the MISSISSIPPI FREEDOM DEMOCRATIC PARTY (MFDP), which was created to give direction to the black voter registration drive and would, it was hoped, gain official recognition at the 1964 Democratic National Convention, to be held in Atlantic City, New Jersey. The MFDP elected a slate of convention delegates, black and white, to compete with the delegates chosen by Mississippi's regular Democratic Party.

Early in Freedom Summer three volunteers—JAMES

Chaney, Andrew Goodman, and Michael Schwerner—were murdered, and throughout the summer marauding whites burned thirty-five black churches. Local authorities, meanwhile, arrested more than a thousand civil rights activists.

In August at the Democratic National Convention the MFDP attempted eloquently but unsuccessfully to be seated as delegates. (See also Hamer, Fannie Lou.)

Suggested Reading

McAdam, Douglas. *Freedom Summer.* New York: Oxford University Press, 1990.

FREE SPEECH

The First Amendment to the Constitution stipulates that "Congress shall make no law respecting an establishment of religion, or prohibiting the free exercise thereof, *or abridging the freedom of speech,* or of the press; or the right of the people peaceably to assemble, and to petition the Government for a redress of grievances" (emphasis added). The italicized phrase, simple and straightforward though it is, has led to endless discussion and debate.

The first federal attempt to limit the First Amendment right to free speech was the Sedition Act of 1798, which made it a crime to "write, print, utter, or publish . . . any false, scandalous, and malicious" expression against the government. The World War I–era Espionage Act of 1917 made it a crime to engage in expression or conduct that might jeopardize the war effort or the security of the nation. In addition to such federal actions, various states, local governments, and institutions have sought to regulate free speech.

The central legal decisions on free speech are those written by Supreme Court associate justice Oliver Wendell Holmes. In 1919 in *Abrams v. United States* and *Schenck v. United States,* Holmes developed the "clear and present danger" test to evaluate any legislation that restricted free speech. Such restrictions, according to Holmes, are constitutionally permissible only when the public interest is under immediate threat. Abstract ideological speech, he argued, must not be restrained, but speech that may cause imminent harm should be. (It was Holmes who pointed out that, for example, free speech does not permit one to yell "Fire!" in a crowded theater.) In subsequent Supreme Court decisions that expanded the "clear and present danger" test, it was argued—under the "fighting words" doctrine—that free speech may be restricted if a particular expression is likely to incite violence. The fighting words doctrine has, in turn, been expanded to encompass what is known as "hate speech," expressions that are likely to foster discrimination against minorities or to incite violence by or against minorities. The Supreme Court has generally held that, in instances of hate speech, where certain expressions vilify or stigmatize an entire class of people (such as African Americans, gays, Hispanic Americans) the equal protection clause of the Fourteenth Amendment outweighs the free speech guarantee of the First Amendment.

Recent technologies, especially the Internet, have introduced new free speech and censorship issues, especially concerning pornography.

A number of court cases have attempted to extend the concept of free speech to nonverbal forms of expression— most importantly, the use of the American flag for commercial purposes or as part of political or social protests. Attempts to introduce local and federal legislation to prohibit burning or otherwise desecrating the flag have been struck down by the courts, most notably by the Supreme Court in *Texas v. Johnson* (1989). (See also Alien and Sedition Acts and flag laws.)

Suggested Reading

Polenberg, Richard. *Fighting Faiths: The Abrams Case, the Supreme Court, and Free Speech.* New York: Penguin, 1989.

Waluchow, Wilfrid J., ed. *Free Expression: Essays in Law and Philosophy.* Oxford, U.K.: Clarendon Press, 1994.

FRIEDAN, BETTY (1921–)

Betty Friedan is an American feminist whose 1963 study of women's discontent with their traditional roles, *The Feminine Mystique,* remains one of the most important documents of modern feminism.

Born Betty Naomi Goldstein, Friedan graduated in 1942 from Smith College with a B.A. in psychology, did graduate work at the University of California, Berkeley, then moved to New York City. She worked until 1947, when she married Carl Friedan (whom she divorced in 1969). She became a homemaker for the next decade, although she occasionally contributed articles to magazines.

In 1957 the responses to a questionnaire that Friedan had created and circulated among her Smith classmates revealed that the majority of these (generally affluent) women were profoundly dissatisfied with their lives. This finding led Friedan to study the nature and roots of this discontent both more broadly and more deeply: the result was *The Feminine Mystique.* An instant and enduring best-seller, the book explored the sense of worthlessness many women felt because they had submerged themselves in complete intellectual, economic, and emotional reliance on a husband. Friedan also explored the ways in which society enforces and reinforces, both overtly and subtly, the continued subordination of women: in large measure by ensuring that, from a very early age, men and women alike perceive such subordination as "normal."

Friedan's book struck a resonant chord among women and gave her the credibility to cofound the NATIONAL ORGANIZATION FOR WOMEN (NOW), a civil rights organization dedicated to achieving equality of opportunity for women. Friedan served as the group's first president and led its campaigns to abolish sex-classified employment ads, to increase the role of women in government, to increase the availability of child care centers for working mothers, and to make BIRTH CONTROL and ABORTION more generally available.

Friedan left the presidency of NOW in 1970 but remained active in the women's movement, organizing a dramatic nationwide Women's Strike for Equality (August 26, 1970) on the fiftieth anniversary of women's suffrage, and assuming leadership of the ultimately unsuccessful effort to obtain ratification of the EQUAL RIGHTS AMENDMENT. In 1971 Friedan became a founder of the National Women's Political Caucus; two years later, she was made a director of the First Women's Bank and Trust Company (which later failed).

In addition to *The Feminine Mystique,* Friedan wrote *It Changed My Life: Writings on the Women's Movement* (1976) and *The Second Stage* (1981), a review of the women's movement at a critical time in its history. In *The Fountain of Age,* (1993) Friedan turned her interest to the psychological and social aspects of aging.

Suggested Reading

Friedan, Betty. *The Feminine Mystique.* 1963. Reprint, New York: Norton, 2001.

FUGITIVE SLAVE ACT (1793)

Article IV, Section 2 of the Constitution guaranteed the right to repossess any "person held to service or labor," thereby giving slave owners the right to recover fugitive slaves. But the Constitution was silent on the mechanism of such recovery. For this reason, on February 12, 1793, the Second Congress passed "An act respecting fugitives from justice, and persons escaping from the service of their masters"—the Fugitive Slave Act of 1793—which authorized the arrest or seizure of fugitives and empowered any magistrate of a county, city or town to rule on the matter. The act authorized levy of a $500 fine against any person who aided a fugitive.

Suggested Reading

Fehrenbacher, Don E. *The Slaveholding Republic: An Account of the United States Government's Relations to Slavery.* Edited by Ward M. McAfee. New York: Oxford University Press, 2001.

Hadden, Sally E. *Slave Patrols: Law and Violence in Virginia and the Carolinas.* Cambridge: Harvard University Press, 2001.

Lively, Donald E. *The Constitution and Race.* New York: Praeger, 1992.

FUGITIVE SLAVE LAW

One of the bills that constituted the COMPROMISE OF 1850, the Fugitive Slave Law required all citizens, whether resident of a free state or a slave-holding state, to assist in the recovery of fugitive slaves. Moreover, the law barred jury trial in cases involving fugitive slaves, requiring instead that such cases be heard by specially appointed commissioners who were paid $5 if an alleged fugitive was released and $10 if the fugitive was returned to the claimant. As if the financial incentive were not enough to facilitate the return of fugitives, the law made it easier for slave owners to file a fugitive slave claim. Nor did the new law rely exclusively on the compliance of citizens and the cupidity of commissioners. Additional federal officials were appointed with responsibility for enforcing the Fugitive Slave Law.

Passage of the law was devastating to slaves who had successfully made their way north, and prompted at least 20,000 to flee to Canada during 1850–1860. Freedmen—blacks who had legally obtained their freedom—were also frequently captured and, on a bogus claim, sent back into SLAVERY. Because they had no recourse to a legitimate trial they were entirely defenseless. However, the law also galvanized the resolve of abolitionists to end slavery and to defy the government by increasing aid to fugitives. The manifest cruelty of the law doubtless recruited many more northerners into the abolitionist camp. (See also ABOLITION MOVEMENT.)

Suggested Reading

Ashworth, John. *Slavery, Capitalism, and Politics in the Antebellum Republic: Commerce and Compromise, 1820–1850.* New York: Cambridge University Press, 1996.

GALLAUDET, THOMAS (1787–1851)

Thomas Gallaudet founded the first American school for the deaf out of a belief that deaf people could be fully educated and that they had a right to such an education.

A graduate of Yale College (1805), Gallaudet began post-graduate work in theology but soon turned to the education of the deaf. He studied institutions for the deaf in England and France and, in France, learned to sign from Abbé Roch-Ambroise Sicard. When he returned to the United States in 1816 Gallaudet founded the American Asylum for Deaf-Mutes in Hartford, Connecticut. The land grant that Gallaudet obtained for this institution from the U.S. Congress was the first instance of federal aid to disabled people. Over the next five decades Gallaudet's school became the nation's principal training center for instructors of the deaf.

In 1830 Gallaudet retired from the American Asylum to accept the first American professorship in the philosophy of education, at New York University. He held the post through 1833.

Gallaudet's 1825 *Plan of a Seminary for the Education of Instructors of Youth* included a proposal for the education of disabled people and for the professional training of teachers of all types of students. Gallaudet published several text-books, including volumes intended for deaf people. In 1856 Amos Kendall founded a small school in Washington, D.C., for deaf people and blind people; it was later headed by Gallaudet's son, Edward Miner Gallaudet, and in 1893 was named Gallaudet College in honor of Thomas Gallaudet. It is now Gallaudet University.

Suggested Reading

Degering, Etta. *Gallaudet, Friend of the Deaf.* 1964. Reprint, Washington, D.C.: Gallaudet University Press, 1982.

GANDHI, MOHANDAS (1869–1948)

Mohandas Gandhi is perhaps better known to the world by the name conferred upon him by his followers, Mahatma (Great Soul) Gandhi; to Indians, he is known simply as Bapu (father). He was not only the father of India's independence from Britain but the leading twentieth-century exponent of nonviolent resistance and nonviolent social change. The great lesson he sought to impart was that people struggling for their rights must not forsake their own respect for life.

Gandhi was born on October 2, 1869, in the Indian province of Gujarat into a family of the Hindu *Bania,* or merchant, caste. His father was the *diwan* (prime minister) of a small Indian state. It was from his mother, who was profoundly religious, that Gandhi absorbed both the religious traditions of Jainism, including its tenet of nonviolence, and the Hindu concept of *ahimsa,* which encompasses religious tolerance, a duty to harm no living being, the practice of vegetarianism, and the observance of fasts as a means of self-purification.

In obedience to tradition Gandhi was betrothed early—to Kasturbai Makanji, at the age of seven—and was married at thirteen. He was well educated in India, then, in 1888, at age nineteen, was sent to London where he studied law at the Inner Temple. On his return to India in 1891 he opened a law practice, but, finding it difficult to earn a living, moved to South Africa in 1893 to work for an Indian firm there.

It was in South Africa that Gandhi awoke to the realities of colonial and racial oppression. As he later wrote, "I discovered that as a man and as an Indian I had no rights." With the encouragement of the Indian community in South Africa, Gandhi began his career as a social activist and moral reformer. From the beginning he pursued this course guided by three unbreakable rules, which he also enforced upon his followers: first came absolute belief in *satyagraha,* or the truth-force, which Gandhi defined as "the method of securing rights by personal suffering; it is the reverse of resistance by arms"; second was *ahimsa,* the doctrine of nonviolence he had imbibed from childhood; third came *brahmacharya,* sexual abstinence. Gandhi said that a "man or woman completely practicing Brahmacharya is absolutely free from passion. Such a one therefore lives nigh unto God, is Godlike" (The Bombay Sarvodaya Mandal, "Philosophy," www.mkgandhi.org/philosophy/index.htm). Through the force of his personality and conviction, Gandhi became well established in South Africa as a lawyer and politician. He founded a number of ashrams (spiritually based communes), the best-known of which were Phoenix Farm, near Durban, and Tolstoy Farm, near Johannesburg. In 1894 he organized the Natal Indian Congress and in 1904 began publishing the *Indian Opinion,* a weekly newspaper. Two years later he undertook his first campaign of civil disobedience, which was intended to begin the process of overcoming discrimination against Indians in South Africa. Gandhi and others were repeatedly imprisoned and beaten, and the campaign attracted worldwide attention.

With his reputation as a leader for Indian rights established, Gandhi left South Africa in July 1914 and returned to India. Immediately he built another ashram, which he envisioned as a model community—one in which neither class nor caste played a part, and all were equal. He demonstrated the principles of the ashram by inviting a family of untouchables—members of the lowest caste in Hindu society, who are considered a source of spiritual pollution—to live alongside the upper-caste Hindus. This was more than a symbolic gesture, for Gandhi knew that a great source of Hindu prejudice against Muslims in India was the fact that many Muslims were the descendants of untouchable converts. In Hindu-dominated society, the untouchables performed work—such as disposing of human waste—that other Hindus would not defile themselves with. In the ashram, however, Gandhi insisted that everyone, himself included, take turns raking the latrines.

During his ashram period Gandhi took up the cause of local Indian peasants and mill workers and in 1918 successfully employed a hunger strike as part of a protest. In 1919 he organized the first all-India nonviolent protest. This protest was marred by mob violence, however, and the response of British administrators led to the infamous Amritsar massacre, in which 379 Indians were killed by British troops dispatched to quell the demonstration.

Profoundly shaken by the massacre, Gandhi began to question his own nonviolent methods. After a period of reflection, however, he decided to use those methods even more resolutely against the British, in the belief that nonviolence would expose the illegitimacy of British rule by force. Once injustice was thoroughly exposed to the world, Gandhi reasoned, it would melt away.

When Gandhi organized a boycott of British cloth, encouraging Indians to weave on their traditional hand looms, the action proved highly effective and made a deep impact on British textile exports. Encouraged, Gandhi extended the boycott to include all British goods. The boycott was just one part of a grand campaign that Gandhi referred to as "noncooperation" with the British. Not only were British goods boycotted but British institutions were likewise shunned: Indian lawyers refused to practice in the British-run courts, and students stopped attending British-run universities.

In 1922, in an attempt to silence Gandhi, colonial authorities imprisoned him on a charge of sedition. Sentenced by the court to six years, he served only two, and was released in 1924. Immediately upon his release he was elected to the presidency of the Indian National Congress. His goal, he announced, was uncompromising: nothing less than home rule for India, which would lead, ultimately, to complete independence. Yet Gandhi never allowed the nationalist goal to overshadow immediate issues of minority rights. As president of the Indian National Congress, he led campaigns for the rights of untouchables and women and campaigned to promote education, to foster the development of village industries, and to improve public health.

Mass action, nonviolent protest, and noncooperation were always at the core of Gandhi's work. In 1930 he led a two-hundred-mile march to protest the British monopoly on salt manufacture. His plan was to lead the marchers to the sea, where he would illegally extract salt from the seawater. The march began at the ashram, with just a few followers, but as the marchers crossed India, more and more people joined them, including foreign newspaper reporters and newsreel crews. Reported worldwide, the Salt Campaign brought much support to the cause of Indian independence and touched off waves of peaceful civil disobedience within India. Imprisoned again in 1932, Gandhi fasted for six days to protest the treatment of the untouchables. In 1933, when he fasted for twenty-one days, officials were so afraid that an insurrection would result if Gandhi died in custody that they released him.

The advent of World War II brought an intermediate set of priorities for Gandhi. Firmly anti-Nazi, he nevertheless led a final campaign against British rule in India—the famous Quit India campaign—for which he and his wife were both imprisoned. He undertook another twenty-one-day fast in 1943. Early in 1944 Kasturbai fell ill with acute bronchitis. Again seeking to avoid popular outrage, British jailers secured a shipment of penicillin for her, but Gandhi believed that the injection of penicillin would be an act of violence, and he insisted instead on using natural medicines and nursing her himself. His wife died, devastating Gandhi. Broken in health and spirit, he was released from prison in May 1944.

At this point, Gandhi saw clearly that independence was inevitable. To prepare for it he focused his efforts on bringing about Hindu-Muslim harmony, but this proved a hopeless task. With independence looming, Gandhi was unable to prevent the violent religious riots that led to partition on August 15, 1947—the creation of a predominantly Hindu India and a predominantly Muslim Pakistan. On January 30, 1948, while he was walking to prayers, Mohandas Gandhi was assassinated by a Hindu extremist. His final act was to bless his assassin.

Gandhi acknowledged an American philosopher, HENRY DAVID THOREAU, as one of his chief inspirations and, in turn, Gandhi inspired new generations of nonviolent human rights and minority rights activists—most notably in America, MARTIN LUTHER KING JR.

Suggested Reading

Chadha, Yogesh. *Gandhi: A Life.* New York: John Wiley, 1999.

Fischer, Louis, ed. *The Essential Gandhi: His Life, Work, and Ideas.* New York: Vintage, 1983.

Merton, Thomas, ed. *Gandhi on Non-Violence.* New York: Norton, 1965.

GARRISON, WILLIAM LLOYD (1805–1879)

William Lloyd Garrison was a fiery abolitionist whose newspaper, the *Liberator* (1831–1865), was the single most influential periodical in the cause of abolition.

Raised in the progressive climate of New England, in 1828 Garrison became editor of the Boston-based *National Philanthropist* and, later in the year, the Bennington, Vermont, *Journal of the Times.* In 1829 he directed his energies more specifically to the cause of abolition when he became coeditor, with Benjamin Lundy, of the Baltimore-based *Genius of Universal Emancipation.* This paper soon proved too moderate for Garrison, however; in 1831, after serving a brief jail term for "libeling" a Newburyport coastal slave trader, Garrison founded the *Liberator,* the most radical of American abolitionist journals.

Garrison's style was confrontational: "I do not wish to think, or speak, or write, with moderation. . . . I will not retreat a single inch—AND I WILL BE HEARD" (John L. Thomas, "William Lloyd Garrison," *Encyclopaedia Britannica 2002,* CD-ROM). Garrison, his colleagues, and his followers called for expiation of the "national sin" of SLAVERY through immediate and unconditional emancipation. To facilitate emancipation, Garrison used his paper as a forum for developing plans to incorporate freed slaves into American society.

In 1832 Garrison founded the New England Anti-Slavery Society, the first abolitionist society to advocate immediate emancipation. The next year he became a founding member of the American Anti-Slavery Society.

In 1837 Garrison took his radicalism yet further, proclaiming his advocacy of "Christian perfectionism," which embraced abolition, supported the rights of women, and called for nonviolent civil disobedience of the laws of a corrupt society. In 1844 he called for the peaceful secession of the free North from the slaveholding South.

Garrison's radicalism created a rift within the American Anti-Slavery Society, and many members left to form a rival group, the American and Foreign Anti-Slavery Society; others joined the Liberty Party, a political party that was independent of Garrison's control. With the relatively few loyalists left to him, Garrison pressed on with the struggle, albeit with diminished influence. The *Liberator* continued to be heard, however; in it, Garrison denounced the COMPROMISE OF 1850, the KANSAS-NEBRASKA ACT, and the DRED SCOTT DECISION, and exalted JOHN BROWN's raid on Harpers Ferry as the work of God.

Garrison's support for Brown's violent action was his first break with pacifism, and when the Civil War broke out, he declared his support of Lincoln's war aims. Although Garrison embraced the EMANCIPATION PROCLAMATION of 1863 as the culmination of his own years of campaigning, once emancipation became a fact he drew back from his earlier call for the immediate integration of freedmen into American society. In 1865 he attempted unsuccessfully to dissolve the American Anti-Slavery Society. In December of that year he published the last issue of the *Liberator* and withdrew entirely from the abolitionist cause. He then largely retired from public life.

Suggested Reading

Mayer, Henry. *All on Fire: William Lloyd Garrison and the Abolition of Slavery.* New York: St. Martin's Press, 1998.

GARVEY, MARCUS (1887–1940)

During 1919–1926 Marcus Garvey founded and organized the first major black nationalist movement in the United States.

Born in Jamaica, Garvey attended school through age fourteen but was mostly self-taught. After traveling in Central

America Garvey settled in London from 1912 to 1914, then returned to Jamaica where, with others, he founded the Universal Negro Improvement and Conservation Association and African Communities League, or Universal Negro Improvement Association (UNIA). The organization's principal goal was to create a black-governed nation in Africa.

Garvey's UNIA enjoyed little success in Jamaica, so in 1916 he took the organization to the United States, establishing branches in New York's Harlem and in black neighborhoods in other northern cities. In the states UNIA attracted great interest, and Garvey was hailed as the "Black Moses." He claimed a following of some two million, although this figure is very much in dispute. What is clear is that Garvey gave blacks a reason to be proud of their heritage; he instilled pride not through rhetoric alone but by publishing in *Negro World,* UNIA's newspaper, stories of black achievement and success.

Nevertheless Garvey believed that blacks would ultimately command respect only through economic autonomy and proposed the creation of what would be, in effect, a separate black economy operating within the larger context of white capitalism. In 1919, to put his proposals into practice, he created the Negro Factories Corporation and the Black Star Line (a steamship company) and opened laundries, a hotel, a printing establishment, and a chain of restaurants and grocery stores.

By 1920 Garvey was at the height of his fame and had attracted an international following: the UNIA convention, held in New York's Liberty Hall, hosted delegates from twenty-five nations. Garvey, however, despite being a visionary, an inspired and inspiring speaker, and a superb propagandist and organizer, was a poor businessman. His enterprises were riddled with fraud and undermined by incompetent management, and in 1922 he and other UNIA members were indicted for mail fraud in connection with the sale of stock for the Black Star Line. Major black leaders had already denounced Garvey because of his advocacy of "racial purity" and separatism (which had led him to applaud such groups as the Ku Klux Klan, which also advocated separation of the races), and Garvey's indictment only hastened the already precipitous decline of his influence.

Garvey was convicted on the mail fraud charges and was sentenced to five years in a federal penitentiary. He had served two years when President Calvin Coolidge commuted his sentence in 1927 and had him deported to Jamaica as an undesirable alien. There were no significant protests. UNIA had collapsed, and Garvey was unable to resurrect the movement. He lived out the rest of his life as an obscure and forgotten exile, and died in London.

Suggested Reading

Cronon, Edmund David. *Black Moses: The Story of Marcus Garvey and the Universal Negro Improvement Association.* Madison: University of Wisconsin Press, 1969.

GAY RIGHTS

Under the laws and mores of the United States, responses to homosexuality have ranged from benign neglect to moral outrage.

Homosexuality has been regarded—including by those in the medical and psychiatric community—as a deviant behavior or as a mental disorder. Openly gay men or women have been shunned or, in some cases, patronizingly or mockingly tolerated. While antigay prejudice in the United States never descended to the depths it reached in Nazi Germany during the 1930s, when homosexuals were forced to wear triangular badges and were deported to concentration camps and often condemned to death, violence against homosexuals has not been not uncommon.

The 1950s: The Beginning of Activism

In 1950 the Mattachine Society—the first major gay advocacy organization in the United States—was founded in Los Angeles. Although its founding may be seen as the earliest beginning of the gay rights movement, the decade of the 1950s was, for the most part, an era of intolerance with regard to homosexuality. In 1952 the American Psychiatric Association formally added homosexuality to its inventory of mental disorders, and the next year President Dwight D. Eisenhower banned gay men and women from federal employment. In 1953 the Mattachine Society began publication of *ONE,* an advocacy journal.

The 1960s: Early Activism

It was not until the 1960s that gay activism truly got under way. When the Homosexual Law Reform Society held its first public meeting in 1960, seeking to bring an end to antihomosexual laws in the United Kingdom, the American homosexual community took note. In 1965 the first frankly homosexual health club was opened in the United States in Cleveland, Ohio. Two years later the *Advocate,* which became the most widely read gay advocacy magazine, began publication in Los Angeles. That same year England and Wales enacted legislation to decriminalize "private consensual sex" between men aged twenty-one and over. (In Scotland and Northern Ireland, homosexual sex continues to be illegal.) In 1968 the Reverend Troy Perry founded the Metropolitan

Community Church in Los Angeles, which openly accepted gay worshipers and became a center for the advocacy of gay rights.

Most students of the history of gay rights in the United States mark June 28, 1969, as the moment that defined the modern gay rights movement. For some years Christopher Street, in New York's Greenwich Village, had been a center of gay social life. The area was subject to continual, almost casual, police harassment, which members of the community felt they had little means of resisting. When early in the morning of June 28 officers raided the Stonewall Inn, a private gay club, they had no reason to anticipate resistance. But the Stonewall raid touched off five days of organized protest and rioting, and inspired gay activism and even militancy. In December the Gay Activists Alliance was founded and became not only the largest gay organization in New York but the most aggressive and high-profile gay advocacy group in the nation.

The 1970s: The Gay Minority and the Mainstream

While the Stonewall Protest galvanized the gay community, the "straight" public was becoming increasingly aware of that community through literature and film, most notably the 1970 movie *The Boys in the Band*. Adapted from a hit Broadway play, the film was the first mainstream Hollywood production with homosexuality as its principal theme.

Also in 1970, on June 28 between two thousand and ten thousand marchers (estimates vary) participated in the first Gay March from Greenwich Village north through Manhattan. In March 1971 the First Annual Gay Conference—an event organized by the Gay Liberation Front—was held at the University of Texas at Austin.

The direction gay rights had taken was first and foremost to emerge from the shadows and declare a gay identity. With the national consciousness heightened, gay advocacy groups sought the repeal of sodomy laws and succeeded in obtaining repeals in Colorado, Hawaii, Idaho, and Oregon in 1971. In the same year a gay Minnesota couple, Jack Baker and James McConnell, were unsuccessful in their suit to obtain a marriage license, although they did succeed in gaining a modicum of legal status for their relationship by persuading a judge to legalize McConnell's adoption of Baker.

In 1972 the U.S. Supreme Court declined to review the case of a man who had been refused a job at the University of Minnesota library because he was openly gay—a decision that in effect upheld the right to refuse employment on the grounds of homosexuality. In that same year, however, Democratic presidential candidate George McGovern went against party regulars by endorsing gay rights; and in 1973 the American Psychiatric Association officially removed homosexuality from its list of mental disorders.

In the course of the 1970s a movement developed to end antigay discrimination in employment. In 1975 Pennsylvania became the first state to ban such discrimination in state employment, although the ban was effected by an executive order of Governor Milton Shapp, not by legislation. Other politicians were equally demonstrative in their opposition to gay rights legislation. On March 2, 1976, for example, George Sullivan, mayor of Anchorage, Alaska, vetoed a gay rights ordinance, but in that same year presidential candidate Jimmy Carter declared that, if elected, he would write executive orders banning antigay discrimination in the military, in housing, in employment, and in immigration.

By the mid-1970s gay rights had become firmly established as a mainstream issue, and a backlash developed in some quarters. Most infamous was the assassination of Harvey Milk, a popular gay San Francisco city supervisor, by his former colleague Dan White, who also shot and killed San Francisco mayor George Moscone. When White was found guilty only of manslaughter and sentenced on May 21, 1979, to five to eight years in prison, a riot broke out, which brought police retaliation not at the site of the riot—city hall—but in the Castro, San Francisco's gay neighborhood.

During the late 1970s a number of conservatives, including singer Anita Bryant, actively campaigned against gay rights, prompting the repeal of gay rights ordinances in Eugene, Oregon; St. Paul, Minnesota; and Wichita, Kansas. However, California voters overwhelmingly rejected the "Briggs initiative," which would have barred gay teachers from the state's classrooms.

The 1980s to the Present

In 1981, amid a generally rising tide of political awareness among gay men and women, news of a "gay plague" began to appear in the media. As the AIDS epidemic unfolded, responses in the straight community were varied, but gay rights organizations rallied together as never before. As people with AIDS and those who were HIV-positive began to be the subjects of discrimination, the disease became a civil rights issue. In the meantime, in 1982 Wisconsin enacted the first state law barring discrimination against gay men and women. It was 1991 before Hawaii and Connecticut followed suit; in 1992, New Jersey and Vermont also banned antigay discrimination.

In 1981 the U.S. Department of Defense came out against gay men and women serving in the military and adopted new regulations to plug the loopholes that had previously allowed some to continue to serve. In 1992 presidential candidate

Bill Clinton promised to overturn this policy, but in 1993 he ended up authorizing a "Don't ask, don't tell" policy under which the military was not permitted to inquire about sexual orientation, but neither were gay and women permitted to live openly as homosexuals.

With respect to "gay marriage," it was the private sector that made the first bold move when, in 1996, Rupert Murdoch, the chief executive officer of Fox Incorporated, announced that his company would extend "domestic partner" benefits to gay employees. Three years later, in 1999, the Vermont Supreme Court ruled that gay couples must be granted the same benefits and protections accorded married couples. Many gay men and women regard legal recognition of the equivalent of marriage as the most important hurdle that must be cleared to attain full social and political equality. As of mid-2002 Vermont is the only state that unconditionally recognizes civil unions between people of the same sex. (See also AIDS and Americans with Disabilities Act.)

Suggested Reading

Clendinen, Dudley, and Adam Nagourney. *Out for Good: The Struggle to Build a Gay Rights Movement in America.* New York: Simon and Schuster, 1999.

Gerstmann, Evan. *The Constitutional Underclass: Gays, Lesbians, and the Failure of Class-Based Equal Protection.* Chicago: University of Chicago Press, 1999.

Marcus, Eric. *Making Gay History: The Half-Century Fight for Lesbian and Gay Equal Rights.* New York: Harper Perennial, 2002.

GAY RIGHTS AND THE MILITARY

See "Don't ask, don't tell" policy.

GENDER BIAS AND DISCRIMINATION

The phrase *gender bias* refers to the separation of the sexes in a way that gives preferential treatment to one sex over the other or that discriminates against one sex. Federal law prohibits gender discrimination. Relevant statutes include the Civil Rights Act of 1964 (Title VII), the Equal Pay Act of 1963, the Pregnancy Disability Act of 1978, and the Family and Medical Leave Act of 1993. Nevertheless, gender bias continues to exist in such areas as the workplace, the schools, and the legal system.

In the Workplace

In 2000 women were paid 73 cents for every dollar men received. Despite legislation, a "glass ceiling" still exists in many industries: although no explicit policy bars women from top management positions, subtle—and largely unstated and unacknowledged—attitudes and policies may effectively deny women access to such positions. Although women now make up almost half of the U.S. workforce, only two Fortune 500 firms are headed by women (U.S. General Accounting Office, "A New Look Through the Glass Ceiling: Where Are the Women?" January 2002, www.house.gov/maloney/issues/womenscaucus/glassceiling.pdf).

In the Schools

Historically, schools have reflected prevailing social values and have therefore tended to treat boys and girls differently, preparing boys for careers and girls for lives as homemakers or for traditionally female occupations, such as teaching and nursing. Since the 1960s this bias has become less and less a matter of deliberate policy, although most observers believe that it persists, to some degree, albeit on a less conscious level. For example, many teachers believe that boys do well in math and girls do well in reading, and the results of achievement tests seem to support this belief (although such tests may themselves be subject to bias), reinforcing teachers' expectations and behavior. In turn, teachers' expectations influence student performance, as students tend to deliver what teachers expect. In many classrooms teachers continue to assign tasks based on sex: girls may be given "housekeeping" duties, whereas boys are assigned to lift heavy things for the teacher. Left to themselves, children in elementary grades tend to self-segregate into male and female groups, and teachers often actively reinforce or passively condone this behavior.

Bias does not stop with the elementary grades. Until well into the twentieth century college populations were overwhelmingly male; although this is no longer the case, many educators continue to believe that achievement tests and college entrance examinations remain biased in favor of young men. A test is gender-biased if men and women with the same level of ability tend to obtain different scores. Bias may be created by the conditions under which a test is administered, the wording of individual test items, and even the student's attitude toward the test. For the Scholastic Achievement Test (SAT), which is widely used for college admissions, the National Center for Fair and Open Testing has reported "a gender gap favoring males [that] persists across all other demographic characteristics, including family income, parental education, grade point average, course work, rank in class, size of high school, size of city, etc." (National Center for Fair and Open Testing, "Gender Bias in College Admissions Tests," www.fairtest.org/facts/genderbias.htm). Educational

Testing Service researchers Howard Wainer and Linda Steinberg found that young men scored thirty-three points higher on the math portion of the SAT than young women who had earned the same grades in the same college math courses (National Center for Fair and Open Testing, "Gender Bias in College Admissions Tests," www.fairtest.org/facts/genderbias.htm).

In the Legal System

On the basis of sentencing statistics it is difficult to avoid the conclusion that the American justice system is characterized by gender bias. On average, men receive prison terms that are 47 percent longer than those assigned to women convicted of the same crime (Marc Angelucci, "Males Get Longer Sentences than Females for Same Crime," *Men's News Daily*, April 29, 2002, www.mensnewsdaily.com/stories/angelucci042902.htm; cites study by Edward Glaeser and Bruce Sacerdote of 2,800 homicide cases randomly drawn from 33 urban counties by the Bureau of Justice Statistics). In the case of sentencing for killing a spouse, the average sentence for a man who kills his wife was recently reported as seventeen and a half years; for a woman who kills her husband, the average sentence was six years (Patrick A. Langan and John M. Dawson, "Spouse Murder Defendants in Large Urban Counties," *U.S. Department of Justice Office of Justice Programs Bureau of Justice Statistics Executive Summary*, September 1995, NCJ-156831).

On the other hand, women who are victims of crime may be subject to bias. It is not unusual, for example, for defense lawyers to attempt to portray rape victims as having brought the rape on themselves by behaving provocatively. In the juvenile justice system offenses committed by boys are sometimes viewed more tolerantly ("boys will be boys"), whereas young female offenders are not similarly excused. (See also GLASS CEILING COMMISSION.)

Suggested Reading

Freidman, Joel, ed. *Law and Gender Bias.* New York: Rothman, 1994.

Sadker, Myra. *Failing at Fairness: How Our Schools Cheat Girls.* New York: Touchstone, 1995.

GENTLEMAN'S AGREEMENT

During the late nineteenth and early twentieth centuries Asian immigrants in the United States—principally, Chinese and Japanese—were often discriminated against, largely because non-Asians feared that their jobs would go to Asian immigrants. In 1880 the United States concluded an exclusion treaty with China; two years later, Congress passed the Chinese Exclusion Act, which barred most new Chinese immigration.

In 1894 the U.S. government concluded a treaty with Japan that guaranteed free immigration, but as the Japanese population in California grew, so did white hostility. In 1900, under diplomatic pressure, Japan agreed not to issue passports to laborers seeking to emigrate to the United States. This policy was easily circumvented, however; immigrants simply traveled via Canada, Hawaii, or Mexico, secured papers in these places, then completed their journey to America.

As the Japanese population continued to grow, a number of community organizations were formed in California to oppose Asian immigration, and on October 11, 1906, the city of San Francisco voted to place all Asian children in a wholly segregated school. The government of Japan was quite willing to cooperate further with the United States on immigration policy, but it was deeply insulted by the discrimination directed toward the Japanese in San Francisco and elsewhere in California. President Theodore Roosevelt intervened, and, in return for a presidential promise that the federal government would act to restrict Japanese immigration, persuaded San Francisco's mayor to rescind the school segregation order.

The promise was kept by means of the 1907 Gentleman's Agreement, by which Japan formalized its policy of denying passports to Japanese who intended to settle in the United States; the policy applied only to laborers and excepted certain classes of businesspeople and professionals. The 1907 agreement also plugged the loophole in the 1900 agreement by asserting the right of the United States to exclude all Japanese immigrants, even those holding passports originally issued for other countries.

The Gentleman's Agreement was signed on February 24, 1907, in Washington, D.C., and went into force on February 18, 1908. (See also CHINESE EXCLUSION TREATY AND ACT.)

Suggested Reading

Ichioka, Yuji. *The Issei: The World of the First Generation Japanese Immigrants, 1885–1924.* New York: Free Press, 1990.

Gulick, Sidney L. *American Democracy and Asiatic Citizenship.* North Stratford, N.H.: Ayer Company Publishers, 1979.

GERRYMANDERING

The term *gerrymandering* refers to the practice of drawing (or redrawing) the boundaries of electoral districts with the purpose of giving one party an unfair advantage over others.

Historically, gerrymandering has been criticized and even found to be illegal because it runs counter to two basic principles of electoral apportionment: compactness of the district and equality of the size of constituencies. Despite a 1964 U.S. SUPREME COURT ruling holding that electoral districts should reflect substantial equality of population, gerrymandering continues to be common. Although gerrymandering is typically carried out by the majority party—the party in power—at the expense of the minority party, the practice has been defended on the grounds that it is sometimes the only means of securing representation for minority groups.

The curious term *gerrymandering* comes from Elbridge Gerry, a Massachusetts governor who in 1812 ushered a law through the state legislature that redrew the senatorial districts, consolidating the waning Federalist Party vote in just a few districts and allowing the emerging Democratic-Republicans to gain disproportionate representation. Journalistic wags of the period observed that the tortured outline of one of the new districts looked like a salamander, and it was a small step to combine "Gerry" with "salamander" to produce "gerrymander."

Suggested Reading

Burke, Christopher Matthew. *The Appearance of Equality: Racial Gerrymandering, Redistricting, and the Supreme Court.* Westport, Conn.: Greenwood Publishing, 1999.

Monmonier, Mark S. *Bushmanders and Bullwinkles: How Politicians Manipulate Electronic Maps and Census Data to Win Elections.* Chicago: University of Chicago Press, 2001.

GILMAN, CHARLOTTE PERKINS (1860–1935)

Born Charlotte Anna Perkins, Gilman was a leading American feminist. Abandoned by her father, she grew up in considerable want and received scant education, but she did study art at the Rhode Island School of Design. After marrying the artist Charles W. Stetson in 1884, she soon discovered that she was ill suited to life as a housewife. Gilman became profoundly depressed and suffered what was described as a nervous collapse, a condition she sought to ameliorate by a trip to California in 1885. In 1888 she settled in Pasadena with her daughter and divorced Stetson. When the artist married one of her friends, Gilman sent her daughter to live with the couple—a daring act at the time.

Gilman began writing fiction and poetry, then moved to San Francisco, where, with Helen Campbell, she edited the *Impress,* the publication of the Pacific Coast Woman's Press Association. During this time—the 1890s—Gilman earned fame as a lecturer on labor and WOMEN'S RIGHTS, and in 1896 she was chosen as a delegate to the International Socialist and Labor Congress in London. Inspired by socialism, in 1898 she published *Women and Economics,* a highly influential call for the economic liberation of women. Flying in the face of the romantic and sentimental idealizations of womanhood and motherhood that were current at the time, Gilman suggested that domesticity was, for many women, a prison. She advocated consigning the care of children to specialists, and thereby freeing women from domestic chores; such ideas were most fully developed in *Concerning Children* (1900) and *The Home* (1903).

She married George H. Gilman, her cousin, in 1900 and continued to write books—some more didactic than others—that developed feminist theory in economic terms. *The Man-Made World* (1911), for example, blamed the vices and miseries of the world on the fact that it had been dominated, historically, by men. Her other mature books include *The Crux* (1911), *Moving the Mountain* (1911), *His Religion and Hers* (1923), and *The Living of Charlotte Perkins Gilman: An Autobiography* (1935). Gilman also published and edited the *Forerunner* (1909–1916), a monthly journal of feminist articles and fiction. In 1915, with JANE ADDAMS, she founded the Woman's Peace Party.

When Gilman developed cancer she sought treatment, but to little avail. Terminally ill, she took matters into her own hands and committed suicide.

Suggested Reading

Gilman, Charlotte Perkins. *The Living of Charlotte Perkins Gilman: An Autobiography.* 1935. Reprint, Madison: University of Wisconsin Press, 1991.

GINSBURG, RUTH BADER (1933–)

President BILL CLINTON nominated Ruth Bader Ginsburg to the U.S. SUPREME COURT in 1993.

Born in Brooklyn, New York, Ginsburg graduated from Cornell University in 1954 and attended Harvard Law School, then transferred to Columbia Law School, from which she received her degree, tying for first place in the 1959 class. Once out of school, however, she quickly discovered that the most desirable firms were unwilling to hire her because she was a woman. After clerking for U.S. District Judge Edmund L. Palmieri (1959–1961), she taught at Rutgers University Law School (1963–1972) and at Columbia Law School (1972–1980); at Columbia Law, she became the first woman to be tenured as a professor.

Ginsburg was active in the women's movement, serving as director of the Women's Rights Project of the AMERICAN CIVIL LIBERTIES UNION. While serving with this organization, Ginsburg argued six major gender-equality cases before the Supreme Court, winning five and effectively establishing the unconstitutionality of gender bias.

President Jimmy Carter appointed Ginsburg to the U.S. Court of Appeals, District of Columbia Circuit, in 1980. Thirteen years later she was appointed to the Supreme Court, where, although on balance a liberal, she has practiced a higher degree of moderation on social issues than might have been expected from a pioneering women's rights attorney. (See also gender bias and discrimination.)

Suggested Reading

Bredeson, Carmen. *Ruth Bader Ginsburg: Supreme Court Justice.* Berkeley Heights, N.J.: Enslow Publishers, 1995.

GLASS CEILING COMMISSION

Glass ceiling is a popular expression that refers to the subtle and unstated—and therefore invisible—barriers that prevent qualified employees from advancing within an organization. Originally specific to women executives, the term referred to the fact that women could go only so far in an organization—and no farther. More recently the term has been extended to include the invisible barriers faced by other minorities.

The federal Glass Ceiling Commission was created pursuant to the Civil Rights Act of 1991. A twenty-one-member body appointed by the president and leaders of Congress and chaired by the secretary of labor, the commission is charged with identifying glass ceilings in the private sector and expanding practices and policies that promote the advancement of minorities and women into positions of responsibility. From 1991 to 1996 the commission focused on three areas: management and decision-making positions; activities to develop and improve skills; and compensation systems.

Having completed its mandate in January 1996, the Glass Ceiling Commission was disbanded. (See also gender bias and discrimination.)

Suggested Reading

Gaskill, Stephen. *Solid Investment: Making Full Use of the Nation's Human Capital, Recommendations of the Federal Glass Ceiling Commission.* Collingdale, Penn.: DIANE Publishing Company, 1995.

GOMPERS, SAMUEL (1850–1924)

Samuel Gompers, a pioneering American labor leader, was the first president of the American Federation of Labor (AFL).

After emigrating from England in 1863, Gompers settled in New York as a cigar maker and was naturalized in 1872. In 1886 Gompers took the national organization of cigar makers out of the Knights of Labor to create the AFL. He served as the federation's president from 1886 to 1924 (except for 1895).

Gompers's approach to labor issues was inherently conservative, and his focus was resolutely apolitical. He advocated what he called "voluntarism," the exertion of influence by means of strictly economic actions, primarily strikes and boycotts. He strove to keep labor focused on economic issues, not political or social goals—and certainly not on revolutionary change. Nevertheless, confronted by federally supported initiatives to encourage open (nonunion) shops and by a barrage of court injunctions that undermined the power of strikes and boycotts, in 1908 Gompers led the AFL in support of Democratic presidential candidate William Jennings Bryan, whose platform included an anti-injunction plank. Bryan was unsuccessful, but, in 1912, another candidate sympathetic to labor, Democrat Woodrow Wilson, won. The Wilson administration ushered in important labor reforms, including those embodied in the Clayton Act (1914), which introduced important amendments to the Sherman Antitrust Act and in the Adamson Act (1916). Wilson also created a cabinet-level secretary of labor.

Suggested Reading

Kaufman, Stuart B., ed. *The Samuel Gompers Papers: The Early Years of the American Federation of Labor, 1887–90.* Champaign–Urbana: University of Illinois Press, 1987.

GOODMAN, ANDREW (1943–1964)

With fellow Congress of Racial Equality (CORE) workers Michael Schwerner and James Chaney, Andrew Goodman was murdered on June 21, 1964, on a back road in Mississippi while participating in CORE's Mississippi Summer Project to register black voters. Goodman had arrived in Mississippi the day before his murder after attending a three-day training session in Ohio for Mississippi Summer volunteers. A native of Manhattan, Goodman was raised by parents who had a passion for liberal causes. In April 1964, after hearing liberal political activist and U.S. congressman Allard Lowenstein, D-N.Y., speak on a strategy for bringing civil rights to Mississippi, Goodman volunteered. (See also Freedom Summer.)

Suggested Reading

Norst, Joel. *Mississippi Burning.* New York: New American Library, 1989.

GRANDFATHER CLAUSE

Between 1895 and 1910 seven southern states enacted laws or constitutional amendments requiring those who wanted to register to vote to pass a LITERACY TEST; several states also required that voters own real property and pay a poll tax. Since relatively few recently freed slaves or their first-generation descendants were either literate, owned property, or could afford to pay a poll tax, the laws effectively barred blacks from the polls. However, because many poor whites also were illiterate, propertyless, and poor, the various laws included "grandfather clauses" to ensure that the voting qualification statutes applied only to blacks. Under the clauses, those who had had the right to vote prior to 1866 or 1867 (and their lineal descendants) would be exempt from all literacy, property, and tax requirements for the franchise. Former slaves, of course, had been excluded from the franchise until the ratification of the FIFTEENTH AMENDMENT in 1870.

In its 1915 decision in *Guinn v. United States,* the SUPREME COURT ruled that grandfather clauses were unconstitutional violations of the equal voting rights guaranteed by the Fifteenth Amendment.

Suggested Reading

Packard, Jerrold P. *American Nightmare: The History of Jim Crow.* New York: St. Martin's Press, 2002.

GRAY PANTHERS

The origin of the Gray Panthers was at an August 1970 meeting of six friends, all of whom were about to retire from national religious and social work organizations. The group had met to discuss the problems commonly faced by retirees, including income loss, social isolation, and the loss of a sense of vocation. In addition to recognizing the problems of retirement, however, the members of the group also realized the freedom that retirement would confer on them, including the freedom to dedicate themselves more fully to activist causes—chiefly, opposition to the Vietnam War.

The name "Gray Panthers," a somewhat tongue-in-cheek play on BLACK PANTHERS, emphasized the gray-haired members' commitment to activism. From the beginning the Gray Panthers' opposition to the Vietnam War created common cause with student groups that were opposed to the war; the group originally called itself the Consultation of Older and Younger Adults for Social Change. (The Gray Panthers name was conferred by the producer of a New York–based television talk show, and not by the group members themselves, although they eventually adopted the title.)

Today the Gray Panthers describe themselves as "an intergenerational advocacy organization." Members work together for social and economic justice, focusing on issues such as universal health care, affordable housing, economic justice, peace, respect for the natural environment, jobs that provide a living wage and the right to organize, access to education, and the preservation of Social Security; the group is also committed to combating ageism, SEXISM, and RACISM.

Beginning in the late 1970s and continuing into the 1980s, the Gray Panthers became a national organization made up of local "networks." In 1985 the Gray Panthers opened its first public policy office in Washington, D.C., and in 1990 formally established this as the organization's national headquarters.

Suggested Reading

Gray Panthers, www.graypanthers.org.

GREAT MIGRATION, THE

Between 1900 and 1960 almost five million AFRICAN AMERICANS left the rural South to settle in the industrial cities of the North—chiefly Chicago, Cleveland, Detroit, Pittsburgh, and New York. The first wave of the Great Migration came between 1915 and 1925 and included the period of America's participation in World War I (1917–1918). Another peak migration period coincided with World War II (1941–1945), when northern factories lost labor to military enlistment, thereby creating more demand and opportunity for African American workers.

Suggested Reading

Lemann, Nicholas. *The Promised Land: The Great Black Migration and How It Changed America.* New York: Vintage, 1992.

GREAT SOCIETY

Several U.S. presidents have been associated with distinctive slogans describing a leading theme or program of their administration. For Theodore Roosevelt it was the Square Deal; for Woodrow Wilson, the New Freedom; for FRANKLIN D. ROOSEVELT, the New Deal; for JOHN F. KENNEDY, the New Frontier; and for LYNDON B. JOHNSON (LBJ), the Great Society.

LBJ first used the phrase in his January 4, 1965, State of the Union message to refer to a program of national reform.

In that speech Johnson not only outlined his vision for the Great Society but declared that, to achieve it, the United States must wage a "war on poverty." Like FDR's New Deal the Great Society encompassed an ambitious program of social welfare legislation, including federal support for education, an expansion of Social Security to provide subsidized medical care for senior citizens (Medicare), and protection against disenfranchisement (in the form of the Voting Rights Act of 1965).

LBJ, who had assumed office in 1963 after Kennedy's assassination, was swept to a landslide victory in his own right in 1964, carrying with him a large Democratic majority in both houses. Although Congress enacted almost all of the Great Society bills on the president's agenda, America's growing involvement in Vietnam created funding scarcities that significantly compromised the Great Society programs and led many to be terminated.

Suggested Reading

Goodwin, Doris Kearns. *Lyndon Johnson and the American Dream.* New York: St. Martin's Press, 1991.

Langston, Thomas. *Lyndon Baines Johnson.* Washington, D.C.: CQ Press, 2002.

GREENSBORO SIT-IN

On February 1, 1960, four black freshmen at North Carolina A&T State University—Ezell Blair Jr., Franklin McCain, Joseph McNeil, and David Richmond, soon to be known as the Greensboro Four—took seats at the whites-only lunch counter of the Woolworth's on South Elm Street in downtown Greensboro. Their intent was to force the issue of integration: peacefully, lawfully, but stubbornly.

At first the other customers and the waitresses ignored them. Then a waitress informed them that blacks were not served at the counter. When they refused to leave, a black employee chided the four for "making trouble" and "hurting race relations." Finally, a store manager walked two blocks to the police station, where Chief Paul Calhoun informed him that as long as the students behaved, he could do nothing except send an officer to keep an eye on the situation. The store manager closed the Woolworth's early. The demonstrators left without having been served and were photographed by a local reporter. The picture quickly gained national circulation.

The next day two more students joined the Greensboro Four to sit at the lunch counter, unserved, from 11 a.m. to 3 p.m. Newspaper, television, and radio coverage began, and over the next several days more students—including white students from other colleges—joined the sit-in, occupying every seat at the counter and forming picket lines outside the store to encourage a boycott of Woolworth's and a Kress variety store. As the protest began to have an economic impact, the city of Greensboro created a committee, headed by Burlington Industries executive Ed Zane, to mediate a solution. Determined to avoid racial violence, both Woolworth's and Kress agreed to integrate their lunch counters. The Greensboro sit-in had succeeded in creating social change peacefully and without government intervention.

Suggested Reading

Schlosser, Jim. "Greensboro Sit-Ins: Launch of a Civil Rights Movement." *Greensboro News & Record,* www.sitins.com.

GREGORY, DICK (1932–)

Dick Gregory earned national attention in the 1960s as an African American stand-up comic whose humor was edged with biting satire attacking racial prejudice. He was among the first African American entertainers to confront white audiences with racially charged satire, which became an effective adjunct to the African American civil rights movement.

Born and raised in a St. Louis ghetto, Richard Claxton Gregory enrolled in Southern Illinois University in 1951 on an athletic scholarship. He was named outstanding student athlete in 1953, but he left to join the army before completing his degree. It was in the military service that Gregory began his show business career, performing stand-up comedy for the troops. After his return to civilian life, Gregory struggled in show business until 1961, when a performance at Chicago's Playboy Club led to television appearances that catapulted him to national fame. From the beginning of his major success Gregory's routines attacked poverty, segregation, and racial discrimination. Off stage he was intensely active in the civil rights movement, participating in many demonstrations and enduring several arrests for civil disobedience. Gregory ran unsuccessfully for mayor of Chicago in 1966 and for president of the United States in 1968.

By the early 1970s Gregory had turned his back on comedy to focus full time on social issues, including not only race relations and racial justice but violence, hunger, capital punishment, drug abuse, and health care reform. His most public form of protest was the hunger strike; until this period, Gregory had been overweight, but he now transformed himself into a lean athlete. He became a vegetarian and made himself an expert on nutrition, creating a nutritional product (the Bahamian Diet) and a company—Dick Gregory Health Enterprises, Inc.—that he hoped would improve the nutritional practices of many black Americans, whose unhealthy diet Gregory believed to be responsible for a life expectancy that is typically shorter than that of white Americans.

Gregory wrote several books, the best known of which are *Nigger: An Autobiography* (1964) and *No More Lies: The Myth and the Reality of American History* (1971).

Suggested Reading

Gregory, Dick. *Nigger: An Autobiography.* 1964. Reprint, New York: Pocket Books, 1995.

Gregory, Dick. *Callus on My Soul: A Memoir.* Atlanta: Longstreet, 2000.

GRIGGS V. DUKE POWER CO.

In 1966, pursuant to Title VII of the Civil Rights Act of 1964, African American employees at a Duke Power generating plant sued the company, challenging Duke's requirement that, as a condition of employment or transfer to the plant, workers had to have a high school diploma or pass intelligence tests. The plaintiffs argued that the company's requirements were not intended to measure the ability to learn to perform a particular job or category of jobs but to exclude blacks, who often lacked the requisite diploma or the educational background to pass the tests.

A district court and appellate court found "no showing of discriminatory purpose in the adoption of the diploma and test requirements," a decision that the Supreme Court overturned in 1971 in *Griggs v. Duke Power Co.*, which held that the Civil Rights Act of 1964 "requires the elimination of artificial, arbitrary, and unnecessary barriers to employment that operate invidiously to discriminate on the basis of race, and if, as here, an employment practice that operates to exclude Negroes cannot be shown to be related to job performance, it is prohibited, notwithstanding the employer's lack of discriminatory intent." The high court's opinion observed that the Civil Rights Act of 1964 "does not preclude the use of testing or measuring procedures, but it does proscribe giving them controlling force unless . . . they are demonstrably a reasonable measure of job performance."

The enduring effect of the decision in *Griggs v. Duke Power Co.* has been to close the door on tests and other requirements and procedures that are clearly discriminatory in *effect,* even if not necessarily in *intent.*

Suggested Reading

Haggard, Thomas R. *Understanding Employment Discrimination.* New York: Lexis, 2001.

Joel, Lewin G. III. *Every Employee's Guide to the Law: Everything You Need to Know about Your Rights in the Workplace and What to Do If They Are Violated.* New York: Pantheon, 1997.

GRIMKÉ, SARAH (1792–1873) AND ANGELINA (1805–1879)

The Grimké sisters were abolitionists and advocates of women's rights.

Born in South Carolina, both came to know the evils of slavery first hand. Early on, Sarah became active in the Society of Friends (Quakers), in Philadelphia; she became a Quaker herself in 1821 and permanently left the South. Her younger sister followed in 1829, settled with Sarah in Philadelphia, and likewise became a Quaker. Angelina formally joined the abolitionist cause in 1835 after writing to radical abolitionist William Lloyd Garrison, who published her letter in the *Liberator;* Sarah soon followed her sister in the cause.

In 1836 Angelina wrote *Appeal to the Christian Women of the South,* in which she urged southern women to use moral suasion to combat slavery. Sarah followed her sister's pamphlet with *An Epistle to the Clergy of the Southern States.* As a consequence of their growing fame as abolitionists, the Grimkés were asked by the American Anti-Slavery Society to make presentations to small groups of women in private homes; the sisters were soon addressing large audiences in public halls.

When the General Association of Congregational Ministers of Massachusetts published a pastoral letter in 1837 denouncing female preachers and reformers, the Grimkés added women's rights to their crusade. They now regularly attracted huge audiences, who were eager to hear their combined message of abolition and equal rights for the sexes. Late in 1837 Angelina published *An Appeal to the Women of the Nominally Free States,* and the following year Sarah issued *Letters on the Equality of the Sexes and the Condition of Woman.* Also in 1838 Angelina married Theodore Dwight Weld, a prominent abolitionist with whom she collaborated on a major book, *Slavery as It Is: Testimony of a Thousand Witnesses* (1839).

Following Angelina's marriage, both of the Grimké sisters withdrew from public life. Weld ran a school located first at Belleville, then at Perth Amboy, New Jersey, and during 1848–1862, the sisters assisted him with teaching. In 1863 all three relocated to West Newton, Massachusetts, and in 1864 settled permanently outside of Boston.

Suggested Reading

Lerner, Gerda. *The Grimké Sisters from South Carolina: Pioneers for Women's Rights and Abolition.* New York: Oxford University Press, 1998.

HABEAS CORPUS

Habeas corpus is a common-law writ of ancient origin by which a judge directs a jailer (or other authority) to "produce the body" of the incarcerated person before the court. Typically, and especially in modern application, a writ of habeas corpus is issued for the purpose of judicial inquiry into the legality of a detention—and, if the detention is found to be unwarranted, to secure the release of the person who has been detained.

In colonial America and in the United States after the Revolution, habeas corpus was considered to be a basic right, which the Constitution subsequently explicitly guaranteed, specifying that habeas corpus "shall not be suspended, unless when in cases of rebellion or invasion the public safety may require it." In 1861, at the beginning of the Civil War, President Abraham Lincoln suspended habeas corpus by executive proclamation—a controversial action that was challenged, in *Ex parte Merryman* (1861), by Chief Justice Roger B. Taney. Taney ordered the proclamation vacated on the grounds that the authority to suspend habeas corpus rested exclusively with Congress. Lincoln ignored the order, but his decision to do so did not create a precedent. Modern opinion holds that congressional consent is required for suspension.

Today, writs of habeas corpus are routinely requested to compel police either to charge a detainee with a crime or release him. Habeas corpus hearings are also held to secure the release of accused persons on the grounds of excessive bail. More rarely, habeas corpus has been used to obtain the release of a prisoner who has been unlawfully detained after his or her sentence has expired, or to challenge arrests made pursuant to a warrant of extradition.

Habeas corpus has application outside of the criminal arena. For example, conflicting claims to the custody of a minor are sometimes adjudicated in habeas corpus, and in some situations and jurisdictions, a writ of habeas corpus may be requested to obtain the release of a patient in a mental hospital to conduct a hearing on the person's sanity.

Suggested Reading

Freedman, Eric M. *Habeas Corpus: Rethinking the Great Writ of Liberty.* New York: New York University Press, 2002.

HAMER, FANNIE LOU (1917–1977)

Sharecropper Fannie Lou Hamer was a leader of the Mississippi Freedom Democratic Party (MFDP) who fought against the Jim Crow laws of Mississippi.

Born Fannie Lou Townsend on October 6, 1917, in Montgomery County, Mississippi, the youngest of twenty children, she worked with her family as a cotton sharecropper and married Perry Hamer in 1944. Hamer was an early member of the Student Nonviolent Coordinating Committee (SNCC), and in 1962 she and seventeen other African Americans attempted to register to vote. She was refused because, according to the registrar, she had failed the literacy test; her employer also warned her to withdraw her application or be fired. When she refused, she was given twenty-four hours' notice to leave the plantation on which she had lived for twenty years. Branded as a troublemaker, Hamer was the victim of many threats (some backed by gunfire) and of official harassment. In June 1963 police officers in Winona, Mississippi, assaulted her after she had attended a citizenship program.

Despite intimidation and attacks, Hamer remained undaunted and became a leader in the cause of civil rights. In 1964 she was one of sixty-eight MFDP delegates sent to the Democratic National Convention in Atlantic City, New Jersey, where she gained national attention by testifying in support of the MFDP's bid for recognition as the only legitimate delegation from Mississippi. To President Lyndon B. Johnson's offer of two at-large convention seats and a promise of future reform, she famously replied, "I'm sick and tired of being sick and tired."

In 1965 Hamer led a challenge to the seating of five white Mississippi congressmen. Throughout the rest of the decade she continued to push for reforms; she started a Project Head Start program in her hometown and in 1968 founded the populist Freedom Farm Corporation, a cooperative farming project. Civil rights activists drew great inspiration from Hamer and regarded her as the personification of the grassroots strength of the movement for minority rights in America.

Suggested Reading

Lee, Chana Kai. *For Freedom's Sake: The Life of Fannie Lou Hamer.* Champaign–Urbana: University of Illinois Press, 2000.

Mills, Kay. *This Little Light of Mine: The Life of Fannie Lou Hamer.* New York: Plume, 1994.

HAMPTON, FRED (1948–1969)

Fred Hampton was a civil rights activist. He was a youth council leader for the West Suburban (Chicago) Branch of the NATIONAL ASSOCIATION FOR THE ADVANCEMENT OF COLORED PEOPLE (NAACP) (1967–1968) and the founder and leader of the Illinois Chapter of the BLACK PANTHER PARTY (1968–1969). Hampton was killed in a 1969 police raid on the Illinois chapter headquarters of the Black Panthers.

Hampton was born and raised in Chicago and attended Triton Junior College in 1966. As the organizer and leader of the Illinois chapter of the Black Panthers, Hampton focused the organization's activities on community activism, including projects such as food pantries, educational programs, and recreational activities for neighborhood children. Recognized within the black community as a valuable mediator among Chicago's rival street gangs, Hampton was regarded by the law enforcement community as a dangerous radical who was committed to the violent overthrow of the white-dominated "establishment." Although the police maintained that they were fired on first, many viewed Hampton's death in a police raid as a politically motivated assassination.

Hampton is given credit for having coined the phrase *rainbow coalition*—later adopted and popularized by the Reverend JESSE JACKSON—at a May 1969 press conference announcing a truce among rival street gangs.

Suggested Reading

Foner, Philip S., ed. *The Black Panthers Speak.* 1970. Reprint, New York: Da Capo Press, 1995.

HARLEM RENAISSANCE

Sometimes called the New Negro Movement, the Harlem Renaissance spanned the 1920s and was centered in the premier black neighborhood of the nation, Manhattan's Harlem. The period was characterized principally by an outpouring of literary works that commanded national attention and by an unprecedented intellectual exchange between black and white writers and intellectuals. To a lesser extent the Harlem Renaissance also fostered the development of black musicians and visual artists.

The most famous figures of the Harlem Renaissance were the novelist and poet James Weldon Johnson (*Autobiography of an Ex-Coloured Man,* 1912; *God's Trombones,* 1927), the novelist and poet Claude McKay (*Harlem Shadows,* 1922; *Home to Harlem,* 1928), the poet Countee Cullen (editor of *Caroling Dusk: An Anthology of Verse by Negro Poets,* 1927), and the poet and novelist Langston Hughes (*The Weary Blues,* 1926; *Not Without Laughter,* 1930). Working together, Wallace Thurman and William Jourden Rapp wrote the 1929 *Harlem,* a highly popular play.

White philanthropic organizations and white writers, especially Carl Van Vechten (*Nigger Heaven,* 1926), did much to support the New Negro movement. Although the Harlem Renaissance did not survive the Great Depression, which largely brought about the dissolution of the black intellectual community in Harlem, the movement nevertheless represented an important early crossing of the COLOR LINE.

Suggested Reading

Lewis, David L., ed. *The Portable Harlem Renaissance Reader.* New York: Penguin, 1995.

HARVARD PROJECT ON SCHOOL DESEGREGATION

Created in 1996 as a program of the Harvard Graduate School of Education and now part of the graduate school's Civil Rights Project, the Harvard Project on School Desegregation has conducted numerous studies of school segregation in the United States and has consistently concluded that de facto school segregation increased during the 1990s.

Suggested Reading

Civil Rights Project, Harvard University, www.law.harvard.edu/civilrights.

HATE SPEECH

Hate speech is language that is likely to foster discrimination against minorities or to incite violence by or against minorities—chiefly, people of color, lesbians, gay men, and members of other historically persecuted groups. Such speech is abusive or threatening in and of itself and often escalates into physical violence.

Hate speech is difficult to address in law because of the adherence, in the United States, to a high standard of FREE SPEECH as guaranteed by the First Amendment. The SUPREME COURT has generally held that expressions that vilify or stigmatize an entire class of people (such as African Americans, gays, Hispanic Americans) violate the equal protection clause of the FOURTEENTH AMENDMENT, which outweighs the free speech guarantee of the First Amendment; however, attempts to introduce comprehensive legislative curbs against hate speech have been, for the most part, disallowed by the Supreme Court as prior restraint of free speech.

Suggested Reading

Delgado, Richard, and Jean Stefancic. *Must We Defend Nazis? Hate Speech, Pornography, and the New First Amendment.* New York: New York University Press, 1999.

Walker, Samuel. *Hate Speech: The History of an American Controversy.* Lincoln: University of Nebraska Press, 1994.

HAYMARKET RIOT

On May 3, 1886, during a strike against the McCormick Harvesting Machine Company—which was part of a larger campaign to secure an eight-hour workday—police moved vigorously to protect strikebreakers, and in the resulting violence one striker was killed and others were injured. The Haymarket Riot occurred the following day. To protest what they regarded as police brutality, the strikers convened a mass demonstration at Haymarket Square on the city's South Side. The demonstration was peaceful until a police unit was called in to break it up. Someone hurled a dynamite bomb, killing seven officers and injuring about sixty others, officers as well as civilians. The rest of the police contingent opened fire on the strikers, some of whom were armed, and shots were exchanged.

Although the bomb thrower was never identified, August Spies and seven others characterized as "anarchist" labor leaders were found guilty of murder on the grounds that they had conspired with, aided, or abetted the unknown bomb thrower. Although the prosecution failed to demonstrate a connection between the unidentified bomber and those convicted, the prevailing public sentiment of hostility toward militant labor organizers and hysteria over the apparent rise of anarchism led to convictions. On November 11, 1887, Spies and three others were hanged. Another man committed suicide in prison. In 1893, after reviewing the convictions of the other three condemned men, Illinois governor John Peter Altgeld pardoned them. It was an act of great moral courage, which, although hailed by liberals and by organized labor, destroyed Altgeld's political career.

The Haymarket affair is frequently cited as an example of the abuse of judiciary power, in that the accused were convicted and punished essentially for their political beliefs.

Suggested Reading

Avrich, Paul. *The Haymarket Tragedy.* 1984. Reprint, Princeton: Princeton University Press, 1986.

HELMS, JESSE A. (1921–)

Longtime senior senator from North Carolina Jesse Helms has represented the right-wing, conservative position on an array of social issues. A lightning rod for liberal criticism of the "conservative agenda," Helms has consistently championed prayer in public schools and has opposed gun control, ABORTION, and government support for the arts.

Helms was born in Monroe, North Carolina, where he attended public schools. He then attended Wingate Junior College and Wake Forest College. He served in the U.S. Navy from 1942 through 1945, then became city editor of the *Raleigh Times* and, later, director of news and programs for the Tobacco Radio Network and Radio Station WRAL in Raleigh. From 1951 to 1953 he was administrative assistant to Sen. Willis Smith and in 1953 served Sen. Alton Lennon in the same capacity. In 1952 he directed the radio-television division of the presidential campaign of Sen. Richard B. Russell of Georgia, and from 1953 through 1960 was executive director of the North Carolina Bankers Association. He returned to broadcasting in 1960, serving as executive vice president, vice chairman of the board, and assistant chief executive officer of Capitol Broadcasting Company in Raleigh from 1960 until his election to the Senate in 1972. In 1996 Helms was elected to his fifth consecutive term in the Senate. He is the ranking minority member of the Committee on Foreign Relations; a member of the Committee on Agriculture, Nutrition and Forestry; and a member of the Rules and Administration Committee. In 2002 he announced that he would not seek a sixth term.

Suggested Reading

Ferguson, Ernest B. *Hard Right: The Rise of Jesse Helms.* New York: Norton, 1986.

HILL, JOE (1879–1915)

Born in Gävle, Sweden, Joel Emmanuel Hägglund immigrated to the United States in 1902 and became known as Joe Hill (sometimes called Joe Hillstrom), a songwriter and organizer for the INDUSTRIAL WORKERS OF THE WORLD (IWW). His highly questionable conviction and subsequent execution for a robbery-murder made him a folk hero and martyr among radicals in the American labor movement.

After Hill reached the United States in 1902 he led an itinerant life before joining the San Pedro (California) local of the IWW in 1910, of which he became secretary. In 1911 his song "The Preacher and the Slave" was published in the IWW's *Little Red Song Book.* The song's most famous verse—"You will eat, bye and bye/In that glorious land above the sky;/Work and pray, live on hay,/You'll get pie in the sky when you die"—is typical of Hill's songwriting style. Focused on the plight of migrant laborers, immigrant sweatshop workers, and railroad laborers, his songs embodied a simplistic Marxist message expressed in a sympathetic but slyly humorous fashion.

In January 1914, while visiting friends in Salt Lake City, Hill was charged with the murder of a grocer and his son, who had been killed in the course of a robbery. The prosecution based its case almost exclusively on circumstantial evidence: Hill had been treated by a physician for a gunshot wound several hours after the murders. Hill's defense was that he had been wounded in a quarrel over a woman, whom he refused to identify out of concern for her honor. Found guilty, he was sentenced to death. Labor interests made many legal appeals on Hill's behalf, all of which failed. His impending execution sparked numerous and widespread protests, as well as accusations that the conviction had been motivated by Hill's radicalism. Even President Woodrow Wilson appealed to the governor of Utah to intervene. Hill was executed by firing squad on November 19, 1915. He telegraphed IWW leader "Big Bill" Haywood the night before his death: "Goodbye Bill. I die like a true rebel. Don't waste time in mourning. Organize." "The Ballad of Joe Hill" ("I thought I saw Joe Hill last night . . ."), composed by Alfred Hays in 1925, became a well-known protest song and was revived in the 1960s by the folk singer Joan Baez.

Suggested Reading

Smith, Gibbs M. *Joe Hill.* Salt Lake City: Gibbs Smith, 1984.

HISPANIC AMERICANS

According to the 2000 national census, Hispanics are the fastest-growing minority in the United States—numbering 35.3 million, or about 13 percent of the population. About 60 percent of Hispanic Americans either come from Mexico or trace their ancestry to that country. Although the overwhelming majority of Hispanic Americans live in Arizona, California, Colorado, New Mexico, and Texas, two-thirds of those of Puerto Rican ancestry live in New York City, and 60 percent of Cuban Americans live in Florida.

Historically, economic opportunity has been the chief reason for Hispanic immigration, although since 1959 CUBAN REFUGEES have come to America largely for political reasons, to escape the repressive regime of Fidel Castro. Since the 1960s many Hispanics from elsewhere in the Caribbean and from Central and South America have also sought political freedom in addition to greater economic opportunity.

Spanish America

In the majority (that is, non-Hispanic) view, early American history was dominated by the English (and English-speaking) traditions associated with the colonial settlement of New England and Virginia; nevertheless, the Spanish exploration, settlement, and colonization of territories that are now encompassed by the United States substantially preceded that of the English.

In 1492 Christopher Columbus, an Italian mariner in the service of Spain, landed on a Caribbean island and claimed for the Spanish monarchs Ferdinand and Isabella the territory that Columbus called Nuéva España—New Spain. Only years later, in 1507, was this new world named America, after the Florentine explorer Amerigo Vespucci, who sailed variously in the service of Spain and Portugal.

Following Columbus's initial voyage a series of Spanish mariners and conquistadors explored, claimed, and colonized the Americas, including much of the territory encompassed by the present United States. In 1513 Spain's Vasco de Nuñez de Balboa crossed the Isthmus of Panama and became the first European to see the Pacific Ocean, thereby establishing a Spanish presence on the Pacific as well as on the Atlantic seaboard.

In 1519 the conquistador Hernan Cortés began the conquest of the Aztec empire of Mexico, which finally fell to him in 1521. It was in Mexico that Spain most thoroughly developed a colonial empire in the New World. From Mexico explorers and settlers pushed northward into what is now the American Southwest. They were accompanied by Franciscan monks, who arrived in Mexico in 1524 and over subsequent years established a system of missions throughout the Spanish colonies.

In 1539 Fray Márcos de Niza led an expedition into New Mexico. From 1539 to 1542, Hernando de Sóto explored what is today the lower South of the United States. In 1540, in a quest for the fabled Cibola, with its Seven Cities of Gold, Francisco Vasquéz de Coronado explored parts of Arizona, California, Kansas, New Mexico, Oklahoma, and Texas. In 1542 Juán Rodríguéz Cabrillo and Bartolome Ferrelo explored the West Coast as far north as Oregon, and in 1565 Pedro Menendez de Aviles founded St. Augustine, Florida, which is today the oldest continuously occupied city in the United States. In 1566, Juan Pardo explored parts of Alabama, Georgia, and Tennessee, and during 1570–1572, a Spanish mission was founded in the Chesapeake Bay area. During 1580–1640 the conquistadors introduced horses to the American Southwest and in 1598 founded the first permanent colony in New Mexico. New Mexico was made a royal province in 1608, and the Palace of the Governors—still in use today—was built in the new capital, Sante Fe, two years later.

During the seventeenth century the Spanish colonial empire spread across the Southwest despite two pueblo revolts (1680 and 1695), in which settlements (pueblos) of subjugated Indians rose up against their Spanish overlords. By the early eighteenth century on the East Coast, English and Spanish interests had begun to clash, and in 1702 British forces from the Carolinas razed St. Augustine. Two years later they destroyed the Spanish missions in North Florida. During the Seven Years War (which Americans refer to as the French and Indian War), Spain allied itself with France; after France's defeat in 1763 Spain ceded Spanish Florida to England.

Hispanics in the American Revolution

Like France, Spain rendered aid to the United States during the American Revolution. The people of New Spain, which included the territory of the present states of Arizona, California, New Mexico, and Texas, helped to finance the Revolution, and Spanish troops fought British troops throughout the Americas. Volunteers from Costa Rica, Cuba, Puerto Rico, Santo Domingo, Spain, Venezuela, and Costa Rica, as well as from territory within the present United States, fought with the Continental Army. In 1784, the Revolution won, the United States permitted Spain to reoccupy Spanish Florida.

Ethnic Friction and Anti-Hispanic Prejudice

Once the common foe, the British, had been defeated, relations between the Hispanic and Anglo American populations began, in many parts of the Republic, to break down. On May 26, 1818, during the First Seminole War (fought against Seminole Indians living adjacent to and within the territory of Spanish Florida), Major General Andrew Jackson, hero of the War of 1812, imperiously and without authorization captured Spanish-held Pensacola, Florida, propelling the United States and Spain into a diplomatic crisis that was resolved only when Spain ceded Florida to the United States.

Increasingly, the predominantly Catholic culture of the American Hispanics conflicted with the predominantly Protestant culture of the Anglo Americans; also increasingly, Hispanics were regarded and treated as an underclass. In Texas, which had been colonized by American entrepreneurs (most notably Moses Austin and his son Stephen) during the 1820s, friction between the Anglo majority and the Mexican minority became a contributing factor to the outbreak of the Texas War of Independence in 1836. A decade later, anti-Mexican prejudice in the Anglo community certainly contributed to the outbreak of the United States–Mexican War.

Throughout the rest of the nineteenth century anti-Hispanic prejudice surfaced frequently, especially in the Southwest, culminating in California's Alien Land Law of 1913 and Alien Land Law of 1920, and in the (albeit slow) development, beginning in the 1920s, of Hispanic American activism.

During the twentieth century the United States witnessed the growth of Hispanic communities whose populations originated in places other than Mexico or the original Spanish territories of the United States.

From Puerto Rico

Puerto Rico was a Spanish possession until the U.S. victory in the Spanish-American War of 1898. Ceded to the United States, Puerto Rico was governed by the U.S. military for a time, then became a territory, but as a result of internal political pressure it was granted an increasing degree of autonomy until it became a quasi-independent commonwealth in 1950.

Puerto Rican immigration to the United States began in 1898. After passage of the Jones Act in 1917, which granted U.S. citizenship to all Puerto Ricans who wished to have it, immigration increased. At first most Puerto Ricans settled in New York City: by 1930 there were 53,000 Puerto Ricans in the United States, 45,000 of whom were in New York. After World War II immigration increased dramatically. Today there are some 2.3 million Puerto Ricans in the United States, almost a million of whom live in New York City.

From Cuba

Cuban immigration to the United States was common during the nineteenth century and into the early twentieth. Most Cubans settled in Florida (especially Key West, Tampa, and West Tampa) and New York City. When Fidel Castro came to power in 1959 there was a sudden influx, with many Cuban immigrants settling in Miami.

Economically, Cuban Americans have generally been the most successful of the Hispanic American minorities. Whereas in 2000 almost 27 percent of Americans of Central and South American origin were living below the poverty line—along with 30 percent of those of Mexican origin and 36.5 percent of those of Puerto Rican origin—little more than 18 percent of Cuban Americans were (U.S. Census Bureau, "Hispanic Population of the United States," Census 2000, www.census.gov/population/www/socdemo/hispanic.html). The Cuban refugees of the Castro era came to well-established Cuban American communities, which were often eager and able to help the new immigrants establish themselves.

From Central and South America and the Caribbean

More than 13 percent of Hispanic Americans are from Central and South America and the Caribbean (especially the Dominican Republic). Political and economic instability in these regions has been largely responsible for the influx of immigrants. The Dominican immigration began in earnest in 1961 after the fall of dictator Rafael Trujillo. Of the approximately one million Dominicans who live in the United States today, most are concentrated in the Manhattan neighborhood of Washington Heights.

Political violence during the 1970s touched off a wave of immigration from El Salvador, Guatemala, and Nicaragua. Salvadorans have favored Los Angeles, which is now sometimes referred to as the Central American capital of the United States. The largest Guatemalan communities in the United States are in California and Florida; Nicaraguans have also settled chiefly in these two states. (For a historical overview of Hispanic Americans from 1910 to the present, see HISPANIC CIVIL RIGHTS MOVEMENT.)

Suggested Reading

Heyck, Denis L., ed. *Barrios and Borderlands: Cultures of Latinos and Latinas in the United States.* New York: Routledge, 1994.

Rodriguez, Richard. *Brown: The Last Discovery of America.* New York: Viking Press, 2002.

Suarez-Orozco, Marcelo M., and Mariela Paez, eds. *Latinos: Remaking America.* Berkeley: University of California Press, 2002.

HISPANIC CIVIL RIGHTS MOVEMENT

The organized Hispanic American civil rights movement may be said to have begun in 1921, when the Orden Hijos de América (Order of the Sons of America) was founded in San Antonio, Texas, to fight unfair wages, anti-Mexican discrimination in education and housing, and general abuses of civil rights. A larger organization, the LEAGUE OF UNITED LATIN AMERICAN CITIZENS, was formed in 1929 with a similar purpose. These organizations and other, smaller groups were created specifically in response to acts of violence against Mexican Americans in the Southwest and to anti-Hispanic legislation such as the ALIEN LAND LAW OF 1913 and ALIEN LAND LAW OF 1920.

Exploitation of Hispanic Immigrants

The first major influx of Mexican immigrants came to the Southwest between 1900 and 1930. Like many recent immigrants, Mexicans found low-paid occupations, largely as laborers and migrant agricultural workers. By 1920, 75 percent of California farm labor was Mexican. By 1928, 75 percent of the construction laborers in Texas were Mexican.

Mexican laborers were paid substantially lower wages than non-Mexicans who did the same jobs, and the Mexican American workforce was subjected to repressive controls. For example, Mexican laborers were often trapped into a kind of indentured servitude by their bosses, who would make loans and advances on wages—at exorbitant interest rates—to force them into debt. Ownership of automobiles was discouraged by employers as well as by police officials, who often singled out Mexican American drivers for traffic tickets.

Immigrants were often denied education. In many places children of Hispanic origin were excluded from public schools—and where this was not the case no provision was made for instruction in Spanish, and little attempt was made to teach English. In many cases the children of agricultural laborers were sent into the fields rather than into the classroom. When Mexican Americans were admitted to secondary education, the boys were shunted into "manual training" courses and the girls into "domestic science."

Beginning during World War I and continuing into the economically flush 1920s, American industry demanded cheap labor, and plant owners and managers actively recruited Mexican workers. With the onset of the Great Depression, however, the need for Mexican labor quickly dried up, and some 400,000 Mexicans were sent back across the border—despite the fact that many were second-generation Mexican Americans and, therefore, U.S. citizens.

Mexican American Labor Movement

During the late 1920s and early 1930s, a Mexican American labor movement began with the formation of two large Hispanic American unions, the Confederation of Mexican Labor Unions and the Imperial Valley Workers' Union. In 1933 farm laborers from both unions went on strike to obtain a wage of one dollar per hundredweight of picked cotton.

The farmers countered with an offer of sixty cents, then prevailed upon local officials to call out the National Guard and the police to break up the strike. Despite the brutality of the encounters between workers and officials, the laborers stood their ground, and the strike was ultimately resolved with a compromise of seventy-five cents per hundredweight.

When America's entry into World War II once again brought a high demand for labor, the U.S. government negotiated the Mexican Farm Labor Supply Program with Mexico, through which thousands of Mexicans were recruited for agricultural work in the United States. The program outlasted the war and did not end until 1964.

The Civil Rights Movement in the 1960s

With the influx of Mexicans into the Southwest came frequent incidents of ethnic violence—especially in urban areas, such as Los Angeles, where the barrios (neighborhoods) were subject to invasion and attack by gangs of whites. Until the 1960s organized protest and activism within the Hispanic American community were centered, for the most part, on local labor issues. Inspired by the emergence of the African American civil rights movement, Cesar Chavez formed the National Farm Workers Association (NFWA) in 1962 and in 1965 staged a nationwide boycott of California wine and table grapes.

Chavez and the NFWA remained a major force in the Hispanic American civil rights movement through the 1980s. However, beginning in the 1960s and continuing into the 1970s, the more militant and culturally focused Chicano movement also developed—which addressed, in addition to political, economic, and civil rights issues, matters of Hispanic identity and pride.

Period of Backlash

The Hispanic community made important political and economic strides during the 1980s, but the end of that decade and the beginning of the 1990s saw a backlash within some sectors of the non-Hispanic majority. First such initiatives as affirmative action were attacked or even struck down. Second, calls to make English the official language of the United States and for the elimination of all bilingual and multilingual educational programs gave dramatic expression to a new xenophobia. Finally, voters in California in 1994 approved Proposition 187, which would have cut off government funding for health care, education, and other state benefits to illegal aliens and their children. A number of politicians even called for a national equivalent of Proposition 187. However, in 1995 a federal district court ruled the California law unconstitutional because it encroached on federal authority in matters of immigration.

(For the history of Hispanic Americans before the 1920s, see Hispanic Americans. For information on specific Hispanic American civil rights organizations, see Alianza Hispano-Americana, American GI Forum, Brown Berets, Mexican-American Legal Defense and Education Fund, Migrant Legal Action Program, National Council of La Raza, and Puerto Rican Legal Defense and Education Fund, Inc. See also English-Only legislation and movements and migrant labor.)

Suggested Reading

Heyck, Denis L., ed. *Barrios and Borderlands: Cultures of Latinos and Latinas in the United States.* New York: Routledge, 1994.

Rodriguez, Richard. *Brown: The Last Discovery of America.* New York: Viking Press, 2002.

Suarez-Orozco, Marcelo M., and Mariela Paez, eds. *Latinos: Remaking America.* Berkeley: University of California Press, 2002.

HOLMES, OLIVER WENDELL, JR. (1841–1935)

One of the most famous names in American jurisprudence, Oliver Wendell Holmes served as an associate justice of the Supreme Court, where he represented the philosophy of judicial restraint, which holds that laws are made by legislative bodies and not by the courts, and that the courts' only concern should be to try the constitutionality of legislation. Holmes was also a vigorous champion of free speech—which, he believed, could be curtailed only in case of a "clear and present danger," as he illustrated memorably in *Abrams v. United States* (1919): "The most stringent protection of free speech would not protect a man in falsely shouting fire in a theatre and causing a panic."

The first child of Oliver Wendell Holmes Sr., who had earned renown as a physician, poet, and essayist, Holmes was born in Boston and educated at a private school and at Harvard College. In 1861, at the outbreak of the Civil War, he left college to enlist as a private in the Union army. He trained, but was not called up. He returned to school and completed his degree, and was then commissioned a first lieutenant in the Twentieth Massachusetts Regiment of Volunteers. Holmes performed heroically, was wounded three times, and left the service as a lieutenant colonel. He entered Harvard Law School in 1864, received his degree in 1866, toured Europe, was admitted to the bar in 1867, and enjoyed fifteen years of successful private practice. Holmes edited the *American Law Review* from 1870 to 1873 and also edited the twelfth edition of James Kent's classic *Commentaries on American Law* (1873). He lectured at Harvard and, during 1880–1881, at the

Lowell Institute in Boston, and his lectures became the basis for his 1881 book, *The Common Law.*

In 1882 Holmes became Weld Professor of Law at Harvard Law School and was named to the Supreme Judicial Court of Massachusetts. He sat on that bench for two decades and became chief justice in 1899. In 1902 President Theodore Roosevelt appointed Holmes to the Supreme Court, where he served until his retirement, shortly before his ninety-first birthday, on January 12, 1932. He was the oldest justice ever to serve.

Suggested Reading

Posner, Richard A. *The Essential Holmes: Selections from the Letters, Speeches, Judicial Opinions, and Other Writings of Oliver Wendell Holmes Jr.* Chicago: University of Chicago Press, 1996.

HOME MORTGAGE DISCLOSURE ACT

The Home Mortgage Disclosure Act (HMDA), which applies to banks, savings associations, credit unions, and other mortgage lending institutions, was enacted by Congress in 1975 and is implemented under the Federal Reserve Board's Regulation C, which requires lending institutions to report data on public loans. This information can help determine whether financial institutions are serving the housing needs of their communities and can assist public officials in distributing public sector investments to attract private investment to areas where it is most needed. Finally, the HMDA makes it easier to identify possibly discriminatory lending patterns.

Suggested Reading

The Federal Financial Institutions Examination Council HMDA information website, www.ffiec.gov/hmda.

HOMESCHOOLING

Homeschooling became increasingly popular during the 1980s and 1990s among parents who, for a variety of reasons, were dissatisfied with the public education system. In many cases parents undertake homeschooling for purely academic reasons, including a conviction that parents and parents' groups can educate children most effectively. In other cases parents have chosen homeschooling out of religious conviction—either because they believe that special religious instruction that is unavailable in public schools should be part of their children's lives, or because they do not wish their children to attend school with those who do not share similar beliefs. Still others opt for homeschooling to avoid sending their children to racially or ethnically mixed public schools.

In 1982 only two states, Nevada and Utah, permitted homeschooling; all other states had mandatory attendance laws, which required schooling in certified schools. Such is the political power of the homeschooling movement that within ten years thirty-five states had passed homeschooling statutes. Standards for accountability, curriculum, and testing vary widely from state to state. (See also EDUCATION RIGHTS.)

Suggested Reading

Guterson, David. *Family Matters: Why Homeschooling Makes Sense.* New York: Harvest Books, 1993.

Stevens, Mitchell L. *Kingdom of Children: Culture and Controversy in the Homeschooling Movement.* Princeton: Princeton University Press, 2001.

HOMESTEAD ACT OF 1862

On May 20, 1862, President ABRAHAM LINCOLN signed into law the Homestead Act, which granted 160 acres of public land free of charge (save for a nominal filing fee) to anyone who was either twenty-one years old or the head of a family and who was either a born or naturalized citizen or who had applied for citizenship. A milestone in human rights, the act represented the first time that a government had granted land to individuals in an entirely nondiscriminatory way. It was also central to the settling of the West.

To perfect the homestead claim the grantee had to live on the land, erect a dwelling on it, and cultivate it for at least five years. Provisions allowed for the acquisition of additional acreage at a low price. Although the act was subject to abuse by railroads and other business interests (which used "dummy entrymen" to file false claims, and to thereby amass land for corporate ownership at public expense), on the whole the legislation worked remarkably well. By the end of the nineteenth century more than eighty million acres had been claimed by some six hundred thousand homestead farmers.

Suggested Reading

Layton, Sanford J. "Homestead Act of 1862." In *Encyclopedia of the American West,* ed. Charles Phillips and Alan Axelrod. New York: Macmillan Reference USA, 1996.

HOOVER, J. EDGAR (1895–1972)

John Edgar Hoover—always known as J. Edgar Hoover—was director of the FEDERAL BUREAU OF INVESTIGATION (FBI) from 1924 until his death in 1972. During this period he transformed the bureau into one of the most highly respected law enforcement agencies in the world; at the same time, however, he ran the agency as something of a personal fiefdom, wielding power that lay outside the Constitution and the system of checks and balances. In particular, Hoover used the FBI to spy on Americans he considered controversial or dangerous—primarily, civil rights activists and prominent liberals and leftists from ELEANOR ROOSEVELT and New York mayor Fiorello LaGuardia to MARTIN LUTHER KING JR.

A Washington, D.C., native, Hoover had intended to enter the ministry but instead enrolled in law school at George Washington University, where he was awarded a bachelor of laws in 1916 and a master of laws in 1917. His first job, which he began in 1917, was as a file reviewer at the Department of Justice, but within two years he was appointed special assistant to Attorney General A. Mitchell Palmer. It was Hoover who zealously directed the PALMER RAIDS—mass roundups (and, in many cases, subsequent deportations) of suspected Bolsheviks during 1919–1920. It was during the era of the Palmer Raids that Hoover began compiling exhaustive files on people he suspected of disloyalty to the United States; during Hoover's forty-eight years as FBI director, these files burgeoned as Hoover waged a continuous—and often very personal—war against communism, communists, fellow travelers, and anyone suspected of being "pink."

In 1922 Hoover was transferred to the Bureau of Investigation as its assistant director. Created in 1905, the bureau was generally feeble and riddled with corruption and inefficiency. In 1924 bureau director William J. Burns was forced out of office, and Hoover was named to direct the agency (his appointment was not officially confirmed until 1931). Hoover immediately reorganized the bureau, renaming it the Federal Bureau of Investigation, and staffed it with agents who held a degree in either law or accounting. The agents were subjected to rigorous professional training and became the most highly respected law enforcement officers in the nation. Hoover also established a scientific crime-detection laboratory and what would become the world's largest fingerprint file, and created the FBI National Academy, a training facility.

In addition to being a brilliant administrator, Hoover was a gifted publicist who created the "Ten Most Wanted" list. Populated by bank robbers and other violent felons whom Hoover avidly demonized, the list drew the excited attention of the public at the same time that it directed the FBI's focus away from the spread of organized crime—which, during the Prohibition era, was taking hold of the nation. FBI manhunts in pursuit of such high-profile criminals as John Dillinger, Pretty Boy Floyd, Baby Face Nelson, and the Barker Gang created an enormously popular and powerful public image for the agency, which received generous funding and grew steadily in size and influence.

Late in the 1930s, as the nation drifted toward war, President FRANKLIN D. ROOSEVELT called on Hoover and the FBI to investigate foreign espionage in the United States, which meant monitoring the activities of Nazis and fascists as well as communists. After World War II, during the cold war, as part of the FBI's intensive surveillance of any and all groups considered to be subversive or on the political fringe, the agency infiltrated both the KU KLUX KLAN and the civil rights movement. Curiously, however, Hoover maintained the same hands-off policy toward organized crime that he had instituted from the earliest days of the bureau. He even stubbornly asserted that the Mafia was nothing more than a popular myth. Not until the late 1960s did the FBI, under tremendous public and political pressure, begin operations against organized crime.

Hoover amassed enormous and closely held files on virtually every public figure and politician. He had a penchant for collecting compromising information, particularly of a sexual nature; by quietly wielding the threat of leaking such information, he succeeded in intimidating those who should have had full authority over him and the bureau. Hoover served under eight presidents and eighteen attorneys general, and none ever dared to act against him.

Suggested Reading

Powers, Richard G. *Secrecy and Power: The Life of J. Edgar Hoover.* New York: Free Press, 1986.

Theoharis, A. G., and J. S. Cox. *The Boss.* New York: Bantam, 1988.

HOSTILE WORK ENVIRONMENT

Although neither federal nor state antidiscrimination laws make explicit use of the phrase *hostile work environment* to refer to harassment in the workplace, the concept has become important in judicial definitions of harassment. Essentially, courts have recognized two forms of harassment: quid pro quo harassment (such as when a manager threatens to fire an employee if she refuses to have sex with him) and harassment that occurs as a consequence of a hostile work environment. This second type of harassment was defined by the U.S. SUPREME COURT in *Meritor Savings Bank v. Vinson* (1986) as a context characterized by speech or conduct related to the plaintiff's race, religion, sex, national origin, age, disability, veteran status (or, in some jurisdictions, sexual orientation, political affiliation, citizenship status, marital status, or personal appearance) that is sufficiently "severe or pervasive" to create a "hostile or abusive work environment."

Defenses against claims of a hostile work environment have sometimes been based on First Amendment rights. For example, claims based, in part, on political statements, religious proselytizing, social commentary, or art may be vulnerable to defense on the grounds of FREE SPEECH. However, no First Amendment defense is possible against claims based on inappropriate physical contact or the use of racial or other slurs.

Suggested Reading

Dobrich, Wanda, et al. *The Manager's Guide to Preventing a Hostile Work Environment.* New York: McGraw-Hill, 2002.

Key cases in sexual harassment include *Harris v. Forklift Systems* (1993), *Burlington Industries, Inc. v. Ellerth* (1998), *Faragher v. City of Boca Raton* (1998), and *Oncale v. Sundowner Offshore Services, Inc.* (1998).

HOUSE UN-AMERICAN ACTIVITIES COMMITTEE

The House Un-American Activities Committee (HUAC) was a committee of the U.S. House of Representatives formed in 1938 and charged with investigating disloyalty and subversive organizations with the object of creating appropriate legislation to prevent and prosecute espionage and sabotage. Although the committee was created on the eve of World War II, from the beginning it was less concerned with investigating fascist and Nazi infiltration of American government and institutions than with rooting out communism. HUAC's first chairman, Martin Dies, employed high-handed and often unscrupulous methods that would mark the committee's work for most of its existence, especially during the cold war years.

To compel witnesses to "name names"—that is, to identify former associates or anyone else with ties to the Communist Party, HUAC freely employed innuendo and intimidation and made vague, sweeping accusations based principally on guilt by association. Anyone who had any connection to a suspect organization was assumed to be disloyal, subversive, or an out-and-out communist, and witnesses who refused to answer were often cited for CONTEMPT OF CONGRESS.

HUAC's highest-profile investigation, undertaken in 1947, was of the entertainment industry. During the investigation a parade of Hollywood notables testified before the committee. Citing the BILL OF RIGHTS, one group—dubbed the Hollywood Ten—refused to name names, and were dealt prison sentences for CONTEMPT of Congress. For conservatives, the Hollywood Ten became a lighting rod for accusations of communist infiltration of the popular media; for liberals, the group became a cause célèbre, dramatic proof of the abuses of a right-wing government out of control.

The next sensational proceeding came in 1948 when journalist Whittaker Chambers accused Alger Hiss, a former official of the Department of State, of spying for the Soviets. It was in connection with this investigation that committee member RICHARD M. NIXON gained his first national exposure as a crusader against communism and a determined cold warrior.

Even during its heyday HUAC had many critics, who accused committee members of trampling the civil liberties of witnesses. Critics also pointed out that although the HUAC's primary charge was to recommend new legislation to combat disloyalty and espionage, the committee had failed to recommend any such legislation.

Beginning in 1950 Sen. JOSEPH MCCARTHY undertook his own Senate investigations of disloyalty and subversive organizations, emulating the tactics of HUAC. From this point until McCarthy was himself disgraced (as a result of the Army-McCarthy Hearings of 1954), the Senate investigation eclipsed HUAC in importance and in the level of public attention it received. HUAC continued to exist in a low-profile role and was renamed the House Internal Security Committee in 1969. It was dissolved entirely in 1975.

Suggested Reading

Bentley, Eric, ed. *Thirty Years of Treason: Excerpts from Hearings before the House Committee on Un-American Activities, 1938–1968.* New York: Thunder's Mouth Press, 2002.

Goodman, Walter. *The Committee: The Extraordinary Career of the House Committee on Un-American Activities.* New York: Farrar, Straus, and Giroux, 1968.

HOUSING RIGHTS

The U.S. Constitution is silent on the subject of housing, but the federal government recognizes a right to "fair housing," which is defined as equal access to housing and bars discrimination in housing because of race, color, national origin, religion, sex, familial status, sexual orientation, or disability. In addition, the federal government and many state governments provide programs to assist members of minority groups and those who meet certain income requirements to obtain housing.

Origins of Housing Laws

By the mid-nineteenth century the influx of immigrant labor into American cities had created overcrowding and slum conditions in some urban neighborhoods. During the 1850s and 1860s some states and municipalities launched (mostly desultory) reform programs, the most important of which was New York State's Tenement House Law of 1867, which set minimal standards for housing in New York City. Although the law was an important precedent, the standards were so low and the enforcement so inadequate that tenement slums continued to proliferate. By 1890, out of a total population of 1.5 million, more than 1 million of New York City's residents were housed in 35,000 tenements, typically under appalling conditions. The majority of tenement dwellers were first- or second-generation immigrants.

Subsidized Housing

In 1890 the New York journalist Jacob Riis, himself an immigrant, published *How the Other Half Lives,* which documented, in words and photographs, New York slum life. Riis's book catalyzed a reform movement that, with regard to housing, took two directions. One direction focused on legislation to restrict immigration. The other led to the creation of the United States Housing Corporation in 1920, which set basic standards for housing and made strictly limited financial aid available. It was not until the early years of the Great Depression, however, during the administration of President Herbert Hoover, that federally subsidized housing began on a large scale, under the aegis of the Reconstruction Finance Corporation. Under President Franklin D. Roosevelt the federal housing program was greatly expanded—first by the Public Works Administration and then in 1934 by the National Housing Act, which created the Federal Housing Administration (FHA). The FHA underwrote mortgage loans by providing mortgage insurance. Although such underwriting did not help the truly poverty stricken, it did put some members of the working poor into houses. It was not until 1937, with passage of the U.S. Housing Act, that the federal government began to subsidize the construction of low-cost apartments for very low-income families. In addition to subsidizing construction, the federal government also subsidized rent, although the tenants paid for operating costs. These depression-era measures laid the foundation of the federal housing subsidy programs that continue to operate today.

Housing Segregation

The lack of decent, affordable housing was not the only housing rights issue of the early twentieth century. In many communities zoning laws or other ordinances were used openly to achieve and maintain ethnic and racial segregation. In 1917, however, the Supreme Court ruled in *Buchanan v. Warley* that it was unconstitutional to use municipal zoning ordinances specifically to regulate where a particular racial group could live. Municipalities responded by passing zoning regulations that were purportedly designed to protect public health, safety, welfare, and even aesthetics, but that often effectively maintained segregation by encouraging the construction of certain housing types in some neighborhoods while banning such housing in other neighborhoods.

Although zoning laws could not be used blatantly to enforce segregation, private covenants could. Under such covenants, landowners in a given area could agree to bar from ownership or tenancy those who were members of certain racial or ethnic groups. However, the 1948 Supreme Court decision in *Shelley v. Kraemer* (argued by lawyers for the National Association for the Advancement of Colored People) put an end to this practice. The decision in *Barrows v. Jackson* (1953), which barred suits against owners who breached prior restrictive covenants by selling their houses to African Americans, ensured that no state court could act to enforce a restrictive covenant.

With zoning and restrictive covenants knocked down as means of enforcing segregation in housing, realtors turned to the practice of "steering" minority clients to particular neighborhoods. Title VIII of the Civil Rights Act of 1968 (which, with the Fair Housing Act of 1988, constitutes the current Fair Housing Act) legally barred realtors from steering prospective tenants or purchasers and also made it illegal to include references to race or ethnicity in advertisements for property. The law did not immediately put an end to steering, but the practice steadily diminished because violators were subject not only to criminal prosecution but to costly civil suits.

Zoning and Public Housing

Although the Supreme Court and other federal courts consistently ruled against discriminatory zoning and real estate practices, in 1971 and 1976 the Court upheld a community's right, in accordance with its zoning ordinances, to approve or disapprove of the construction of public housing projects. In many cases, such decisions had the effect of enforcing racial segregation by barring (for example) the type of construction used to create public housing projects.

Municipal governments are free to enact zoning restrictions that limit the number of bedrooms in a structure, specify the minimum and maximum sizes of dwellings, prohibit certain types of construction (including apartment houses), and set construction standards that may make certain structures financially infeasible. When such ordinances are legally challenged, the courts must decide whether the intent of the zoning ordinances in question is racially or ethnically exclusionary. The issue of exclusionary zoning remains an exceedingly complex and difficult one. See also DEPARTMENT OF HOUSING AND URBAN DEVELOPMENT, U.S., FAIR HOUSING ACT, and *MOUNT LAUREL* CASES.

Suggested Reading

Spada, Marcia Darvin. *Fair Housing.* Cincinnati, Ohio: South-Western Publishing, 2001.

HOWARD, OLIVER O. (1830–1909)

To military historians, O. O. Howard is best known as a heroic Civil War general who lost an arm after a grievous wound and as the vigorous commander of army operations against the Nez Perce and the Bannock Indians. He was also a committed abolitionist who was earnestly concerned about the welfare of the liberated slaves. From May 1865 through June 1872 Howard served as commissioner of the FREEDMEN'S BUREAU, the agency charged with assisting blacks. In 1867 Howard founded (and subsequently became president of) Howard University in Washington, D. C., which remains the leading American institution of black higher education.

Born and raised in rural Leeds, Maine, Howard graduated from Bowdoin College in 1850 and from West Point in 1854. He was commissioned a second lieutenant and was assigned as an artillerist, then returned to West Point as a mathematics instructor. In June of 1861, with the outbreak of the Civil War, he was appointed colonel of the Third Maine Volunteers. By the time of the first Battle of Bull Run, on July 21, 1861, he was a brigade commander and in September was appointed brigadier general of volunteers. Howard served in the Peninsula campaign, fighting at Fair Oaks on May 31, 1862, where he lost his right arm. Returning to combat, he fought at South Mountain on September 14 and at Antietam on September 17. In November 1862, he was promoted to major general of volunteers and divisional commander. He led II Corps at Fredericksburg on December 13, then was assigned command of XI Corps on April 2, 1863. At Chancellorsville during May 2–4, 1863, he was routed by Thomas "Stonewall" Jackson, but redeemed himself at Gettysburg (July 1–3) when his unit performed with such distinction that it received the special thanks of Congress.

In September 1863 Howard transferred to the Army of the Cumberland and fought at Chattanooga (November 24–25) and in the Atlanta campaign (May–August 1864) before he was given command of the Army of the Tennessee. He accompanied General William Tecumseh Sherman on his infamous "march to the sea" during September–December 1864 and was subsequently promoted to brigadier general of regulars and breveted to major general.

After the war, in addition to his work with the Freedmen's Bureau and Howard University, Howard was closely involved in Indian affairs. In 1872 he negotiated with Cochise for the return of the Chiricahua Apaches to their reservation, and, two years later, returned to active military duty as commander of the Department of the Columbia. In this capacity he attempted to negotiate with a faction of the Nez Perce to abandon lands that the federal government wanted. When the negotiations failed, Howard commanded an exhausting but successful military campaign against the tribe. After the defeat of the Nez Perce Howard petitioned the president and Congress for permission to resettle the tribe on the land they had fought to occupy. The petition was unsuccessful.

During 1878 Howard campaigned against the Bannock Indians, who were raiding in the Northwest. After this debilitating and mostly fruitless exercise, he returned to the East and in 1881 was appointed superintendent of West Point. The following year he was named commander of the Department of the Platte (1882–1886) and then the Division of the East (March 1886–November 1894). In 1893 Howard was honored with the Medal of Honor for his action at Fair Oaks during the Civil War.

Howard retired from the military in 1894 and in 1895 founded another black institution of higher learning, Lincoln Memorial University in Tennessee. He devoted his final years to writing military history and an autobiography.

Suggested Reading

Howard, Oliver O. *Autobiography of Oliver Otis Howard.* 1907. Reprint, New York: Ayer, 1977.

HUGHES, LANGSTON (1902–1967)

Langston Hughes, an African American writer who became a prominent figure in the HARLEM RENAISSANCE, was regarded by both blacks and whites as one of the major interpreters of what it meant to be black in the United States.

Hughes was born in Joplin, Missouri, and was raised by his mother (after she separated from his father) and grandmother. Following the death of his grandmother, Hughes and his mother moved to six different cities before settling in Cleveland, Ohio. In 1921, after graduating from high school, Hughes wrote "The Negro Speaks of Rivers," which was published in the *CRISIS;* it marked him as an important new voice and became one of his best-known poems.

Hughes enrolled in Columbia University, but he left in 1922 to taste life in Harlem and at sea, where he worked as a steward on an Africa-bound freighter. He wandered in Europe for a time, winning a prestigious poetry prize in 1925 and, in 1926, after returning to the United States, the Witter Bynner Undergraduate Poetry Award from Lincoln University. In a stroke of self-promotional brilliance, Hughes—who was working as a busboy in a Washington, D.C., hotel—placed three of his poems beside the plate of Vachel Lindsay, a popular (white) poet who was a guest in the hotel dining room. The very next day, journalists reported that Lindsay had "discovered" a Negro busboy poet. Hughes received a scholarship to Pennsylvania's Lincoln University, from which he graduated in 1929, having already published two volumes of verse: *The Weary Blues* (1926) and *Fine Clothes to the Jew* (1927). *Not without Laughter,* a work of autobiographical prose, came out in 1930.

Hughes's initial successes were warmly greeted by white as well as by black readers. However, the commercial success notwithstanding, Hughes became increasingly militant in matters of racial justice and also increasingly committed to the political left. He toured Haiti, Japan, and the Soviet Union and served during 1937 as a newspaper correspondent in the Spanish Civil War, in which his sentiments clearly lay with the anti-fascist Loyalists. In 1934 he published his first collection of short stories, *The Ways of White Folks,* and in 1940 *The Big Sea,* an autobiography to age twenty-eight. (His later years would be addressed in *I Wonder as I Wander,* which was published in 1956.)

In 1949 Hughes edited a major anthology of African American literary expression, *The Poetry of the Negro,* and in 1958, with Arna Bontemps, *The Book of Negro Folklore.* Hughes also wrote for the stage and translated from Spanish the poetry of Federico García Lorca and Gabriela Mistral. Only after Hughes's death was the more strident poetry of *The Panther and the Lash* published by his family.

Suggested Reading

Hughes, Langston. *The Collected Poems.* New York: Vintage, 1995.

Rampersad, Arnold. *The Life of Langston Hughes.* New York: Oxford University Press, 2002.

HULL HOUSE

Founded in Chicago in 1889 by Jane Addams and Ellen Starr, Hull House was a pioneering "social settlement"—a center where the city's recent immigrants could obtain immediate aid as well as education and training for self-betterment. The core of Hull House was the abandoned residence of Charles G. Hull (at 800 South Halsted Street, Chicago), to which, eventually, a dozen buildings and a playground were added (as well as a summer camp, which was located in rural Wisconsin).

Hull House was inspired by Toynbee Hall, a settlement in the slums of London founded by Samuel A. Barnett. Although its original function was as a kindergarten, Hull House grew, through private donations, to include a day nursery and a school that offered secondary- and college-level extension classes, as well as evening classes devoted to civil rights and citizenship. Hull House's influence, however, extended far beyond Chicago's poor South Side, and it became a center of national social change. Working from Hull House, Addams and Starr promoted the passage of state child labor laws, the establishment of separate courts for juvenile offenders, and the creation of special agencies for the protection of children. Hull House also became a hotbed of trade union organization, grassroots social welfare programs, and women's suffrage; during World War I it became the center of a controversial campaign for world peace.

In the early 1960s much of the Hull House complex was leveled to make way for the construction of the Chicago Circle Campus of the University of Illinois, but the original Hull residence and an adjoining dining hall were retained as museums. Hull House activities, though decentralized, still continue.

Suggested Reading

Addams, Jane. *Twenty Years at Hull-House.* 1910. Reprint, New York: Signet, 1999.

Davis, Allen F. *American Heroine: The Life and Legend of Jane Addams.* New York: Oxford University Press, 1973.

HUMAN RIGHTS WATCH

Human Rights Watch, the largest human rights organization based in the United States, is staffed by lawyers, journalists, academics, and experts of many nationalities who investigate human rights abuses all over the world. The organization publishes its findings annually through books and reports, generating extensive media coverage. The object of the publicity is to embarrass governments (and other entities) that commit abuses, not only in the eyes of their citizens but in the eyes of the world.

In addition to bringing human rights abuses to light and creating national and international pressure to stop them, Human Rights Watch representatives work with government officials at the United Nations, in the European Union, in Washington, D.C., and in capitals around the world to urge changes in policy and practice. In some circumstances Human Rights Watch has campaigned for the withdrawal of military and economic support from certain governments; in times of crisis, the organization endeavors to provide timely information from the front. For example, refugee accounts that were collected, synthesized, and cross-corroborated by Human Rights Watch were instrumental in motivating the international community's response to the wars in Chechnya (1994–1996) and Kosovo (1998).

Human Rights Watch was founded in 1978 as Helsinki Watch, specifically to monitor the compliance of Soviet bloc countries with the human rights provisions of the landmark Helsinki Accords. In 1981 Americas Watch was created in response to the human rights abuses that accompanied the struggle between left and right in Central America. During the 1980s the "watch" committees grew to cover other regions of the world, and in 1988 the committees were united as Human Rights Watch.

Headquartered in New York, Human Rights Watch has major offices in Brussels, Hong Kong, London, Moscow, Los Angeles, and Washington. The organization also sets up ad hoc offices wherever intensive investigations are being conducted. Currently, the organization tracks developments in more than seventy countries, focusing on issues such as WOMEN'S RIGHTS, CHILDREN'S RIGHTS, and the flow of arms to forces that commit abuses. In recent years, Human Rights Watch has also addressed academic freedom, the human rights responsibilities of corporations, international justice, prisons, drugs, and refugees. Any and all parties to conflict—from legitimately elected governments to rebel forces—may find themselves the target of Human Rights Watch investigations.

Domestically the organization has reported on human rights issues related to prison conditions, law enforcement (police abuses), immigration (the indefinite detention of immigrants), and the criminal justice system (the execution of juvenile offenders and mentally retarded people).

Suggested Reading

Human Rights Watch. *Human Rights Watch World Report 2001.* New York: Human Rights Watch, 2002.

HUTCHINSON, ANNE (1591–1643)

Anne Hutchinson is celebrated as an early American pioneer in the struggle for human rights, religious freedom, freedom of individual conscience, and WOMEN'S RIGHTS.

She was born Anne Marbury in 1591 to the Reverend Francis Marbury and his wife, Bridget, in Alford, Lincolnshire, England. On August 9, 1612, in London, she married the merchant William Hutchinson, and in 1634 the couple immigrated to America with a group led by the Reverend John Lothrop. They settled in Boston.

Hutchinson had come of age in England during an era of religious persecution. Twice her own father had been imprisoned for preaching about the incompetence of English ministers. Hutchinson gravitated toward the Puritan point of view, and when the minister she most respected, the Reverend John Cotton, left for New England, she declared that she "could not be at rest but I must come hither." To her profound dismay, what she found in the Massachusetts Bay Colony was not religious freedom but narrow dedication to prayer and self-discipline. Searching for more, Hutchinson invited women to meet in her home after church to discuss religion. These meetings soon evolved from discussions of that day's sermon to sessions in which Hutchinson eloquently shared her own beliefs. Although she was well educated in matters of theology, Hutchinson espoused the radical point of view that mere conformity to religious laws was neither proof nor expression of personal godliness. In her view, true spirituality flowed not from sermons or the Bible but from an inner experience of the Holy Spirit.

Hutchinson's message of inner revelation, spiritual liberty, and freedom of conscience attracted a following not only among women but among prominent New England men. Hutchinson's growing popularity and influence drew protests from the Reverend John Wilson, the local pastor, and, when Governor John Winthrop joined him in opposing Hutchinson, a major schism developed in the Puritan church, threatening the political stability of the entire Massachusetts Bay Colony. Hutchinson was condemned as an antinomian—one who adheres to the heretical doctrine that Christians are not bound by moral law—and in August 1637 Winthrop banned all private religious meetings. When Hutchinson defied the ban, Winthrop and his supporters filed charges against her, and she was tried for heresy before a meeting of the General Court. Winthrop described Hutchinson's meetings as "a thing not tolerable nor comely in the sight of God, nor fitting for your sex," and he accused her of breaking the Fifth Commandment by not honoring her father and mother—by which he meant, metaphorically, the magistrates of the colony. Hutchinson conducted an intellectually brilliant defense and came close to clearing herself of all charges, until she let it slip that the Lord had revealed Himself to her in a personal vision. Winthrop declared, "I am persuaded that the revelation she brings forth is delusion," and the court voted to banish her from the colony (James Kendall Hosmer, ed., *Winthrop's Journal,* New York: Barnes and Noble, 1959, 284).

On March 15, 1638, Hutchinson was also tried by the church and excommunicated. Hutchinson responded: "The

Lord judgeth not as man judgeth. Better to be cast out of the church than to deny Christ." She found refuge in the Rhode Island colony founded by ROGER WILLIAMS, who advocated what he called "soul liberty," in the name of which he counseled toleration of all faiths. In Rhode Island Hutchinson and her husband, fifteen children, and sixty followers settled on the island of Aquidneck, which she called Peaceable Island. In 1638 they founded the town of Pocasset, which was renamed Portsmouth the following year. When her husband died in 1642 Hutchinson took her unmarried children to the Dutch colony in New York, where she built a home on Pelham Bay (now in the Bronx). There in August 1643 she perished, along with five of her youngest children, in a Mahican raid. (See also RELIGION, FREEDOM OF.)

Suggested Reading

Hall, David D., ed. *The Antinomian Controversy 1636–1638: A Documentary History.* Durham: Duke University Press, 1990.

"I HAVE A DREAM" SPEECH (MARTIN LUTHER KING JR.)

On August 28, 1963, from the steps of the Lincoln Memorial, MARTIN LUTHER KING JR. delivered one of the greatest speeches in the history of the nation and in the history of minority rights. Addressed to a crowd of more than 200,000 who had marched on Washington—in what was the largest demonstration in American history up to that time—the speech did much to galvanize the civil rights movement and has remained the movement's most compelling single expression. (The speech is widely reproduced. It may be heard online at www.historychannel.com. See also MARCH ON WASHINGTON.)

Suggested Reading

Washington, James Melvin, ed. *I Have a Dream: Writings and Speeches That Changed the World.* San Francisco: Harper San Francisco, 1992.

IMMIGRATION ACT OF 1917

The Immigration Act of February 5, 1917 (39 *Statutes at Large* 874), codified all exclusion provisions enacted in previous immigration legislation. It forbade immigration of Asian persons from the "barred zone" (known as the Asia-Pacific triangle) and added the following controversial exclusions:

> All idiots, imbeciles, feeble-minded persons, epileptics, insane persons; persons who have had one or more attacks of insanity at any time previously; persons of constitutional psychopathic inferiority; persons with chronic alcoholism; paupers; professional beggars; vagrants; persons afflicted with tuberculosis in any form or with a loathsome or dangerous contagious disease; persons not comprehended within any of the foregoing excluded classes who are found to be and are certified by the examining surgeon as being mentally or physically defective, such physical defect being of a nature which may affect the ability of such alien to earn a living; persons who have been convicted of or admit having committed a felony or other crime or misdemeanor involving moral turpitude; polygamists, or persons who practice polygamy or believe in or advocate the practice of polygamy; anarchists, or persons who believe in or advocate the overthrow by force or violence of the Government of the United States.

In addition the act broadened the classes of aliens who could be summarily deported and abolished the statute of limitation governing deportation in certain more serious cases. President Woodrow Wilson objected to much of the act as too restrictive and vetoed it, but Congress passed it over the president's veto.

Suggested Reading

Hutchinson, Edward Prince. *Legislative History of American Immigration Policy: 1798–1965.* Philadelphia: University of Pennsylvania Press, 1981.

IMMIGRATION ACT OF 1924

The Immigration Act of May 26, 1924, established the first permanent limitation on immigration and created the "national origins quota system." It did not supplant, but worked in conjunction with, the IMMIGRATION ACT OF 1917 to govern U.S. immigration policy until passage of the IMMIGRATION AND NATURALIZATION ACT OF 1952. (See Appendix A for additional details on the Immigration Act of 1924.)

Suggested Reading

Hutchinson, Edward Prince. *Legislative History of American Immigration Policy: 1798–1965.* Philadelphia: University of Pennsylvania Press, 1981.

IMMIGRATION ACT OF 1965

Officially, the Immigration and Nationality Act Amendments of October 3, 1965, generally known as the Immigration Act of 1965, substantially liberalized U.S.

immigration policy. (See Appendix A for the text of the Immigration Act of 1965.)

Suggested Reading

Hutchinson, Edward Prince. *Legislative History of American Immigration Policy: 1798–1965.* Philadelphia: University of Pennsylvania Press, 1981.

IMMIGRATION AND NATURALIZATION ACT OF 1952

The Immigration and Naturalization Act of June 27, 1952, incorporated into a single comprehensive statute the multiple laws that had governed immigration and naturalization in the United States. For the most part the law perpetuated immigration policies from earlier statutes. (See Appendix A for additional details about the Immigration and Naturalization Act of 1952. See also IMMIGRATION ACT OF 1917 and IMMIGRATION ACT OF 1924.)

Suggested Reading

Hutchinson, Edward Prince. *Legislative History of American Immigration Policy: 1798–1965.* Philadelphia: University of Pennsylvania Press, 1981.

IMMIGRATION REFORM AND CONTROL ACT

The Immigration Reform and Control Act of November 6, 1986, provided legalization (that is, temporary and then permanent resident status) for aliens who had resided in the United States in an unlawful status since January 1, 1982 and sanctioned employers who knowingly hire illegal aliens. The act also provided for increased immigration enforcement at U.S. borders. (See Appendix A for details about the Immigration Reform and Control Act.)

Suggested Reading

Hutchinson, Edward Prince. *Legislative History of American Immigration Policy: 1798–1965.* Philadelphia: University of Pennsylvania Press, 1981.

IMMIGRATION RIGHTS, STATUTES, AND RESTRICTIONS

See CHINESE EXCLUSION REPEAL ACT, CHINESE EXCLUSION TREATY AND ACT, GENTLEMAN'S AGREEMENT, IMMIGRATION ACT OF 1917, IMMIGRATION ACT OF 1924, IMMIGRATION ACT OF 1965, IMMIGRATION AND NATURALIZATION ACT OF 1952; and IMMIGRATION REFORM AND CONTROL ACT.

INDENTURED SERVITUDE

The system of indentured servitude was introduced into colonial America in 1610 by the Virginia Company as a means of financing the transportation of workers from England to the colony. In exchange for passage and for maintenance during their period of service, workers indentured (bound) themselves to masters for fixed periods (typically, seven to fourteen years). The practice may be seen as a limited form of enslavement or, more benignly, as an extension of the traditional apprentice system. Between 200,000 and 300,000 British immigrants came to North America as indentured servants, accounting for one-half to two-thirds of early European immigration.

Indentured servitude was all but dead as an institution by the end of the eighteenth century, although isolated instances were reported as late as 1830.

Suggested Reading

Smith, Abbot Emerson. *Colonists in Bondage: White Servitude and Convict Labor in America, 1607–1776.* Baltimore: Clearfield Company, 2000.

INDIAN CHILD WELFARE ACT OF 1978

U.S. Code Title 25, Indians Chapter 21, is familiarly known as the Indian Child Welfare Act of 1978 and is intended "to protect the best interests of Indian children and to promote the stability and security of Indian tribes and families by the establishment of minimum Federal standards for the removal of Indian children from their families and the placement of such children in foster or adoptive homes which will reflect the unique values of Indian culture." (See Appendix A for major provisions and additional details of the Indian Child Welfare Act of 1978.)

Suggested Reading

Jones, B. J. *The Indian Child Welfare Act Handbook: A Legal Guide to the Custody and Adoption of Native American Children.* Washington, D.C.: Section of Family Law, American Bar Association, 1978.

INDIAN CITIZENSHIP ACT

Enacted in 1924, the Indian Citizenship Act is formally known as "An Act to Authorize the Secretary of the Interior to Issue Certificates of Citizenship to Indians." The act unilaterally declared all NATIVE AMERICANS to be citizens of the United States. (See Appendix A for the enactment clause of the Indian Citizenship Act. See also DAWES SEVERALTY ACT.)

Suggested Reading

Hoxie, Frederick E. *A Final Promise: The Campaign to Assimilate the Indians, 1880–1920.* Lincoln: University of Nebraska Press, 1984.

McDonnell, Janet. *The Dispossession of the American Indian.* Bloomington: Indiana University Press, 1991.

INDIAN CIVIL RIGHTS ACT

The Indian Civil Rights Act of 1968 (ICRA) prohibits Indian tribal governments from enacting or enforcing laws that violate certain individual rights. ICRA essentially recapitulates the U.S. Constitution's BILL OF RIGHTS, but because the Bill of Rights does not specifically apply to tribal governments, which are considered sovereign, Congress deemed desirable the adoption of ICRA.

In addition to recapitulating the Bill of Rights, ICRA reflects a limitation on legal penalties a tribe may adjudge. For conviction of any one offense there can be no punishment greater than imprisonment for one year and a fine of $5,000, or both. (More serious crimes are in the jurisdiction of federal courts, per the INDIAN COUNTRY CRIMES ACT.)

Suggested Reading

French, Laurence. *Indians and Criminal Justice.* New York: Rowman and Littlefield, 1982.

INDIAN COUNTRY CRIMES ACT

The Indian Country Crimes Act (also known as the General Crimes Act [18 USC 1152]) creates federal court jurisdiction for certain types of offenses committed by Indians against non-Indians and for all offenses committed by non-Indians against Indians. (See also INDIAN MAJOR CRIMES ACT.)

Suggested Reading

French, Laurence. *Indians and Criminal Justice.* New York: Rowman and Littlefield, 1982.

INDIAN FREEDOM OF RELIGION ACT

See AMERICAN INDIAN RELIGIOUS FREEDOM ACT OF 1978.

INDIAN MAJOR CRIMES ACT

The Indian Major Crimes Act is the most important of several acts that deal with jurisdiction in cases of "offenses committed within Indian country." The act specifies that major felonies are to be tried exclusively in federal court and not under tribal jurisdiction.

The INDIAN COUNTRY CRIMES ACT (also known as the General Crimes Act) creates federal court jurisdiction for certain types of offenses committed by Indians against non-Indians and for all offenses committed by non-Indians against Indians. A portion of the INDIAN CIVIL RIGHTS ACT (25 USC 1302[7]) limits the criminal jurisdiction of tribal courts to offenses that carry a maximum penalty of no more than one year imprisonment—that is, to misdemeanors. (See Appendix A for the major provisions of the Indian Major Crimes Act.)

Suggested Reading

French, Laurence. *Indians and Criminal Justice.* New York: Rowman and Littlefield, 1982.

INDIAN REMOVAL ACT OF 1830

The Indian Removal Act of 1830, officially titled "An Act to Provide for an Exchange of Lands with the Indians Residing in Any of the States or Territories, and for Their Removal West of the River Mississippi," was signed into law by President ANDREW JACKSON on May 28, 1830, and authorized the president to grant Indian tribes certain western lands in exchange for Indian lands within state borders, mainly in the Southeast, from which the tribes would then be permanently "removed."

Jackson was not the first to come up with such an idea. GEORGE WASHINGTON had spoken of creating the political equivalent of what he called a "Chinese Wall" to separate Indians and settlers, and Thomas Jefferson had concluded the Louisiana Purchase, in part, to acquire a western territory into which the Indians could be moved. JAMES MADISON had considered a scheme to exchange newly acquired western lands for the Indians' eastern holdings, and it was James Monroe's secretary of war, JOHN C. CALHOUN, who first proposed an act of Congress to mandate removal. Monroe's successor, John Quincy Adams, laid the groundwork for the removal legislation, which was enacted during the administration of his successor, Jackson.

As described in this law, the removal was to occur through a voluntary exchange of eastern lands for western ones. In practice, however, government officials unilaterally identified tribal "leaders" and secured their agreement, then declared the arrangement binding on all members of the tribe, regardless of whether a majority concurred. Once such an agreement was concluded, the government moved the Indians off the land, often by force.

Although some northern tribes were peacefully resettled on western lands (collectively referred to as Indian Territory, the lands centered on present-day Oklahoma and included parts of adjacent states), the so-called Five Civilized Tribes of the Southeast—the Cherokee, Chickasaw, Choctaw, Creek, and Seminole—resisted removal. During the 1830s some 100,000 members of these tribes were moved to Indian Territory by military force and about 25,000 died en route. The most infamous removal, known as the Trail of Tears, was that to which the Cherokee were subjected during 1838–1839.

Of all the tribes that were removed, none resisted more effectively than the Seminoles (and closely allied members of the Creek tribe) who lived in or near Florida. The Second Seminole War (1835–1842) was fought because of the Seminoles' refusal to leave their lands; and many Seminoles were, in fact, never removed from Florida. (See Appendix A for the major provisions of the Indian Removal Act of 1830.)

Suggested Reading

Axelrod, Alan. *Chronicle of the Indian Wars: From Colonial Times to Wounded Knee.* New York: Macmillan, 1993.

Prucha, Francis Paul. *Documents of United States Indian Policy.* 2d ed. Lincoln: University of Nebraska Press, 1990.

INDIAN REORGANIZATION ACT

Signed into law on June 18, 1934, the Indian Reorganization Act—or the Wheeler-Howard Indian Reorganization Act—reversed the attempt at assimilation promoted by the DAWES SEVERALTY ACT and fostered instead a return to tribal organization. Allotments under the Dawes legislation were stopped, and unsold "surplus" lands were returned to the tribes. In addition, the Indian Reorganization Act promoted tribal self-government by encouraging tribes to write constitutions and to assume the management of their own affairs. To aid in reorganization, the act created a loan program for tribal land purchases, for education, and for general assistance with the development of tribal government. The 1934 act remains the basis for federal policy and legislation concerning Indian affairs.

Suggested Reading

Hoxie, Frederick E. *A Final Promise: The Campaign to Assimilate the Indians, 1880–1920.* Lincoln: University of Nebraska Press, 1984.

McDonnell, Janet. *The Dispossession of the American Indian.* Bloomington: Indiana University Press, 1991.

INDIAN RESOURCE LAW CENTER

The Indian Resource Law Center, founded and directed by NATIVE AMERICANS, is "dedicated to protecting the right of indigenous peoples to live with dignity and respect according to the ways of their ancestors." The principal goal of the organization is the "survival of indigenous peoples, including protection of their land rights, environment, and right to self-determination." To assist in achieving this goal, the organization provides legal and technical support to indigenous communities and also works to reform national and international laws to recognize the human rights of indigenous peoples.

Suggested Reading

Pevar, Stephen L. *The Rights of Indians and Tribes: The Basic ACLU Guide to Indian Tribal Rights.* 2d ed. Carbondale: Southern Illinois University Press, 1992.

INDIAN SELF-DETERMINATION ACT

The Indian Self-Determination Act, which was passed in 1975, is designed primarily to grant tribes the right to administer federal assistance programs. That is, the act eliminated centralized control of such programs and placed it in the hands of the individual tribes. The complex legislation has been amended frequently. (See Appendix A for the rationale for the act and its major provisions.)

Suggested Reading

Castile, George Pierre. *To Show Heart: Native American Self-Determination and Federal Indian Policy, 1960–1975.* Tempe: University of Arizona Press, 1998.

INDIAN TRADE AND INTERCOURSE ACTS

Between 1790 and 1799 Congress passed four Trade and Intercourse Acts to regulate commerce with Indians and to preserve the Indians' possession of their lands. These acts provided for the appointment of Indian agents and for the licensing of federal traders who were authorized to barter with the Indians for furs and other goods. In 1802 a final Trade and Intercourse Act codified the four earlier ones.

The Indian Trade and Intercourse Acts, particularly sections five and eight of the 1793 act, were introduced in a number of twentieth-century lawsuits seeking recovery of tribal lands. For example, from 1795 through 1846 about twenty-five treaties were executed between the Oneida tribe and the state of New York, resulting in the purchase of approximately 270,000 acres of land from the Oneidas. The plaintiffs in recent litigation claim that because only two of the treaties had the participation of the federal government, the rest, made without federal authority, were violations of the Indian Trade and Intercourse Acts, and are therefore invalid. (See Appendix A for the text of the 1793 act.)

Suggested Reading

Kuklinski, Joan. *American Indian Land Claims: A Selected Bibliography.* Monticello, Ill.: Vance Bibliographies, 1982.

Shattuck, George C. *The Oneida Land Claims: A Legal History.* Syracuse: Syracuse University Press, 1991.

INDIAN WARS

As defined by the U.S. Army, the Indian Wars spanned twenty-five years from 1866 to 1891; however, warfare became endemic to the North American continent beginning in 1493 when a Spanish garrison of thirty-nine men, whom Christopher Columbus deposited on La Navidad (a small colony on the island of Hispaniola), were killed by Indians in retaliation for the garrison's depredations, including looting and rape. Within the territory of the present United States, major Indian wars since 1493 include

1599: Acoma Pueblo Revolt—against the Spanish in New Mexico.

1622–1644: Powhatan War—between the tribes of the Powhatan Confederacy and the English settlers of Virginia.

1636–1637: Pequot War—between the Pequots (and allied tribes) and the English settlers of the New England region.

1639–1664: Dutch-Indian Wars—between various tribes and the Dutch, chiefly in New York and New Jersey.

1675–1676: Indian War of 1675–1676—between Nanticokes and Susquehannocks and settlers in Maryland and Virginia.

1675–1676: King Philip's War—between Wampanoags (and allied tribes) and settlers of New England; in proportion to the population on both sides, the deadliest war in American history.

1688–1697: King William's War—between various New England tribes and New England settlers. The Abnaki War coincided with it, but was concentrated in extreme northern New England.

1680, 1688–1689, and 1692: Popé's Rebellion—an uprising against the Spanish in the Southwest. Popé, of the Tewa Pueblo, led a successful uprising then assumed dictatorial power. After his death in 1688 the Spanish began retaking the pueblos and completed their reconquest in 1692.

1695: First Pima Revolt—between the Pimas of lower Pimeria Alta (northern Mexico and southern Arizona) and the Spanish.

1702–1713: Queen Anne's War—between French-allied Indians and English colonists in the Canadian maritime region and in Florida, Maine, Massachusetts, and South Carolina.

1711–1713: Tuscarora War—between the Tuscaroras and settlers in North Carolina.

1712–1733: Fox Resistance—between the Fox Indians and French colonists (and their Indian allies) in the lower Mississippi River region.

1715–1716: Yamasee War—between Yamasees, Catawbas, and other tribes and settlers in Georgia and South Carolina.

1720–1724: Chickasaw Resistance—between the Chickasaws and French (and French Choctaw allies) in the lower Mississippi Valley.

1740–1748: King George's War—between English and French colonial interests and their Indian allies in Nova Scotia and northern New England.

1751: Second Pima Revolt—between the Pima and the Spanish in northern Mexico and southern Arizona.

1754–1763: French and Indian War—the North American phase of Europe's Seven Years' War; in America, fought between the British (with a few Indian allies) and the French (with many Indian allies). Numerous tribes were involved, and the conflict ranged from the East Coast to the Ohio Country and the upper Midwest.

1762: Cherokee Uprising—between the Cherokees and settlers in the Southeast, in which the Cherokees were forced to cede much of their land in Georgia and the Carolinas.

1763–1764: Pontiac's Rebellion—a coda to the French and Indian War, in which the Ottawa and allied tribes fought the English, principally in the Ohio Country and the upper Midwest.

1773–1774: Lord Dunmore's War—between Shawnees and settlers in Virginia.

1775–1783: American Revolution—as in the French and Indian War, Indians played a major role. Of the tribes that did not remain neutral, most were allied with the British against the Americans.

1786–1794: Little Turtle's War—between Shawnees, Miamis, and Ottawas and American settlers, militia, and regular army in the Ohio Country.

1812–1815: War of 1812—between the United States and Britain, which used many Indian allies (especially the Shawnee, who were led by Tecumseh). Combat involving Indians was mainly in the Old Northwest and the upper Midwest and in Alabama, the Carolinas, Florida, and Georgia. The war also spawned conflict between U.S. forces and the Red Stick Creeks in the South.

1816–1818: First Seminole War—between Seminoles and Red Stick Creeks and the U.S. army and militia, mainly in Florida.

1829–1832: Black Hawk War—between Sac and Fox and federal authorities in the upper Midwest, along the Mississippi River .

1830–1839: Indian Removal —violent clashes between the U.S. Army and tribes removed from the East and forcibly relocated to territory west of the Mississippi River.

1835–1842: Second Seminole War—between Seminoles (and Creeks) and federal authorities, who attempted to remove the tribe from Florida pursuant to the Indian Removal Act of 1830.

1850–1851: Mariposa War—between Miwoks and Yokuts and California gold miners.

1851–1852: Yuma and Mojave Uprising—a revolt against California authorities and the U.S. Army.

1853–1855: General conflict between the U.S. Army and the Utes and Jicarilla Apaches in New Mexico and Colorado.

1855–1856: Yakima War—between the Yakimas and the U.S. Army in the Northwest.

1855–1856: Rogue River War—between the Takelmas and Tutunis (tribes the whites collectively called "Rogues") and the U.S. Army, along the Oregon-California border.

1856–1857: General conflict between the Cheyennes (and Pawnees) and the U.S. Army, in the region of the Platte River.

1858–1859: Coeur d'Alene War—between the Coeur d'Alenes and the U.S. Army, in Washington State.

1860s: General warfare between the Navajos and the U.S. Army, militia, and settlers, in the Southwest.

1860: Paiute War (Pyramid Lake War)—violence between local militia and Paiutes, along the California Trail.

1860–1863: Apache Uprising—led by Mangas Coloradas, in the Southwest.

1861–1865: Civil War—battles in the far West sometimes involved Indians, who were usually allied with the Confederates; with the reduction of the U.S. Army presence in the Southwest, Indian raiding increased.

1862–1863: Santee Sioux Uprising—major and widespread uprising in Minnesota by the Santee Sioux against settlers in the region, with heavy loss of life.

1863: Shoshoni War—between the Shoshoni and the U.S. Army along the Bear River, mainly in Idaho.

1863–1864: Navajo War—resistance to confinement on reservations ignited warfare in the Southwest.

1864–1865: Cheyenne-Arapaho War—between the Sioux and Cheyenne and the U.S. Army and state forces, mainly in Colorado; triggered by the Sand Creek Massacre of November 28, 1864.

1866–1868: War for the Bozeman Trail—between the Teton Sioux and others and the U.S. Army, along the Bozeman Trail in Montana.

1866–1868: Snake War—pursuit, by the U.S. Army, of the Northern Paiutes of southeastern Oregon and southwestern Idaho.

1867: Hancock's Campaign—between the Cheyenne and Sioux and the U.S. Army in Indian Territory (Oklahoma) and Texas.

1868–1869: Sheridan's Campaign—between the U.S. Army and the Cheyenne, Comanche, Kiowa, and Oglala Sioux "hostiles."

1871–1877: Apache Wars—Series of running conflicts throughout the Southwest.

1872–1873: Modoc War—between a tiny California tribe and the U.S. Army in northern California.

1874: Red River War—between the Kiowas and the Comanches and the U.S. Army in Texas.

1875–1877: Sioux War for the Black Hills—between Sioux militants defending the sacred Black Hills and the U.S. Army.

1877: Pursuit of the Nez Perces—a pursuit by the U.S. Army of Chief Joseph's band of resisters, in the Northwest.

1878: Bannock War—Running warfare between the Bannocks and the U.S. Army in southern Idaho.

1878–1879: Pursuit of the Northern Cheyenne—an army campaign to force the tribe's removal to Indian Territory.

1879: Sheepeater War—between renegade Shoshonis and Bannocks and the U.S. Army in Idaho.

1879: Ute War—a short, violent war in Colorado between the Utes and settlers and the U.S. Army that resulted from heavy-handed treatment of the Indians on a reservation.

1881–1884: Geronimo's Resistance—raids by the legendary warrior in Mexico and the Southwest; he repeatedly evaded capture.

1890: Ghost Dance Uprising and Wounded Knee—final efforts of organized, militant Sioux resistance.

In 1891 the surrender of the Sioux Nation ended four hundred years of warfare in North America.

Suggested Reading

Axelrod, Alan. *Chronicle of the Indian Wars: From Colonial Times to Wounded Knee.* New York: Macmillan, 1993.

INDIVIDUALS WITH DISABILITIES EDUCATION ACT

In the mid-1970s Congress passed the Education for All Handicapped Children Act (P.L. 94B142). In 1990 the name of the act was changed to the Individuals with Disabilities Education Act (IDEA), and in 1997 the act was renewed and extensively amended. The purpose of the act is to provide full educational opportunity for everyone, regardless of disability. (See Appendix A for the rationale for the act, in its 1997 version, which is embodied in the text of the law.)

Suggested Reading

Office of Special Education and Rehabilitative Services, www.ed.gov/offices/OSERS/Policy/IDEA/the_law.html.

INDUSTRIAL WORKERS OF THE WORLD

The Industrial Workers of the World (IWW)—later nicknamed "the Wobblies"—was founded in Chicago in 1905 by representatives of forty-three groups that were opposed to the more mainstream labor movements, especially the AMERICAN FEDERATION OF LABOR, which restricted union membership to skilled workers (excluding unskilled, "industrial" labor) and, the IWW believed, "compromised" with capitalism.

Chief among the IWW founders were William D. "Big Bill" Haywood (Western Federation of Miners), Daniel De Leon (Socialist Labor Party), and EUGENE V. DEBS (Socialist Party). A radical organization from the beginning, the IWW splintered into two factions in 1908: one favored political action to further the cause of industrial labor, and the other rejected politics in favor of action—primarily strikes, boycotts, and even sabotage. It was this militant faction, led by Haywood, that came to dominate the IWW, transforming it from a labor movement into what was essentially a Marxist revolutionary organization whose goal was to overthrow capitalism and bring the means of production into the hands of the workers.

In its most radical form the IWW was associated in the public mind with anarchy, terrorism, and communism. Law enforcement targeted the group and its members, and violent confrontations with police as well as private security forces were frequent. Most notorious was the arrest, trial, and execution of IWW activist JOE HILL, in 1915, on a highly questionable murder charge. Hill became an IWW icon—a martyr to the cause of labor under the heel of capital.

In keeping with its radical political stance, the IWW opposed U.S. entry into World War I, which gave the government ample opportunity to pursue and prosecute IWW members under the wartime ESPIONAGE ACT, especially after IWW actions were directed at halting the mining of copper, a vital wartime commodity.

In the antiradical, anti-red climate of the postwar years, the IWW was subject to continuous persecution and eventually succumbed to the government's war of attrition. As a labor organization the IWW never became a great force, although its influence among workers in the mining and lumber industries of the Pacific Northwest was significant for a time. By the mid-1920s the IWW was a ghost of itself, although it continued—and continues—to exist.

Suggested Reading

Bird, Stewart, Dan Georgakas, and Deborah Shaffer. *Solidarity Forever: An Oral History of the IWW.* Chicago: Lake View Press, 1985.

INSULAR CASES

As a result of the Spanish-American War, the United States acquired Atlantic and Pacific possessions, including Puerto Rico and the Philippines. When Congress enacted tariffs on goods entering the mainland United States from the new U.S. territories, a number of lawsuits were brought, arguing that the tariffs were unconstitutional and that the new territories were entitled to the same constitutional guarantees that applied to citizens of the United States. In a series of closely related decisions—*Downes v. Bidwell* (1901), *Dorr v. United States* (1904), and *Balzac v. Porto Rico* (1922), collectively called the Insular Cases—the SUPREME COURT held that the "Constitution does not follow the flag"; that is, Congress has the power to exert direct control over any U.S. possessions or colonies.

The Insular Cases marked a turning point in American expansionism. In the past such expansion had always occurred under the assumption that, in the course of time, the acquired territories would become states, and the territories were therefore accorded many of the rights of states from the time of acquisition. The territories acquired as a result of the Spanish-American War, however, were perceived as too different from the mainland United States—in terms of race, religion, language, and customs—ever to be considered candidates for statehood, and were thus excluded by U.S. statute and policy from enjoyment of full constitutional rights. The populations of Puerto Rico and the Philippines were regarded by the federal government in much the same way as American Indians—as aboriginal peoples entitled to whatever rights Congress chose to grant and respect.

Suggested Reading

Kerr, Edward. *The Insular Cases: The Role of the Judiciary in American Expansionism.* Port Washington, N.Y.: Kennikat Press, 1982.

INTEGRATION

See DESEGREGATION.

INTERAGENCY COUNCIL ON THE HOMELESS

The Interagency Council on the Homeless was created by Congress in 1987 as part of the Stewart B. McKinney Homeless Assistance Act. The council was reorganized in 1993, and its role was assumed by the Working Group of the White House Domestic Policy Council. The mission of the Interagency Council is to provide federal leadership for efforts to assist homeless families and individuals.

The council is chaired by the secretary of Housing and Urban Development and includes the heads of other federal departments such as agriculture, commerce, defense, education, energy, interior, justice, labor, and transportation, as well as the heads of independent agencies (the Corporation for National and Community Service, the Federal Emergency Management Agency, the General Services Administration, the Social Security Administration, and the Postal Service), and the head of the Office of Management and Budget.

The council plans and coordinates the federal government's actions and programs to assist homeless people; monitors and evaluates the assistance to homeless people provided by all levels of government and the private sector; ensures that technical assistance is available to help community and other organizations effectively assist homeless people; and disseminates information on federal resources available to assist the homeless population.

Suggested Reading

Interagency Council on the Homeless Fact Sheet, www.wmpenn.edu/PennWeb/LTP/organization/InterCouncil.html.

INTERNATIONAL LADIES GARMENT WORKERS UNION

The International Ladies Garment Workers Union (ILGWU), created in 1900 through the amalgamation of seven local garment workers' unions, was one of the first and most important organizations through which immigrants gained a social and political voice. The union's early years were marked by a strong association with radical politics (many members were Russian immigrants), which caused much dissension within union ranks. A management association, the National Association of Manufacturers, attempted to kill the ILGWU by introducing an open-shop movement, and by 1908 there was much discussion of merging with the United Garment Workers, an American Federation of Labor union of men's tailors. The prospect of submersion in a merger energized the ILGWU, which staged two highly effective mass strikes in 1909 and 1911, paralyzing New York City's garment district and forcing dress manufacturers to bargain with the union. Louis D. Brandeis hammered out a Protocol of Peace between the ILGWU and management that became a model of cooperation between labor and management. The arrangement was so effective that during the 1920s Communist attempts to gain control of the union were defeated.

Led by longtime president David Dubinsky, the ILGWU became one of the nation's most powerful unions, offering members a broad range of benefits. Moreover, a high degree of cooperation existed between the union and the manufacturers. However, beginning in 1968 and continuing well into the early 1990s, American clothing manufacturers relied increasingly on imports and on off-shore labor, and the ILGWU lost large numbers of members. In 1995 it merged with the Amalgamated Clothing and Textile Workers' Union to form the Union of Needletrades, Industrial and Textile Employees (UNITE).

Suggested Reading

Tyler, Gus. *Look for the Union Label: A History of the International Ladies' Garment Workers' Union*. Armonk, N.Y.: M. E. Sharpe, 1995.

ISLAM, NATION OF

Popularly known as the Black Muslims and also known as the American Muslim Mission, the Nation of Islam was founded by Wallace Fard Muhammad (also known as W. D. Fard or Wali Farad). He claimed to be an orthodox Muslim who had been born in Mecca and immigrated to the United States in 1930. In 1931 he founded a mosque in Detroit that attracted a following of black migrants from the southern United States. These followers regarded Fard as an incarnation of Allah, who had come to liberate what Fard called the "Lost-Found Nation of Islam in the West." Fard offered the hope of liberation from racial oppression and of ascent into dignity and self-sufficiency.

In 1934 Fard mysteriously disappeared, and leadership of the Black Muslim movement passed to Elijah Muhammad, who soon founded a second temple in Chicago which became his headquarters. It was not until the end of World War II, however, that the Nation of Islam began to grow substantially. Although he counseled strict nonviolence, Elijah

Muhammad's message became increasingly militant, and he preached not of the equality of blacks and whites but of the racial superiority of blacks—specifically, black men—who were, he said, destined by Allah to become the cultural and political leaders of the world. Muhammad portrayed Christianity as the religion of enslavement, foisted upon the black population by whites—who were nothing less than a race of devils, doomed soon to topple from the dominance they had so long enjoyed.

The Black Muslim leadership did not counsel its followers to wait patiently for the great black millennium to arrive. Instead, black men were urged to work toward the ultimate goal of black supremacy by laboring together in the present to uplift the race, especially those members who had fallen into lives of crime and drug addiction. The Nation of Islam established many programs to teach African and African American history and culture to instill racial and cultural pride.

The Black Muslim movement achieved its greatest prominence and influence—and, among whites, its greatest notoriety—during the 1960s when MALCOLM X emerged as Elijah Muhammad's chief spokesman. Within the Nation of Islam, however, Malcolm X became so popular that power struggles, jealousies, and internal turmoil arose. When he was suspended from the Black Muslims, Malcolm X founded a rival organization, the Muslim Mosque, Inc. Malcolm X was assassinated by Black Muslims in 1965.

During the late 1970s Elijah Muhammad's son Warith Deen (Wallace D.) Muhammad assumed leadership of the Nation of Islam and sought reconciliation with the white establishment, repudiating much prior doctrine. To sever the organization from its past, Muhammad renamed it the American Muslim Mission. When Muhammad dissolved the Nation of Islam in 1985 so that its members could simply enter the international orthodox Islamic community, a splinter group arose under the leadership of LOUIS FARRAKHAN, which attempted to revive the racially charged spirit and uncompromising doctrine of the original Nation of Islam. (See also GREAT MIGRATION.)

Suggested Reading

Banks, William H., Jr. *The Black Muslims.* New York: Chelsea House, 1996.

ISSEI

The term *issei,* which means first generation, refers to a Japanese immigrant, especially an immigrant to the United States. (See also NISEI.)

JACKSON, ANDREW (1767–1845)

A frontier military commander who became the seventh president of the United States, Andrew Jackson was seen in his day as the champion of the common man. This view has been moderated over the years, however, by historical analysis; in particular, Jackson's political reputation has suffered because of his association with the policy of "Indian removal," which was carried out high-handedly and often with great brutality.

Jackson was born in Waxhaws, on the border of South and North Carolina. His childhood was torn by the American Revolution and the British invasion of the Carolinas in 1789. His father had died before he was born, and his brothers, fighting in the Revolution, were captured at the Battle of Hanging Rock, on August 1, 1780 (one of them, Robert, died in captivity). Too young to join the militia or the Continental Army, Jackson served as a partisan and was captured, then severely wounded when an officer struck him with the flat of his sword after he refused to black the man's boots. In the meantime Jackson's mother, who had volunteered to nurse American prisoners of war confined in a prison hulk anchored in Charleston Harbor, died of prison fever, leaving the fourteen-year-old Jackson an orphan. After he had spent his modest inheritance Jackson studied law, gained admission to the North Carolina bar, then moved to Nashville, Tennessee, where in 1791 he became attorney general for the Southwest Territory and later circuit-riding solicitor in the area surrounding Nashville.

While serving the territory Jackson also took on private clients, many of whom were merchants who had suffered ruinous financial losses as a result of the extension of federal authority over the Tennessee territory. By representing these clients Jackson acquired a reputation as a foe of federal tyranny—a stance that made him highly popular in Tennessee.

In 1791 Jackson married Rachel Donelson Robards. She had been married earlier, but both she and Jackson believed that this union had been legally dissolved. When this proved not to be the case, the couple remarried, in 1794, but the implication of dishonor haunted Jackson's private and political life for many years, and led to an 1806 duel in which Jackson was wounded and his opponent slain.

Jackson served as a delegate to the Tennessee constitutional convention in 1796 and was elected to Congress when Tennessee was admitted to the union. He served from 1796 to 1797, when he was appointed to serve out the senatorial term of his political mentor, William Blount, who had been expelled from the Senate because he had been implicated in a British plan to seize Florida and Louisiana from Spain. Financial problems prompted Jackson's resignation from the Senate in 1798, and he returned to Tennessee to rebuild his fortune. He succeeded in doing so, but he became embroiled in scandal through his association with Aaron Burr and Burr's scheme to create an empire stretching from the Ohio River to Mexico.

Between the Burr scandal and the 1806 duel, Jackson's political career seemed doomed until Governor William Blount of Tennessee commissioned him a major general of volunteers in the War of 1812. In 1814 Jackson marched against the pro-British Red Stick Creek Indians, defeating them decisively at the Battle of Horseshoe Bend on March 27. Jackson forced upon all the Indians of the region a treaty that ceded to the government large tracts in Alabama and Georgia. After this success Jackson was appointed to command the defense of New Orleans—which he did with great brilliance, defeating the British on January 8, 1815. Although by this time the War of 1812 had been ended by the Treaty of Ghent (December 24, 1814), word of the treaty did not reach Jackson or the British commander before the battle. The effect of Jackson's victory was to make the war, which had been largely disastrous for the United States, seem like an American triumph. Jackson instantly became a national hero.

In 1817 Jackson led the nation's first war against the Seminole Indians, evicting them from their tribal homelands and pursuing them deep into Spanish Florida through the spring of 1818. While in Florida Jackson decided (without authorization) to seize the territory from Spain. On May 26,

1818, he took Spanish-held Pensacola, precipitating a diplomatic crisis that was resolved by the Adams-Oñis Treaty of 1819, by which Spain formally ceded Florida to the United States.

In 1821 Jackson resigned his army commission to become provisional territorial governor of Florida. The following year the Tennessee legislature nominated him for the presidency, then, in 1823, elected him to the U.S. Senate. In 1824 Jackson ran for president but was defeated by John Quincy Adams in a contest so close that its outcome had to be decided by the House of Representatives. When Jackson ran again in 1828 he won by a comfortable margin.

As president Jackson introduced an unprecedented degree of egalitarian democracy. Following Jackson's leadership, most states abandoned property ownership as a prerequisite for eligibility to vote. Jackson also introduced a policy of rotation in federal jobs, which, although intended to be equitable, gave rise to the infamous spoils system—blatant political patronage. Jackson vehemently opposed a program of internal improvements that had been sponsored by Speaker of the House Henry Clay and former president John Quincy Adams, who was then representing Massachusetts in the House. Jackson protested that the plan favored the wealthy. A firm believer in preserving the Union at all costs, Jackson was prepared to respond militarily to the Nullification Crisis of 1832.

Jackson also led opposition to the Second Bank of the United States. The bank's strategy was to stabilize the economy by tightening credit and recentering U.S. currency on gold and silver; tight credit, however, worked a great hardship on small merchants, farmers, and, indeed, the "common man" generally. When the bank's charter came up for renewal Jackson vetoed a recharter bill. In 1832, after he won election to a second term, Jackson issued an executive order withdrawing all federal deposits from the bank; the institution never recovered from this blow, and it dissolved altogether when its charter expired in 1836. Although Jackson's action made credit more plentiful, spurring western settlement, the economy became dangerously unstable—a condition that would endure throughout the entire nineteenth century.

In 1830 Jackson endorsed and enthusiastically enforced the Indian Removal Act, one of the many low points in the history of Indian relations—and, as executed, a brutal violation of the Indians' human rights. Jackson's presidency thus stands as a contradiction: he simultaneously empowered and economically imperiled the common people. He broadly expanded the application of democracy, but he is most closely associated with the trampling of the rights of the Indian minority.

The president's later years were plagued by ill health. After his second term as president he retired to the Hermitage, his beloved estate outside of Nashville. There he remained a powerful force in the Democratic party until his death in 1845. (See also Calhoun, John C.)

Suggested Reading

Schlesinger, Arthur Meier, Jr. *The Age of Jackson*.1945. Reprint, Boston: Little Brown, 1988.

JACKSON, JESSE LOUIS (1941–)

Born into a poor African American family in Greenville, South Carolina, Jesse Jackson earned a scholarship that sent him to the University of Illinois during 1959–1960, but he completed his undergraduate degree (in sociology) in 1964 at the Agricultural and Technical College of North Carolina, a mainly black institution. Jackson went on to postgraduate study at Chicago Theological Seminary and was ordained as a Baptist minister in 1968.

During his undergraduate years, Jackson became involved in the African American civil rights movement and participated in the Selma SNCC–SCLC demonstration. He was inspired by Martin Luther King Jr., who encouraged him to become active in the Southern Christian Leadership Conference (SCLC). In 1966, under the auspices of the SCLC, Jackson was instrumental in starting the Chicago branch of Operation Breadbasket, the economic aid operation of the SCLC. From 1967 to 1971 Jackson served as the national director of Operation Breadbasket, then left to found Chicago's Operation PUSH (People United to Save Humanity), an organization to promote black self-help and self-sufficiency. During the 1970s and 1980s Jackson emerged as one of the highest-profile leaders of the civil rights movement. In Chicago he led a voter registration program that helped elect the city's first black mayor, Harold Washington, in April 1983. From this point on Jackson was directly active in politics, both on a national and an international level. He offered himself as a presidential candidate, and he has enjoyed repeated success as an unofficial negotiator in several international crises.

In 1989 Jackson declared himself a resident of Washington, D.C., and the following year was elected to the office of "statehood senator," a position from which he lobbied Congress to obtain statehood for the District of Columbia, which does not send voting representatives to Congress. He continues to be active in the fields of civil rights and human rights and to be involved in advocacy for the poor.

Suggested Reading

Frady, Marshall. *Jesse Jackson: A Biography.* New York: Random House, 1996.

JACKSON, MAHALIA (1911–1972)

A performer whose talent and magnetism crossed racial lines, Mahalia Jackson was the foremost female American gospel music singer of her time.

Raised in a straitlaced religious family, she imbibed the traditions of gospel singing but also—secretly—listened to recordings of blues great Bessie Smith and opera immortal Enrico Caruso, whose diverse styles she incorporated into her own gospel singing. At age sixteen she joined Chicago's Greater Salem Baptist Church choir, where she earned local renown as a soloist. When she participated in a national tour of the choir during the 1930s she became known to a much wider audience, and in 1934 she began to record.

Although Jackson's performances were always flavored with the blues, she sang only religious music, performing not only in churches but on radio and on television; beginning in 1950 she sang annually in New York's Carnegie Hall. She brought the African American gospel tradition to a broad audience, including whites.

Beginning in 1955, Jackson became active in the civil rights movement, giving benefit concerts and lending her voice to the cause. Her popularity with whites was doubtless of great value in winning acceptance for the movement. In January 1961 Jackson sang at the inauguration of President John F. Kennedy. She was the first African American performer to participate in such an event.

Suggested Reading

Orgill, Roxane. *Mahalia: A Life in Gospel Music.* Cambridge, Mass.: Candlewick Press, 2002.

JAPANESE AMERICAN EVACUATION CLAIMS ACT

Passed by Congress on July 2, 1948, the Japanese American Evacuation Claims Act gave Japanese Americans who were interned during World War II until January 3, 1950, to file claims against the federal government for damages to or loss of real or personal property in consequence of their internment. Pursuant to such claims the federal government paid a total of $31 million to former internees—which, by best estimates, represented less than ten cents for every dollar lost (Japanese American National Museum, "Japanese American Incarceration Facts," www.janm.org/nrc/internfs.html). (See also Japanese internment.)

Suggested Reading

Irons, Peter H., ed. *Justice Delayed: The Record of the Japanese American Internment Cases.* Middletown: Wesleyan University Press, 1989.

Ng, Wendy L. *Japanese American Internment During World War II: A History and Reference Guide.* Westport, Conn.: Greenwood, 2002.

JAPANESE EXCLUSION LEAGUE

The Japanese Exclusion League, also called the Japanese and Korean Exclusion League, was founded in San Francisco in 1905 and was later reconstituted as the Asiatic Exclusion League. For the most part league members were affiliated with labor unions, which feared loss of employment to Japanese and other Asian immigrants. The league opposed not only immigration but also intermarriage. The founding of the league was part of a general anti-Asian movement in San Francisco, which led, ultimately, to the Gentleman's Agreement.

Suggested Reading

Daniels, Roger. *The Politics of Prejudice: The Anti-Japanese Movement in California and the Struggle for Japanese Exclusion.* Berkeley: University of California Press, 1978.

JAPANESE INTERNMENT

At the time of the attack on Pearl Harbor on December 7, 1941, some 120,000 people of immediate Japanese descent were resident in the United States. Of these about 80,000 had been born in this country and were citizens. Within four days of Pearl Harbor the Federal Bureau of Investigation (FBI) had arrested and detained 1,370 Japanese Americans as "dangerous enemy aliens," despite the fact that they were citizens. On December 22 came the first public call—from the Agriculture Committee of the Los Angeles Chamber of Commerce—to put Japanese Americans under federal control. For years Japanese Americans had been successfully farming in California, Oregon, and Washington, creating stiff competition for Anglo farmers. Although many Americans no doubt feared that Japanese Americans would align with their country of origin or ancestry and commit acts of sabotage, the war also provided a convenient excuse for bringing years of agricultural competition to an end.

On January 5, 1942, U.S. draft boards summarily classified all Japanese American selective service registrants as enemy aliens, and many Japanese Americans who were already serving were discharged or restricted to menial duties. On January 6 Leland Ford, who represented the district that encompassed Los Angeles, sent a telegram to Secretary of State Cordell Hull asking that all Japanese Americans be removed from the West Coast: "I do not believe that we could be any too strict in our consideration of the Japanese in the face of the treacherous way in which they do things" (Roger Daniels et al., eds., *Japanese Americans: From Relocation to Redress,* Salt Lake City: University of Utah Press, 1986, 24). Before the end of the month the California State Personnel Board voted to bar from civil service positions all "descendants of natives with whom the United States [is] at war." Although in principle this group included descendants of Germans and Italians, the ban was actually instituted only against Japanese Americans.

On January 29 U.S. Attorney General Francis Biddle established "prohibited zones"—areas forbidden to all enemy aliens. Accordingly, German and Italian as well as Japanese aliens were ordered to leave San Francisco waterfront areas. The next day California attorney general EARL WARREN—who in the 1950s would gain national prominence as the civil libertarian chief justice of the United States—issued an urgent statement calling for preemptive action to prevent a repetition of Pearl Harbor. Early the following month the U.S. Army designated twelve "restricted areas" within which enemy aliens were permitted to travel only to and from work (and even then, only if their jobs were located no more than five miles from their homes) and were subject to a curfew from 9 p.m. to 6 a.m.

The first mention of "removal" of enemy aliens came on February 6, 1942, from a Portland, Oregon, American Legion post; it was followed a week later by an appeal from the entire West Coast congressional delegation to President FRANKLIN D. ROOSEVELT asking that he order the removal of "all persons of Japanese lineage . . . aliens and citizens alike, from the strategic areas of California, Oregon and Washington" (Daniels, et al., 36). On February 16 the California Joint Immigration Committee urged that all Japanese Americans be removed from the Pacific Coast and other vital areas.

By February 19 the FBI held 2,192 Japanese Americans, and on that day President Roosevelt signed Executive Order 9066 authorizing the secretary of war to define military areas "from which any or all persons may be excluded as deemed necessary or desirable." As interpreted and executed by Secretary of War Henry Stimson and the man he put in charge of the operations, Lieutenant General John DeWitt, this meant that Japanese Americans—citizens and noncitizens alike—living within two hundred miles of the Pacific Coast were "evacuated."

In all, more than one hundred thousand people were moved to internment camps in Arizona, Arkansas, California, Colorado, Idaho, Utah, and Wyoming. Although postwar comparisons of these facilities to Nazi concentration camps were unfounded—conditions were neither inhuman nor inhumane—the camps were spartan, and many internees suffered significant, and in some cases catastrophic, financial hardship and loss.

Another significant injury was to the Constitution and the BILL OF RIGHTS. Nevertheless, the only significant opposition to the removal came from Quaker activists and the AMERICAN CIVIL LIBERTIES UNION (ACLU). ACLU–backed suits brought before the Supreme Court—most notably, *Hirabayashi v. United States* (1943) and *Korematsu v. United States* (1944)—failed, however; the high court upheld the constitutionality of the executive order.

During their confinement some 1,200 young Japanese men secured release from the camps by enlisting in the U.S. Army, where they were segregated in the 442nd Regimental Combat Team, which also included about 10,000 Japanese-Hawaiian volunteers. (Japanese-Hawaiians had not been subject to the removal order.) The 442nd was sent to Europe and fought valiantly in Italy, France, and Germany, emerging from the war as the most highly decorated unit (for its size and length of service) in American military history.

On December 17, 1944, Maj. Gen. Henry C. Pratt issued Public Proclamation No. 21, which, effective January 2, 1945, permitted the "evacuees" to return to their homes. Many, with difficulty, took up their lives where they had left them, but many others were financially and emotionally devastated. In 1948 Congress passed the JAPANESE AMERICAN EVACUATION CLAIMS ACT, which paid out some $31 million in claims—a fraction of the actual financial losses incurred. All court cases seeking additional compensation failed until 1968, when a new congressional act reimbursed some internees who had lost property because of their relocation. Twenty years later, in 1988, Congress appropriated more funds to pay a lump sum of $20,000 to each of the sixty thousand surviving Japanese American internees.

Suggested Reading

Irons, Peter H., ed. *Justice Delayed: The Record of the Japanese American Internment Cases.* Middletown: Wesleyan University Press, 1989.

Ng, Wendy L. *Japanese American Internment During World War II: A History and Reference Guide.* Westport, Conn.: Greenwood, 2002.

JEFFERSON, THOMAS (1743–1826)

Thomas Jefferson was an astounding "man of many parts"—a brilliant lawyer, legal reformer, champion of freedom of religion, architect, inventor, farmer, naturalist, author, violinist, educator, and, of course, a politician and statesman. He wrote the first draft of the DECLARATION OF INDEPENDENCE, served in the cabinet of GEORGE WASHINGTON as the first secretary of state (1789–1794), and under John Adams was the nation's second vice president (1797–1801). Although he and Adams were friends, they drifted far apart in their politics: Adams became a conservative Federalist, and Jefferson created the liberal Democratic-Republican Party. While serving as vice president, Jefferson opposed the ALIEN AND SEDITION ACTS (which the Adams administration had sponsored) by writing with JAMES MADISON the *Virginia and Kentucky Resolutions* (1798–1799).

From 1801 to 1809 Thomas Jefferson was the third president of the United States. During his presidency he made the Louisiana Purchase, successfully fought piracy off the Barbary Coast, oversaw the dismantling of the most pernicious of the ALIEN AND SEDITION ACTS, and countered Federalism by promoting individual freedom as the core value of the new American democracy.

Jefferson was born in rural Albemarle County, Virginia, to a prosperous—although by no means wealthy—planter. His Piedmont background always prompted him to identify with the frontier—"the West"—more closely than with the Tidewater establishment of political conservatism and privilege. His commitment to the Piedmont was evident in his early decision to design and build a noble house atop a mountain. Monticello, a lifelong labor of love, not only became one of the most beautiful buildings of late-eighteenth-century America but symbolically embodied Jefferson's guiding ideals. An aesthetic expression of Enlightenment principles and the values of urbane civilization, it was nevertheless built on the edge of the wilderness, and its front door looked toward the West.

In 1768 Jefferson, having begun the practice of law, successfully stood as a candidate for Virginia's House of Burgesses and became a supporter of resolutions opposing Parliament's authority over the colonies. In 1772 he made a loving and socially advantageous marriage to Martha Wayles Skelton; two years later, he wrote his first important revolutionary political tract, *A Summary View of the Rights of British America,* in which he advanced the idea that the bonds that tied the American colonies to England were entirely voluntary. The document earned him national notice, and in 1775 the Virginia legislature sent him to Philadelphia as a delegate to the Second Continental Congress. Although he did not participate vigorously in debates, his genius as a writer was recognized, and he was tapped to compose the Declaration of Independence.

The document was intended to list grievances against King George III, to justify to the world a revolution, and, generally, to express (as Jefferson himself said) "the American mind." However, Jefferson stepped beyond his assignment in two ways. One—his condemnation of slavery—Congress edited out; the other it let stand: "We hold these truths to be self-evident; that all men are created equal; that they are endowed by their Creator with certain inalienable rights; that among these are life, liberty and the pursuit of happiness; that to secure these rights, governments are instituted among men, deriving their just powers from the consent of the governed." This brief passage of political philosophy may be taken as the cornerstone statement of the American ideal of democratic government.

In October 1776 Jefferson returned to Virginia to undertake the monumental task of reforming the state's archaic legal code to bring it into line with the principles of the Revolution. By ending the feudal traditions of primogeniture (exclusive inheritance by the oldest son) and entail (statutory limitation of inheritance), Jefferson made possible a broad redistribution of land. In the belief—held lifelong—that democracy required an educated citizenry, Jefferson proposed a plan of extensive public education. He also crafted a law that prohibited the establishment of any state-sanctioned religion and mandated the absolute separation of church and state. The reform of Virginia's body of laws foreshadowed the legal philosophy that Jefferson would attempt to implement on the national level.

In 1779 Jefferson was elected governor of Virginia—at that time, an office with frustratingly little authority. In 1780, unable to organize an adequate defense against British invasion, he was forced, somewhat ignominiously, to take flight to avoid capture.

Amid criticism for his leadership during the invasion of Virginia and following the death of his five-month-old daughter in 1781 and that of his wife the following year, Jefferson sank into depression and resolved to avoid politics. However, later in 1782, he could not resist the call to serve again as a delegate to the Continental Congress. There he championed the rights of the western territories, successfully arguing that, as their population and other conditions warranted, they should be admitted to the Union on an equal footing with the original thirteen states.

In 1784 Jefferson was sent to Paris to replace the aging Benjamin Franklin as American minister to France. Jefferson spent five years abroad—trying, mostly in vain, to conclude trade and commerce treaties with the nations of Europe. Nevertheless, Jefferson's years in Europe increased his sophistication—and, for better or worse, his intimacy with the developing events of the French Revolution committed him more thoroughly to radical democracy. (Some scholars have argued that it was at this time that Jefferson had a sexual liaison with Sally Hemings, one of his slaves. Although recent studies based on DNA evidence strongly suggest that Jefferson did have children by one or more of his slaves, the evidence regarding Hemings is by no means conclusive.)

Jefferson returned to the United States in 1789 to serve as the first secretary of state under President George Washington. As one of the Founders of the new Republic, Jefferson was concerned that the new Constitution (which had been written while he was in France) lacked a bill of rights. He wanted to ensure that the Constitution strictly defined those areas of conduct and law over which the federal government had jurisdiction, and that it explicitly left everything else to the states and to the people. Accordingly, he supported James Madison in the drafting of the Bill of Rights.

As secretary of state Jefferson bore the responsibility of advising on foreign relations, but his partisan attitude toward France came sharply into conflict with the absolute neutrality advocated by President Washington, Secretary of the Treasury Alexander Hamilton, and Vice President John Adams. Indeed, Jefferson found himself increasingly at odds with the president and his cabinet. Jefferson saw Federalism, with its emphasis on a powerful central government, as undermining the principles for which the American Revolution had been fought, and with James Madison he began, behind the scenes, to create an opposition party, the Democratic-Republicans.

In 1796 Jefferson ran for the presidency against Adams. He lost narrowly—and by the rules of the Constitution at that time he became (after much congressional wrangling) vice president. While in this office he eloquently opposed the Alien and Sedition Acts. In 1800 he ran against Adams again, this time defeating him by an ample margin. Perhaps surprisingly, Jefferson entered office on a conciliatory note, but he soon began a vigorous drive to transform the government by sweeping away as many Federalist officeholders as possible. His goal was to decentralize government and entrust the bulk of authority to "the people."

Whatever else Jefferson achieved as president, the greatest single accomplishment of his administration was the Louisiana Purchase, which added a vast territory to the nation, gave it a claim to truly continental status, and removed threats and encroachments from Spanish, French, and British interests in North America. Unfortunately, the Louisiana Purchase was also the high-water mark of Jefferson's two terms. Despite his vaunted advocacy of a free press, he countered criticism of his policies not with reasoned argument but by vigorously prosecuting some journalists for libel. Worse, the Embargo Act of 1807, which Jefferson intended as an alternative to warring with England and France, closed American ports to all foreign imports and American exports, crippling the American economy.

Jefferson left office in 1809, exhausted and generally disappointed by his second term. His years of retirement, however, were hardly years of idle leisure. He designed a second house for himself, and he completed work on Monticello. Most significantly, he designed the campus and principal buildings of the University of Virginia and served as its first rector, taking major responsibility for creating the institution's curriculum and hiring its faculty. Jefferson also reconciled with his longtime political adversary and erstwhile friend, John Adams, with whom he conducted an important and eloquent political and personal correspondence. Jefferson died on the fourth of July 1826.

Suggested Reading

Axelrod, Alan. *The Life and Work of Thomas Jefferson.* New York: Alpha, 2001.

Brown, David S. *Thomas Jefferson: A Biographical Companion.* Santa Barbara, Calif.: ABC-CLIO, 1998.

Malone, Dumas. *Jefferson and His Time.* 6 vols. Boston: Little, Brown, 1948–1981.

JEHOVAH'S WITNESSES, SUPREME COURT RULINGS CONCERNING

The Jehovah's Witnesses, a Christian sect, has been a party in a number of important Supreme Court decisions concerning free speech and religious liberties.

Chaplinsky v. New Hampshire (1940)

A Jehovah's Witness named Chaplinsky was preaching on a Rochester, New York, street corner. A citizen complained to local law enforcement, and a city marshal asked Chaplinsky to "slow down," meaning to moderate his presentation because he was creating a nuisance. Chaplinsky responded with outrage, calling the officer a "Goddamned racketeer" and a "damned fascist," among other things. Chaplinsky was arrested and convicted of violating a statute prohibiting addressing "any offensive, derisive or annoying word to any other person . . . or calling that person by any offensive or derisive name." The case was ultimately appealed to the Supreme Court on the grounds that the statute violated the First Amendment guarantee of free speech. The majority of the justices upheld the conviction, declaring that the "lewd and the obscene, the libelous, and . . . insulting or 'fighting' words . . . are no essential part of any exposition of ideas, and are of such slight social value as a step to truth that any benefit that may be derived from them is clearly outweighed by the social interest of order and morality."

Cantwell v. Connecticut (1940)

In *Cantwell v. Connecticut* (1940), the high court ruled that a statute requiring a license to solicit for religious purposes constituted a "prior restraint" that vested the state with excessive power in determining which groups must obtain a license. Pursuant to the decision, Jehovah's Witnesses were permitted to solicit membership and donations without a special license.

Minersville School District v. Gobitis (1940)

Objecting to a school's requirement that students salute the U.S. flag, Jehovah's witnesses argued that to do so was to treat the flag as a graven image—which, according to their interpretation of the Bible, was a sin. With a single dissenting vote, the Supreme Court ruled that the school district's interest in creating "national unity" was sufficient cause to allow the district to require that students salute the flag.

Cox v. New Hampshire (1941)

In *Cox v. New Hampshire* (1941) the Supreme Court unanimously upheld the convictions of Jehovah's Witnesses who had engaged in a public parade without a license.

Jones v. Opelika (1942)

In *Jones v. Opelika* (1942), which involved the sale of Jehovah's Witness literature, the Supreme Court upheld an Opelika, Florida, ordinance prohibiting the sale of literature without a license. The court noted that the ordinance did not apply to persons or groups observing a religious ritual, but only to individuals engaged in a commercial activity. The court held that even though the content of the product was religious, the Jehovah's Witnesses were engaged in such an activity.

Jones v. Opelika (1943)

In *Jones v. Opelika* (1943), the Supreme Court ruled that the practice of charging a flat fee for a license to distribute literature is unconstitutional because it restricts the freedom of the press to those who can afford to pay the licensing fee.

Murdock v. Pennsylvania (1943)

In *Murdock v. Pennsylvania* (1943), the Supreme Court ruled that a local ordinance requiring solicitors to purchase a license was an unconstitutional tax on the right of Jehovah's Witnesses to exercise their religion freely.

West Virginia State Board of Education v. Barnette (1943)

In *West Virginia State Board of Education v. Barnette* (1943), in an 8–1 decision, the Court ruled that a school district had violated the rights of students by forcing them to salute the American flag. As in *Minersville School District v. Gobitis* (1940), Jehovah's Witnesses had objected to the requirement as an affront to their religious beliefs. This decision ran counter to *Minersville School District v. Gobitis* (1940).

Prince v. Massachusetts (1944)

In *Prince v. Massachusetts* (1944), in a close decision (5–4), the Supreme Court upheld a Massachusetts statute regulating and restricting the sale of religious literature by children.

Watchtower Society v. Village of Stratton (2001)

In 1998 Jehovah's Witnesses were convicted of violating a Stratton, Ohio, requirement that door-to-door solicitors obtain a permit, and the Sixth Circuit Court upheld the ordinance. As of late 2002 a Supreme Court decision on *Watchtower Society v. Village of Stratton* (2001) was still pending.

Suggested Reading

Finkelman, Paul, and Melvin I. Urofsky. *Landmark Decisions of the U.S. Supreme Court.* Washington, D.C.: CQ Press, 2002.

Peters, Shawn Francis. *Judging Jehovah's Witnesses: Religious Persecution and the Dawn of the Rights Revolution.* Lawrence: University Press of Kansas, 2000.

JIM CROW LAWS

"Jim Crow" was the name of a song and dance, as well as a character, created in 1829 by Thomas "Daddy" Rice, one of the originators of the tradition of blackface minstrel shows. The phrase *Jim Crow* was thus associated with a belittling racial stereotype, and *Jim Crow laws* became the general term for state legislation, in effect roughly from the 1880s through the 1960s, intended to enforce racial segregation.

Although Jim Crow laws were most numerous and persistent in the South, they also existed on the books of many northern states and municipalities. Most of the laws barred miscegenation (marriage, cohabitation, or sexual intercourse across racial lines) and required business owners and public institutions to provide separate accommodations for black and white customers. In many cases white businesses that could not afford to provide separate facilities simply turned away black job applicants and refused to serve black patrons.

Examples of Alabama's Jim Crow laws include a statute barring hospitals from requiring white female nurses to work in wards or rooms in which black men are placed; a requirement that bus operators provide separate waiting rooms or spaces and separate ticket windows "for the white and colored races"; a requirement that railroad passenger cars be partitioned into white and black sections; a requirement that white and black restaurant patrons be separated by room or partition; and a prohibition against blacks and whites playing "together or in company with each other at any game of pool or billiards."

An Arizona statute held "null and void" any "marriage of a person of Caucasian blood with a Negro, Mongolian, Malay, or Hindu," and a Florida law prohibited "all marriages between a white person and a negro, or between a white person and a person of negro descent to the fourth generation inclusive." Florida law also barred cohabitation: "Any negro man and white woman, or any white man and negro woman, who are not married to each other, who shall habitually live in and occupy in the nighttime the same room shall each be punished by imprisonment not exceeding twelve (12) months, or by fine not exceeding five hundred ($500.00) dollars." As was typical of southern states, Florida's Jim Crow laws also mandated that "the schools for white children and the schools for negro children shall be conducted separately," that black and white juvenile delinquents be held in "separate buildings, not nearer than one-fourth mile to each other"; and that black and white patients be segregated in all mental hospitals.

In Georgia, "No colored barber shall serve as a barber [to] white women or girls," and the "officer in charge shall not bury, or allow to be buried, any colored persons upon ground set apart or used for the burial of white persons." Even amateur sport was regulated in Georgia: "It shall be unlawful for any amateur white baseball team to play baseball on any vacant lot or baseball diamond within two blocks of a playground devoted to the Negro race, and it shall be unlawful for any amateur colored baseball team to play baseball in any vacant lot or baseball diamond within two blocks of any playground devoted to the white race." Parks were similarly segregated: "It shall be unlawful for colored people to frequent any park owned or maintained by the city for the benefit, use and enjoyment of white persons . . . and unlawful for any white person to frequent any park owned or maintained by the city for the use and benefit of colored persons." (Statutes quoted in "Jim Crow Laws," www.nilevalley.net/history/jim_crow_laws.html.)

Suggested Reading

Chafe, William Henry et al., eds. *Remembering Jim Crow: African Americans Tell about Life in the Segregated South*. New York: New Press, 2001.

Woodward, C. Vann. *The Strange Career of Jim Crow*. 1965. Reprint, New York: Oxford University Press, 2001.

JOB CORPS

The Job Corps, the nation's principal residential employment and training program for at-risk young adults, was created in 1964 as part of LYNDON JOHNSON'S GREAT SOCIETY and is currently authorized by Title I-C of the Workforce Investment Act of 1998. Funded by Congress and administered by the U.S. DEPARTMENT OF LABOR, the Job Corps operates through a nationwide network of campuses, is open to at-risk women and men ages sixteen to twenty-four, and currently serves about seventy thousand young people annually.

The mission of the Job Corps is to draw eligible young adults into a career path that will enable them to acquire vocational skills. The Job Corps also assists with after-program placement. Targeted youth are socially or economically disadvantaged—typically, poor or unemployed, high school dropouts, or members of minority groups.

Suggested Reading

"Background on the Job Corps," http://jobcorps.doleta.gov/

JOB TRAINING PARTNERSHIP ACT

The Job Training Partnership Act (JTPA), which became effective on October 1, 1983, provides job-training services for economically disadvantaged adults and youth, dislocated workers, and others who face significant employment barriers. Under the JTPA state and local governments, in partnership with the private sector, take primary responsibility for developing, managing, and administering training programs.

Title I of the JTPA lays out the system of coordination among state and local governments and the business community; the principal elements of that system are State Job Training Coordinating Councils, Human Resource Investment Councils, Service Delivery Areas, and Private Industry Councils. Title II-A authorizes training and services for the economically disadvantaged and others who face significant employment barriers. Training is afforded through grants to states for local training and employment programs. Title II-B offers economically disadvantaged young people jobs and training during the summer, including basic and remedial education; work-experience programs; and support services, such as transportation. Title II-C provides year-round training and employment programs for youth.

Title III of the JTPA, the Economic Dislocation and Worker Adjustment Assistance Act, authorizes employment and training help for dislocated workers—those who have lost their jobs in mass layoffs or plant closings, and others who have been laid off and are unlikely to return to their jobs. Title III also encompasses the Worker Adjustment and Retraining Notification Act (WARN), which requires advance notice of plant closing or mass layoffs. Title IV authorizes federal programs for Native Americans, migrant and seasonal farmworkers, and veterans.

Suggested Reading

"Job Training Partnership Act," www.doleta.gov/archives/jtpa.asp.

JOHNSON, LYNDON B. (1908–1973)

The thirty-sixth president of the United States, Lyndon B. Johnson (LBJ) came to office in 1963 following the assassination of John F. Kennedy and was reelected in his own right in 1964. LBJ is most closely associated with the sweeping social welfare programs of the Great Society and with the passage of the momentous Civil Rights Act of 1964 and the Voting Rights Act of 1965. He was also the president who vastly expanded U.S. involvement in the Vietnam War, creating a tremendous economic burden that greatly compromised the Great Society programs.

Johnson was born in modest circumstances in southwestern Texas and was educated at Southwest Texas State Teachers College in San Marcos. At his first teaching job, at a predominantly Mexican American school in Cotulla, Texas, his social consciousness was awakened, and he developed an abiding concern for the needs of the underprivileged.

Johnson became involved in politics when he worked on the congressional campaign of Democrat Richard Kleberg in 1930 and subsequently served as his legislative assistant. In 1934 Johnson married Claudia Alta Taylor, "Lady Bird." During this time he began a friendship and working relationship with Sam Rayburn, who was then the chairman of the Committee on Interstate and Foreign Commerce and later became Democratic leader of the House of Representatives and Speaker of the House. During 1935–1937 LBJ directed the National Youth Administration in Texas, then won election to Congress, serving for most of the next twelve years, except for six months in the U.S. Navy during 1941–1942. Johnson was the first member of Congress to see active duty in World War II.

In 1948 Johnson won election to the Senate, where he served for twelve years, rising rapidly to become Democratic whip in 1951, minority leader in 1953, and majority leader in 1955. As a party leader he was famous—or infamous—for creating consensus, often by forcible methods. It was Johnson who secured Senate passage of the Civil Rights Act of 1957 and, in 1960, other important civil rights measures.

Chosen as John F. Kennedy's running mate, in 1960 LBJ became vice president and, after Kennedy was assassinated in Dallas on November 22, 1963, Johnson took the oath of office that afternoon.

In a manner that recalled Harry S. Truman's takeover after the sudden death of Franklin D. Roosevelt (FDR), Johnson handled the transition masterfully. Also masterful was Johnson's reference to Kennedy as a "martyr" in his efforts to achieve passage of the social legislation that Kennedy had introduced—most importantly the Civil Rights Act, signed into law on July 2, 1964.

Shortly before passage of the act Johnson had presented to the nation his domestic agenda for the Great Society, which eclipsed FDR's New Deal in scope and magnitude. Great Society measures included the War on Poverty and the establishment of the Job Corps and of the Head Start program for preschool children. In 1965 the LBJ–sponsored Voting Rights Act outlawed literacy tests and other discriminatory ploys to prevent African Americans from voting. The LBJ presidency also saw passage of Medicare and Medicaid and of a series of measures addressing education, housing, urban development, and immigration.

Johnson's commitment to defeating communism in Vietnam led to a continued escalation of that conflict until, by 1968, more than half a million U.S. troops were involved in the war. The cost in lives and treasure was staggering and failed utterly to defeat the communists. By the mid-1960s an antiwar movement was gathering strength, and in 1968 civil disturbances and riots—related to the war and to racial issues—shook the nation. Facing reelection to a second term in his own right, Johnson found himself opposed by two fellow Democrats, Robert Kennedy and Sen. Eugene McCarthy. Fearing that the Democratic Party would be torn apart and that his own candidacy would sabotage any effort to negotiate peace in Vietnam, LBJ announced, in a speech televised on March 31, 1968, that he had ordered reductions in the bombing of North Vietnam, that he was calling for peace talks, and that he would not accept his party's renomination.

A tumultuous and troubled Democratic National Convention nominated LBJ's vice president, Hubert H. Humphrey, in August 1968. He was defeated by Republican Richard Nixon, and Johnson retired to the LBJ Ranch near Johnson City, Texas. He wrote a volume of memoirs, *The Vantage Point: Perspectives of the Presidency, 1963–1969* (1971), and died of a heart attack in 1973. (See LITERACY TESTS FOR VOTING.)

Suggested Reading

Langston, Thomas. *Lyndon Baines Johnson*. American Presidents Reference Series. Washington, D.C.: CQ Press, 2002.

Unger, Irwin, and Debi Unger. *LBJ: A Life*. New York: Wiley, 1999.

JONES, MARY HARRIS ("MOTHER JONES," 1830–1930)

Born Mary Harris in Cork, Ireland, Mary Harris Jones immigrated to the United States with her husband, an iron molder. When he died in an 1867 epidemic in Memphis, Tennessee, Jones moved to Chicago only to lose everything she owned in the Great Chicago Fire of 1871. Prompted by the catastrophe to call on the Knights of Labor for aid, Jones received her introduction to the labor movement and became an activist. By 1890 she achieved national prominence as a fiery speaker and organizer, working primarily for the United Mine Workers. By then known as Mother Jones, she ended each talk by urging her audience: "Join the union, boys."

Jones was active in the movement to end child labor, and in 1898 she was a founding member of the radical Social Democratic Party and of the INDUSTRIAL WORKERS OF THE WORLD in 1905. Her 1925 *Autobiography of Mother Jones* was—and is—regarded as an inspirational handbook by labor organizers and advocates for the disadvantaged.

Suggested Reading

Gorn, Elliott J. *Mother Jones: The Most Dangerous Woman in America*. New York: Farrar, Straus, and Giroux, 2002.

JOURNEY OF RECONCILIATION

In 1947 the CONGRESS OF RACIAL EQUALITY (CORE) resolved to send eight white and eight black men on a two-week journey through Kentucky, North Carolina, Tennessee, and Virginia to test the SUPREME COURT ruling that had declared segregation in interstate travel unconstitutional. This program, organized by George Houser and BAYARD RUSTIN, was called the Journey of Reconciliation.

The Journey of Reconciliation began on April 9 and included, in addition to Houser and Rustin, Louis Adams, Dennis Banks, Joseph Felmet, Homer Jack, Andrew Johnson, Conrad Lynn, Wallace Nelson, James Peck, Worth Randle, Igal Roodenko, Eugene Stanley, William Worthy, and Nathan Wright. A number of these activists were arrested, often more than once, and in North Carolina Rustin and Johnson, both black, were convicted of having violated a JIM CROW bus statute and were sentenced to thirty days on a chain gang. The judge treated the two white men arrested, Roodenko and Felmet, even more harshly, sentencing them to ninety days at chain gang labor.

The Journey of Reconciliation was a prelude to the civil rights movement that by the mid-1950s had begun to mature, and it was the beginning of what became a long campaign of "direct action" by CORE. (See also FREEDOM RIDES.)

Suggested Reading

Anderson, Jervis. *Bayard Rustin: Troubles I've Seen*. New York: HarperCollins, 1997.

Haskins, James. *Bayard Ruskin: Behind the Scenes of the Civil Rights Movement*. New York: Hyperion, 1997.

Levine, Daniel. *Bayard Rustin and the Civil Rights Movement*. New Brunswick: Rutgers University Press, 1999.

KANSAS-NEBRASKA ACT

In the early 1800s the SLAVERY issue was so contentious that a series of tortured compromises were offered to avoid national disunity and even civil war. The MISSOURI COMPROMISE, hammered out in 1820, sought to limit the expansion of slavery geographically, and the COMPROMISE OF 1850 added the element of popular sovereignty, whereby the territories acquired as a result of the UNITED STATES–MEXICAN WAR would be permitted to vote themselves slave or free without federal intervention.

In 1854, when the territories of Nebraska and Kansas applied for statehood, Congress repealed the Compromise of 1850 and replaced it with the Kansas-Nebraska Act. The act applied popular sovereignty to Kansas and Nebraska but also extended it beyond those territories, thereby eliminating the geographical barrier to the expansion of slavery that had been created by the Missouri Compromise. In effect the federal government abandoned the objective of limiting the expansion of slavery in the territories.

Intended, as all the compromises were, to defuse tensions and stave off civil war, the Kansas-Nebraska Act had the opposite effect. There was no doubt that Nebraskans, who were predominantly free-soil northerners, would vote themselves a free territory and state. But Kansas, to the south of Nebraska, was up for grabs. On the eve of statehood, proslavery Missourians and antislavery Iowans streamed into the territory in often violent competition with one another to create a majority for the popular sovereignty vote. As more Missourians poured in, they soon outnumbered the Iowans and were able to elect a proslavery territorial legislature, which duly designated Kansas as slave territory. Once their goal was accomplished, many of the Missourians returned to their home state, while most of the Iowans remained, rendering Kansas a slave territory with an abolitionist majority. The cycle of arson, murder, and revenge between the slavery and free-soil factions became so commonplace that the nation took to calling the territory "Bleeding Kansas." When Kansas was finally admitted to the Union in 1861 its proslavery legislature had been largely replaced, and it entered as a free state but continued to be plagued by guerilla violence throughout the Civil War. (See also BROWN, JOHN, and the THREE-FIFTHS COMPROMISE.)

Suggested Reading

Goodrich, Thomas. *War to the Knife: Bleeding Kansas, 1854–1861*. Mechanicsburg, Pa.: Stackpole Books, 1998.

KELLER, HELEN (1880–1968)

Born in Tuscumbia, Alabama, Helen Adams Keller was stricken with a high fever (presumably scarlet fever) when she was nineteen months old, leaving her blind, deaf, and mute. Alexander Graham Bell, the inventor of the telephone and a prominent educator of the deaf, examined her when she was six and recommended that the family send her to Anne Sullivan, a member of the faculty at the Perkins Institution for the Blind, a Boston-based school run by Bell's son-in-law. This was the beginning of an extraordinary relationship that lasted from 1887 until Sullivan's death in 1936. Thanks to Sullivan, Keller, who proved highly intelligent, learned to feel objects and to associate them with words—which, using finger signals, Sullivan spelled out on Keller's palm. Later, Keller learned to read by feeling raised words on cardboard, and to construct her own sentences by arranging tactile words in a special frame. Sullivan's teaching was supplemented by instruction in braille at the Perkins Institution (1888–1890) and by speech lessons under Sarah Fuller of Boston's Horace Mann School for the Deaf. Eventually Keller was able to understand speech if she placed her fingers on the lips and throat of the speaker while the words were simultaneously spelled out on her palm.

At fourteen Keller enrolled in the Wright-Humason School for the Deaf in New York City; two years later she became a student at the Cambridge (Massachusetts) School for Young Ladies, and was admitted to Radcliffe College in 1900. Keller graduated cum laude in 1904.

Given the severity of her disabilities, Keller had acquired extraordinary skills, and she wanted to share her experience—not only to help and to inspire other disabled people but to demonstrate to the sighted and hearing world that her disabilities diminished neither her intellectual capacity nor her humanity. She began by contributing articles on blindness to the *Ladies' Home Journal* and other major national magazines. In 1902 she published an autobiography, *The Story of My Life*, which was followed by *Optimism* (1903), *The World I Live In* (1908), *My Religion* (1927), *Helen Keller's Journal* (1938), and *The Open Door* (1957). Although years of training had given her considerable power of speech, Keller still used an interpreter when speaking before hearing audiences, and, in this way, she became a celebrated lecturer. An activist on behalf of the AMERICAN FOUNDATION FOR THE BLIND, Keller also contributed a substantial endowment to that organization.

Keller's example, writings, and activism greatly improved the treatment of the deaf and the blind in the United States and elsewhere. Most important, people who were deaf or blind were removed from demoralizing and debilitating segregation in asylums. Keller's work also led, in many states, to the creation of official commissions for the blind.

As popular as Keller's articles and books were, it was *The Miracle Worker* (1959), William Gibson's Pulitzer Prize–winning dramatization of Keller's early work with Sullivan, that brought Keller's experience to its widest audience. In 1962 the play was brought to the screen as an Academy Award–winning motion picture.

Suggested Reading

Herrmann, Dorothy. *Helen Keller: A Life*. New York: Knopf, 1998.

Lash, Joseph P. *Helen and Teacher: The Story of Helen Keller and Anne Sullivan Macy*. New York: Perseus Press, 1997.

KENNEDY, JOHN FITZGERALD (1917–1963)

When he took the oath of office at age forty-three, John F. Kennedy (JFK) became the nation's youngest elected president. His assassination on November 22, 1963, during a visit to Dallas, Texas, also made him the youngest to die. Youth—and the determination, idealism, and optimism of youth—were very much at the center of the Kennedy presidency, which saw the beginning of a new commitment to minority rights. Indeed, although born into wealth and privilege, Kennedy entered office as the member of a minority: he was the nation's first Catholic president. Nevertheless, with respect to minority rights, the early promise of Kennedy's administration was not realized until the presidency of Kennedy's successor, LYNDON JOHNSON.

Although Kennedy inspired the nation with his wit, eloquence, and intelligence, as well as his ability to draw those around him toward noble aspirations, the Kennedy legacy is also a troubled one. The president was rarely able to create a working consensus with Congress, and, at the time of assassination, his social agenda had yet to get off the ground.

Kennedy was born in Brookline, Massachusetts, the son of a large Irish-American political family. He was educated at Harvard, graduated in 1940, and joined the navy during World War II, volunteering for hazardous duty as the skipper of a PT boat. On the night of August 2, 1943, a Japanese destroyer rammed PT-109, cutting it in two. Two of Kennedy's men were killed instantly by the collision, but the others managed to leap into the water. Kennedy rescued Patrick McMahon, who had been badly burned, by pulling him to a small island, clenching the strap of McMahon's life jacket between his teeth as he swam. Kennedy was awarded the Navy and Marine Corps Medal for his leadership and courage.

In 1946 Kennedy successfully ran for Congress on the Democratic ticket. He served three terms, was very popular, and advanced to the Senate in 1953. That same year he married Jacqueline Bouvier, whose beauty and intelligence would prove to be enormous political assets.

A college football injury had left Kennedy with cripplingly painful back problems that were aggravated by the PT-109 disaster. In 1955, while recovering from two major, life-threatening surgeries, he wrote the best-selling, Pulitzer Prize–winning *Profiles in Courage,* a collection of biographies of American political leaders who had risked everything in defense of their ideals.

Kennedy failed to win the Democratic nomination for vice president in 1956, but four years later decided to run for president. In 1960 he won the nomination on the first ballot, then went on to defeat RICHARD M. NIXON in an extremely close race. Nixon had been two-term vice president under the very popular DWIGHT D. EISENHOWER and had a reputation as an uncompromising cold warrior and anticommunist. Kennedy's relative youth and inexperience, in contrast, raised concerns among some voters, while others feared that a Roman Catholic would somehow tie the nation to the service of the Pope.

JFK's inaugural address set the tone of high idealism that he hoped would define his administration. "Ask not," he memorably proclaimed, "what your country can do for you—ask what you can do for your country." On the economic front, Kennedy introduced a number of initiatives that certainly helped to propel the nation into its longest sustained economic expansion since World War II. He stumbled badly in the conduct of the Bay of Pigs invasion of Castro's Cuba, but his subsequent management of the Cuban Missile Crisis was masterful. Not only was a nuclear Armageddon averted, but the Soviet Union, in agreeing to remove nuclear missiles from Cuba, was maneuvered into an important cold war defeat.

Kennedy's foreign policy was not exclusively concentrated on the cold war. He sponsored the Alliance for Progress, which extended economic and humanitarian assistance to the impoverished nations of Latin America, and he fostered the creation and development of the Peace Corps, a practical means of putting the idealism of America's young men and women to work in aid of the world's poorest peoples. At home JFK backed important and comprehensive initiatives against poverty, and, with some initial reluctance, his administration promoted the cause of civil rights. Congress resisted most of Kennedy's social agenda, however, and the president proved unable to break the logjam. Kennedy's assassination in Dallas—which Johnson referred to as a "martyrdom"—gave his successor the moral authority necessary to secure passage of the CIVIL RIGHTS ACT OF 1964 and the VOTING RIGHTS ACT OF 1965, as well as the programs of the GREAT SOCIETY.

Whatever the Kennedy administration's failures, it generally raised the tone of the American national agenda. If practical results were disappointing in the arena of civil rights, the administration did give the movement something of tremendous value: hope and an incentive to aspire. Measured strictly in terms of the legislation enacted during his administration, the Kennedy legacy in the area of minority rights is not impressive; however, he emerged as an icon of all that is best in the American character, and his memory was doubtless instrumental in propelling to passage the momentous legislation of the Johnson years.

Suggested Reading

Bernstein, Irving. *Promises Kept: John F. Kennedy's New Frontier.* New York: Oxford University Press, 1991.

Schlesinger, Arthur M., Jr. *A Thousand Days: John F. Kennedy in the White House.* New York: Random House, 1984.

KENNEDY, ROBERT F. (1925–1968)

Brother of JOHN F. KENNEDY, Robert F. Kennedy (RFK) served as attorney general in the Kennedy cabinet and was also his brother's most trusted adviser. In 1965 he became a U.S. senator and in 1968 began a campaign for the Democratic presidential nomination. He was assassinated after winning the California primary.

Robert Kennedy was born into a prominent Boston political family and, like his brother, studied at Harvard University. He interrupted his studies to serve—again, like JFK—in the navy during World War II, then completed his degree in 1948. He went on to the University of Virginia Law School, taking his degree in 1951. Although he managed JFK's successful run at the Senate, Robert Kennedy did not enter the public spotlight in his own right until 1953, when he served as assistant counsel to the Senate Permanent Subcommittee on Investigations, which was headed by Sen. JOSEPH R. MCCARTHY, R-Wisc. Resigning after less than a year, Kennedy returned the following year as counsel to the Democratic minority. He achieved even more prominence in 1957 when, as chief counsel to the Senate select committee conducting investigations into labor racketeering, he pressed Teamster's Union president James R. "Jimmy" Hoffa on the union's links to organized crime.

Kennedy stepped down from the select committee in 1960 to run JFK's presidential campaign. Appointed attorney general, he took charge of enforcing federal policy and SUPREME COURT rulings concerning the integration of public facilities, schools, and universities. It was RFK who dispatched four hundred U.S. marshals in May 1961 to protect MARTIN LUTHER KING JR. and his supporters in a march on Montgomery, Alabama. In most cases, however, Kennedy tried to avoid using federal forces and instead made persuasive long-distance telephone calls to southern governors, mayors, and law enforcement officials to work out strategies to avoid confrontation and violence. Some civil rights activists supported Kennedy's approach, while others believed that confrontation was necessary to achieve their ends and that RFK's "deals" with local authorities compromised civil rights actions. Segregationists universally criticized him for usurping state's rights.

Although RFK did not immediately resign as attorney general after JFK's assassination, he was no admirer of LYNDON JOHNSON, and he stepped down in September 1964. Deeply depressed for a time, he nevertheless won election in 1964 as U.S. senator from New York. In the Senate he became a leading liberal voice, effectively opposing Lyndon Johnson on the Vietnam War. In 1968 he began a campaign to capture the Democratic presidential nomination, and by June 4, after a victory in California, had won five out of six primaries. On June 5, just after midnight, he addressed supporters at Los Angeles's Ambassador Hotel. As he left, he cut through a kitchen hallway where he was shot by Sirhan Bishara Sirhan, a Palestinian immigrant, and died almost immediately.

Suggested Reading

Thomas, Evan. *Robert Kennedy: His Life.* New York: Simon and Schuster, 2000.

KING, MARTIN LUTHER, JR. (1929–1968)

Martin Luther King Jr. was born in Atlanta, Georgia, the son of a prominent African American Baptist minister who was himself the son of a minister. A gifted student, King entered Atlanta's Morehouse College at age fifteen and received a B.A. in 1948. He had intended to pursue a career in medicine or law but, shortly before he graduated, decided instead to enter the ministry. He earned a bachelor of divinity degree from Crozer Theological Seminary in 1951 and began reading about Mohandas Gandhi's philosophy of nonviolent protest. After graduating from Crozer, King enrolled in Boston University where he earned a doctorate in theology in 1955.

King became pastor of the Dexter Avenue Baptist Church in Montgomery, Alabama, and was serving in this capacity when, on December 1, 1955, Rosa Parks was arrested for violating Montgomery's Jim Crow laws by refusing to give up her bus seat to a white passenger. In response local black activists formed the Montgomery Improvement Association, chose King to lead the organization, and with his guidance organized the Montgomery Bus Boycott.

King's leadership of the boycott—in particular, his eloquence in explaining it not only to blacks but to white America—gave it an impact that reached far beyond Montgomery. Thanks in large part to King, the boycott essentially launched the African American civil rights movement. King, however, paid a price. His home was attacked and dynamited, and his family threatened. Relying on his faith in God, on his conviction of the rightness of his cause, and on Gandhi's nonviolent example, King endured. So did the boycott, which, in little more than a year, won the desegregation of the Montgomery city buses.

Determined to build upon the success of the Montgomery boycott, King organized the Southern Christian Leadership Conference (SCLC), which was intended as a base of operations and a forum from which he could deliver his message nationally. Under the auspices of the SCLC, King quickly became a nationally known figure, a sought-after lecturer, and, for most Americans, black and white alike, the primary spokesman for civil rights. In February 1959 he and other members of the SCLC traveled to India, where King discussed Gandhi's philosophy with Indian prime minister Jawaharlal Nehru—an experience that crystallized King's understanding of and commitment to the nonviolent approach.

In 1960, with his father, King was named copastor of Atlanta's Ebenezer Baptist Church. He continued to lead and participate in nonviolent protest and in October 1960 was arrested, along with thirty-three others, while protesting segregation at the lunch counter of an Atlanta department store. Although the charges in this case were dropped, King was sentenced to a term at the state prison farm on trumped-up traffic charges. By this time King had become a prominent national figure, and the sentence provoked widespread outrage. President Dwight D. Eisenhower declined to intercede, but presidential candidate John F. Kennedy did make a successful appeal—an act that gained him significant and much-needed black support in the election. Throughout the 1960s King's commitment to nonviolence earned him the ongoing gratitude and support of President Kennedy and his successor, Lyndon Johnson—and, for the most part, the allegiance of other black civil rights activists, at least until the rise of the Black Power movement later in the decade.

In 1963 in Birmingham, Alabama, King led a campaign to end segregation in hiring and at facilities such as lunch counters. The protestors were, as usual, nonviolent; however, the police reaction was brutal—and nationally televised—and King was jailed, along with many other protesters. When some of Birmingham's black clergy joined with some of the city's white clergy in denouncing King and the demonstrations, King issued his famous "Letter from Birmingham Jail," which eloquently explained and justified his methods and goals.

On August 28, 1963, in Washington, D.C., King addressed a crowd of more than 200,000 who had gathered in front of the Lincoln Memorial and delivered his "I Have a Dream" speech, which became the single most important statement of the entire civil rights era and undoubtedly helped to swell the tide that carried the Civil Rights Act of 1964 to passage. In December 1964 King was awarded the Nobel Peace Prize.

The Nobel prize was the high point of King's virtually unquestioned leadership of the civil rights movement. King's involvement in the Selma SNCC–SCLC demonstration in 1965 marked the beginning of a decline in his influence.

When the first Selma march was beaten back by local police and state troopers, King stepped in to lead a second in March 1965. However, he refused to confront a phalanx of state troopers directly. Before the procession reached the troopers, King asked the demonstrators to kneel in prayer. Then, instead of leading them onward, as they expected, he led them in retreat. In one very important sense, this demonstration was successful, in that it prompted passage of the Voting Rights Act of 1965 later that year while also avoiding bloodshed. Yet young activists accused King of having become overly cautious, and some even suggested that he had avoided confrontation because of a prearrangement with white officials. From roughly this point, a militant wing steadily gained influence within the civil rights movement, posing an increasingly serious challenge to the nonviolent approach. The summer of 1965 saw the Watts race riot in Los Angeles and marked the beginning of a succession of "long hot summers" in which racial violence became commonplace in American cities.

Partially in response to rising urban militancy, King took his message into the cities of the North. In 1966 he began a campaign against racial discrimination in Chicago, focusing especially on the highly explosive area of housing. Although King, working with a coalition that included black and white activists as well as labor organizations, succeeded in hammering out an agreement calling for an end to housing discrimination, little of practical or enduring value was achieved, and King and his methods were, once again, challenged by the younger activists.

On April 4, 1967, speaking at New York's Riverside Church, King announced his opposition to the Vietnam War—a stance that met with objections from blacks who felt that it diluted the focus on domestic civil rights, and that also weakened President Johnson's support for King. At this time King also attempted to broaden the struggle for black civil rights to encompass all people, especially poor people, regardless of race. Once again younger black activists objected. Nevertheless, King planned the Poor People's Campaign and the March on Washington, both of which were intended to be multiracial. He decided first, however, to lend his personal support to striking sanitation workers in Memphis, Tennessee. There, on April 4, 1968, he was assassinated by James Earle Ray.

Despite disappointments after 1965, Martin Luther King Jr. was the one leader who succeeding in transforming separate protest efforts into a unified national crusade—a crusade that not only forced changes in law, policy, and government but that spoke directly to the consciousness and conscience of both black and white America. With his genius for translating local issues into timeless concerns of universal morality, King elevated the struggle for black civil rights to a crusade for right and for humanity. (See also Birmingham SCLC protests.)

Suggested Reading

Archer, Jules. *They Had a Dream: The Civil Rights Struggle from Frederick Douglass to Marcus Garvey to Martin Luther King and Malcolm X.* New York: Viking Press, 1993.

Carson, Clayborne, ed. *The Autobiography of Martin Luther King, Jr.* New York: Warner Books, 2001.

Washington, James Melvin, ed. *A Testament of Hope: The Essential Writings and Speeches of Martin Luther King, Jr.* San Francisco: Harper San Francisco, 1991.

KING, RODNEY, CASE

On March 3, 1991, Los Angeles police stopped Rodney King, a black motorist, on a freeway. In the course of arresting him, four white officers beat King, kicking him and hitting him with their batons. Unknown to the officers, an onlooker with a home video camera recorded most of the event. The video—broadcast repeatedly on national television—provoked outrage at the brutality and apparent racism of the police.

In an April 1992 trial held in Simi Valley, California (defense attorneys had successfully argued for a change of venue out of Los Angeles), the four officers, who contended that King had menaced them and posed what they believed was a danger, were acquitted of assault, a decision that ignited in Los Angeles the worst riots in the United States since the New York Draft Riots during the Civil War. When the rioting was finally quelled on May 2, 1992, fifty-five people were dead, 2,383 were injured, and more than $1 billion in property had been lost. Daryl Gates, the controversial chief of the Los Angeles Police Department, was also forced to step down.

In August a federal grand jury indicted the officers on federal civil rights charges. Two of the four were subsequently found guilty of having violated King's civil rights.

For many Americans, black and white, the Rodney King case was a shocking revelation of the racial gulf that has endured despite years of demonstrated progress in the African American civil rights movement.

Suggested Reading

Jacobs, Ronald N. *Race, Media, and the Crisis of Civil Society: From Watts to Rodney King.* New York: Cambridge University Press, 2000.

KNOW-NOTHING PARTY

The Know-Nothing Party grew out of a secret society, founded in New York City, in 1849, that called itself the Star-Spangled Banner. The organization and the party it spawned were anti-Catholic and nativist, or anti-immigrant. The political party retained the trappings of a secret society: its members were cautioned to reply to all questions about the organization by replying, "I know nothing," and so the party acquired its familiar name. By the mid-1850s, however, its official (but little-used) name was the American Party.

The Know-Nothings called for sharp curbs on immigration, for the restriction of the vote to native-born citizens; for the exclusion of all foreign-born residents from public office; and for a drastic increase in the residency requirement for naturalization, from five to twenty-one years. During the early 1850s, when an influx of immigration seemed to many to threaten jobs and the American identity, the Know-Nothing Party enjoyed tremendous growth and succeeded in putting a number of state and local candidates into office. In a move that attracted conservatives who were unwilling to come out in support of either the proslavery Democrats or the antislavery Republicans, the party supported the Kansas-Nebraska Act of 1854. As of 1855, when the party was at its most successful, forty-three U.S. representatives were Know-Nothings. The following year, however, at the Know-Nothing convention in Philadelphia, the party was torn apart when southern delegates successfully championed a proslavery platform. Know-Nothing presidential candidate Millard Fillmore carried only a single state (Maryland), and only a dozen Know-Nothings remained in Congress. Almost immediately after the 1856 elections, the party effectively dissolved.

Suggested Reading

Mulkern, John R. *The Know-Nothing Party in Massachusetts: The Rise and Fall of a People's Party.* Boston: Northeastern University Press, 1990.

KOREAN EXCLUSION LEAGUE

See Asiatic Exclusion League and Japanese Exclusion League.

KU KLUX KLAN

Until the advent of the Aryan Nations, the Ku Klux Klan (KKK) was the best-known "secret" militant white supremacist organization in the United States. It is also anti-Catholic, anti-Jewish, and anti-immigrant. The origin of the name is uncertain, but it is believed that the "Ku Klux" is derived from the word *kyklos,* which is Greek for circle, and that "Klan" made for an appropriately alliterative addition.

The KKK was originally founded in Pulaski, Tennessee, as a secret society and social club whose members were Confederate veterans. Almost immediately, the KKK became a means of mounting resistance to Reconstruction. During the Reconstruction period, other white supremacist organizations were also formed on the model of the KKK (most notably the Knights of the White Camelia, which was founded in Louisiana in 1867); indeed, in many localities, such organizations constituted a kind of shadow government.

Although KKK apologists, consisting mainly of those nostalgic for the "Old South," claim that members were frequently called upon to defend their homes and those of their neighbors from marauding blacks and vengeful northern whites, most historians believe that while the KKK may indeed have played a defensive role, it was also dedicated, from the beginning, to restoring white supremacy in the South—and, toward that end, engaged in campaigns of violence and intimidation against former slaves.

In 1867, the KKK met in convention in Nashville, Tennessee, where it officially constituted itself as the Invisible Empire of the South. Its first leader, called the grand wizard, was probably the Confederate cavalry commander Nathan Bedford Forrest. Like many other secret societies of the day, the KKK rapidly evolved a complex hierarchy of offices—which extended, in this case, from the grand wizard to grand dragons, grand titans, and grand cyclopses. Again like the members of other secret societies, KKK members dressed in special clothing, although it is also likely that the robes, hoods, and sheets members wore were specifically intended both to terrorize uneducated (and typically superstitious) former slaves and to hide members' identities, enabling them to elude the military governments of the Reconstruction South.

By the late 1860s, with the goal of keeping the newly freed blacks "in their place," KKK "night riders" were staging raids throughout the South, whipping, beating, and lynching freedmen as well as any whites who supported them. Although the KKK was probably chiefly responsible for restoring white southern rule in Georgia, North Carolina, and Tennessee, by 1869 the organization's methods had become so brutal that Forrest himself ordered it dissolved. Once the central organization had ceased to exist, however, local "klavens" (branches) continued to operate independently, and the ongoing KKK activity led first to the Force Act, in 1870, and then to the Ku Klux Klan Act, in 1871—bills that authorized the president to suspend the writ of habeas corpus and to use federal forces to suppress and punish terrorist organizations. Although in 1882, in *United States v. Harris,* the Supreme Court declared the Ku Klux Act unconstitutional, the decision was by then largely moot. With the brokered election of Rutherford B. Hayes as president in 1876, Reconstruction came to an abrupt end throughout the South, and there was no longer any need for a secret organization to intimidate blacks.

The KKK remained dormant until 1915, when, inspired by Thomas Dixon's 1905 novel *The Clansman* and the 1915 film that drew upon it, D. W. Griffith's The Birth of a Nation, both of which mythologized the Reconstruction-era KKK, Colonel William J. Simmons revived the organization at a rally held at Stone Mountain, near Atlanta, Georgia. By the early 1920s, driven by a combination of post–World War I xenophobia and nativism, a belief in white supremacy, and nostalgia for the Old South, the KKK expanded rapidly, mostly in small-town Protestant America, especially in the South and Midwest. By the mid-twenties, KKK membership exceeded four million. It was at this time that the burning cross became a pervasive Klan symbol.

During the 1930s, with the onset of the Great Depression, KKK membership and influence declined once again, and became virtually nonexistent during World War II. It was the African American civil rights movement that prompted a revival of the KKK—almost exclusively in the South—during the 1960s. Once again, the organization became a vehicle for intimidating blacks as well as white activists from the North. Violence came in the form of domestic terrorism: beatings, shootings, bombings, and acts of arson. The KKK continues to exist today, albeit in fragmented, small, and typically surreptitious units, some of which are aligned and allied with the Aryan Nations and other far-right extremist groups.

Suggested Reading

Chalmers, David Mark. *Hooded Americanism: The History of the Ku Klux Klan.* 3d ed. Durham: Duke University Press, 1987.

LABOR RIGHTS

The U.S. Constitution guarantees labor only one right: to organize for the promotion of its collective self-interest. This guarantee is included in the First Amendment, which also guarantees the rights of FREE SPEECH and freedom of peaceable assembly. Subsequent federal legislation prohibits discrimination in employment on the basis of race, religion, national origin, gender, age, and disability. COLLECTIVE BARGAINING, the process in which representatives of workers and management negotiate to determine the conditions of employment, is principally governed by the National Labor Relations Act (NLRA) of 1935, with subsequent amendments. Although collective bargaining does not flow directly from the Constitution, the NLRA was enacted on the basis of Congress's power to regulate interstate commerce, as stipulated by Article I, Section 8. The NLRA created the National Labor Relations Board (NLRB), which makes decisions and sets regulations to supplement and define the provisions of the act. Various states also have laws governing collective bargaining, but where state and federal law overlap, federal law takes precedence.

In contrast to the constitutions of some nations, that of the United States neither guarantees the right to work nor defines work as an obligation. (Article 28 of the Japanese constitution, for example, stipulates that "All people shall have the right and the obligation of work.") From time to time, many legal philosophers—and a handful of politicians—have proposed adding the right to work to the list of American constitutional rights. (State "right to work" laws have nothing to do with guaranteeing employment; they merely bar or curb exclusive union bargaining arrangements, thereby ensuring that no worker is required to join a union as a condition of employment.)

(See also AFFIRMATIVE ACTION; AGE DISCRIMINATION; AGE DISCRIMINATION ACT OF 1975; AGE DISCRIMINATION IN EMPLOYMENT ACT OF 1967; AIDS; AMERICAN FEDERATION OF LABOR; AMERICANS WITH DISABILITIES ACT; BROTHERHOOD OF SLEEPING CAR PORTERS; CHINESE FOR AFFIRMATIVE ACTION; COCA-COLA COMPANY, CLASS ACTION SUIT AGAINST; COUNCIL OF FEDERATED ORGANIZATIONS; DEBS, EUGENE V.; DEPARTMENT OF LABOR, U.S.; DRUG TESTING; EQUAL EMPLOYMENT OPPORTUNITY COMMISSION, U.S.; EQUAL PAY ACT OF 1963; FAIR EMPLOYMENT PRACTICES COMMITTEE; FAIR LABOR STANDARDS ACT; FAMILY AND MEDICAL LEAVE ACT; FARM LABOR RIGHTS; GENDER BIAS AND DISCRIMINATION; GLASS CEILING COMMISSION; GOMPERS, SAMUEL; GRAY PANTHERS; HOSTILE WORK ENVIRONMENT; INDENTURED SERVITUDE; INDUSTRIAL WORKERS OF THE WORLD; INTERNATIONAL LADIES GARMENT WORKERS UNION; JOB TRAINING PARTNERSHIP ACT; MIGRANT LABOR; MIGRANT LEGAL ACTION PROGRAM; NATIONAL FARM WORKERS ASSOCIATION; OCCUPATIONAL SAFETY AND HEALTH ACT; OFFICE OF FEDERAL CONTRACT COMPLIANCE PROGRAM; TRIANGLE SHIRTWAIST FIRE.)

Suggested Reading

Fick, Barbara J. *The American Bar Association Guide to Workplace Law: Everything You Need to Know about Your Rights as an Employee or Employer.* New York: Times Books, 1997.

Lichtenstein, Nelson. *State of the Union: A Century of American Labor.* Princeton: Princeton University Press, 2002.

LA FOLLETTE, ROBERT M. (1855–1925)

Robert La Follette was the most vocal leader of the Progressive Movement of the late nineteenth and early twentieth centuries.

He was born in Primrose, Wisconsin, and graduated from the University of Wisconsin in 1879. In 1880 he was elected district attorney, and four years later he was elected to the first of three terms in the House of Representatives. Nominally a Republican, La Follette was in fact independent, a strong and often strident voice for reform.

Defeated in an 1890 bid for a fourth term in Congress, "Fighting Bob" returned to Madison, Wisconsin, to practice law, but reentered politics and was elected governor in 1900, serving until 1906. From the statehouse he successfully sponsored a sweeping program of popular reforms that became known collectively as "the Wisconsin idea." These reforms included campaign spending limits and direct primary elections, both of which were intended to empower the people by weakening the party establishment. La Follette also created state commissions on railroad regulation, transportation, the environment, taxes, and the civil service. Commission seats were filled largely by university-educated experts.

In 1906 La Follette was elected to the U.S. Senate, in which he served three terms. In 1909 he founded *La Follette's Weekly Magazine,* which was subsequently renamed the *Progressive* and is still published. In 1924 La Follette ran unsuccessfully for president on the Progressive Party ticket, capturing five million votes—almost one-sixth of the total cast.

Suggested Reading

Unger, Nancy C. *Fighting Bob La Follette: The Righteous Reformer.* Chapel Hill: University of North Carolina Press, 2000.

LAS CASAS, BARTOLOMÉ DE (1474–1566)

Bartolomé de Las Casas, a Spanish missionary in the Americas, was perhaps the earliest advocate of minority rights. He acted both as a historian of the Spanish experience in the New World and as a reformer, documenting the oppression of NATIVE AMERICANS by the conquistadors and other Europeans and issuing a plea for the abolition of Indian SLAVERY. His most important work is the *Historia de las Indias,* written and circulated in the 1500s but not printed until 1875.

Las Casas was the son of a minor merchant and may have served as a soldier in Grenada in 1497. After a Latin education in the academy of the cathedral in Seville, he embarked for Hispaniola in the West Indies in 1502 and participated in several expeditions. For his services to the crown he was granted an *encomienda*—a royal gift, which included land and the labor of the Indians who inhabited it. Las Casas soon began to serve as a lay missionary among "his" Indians and was ordained a priest in 1512 or 1513, almost certainly becoming the first person to receive holy orders in America.

In 1513 Las Casas participated in the brutal conquest of Cuba, earning another *encomienda.* On August 15, 1514, he preached a sermon in which he denounced slavery and announced that he was returning the Indians he had received as part of his *encomienda* to the governor. Las Casas subsequently decided that to effect real change in Spanish colonial policy toward the Indians he would have to take his case personally to the Spanish court. With the support of Francisco Jiménez de Cisneros, archbishop of Toledo, Las Casas drew up and promoted the *Plan para la reformación de las Indias.* On the strength of this document Las Casas was appointed priest-procurator of the Indies and given leadership of a commission to investigate the status of the Indians. In this official capacity he went back to America in November 1516, then returned to Spain the following year.

In Spain Las Casas described in detail the mistreatment of the Indians and presented a plan for their peaceful colonization. In December 1519 he managed to persuade King Charles I to permit the founding of "towns of free Indians," which were to foster a collaborative civilization where Spaniards and Indians lived as equals. (The colony of which these towns would be a part was to be located in present-day Venezuela.) Las Casas set off in December 1520 to start the project, but he was unable to recruit a sufficient number of farmers. Moreover, he was bitterly opposed by the *encomienderos* of Santo Domingo and by many Indians as well. The project was abandoned in January 1522.

Las Casas now became a priest in earnest, joining the Dominicans in 1523 and withdrawing into a quiet, pious life. In 1527 he began writing *Historia apologética,* which led to his major work, *Historia de las Indias.* This volume combined historical chronicle with a prediction of disaster for Spain as retribution for its unjust and brutal treatment of the Indians. While writing *Historia de las Indias,* Las Casas sent three letters (1531, 1534, and 1535) to the Council of the Indies in Madrid, accusing various individuals and institutions of oppressing the Indians. He generally condemned the *encomienda* system and called instead for the peaceful evangelization of the Indians. In 1542 Las Casas wrote *Brevísima relación de la destrucción de las Indias* ("A Brief Report on the Destruction of the Indians"), condemning the Spanish colonizers for sacrificing the Indians' lives and souls to their lust for gold.

Shortly after the circulation of *Brevísima relación,* Spain's King Charles enacted the *Leyes Nuevas* (New Laws), which ended the *encomienda* as a hereditary grant, mandating instead that the Indians on the land would be liberated upon the death of the original grantee. Las Casas was named bishop of Chiapas, in Guatemala, and in July 1544, with forty-four Dominicans, sailed for America to oversee the implementation of the *Leyes Nuevas.* Arriving in January 1545 he promulgated *Avisos y reglas para confesores de españoles* ("Admonitions and regulations for the confessors of Spaniards"), which forbade absolution to those who held Indians in *encomienda.*

Las Casas was so unrelenting in his administration of the New Laws that he was effectively driven out of office.

He returned to Spain in 1547 where he became influential in the royal court and continued working to secure just treatment for the Indians. Although he failed to bring Indian serfdom to an end, it is likely that his efforts did somewhat ameliorate the Indians' situation.

Suggested Reading

Las Casas, Bartolomé de. *Short Account of the Destruction of the West Indies.* 1552. Translated by Nigel Griffin, New York: Penguin, 1999.

Traboulay, David M. *Columbus and Las Casas: The Conquest and Christianization of America 1492–1566.* Lanham, Md.: University Press of America, 1994.

LEADERSHIP CONFERENCE ON CIVIL RIGHTS

The Leadership Conference on Civil Rights (LCCR) was founded in 1950 by A. Philip Randolph, founder of the Brotherhood of Sleeping Car Porters; Roy Wilkins, executive secretary of the National Association for the Advancement of Colored People; and Arnold Aronson, a leader of the National Jewish Community Relations Advisory Council. The organization was inspired by the early civil rights initiatives of the administration of Harry S. Truman.

The LCCR, which began by coordinating the efforts of thirty organizations, mostly civil rights and labor groups, currently consists of more than 185 national organizations, including civil liberties and rights groups, that represent people of color, women, children, labor, people with disabilities, older Americans, religious groups, and gay men and women—some fifty million Americans in all. The LCCR advocates census reform to ensure that all are counted; a strong "elementary and secondary education act" to ensure that no child is left behind; adequate funding for full enforcement of the nation's civil rights laws; the appointment of qualified and diverse federal judges; effective federal policy against hate crimes; affirmative action for women and minorities; workplace antidiscrimination policies for gay men and women; equity in the criminal justice system; a fair and just minimum wage; due process and civil rights protections in immigration laws; and the guarantee of religious freedom and accommodation for all Americans.

Suggested Reading

The Leadership Conference on Civil Rights, www.civilrights.org/lccr/.

LEAGUE OF NATIONS

Appended to the Treaty of Versailles (1919), which formally concluded World War I, was the Covenant of the League of Nations. The covenant created an international body of cooperation and adjudication founded on the principles of "collective security" (joint action by members against any aggressor), arbitration of international disputes, reduction of armaments, and open diplomacy. Although the league was an organization of nations, it was also concerned to protect the rights of minorities and, specifically, to prevent government persecution of minorities. Also subject to protection were the rights of smaller, weaker nations when threatened by larger, more powerful ones.

A noble experiment in principle, the League of Nations failed in practice, in large part because the U.S. Congress chose not to ratify the Treaty of Versailles and, therefore, not to join the league. Without U.S. influence, the league was weak. During the 1930s powerful aggressor nations—especially Germany, Italy, and Japan—simply ignored league sanctions and ultimately withdrew from the organization. The League of Nations failed to prevent World War II and, in fact, virtually dissolved during the conflict.

Despite the failure of the league it did inspire the creation of the United Nations (UN) in 1946. That organization was not only more powerful but had the full support of the United States; over the years the UN has directed a large proportion of its resources to protecting minorities and to supporting human rights generally.

Suggested Reading

Knock, Thomas J. *To End All Wars.* Princeton: Princeton University Press, 1995.

LEAGUE OF UNITED LATIN AMERICAN CITIZENS

With approximately 115,000 members throughout the United States and Puerto Rico, the League of United Latin American Citizens (LULAC) is the largest and oldest Hispanic organization in the nation. Its mission is to advance the economic condition, educational attainment, political influence, health, and civil rights of Hispanic Americans through community-based programs that operate at more than six hundred LULAC councils nationwide. These councils provide more than $500,000 in scholarships for Hispanic students each year. The organization also conducts citizenship and voter registration drives, develops low-income housing, conducts youth leadership training programs, and generally works to empower the Hispanic community at the local, state, and national levels. LULAC operates sixteen National Educational Service Centers, which provide counseling to more than 18,000 Hispanic students annually. SER—Jobs for Progress, LULAC's employment arm, provides job skills and literacy training to the Hispanic community through more than forty-eight employment training centers throughout the United States, and the LULAC Corporate Alliance, an advisory board of Fortune 500 companies, fosters partnerships between corporations and the Hispanic community.

LULAC was founded by three organizations: the Knights of America, Council Number 4 of the Order of the Sons of America, and the League of Latin American Citizens. At the invitation of the league the Knights and the Sons of America met at Harlingen, Texas, on August 14, 1927. The idea of merging into one large organization was discussed and debated, and after a long process the united organization was created on February 17, 1929, in Corpus Christi.

LULAC grew rapidly throughout Texas and by 1932 had spread into Arizona, California, Colorado, and New Mexico. Today it is established in forty-eight states, Puerto Rico, and Mexico. Under the auspices of LULAC various specialized organizations have been formed, including the American GI Forum, which addresses the rights of Hispanic veterans; the Mexican-American Legal Defense and Education Fund; and SER—Jobs for Progress, Inc. LULAC is an important lobbying presence in Washington, D.C.

Suggested Reading

The League of United Latin American Citizens, www.lulac.org.

LEGAL SERVICES FOR PRISONERS WITH CHILDREN

Legal Services for Prisoners with Children (LSPC) was founded in 1978 to challenge "the expansion of the prison industrial complex and the concomitant damage that this expansion has wrought on low income communities and communities of color generally, and on women and their children specifically." The organization focuses on legal and social policy issues affecting incarcerated mothers and their children, parents in prison, and family members and others who are caring for the children of incarcerated parents. By providing information, training, technical assistance, and litigation, the LSPC advocates for the civil rights and empowerment of incarcerated parents, their children, and their family members and of people at risk for incarceration.

Suggested Reading

Legal Services for Prisoners with Children, www.prisonerswithchildren.org.

"LETTER FROM BIRMINGHAM JAIL" (MARTIN LUTHER KING JR.)

During the Birmingham SCLC protests, Martin Luther King Jr. was jailed. On April 12, 1963, a group of eight Alabama clergymen, white and black, denounced the "series of demonstrations by some of our Negro citizens, directed and led in part by outsiders" as "unwise and untimely" ("Statement by Alabama Clergymen," April 12, 1963, at http://almaz.com/nobel/peace/MLK-jail.html). From jail King replied to the statement on April 16, 1963. What he wrote reveals his own conception of nonviolent protest; of his role in the civil rights movement; and of the moral, social, and political meaning of that movement. (The text of the "Letter from Birmingham Jail" may be accessed online at http://almaz.com/nobel/peace/MLK-jail.html.)

Suggested Reading

Carson, Clayborne, ed. *The Autobiography of Martin Luther King, Jr.* New York: Warner Books, 2001.

Washington, James Melvin, ed. *A Testament of Hope: The Essential Writings and Speeches of Martin Luther King, Jr.* San Francisco: Harper San Francisco, 1991.

LEWISBURG PRISON PROJECT

The Lewisburg Prison Project, Inc. (LPP), is an advocacy organization "dedicated to the principle that prisoners are persons with incontestable rights to justice and compassion." Through legal and other assistance, the LPP works to safeguard the constitutional and human rights of prisoners in central Pennsylvania.

Founded in 1973 by a group of Lewisburg citizens, the LPP counsels and assists prisoners in four federal institutions (Allenwood, Lewisburg, McKean, and Schuylkill), eleven Pennsylvania state prisons, and thirty-four county jails. LPP workers visit inmates and assist them by intervening with prison authorities, furnishing legal materials, and evaluating their cases for possible litigation. The LPP also distributes publications to inmates nationwide, including material on legal research, religious rights, the First Amendment, access to courts, administrative remedies, disciplinary hearings, racial and religious discrimination, assaults, and medical rights.

Suggested Reading

Lewisburg Prison Project, www.eg.bucknell.edu/~mligare/LPP.html.

LEWIS, JOHN (1940–)

A major civil rights activist, John Lewis served as chairman of the STUDENT NONVIOLENT COORDINATING COMMITTEE (SNCC) throughout the mid-1960s and has represented Georgia in the U.S. Congress since 1986.

Lewis was born to sharecroppers on February 21, 1940, outside of Troy, Alabama, grew up on the family's farm, and attended segregated public schools in Pike County, Alabama. He earned a B.A. in religion and philosophy from Fisk University and also graduated from the American Baptist Theological Seminary in Nashville, Tennessee (1957). While a student in Nashville, Lewis organized SIT-INS at the city's segregated lunch counters. In 1961 he became one of the original FREEDOM RIDERS—setting off, on May 4, 1961, to desegregate interstate transportation in the South by traveling from Washington, D.C., to New Orleans. At Rock Hill, South Carolina, Lewis was severely beaten by a white mob and, a few days later, in Montgomery, Alabama, was assaulted again. Photographs of the bloodied Lewis were widely published, bringing national attention to the Freedom Rides and to the violent injustice of segregation.

In 1963 Lewis was elected chairman of SNCC, which he had helped to form, and, at twenty-three was recognized as one of the "Big Six" leaders of the civil rights movement, taking his place alongside JAMES FARMER, MARTIN LUTHER KING JR., A. PHILLIP RANDOLPH, ROY WILKINS, and WHITNEY YOUNG. Lewis was one of the planners of the MARCH ON WASHINGTON in August 1963 and delivered one of the keynote addresses. The following year he coordinated SNCC efforts to organize voter registration drives and community action programs during Mississippi's FREEDOM SUMMER.

On March 7, 1965, with fellow activist Hosea Williams, Lewis led more than six hundred marchers across the Edmund Pettus Bridge in Selma, Alabama. When Alabama state troopers attacked the marchers, the result was the infamous "BLOODY SUNDAY"—which, along with the later march from Selma to Montgomery, led to passage of the VOTING RIGHTS ACT OF 1965.

After he left SNCC in 1966 Lewis remained active in the civil rights movement as associate director of the Field Foundation and through his participation in the Southern Regional Council's voter registration programs. As director of the Voter Education Project, Lewis was instrumental in adding nearly four million minority voters to the voting rolls. In 1977 President JIMMY CARTER appointed Lewis to direct the more than 250,000 volunteers of ACTION, the federal volunteer agency. He left that agency in 1980 to become the community affairs director of the National Consumer Co-op Bank in Atlanta and was elected to the Atlanta City Council the following year. He resigned from the council in 1986 to run for Congress and since then has represented Georgia's Fifth Congressional District, encompassing the entire city of Atlanta and parts of Fulton, DeKalb, and Clayton Counties. In the 107th Congress Lewis was a member of the House Committee on Ways and Means, where he served on the Subcommittee on Health and Subcommittee on Oversight. Since 1991 he has served as Chief Deputy Democratic Whip. (See also SELMA SNCC-SCLC DEMONSTRATION.)

Suggested Reading

Lewis, John, with Michael D'Orso. *Walking with the Wind: A Memoir of the Movement*. New York: Simon and Schuster, 1998.

LINCOLN, ABRAHAM (1809–1865)

The sixteenth and perhaps greatest president of the United States, Abraham Lincoln led the nation through the Civil War and selectively emancipated the slaves.

Born in humble circumstances near Hodgenville, Kentucky, on February 12, 1809, and indifferently educated as a child, Lincoln became an avid reader in his youth and gave himself a remarkable education. At nineteen, he moved with his family to Illinois, settling west of Decatur on the north bank of the Sangamon River. There he worked on a flatboat carrying cargo to New Orleans, where he witnessed his first slave auction. Although he did not become an outright abolitionist, Lincoln was personally repelled by what he saw.

Back in Illinois, Lincoln worked as a store clerk in the village of New Salem and soon built a local reputation as an athlete and as a young man with a future. With the aid of a local schoolmaster he continued his education. In 1832 he left home briefly to serve in the militia during the Black Hawk War, and when he returned to New Salem he sought election to the state legislature. Locally, he polled impressive numbers, but because he was unknown outside the village, he lost the election. Disappointed in politics, Lincoln, along with a partner, bought a store that quickly failed. He next found work as a surveyor, as postmaster, and as a doer of odd jobs. In 1834 he ran again for the Illinois House of Representatives and this time was elected. Lincoln was reelected in 1836, 1838, and 1840. During this period he also studied law, obtaining his license to practice in 1836.

In 1837 Lincoln moved to Springfield, the new state capital, and opened a law office. As his practice became increasingly successful he worked so diligently to pay off the debts that he had incurred when his store failed that he earned the nickname "Honest Abe"—along with a reputation that would serve him well in his subsequent political career. As part of his law practice Lincoln was a circuit rider covering some 12,000 square miles of the Eighth Judicial Circuit, an experience that introduced him to a large portion of Illinois.

Lincoln married Mary Todd on November 4, 1842 and in 1846 was elected to the U.S. Congress on the Whig ticket. Two years later, after failing to obtain the hoped-for patronage office of commissioner of the General Land Office, he returned to Springfield where he resumed his law practice and became one of the state's most sought-after attorneys.

In 1856 the Republican Party was created from a collection of smaller antislavery parties, and in 1858 Lincoln, running as a Republican, opposed the incumbent Stephen A. Douglas in the race for the U.S. Senate. Lincoln was never an abolitionist activist, but he did believe that SLAVERY was inherently unjust and opposed its extension, which Douglas had fostered through his advocacy of the KANSAS-NEBRASKA ACT. Lincoln thus became a moderate campaigner against slavery, opening his 1858 Senate run with the celebrated declaration, " 'A house divided against itself cannot stand.' I believe this government cannot endure permanently half slave and half free" (*Speech at the Republican State Convention, Springfield, Illinois,* June 16, 1858). Lincoln challenged Douglas to a series of seven debates in which Lincoln defined slavery as a moral issue but also offered a compromise: tolerate slavery where it existed, but bring about its ultimate extinction by preventing its spread. Although Douglas narrowly defeated Lincoln, the debates attracted national attention, and in 1860 Lincoln became the Republican candidate for the presidency. The splintering of the Democratic Party on the eve of the Civil War brought Lincoln a plurality in the general election.

When Lincoln took office, the southern states had already begun to secede from the Union. His firm purpose in fighting a civil war was not to free the slaves but to restore and preserve the Union—in the belief, he said, that a free and unified United States was "the last, best hope of earth" (*First Inaugural Address,* March 4, 1861). Lincoln took a very personal hand in directing the war, at times assuming nearly dictatorial powers—including, most notoriously, his decision to suspend HABEAS CORPUS. Yet Lincoln never comported himself as a tyrant. The force of his personality was revealed instead through a strength of character, an eloquence both passionate and compassionate, and a fierce courage and determination. Lincoln was highly effective at making the moral purpose of the war clear to all.

Nevertheless, Lincoln was no mere idealist. The EMANCIPATION PROCLAMATION, for example, was a bold compromise. Issued in preliminary form on September 22, 1862, and in final form on January 1, 1863, the document did not free all slaves but exempted from liberation those slaves in the border states (slave states still loyal to the Union) and in all Confederate territory already under the control of Union armies. Lincoln did not want to invite the SUPREME COURT to declare the proclamation an unconstitutional seizure of property, and he wanted even less to offend the border states (and perhaps prompt them to secede) or to provoke renewed rebellion in the occupied portions of the Confederacy.

Lincoln not only sustained the war effort but did so without losing sight of the humanity of the enemy and the fact that the Confederates were fellow Americans, albeit in rebellion. Reelected to a second term he delivered an inaugural address that called for "binding up the nation's wounds" and acting "with malice toward none and charity for all" (*Second Inaugural Address,* March 4, 1865). One of the most tragic and destructive aspects of Lincoln's assassination by John Wilkes Booth on April 14, 1865, is that the nation, especially the South, was deprived of Lincoln's healing hand and the promise of an equitable approach to postwar RECONSTRUCTION, which, doubtless, would have eased the lot of white and black southerners alike.

Suggested Reading

Fehrenbacher, Don E. *Abraham Lincoln: Speeches and Writings 1832–1858.* New York: Library of America, 1989.

Oates, Stephen B. *With Malice toward None: A Life of Abraham Lincoln.* New York: Harper Perennial, 1994.

Pinsker, Matthew. *Abraham Lincoln.* American Presidents Reference Series. Washington, D.C.: CQ Press, 2002.

LITERACY TESTS FOR VOTING

The passage of the Fifteenth Amendment in 1870 explicitly enfranchised blacks, but once RECONSTRUCTION ended in 1877 southern states and local jurisdictions employed various means to prevent blacks from voting. In 1890 Mississippi became the first state to require that prospective voters pass a literacy test, and other southern states soon followed suit. Since most former slaves were illiterate, the requirement effectively barred them from the polls; the GRANDFATHER CLAUSE, meanwhile, ensured that most illiterate whites retained the franchise. Over the years, as more blacks achieved literacy, states and individual jurisdictions managed to administer literacy tests in such a way as to ensure that blacks would still fail them. For example, neither the tests nor the scoring was standardized, but were subject instead to the whims of polling-place officials.

The CIVIL RIGHTS ACT OF 1964 required states to hold all potential voters to the same standards; to refrain from denying anyone the right to vote on the basis of trivial errors on an application card; to administer all literacy tests in writing; and to accept a sixth-grade education, in English, as functional literacy for all voters. The VOTING RIGHTS ACT OF 1965 addressed the use of literacy tests more stringently, summarily suspending, for five years, literacy tests and other similar preconditions to voting. The act also indefinitely suspended literacy tests in states in which less than 50 percent of the voting-age population had been registered or had voted in the 1964 election. Congress was empowered to authorize the Civil Service Commission to appoint federal voting examiners when requested to do so by a federal court, or when the U.S. attorney general reported that twenty or more residents of a given area had filed complaints regarding voting rights. Examiners were also automatically sent to areas that regularly used literacy tests or similar procedures, or where less than 50 percent of the voting-age population had voted in 1964.

The 1965 law was amplified in 1970 by voting-rights legislation that, among other things, banned outright the use of literacy tests in twenty states, including some northern states. In the North the issue was less one of discrimination against blacks than against citizens who either did not speak English or who spoke it marginally. Voting-rights legislation passed in 1975 explicitly provided for language assistance to minority voters, effectively barring states or local jurisdictions from preventing non-English-speaking citizens from voting.

Suggested Reading

Davidson, Chandler. *Controversies in Minority Voting: The Voting Rights Act in Perspective.* Washington, D.C.: Brookings Institution, 1992.

Davidson, Chandler, and Bernard Grofman. *Quiet Revolution in the South: The Impact of the Voting Rights Act, 1965–1990.* Princeton: Princeton University Press, 1994.

Lawson, Steven F. *Black Ballots: Voting Rights in the South, 1944–1969.* New York: Columbia University Press, 1976.

LITTLE ROCK SCHOOL CRISIS

During the 1950s many southern towns conducted active and organized resistance to federal attempts to abolish JIM CROW LAWS. By the mid-1950s, however, Little Rock, Arkansas, had proven itself moderately progressive by desegregating its public buses, libraries, and parks. Blacks were recruited for the police force, and some Little Rock neighborhoods had been successfully integrated. A plan for the gradual DESEGREGATION of the public schools had also been introduced, to commence with the enrollment of nine black students at Central High School in the fall of 1957. During the summer, however, opposition to the plan grew, and Arkansas governor ORVAL FAUBUS—up to this point a moderate on desegregation issues—announced that he disapproved of "any attempt to force acceptance of change to which the people are so overwhelmingly opposed" (Daisy Bates, *The Long Shadow of Little Rock: A Memoir.* New York: David McKay, 1962, p. 49). After this announcement the state senate voted a resolution declaring its opposition to the desegregation of the public schools. In response to the governor's statement and the senate resolution, Daisy Bates, the local leader of the NATIONAL ASSOCIATION FOR THE ADVANCEMENT OF COLORED PEOPLE (NAACP), enlisted the NAACP's aid to obtain a court order compelling the Little Rock Board of Education to abide by its promised plan.

On the first day of classes Elizabeth Eckford, one of the nine black students who had been enrolled, arrived at Central High and was met by a menacing white mob and by National Guardsmen who had been dispatched by Faubus. A guardsman barred Eckford's entry into the school, and the mob began shouting racial slurs and threats, including calls for LYNCHING. A lone sympathetic white woman, Grace Lorch, took Eckford in hand and whisked her to the safety of a city bus.

President DWIGHT D. EISENHOWER had earlier voiced his support for the SUPREME COURT's desegregation decision, *BROWN V. BOARD OF EDUCATION OF TOPEKA, KANSAS,* but he did not favor federal intervention in forcing desegregation on the South. Faubus's action in calling out the National Guard, however, together with the threat of mob violence, forced Eisenhower's hand. After meeting with Faubus on September 14, 1957, Eisenhower believed that he had secured the governor's promise to abide by the federal court order. Although Faubus did indeed withdraw the National Guard, he refused to dispatch state troopers to protect the nine black students, whom the press referred to as the Little Rock Nine. On September 25, after a white mob again menaced the students, Eisenhower put the Arkansas National Guard under federal command and dispatched a thousand regular army troops, of the 101st Airborne Division, to Little Rock. Throughout the remainder of the school year, regular army troops (in reduced numbers) remained in Little Rock, acting as escorts for the Little Rock Nine and providing protection during the school day.

On May 29, 1958, Ernest Green, the only senior among the nine, graduated from Central High. Supporters of civil rights—and of federal intervention in support of civil rights—celebrated Green's graduation as a triumph, but Little Rock responded by defiantly closing its schools in the fall of 1958. Throughout the South a number of school districts followed suit, provoking the Supreme Court and other federal courts to order the schools to reopen. In some school districts white parents were encouraged, by means of state and local subsidies for textbooks and other materials, to transfer their children to private academies (at the time exempt from the *Brown* decision). (See also "SEPARATE BUT EQUAL" DOCTRINE.)

Suggested Reading

Armor, David J. *Forced Justice: School Desegregation and the Law.* New York: Oxford University Press, 1995.

Counts, I. Wilmer, Will Campbell, Ernest Dumas, Will Counts, and Robert S. McCord. *A Life Is More Than a Moment: The Desegregation of Little Rock's Central High.* Bloomington: Indiana University Press, 1999.

Jacoway, Elizabeth, and C. Fred Williams, eds. *Understanding the Little Rock Crisis: An Exercise in Remembrance and Reconciliation.* Little Rock: University of Arkansas Press, 1999.

LOCAL 93 INTERNATIONAL ASSOCIATION OF FIREFIGHTERS AFL-CIO V. CLEVELAND

The SUPREME COURT decision in *Local 93 International Association of Firefighters AFL-CIO v. Cleveland* (1986) held that a federal court could enforce a voluntary agreement to give minorities preference in hiring and promotion. The high court ruled that under Title VII of the CIVIL RIGHTS ACT OF 1964, a voluntary public sector AFFIRMATIVE ACTION plan is valid when contained in a consent decree.

Suggested Reading

Curry, George E., and Cornel West, eds. *The Affirmative Action Debate.* New York: Perseus, 1996.

Jost, Kenneth. "Affirmative Action," *CQ Researcher,* September 21, 2001, 737–760.

LOS ANGELES RACE RIOT

On March 3, 1991, police officers stopped an African American motorist, RODNEY KING, for speeding. The officers reported that King menaced them. In the course of making an arrest, they beat King severely. A bystander with a home video camera recorded the beating, which was broadcast nationally. Four officers were subsequently tried—in accordance with a change of venue decree—by a predominantly white jury in Simi Valley outside of Los Angeles. On April 29, 1992, all four men were acquitted. Shortly after the verdict was announced a riot broke out, centered on the corner of Florence and Normandie Streets in South Central Los Angeles, a predominantly black neighborhood. The riot spread quickly through the night and into the next day, ultimately covering fifty square miles in South Central and triggering smaller disturbances in Atlanta, Pittsburgh, San Francisco, and Seattle. Police in Los Angeles were slow to respond, and President George H.W. Bush sent 4,500 U.S. Army troops to South Central. When the violence was finally quelled on May 2, 55 people were dead and 2,383 injured, and more than $1 billion in property had been lost. Some 17,000 arrests were made.

Most of the victims of the violence were African Americans, although Korean shopkeepers in the neighborhood were also targeted. As a result of the riots Daryl Gates, the controversial chief of the Los Angeles Police Department, was forced to step down. For many in the nation the violence—the worst riot in the United States since the New York City Draft Riots of the Civil War—revealed that racial tension and a sense of social injustice were still very much a part of American life.

Suggested Reading

Jacobs, Ronald N. *Race, Media, and the Crisis of Civil Society: From Watts to Rodney King.* New York: Cambridge University Press, 2000.

LOUIS, JOE (1914–1981)

Born Joseph Louis Barrow in Lafayette, Alabama, Joe Louis—the Brown Bomber—reigned as world heavyweight boxing champion from June 22, 1937 (when he knocked out James J. Braddock) until his temporary retirement on March 1, 1949. Louis was a magnificent boxer who held the title longer than anyone ever has and who successfully defended it twenty-five times—twenty-one by knockouts. He was the first black professional athlete since Jack Johnson (who had won the world heavyweight title in 1908) to achieve wide national fame among whites as well as blacks, and he was almost universally regarded in the black community as a source of racial pride and as proof that AFRICAN AMERICANS could perform on a par with (or better than) whites. Louis defeated a series of outstanding white fighters.

Louis began his boxing career in Detroit and in 1934 won both the Golden Gloves and the U.S. Amateur Athletic Union 175-pound championship. His first professional fight came on July 4 of that year, and he subsequently knocked out such greats as Max Baer, James J. Braddock, Primo Carnera (of Mussolini's Italy), Max Schmeling (of Hitler's Germany), Jack Sharkey, and Jersey Joe Walcott. Louis did not lose a professional fight until 1936, when he fell to Schmeling, whom he subsequently and spectacularly defeated in 1938 after taking the heavyweight crown from Braddock the year before.

In 1942 Louis was drafted into the U.S. Army. He returned to boxing after the war, retiring in 1949 as the undefeated champion. Louis returned to challenge Ezzard Charles on September 27, 1950, but lost a decision to him. On October 26, 1951, Rocky Marciano knocked Louis out in what proved to be Louis's last major fight. Louis fought seventy-one bouts in his professional career, winning all but three; fifty-four of his victories were by knockout.

Louis's later years were troubled. Like many fighters, he had been poorly and unethically managed and, as a result, suffered from financial difficulties, which were compounded in his case by federal income tax problems. He managed to use his celebrity to obtain employment as a greeter for the Caesar's Palace casino in Las Vegas.

Suggested Reading

Mead, Christopher. *Champion: Joe Louis, Black Hero in a White World.* New York: Scribner, 1985.

LOVING V. VIRGINIA

The 1967 SUPREME COURT decision in *Loving v. Virginia* ruled unconstitutional all state miscegenation laws (laws barring interracial marriage, cohabitation, or sexual intercourse).

In 1958 Richard Loving, a white man, and Mildred Bean, a black woman, went to Washington, D.C., to be married because their home state, Virginia, enforced a miscegenation statute. Once married they returned to Virginia and lived in Caroline County. They were arrested in 1959 and found guilty of violating the state statute. Sentenced to a year in prison, they agreed to accept a suspended sentence in return for leaving the state and promising not to return for twenty-five years. Resettled in Washington, D.C., the Lovings brought suit in 1963, challenging the constitutionality of the Virginia statute. In March 1966 the Virginia Supreme Court of Appeals upheld the law, and the case proceeded to the U.S. Supreme Court, which on June 12, 1967, unanimously overturned the state court's decision and ruled the law unconstitutional on the grounds that it violated the FOURTEENTH AMENDMENT. This decision effectively nullified the miscegenation laws of the sixteen states that, at the time, retained them.

Suggested Reading

Sollors, Werner. *Interracialism: Black-White Intermarriage in American History, Literature, and Law.* New York: Oxford University Press, 2000.

LYNCHING

Lynching is an act of "vigilante justice" in which a person is seized or abducted and, without any semblance of DUE PROCESS of law, executed, typically by hanging. People have been lynched for violating local mores, customs, or sensibilities as well as for specific alleged crimes.

According to many authorities the practice of lynching got its name from Virginia militia colonel Charles Lynch, who during the American Revolution meted out summary "justice" to local loyalists. Lynch law certainly prevailed in many American frontier communities during the eighteenth and early nineteenth centuries, but beginning about 1880 the victims of lynching were most often blacks, especially those regarded as having "stepped out of place" by violating social custom (for example, talking "improperly" to a white woman or demanding basic rights). In some communities Asians, Jews, Hispanics, Native Americans, or members of other minorities were targeted. Those who held unpopular beliefs—political radicals, for instance, or white advocates of civil rights—have also been the victims of lethal mob violence.

The first reliable statistics on lynching date from 1882. Between that year and 1968, when lynching (but not all racially motivated violence) virtually disappeared, 4,743 people were killed by lynch mobs, of whom 3,446 were blacks. During this period Mississippi had 539 black lynch victims and 42 whites; Georgia, 492 blacks, 39 whites; Texas, 352 blacks, 141 whites; Louisiana, 335 blacks, 56 whites; and Alabama, 299 blacks, 48 whites (University of Missouri-Kansas City School of Law, "Lynching in America: Statistics, Information, Images," at www.law.umkc.edu/faculty/projects/ftrials/shipp/lynchstats.html). These numbers account only for lynchings actually recorded; doubtless, many other people were lynched during this period.

Lynchings were mob affairs, sometimes carried out in the dead of night but sometimes performed openly as public spectacle. In extreme cases local newspapers actually announced an upcoming lynching. Torture and mutilation were sometimes part of the lynching, and, in some cases, the corpse of the victim was dismembered and various parts were distributed as souvenirs.

While many lynchings were carried out only with the connivance of law enforcement authorities, many others were actively initiated or instigated by local authorities. (See also TILL, EMMETT.)

Suggested Reading

Dray, Philip. *At the Hands of Persons Unknown: The Lynching of Black America.* New York: Random House, 2002.
Moses, Norton H. *Lynching and Vigilantism in the United States: An Annotated Bibliography.* Westport, Conn.: Greenwood Publishing, 1997.

MADISON, JAMES (1751–1836)

The fourth president of the United States, serving from 1809 to 1817, James Madison was a political protégé of THOMAS JEFFERSON, a central voice in the creation of the Constitution, chief sponsor of the BILL OF RIGHTS, and, with Alexander Hamilton and John Jay, coauthor of *THE FEDERALIST PAPERS*. Before becoming president, Madison served as Jefferson's secretary of state.

Madison was born on Montpelier, a plantation in Virginia's Blue Ridge foothills. A brilliant student, he earned his degree from the College of New Jersey (later Princeton University) in only two years, then went on to become a fervent advocate of independence. Elected to Virginia's convention of 1776, where he drafted the state's guarantee of religious freedom, Madison was then sent by Virginia to the Continental Congress in 1780. When the ARTICLES OF CONFEDERATION were ratified in 1781, Madison—a steadfast advocate of federal government and a strong Union—attempted to compensate for the weak federal union created by the articles by asserting that Congress had the implied power to enforce financial requisitions upon the states—by military coercion, if necessary. When this argument failed he continued to fight for an amendment to strengthen the federal government.

A prime mover behind the call for a constitutional convention in 1787, Madison set out at the convention to replace the articles with a new constitution that would give the federal government the power of taxation and create a genuine union of states rather than a loose confederation of individual sovereignties. The essence of his "Virginia Plan," which provided the basic skeleton for what became the Constitution, was a strong government, yet one in which powers were shared, checked, and balanced among distinct branches.

Ratification of the Constitution was an uphill struggle, which Madison approached by collaborating with Alexander Hamilton and John Jay on *The Federalist Papers.* Most scholars agree that Madison wrote twenty-nine out of the eighty-five *Federalist* essays, and his contribution forms a constitutional commentary that is still used by legal scholars today.

After election to the new House of Representatives created by the Constitution, Madison sponsored the first twelve proposed constitutional amendments, ten of which were enacted as the Bill of Rights, on which the individual rights of all Americans are based.

Like Jefferson, Madison vehemently disagreed with GEORGE WASHINGTON's secretary of the treasury, Alexander Hamilton, on financial matters, a conflict that led Madison—again, like Jefferson—to become a "strict constructionist" with regard to the Constitution; that is, to deny the existence of "implied power" for the federal government and to hold instead that all powers not explicitly assigned to the federal government are the province of the states and the people. In taking this position Madison modified his earlier advocacy of a powerful central government.

Madison married Dolley Payne Todd in 1794, a widow seventeen years his junior who, because Jefferson was a widower, served as hostess at White House social functions. With the election of her husband to the presidency, Dolley Madison would effectively create the role of first lady.

In 1798 both Madison and Jefferson protested the ALIEN AND SEDITION ACTS. In the Virginia Resolutions Madison argued that the acts violated the First Amendment. Although Jefferson's Kentucky Resolutions put the case for nullification—the right of any state to nullify any federal law it deemed unconstitutional—more directly, Madison's Virginia Resolutions were consonant with the same doctrine.

As Jefferson's secretary of state (1801–1809), Madison was highly influential. After he published his diplomatic dispatches, he won widespread public approval and easily won the presidency in 1808. Madison took a strong hand with France and England, a course that ultimately led to the War of 1812. His conduct of that war was hampered by a parsimonious Congress that repeatedly refused to finance the war adequately. Unwisely, Madison also put the army in the command of superannuated veterans of the American Revolution. Despite prodigies performed by the U.S. Navy, the ground war was for the most part a disaster, culminating in the burning of Washington, which Madison and his wife—along with most of Congress—were forced to flee. However, because ANDREW JACKSON's victory at the Battle of New Orleans ended the war on a rather misleading note of American triumph, Madison left office a very popular figure.

Madison retired to Montpelier to become a technologically progressive farmer. Although a southerner and slave owner, he abhorred SLAVERY and was active in efforts to encourage the federal government to purchase slaves and resettle them in the African territory that would become Liberia. Madison also collaborated with his former mentor, Jefferson, in the creation of the University of Virginia, and later served as its rector. (See also RELIGION, FREEDOM OF.)

Suggested Reading

Banning, Lance. *The Sacred Fire of Liberty: James Madison and the Founding of the Federal Republic.* Ithaca: Cornell University Press, 1995.

Wills, Gary. *James Madison.* New York: Henry Holt, 2002.

MAGNA CARTA

The Magna Carta was issued, under pressure from the English barons, by King John of England at Runneymede. A cornerstone of English COMMON LAW, it is also by definition a cornerstone of U.S. law. The heart of the document is the king's renunciation of absolute, arbitrary power and a guarantee of certain individual liberties; therefore, it is rightly viewed as the foundation of basic Anglo-American concepts of government. (See Appendix A for excerpts from the Magna Carta.)

Suggested Reading

Howard, A. E. Dick. *Magna Carta: Text and Commentary.* Charlottesville: University Press of Virginia, 1997.

MALCOLM X (EL-HAJJ MALIK EL-SHABAZZ; 1925–1965)

Thanks to his own charisma and to the extraordinary *Autobiography of Malcolm X* (a collaboration with Alex Haley, published posthumously in 1965), Malcolm X is remembered as the nation's most famous black radical, a herald of the BLACK POWER MOVEMENT, and a strong symbol of awakened black pride—as well as black rage and defiance.

He was born Malcolm Little in Omaha, Nebraska, on February 21, 1925, the son of Rev. Earl Little, a preacher and a follower of black nationalist MARCUS GARVEY. When the KU KLUX KLAN ran Little and his family out of Omaha, they resettled in Milwaukee, Wisconsin, in 1926. Two years later Earl Little purchased a house in Lansing, Michigan, and on November 7, 1929, the house burned to the ground in a fire that was allegedly set by white racists. The family moved to another house in East Lansing the following month. On September 28, 1931, Malcolm's father was struck and killed by a streetcar. It was rumored (and Malcolm X believed) that Earl Little had been assaulted by members of the BLACK LEGIONNAIRES, a white supremacist organization, and thrown onto the car tracks.

Left destitute by her husband's death, Malcolm's mother was unable to support her eight children and sent Malcolm to a foster home in East Lansing. Young Malcolm proved a very bright and eager student—until a favorite teacher responded to his announced ambition to become a lawyer with "that's no realistic goal for a nigger" (*Autobiography of Malcolm X.* 1965. Reprint, New York: Ballantine, 1992, p. 28). Malcolm left school in 1939 after completing the seventh grade, then briefly attended high school.

As a teenager Malcolm held various menial jobs and lived in a number of foster homes until 1941, when he moved to Boston to live with his half-sister, Ella. There he became involved in street gangs, crime, and narcotics use. For several years he worked for the New York, New Haven, and Hartford Railroad as a Pullman porter, then moved back to Michigan briefly. In 1943 he settled in Harlem, where, as "Big Red" (he had red hair), he quickly earned a reputation as a ruthless, reckless street hustler, thief, gambler, dope pusher, and all-around criminal. In 1946, when he was twenty-one, he was arrested after attempting to reclaim a stolen watch he had left for repair at a Boston jewelry store. His subsequent conviction—for carrying firearms, breaking and entering, and larceny—brought his criminal career to a halt.

Malcolm Little was sentenced to eight to ten years imprisonment. While in prison he studied in the prison library, gaining for himself the education he had failed to receive in school, and he learned from his brother Reginald about the Nation of Islam (NOI) and the teachings of Elijah Muhammad. Paroled in August 1952, Little found employment in a Detroit furniture store and then at the Ford Motor Company. By 1953 he was also attending Nation of Islam meetings, and in February of that year he moved to Chicago to live with Elijah Muhammad and study for the NOI ministry. In September 1953 Malcolm Little—who had, in Black Muslim fashion, rejected his "slave name" and chosen a new name, Malcolm X—became the first minister of Boston's NOI Temple No. 11. During the 1950s Malcolm X emerged as the NOI's leading spokesman. Charismatic, eloquent, fiery, and anger-charged, he converted thousands of African Americans to the Black Muslim faith, and his fame soon eclipsed that of Elijah Muhammad himself.

Unsparing in his criticism of white America, Malcolm X referred to the white man as "the devil" and, as part of a program of black nationalism, advocated absolute segregation and avoidance of all contact with whites. He established the Organization of Afro-American Unity, which demanded an investigation of RACISM in the United States by the United Nations Commission on Human Rights. Malcolm X both terrified and outraged white America by telling black audiences that they had to attain their freedom by "any means necessary"—including not only political and economic self-determination but violent self-defense.

By the early 1960s it was clear that Malcolm X was coming into conflict with NOI leaders, including Elijah Muhammad. In December 1963, after Malcolm X violated Elijah Muhammad's directive that no NOI minister should comment on the recent assassination of President JOHN F. KENNEDY (Malcolm X had told reporters that Kennedy had failed to foresee that "the chickens would come home to roost so soon") he was suspended and "silenced" by Elijah Muhammad for ninety days. This action widened a growing gulf between Malcolm X and Elijah Muhammad, whose luxurious lifestyle and marital infidelity Malcolm X found greatly disturbing. By early 1964 Malcolm X had parted from the NOI and begun to develop Muslim Mosque, Inc., a breakaway ministry. He embarked on a pilgrimage to Mecca and a tour of the Middle East and Africa. As a result of this experience of the traditional core of Islam, Malcolm X began to shed his absolutist views concerning segregation, although he remained a black nationalist and a pan-Africanist, founding the Organization of Afro-American Unity (OAAU). He sought reconciliation with Elijah Muhammad and solidarity with MARTIN LUTHER KING JR., with whom the popular press often contrasted him, portraying King as the apostle of nonviolence and Malcolm X as the advocate of militancy. Malcolm X signaled his newfound personal and philosophical peace by adopting the Islamic name El-Hajj Malik El-Shabazz.

During the last two years of his life, Malcolm X was often the target of threats, and on February 21, 1965, as he began to address an OAAU rally at the Audubon Ballroom in Harlem, he was shot to death. Two NOI members, Talmadge Hayer and Reuben X, were convicted of the crime, but many believe that the FEDERAL BUREAU OF INVESTIGATION and other government agencies may have played a role in his murder. (See also ISLAM, NATION OF.)

Suggested Reading

Carson, Clayborne. *Malcolm X: The FBI File.* New York: Carroll and Graf, 1991.

Clarke, John Henrik. *Malcolm X: The Man and His Times.* New York: Macmillan, 1969.

Davis, Lenwood. *Malcolm X: A Selected Bibliography.* Westport, Conn. Greenwood, 1984.

DeCaro, Louis. *Malcolm and the Cross: The Nation of Islam, Malcolm X, and Christianity.* New York: New York University Press, 1998.

Johnson, Timothy V. *Malcolm X: A Comprehensive Annotated Bibliography.* New York: Garland, 1986.

MANDELA, NELSON (1918–)

Nelson Mandela earned worldwide fame as a South African black nationalist who was imprisoned by the white government from 1962 to 1990, then elected president in 1994 after the end of the apartheid (strict segregationist) government. A symbol of the struggle for human rights not only in South Africa but throughout the world, Mandela was a continuing inspiration to activists in the AFRICAN AMERICAN CIVIL RIGHTS MOVEMENT.

The son of Henry Mandela, chief of the Xhosa-speaking Tembu people, Mandela renounced his claim to succeed his father as chief and decided to study law, earning his degree at the University of South Africa in 1942. He joined the African National Congress (ANC), a black nationalist group, in 1944 and rose to a leadership position by 1949. Under Mandela's direction the campaign for the liberation of South Africa's oppressed black majority became increasingly militant. Tried for treason during 1956–1961, Mandela was acquitted. But in the wake of the massacre of black Africans by police forces at Sharpeville in 1960, and the subsequent government ban on the ANC, Mandela called for outright acts of sabotage against the white South African regime, an action that led to his imprisonment in 1962. Initially sentenced to five years, he was subsequently tried (in what was known as the Rivonia Trial) on charges of sabotage, treason, and violent conspiracy and on June 12, 1964, was sentenced to life imprisonment.

During his long incarceration Mandela remained the spiritual leader of South Africa's black nationalist movement. He also became an international symbol of the evils of apartheid. Citing South African injustices—and often invoking Mandela's name—many nations shunned South Africa economically and politically as a gesture of moral protest. At last, on February 11, 1990, South African president F. W. de Klerk ordered Mandela's release. The next month, Mandela was named deputy president of the ANC and became ANC president in July 1991. He worked with de Klerk to end apartheid and to transform the South African government into a nonracial democracy. In 1993 the two men were jointly awarded the Nobel Peace Prize.

Elected president of South Africa in 1994, Mandela instituted widespread programs of reform and improvement and created the Truth and Reconciliation Commission, which investigated human rights violations under apartheid. In 1999 Mandela decided not to seek a second term as president and retired from public life.

Suggested Reading

Mandela, Nelson. *Long Walk to Freedom: The Autobiography of Nelson Mandela.* New York: Little, Brown, 1995.

MARCH AGAINST FEAR

In 1966 James Meredith, the student who had integrated the University of Mississippi four years earlier, decided to march from Memphis, Tennessee, to Jackson, Mississippi. The object of what he called the March Against Fear was to assert the right of African Americans to move freely and safely across the South. Meredith also intended to encourage people along the march route to register to vote.

Meredith set off from Memphis on June 5, 1966. Soon after he had begun, he was shot and wounded by a sniper and had to be hospitalized. On hearing of the shooting, other civil rights leaders, most notably Stokely Carmichael, Martin Luther King Jr., and Floyd McKissick, took up the march, renaming it the Meredith March. At Greenwood, Mississippi, Carmichael delivered his Black Power speech, which signaled a splintering in the African American civil rights movement between those who, like King, subscribed to nonviolence, and those who took a more militant stance. As for Meredith, after he was released from the hospital on June 25 he rejoined the march and arrived with the others at Jackson, Mississippi. (See also Mississippi, University of.)

Suggested Reading

Meredith, James. *Three Years in Mississippi.* Bloomington: Indiana University Press, 1966.

MARCH ON WASHINGTON

In 1963 a coalition of civil rights groups and figures—most prominently the Congress of Racial Equality, the National Association for the Advancement of Colored People, the National Urban League, the Negro American Labor Committee, the Southern Christian Leadership Conference, the Student Nonviolent Coordinating Committee, A. Philip Randolph, and Bayard Rustin—organized a "march for jobs and freedom" to Washington, D.C. In large part the objective of the march was to create the momentum necessary for passage of the pending Civil Rights Bill. Word of the march spread quickly through local civil rights and church groups, and organizers provided transportation to Washington from all over the country. More than thirty special "freedom trains" and two thousand chartered "freedom buses" brought some 250,000 people to the capital, an estimated 60,000 of whom were white.

As the magnitude of the march became apparent, the national media devoted extensive coverage to it. Experts predicted—correctly, as it turned out—that the March on Washington would be the largest demonstration ever seen in the United States to that time. All 2,900 members of the Washington, D.C., police force were mustered, and 1,000 additional police officers were called in from suburban areas. Along with U.S. Army units, 2,000 National Guardsmen were put on alert. No one was more concerned about security and order than the march organizers themselves, who designated 2,000 marchers as civilian "marshals." Fifteen hundred black officers from the New York City Police Department took a day's leave to assist with security.

In addition to security, city officials and parade organizers had to manage a massive project in logistics—coordinating the special trains, chartered buses, and special airline flights, most of which were expected to arrive between six and eleven A.M. on August 28. Once the marchers were in place there was the question of where they would sleep. Families opened their homes to the visitors, and churches volunteered space as dormitories.

The organizational effort paid off in a massive—and entirely peaceful—demonstration that began with A. Philip Randolph speaking before the Lincoln Memorial:

> Fellow Americans, we are gathered here in the largest demonstration in the history of this nation. Let the nation and the world know the meaning of our numbers. We are not a pressure group, we are not an organization or a group of organizations, we are not a mob. We are the advance guard of a massive moral revolution for jobs and freedom ("The March on Washington," www.angelfire.com/pa/marchonwashington/march.html).

In addition to speeches there were performances by prominent and socially conscious musicians, including Josh White; Odetta; Mahalia Jackson ; Joan Baez; Bob Dylan; and Peter, Paul, and Mary.

Speakers represented a broad spectrum of positions. John

LEWIS, the most assertive, believed that the pending Civil Rights Bill was too little too late. Although King and Randolph had persuaded him to tone down the speech he planned to make, Lewis's language remained stern: "By the force of our demands, our determination and our numbers, we shall splinter the segregated South into a thousand pieces, and put them back together in the image of God and Democracy" ("The March on Washington," www.angelfire.com/pa/marchonwashington/march.html).

Of all the speeches, however, the most memorable was King's "I HAVE A DREAM" SPEECH, which was widely broadcast and has stood as one of the great monuments of the civil rights movement and of the history of the general struggle for human rights.

The March on Washington was a great success in that it awakened many Americans to the civil rights movement and to the essential rightness of the demand for equality and justice. It was also a triumph of nonviolence. In more specific terms, the march advanced what *U.S. News and World Report* (September 9, 1963) identified as seven demands:

1. Immediate passage of "meaningful" civil rights legislation
2. Immediate elimination of all racial segregation in public schools throughout the nation
3. Protection from police "brutality" for civil rights demonstrations everywhere
4. A major program of public works to provide jobs for all the nation's unemployed
5. A federal law prohibiting racial discrimination in all hiring
6. A national minimum wage of two dollars an hour
7. Self-government for the District of Columbia (which was 57 percent black at the time).

(See also CIVIL RIGHTS ACT OF 1964.)

Suggested Reading

Pfeffer, Paula A. *A. Philip Randolph: Pioneer of the Civil Rights Movement*. Baton Rouge: Louisiana State University Press, 1996.

MARGOLD REPORT

In 1930 the NATIONAL ASSOCIATION FOR THE ADVANCEMENT OF COLORED PEOPLE (NAACP) commissioned an attorney, Nathan Ross Margold, to study the problem of overturning *PLESSY V. FERGUSON* and bringing to an end the "SEPARATE BUT EQUAL" DOCTRINE as a legal defense of segregation. The Margold Report, issued in 1933, argued that the NAACP should file a strategic set of lawsuits demonstrating that southern states and municipalities had not, in fact, established separate but *equal* facilities. After this case was successfully made, the report continued, the NAACP should then challenge the separate but equal doctrine itself on the grounds that it violated the equal protection clause of the FOURTEENTH AMENDMENT.

Two black attorneys, Charles H. Houston and THURGOOD MARSHALL, used the strategy recommended in the Margold Report to argue a series of cases before the SUPREME COURT, culminating in *BROWN V. BOARD OF EDUCATION OF TOPEKA, KANSAS,* which finally overturned *Plessy v. Ferguson* and ended racial segregation in public education.

Suggested Reading

Kluger, Richard. *Simple Justice: The History of Brown v. Board of Education and Black America's Struggle for Equality.* New York: Random House, 1977.
Patterson, James T. *Brown v. Board of Education: A Civil Rights Milestone and Its Troubled Legacy.* New York: Oxford University Press, 2001.

MARSHALL, THURGOOD (1908–1993)

The first African American associate justice of the U.S. SUPREME COURT, Thurgood Marshall began his legal career as the lead attorney for the NATIONAL ASSOCIATION FOR THE ADVANCEMENT OF COLORED PEOPLE (NAACP), heading up that organization's legal fight against JIM CROW LAWS. Later, as U.S. solicitor general in the administration of LYNDON B. JOHNSON, Marshall successfully defended the constitutionality of the CIVIL RIGHTS ACT OF 1964 and other landmark civil rights legislation.

Marshall was born in Baltimore on July 2, 1908, the son of a boat-club steward and a teacher (his mother taught in Baltimore's segregated elementary schools). Marshall graduated from Lincoln University in 1930 and then, at the top of his class, from Howard University Law School in 1933. His principal mentor at Howard, Charles Houston, introduced him to the NAACP, and for some twenty-five years Marshall served as director of the NAACP's Legal Defense and Educational Fund. During his tenure with the NAACP, Marshall argued thirty-two cases before the Supreme Court, winning twenty-nine, including the great legal landmarks of the civil rights movement: *Smith v. Allwright* (1944); *MORGAN V. VIRGINIA* (1946); *SWEATT V. PAINTER* (1950); and, most momentous of all, *BROWN V. BOARD OF EDUCATION OF TOPEKA, KANSAS* (1954), which overturned *PLESSY V. FERGUSON* (1896), long the legal basis of segregation. Marshall successfully argued that, in the instance of public education, the "SEPARATE BUT EQUAL" DOCTRINE governing public facilities was inherently flawed because separate schooling denied blacks a full educational experience.

In 1961 Marshall was appointed to the U.S. Court of Appeals, a post he resigned in 1965 to become President Johnson's solicitor general. In 1967 Johnson appointed Marshall to the Supreme Court, and for the next quarter-century Marshall was the court's leading champion of minority rights. Liberal, plainspoken, outspoken, and always a civil libertarian, Marshall upheld not only the rights of African Americans and other racial and ethnic minorities but was also a proponent of a woman's right to ABORTION and an opponent of CAPITAL PUNISHMENT and attempts to curtail freedom of speech. A liberal voice on the court during its most liberal years as well as during its more conservative transformation in the 1970s and 1980s, Marshall stepped down shortly before his death. He died on January 24, 1993.

Suggested Reading

Tushnet, Mark V. *Making Civil Rights Law: Thurgood Marshall and the Supreme Court, 1936–1961*. New York: Oxford University Press, 1996.

———. *Making Constitutional Law: Thurgood Marshall and the Supreme Court, 1961–1991*. New York: Oxford University Press, 1997.

Williams, Juan. *Thurgood Marshall: American Revolutionary*. New York: Times Books, 2000.

MARTIN LUTHER KING DAY

On November 2, 1983, President RONALD REAGAN signed into law a bill proclaiming the third Monday in January a national holiday to commemorate the birth of MARTIN LUTHER KING JR.

A bill had been introduced in the House of Representatives as early as 1968, just four days after King's assassination, by Rep. John Conyers, D-Mich. When the bill stalled in committee, petitions—with six million signatures endorsing the holiday—were submitted to Congress. On the strength of continued popular support, Conyers and Rep. Shirley Chisholm, D-N.Y., resubmitted the legislation repeatedly over the years, and the public continued to press for a King commemorative holiday (the call became most sharply focused during civil rights marches in Washington during 1982 and 1983). After a compromise was reached on the date of the holiday (there were objections that it was too close to Christmas and New Year's), the bill finally passed in both houses; instead of being held on January 15, King's birthday, the holiday is observed on the third Monday in January.

Acceptance of the King holiday was neither immediate nor universal. Some states refused to observe it, and some southern states introduced celebrations commemorating various Confederate generals on that day. Utah designated the holiday Human Rights Day rather than Martin Luther King Day, and Arizona approved the holiday only in 1992 in response to a threatened tourist boycott. New Hampshire called the holiday Civil Rights Day until 1999, when the legislature officially acknowledged it as Martin Luther King Jr. Day.

Suggested Reading

Baldwin, Lewis V. *To Make the Wounded Whole: The Cultural Legacy of Martin Luther King Jr.* Minneapolis: Fortress, 1992.

MARTIN LUTHER KING JR. CENTER FOR SOCIAL CHANGE

The King Center for Social Change was established in 1968 by Coretta Scott King, widow of MARTIN LUTHER KING JR., as a living memorial to her husband. Located within the Martin Luther King Jr. National Historic Site in Atlanta, Georgia, the center encompasses both the house in which King was born and the site of his grave. The center offers exhibits illustrating King's life and teachings, as well as a library and archives, and sponsors projects and activities focused on the following:

Developing and disseminating programs based on King's philosophy of nonviolence

Creating an international network of organizations to raise awareness and understanding of King's legacy

Administering permissions to other nonprofit organizations and government agencies that use King's writings for their programs

Monitoring and reporting on the impact of King's legacy throughout the world.

Suggested Reading

King Center for Social Change, www.thekingcenter.org.

MARYLAND COLONY

With RHODE ISLAND and PENNSYLVANIA, the colony of Maryland was among the first American governments to guarantee at least a modicum of religious freedom. From the beginning, moreover, the Maryland colony endeavored, through trade and mutual respect, to create peaceful relations with the local Indians.

Leonard Calvert, younger brother of Lord Baltimore, led the colony's founding expedition to St. Clement's Island (present-day Blakistone Island), in the lower Potomac River, landing there in March 1634. Under Calvert's direction colonists quickly created friendly trading relations with the Indians. The first colonists included indentured servants and, beginning about 1639, African slaves.

The Calverts, Catholics in Anglican England, decreed freedom of religion, albeit within Trinitarian Christianity, a guarantee that was formalized by the colony's general assembly in the Act Concerning Religion (1649), later known as the Act of Religious Toleration. When government of the colony was taken over by the crown in 1692, the Church of England was officially established; however, the colony preserved its traditional role as a safe haven for religious dissidents and exiles from other, less tolerant colonies. (See also RELIGION, FREEDOM OF, and INDENTURED SERVITUDE.)

Suggested Reading

Brugger, Robert J. *Maryland: A Middle Temperament, 1634–1980.* 1988. Reprint, Baltimore: Johns Hopkins University Press, 1996.

MASSACHUSETTS *BODY OF LIBERTIES*

The Massachusetts *Body of Liberties* (1641) was the first code of law enacted in New England. The laws given in this document afforded a significantly greater degree of liberty than the laws in force in England at the time. (See Appendix A for excerpts from the Massachusetts *Body of Liberties.*)

Suggested Reading

The Colonial Laws of Massachusetts: Reprinted from the Edition of 1660, with the Supplements to 1672 : Containing Also, the Body of Liberties of 1641. Littleton, Colo.: Fred B. Rothman, 1995.

MATTACHINE SOCIETY

The founding of the Mattachine Society in Los Angeles in 1951 is generally considered to be the starting point of the organized GAY RIGHTS movement in the United States. Its principal founder was an activist named Harry Hay, who, with other charter members of the society, published *One,* the first widely circulated gay periodical in the United States. Monthly publication began in 1952; the magazine featured articles on the Mattachine Society as well as a variety of personal essays. Soon after the organization's founding in Los Angeles, Mattachine Society chapters also formed in Boston, Chicago, Denver, New York, Philadelphia, and Washington, D.C.

The origin of the name *Mattachine* is a bit obscure. Some authorities believe that it is a references to Mattacino, a traditional character in Renaissance Venetian comedy (*commedia dell'arte*). Mattacino was typically a court jester or fool who spoke the truth to the king when no one else dared. Others believe that the Mattachine character type was drawn from medieval French cultural tradition and refers to the court jesters who always wore masks in public.

The purpose of the Mattachine Society was to serve the gay community by providing legal and counseling referrals and by lobbying for the repeal of sodomy laws and other discriminatory measures. During the early 1960s the Mattachine Society was the most vocal and widely recognized gay rights organization in the United States. However, after the STONEWALL PROTEST of 1969, events seemed to outpace the Mattachine Society, which was perceived as insufficiently aggressive. The organization lost members, suffered a financial crisis, and was disbanded early in 1987.

Suggested Reading

Roscoe, Will, ed. *Radically Gay: Gay Liberation in the Words of Its Founder.* Boston: Beacon Press, 1997.

MCCARTHY, JOSEPH (1908–1957)

During the anti-Communist "witch-hunts" led by Joseph McCarthy in the early 1950s, the Republican senator from Wisconsin became notorious for trampling the rights of DUE PROCESS and generally circumventing the Constitution. His approach—based on vague accusations and guilt by association—deeply tainted the times, which became known as the "McCarthy era."

Joseph McCarthy was born near Appleton, Wisconsin, became an attorney, and served as a circuit judge (1940–1942) before enlisting in the U.S. Marines during World War II. Elected to the Senate in 1946 on the Republican ticket, McCarthy had an undistinguished senatorial career until February 1950 when he charged, at a Republican women's club meeting in Wheeling, West Virginia, that he had the names of 205 Communists who had infiltrated the U.S. Department of State. His assertion created a media frenzy and instantly elevated McCarthy to public attention. Called to testify before the Senate Committee on Foreign Relations, he was unable to produce the name of any Communist in any government department—but the public, frustrated by the cold war and the Korean War, enthusiastically supported his campaign to root out Communists in American government and life. On the strength of his popular image as a bold cold warrior and crusader against Communism, McCarthy was elected to a second senatorial term in 1952 and secured the chairmanship of the Senate's Government Committee on Operations, as well as of its permanent subcommittee on investigations. From this position McCarthy dedicated the next two years to high-handed investigations of government departments, questioning a seemingly endless string of witnesses concerning suspected Communist affiliations. Although the Soviets and other Communist powers undoubtedly practiced espionage in the United States, McCarthy never made a legitimate case against anyone brought before his committee. Nevertheless, the mere fact of being brought up for questioning was enough to ruin lives and careers.

Eventually, McCarthy turned on members of his own party, including President DWIGHT D. EISENHOWER. When in 1954 he charged that the U.S. Army was widely and deeply infiltrated by Communists, the thirty-six-day Army-McCarthy Hearings—which were nationally televised—revealed to a national audience a McCarthy who was not a valiant crusader but an irresponsible, self-serving bully. Thoroughly discredited by the hearings, McCarthy immediately fell out of favor with the public. He lost his chairmanship of the Government Committee on Operations and its subcommittee on investigations, and, on December 2, 1954, was formally censured by the Senate for conduct "contrary to Senate traditions." From this point forward McCarthy was frozen out by colleagues and the public alike. Always a heavy drinker, he retreated into alcoholism and died prematurely and in disrepute.

Suggested Reading

Herman, Arthur. *Joseph McCarthy: Reexamining the Life and Legacy of America's Most Hated Senator.* New York: Free Press, 1999.

Rovere, Richard H. *Senator Joe McCarthy.* 1959. Reprint, Berkeley: University of California Press, 1996.

MCKINLEY HOMELESS ASSISTANCE ACT

The Steward B. McKinley Homeless Assistance Act (Public Law 100-77), passed in 1987, defines a homeless person as one "who lacks a fixed, regular and adequate nighttime residence." The act created the Interagency Council on the Homeless as an independent agency in the executive branch; however, funding for the agency was stopped in 1994, and its role was assumed by the Working Group of the White House Domestic Policy Council, a collection of seventeen agencies chaired by the secretary of housing and urban development.

The McKinley Act also established a grant program for services to the mentally ill and for demonstration projects providing community services to the homeless. The act continues to provide important funding directly to communities that create programs to aid the homeless.

Suggested Reading

Jencks, Christopher. *The Homeless.* Cambridge: Harvard University Press, 1994.

MCLAURIN V. OKLAHOMA STATE REGENTS

McLaurin v. Oklahoma State Regents was argued in the SUPREME COURT during April 3–4, 1950, and decided on June 5 of that year. The appellant, George W. McLaurin, was an African American citizen with a master's degree living in Oklahoma. He applied to the University of Oklahoma, at the time an all-white institution, for additional graduate study and, pursuant to Oklahoma statute, was rejected because of his race. He sued in district court, alleging that the statute was unconstitutional because it deprived him of the equal protection of the laws. The court decided in his favor, whereupon the Oklahoma legislature amended the segregation statutes to permit the admission of blacks to institutions of higher learning that were attended by white students, but only in cases where such institutions offered courses not available in the state's black schools; the legislation further stipulated that, in such cases, the program of instruction "shall be given at such colleges or institutions of higher education upon a segregated basis." McLaurin was thus assigned to a seat in the classroom in a row specified for black students, assigned a special table in the library, and, although permitted to eat in the cafeteria, was assigned to a special table there. The Supreme Court held that the "conditions under which appellant is required to receive his education deprive him of his personal and present right to the equal protection of the laws; and the Fourteenth Amendment precludes such differences in treatment by the State based upon race." (See also FOURTEENTH AMENDMENT RIGHTS.)

Suggested Reading

Kluger, Richard. *Simple Justice: The History of Brown v. Board of Education and Black America's Struggle for Equality.* New York: Random House, 1977.

MEDICAID AND MEDICARE

Medicaid and Medicare are federal programs that guarantee health insurance for the elderly (Medicare) and for the poor (Medicaid). They were enacted in 1965 as amendments (Titles XVIII and XIX, respectively) to the

Social Security Act of 1935 and went into effect in 1966 as central legislation in President Lyndon Johnson's Great Society program.

Medicare applies to most people aged sixty-five or older and provides two related health insurance plans: Part A, a hospital insurance plan, and Part B, a supplementary medical insurance plan. The hospital plan contributes to payment for inpatient hospital care, skilled in-home nursing care, and some additional home health services. Subject to various rules, a person is eligible for ninety days of hospitalization and, after that, one hundred days of nursing care within any benefit period. Additional care requires a substantial copayment. Part B, the supplementary medical insurance plan, requires payment of a monthly premium and pays 80 percent of most medical bills.

Medicaid covers low-income people under age sixty-five and those over age sixty-five who have exhausted their Medicare benefits. Medicaid funding comes from federal and state sources, and states are required to offer Medicaid to all residents on public assistance. Beyond this single requirement, eligibility guidelines for enrollment in Medicaid are determined by the states individually. Hospital care, physicians' services, nursing, home health services, and diagnostic screening are covered.

Both Medicare and Medicaid legislation have been amended, particularly with the goal of "cost containment." During the 1980s, as reimbursement levels were increasingly restricted, many physicians declined to accept Medicaid patients. Both Medicare and Medicaid have been subject to serious fraud and abuse, not only by bogus patients and corrupt physicians but by suppliers of medical products. Nevertheless, the programs continue to be important elements in the nation's social safety net.

Suggested Reading

Marmor, Theodore. *The Politics of Medicare.* 2d ed. New York: Aldine de Gruyter, 2000.

MEIKLEJOHN CIVIL LIBERTIES INSTITUTE

Founded by Ann Fagan Ginger in 1965 as a means of creating and sharing effective, innovative legal research, writing, and courtroom strategies in the fields of constitutional law and civil liberties, the Meiklejohn Civil Liberties Institute (MCLI) advocates for human rights and peace law by reporting on violations of U.S. laws and of the treaties, conventions, and resolutions of the United Nations. The MCLI trains interns and publishes and distributes the *Human Rights and Peace Law Docket,* the *Human Rights Organizations and Periodicals Directory,* "peace law packets," a newsletter, and other publications.

In 1964 Ginger secured the permission of the noted civil libertarian Alexander Meiklejohn to use his name, and in 1965 the MCLI opened the Meiklejohn Civil Liberties Library, in Berkeley, California. Within a year the library became the Meiklejohn Civil Liberties Institute and began publishing books, sponsoring speakers, and presenting testimony in Congress.

Suggested Reading

Meiklejohn Civil Liberties Institute, www.sfsu.edu/~mclicfc/index.html.

MELTING POT CONCEPT

During the late nineteenth and early twentieth centuries, politicians as well as social activists believed that American society functioned as a great "melting pot" that would ultimately assimilate people of all ethnic backgrounds and, in the end, produce more or less uniform "Americans." (The earliest documented use of the actual phrase "melting pot" came in 1912.) Thus the ideal to be pursued in the immigration and naturalization process was the gradual replacement of cultural distinctions with assimilation and homogeneity. Although, in a sense, the melting pot concept promoted the acceptance of a wide variety of immigrants, it also called for full assimilation. To the extent that it demanded the subordination of "foreign" cultural identity, the melting pot concept—which dominated U.S. immigration policy for many years—posed a threat to minority rights.

Suggested Reading

Glazer, Nathan, and Daniel Patrick Moynihan. *Beyond the Melting Pot.* 2d rev. ed. Cambridge: MIT Press, 1970.

MENTALLY ILL, RIGHTS OF THE

Before the introduction in the 1960s of effective pharmacological treatments for severe mental illness, most people who were severely mentally ill were incarcerated in public or private institutions or asylums. These facilities were subject to laws prescribing minimum standards of humane treatment, but, in many cases, were understaffed, underfunded, and overcrowded.

Although institutions and asylums continued to exist and to treat patients, the introduction of new medications permitted the deinstitutionalization of many mentally ill people, greatly reducing the patient populations of such facilities; however, community-based outpatient facilities were—and are—often lacking or inadequate. Many unsupervised or undersupervised mentally ill people are unable to support themselves, and in many cases become homeless. Once homeless, such people often fall afoul of the police and are taken into the criminal justice system. To an extent, prisons have thus replaced psychiatric hospitals: it is estimated that 6–8 percent of prison inmates suffer from severe mental illness (versus 2.8 percent in the general population) (Open Society Institute, "Mental Illness in US Jails: Diverting the Nonviolent, Low-level Offender," Occasional Paper Series, No. 1, November 1996, www.soros.org/crime/research_brief__1.html). Although all states have statutes defining the legal rights of people who are identified as mentally ill, most authorities on mental illness—and many social activists—believe that the lack of community-based treatment facilities has created a crisis that violates the rights of the mentally ill.

The AMERICANS WITH DISABILITIES ACT, enacted on July 26, 1990, as Public Law 101–336, defines people with many types of mental illness as disabled and therefore legally protected against all forms of discrimination. On January 1, 1998, the Mental Health Parity Act went into effect, which required companies with more than fifty workers and that offer mental health benefits as part of their health package to provide annual and lifetime benefits devoted to mental health care that are the same as those devoted to the treatment of physical illnesses. (See Appendix A for an example of legislation defining the legal rights of the mentally ill.)

Suggested Reading

Rector Press. *Mentally Ill: Their Rights.* Leverett, Mass.: Rector Press, 1994.

MEREDITH, JAMES HOWARD (1933–)

James Meredith gained national fame through his struggle in 1962 to gain admission to the segregated University of Mississippi. His ultimate success was a major victory over southern segregation.

Born in Kosciusko, Mississippi, on June 25, 1933, Meredith attended the all-black Jackson State College from 1960 to 1962. In 1961 he twice applied for admission to the University of Mississippi and was twice rejected. He filed a complaint with the federal district court on May 31, 1961, alleging that he had been denied admission because of his race. The court rejected his complaint, but on appeal the Fifth Judicial Circuit Court reversed the lower court's ruling, deciding by a 2–1 vote that Meredith had been refused admission solely because of his race and that Mississippi was illegally maintaining a policy of educational segregation, in violation of the SUPREME COURT's ruling on racial segregation in *BROWN V. BOARD OF EDUCATION OF TOPEKA, KANSAS* (1954). Meredith's legal efforts were supported by MEDGAR EVERS and the NATIONAL ASSOCIATION FOR THE ADVANCEMENT OF COLORED PEOPLE. Despite a federal court order to admit Meredith, Mississippi's governor, ROSS BARNETT, vowed that he would personally prevent Meredith from enrolling. Reluctantly, U.S. Attorney General ROBERT F. KENNEDY sent federal marshals to escort Meredith through registration and into class and to continue to protect him. During the riots that followed Kennedy's decision, 160 marshals were wounded (twenty-eight by gunfire) and two bystanders (one a French journalist) were killed.

For more than a year Meredith studied as the only AFRICAN AMERICAN in the university. He endured threats and ostracism, but he graduated in 1964 and, two years later, wrote of his experience in *Three Years in Mississippi* (1966). On June 5, 1966, to protest RACISM, Meredith started his MARCH AGAINST FEAR from Memphis, Tennessee, to Jackson, Mississippi. Two days into the march he was felled by a sniper's bullet and left for dead by the roadside. Hospitalized, he ultimately recovered. But news of his shooting energized the CONGRESS OF RACIAL EQUALITY, the SOUTHERN CHRISTIAN LEADERSHIP CONFERENCE, and the STUDENT NONVIOLENT COORDINATING COMMITTEE, as well as STOKELY CARMICHAEL, MARTIN LUTHER KING JR., and Floyd McKissick, all of whom banded together to continue the march in Meredith's name. At Greenwood, Mississippi, Carmichael delivered his famous BLACK POWER speech, coining the term and calling on African Americans "to unite, to recognize their heritage, and to build a sense of community" (Stokeley Carmichael, "Berkeley Speech," in *Contemporary American Voices,* ed. James R. Andrews and David Zarefsky. White Plains, N.Y.: Longman, 100–107). On Meredith's release from the hospital on June 25, 1966, he rejoined the march.

After graduating from the UNIVERSITY OF MISSISSIPPI, Meredith attended the University of Ibadan in Nigeria (1964–1965) and Columbia University (1966–1968) in New York. During the late 1960s, however, Meredith turned away from civil rights activism, became a stockbroker, and joined the Republican Party. In 1972 he made an unsuccessful run for Congress, and, as time went on, became increasingly conservative. In 1988 he accused liberal whites of being an enemy of African Americans and, in 1989, joined the staff of Jesse

Helms, the deeply conservative senator from North Carolina. Meredith was vocal in his opposition to economic sanctions against South Africa during the final years of apartheid and opposed legislation to make the birthday of Martin Luther King Jr. (whom he accused of being a communist) a national holiday. (See also MISSISSIPPI, UNIVERSITY OF.)

Suggested Reading

Meredith, James. *Three Years in Mississippi*. Bloomington: Indiana University Press, 1966.

MEREDITH MARCH

See MARCH AGAINST FEAR; MEREDITH, JAMES HOWARD.

MEXICAN-AMERICAN LEGAL DEFENSE AND EDUCATION FUND

The Mexican-American Legal Defense and Education Fund (MALDEF) was founded in 1968 in San Antonio, Texas, and is now the leading nonprofit Latino litigation, advocacy, and educational outreach institution in the United States. The organization defines its mission as fostering sound public policies, laws, and programs to safeguard the civil rights of the thirty-five million Latinos living in the United States and, further, "to empower the Latino community to fully participate in our society." The organization focuses its efforts on employment, education, immigration, political access, language, and equitable access to public resources and accomplishes its goals by means of advocacy, community education, collaboration with other groups and individuals, a program of higher education scholarships in law and communications, and, when necessary, litigation.

Suggested Reading

Martinez, Oscar J. *Mexican-Origin People in the United States: A Topical History*. Tucson: University of Arizona Press, 2001.
Meier, Matt S., and Margo Gutierrez, eds. *Encyclopedia of the Mexican American Civil Rights Movement*. Westport, Conn.: Greenwood, 2000.

MEXICAN WAR

See UNITED STATES-MEXICAN WAR.

MFUME, KWEISI (1948–)

Born Frizzell Gray outside of Baltimore, Mfume dropped out of high school following the death of his mother in 1960 and began working to support his three sisters. He led the life of a young delinquent until, at age twenty-two, he earned a high school equivalency diploma, then enrolled at Morgan State University, graduating magna cum laude in 1976. While studying at Morgan State he also began working as a disc jockey and developed an interest in politics. He adopted the name Kweisi Mfume ("conquering son of kings," in the Ibgo language) and in 1978 won election to a seat on the Baltimore City Council. He also earned a master's degree in liberal arts from the Johns Hopkins University.

Mfume served on Baltimore's city council until 1986, when he was elected to the U.S. House of Representatives from Maryland's Seventh District. He led the Congressional Black Caucus from 1992 to 1994. Mfume left Congress in 1996 to accept the presidency of the NATIONAL ASSOCIATION FOR THE ADVANCEMENT OF COLORED PEOPLE (NAACP). He revitalized the organization, engineering the reduction and ultimate elimination of its six-figure debt. In an effort to refocus the energies of the civil rights movement, Mfume has concentrated on raising what had become, in recent years, the flagging expectations of NAACP local branches. He is the author of an autobiography, *No Free Ride* (1996).

Suggested Reading

Mfume, Kweisi. *No Free Ride: From the Mean Streets to the Mainstream*. New York: Ballantine, 1996.

MIGRANT LABOR

The term *migrant labor* is used to refer to people who enter the United States, legally or illegally, as temporary or seasonal workers, typically in agriculture or in semiskilled or unskilled industry. The expansion of international trade, continued population growth, and economic and political oppression, especially in Latin America, have prompted the migration of labor to the United States and other industrialized nations. The International Labour Organization (ILO), a UNITED NATIONS (UN) agency, estimates the number of migrant workers in the world today to be between 36 million and 42 million. In all, some fifty-five countries are significant "exporters" of migrant laborers, and sixty-seven are significant "importers" (International Labour Organization, *Migrant Workers*, ILOLEX General Surveys, "1999, Migrant

Workers: Introduction," http://ilolex.ilo.ch:1567/english/surveyq.htm).

Migrant workers in low-skilled and low-paying jobs are vulnerable to exploitation and discrimination, and pay and other employment conditions are typically not equivalent to those enjoyed by resident workers. Unscrupulous employers may defraud workers by requiring them to post monetary "deposits" (to pay for housing, clothing, equipment, and so on) against their future wages or to surrender their passports, effectively binding them to serve for a certain time. Women migrant workers are often vulnerable to physical and SEXUAL HARASSMENT. Other abuses include forced labor, excessive overtime, denial of access to public benefits, and discrimination.

Socially conscious Americans are concerned not only about the migrant-labor policies of American companies that import labor into the United States but about the policies of U.S.–based companies that use migrant labor in other countries. In recent years corporations have been embarrassed by the public attention focused on their migrant-labor policies. In some cases lawsuits have been filed against companies for violating laws and standards designed to protect migrant workers from discrimination and other abuses. In January 1999, for example, U.S. advocacy groups filed a $1 billion series of class action lawsuits on behalf of garment workers in the U.S. territory of Saipan, Northern Marianas Islands, against several major American companies. Most workers in Saipan's factories are migrants from other Asian countries, especially China. The suits alleged excessive recruitment fees, illegal employment contracts, oppressive working conditions, sexual harassment, and forced abortions. As a result of the suits, various companies canceled or reduced contracts on the island, motivating the Saipan Garment Manufacturers Association to adopt a code of conduct and a monitoring system to prevent future abuses.

Other recent actions include the Dole Citrus lawsuit and the El Monte Factory lawsuits. Filed in January 2000 on behalf of more than a hundred migrant fruit harvesters from Mexico and Guatemala, the Dole Citrus lawsuit accuses agricultural giant Dole Citrus of failing to keep accurate wage records and underpaying the workers for labor performed during 1997–1999. As of fall 2002 the outcome of the suit was still pending.

The El Monte Factory lawsuits alleged that the owners of Los Angeles's El Monte garment factory held migrant workers from Thailand in indentured servitude. The workers were freed from the factory in 1995 and in 1999 were awarded $1.2 million in settlement of the final lawsuit, which was against Tomato, Inc., the clothing retailer that had originally hired the factory. The total judgment awarded to the workers amounted to more than $4 million. In related settlements, BUM International, LF Sportswear, Mervyn's, and Montgomery Ward paid a total of $2 million. Hub Distributing/Miller's Outpost settled for an additional, undisclosed amount.

The ILO administers two principal conventions designed to protect migrant workers: the Migration for Employment Convention (Revised) of 1949, and the Migrant Workers (Supplementary Provisions) Convention of 1975. These conventions govern recruitment, access to information, contract conditions, medical examinations, assistance in settling into the new environment, vocational training, promotion, job security, liberty of movement, and the right to appeal termination. Most important, the conventions attempt to secure equality of opportunity and treatment for migrant and resident workers. In 1990 the UN adopted the Convention on Protection of the Rights of All Migrant Workers, which requires the protection of the human rights of migrant workers and their families, regardless of their legal status in the host country. The convention also calls for legally resident migrants to receive parity of treatment with nationals of the host country in various legal, political, economic, social, and cultural areas. As of 2002 the 1990 convention had been ratified by only a small minority of UN member nations, so it has not yet come into effect.

In the meantime, however, individual nations and organizations have adopted their own standards. For example, the Maquiladora Standards of Conduct were developed by the Coalition for Justice in the Maquiladoras, a coalition of nongovernmental agencies that works to bring justice to maquiladora (border-area factory) workers in Mexico. Addressed to all U.S. corporations that operate in or use workers in Mexico, the standards seek to ensure a safe environment, safe working conditions, and an adequate standard of living.

Legislation governing the North American Free Trade Agreement, enacted during the 1990s to create a North American free trade zone among Mexico, the United States, and Canada, also seeks to protect the welfare of migrant labor. (See also INDENTURED SERVITUDE.)

Suggested Reading

Business for Social Responsibility, "Migrant Labor," www.bsr.org/BSRResources/WhitePaperDetail.cfm?DocumentID=519.

Cholewinski, Ryszard. *Migrant Workers in International Human Rights Law: Their Protection in Countries of Employment*. Oxford, U.K.: Clarendon, 1997.

MIGRANT LEGAL ACTION PROGRAM

The Migrant Legal Action Program (MLAP) is an advocacy and support organization established in 1970 to protect and promote the rights and interests of migrant farmworkers. The MLAP is not a membership organization but provides numerous private attorneys, more than fifty field programs, and various advocacy groups with resource materials; technical assistance; policy development; litigation support; public education; and training on housing, labor conditions, and education for farmworkers.

Suggested Reading

McWilliams, Carey, and Douglas C. Sackman. *Factories in the Field: The Story of Migratory Farm Labor in California*. Berkeley: University of California Press, 2000.

MILITARY, DESEGREGATION OF THE

During the nineteenth and much of the twentieth century, the U.S. military was racially segregated. In the army separate black units were for the most part commanded by white officers. In the navy black and white sailors served aboard the same ships, but black sailors invariably served as stokers (in the days of coal-fired steam boilers) and as mess boys—cooks, waiters, and stewards; they were not combat sailors, and none were officers.

On July 26, 1948, President HARRY S. TRUMAN issued Executive Order 9981, which directed that "all persons in the Armed Services" were to receive "equality of treatment and opportunity . . . without regard to race." Although the order did not explicitly mention integration, when a reporter asked President Truman if that is what the order meant, he replied with a simple yes.

In practice Executive Order 9981 did not result in the immediate integration of the services, especially in the South, but it did set the process into rapid motion. Moreover, the order reached beyond the sphere of military authority and into the general community. When businesses in communities adjacent to military bases refused to serve black soldiers, airmen, or sailors, black and white troops would often cooperate to force integration by going into local segregated businesses and demanding that they both be served. Commanders of military installations informed local segregated businesses that they would be declared off limits to *all* personnel if *all* personnel were not served equally.

Thanks to Truman's executive order, the U.S. military became the wedge that helped make way for integration in civilian society.

Suggested Reading

Moskos, Charles C., and John Sibley Butler. *All That We Can Be: Black Leadership and Racial Integration the Army Way*. New York: Basic, 1996.

MILLION MAN MARCH

Organized by LOUIS FARRAKHAN, leader of the Nation of Islam, and Benjamin Chavis Jr., former executive director of the NATIONAL ASSOCIATION FOR THE ADVANCEMENT OF COLORED PEOPLE, the Million Man March was a nationwide, grassroots mobilization of African American men who traveled to Washington, D.C., for what organizers described as a mass spiritual and social transformation. The day of the march, October 16, 1995, was to be a "holy day of atonement and reconciliation" that would also see the dissemination of a political "manifesto" intended to advance the cause of black America (Institute for Global Communications, "Million Man March Fact Sheet, October 16, 1995," www.igc.org/africanam/hot/facts.html). March organizers also called on marchers to register to vote.

The day-long event began at 5 a.m., with the "Early Morning Glory Service" at the West Front of the U.S. Capitol. From 7 a.m. to 11 a.m. a program entitled "Sankofa: Lessons from the Past—Linkages to the Future" was presented, followed from 11 a.m. to 4 p.m. by a program entitled "Affirmation/Responsibility, Atonement/Reconciliation." From 4 p.m. to 7 p.m. the "Post March Celebration" was held, followed by religious services until 10 p.m. The National Park Service estimated attendance at 850,000, the Nation of Islam at 1.5 million.

The Million Man March was a peaceful demonstration that produced mixed responses in the black as well as white communities. While many blacks and whites applauded the demonstration and its celebration of black pride and self-determination, many also objected to the association of the march with Farrakhan, who had been widely criticized for anti-Semitism and racially polarizing rhetoric. Others objected to the fact that the event was a million *man* march—exclusively for men. (See also ISLAM, NATION OF.)

Suggested Reading

Madhubuti, Haki R., and Maulana Karenga, eds. *Million Man March/Day of Absence: A Commemorative Anthology*. Chicago: Third World Press, 1996.

MIRANDA V. ARIZONA

Born in 1940 in Mesa, Arizona, Ernesto Miranda became a career criminal, committing his first felony—grand theft auto—at age fourteen and, at sixteen, attempting his first rape. By the time he was twenty-one Miranda had been charged with numerous felonies and misdemeanors committed when he was not serving time in custody. In the early 1960s, however, Miranda was living in Mesa and finally had steady employment. On March 13, 1963, he was arrested and taken into custody for the kidnapping and rape of Lois Ann Jameson. When he was put in a lineup, the victim failed to identify him positively, but the police told him that he had been identified, and he was then taken into an interrogation room, where, after two hours of questioning, he confessed to the rape. The confession was not extracted by means of physical coercion, but Miranda was not permitted to consult an attorney before making his confession.

Despite his lawyer's argument that most of the evidence against him was inadmissible, because Miranda had been questioned without having been apprised of his rights or provided with legal counsel (which would have preserved his FIFTH AMENDMENT right to freedom from self-incrimination), Miranda was convicted. His conviction, appealed to the SUPREME COURT in 1966, was overturned.

The decision in *Miranda v. Arizona* was assailed by law enforcement advocates nationwide, who declared that the interrogation room was the domain of the police alone, and that the decision would severely hinder attempts to bring criminals to justice. Two years after *Miranda v. Arizona* was handed down, Congress passed 18 USC Section 3501, which blunted the effects of the decision by stipulating that the provision of "Miranda warnings" was only one factor among many in determining the admissibility of a confession. (As specified in the original *Miranda* decision, an arrestee must be clearly warned that anything he says can be used against him in a court of law; he must be advised of his constitutional right to remain silent and to obtain legal counsel before speaking to police; he must be further advised that counsel will be provided at no charge, if he cannot afford an attorney.) More important, the law stated that if any one of the factors that determined the voluntariness of a confession had been breached (including the absence of Miranda warnings), the confession could still be defined as voluntary and would therefore be admissible. Interestingly, because Justice Department and police officials assumed it was unconstitutional, the 1968 law was rarely used, which also meant that the Supreme Court had no opportunity to rule on it—until *Dickerson v. United States* in 2000.

Charles Dickerson was held by the FEDERAL BUREAU OF INVESTIGATION for questioning about a bank robbery in Alexandria, Virginia. He was interviewed twice: during the first interview he was not advised of his Miranda rights; the circumstances of the second interview were in dispute. Dickerson confessed, leading police to search his apartment and to arrest his cohorts. His confession was suppressed at the trial, but the Fourth Circuit of Appeals overruled the suppression on grounds of Section 3501 of the 1968 law. The case then went to the U.S. Supreme Court, which, as a result, revisited *Miranda v. Arizona*. Chief Justice Rehnquist delivered the majority opinion of the court to let the 1968 Miranda law stand.

Finally, as to the fate of Ernesto Miranda: after the 1966 Supreme Court ruling, he was retried, again convicted, and served a prison term until 1972. In 1976, he was stabbed to death in a bar in Phoenix, Arizona, following an argument over a poker game. (See Appendix A for excerpts from the ruling overturning the Miranda conviction.)

Suggested Reading

Wice, Paul B. *Miranda v. Arizona: "You Have the Right to Remain Silent."* New York: Franklin Watts, 1996.

MISCEGENATION LAWS

Miscegenation is marriage, cohabitation, or sexual intercourse across racial lines. Thirty states carried miscegenation laws on their books well into the twentieth century; sixteen—Alabama, Arkansas, Delaware, Florida, Georgia, Kentucky, Louisiana, Mississippi, Missouri, North Carolina, Oklahoma, South Carolina, Tennessee, Texas, Virginia and West Virginia—retained miscegenation laws until 1967, when, in *LOVING V. VIRGINIA,* the U.S. SUPREME COURT ruled such legislation unconstitutional. Fourteen states—Arizona, California, Colorado, Idaho, Indiana, Maryland, Montana, Nebraska, Nevada, North Dakota, Oregon, South Dakota, Utah, and Wyoming—had repealed their miscegenation laws during the 1950s and 1960s before the high court's decision.

Virginia's Racial Integrity Act of 1924, which was typical of state miscegenation laws, made it "unlawful for any white person in this state to marry any save a white person, or a person with no other admixture of blood than white and American Indian." The law voided all marriages between whites and blacks, and barred couples from leaving the state to get married and then returning. The penalty for violating the statute was severe: "If any white person intermarry with a colored person, or any colored person intermarry with a white person, he shall be guilty of a felony and shall be punished by confinement in the penitentiary for not less than one nor more than five years." Appeals to the state supreme court were in vain. In 1955 that court declared that the statute was valuable inasmuch as it "preserve[s] the racial integrity of [Virginia] citizens" and prevents "the corruption of blood," the creation of "a mongrel breed of citizens," and "the obliteration of racial pride." In the *Loving* case, the Virginia trial judge who had accepted the couple's guilty plea to the charge of miscegenation (sentencing them to a year in jail or a twenty-five-year exile from Virginia) declared that "Almighty God created the races white, black, yellow, Malay and red, and he placed them on separate continents. And but for the interference with his arrangement there would be no cause for such marriages. The fact that he separated the races shows that he did not intend for the races to mix" (www.eugenics-watch.com/roots/chap07.html).

During the colonial era, miscegenation, chiefly between white men and black women, was common and often—but not always—overlooked. In *In Re Davis* (1630) and *Re Sweet* (1640), for example, white men were punished for "fornicating" with black women. Virginia colonial laws were typical. White men who had sexual relationships with black women did risk punishment, but if children resulted, the fathers were not obligated to support either the children nor their mother; the law thus tended to condone *illicit*—that is, extramarital—miscegenation. In 1691 a Virginia statute explicitly barred interracial marriage and levied a fine against any white woman who had a child with a black man; if she could not pay, the woman was to be bound to servitude for a period of time, as was her child.

The Virginia General Assembly passed additional miscegenation laws in 1705, 1748, and 1753, and after the Revolution, in 1792. The focus of all these laws was on interracial marriage rather than interracial sex: in the antebellum South, well into the nineteenth century, sexual relationships between white men and slave women were common, publicly condemned, but not prosecuted by law. Social sanctions against interracial sex increased after the Civil War, and miscegenation laws became more stringent, although the emphasis continued to be on marriage rather than on sex outside of marriage.

Suggested Reading

Moran, Rachel R. *Interracial Intimacy: The Regulation of Race and Romance.* Chicago: University of Chicago Press, 2001.

MISSISSIPPI FREEDOM DEMOCRATIC PARTY

The Mississippi Freedom Democratic Party (MFDP) was founded in April 1964 at the monthly Mississippi convention of the COUNCIL OF FEDERATED ORGANIZATIONS to challenge the state's regular Democratic party—the party that had actively barred AFRICAN AMERICANS from the polls and from any participation in the electoral process.

An MFDP contingent traveled to the 1964 Democratic National Convention in Atlantic City, New Jersey, in the hope of unseating the regular contingent of Mississippi delegates. President LYNDON JOHNSON attempted unsuccessfully to hammer out a compromise prior to the convention and, it is alleged, ordered the FEDERAL BUREAU OF INVESTIGATION to infiltrate and monitor MFDP strategy meetings. When MFDP delegate FANNIE LOU HAMER stood on the convention floor to deliver an eloquent speech to the credentials committee, seeking official recognition of the MFDP delegation, Johnson attempted to preempt the national television audience by scheduling an "urgent" speech of his own. In the end, Democratic Party leaders offered the MFDP two seats "at large," without power to vote. The MFDP refused the compromise.

The appearance of the MFDP at the convention and Hamer's speech were the high points of the organization's short life. Although the party did succeed in involving some Mississippi blacks in the electoral process, its failure to secure official recognition at the convention signaled the diminishing influence of the AFRICAN AMERICAN CIVIL RIGHTS MOVEMENT in Mississippi and the rise of the BLACK POWER MOVEMENT there.

Suggested Reading

Lee, Chana Kai. *For Freedom's Sake: The Life of Fannie Lou Hamer.* Champaign-Urbana: University of Illinois Press, 2000.

Mills, Kay. *This Little Light of Mine: The Life of Fannie Lou Hamer.* New York: Plume, 1994.

MISSISSIPPI, UNIVERSITY OF

Early in 1961 JAMES MEREDITH informed MEDGAR EVERS, of the NATIONAL ASSOCIATION FOR THE ADVANCEMENT OF COLORED PEOPLE (NAACP), that he wanted to enroll in the all-white University of Mississippi. On Evers's recommendation, Meredith secured the advice and support of the director of the NAACP Legal Defense Fund, THURGOOD MARSHALL. Meredith had chosen to integrate a symbol of the Old South, and he knew that he was about to precipitate a showdown.

At the time that the NAACP obtained a federal district court order to compel "Ole Miss" to admit Meredith, Mississippi governor Ross Barnett was rallying support for segregation. "There is no case in history," he declared, "where the Caucasian race has survived social integration." In a halftime speech at an Ole Miss football game, on the eve of the fall semester, Barnett proclaimed: "I love Mississippi. I love her people, her customs! And I love and respect her heritage." The crowd cheered, chanting, "Never shall our emblem go, from Colonel Reb to Old Black Joe!"

On Sunday September 30, 1962, the day after the game, while students returned from the stadium in Jackson to the university campus in Oxford, federal marshals, acting on orders from U.S. Attorney General Robert F. Kennedy, secretly escorted Meredith onto campus. The plan was to register him on Monday. Word of Meredith's presence leaked out, however, and students (as well as others) appeared on campus, lit bonfires, and staged demonstrations. The demonstrations soon grew into a riot, overwhelming the federal marshals on the scene. President John F. Kennedy delivered an urgent television address in which he declared that "Americans are free . . . to disagree with the law, but not to disobey it." By daybreak on Monday, 160 marshals had been injured, twenty-eight of whom had been shot; two civilians, including a French journalist, had been killed. Federal troops were sent in, and order was restored by 8 a.m., in time for Meredith to register as a full-time student. He attended his first class—fittingly, in American history—just one hour later. The university took no disciplinary action against the rioters. Meredith graduated in 1964 after enduring isolation and continual harassment (Peter B. Levy, *The Civil Rights Movement,* Westport, Conn.: Greenwood, 1998, p. 67).

Suggested Reading

Meredith, James. *Three Years in Mississippi.* Bloomington: Indiana University Press, 1966.

MISSOURI COMPROMISE

Early in the nineteenth century, as the United States acquired new western territories, legislators were well aware that the new lands would eventually be divided into states, potentially threatening the precarious legislative balance between free and slave states.

With regard to the lands gained through the Louisiana Purchase, northern abolitionists argued that the Northwest Ordinance of 1787, which had barred the introduction of slavery into the Ohio Territory, had established a free-soil precedent for *all* new territories. Slavery advocates countered that the Constitution, which took precedence over the Northwest Ordinance, actively protected slavery by means of the Fourth Amendment, which guaranteed the security of property—and, moreover, that the Constitution's Three-Fifths Compromise confirmed the legality of slavery. The South's crowning argument against federal intervention in slavery, however, was the fact that the Constitution gave the individual states all power and authority not specifically reserved to the federal government. Since the Constitution did not reserve to federal authority the regulation of slavery, slavery must be under individual state jurisdiction. Thus, those states that were opposed to slavery were free to forbid it within their own borders, while those states that favored slavery were equally free to permit and protect it within *their* borders.

Here the argument stood, precariously, until 1819, when the territory of Missouri petitioned Congress for admission as a slaveholding state, which would have given the Senate a slaveholding majority. To forestall this result, New York representative James Tallmadge responded to Missouri's petition by introducing an amendment to the statehood bill under which the further introduction of slavery into the state would be banned, slaves currently living in the territory would remain slaves after the transition to statehood, and all slaves born in the state would be emancipated when they reached twenty-five years of age. The idea was to eliminate slavery from Missouri by attrition. The House passed the Tallmadge amendment, but the Senate rejected it, then adjourned without deciding the matter of Missouri statehood. When the Senate reconvened, a rancorous debate ensued, with northern senators arguing that Congress had the right to ban slavery in new states and Southerners arguing that new states had the same rights as the original thirteen, including the right to decide whether to allow slavery.

At last, in March 1820 Sen. Jesse B. Thomas of Illinois proposed a compromise: two months earlier, a bill to admit Maine as a state separate from Massachusetts (of which it had long been a part) had passed the House. Thomas proposed that Missouri enter the union as a slave state, but that, simultaneously, Maine be admitted as a free state, thereby preserving (for the time being) the balance between free and slave representation in the Senate. Promoted eloquently by Speaker of the House Henry B. Clay of Kentucky (who thereby earned the somewhat dubious epithet of the Great Compromiser), the Missouri Compromise was passed, supplanting further consideration of the Tallmadge amendment. The Missouri Compromise permitted slavery in Missouri but also drew a line across the Louisiana Territory—at a latitude of 36 degrees, 30 minutes—north of which slavery would be permanently banned, except in the single case of Missouri.

The Missouri Compromise doubtless prevented the immediate outbreak of civil war, but few politicians believed that it was a permanent solution to the slavery issue.

Suggested Reading

Dixon, Susan B. *History of the Missouri Compromise and Slavery in American Politics.* 1903. Reprint, New York: Johnson Reprint Corporation, 1970.

MISSOURI EX REL. GAINES V. CANADA

Missouri ex rel. Gaines v. Canada was argued before the U.S. SUPREME COURT by attorneys from the NATIONAL ASSOCIATION FOR THE ADVANCEMENT OF COLORED PEOPLE on November 9, 1938, on behalf of Lloyd Gaines, an African American who had been refused admission to the School of Law of the University of Missouri. Because of the earlier decision in *PLESSY V. FERGUSON,* in which the Supreme Court had upheld the "SEPARATE BUT EQUAL" DOCTRINE, there was little hope of summarily integrating the School of Law; however, because the state of Missouri did not provide a law school for AFRICAN AMERICANS, the high court held, on December 12, 1938, that the state had either to admit Gaines to the law school or provide him with "separate but equal" education in the form of a law school that admitted blacks. The court permitted the state to arrange for Gaines to attend an integrated law school in a neighboring state until such a law school was opened at Lincoln University, the all-black institution in Missouri.

Suggested Reading

Tushnet, Mark V. *The NAACP's Legal Strategy against Segregated Education, 1925–1950.* Chapel Hill: University of North Carolina Press, 1987.

MONTGOMERY BUS BOYCOTT

On Thursday, December 1, 1955, ROSA PARKS, a black department store seamstress and tailor, boarded a Montgomery, Alabama, city bus on her way home from work. She sat with three other blacks in the fifth row—the first row that blacks, by city ordinance, were permitted to occupy. After the bus had progressed through a few more stops, the four front rows were filled with whites, and one white man was left standing. According to a Montgomery city ordinance, a black person was to surrender a seat to a white person if asked; however, the ordinance also barred blacks and whites from occupying the same row. Accordingly, the bus driver asked all four of the blacks seated in the fifth row to move. Three did so, but Parks refused, and the driver summoned police, who arrested her.

The arrest was no accident. Montgomery's African American activist community had for some time been contemplating a boycott to achieve integration of the city's buses. Parks was active in the NATIONAL ASSOCIATION FOR THE ADVANCEMENT OF COLORED PEOPLE (NAACP), and when E. D. Nixon, director of the local NAACP chapter, heard of Parks's arrest, he posted bond for Parks, then enlisted her cooperation in initiating the boycott. Another NAACP activist, Jo Ann Robinson, mimeographed and distributed flyers urging a one-day boycott of the buses on the day that the Parks case was to be heard. Local black ministers, including MARTIN LUTHER KING JR. agreed to spread the word in their Sunday sermons. King had hoped for 60 percent cooperation with the boycott; to his astonished delight, Montgomery buses were almost completely empty on Monday.

As a result of the initial success of the boycott, King and other activists formed the MONTGOMERY IMPROVEMENT ASSOCIATION (MIA), with King as president. After some debate it was decided that the question of whether to continue the boycott should be put to a mass meeting. The decision at that meeting was unanimous, and the boycott continued.

On December 8, the fourth day of the boycott, King and other MIA members met with the city commissioners and representatives of the local bus company. The MIA presented a DESEGREGATION plan, which the bus company summarily rejected. City officials, moreover, informed the MIA representatives that any city cab driver who charged less than the authorized minimum fare of forty-five cents would be prosecuted. (Black taxi services had begun charging blacks a dime, the same as the bus fare.) The MIA responded with a highly effective expedient: a "private taxi" system—a precisely organized car pool—to get blacks to and from work.

Throughout the boycott, city commissioners and others repeatedly approached various leaders of the black community in an effort to sabotage the undertaking. When these peaceful—if underhanded—efforts failed, some whites resorted to violence. King's home was bombed on January 30, 1956, and Nixon's on February 1. When this intimidation failed, officials obtained an indictment later in the month of eighty-nine blacks under a rarely used statute prohibiting boycotts. King, the first to be tried, was given the choice of paying a $500 fine and $500 in court costs or spending 386 days in the state penitentiary.

The "private taxi" system also came under various forms of attack. For example, insurance companies canceled the liability insurance on church-owned station wagons. (In response, King secured insurance through a black agent in Atlanta, who obtained underwriting from no less a firm than Lloyd's of London, specialists in underwriting high-risk insurance.) The police also arrested drivers for minor and trumped-up traffic offenses. Despite the harassment, pressure, and physical danger, the boycott not only continued but expanded, costing the Montgomery business community dearly—as blacks, unwilling to ride the bus, stopped patronizing downtown stores. Moved by economic necessity, business owners formed a group called the Men of Montgomery in an attempt to negotiate directly with the MIA. The negotiations stalled.

In the meantime, representatives of the boycott took the city and the bus company to federal court, securing a ruling that declared segregation on buses unconstitutional. When the city appealed, the U.S. SUPREME COURT, on November 13, 1956, upheld the lower court's ruling. Although the decision officially ended the Montgomery Bus Boycott on a note of high triumph, blacks did not return to the buses until December 21, 1956, when the court's mandate came into force.

The transition to integrated buses was not an easy one. There were sniper incidents, which forced the suspension of bus operations after 5 P.M. A white group attempted unsuccessfully to inaugurate a whites-only bus service. Extremists bombed the homes of three black families, four Baptist churches, and the People's Service Station and Cab Stand, and an unexploded bomb was removed from King's own front porch. Of the seven white men arrested for the bombings, five were indicted. Two defendants, Raymond D. York and Sonny Kyle Livingston, were found not guilty, despite having signed confessions. The other cases were dismissed in a compromise agreement that dropped the cases against the blacks who had been arrested under the antiboycott laws.

Suggested Reading

Jo Ann Robinson. *The Montgomery Bus Boycott and the Women Who Started It.* Knoxville: University of Tennessee Press, 1987.

MONTGOMERY IMPROVEMENT ASSOCIATION

The Montgomery Improvement Association (MIA) was formed in 1955 by African American activists in Montgomery, Alabama, to organize and administer the MONTGOMERY BUS BOYCOTT. Its president was MARTIN LUTHER KING JR.. The MIA also represented the boycott and the black community in negotiations with bus company officials and the Montgomery city government. Simultaneously, the organization retained attorney Fred Gray, who, on February 1, 1956, filed a petition in federal court to declare segregated seating on buses unconstitutional. The ruling was secured, and, when the city appealed, the U.S. SUPREME COURT weighed in, in November, with a decision that legally brought an end to segregated seating on public buses.

After the triumph of the Montgomery Bus Boycott, the MIA became the principal founding group of the SOUTHERN CHRISTIAN LEADERSHIP CONFERENCE (SCLC). With the ascendancy of the SCLC, the MIA was relegated to a secondary role but continued to engage in civil rights activism in Montgomery, including a voter-registration drive and an unsuccessful attempt to integrate the city's parks. The organization succeeded, however, in 1962, in pressuring the Montgomery bus company to hire black drivers.

Suggested Reading

Jo Ann Robinson. *The Montgomery Bus Boycott and the Women Who Started It.* Knoxville: University of Tennessee Press, 1987.

MORGAN V. VIRGINIA

In *Morgan v. Virginia* (1946), the U.S. SUPREME COURT, after hearing arguments by THURGOOD MARSHALL and William H. Hastie, attorneys from the NATIONAL ASSOCIATION FOR THE ADVANCEMENT OF COLORED PEOPLE, struck down as unconstitutional state laws requiring segregated seating on interstate buses.

The case came about when Irene Morgan boarded a Greyhound bus in Gloucester, Virginia, bound for Baltimore, Maryland, in July 1944. Morgan, who was recovering from a recent miscarriage, found a seat in the rear section that was reserved for blacks. When a white couple boarded about a half hour later, the driver ordered Morgan and the black woman seated next to her, who was holding an infant, to relinquish their seats to the couple. Morgan refused and was arrested. She subsequently pleaded guilty to a charge of resisting arrest, for which she was fined $100; however, she refused to plead guilty to having violated Virginia's segregation law. Her stance allowed her attorney, Spottswood Robinson III, to argue that segregation laws unfairly impeded interstate commerce. Found guilty nonetheless, Morgan was fined $10. Robinson, joined by Thurgood Marshall, appealed the case up through the U.S. SUPREME COURT, which decided that the Virginia statute caused such inconvenience to passengers as to unfairly impede interstate commerce, and was therefore in violation of the Constitution.

The widely publicized decision inspired in 1947 the JOURNEY OF RECONCILIATION and, subsequently, the first FREEDOM RIDE.

Suggested Reading

Levy, Peter B. *The Civil Rights Movement.* Westport, Conn.: Greenwood, 1998.

MORMON CHURCH

In March 1830 young Joseph Smith Jr. published *The Book of Mormon,* and in April of that year founded a religion—with six initial adherents—that was based on the book. *The Book of Mormon* relates how, in 1820, Smith, then fifteen, was visited by God the Father and Jesus Christ near his family's farm in upstate New York. In 1823 he was visited again, this time by an angel named Moroni, who instructed him to dig in a certain place on a nearby hill. There Smith unearthed a book that consisted of beaten gold plates engraved with the words of Moroni's father, Mormon. The book told of a struggle between a tribe of evil and a tribe of good, a combat that had taken place in the New World long before the days of Columbus. From this conflict, Moroni had emerged as the only survivor of the tribe of the good; whoever recovered his book was charged with restoring to the world the true Church of Christ.

The Church of Jesus Christ of Latter-Day Saints—popularly called the Mormon Church—grew very rapidly. By 1844, when Smith and his followers settled in Nauvoo, Illinois, a separatist community they built themselves, it had swelled from 6 to 15,000 members. Although they sought to live apart, Mormons were persecuted wherever they went, and the existence of their religion would sorely test the limits of freedom of religion in the United States.

Most repugnant to gentiles (as Mormons called those outside the faith) was the Mormon practice of polygamy. Opposition to the Mormons and to polygamy often became violent, and, on June 27, 1844, Joseph Smith and his brother were murdered by a mob, prompting Smith's second-in-command, Brigham Young, to move the faithful from Nauvoo to a remote location in the far West. The Mormon Trek spanned the 1840s and 1850s, carrying Mormons to the shore of the Great Salt Lake, where they built Salt Lake City.

Young had settled his followers in the remote desert in the belief that no one else would covet the country and that the members of his church would be left to themselves to practice their religion as they pleased. However, as non-Mormon settlers arrived and as travelers bound for California passed through, violent clashes became frequent. Polygamy was typically the major issue. In 1870 the U.S. Congress passed several laws barring polygamy, and in 1873 passed the Poland Act, which gave Congress the power to prosecute Mormons for the practice. The Edmunds Act, also of 1873, summarily disenfranchised all Mormons who practiced polygamy.

The Mormon Church chose one of its leaders, George Reynolds, to bring the antipolygamy laws to a test in the U.S. SUPREME COURT. Convicted of polygamy in territorial district court, Reynolds appealed to the Utah Territorial Supreme Court, which upheld the conviction, and appealed next to the U.S. Supreme Court, which heard the case in 1879 and unanimously upheld the conviction and the federal antibigamy statutes under which the conviction had been made. The high court specifically ruled polygamy to be beyond the protections of the First Amendment. While the court acknowledged that polygamy was an expression of a sincere religious belief, it held that the right of this expression failed to outweigh the greater public interest—in this case, protecting the fabric of society from the destructive practice of having multiple wives. The court also ruled that making a special exception to permit Mormons to practice polygamy would tear down the wall separating church and state.

The decision in *Reynolds v. United States* (1879) was important not only to the Mormon Church and as a definition of the limits of religious freedom, but has also figured as a precedent in legal debate over other issues, including CIVIL UNIONS and the use of hallucinogens in Native American religious rituals. Following the decision in *Reynolds,* the mainstream of the Church of Jesus Christ of Latter-Day Saints proved increasingly willing to renounce the doctrine and practice of polygamy, and in 1890 the church issued a manifesto officially abandoning polygamous marriage; however, some Mormons continue to practice polygamy, in defiance of both the church and the law. (See also RELIGION, FREEDOM OF.)

Suggested Reading

Van Wagoner, Richard S. *Mormon Polygamy: A History.* New York: Signature, 1992.

MOSES, ROBERT PARRIS (1935–)

Robert Moses headed the organizing efforts of the STUDENT NONVIOLENT COORDINATING COMMITTEE (SNCC) in Mississippi during the early 1960s, including, most notably, FREEDOM SUMMER.

Born in New York City on January 23, 1935, the son of a janitor, Moses excelled in school, earning a B.A. from Hamilton College (1956) and an M.A. in philosophy from

Harvard (1957). He was about to pursue a Ph.D. in mathematics at Harvard when his father fell ill, and Moses returned to New York to care for him. While supporting himself and his father by teaching high school mathematics, Moses closely followed the SIT-INS that were occurring as part of a general DESEGREGATION campaign in the South, and he felt compelled to go to Atlanta to join the civil rights movement. There he became associated with SNCC and then traveled to Mississippi, where he began organizing a voter education campaign.

Although Moses was committed to the idea of a local, grassroots movement, he came to realize that RACISM was so institutionalized in the South that only a crusade of national scope would begin to erode it. From this insight, FREEDOM SUMMER and the MISSISSIPPI FREEDOM DEMOCRATIC PARTY grew.

Although in 1965 Moses delivered a keynote address at an anti–Vietnam War demonstration organized by STUDENTS FOR A DEMOCRATIC SOCIETY, he became disillusioned with liberalism, dropped out of the civil rights movement, and even adopted Parris (his mother's maiden name) as his last name in an effort to divorce himself from the recognition he had gained as a civil rights activist. Moses traveled to Africa during the 1970s and returned to the United States in 1976 to resume his mathematics studies. In 1980 he combined mathematics with a revival of his earlier activism and devised the ALGEBRA PROJECT to teach mathematics to underprivileged youth. In 1992 he took the project to rural Mississippi as the Delta Algebra Project.

Suggested Reading

Moses, Robert P., and Charles E. Cobb Jr. *Radical Equations: Math Literacy and Civil Rights.* New York: Beacon, 2000.

MOUNT LAUREL CASES

In 1971 Ethel Lawrence sued Mt. Laurel, a predominantly white, upper-middle-class suburban New Jersey township that had used exclusionary zoning to block plans for an apartment complex that would have accommodated lower-income residents—presumably including black residents. Like many other communities, Mt. Laurel used its zoning power to create and enforce de facto segregation. By zoning for low-density development only, a suburb can effectively exclude those who cannot afford to purchase single-family dwellings—specifically, renters, lower-income residents, and minority residents.

The Lawrence case led to the first *Mount Laurel* case, *Southern Burlington County NAACP v. Mount Laurel,* in which the New Jersey Supreme Court ruled that Mt. Laurel's zoning ordinances violated the state constitution's guarantee of equal protection of the laws. The court's reasoning was that municipalities were constitutionally obligated to provide for the general welfare and were therefore obliged to consider regional as well as local welfare in making zoning decisions. More specifically, the court ruled that every community has an obligation to use its zoning authority in a positive manner—and that this obligation includes affording the opportunity to construct low- and moderate-income housing.

The *Southern Burlington County NAACP v. Mount Laurel* decision recognized that suburban development often occurs adjacent to relatively poor inner cities, and that exclusionary zoning effectively prevented inner city residents from moving into the newly developed suburbs—thus effectively denying some residents of a given region equal access to the dwelling, educational, and commercial advantages of the suburbs of that region.

As compelling as the first *Mount Laurel* decision was, many New Jersey municipalities refused to comply, prompting a second state supreme court decision in 1983, in *South Burlington County NAACP v. Township of Mount Laurel* popularly known as *Mount Laurel II,* which specified more stringent guidelines for the provision of affordable housing. Pursuant to *Mount Laurel II,* the New Jersey state legislature enacted laws providing funding to encourage the construction of low- and moderate-income housing in desirable areas.

Suggested Reading

Kirp, David L. *Our Town: Race, Housing, and the Soul of Suburbia.* New Brunswick: Rutgers University Press, 1996.

NASHVILLE STUDENT MOVEMENT

In 1958 black leaders in Nashville, Tennessee, founded the Nashville Christian Leadership Conference (NCLC), an affiliate organization of the SOUTHERN CHRISTIAN LEADERSHIP CONFERENCE. During much of that year, NCLC members—under the direction of Rev. Kelly Miller Smith, president of the NCLC and pastor of the First Colored Baptist Church—studied and discussed nonviolent approaches to segregation. In 1959 the organization began a movement to desegregate downtown Nashville. In November and December Smith and Rev. James M. Lawson Jr., as well as students from Nashville's black colleges—including Marion Barry, James Bevel, JOHN LEWIS, Diane Nash, and others—attempted to buy goods at segregated department stores and to eat at segregated lunch counters. During 1958–1959 increasing numbers of black students—from the American Baptist Theological Seminary, Fisk University, Meharry Medical College, and Tennessee A & I State University, all Nashville-area black institutions—were trained in methods of nonviolent protest. By the beginning of 1960 the Nashville student movement was under way.

On February 13, 1960, twelve days after the GREENSBORO SIT-IN, the Nashville student movement began its first SIT-INS, entering the Kress, Woolworth, and McClellan stores simultaneously, at about 12:40 p.m. After making purchases the students occupied seats at the lunch counters. About two hours later all the stores closed their lunch counters without having served the students. During the next three months the sit-ins continued, not only at the three stores initially targeted but at the Greyhound and Trailways bus terminals, a Grant's variety store, a Walgreen drugstore, and two major Nashville department stores, Cain-Sloan and Harvey.

On February 27 a group of whites attacked the demonstrators, and in the ensuing melee many students were arrested. Two days later, eighty-one were found guilty of disorderly conduct. They refused to pay the fines levied against them, choosing instead to serve time in jail. Lawson, a student at the time, was expelled from Vanderbilt University's divinity school.

Not only did Nashville's black community rally behind the demonstrators, but on March 3 Mayor Ben West appointed a biracial committee to investigate segregation in the city. When on April 5 the committee recommended that lunch counters be divided into white and black sections, the NCLC (acting on behalf of the Nashville student movement) rejected the proposal; the result was a standoff. On April 19 the home of Z. Alexander Looby, attorney for the demonstrators, was destroyed by a bomb, triggering a mass march to city hall. The march was followed by a new round of talks, and at last city officials determined that lunch counters should be unconditionally desegregated. On May 10, 1960, Nashville became the first major southern city to desegregate its public facilities.

The success of the Greensboro and Nashville protests inspired numerous student protests throughout the South, and the Nashville students' carefully crafted principles of direct nonviolent protest, which included specific rules of conduct, were used as models in subsequent actions.

Suggested Reading

Lewis, John, with Michael D'Orso. *Walking with the Wind: A Memoir of the Movement*. 1998. Reprint, New York: Harvest, 1999.

Wynn, Linda T. "Nashville Sit-Ins (1959–1961)," www.tnstate.edu/library/digital/nash.htm.

NATIONAL ABORTION RIGHTS ACTION LEAGUE

In 1969, in an effort to bring national unity to the initiatives of various state groups, a group of abortion-rights activists, including BETTY FRIEDAN, founded the National Association for the Repeal of Abortion Laws. In 1973, when the SUPREME COURT's ruling in *ROE V. WADE* secured the right to abortion, the National Association for the Repeal of Abortion Laws renamed itself the National Abortion Rights

Action League (NARAL). Including its many state affiliates, NARAL has about 300,000 members.

NARAL works both as a public outreach organization, providing information on reproductive rights and health issues, and as a political organization, working to elect prochoice candidates at all levels of government. In recent years NARAL has added to its mission the promotion of policies and programs designed to enable women and men to make responsible and informed decisions about sexuality, contraception, pregnancy, childbirth, and ABORTION. The purpose of this new direction is to make abortion less necessary.

NARAL encompasses three organizations:

- NARAL, Inc., a nonprofit corporation, operates through the political and legislative systems to advocate for comprehensive reproductive health policies and to secure reproductive choice for all Americans.
- NARAL-PAC, a political action committee, directly supports prochoice candidates through advertising campaigns, get-out-the-vote efforts, and financial contributions.
- The NARAL Foundation is a charitable organization founded in 1977 that supports and performs research and legal work, publishes policy reports, conducts public education campaigns, and provides leadership training for grassroots activists nationwide.

Suggested Reading

NARAL, www.naral.org.

NATIONAL ADVISORY COMMISSION ON CIVIL DISORDERS, REPORT OF

In response to widespread race riots during the middle to late 1960s, President LYNDON B. JOHNSON appointed the National Advisory Commission on Civil Disorders, under the chairmanship of Illinois governor Otto Kerner, to investigate the causes of the rioting and to recommend remedies. The commission (commonly known as the Kerner Commission) concluded that the riots were the product of the urban black ghetto—an environment that had been created by white RACISM. The commission recommended a program of federal spending to alleviate adverse economic conditions in the ghetto and to promote the full integration of AFRICAN AMERICANS into mainstream American life. The most chilling conclusion of the commission was contained in a single italicized sentence: *"Our nation is moving toward two societies, one black, one white—separate and unequal."* (See Appendix A for excerpts from the *Report of the National Advisory Commission on Civil Disorders.*).

Suggested Reading

National Advisory Commission on Civil Disorders. *Report of the National Advisory Commission Civil Disorders.* New York: New York Times Company, 1968.

NATIONAL AFFORDABLE HOUSING ACT

The National Affordable Housing Act was passed in 1990. Comprehensive and complex, the law begins by stating that "The Congress affirms the national goal that every American family be able to afford a decent home in a suitable environment." Toward this end, the act sets forth a national housing policy.

The act provides for government investment in affordable housing, which takes two principal forms: investment partnerships with states, municipalities, and the private sector; and direct grants to first-time home buyers, which are made through the National Homeownership Trust. A program called Youthbuild provides grants to disadvantaged young people who assist in the construction of low-income housing, chiefly for the homeless.

While the National Affordable Housing Act has increased the availability of housing for the elderly and for low-income families, many of its programs have never been fully funded or implemented. (See Appendix A for the portions of the law that set out a national housing policy.)

Suggested Reading

U.S. Senate. *The Nation's Affordable Housing Crisis: Hearing before the Subcommittee on Housing and Urban Affairs of the Committee on Banking, Housing, and Urban Affairs, March 6, 1992.* Washington, D.C.: U.S. Government Printing Office, 1992.

NATIONAL AMERICAN WOMAN SUFFRAGE ASSOCIATION

The National American Woman Suffrage Association (NAWSA) was created in 1890 through the merger of two rival groups, the National Woman Suffrage Association (NWSA), led by ELIZABETH CADY STANTON and SUSAN B. ANTHONY, and the American Woman Suffrage Association (AWSA), led by Lucy Stone, Henry Blackwell, and Julia Ward Howe. Both of the older organizations had been established in the late 1860s; the NWSA focused on obtaining the franchise for women by means of a constitutional amendment, and the AWSA favored state-by-state campaigns rather than federal change. The merger of the groups into the NAWSA also merged the two strategies.

After passage of the Nineteenth Amendment in 1920, which secured the vote for women, the NAWSA became the basis for the League of Women Voters.

Suggested Reading

Kraditor, Aileen S. *The Ideas of the Woman Suffrage Movement, 1890–1920.* New York: Norton, 1981.

Wheeler, Marjorie Spruill, ed. *One Woman, One Vote: Rediscovering the Woman Suffrage Movement.* Troutdale, Ore.: Newsage, 1995.

NATIONAL ASSOCIATION FOR THE ADVANCEMENT OF COLORED PEOPLE

The National Association for the Advancement of Colored People (NAACP) was founded in 1909 as an outgrowth of the Niagara Movement, which was led primarily by W.E.B. Du Bois. Interracial from the beginning, the NAACP was dedicated to ending segregation and discrimination in areas such as education, housing, employment, transportation, and voting. As a more general goal, the NAACP sought, through advocacy efforts, to ensure that blacks enjoyed all constitutionally guaranteed rights.

During 1909–1934, when Du Bois was active as the NAACP's director of research and as editor of its magazine, the *Crisis,* the NAACP became the single most influential civil rights organization. Under the leadership of Du Bois and the other founders of the Niagara Movement, the organization opposed Booker T. Washington's philosophy of accommodationism, which called for blacks to defer the quest for social and political equality in exchange for achieving a measure of black economic self-determination; to the NAACP, equality and economic self-determination were inseparable. Thanks in large part to the expanding influence of the NAACP, accommodationism ultimately passed out of favor.

From its inception the NAACP has been most influential—and most successful—in its advocacy work and in its management of civil rights litigation. In 1939 the organization created, as an independent entity, the NAACP Legal Defense and Education Fund—which was, in effect, the legal arm of the African American civil rights movement. Especially during the late 1940s and early 1950s, fund lawyers (most notably Thurgood Marshall) argued a series of landmark cases before the U.S. Supreme Court, most of which were aimed at overturning *Plessy v. Ferguson,* the legal basis for the "separate but equal" doctrine, which had supplied the foundation for enduring segregation, especially in the South. The culmination of this series of cases was *Brown v. Board of Education of Topeka, Kansas,* in which the Supreme Court found that separate educational facilities were inherently unequal, and therefore unconstitutional.

In addition to engaging in litigation, the NAACP works as a lobbying organization to secure the enactment of civil rights legislation. As an outreach organization, the NAACP creates and supports education and public information programs.

Suggested Reading

Hughes, Langston. *Fight for Freedom: The Story of the NAACP.* New York: Norton, 1962.

NATIONAL ASSOCIATION OF COLORED WOMEN

The National Association of Colored Women (NACW) was founded at an 1896 convention in Washington, D.C., when the National Federation of Afro-American Women and the National League of Colored Women merged. The organization's founders included Ida Bell Wells-Barnett, Frances E.W. Harper, Harriet Tubman, and Mary Church Terrell, who was elected the NACW's first president.

The organization's motto, "Lifting As We Climb," reflected its goal of improving both the lot of its members and of blacks in general, especially black women. Under Terrell's leadership, the NACW undertook projects related to job training, wage equity, and child care; the organization also funded and established kindergartens, vocational schools, summer camps, and retirement homes. The NACW was in the forefront of opposition to segregated public transportation and was active in raising public awareness of lynching and combating the practice.

In 1912 the NACW established a national college scholarship fund for black women and, in the same year, endorsed the women's suffrage movement—two years before the General Federation of Women's Clubs, the NACW's white counterpart, would make the same endorsement.

The period of most intense and influential NACW activity was in the late 1910s, when national membership reached more than 300,000, but even by the mid-twentieth century, when the NACW role was somewhat diminished, the organization had chapters in most states, as the organization shifted focus from national to local, community-based service projects.

Suggested Reading

Sudbury, Julia. *Other Kinds of Dreams: Black Women's Organizations and the Politics of Transformation.* New York: Routledge, 1998.

White, Deborah Gray. *Too Heavy a Load: Black Women in Defense of Themselves, 1894–1994.* New York: Norton, 1998.

NATIONAL CENTER FOR LESBIAN RIGHTS

Founded in 1977, the National Center for Lesbian Rights (NCLR) is a legal center dedicated to advancing the rights and safety of lesbians and their families. Through both litigation and advocacy, the NCLR works to eliminate discriminatory laws and to create new laws and policies. Central issues include child custody, same-sex adoption, and CIVIL UNIONS.

Based in San Francisco, the NCLR operates in all fifty states through a network of volunteer attorneys.

Suggested Reading

National Center for Lesbian Rights, www.nclrights.org.

NATIONAL CENTER FOR YOUTH LAW

The goal of the National Center for Youth Law (NCYL), a private nonprofit law office founded in 1978, is to use the law to protect children from the damage caused by poverty and to improve the lives of those children who do live in poverty. The NCYL advocates to expand health care and social programs and to increase access to housing for families with children; it works within the existing welfare system to secure public benefits to meet the special needs of children; and it works with advocates, foster parents, and others to reform state child-welfare systems. In California, through a program of public information and advocacy, the NCYL works to improve the collection of child support.

NCYL advocacy efforts include the publication and distribution of articles, manuals, and books, and of a bimonthly journal, *Youth Law News.* The organization furnishes technical assistance and training, and generally assists legal advocates for poor children. As appropriate, the NCYL also lobbies for legislative reform.

Suggested Reading

National Center for Youth Law, www.ncyl.org.

NATIONAL CLEARINGHOUSE FOR THE DEFENSE OF BATTERED WOMEN

The National Clearinghouse for the Defense of Battered Women, a national organization based in Philadelphia, helps battered women—those faced with life-threatening violence from their abusers—by providing technical and legal assistance, support, resources, networking, and training.

Suggested Reading

Bradley Berry, Dawn. *Domestic Violence Sourcebook.* New York: McGraw-Hill, 2000.

Gosselin, Denise Kindschi. *Heavy Hands: An Introduction to the Crimes of Domestic Violence.* Paramus, N.J.: Prentice Hall, 2000.

NATIONAL CONGRESS OF AMERICAN INDIANS

The National Congress of American Indians (NCAI) was founded in 1944 to foster unity and cooperation among tribal governments and to protect treaty rights and sovereign rights; the organization was established in response to the termination of tribal ownership of lands and other assimilation policies that the U.S. federal government had forced on tribal governments.

The NCAI now includes 250 member tribes from all over the United States and is the nation's leading tribal government organization. Its central goals are to protect programs and services that benefit Native American families, especially programs for youth and elders; to support Native American education, including Head Start, elementary, postsecondary, and adult programs; to improve health care for Native Americans—in particular, to prevent juvenile substance abuse, HIV-AIDS, and other major diseases; to support environmental protection and natural resources management; to protect Native American cultural resources and religious freedoms; to promote economic opportunity for Native Americans on and off the reservations; and to protect the right to decent, safe, and affordable housing.

Suggested Reading

National Congress of American Indians, www.ncai.org.

NATIONAL COUNCIL OF LA RAZA

The National Council of La Raza (NCLR) was established in 1968 as a private, nonprofit, nonpartisan organization whose goal is to reduce poverty and discrimination and to improve opportunities for Hispanic Americans. The organization assists community-based Hispanic organizations by providing assistance in management, governance, program operations, and resource development. The NCLR also supports and conducts research, policy analysis, and advocacy to provide a Hispanic perspective on national and local issues such as education, immigration, housing, health, employment and training, and civil rights. The organization works to increase understanding of Hispanic needs among the general public and policy makers alike.

The largest constituency-based national Hispanic organization in the United States, the NCLR has more than 270 formal affiliates in forty states, Puerto Rico, and the District of Columbia. Through a broader network of informal affiliates, it is linked to some thirty thousand groups and individuals nationwide. The organization publishes a quarterly newsletter, *Agenda,* and issues policy reports and training modules.

Suggested Reading

National Council of La Raza, www.nclr.org.

NATIONAL COUNCIL OF SENIOR CITIZENS

The National Council of Senior Citizens (NCSC) was founded in 1961 by the Democratic National Committee and the American Federation of Labor–Congress of Industrial Organizations—and, until December 31, 2000, when it ceased operations as a membership organization, received substantial funding from the federal government. The NCSC was an important advocate and lobbying group for the preservation of Medicare and Social Security and for the enactment of a national health care plan that would have included long-term care, reduced drug costs, and housing assistance for seniors.

Suggested Reading

Powell, Lawrence Alfred, Kenneth J. Branco, and John B. Williamson. *The Senior Rights Movement: Framing the Policy Debate in America.* New York: Twayne, 1996.

NATIONAL FARM WORKERS ASSOCIATION

Migrant leader Cesar Chavez founded the National Farm Workers Association (NFWA) in 1962 to unify migrant agricultural workers so that they could mount effective labor actions. In 1965, under Chavez's leadership, the NFWA organized a strike of California grape pickers to demand higher wages. A unique component of the strike was a nationwide appeal to consumers to boycott California table grapes as a show of support for the strikers. Together, the strike and boycott were highly effective. In 1966 the NFWA merged with a branch of the American Federation of Labor–Congress of Industrial Organizations to become the United Farm Workers.

Suggested Reading

Ferriss, Susan, and Ricardo Sandoval. *The Fight in the Fields: Cesar Chavez and the Farmworkers Movement.* New York: Harcourt Brace, 1997.

NATIONAL GAY AND LESBIAN TASK FORCE

The National Gay and Lesbian Task Force (NGLTF) was founded in 1973 to secure the civil rights of gay, lesbian, bisexual, and transgendered people and to provide a vehicle for a powerful political movement. In that same year the organization was instrumental in persuading the American Psychiatric Association to discontinue its practice of classifying homosexuality as a mental illness. In 1975 NGLTF lobbying efforts helped to secure a ruling from the U.S. Civil Service Commission that allowed gay men and women to serve in government employment. That same year, working with Representative Bella Abzug, D.-N.Y., the organization crafted the first gay rights bill to be brought before Congress. The NGLTF has sponsored national educational campaigns concerning gay rights, and in 1978 it released the first-ever study of discrimination in the private sector on the basis of sexual orientation.

In the 1980s the NGLTF increasingly focused on the issue of antigay violence, issuing a comprehensive national report on the subject in 1984. In 1990 the organization was in the forefront of efforts to secure passage of the Hate Crimes Statistic Act (28 USC 534). The NGLTF continued to fight antigay discrimination throughout the 1990s, and in 1991, in conjunction with the National Center for Lesbian Rights, launched the Families Project to promote the rights of gay and lesbian parents, especially in adoption situations. That same year the NGLTF developed the Fight the Right Project to educate activists and to assist local organizers in combating antigay ballot initiatives. In 1997 the NGLTF launched the Federation of Lesbian, Gay, Bisexual and Transgender Political Statewide Organizations, and in 1999 it created the Legislative Lawyering Project to promote progressive legislation at the state and federal levels.

Suggested Reading

National Gay and Lesbian Task Force, www.ngltf.org.

NATIONAL HOUSING LAW PROJECT

The National Housing Law Project (NHLP), a national housing and legal advocacy center, was established in 1968 to provide specialized legal assistance to attorneys dealing with issues related to housing and urban development. Since its founding the organization has enlarged its mission to advance housing justice for poor people by working to preserve and increase the supply of affordable housing, to improve existing housing conditions, to expand and enforce the rights of low-income tenants and homeowners, and to increase housing opportunities for racial and ethnic minorities. The organization also provides advocacy for individuals and groups and lobbies for progressive housing laws.

Suggested Reading

National Housing Law Project, www.nhlp.org.

NATIONAL IMMIGRATION PROJECT

Created in 1974, the National Immigration Project is part of the National Lawyers Guild, an organization that was founded in 1937 as the nation's first racially integrated bar association. The National Immigration Project is a network of immigration lawyers, law students, and others in the legal field who work to end unlawful immigration practices, to recognize the contributions of immigrants in this country, to promote fair immigration practices, and to expand the civil and human rights of all immigrants in the United States, regardless of their legal status.

The National Immigration Project provides technical assistance, advice, and resources to lawyers and community groups; participates directly in litigation; and works to create new legal strategies for advancing the rights of immigrants. It also sponsors seminars and produces publications to develop and improve legal and advocacy skills in the area of immigration law. Special areas of focus include battered immigrant women, border violence, HIV-AIDS, the rights of incarcerated noncitizen defendants, and Immigration and Naturalization Service raids and enforcement practices.

Suggested Reading

National Immigration Project, www.nationalimmigrationproject.org.

NATIONAL LAWYERS GUILD

The National Lawyers Guild (NLG) was founded in 1937 as an alternative to the conservative—and, at the time, racially segregated—American Bar Association. The NLG is dedicated to the proposition that human rights are more sacred than property interests. Guild members include lawyers, law students, legal workers, and jailhouse lawyers.

As part of its commitment to the rights of both working people and the unemployed, the NLG supported and promoted President Franklin D. Roosevelt's New Deal. During the 1940s the NLG assisted with union organizing campaigns, opposed racial discrimination, fought against state poll taxes (which were aimed primarily at disenfranchising black voters), and investigated race riots. Following World War II NLG members were active at the Nuremberg trials, which heard the cases of Nazi war criminals, and they participated in the founding of the United Nations. In the 1950s, during the early years of the Cold War, as the NLG took on the defense of labor leaders, political activists, and others accused of being communists or fellow travelers, the organization found itself under attack by the House Un-American Activities Committee and the forces of Sen. Joseph McCarthy.

During the 1960s the NLG took an active role in the burgeoning African American civil rights movement, creating the Committee to Aid Southern Lawyers and opening offices in Jackson, Mississippi, and other southern cities. In the 1970s the organization turned its attention to providing legal counsel to draft resisters and antiwar activists, and in 1971 the guild opened offices in Southeast Asia to provide legal defense for American soldiers resisting the Vietnam War. During this period the NLG also became active in promoting affirmative action, gay rights, and women's rights, and organized defense teams for prisoners who were involved in the Attica Prison riot and for protesters who were involved in the siege at Wounded Knee.

In the 1980s, during the conservative backlash that accompanied the administration of President Ronald Reagan, the NLG mounted a legal campaign in support of affirmative action, especially in law schools, and came to the defense of other civil rights gains then under attack. The 1990s saw a renewed focus on workers' rights, this time both in the United States and abroad.

Suggested Reading

Ginger, Ann Fagan. *The National Lawyers Guild: From Roosevelt through Reagan.* Philadelphia: Temple University Press, 1988.

NATIONAL NEGRO CONFERENCE

The National Negro Conference (NNC) was a Great Depression–era organization, founded in 1936, that provided the foundation for the Southern Negro Youth Congress, founded in 1937. The NNC was highly political and embraced socialism, and, after World War II, was listed by the U.S. attorney general as a subversive organization. As a force for practical social change, the NNC was never very powerful, and it dissolved during the early 1950s.

Suggested Reading

Reggio, Michael H. "Human Rights in Twentieth-Century United States." In *Civil Rights in America, 1500 to the Present,* ed. Michael H. Reggio. Detroit: Gale Research, 1998.

NATIONAL ORGANIZATION FOR WOMEN

The National Organization for Women (NOW, Inc.) was established on June 30, 1966, in Washington, D.C., by women attending the Third National Conference of the Commission on the Status of Women. Created in 1961 by order of President John F. Kennedy to investigate and report on the status of women in the United States, the commission issued a report in 1963, which concluded that women were consistently discriminated against in most aspects of American life. Among the twenty-eight women who founded NOW was its first president, Betty Friedan, author of *The Feminine Mystique* (1963), a groundbreaking study of women's social disaffection.

NOW's principal goal has always been to bring about equality for all women. To that end, the organization has lobbied for legislation; sponsored litigation; and organized rallies, mass marches, pickets, and nonviolent civil disobedience.

Throughout its history, NOW has initiated or supported important lawsuits against sex discrimination in employment, and has been highly successful in this arena. In 1969, in *Weeks v. Southern Bell,* attorney Sylvia Roberts, NOW's southern regional director, won a ruling from the U.S. Fifth Circuit Court that held that the company had violated Title VII of the Civil Rights Act of 1964 by barring women from jobs that required lifting more than thirty pounds. This decision was the first to apply Title VII to sex discrimination. During the 1970s NOW organized lobbying efforts and pickets of newspapers to win a ruling from the Equal Employment Opportunity Commission that compelled newspapers to eliminate sex-segregated help-wanted ads.

NOW was a major supporter of the Equal Rights Amendment (ERA) and continues to be a major force in efforts to protect abortion rights. In 1995 NOW organized the first mass demonstration to focus on the issue of violence against women, drawing 250,000 demonstrators to the National Mall in Washington, D.C.

With 500,000 contributing members in 550 chapters in all fifty states and the District of Columbia, NOW is the largest feminist organization in the United States. The organization's official priorities include winning economic equality for women and securing it through the ERA; championing abortion rights, reproductive freedom, and other women's health issues; opposing racism; fighting bigotry against lesbians and gay men; and ending all violence against women. (See also NOW Legal Defense and Education Fund.)

Suggested Reading

Freedman, Estelle B. *No Turning Back: The History of Feminism and the Future of Women.* New York: Ballantine, 2002.

NATIONAL URBAN LEAGUE

The National Urban League, often simply called the Urban League, is the oldest and largest community-based organization devoted to empowering blacks to enter the economic and social mainstream. Its goal is to enable African Americans "to secure economic self-reliance, parity and power and civil rights."

The Urban League's predecessor organization, the Committee on Urban Conditions among Negroes, was established in New York City on September 29, 1910, at the time of the Great Migration of southern rural blacks to the North. Although racism was not sanctioned by law in the North as it was in the South, black newcomers were nevertheless confronted by racial discrimination—barred from all but menial employment, housed poorly, and educated inadequately. The Committee on Urban Conditions among Negroes sought to ease the transition to the urban North and to improve economic and social conditions there.

In 1911 the Committee on Urban Conditions among Negroes merged with the Committee for the Improvement of Industrial Conditions among Negroes in New York (which had been founded in 1906) and the National League for the Protection of Colored Women (founded in 1905) to become the National League on Urban Conditions among Negroes. That name was shortened in 1920 to the National Urban League.

The Urban League counseled black migrants from the South, helped to train black social workers, and worked with businesses and community leaders to create educational and employment opportunities for blacks. The organization also conducted research into the problems blacks faced in employment, recreation, housing, health and sanitation, and education. Need spurred rapid growth, and by 1918 the organization had eighty-one staff members working in thirty cities. The Urban League's board of directors was (and remains) interracial.

During the 1920s the Urban League became increasingly activist, deliberately campaigning to break the barriers to black employment. Negotiation was combined with boycotts against firms that refused to employ blacks. Lobbying efforts were instituted, becoming most intensive during the era of the New Deal. When World War II created a vast demand for labor, the Urban League responded with a successful effort to integrate segregated trade unions in defense plants and to institute programs to train black youths for skilled blue-collar employment. After the war the Urban League created a program to induce Fortune 500 companies to hold career conferences on black college campuses and to begin to place African Americans in hitherto unattainable white-collar positions.

In 1961, as the AFRICAN AMERICAN CIVIL RIGHTS MOVEMENT entered its most important phase, WHITNEY MOORE YOUNG JR. became the new executive director of the Urban League. Young vigorously ushered the organization into the mainstream of the civil rights movement and opened its New York headquarters to meetings of civil rights leaders. Young also called for a "domestic Marshall Plan," an economic aid program designed to narrow the social and economic gap between black and white Americans. This initiative was influential in the formulation of LYNDON B. JOHNSON'S GREAT SOCIETY and WAR ON POVERTY.

Young, who died in 1971 in a drowning accident, was succeeded by Vernon E. Jordan Jr., the former executive director of the United Negro College Fund. Under Jordan the Urban League worked more closely with the federal government to administer programs and deliver services to urban communities. The Urban League's citizenship education program sought to heighten black political awareness and to increase the black vote. The organization also undertook efforts to increase employment opportunities for women of color.

John E. Jacob succeeded Jordan in 1982 and created a series of programs to aid those who work for and with the league: the Whitney M. Young, Jr., Training Center, to provide training and leadership development opportunities for both staff and volunteers; the Whitney M. Young, Jr., Race Relations Program, which recognizes affiliates doing exemplary work in race relations; and the Whitney M. Young, Jr., Commemoration Ceremony, which honors and pays tribute to long-term staff and volunteers who have made extraordinary contributions to what National Urban League members call the "Urban League Movement."

Jacob was succeeded in 1994 by Hugh B. Price. Since then the league has focused more intensively on education and youth development, economic empowerment, and the advocacy of AFFIRMATIVE ACTION, a principle and policy often under attack since the 1980s.

Suggested Reading

Parris, Guichard. *Blacks in the City: A History of the National Urban League.* Boston: Little Brown, 1971.

Young, Whitney M., Jr. *Beyond Racism: Building an Open Society.* New York: McGraw-Hill, 1961.

NATIONAL WOMAN'S PARTY

The National Woman's Party (NWP) was founded in 1913 as the Congressional Union for Woman Suffrage and was headed by feminists Lucy Burns and Alice Paul (who in 1923 would author the EQUAL RIGHTS AMENDMENT). The Congressional Union consisted primarily of women who had left the National American Woman Suffrage Association (NAWSA) because of its insistence on confining the campaign for enfranchisement to the local and state levels. Both the Congressional Union and the organization it became in 1916, the National Woman's Party, sought nothing less than a constitutional amendment giving women the vote. Abandoning the genteel lobbying tactics of the NAWSA, the NWP used confrontation and direct action—picketing the White House (it was the first group in American history to do so), conducting suffrage marches, and engaging freely in acts of civil disobedience. Many NWP members were jailed—and, once in jail, many staged hunger strikes.

The NWP was so uncompromising that it often alienated other, more moderate suffragist groups. The party opposed the United States' entry into World War I, and denounced President Woodrow Wilson, not only for the war but for failing to secure the vote for women. Nevertheless, it was Wilson's endorsement of the Nineteenth Amendment (which he referred to as a vital war measure) that spurred its passage in 1920. Some historians argue that the radicalism and confrontational tactics of the NWP were crucial in securing passage of the amendment, while others believe that the NWP's extremism made other suffragist organizations seem reasonable and moderate by comparison, and thereby gained support for *those organizations*—and, ultimately, for the amendment.

In 1921 the NWP refocused its efforts on discrimination against women in American society. It began publishing a journal, *Equal Rights,* and in 1923 it brought forward Alice Paul's proposed equal rights amendment, which was first introduced into Congress in that year. However, torn by internal dissension and shunned by mainstream feminists, the NWP failed to gain a large following. Before the decade was out, it had faded into a marginal presence. (See also women's suffrage movement.)

Suggested Reading

Lunardini, Catherine A. *From Equal Suffrage to Equal Rights: Alice Paul and the National Woman's Party, 1910–1928.* Lincoln, Neb.: iUniverse.com, 2000.

NATIONAL WOMEN'S LAW CENTER

The National Women's Law Center (NWLC) was founded in 1972 to protect and advance the progress of women and girls at work, in education, and in other aspects of their lives. The organization works by researching, monitoring, and analyzing public policy and through litigation, advocacy, coalition building, and public education. In recent years the NWLC has focused on family economic security, and, through the reform of law and public policy, has attempted to improve the economic security of women, especially low-income women. In the area of health the NWLC works to improve national policy on family planning and reproductive health services. In the field of employment it promotes legislation to ensure high-quality child care for working women. The organization is also active in strengthening and enforcing laws and policies against discrimination in the workplace.

Suggested Reading

National Women's Law Center, www.nwlc.org.

NATION OF ISLAM

See Islam, Nation of.

NATIVE AMERICAN CHURCH

The Native American Church, an indigenous religious movement among Native Americans, is often called (chiefly by outsiders) Peyotism or Peyote Religion. At least fifty tribes are currently associated with the Native American Church, and although no hard statistics exist, the church is believed to have approximately a quarter of a million members.

Peyote is a type of spineless cactus, the top of which contains mescaline, a hallucinogenic drug. In pre-Columbian Mexico, the Huichol Indians used peyote both as a medicine and as a means of experiencing spiritual visions. By the middle of the nineteenth century, peyote-based rituals had penetrated well into the American Great Plains and, by the 1880s, had come to be an important part of the religions practiced by the Kiowa and Comanche tribes of Oklahoma. During the 1890s peyote use spread into the northern plains, then well into Canada.

The Native American Church encompasses a wide range of theological tenets and practices, but all rituals combine, in some form or other, Christian elements with the spiritual veneration of peyote, which, the faithful believe, enables them to commune with God and with the spirits through which God interacts with human beings. Church members also believe that peyote consumption permits communion with the spirits of tribal ancestors and relatives who have died. Members of the Native American Church believe in one God, or Great Spirit, and in numerous lesser spirits through which God makes himself manifest. For some believers peyote is the incarnation of the Peyote Spirit, which may be regarded as analogous to Jesus Christ—that is, as both God and intercessor; for others, Peyote is simply a powerful guardian spirit.

Because the Native American Church is based upon the use of peyote, which Bureau of Indian Affairs officials regarded as a dangerous intoxicant, it was banned by an administrative directive in 1888. Apparently to reinforce the federal directive, fifteen states subsequently enacted formal statutes banning the use of peyote. During the twentieth century, numerous efforts were made to enact federal legislation banning peyote use, but the efforts repeatedly failed. Seeking to obtain legal legitimacy for peyote worship, various Native American peyote groups incorporated as religious organizations under state laws. In 1914 the First-Born Church of Jesus Christ incorporated in Oklahoma and was reincorporated four years later as the Native American Church.

By 1960 the Native American Church was legally incorporated in eleven states. Nevertheless, the church was still under threat from state and federal lawmakers, and during the 1960s church members mounted court appeals on constitutional grounds, claiming that ritual peyote use was protected by the guarantee of freedom of religion—a position that was repeatedly upheld in the supreme courts of several states. Although during the 1960s and 1970s the U.S. SUPREME COURT had limited the authority of governments to pass restrictive legislation against specific religions and religious practices (*Sherbert v. Verner,* 1963; *Wisconsin v. Yoder,* 1972), its decision in *Employment Division v. Smith* (1990) held that the religious use of peyote was not a constitutionally protected right.

This decision prompted more than sixty religious and civil liberties organizations to form the Coalition for the Free Exercise of Religion and to lobby for the federal Religious Freedom Restoration Act (RFRA), which was signed into law by President BILL CLINTON on November 16, 1993. The legislation permits governments to limit religious freedom only if there is a compelling societal reason to do so—and requires them, in such cases, to impose restrictions using the least intrusive method possible. The RFRA was intended, among other things, to protect the Native American Church.

On June 25, 1997, in *Boerne v. Flores,* the U.S. Supreme Court overturned the RFRA as unconstitutional. In the case in question, the Roman Catholic archbishop of San Antonio, Texas, had sued the city of Boerne for refusing to issue a construction permit that would have allowed the church to expand into a historic district. The high court ruled that the RFRA failed to maintain the separation of powers and the federal-state balance of powers. Since this ruling, ten states—Alabama, Arizona, Connecticut, Florida, Idaho, Illinois, New Mexico, Rhode Island, South Carolina, and Texas—have passed state versions of the RFRA, and, on September 22, 2000, President Clinton signed into law the Religious Land Use and Institutionalized Persons Act, which restricts governments from interfering with the religious use of land and guarantees religious freedom to inmates of institutions. What protection the law affords the Native American Church is open to question; however, no recent attempts have been made to restrict the church or its use of peyote. (See also RELIGION, FREEDOM OF.)

Suggested Reading

Smith, Huston, and Reuben Snake, eds. *One Nation under God: The Triumph of the Native American Church.* Santa Fe, N.M.: Clear Light, 1998.

NATIVE AMERICAN CIVIL RIGHTS MOVEMENT

This article discusses Native American participation in the civil rights movement beginning in the 1960s. For an overview of Native Americans and Native American rights before 1960, see NATIVE AMERICANS.

In the 1960s, during the height of the AFRICAN AMERICAN CIVIL RIGHTS MOVEMENT, Native American activists made common cause with black activists insofar as both groups were seeking full and equal citizenship rights. To Native Americans, however, civil rights included the preservation of their *separate* cultural and political communities, as well as a high degree of political sovereignty.

During the civil rights era Native American rights achieved high visibility, and as a consequence the landmark legislation of the period—the VOTING RIGHTS ACT OF 1965, the FAIR HOUSING ACT, and the EQUAL EMPLOYMENT OPPORTUNITY ACT—specifically included Native Americans. At the same time, social legislation acknowledged the cultural identity and separateness of Native Americans; for example, Indian tribal governments were permitted a voice in the administration of federally funded social programs.

The INDIAN CIVIL RIGHTS ACT of 1968 prohibits tribal governments from enacting or enforcing laws that violate certain individual rights (the act essentially recapitulates the BILL OF RIGHTS and applies it explicitly to Native Americans); however, in 1978 the U.S. SUPREME COURT decided in *Santa Clara Pueblo v. Martinez* that tribal governments retain sovereign immunity and are therefore immune from lawsuits. The high court further held that it was the province of tribal governments, not the federal government, to protect the rights of individuals under the Indian Civil Rights Act, thereby acknowledging a highly significant degree of tribal self-determination and sovereignty.

In the case of African Americans, the 1960s are generally regarded as the great era of civil rights progress. For Native Americans, the 1960s were just the beginning. Although 1960s legislation secured (at least in law) the individual rights of Native Americans as citizens, during the decade that followed Native American activists increasingly pursued rights not as citizens but as members of tribal nations: the focus shifted from obtaining individual rights to achieving increased political and social self-determination and to compelling the federal government to uphold rights that it had granted during the nineteenth century through a series of treaties. Native American activists conducted their campaigns in the courts, through legislative lobbying, and through the militant action of groups such as the American Indian Movement (AIM). In 1973 AIM laid siege to Wounded Knee, South Dakota, to protest treaty violations that had deprived the Lakota (mainly Oglala Sioux) of the sacred Black Hills.

There can be no doubt that the Native American civil rights movement improved the lives of most Native Americans. Not only did Native Americans gain legislative recognition and protection of their rights as American citizens, but tribal governments achieved a significant measure of sovereignty and self-determination. Nevertheless, Native Americans remain the poorest minority in the United States, with the lowest per capita income, the highest unemployment, the shortest life expectancy, and the worst health and housing of any American ethnic group. (See also Siege at Wounded Knee.)

Suggested Reading

Grinde, Donald A., Jr. *Native Americans.* Washington, D.C.: CQ Press, 2002.
Lazarus, Edward. *Black Hills, White Justice: The Sioux Nation versus the United States, 1775 to the Present.* New York: HarperCollins, 1991.

NATIVE AMERICAN RIGHTS FUND

The Native American Rights Fund (NARF), a national nonprofit organization, provides legal representation and technical assistance to Native American tribes, organizations, and individuals. The organization is dedicated to preserving tribal existence, protecting tribal natural resources, promoting human rights, ensuring government accountability, developing Indian law, and educating the public about Indian rights, laws, and issues.

NARF is rooted in the War on Poverty of the 1960s, when the federal government funded an ambitious set of legal services programs for the poor. A number of these programs were located on or near Indian reservations, and it became clear that few lawyers were familiar with the special legal needs of Native American clients. Thus in 1970 the Ford Foundation collaborated with California Indian Legal Services (a federally funded agency) to create a pilot project: the goal was to create a national organization of Native American advocates with experience and expertise in so-called Indian law. Originally known as the Native American Rights Fund, the program became independent of California Indian Legal Services in 1971 and relocated to Boulder, Colorado, where it incorporated separately, with an all-Indian board of directors, and grew into a major advocacy organization. In addition to providing legal assistance and services to Native American individuals and tribes, NARF maintains the National Indian Law Library at Boulder.

Suggested Reading

Native American Rights Fund, www.narf.org.

NATIVE AMERICANS

This article surveys the status of Native Americans in the United States up to the civil rights movement, which had begun in earnest by about 1960. For a discussion of Native American participation in the civil rights movement, beginning in the 1960s, see Native American civil rights movement.

When Columbus returned to Spain after his first voyage to America in 1492, he left behind on the island he called La Navidad a small garrison of Spaniards. Shortly after Columbus left the island, the garrison began pillaging Indian goods and raping Indian women. The Indians retaliated by killing the Spaniards. This exchange, which occurred sometime in 1493, marked the beginning of four hundred years of chronic—and, in some places, virtually continuous—warfare, which did not end until shortly after the massacre at Wounded Knee, South Dakota, on December 29, 1890.

Outright warfare was not the only evidence of hostile relations. Both before and after the American Revolution, Indians were often treated with contempt, not only by European settlers but by local, state, and federal governments. Land grabs, swindles, and discrimination (often legally sanctioned) were common, even when trade between settlers and Indians was of great importance to both groups. Activist rhetoric notwithstanding, it was never U.S. policy to "exterminate" the Indians; it *was* federal policy, however, to confine Indians to designated territories or reservations—which led, in the West, to more or less continuous small-scale warfare from the 1850s to 1891.

Even during times of greatest hostility, people of goodwill among the tribes and in the federal government attempted to create equitable, peaceful relations, which were often codified in treaties. Nevertheless, the terms of such treaties were rarely honored by either side. If whites chose, for example, to settle in a territory that had been pledged exclusively to Indians, the federal government was generally unwilling to call out the army against the settlers. For their part, not all members of a tribe felt obligated to honor treaties that had been concluded with a few tribal representatives. Thus signatories on both sides had little capacity—and, sometimes, little incentive—to enforce treaties.

A more general problem was a prevailing ambiguity in the relations between the United States and the tribes. Were Indians to be regarded as citizens of the United States, as citizens of sovereign nations, or as something else? In 1871 the Indian Appropriations Act forcefully resolved this ambiguity by bringing an end to all treaty making between the federal government and the tribes and making all Indian affairs subject to ordinary federal legislation. Furthermore, any tribes or individual Indians who chose not to become American citizens were barred from making any contracts related to Indian lands and were also barred from bringing claims against the federal government unless they first received the approval of the secretary of the interior. In effect, among other things, the act gave Indians the option of becoming American citizens but also penalized them for not exercising that option. Noncitizen Indians were regarded as wards of the government—subject to federal protection, but also without civil rights. In effect, federal legislative power over Native Americans became absolute.

Passage of the DAWES SEVERALTY ACT on February 8, 1887, sought to change the status of Indians—but at even heavier cost to Indian tribal sovereignty and cultural identity. Although the act was intended to integrate Indians into the political and cultural mainstream of white American society, its immediate practical effect was to break up tribal land holdings. Under the act tribal holdings were dissolved, and individual Indians were granted plots ("allotments"); in receiving their allotments, the Indians became United States citizens; those who had already separated from their tribes and lived in white communities were immediately declared citizens. But because so many Indians were impoverished, they were forced to sell off the land that they had acquired—thus transferring what had once been tribal lands into non-Indian hands.

The Dawes Act did not by any means dissolve all tribal lands, nor did it make all Indians citizens. The American Indian Citizenship Act of 1924, however, did impose citizenship on all Indians. Although the act did not dissolve tribal government or abrogate Indian tribal citizenship, the framers of the legislation believed—and hoped—that American citizenship would bring about the eventual dissolution of the tribes. In fact, most tribal governments did not disappear, and Indians who had not already become U.S. citizens lived under a kind of dual citizenship, which endures to this day.

In the atmosphere of general social reform ushered in by FRANKLIN D. ROOSEVELT'S New Deal, the federal government reexamined its Indian policy—and its effects—and concluded that the policy under the Dawes Act and the Indian Citizenship Act of 1924 had been a dismal failure: a majority of Indians lived in poverty, lacked rudimentary health care, died young, and were housed miserably. On June 18, 1934, the INDIAN REORGANIZATION ACT reversed the Dawes Act and encouraged a return to tribal organization. Not only were allotments under the Dawes legislation halted, but unsold "surplus" Indian lands were returned to the tribes. The Indian Reorganization Act actively promoted tribal self-government by encouraging tribes to write constitutions and to assume the management of their own affairs. A loan program for tribal land purchases, for education, and for the development of tribal government was put into effect.

With the end of the Great Depression and the entry of the United States into World War II, many of the New Deal programs came to an end. No government agency was hit harder than the Department of the Interior's Bureau of Indian Affairs, and no government program was cut more severely than the funding for the Indian Reorganization Act. The postwar years also saw a backlash against the self-determination that had been supported by the Indian Reorganization Act. Amid the anti-Communist hysteria of the early 1950s, some legislators criticized Indian self-government and culture as un-American and communist in spirit. Once again, there was a call to integrate Indians into mainstream American culture, and the federal government instituted a policy of "termination"—that is, the termination of treaty rights and tribal governments. Indians were to be "assimilated," and thousands of acres of Indian lands, formerly protected by treaty, were seized as public land. Many hundreds of families were displaced.

It was at this new low point in relations between the federal government and Native Americans that Indian activists joined the civil rights movement of the 1960s. Their activism fortuitously coincided with a growing recognition among legislators that the policies of termination and assimilation were ineffective at best and disastrous at worst. As it had been in the 1930s, Indian policy was poised for dramatic reform at the beginning of the 1960s. (See also INDIAN REMOVAL ACT OF 1830 and INDIAN WARS.)

Suggested Reading

Hoxie, Frederick E. *A Final Promise: The Campaign to Assimilate the Indians, 1880–1920*. Lincoln: University of Nebraska Press, 1984.

Grinde, Donald A., Jr. *Native Americans*. Washington, D.C.: CQ Press, 2002.

McDonnell, Janet. *The Dispossession of the American Indian*. Bloomington: Indiana University Press, 1991.

NATIVISM

Nativism is anti-immigrant sentiment, and it often motivates anti-immigrant policy and laws. It is one of the enduring paradoxes of U.S. history that this nation of immigrants has frequently undergone spasms of nativism. Although the Alien Acts of 1798 may be regarded as the first overtly nativist federal legislation, the nineteenth century saw the sharpest rise in nativism—much of it directed against Catholic immigrants, who were regarded by many in the Protestant American majority as putting their allegiance to the foreign pope before their allegiance to the United States and its democracy. This ideological concern dovetailed neatly with the fears of workingmen, who worried about losing their jobs to cheaper immigrant laborers.

During the nineteenth century a number of political parties developed nativist platforms. The most famous was the KNOW-NOTHING PARTY, which was specifically anti-Catholic as well as more generally anti-immigrant. By 1855 the Know-Nothings had sent more than a hundred men to Congress; however, after the overwhelming defeat in 1856 of their presidential candidate, Millard Fillmore, the party rapidly disintegrated.

By the late nineteenth century and the beginning of the twentieth, nativists had turned their attention away from Catholics and focused it instead on foreign radicals—anarchists, socialists, and, eventually, communists. Asians and immigrants from eastern Europe were also targeted. Antiradical expressions of nativism became more intense after World War I and the success of the Bolshevik Revolution in Russia. The IMMIGRATION ACT OF 1924 set quotas that favored western Europeans and discriminated against those from southern and eastern Europe and excluded Asians almost completely. (See also ALIEN AND SEDITION ACTS, ASIATIC EXCLUSION LEAGUE, and CHINESE EXCLUSION TREATY AND ACT. For a discussion of the evolution of U.S. immigration policy after 1924, see IMMIGRATION AND NATURALIZATION ACT OF 1952; IMMIGRATION ACT OF 1965; IMMIGRATION REFORM AND CONTROL ACT; AND IMMIGRATION RIGHTS, STATUTES, AND RESTRICTIONS.)

Suggested Reading

Michaels, Walter Benn. *Our America: Nativism, Modernism and Pluralism.* Durham: Duke University Press, 1997.

NATURALIZATION ACT OF 1870

The first important piece of legislation restricting Asian immigration into the United States, the Naturalization Act of 1870 barred Chinese immigrants from becoming U.S. citizens and prohibited the wives of Chinese laborers from entering the country with their husbands. (See also CHINESE EXCLUSION TREATY AND ACT.)

Suggested Reading

Gyory, Andrew. *Closing the Gate: Race, Politics, and the Chinese Exclusion Act.* Chapel Hill: University of North Carolina Press, 1998.

NATURAL RIGHTS

When THOMAS JEFFERSON, in the DECLARATION OF INDEPENDENCE, wrote of the "self-evident" truth that human beings are "endowed by their creator with certain inalienable rights," he demonstrated his belief, typical of eighteenth-century idealists, in natural law and the concept of natural rights.

The first to thoroughly examine natural rights was Aristotle, who distinguished between what was "just by nature" and what was "just by law," and who described a natural justice that transcended the laws of society. Later, Roman law seemed to acknowledge, if not always to embody, the concept of natural law. The early fathers of the Christian church, most notably St. Augustine of Hippo, also refer to natural law, which is described as having been sufficient before the fall of Adam and Eve, but as requiring augmentation—through religion and human law—since the introduction of original sin. Later Christian philosophers, such as St. Thomas Aquinas, treated natural law and natural rights as the imperfect but valuable physical expression of God's mind.

The English philosopher Thomas Hobbes (1588–1679) reinterpreted natural right as the right to self-defense, and defined natural law as a precept forbidding a person from doing anything destructive to his own life. Hobbes may be regarded as the intellectual founder of the "school of natural law," which endeavored, by rational deduction, to derive social law from what was posited as natural right and natural law.

In writing the Declaration of Independence, Jefferson was influenced most directly by John Locke (1632–1704), who held that a just society was one in which free and equal people observed natural law. The French philosopher Jean-Jacques Rousseau (1712–1778), another influence on Jefferson, went even further, postulating the existence of the "noble savage"—the wholly virtuous human being who, living apart from society, was guided by two principles existing apart from and prior to reason: self-preservation and compassion (which Rousseau defined as a natural, inborn revulsion at the suffering of others).

Today the sense that certain rights transcend society and the laws of any particular time and place pervades international politics, although the rights themselves are referred to as "human rights" rather than as natural rights. The concept of human rights is, indeed, generally held to be "self-evident" (to borrow Jefferson's phrase), in the sense that little effort is expended in defining a philosophical basis or rationale for such rights. Instead, the modern defense of human rights has taken place on a practical rather than a philosophical plane, through the repeated effort—evident, for example, in any number of United Nations conventions, resolutions, and treaties—to enumerate a set of absolutely "inalienable" human rights.

Suggested Reading

Tuck, Richard. *Natural Rights Theories.* Cambridge, U.K.: Cambridge University Press, 1982.

NEWTON, HUEY P. (1942–1989)

With Bobby Seale, Huey Newton founded the Black Panther Party in October 1966.

Newton was born in Monroe, Louisiana, on February 17, 1942, and moved with his parents to Oakland, California, where he grew up. At Merritt College Newton and Seale founded the Black Panther Party for Self-Defense (later shortened to the Black Panther Party) as a radical organization aimed primarily at black urban youth, who were impatient and dissatisfied with the mainstream African American civil rights movement. Black Panther branches developed in many American cities. The tough, militant image projected by members caused many whites, as well as middle-class blacks and blacks in the mainstream civil rights movement, to equate the Panthers with the street gangs common to the ghettoes. However, Newton's vision of the Black Panthers was as a community-based and community-oriented self-help organization. Under Newton's leadership the Panthers introduced day care and other programs to serve their neighborhoods, and they patrolled their communities to protect residents from crime as well as police brutality. It was these patrols that routinely led to clashes with authorities.

On October 28, 1967, Newton was involved in a shootout with police and was arrested for murder. The Newton trial became a popular radical and liberal cause, and the slogan "Free Huey!" was a rallying cry of a turbulent 1968. Newton was convicted on a lesser charge of manslaughter, but in 1970 the conviction was overturned on appeal, and Newton was released from prison. He returned to the Black Panther Party but found that, in his absence, it had splintered into two factions: one that followed Eldridge Cleaver, an advocate of international revolution, and one that followed Newton himself, who saw the Black Panthers as a viable American political party that could sponsor candidates for elective office and continue to operate community services. Newton discovered that the party was too severely split to restore to its original effectiveness. Worse, in 1974 he was charged with the murder of a woman; he left the party and fled to Cuba. Three years later he returned to the United States to face the charges. Two trials resulted in hung juries, and Newton enrolled at the University of California, Santa Cruz, from which he earned a Ph.D. in social philosophy in 1980 with a dissertation titled "War Against the Panthers: A Study of Repression in America."

In 1982 the Black Panther Party officially disbanded, and in March 1989 Newton was sentenced to a six-month prison term for misappropriating public funds intended for a Black Panther–founded Oakland school. He was also convicted of the illegal possession of firearms. On August 22, 1898, he was shot to death by a drug dealer on the streets of Oakland.

Suggested Reading

Foner, Philip S. *The Black Panthers Speak.* 1970. Reprint, New York: Da Capo, 1995.

Newton, Huey P. *To Die for the People: The Writings of Huey P. Newton.* 1972. Reprint, New York: Writers and Readers, 1995.

———. *Revolutionary Suicide.* 1973. Reprint, New York: Writers and Readers, 1995.

NEW YORK ASSOCIATION FOR IMPROVING THE CONDITIONS OF THE POOR

The New York Association for Improving the Conditions of the Poor (known as the AICP) was founded in 1843 by prosperous New York City merchants and businessmen who were appalled by tenement and slum life, and who were determined to improve the conditions that caused disease, crime, and vice among the poor. In part the AICP's efforts took the form of a moral (and moralistic) crusade to reform the character of the poor themselves, who were seen as improvident or simply lazy. However, the AICP also campaigned among city and state lawmakers to alleviate the overcrowded and inadequate housing conditions in New York City and Brooklyn (which was, during most of the nineteenth century, a city separate from New York). The AICP's lobbying was mostly in vain until 1856, when state legislators created a committee to inspect the "tenement houses" of New York and Brooklyn. The committee members, duly shocked by what they saw, called for legislation—which, however, was not forthcoming until 1867, when the state of

New York enacted the Tenement House Law, a set of very minimal housing standards.

With the continued support of wealthy New Yorkers, most notably Frederick Vanderbilt, the AICP continued to lobby for reform of slum conditions through the end of the nineteenth century. (See also HOUSING RIGHTS.)

Suggested Reading

Riis, Jacob A. *How the Other Half Lives: Studies among the Tenements of New York.* 1890. Reprint, New York: Penguin, 1997.

NEW YORK CHILDREN'S AID SOCIETY

In 1853 the social reformer Charles Loring Brace assembled a group of reform-minded men and women to create the New York Children's Aid Society as an alternative to the miserable and typically heartless orphan asylums and almshouses that, during the period, served poor, homeless, and orphaned children. Brace sought to offer services not only to children (including disabled children) but to working women and impoverished families. Brace believed that slum conditions could be improved only through the provision of material aid to disadvantaged children and their families.

By the end of the nineteenth century the Children's Aid Society had sponsored the first industrial schools, the first parent-teacher associations, the first visiting nurse service, the first free school lunch programs, the first free dental clinics, the first day schools for disabled children, and programs that anticipated modern forms of foster care, kindergarten, and "fresh air" vacations—"Orphan Train" excursions to the country.

Today, the society serves more than 120,000 children and their families annually, working in collaboration with community centers, camps, public schools, courts, and parents. The society's efforts are concentrated chiefly in New York City, but it also sponsors a national outreach program in teen pregnancy prevention.

Suggested Reading

Brace, Charles Loring. *The Life of Charles Loring Brace.* New York: Charles Scribner's Sons, 1894.

NIAGARA MOVEMENT

In the summer of 1905 W.E.B. DUBOIS and a group of twenty-nine other social activists met secretly in Niagara Falls, Ontario, to hammer out an organized response to the accommodationist policies promulgated by the nation's most highly visible black reformer, BOOKER T. WASHINGTON, in his "ATLANTA COMPROMISE" SPEECH. The result was a set of resolutions that led to the founding of the Niagara Movement and to the creation of a formal manifesto that demanded full civil liberties for blacks, an end to racial discrimination, and an acknowledgment of the brotherhood of all races.

Although the Niagara Movement grew quickly, adding thirty branches nationally within little more than a year, it began to disintegrate almost as rapidly, mostly as the result of poor funding and weak organization. Then in August 1908 thousands of white residents descended upon the black community of Springfield, Illinois, after a black prisoner who had been charged with raping a white woman was transferred to another prison. The white mob assaulted and killed black residents, burned homes and buildings, and lynched two elderly black men before the Illinois state militia succeeded in restoring order. After the riot most white Americans voiced no remorse; indeed, some were vocal in their approval of what they deemed an action that would serve to keep blacks "in their place." (Charges against the accused rapist were subsequently withdrawn as groundless.) This so-called Race War of the North prompted a number of white liberals to join with members of the Niagara group to create the NATIONAL ASSOCIATION FOR THE ADVANCEMENT OF COLORED PEOPLE in 1909. With the founding of that organization the Niagara Movement formally disbanded in 1910.

Suggested Reading

Kellogg, Charles Flint. *NAACP: A History of the National Association for the Advancement of Colored People.* Baltimore: Johns Hopkins University Press, 1973.

Senechal, Roberta. *The Sociogenesis of a Race Riot: Springfield, Illinois, in 1908.* Champaign-Urbana: University of Illinois Press, 1990.

NISEI

The term *nisei* refers to a person who is born in America (and who is therefore an American citizen) of parents born in Japan. (See also ISSEI.)

NIXON, RICHARD M. (1913–1994)

The thirty-seventh president of the United States (1969–1974), Richard Milhous Nixon was the only chief executive in American history to resign from office. Although he may be credited with important progress in international relations—in particular, improved relations with both China and the Soviet Union—his disregard for DUE PROCESS and for the separation of powers, and his attempt to create what was, essentially, an imperial presidency, seriously threatened rights under the Constitution.

Nixon was raised in modest circumstances in Yorba Linda, California, at that time a farming community not far from Los Angeles. His father was a marginally successful grocer, and his mother, a devout Quaker, took a strong hand in raising her son. After graduating from Whittier College, in Whittier, California, in 1934, Nixon attended Duke University Law School and was awarded a law degree in 1937. He returned to Whittier to practice law, married Thelma Catherine ("Pat") Ryan, then entered government as an attorney in the Office of Price Administration in Washington, D.C. In 1942, during World War II, Nixon served in the U.S. Navy as an aviation ground officer. After the war, in 1946, he was elected to the U.S. House of Representatives on the Republican ticket after having attacked five-term liberal Democratic incumbent Jerry Voorhis as a communist sympathizer. This first campaign foreshadowed the Nixon political style, which was characterized by a ruthless desire to win at any cost and a willingness to equate liberalism with communism—and to ensure that the electorate made the same equation.

The formula was highly effective. In his 1948 bid for reelection Nixon, in a highly unorthodox move, entered the Democratic as well as the Republican primaries. He won both, and he assumed a seat on the powerful HOUSE UN-AMERICAN ACTIVITIES COMMITTEE. From this post, during 1948–1950, Nixon spearheaded the investigation of Alger Hiss, a former State Department official who had been accused of spying for the Soviet Union. Nixon pressed the investigation so doggedly and pursued Hiss with such relish that he earned a national reputation as a valiant anticommunist. (Hiss was never convicted of espionage, but he did serve prison time for perjury.)

Building on his reputation, Nixon defeated Democrat Helen Gahagan Douglas for a Senate seat in 1950, accusing her of being "pink, right down to her underwear." When he distributed "pink sheets" that compared Douglas's voting record to that of Vito Marcantonio, an openly leftist representative from New York, the *Independent Review,* a small California paper, dubbed Nixon "Tricky Dick," an epithet he was never able to shed.

The Republican Party tapped Nixon's anticommunist credentials in 1952 when it nominated him as the vice presidential candidate on DWIGHT D. EISENHOWER's ticket. When a scandal over a secret Nixon "slush fund" threatened to derail the campaign, Nixon delivered a televised speech on September 23, 1952, in which he denied ever having accepted gifts or money from outside interests, except for a cocker spaniel given to his six-year-old daughter Tricia. "Regardless of what they say about it," Nixon said, "we are going to keep it." The dog was named Checkers, and the speech became known as the Checkers Speech. It saved the Nixon candidacy and helped propel Eisenhower to the White House by a landslide margin over Democrat Adlai E. Stevenson.

Nixon was not an exceptional vice president, but during 1955–1957 when Eisenhower suffered a heart attack, then, later, an attack of ileitis and after that a mild stroke, Nixon performed well as chair of cabinet sessions and National Security Council meetings. (The agreement Eisenhower and Nixon concluded regarding the responsibilities and authority of the vice president in the event of presidential disability was later formalized, in 1967, as the Twenty-Fifth Amendment to the Constitution.)

After two terms as vice president Nixon was nominated in 1960 as the Republican candidate for president. Democrat JOHN F. KENNEDY defeated him in an extremely close election. Nixon returned to his California home, wrote a best-selling memoir, *Six Crises* (1961), then ran unsuccessfully for governor of California in 1962. At a press conference after the defeat he bitterly announced his retirement from politics, lashing out at the press with the famous remark that journalists would not "have Dick Nixon to kick around anymore."

After successfully practicing law in New York City he received the Republican nomination for president in 1968, having brokered a deal with traditionally Democratic southern conservatives by promising that he would appoint "strict constructionists" to the federal courts and name a southerner to the Supreme Court. In other words, Nixon pledged that, if elected, he would turn the tide against such civil rights measures as court-ordered busing and other federal initiatives to force racial integration.

Nixon's defeat of Democrat Hubert H. Humphrey was based largely on the vague promise of a plan to bring "peace with honor" to the Vietnam War. To a nation torn by civil dissent and racial unrest, he further pledged an administration of law and order, an aggressive policy against illegal drug use, and an end to the highly unpopular military draft. Appealing to what he called the "great Silent Majority" of Americans, Nixon won by a slim popular margin.

As president Nixon widened the scope of the bombing in Vietnam, but in response to popular protest he also accelerated the process of "Vietnamization," pulling out U.S. ground troops and turning over increasing responsibility to South Vietnamese forces. Despite Nixon's hostility toward antiwar protesters and others he characterized as leftists, the anticipated wholesale repression of dissent never came to pass, especially as Nixon's judicial appointees declined, for the most part, to become political or ideological tools of the administration. In some respects Nixon adopted surprisingly liberal policies, especially with regard to environmental legislation. And in the diplomatic arena, Nixon and his foreign policy adviser Henry Kissinger (later secretary of state) greatly eased long-time Cold War tensions through adept—and sometimes brilliant—diplomacy with the Soviet Union and China.

In 1972 Nixon ran for a second term, defeating Democratic senator George S. McGovern in a spectacular landslide—47.1 million votes to 29.1 million, and 520 electoral votes to 17. Yet in a series of revelations that had begun even before the reelection victory, it became clear that Nixon had masterminded a massively illegal campaign, including burglarizing and wiretapping the national headquarters of the Democratic Party at the Watergate office complex in Washington, D.C. The Watergate scandal came to represent what was eventually revealed to be a long catalogue of presidential misdeeds, including the illegal use of the Federal Bureau of Investigation (FBI) for internal espionage against political enemies; the use of the Internal Revenue Service to intimidate, harass, and even financially ruin opponents; and the use of various frauds (called "dirty tricks" by the Committee to Re-Elect the President) to embarrass other candidates—among them Maine senator Edmund Muskie, a popular presidential challenger—during the Democratic primaries. Indeed, the list of violations of the Constitution, of due process, and of the separation of powers grew formidably, first through a series of stories in the *Washington Post,* and then during months of televised Senate hearings. Moreover, it was revealed that the Nixon White House had attempted to cover up its involvement in the Watergate break-in by issuing instructions to the FBI not to investigate certain matters and paying hush money to the Watergate burglars. During the course of the Senate hearings, Nixon's top aides and advisors admitted, one by one, to wrongdoing at the behest of a higher authority—ultimately, the president himself. Another outcome of the hearings was the revelation that Nixon had maintained an "enemies list"—of politicians, journalists, entertainers, intellectuals, and civil rights activists—whom he had targeted for surveillance and harassment.

In July 1974 the Senate committee learned that the Oval Office had a tape-recording system. Archibald Cox, the special prosecutor appointed to investigate Watergate, subpoenaed the tapes. When Nixon refused to give them up, Cox again demanded the tapes, and Nixon responded by ordering Attorney General Elliot Richardson to dismiss Cox. Indignant, Richardson resigned in protest, and when Richardson's assistant, William Ruckelshaus, also refused to fire Cox, he was dismissed. Nixon's solicitor general, Robert Bork, readily complied.

What became known as the Saturday Night Massacre only pointed to the degree of desperation in the Nixon White House. Calls for impeachment became louder and more numerous. Nixon acquiesced to the appointment of a new special prosecutor, Leon Jaworski, and released seven of the nine tapes Cox had subpoenaed. Jaworski subsequently obtained many more in addition to those originally subpoenaed, but by this time the House Judiciary Committee had already drawn up articles of impeachment. On August 5, 1974, Nixon reluctantly turned over the transcript of a conversation taped on June 23, 1972, in which he discussed using the Central Intelligence Agency to block the FBI's investigation of the Watergate break-in. This transcript provided the proverbial smoking gun and made impeachment inevitable. Three days later Nixon made a televised speech in which he announced his resignation, effective at noon on August 9.

The presidency now fell to Gerald R. Ford, who had been appointed vice president the previous year after Vice President Spiro T. Agnew had resigned in the face of charges of bribery, extortion, and income tax evasion dating back to his time as governor of Maryland. In a highly controversial act of dubious legality, President Ford, on September 8, 1974, preemptively pardoned Nixon for any crimes he committed or may have committed.

Nixon retired from public life and turned to writing memoirs and books on international affairs. In the years before his death in 1994 he significantly rehabilitated his image and was even looked on by some politicians as a kind of elder statesman.

Suggested Reading

Bernstein, Carl, and Bob Woodward. *All the President's Men.* 1974. Reprint, New York: Touchstone, 1994.

Nixon, Richard M. *RN: The Memoirs of Richard Nixon.* 1978. Reprint, New York: Touchstone, 1990.

NONVIOLENCE DOCTRINE

From the beginning of his involvement in the African American civil rights movement, the Reverend Martin Luther King Jr. counseled and taught an approach based on absolute nonviolence, including nonviolent civil disobedience. King proved himself a master of nonviolent tactics, which rely on moral suasion: the goal is the persistent demonstration of the contrast between what is right and what is wrong, even if a majority in a particular time and place practice what is wrong. To give in to violence, King believed, was to adopt the values of those who adhered to injustice.

King's nonviolence doctrine was based on a combination of Christian teachings, the writings of HENRY DAVID THOREAU (especially "Civil Disobedience"), and, most immediately, the writings and example of MOHANDAS GANDHI. It was Gandhi who had most fully articulated the role of nonviolence in effecting social and political change. Gandhi's doctrine was founded in large measure on his religious beliefs, which were a combination of Jainism and Hinduism. Jainism emphasizes *satyagraha,* the truth-force, which Gandhi personally defined as a method of securing rights by personal suffering. Hinduism includes the concept of *ahimsa,*, an absolute resolve to harm no living being.

Nonviolence proved highly effective in the civil rights movement, although, by about 1965, the rise of the BLACK POWER MOVEMENT came as a serious challenge to the nonviolent approach.

Suggested Reading

Fahey, Joseph J., and Richard Armstrong, eds. *A Peace Reader: Essential Readings on War, Justice, Non-Violence, and World Order.* Rev. ed. Mahwah, N.J.: Paulist Press, 1992.

Merton, Thomas, ed. *Gandhi on Non-Violence.* New York: Norton, 1965.

NOW LEGAL DEFENSE AND EDUCATION FUND

Founded in 1970, the NOW Legal Defense and Education Fund uses litigation, education, and public information programs to pursue equality for women and girls in the workplace, in schools, in their families, and in the courts. In addition, the fund provides technical assistance to Congress and state legislatures and works to organize national grassroots coalitions to promote and sustain women's equality.

The organization was established by the founders of the NATIONAL ORGANIZATION FOR WOMEN but operates separately and independently. Recent areas of special emphasis include child care, reproductive rights, violence against women, education, poverty and welfare, workplace rights and equality, the rights of immigrant women, and women's human rights.

Suggested Reading

NOW Legal Defense and Educational Fund, www.nowldef.org.

OCCUPATIONAL SAFETY AND HEALTH ACT

The Occupational Safety and Health Act (OSH Act) of 1970 was an ambitious, comprehensive, and complex piece of legislation. It was designed, in the words of the introduction to the act, to "assure safe and healthful working conditions for working men and women; by authorizing enforcement of the standards developed under the Act; by assisting and encouraging the States in their efforts to assure safe and healthful working conditions" and "by providing for research, information, education, and training in the field of occupational safety and health."

As published in the act, Congress concluded "that personal injuries and illnesses arising out of work situations impose a substantial burden upon, and are a hindrance to, interstate commerce in terms of lost production, wage loss, medical expenses, and disability compensation payments"; therefore, the OSH Act specifically addresses occupational safety and health standards; inspections, investigations, and record keeping; enforcement and penalties; safety programs; research; training and employee education; and other issues. The act created, within the DEPARTMENT OF LABOR, the National Institute for Occupational Safety and Health and the Occupational Safety and Health Administration. (See Appendix A for a portion of the OSH Act.)

Suggested Reading

Occupational Safety and Health Administration, www.osha.gov.

O'CONNOR, SANDRA DAY (1930–)

The first woman to be appointed to the U.S. SUPREME COURT, Sandra Day O'Connor was born in El Paso, Texas, and grew up on a large family ranch near Duncan, Arizona. She graduated from Stanford University (1950) and Stanford Law School (1952), married classmate John Jay O'Connor III, then returned to Arizona, where she practiced in the town of Maryville. O'Connor served as assistant attorney general for Arizona during 1965–1969 and was then elected to the Arizona Senate as a Republican, serving from 1969 to 1974. She became majority leader of the state senate and was the first woman in the United States to hold such a position.

In 1974 O'Connor was elected a judge of the Superior Court in Maricopa County, then in 1979 was appointed to the Arizona Court of Appeals. President RONALD REAGAN appointed her to the U.S. Supreme Court in 1981.

Although O'Connor was expected to be a conservative justice, her opinions have tended to defy easy categorization. For the most part her views have been moderate rather than conservative, and her opinions have been pragmatic and dispassionate. Critics and admirers alike note the care with which she researches her opinions, such as that in *Lynch v. Donnelly* (1984), which established the legal standard for determining when religious or quasi-religious displays (in this case, a government-sponsored nativity scene) violate the constitutional separation of church and state. Her opinion in *CITY OF RICHMOND V. J.A. CROSON CO.* (1989), held that government programs that set aside a fixed percentage of public contracts for minority businesses violated the guarantee of equal protection. In *Planned Parenthood of Southeastern Pennsylvania v. Casey,* O'Connor joined a judicial plurality in criticizing the constitutional foundation for *ROE V. WADE,* the high court's momentous 1973 decision upholding the right of ABORTION. While critical of *Roe v. Wade, Planned Parenthood of Southeastern Pennsylvania v. Casey* did not overturn it.

Suggested Reading

Huber, Peter William. *Sandra Day O'Connor.* New York: Chelsea House, 1990.
O'Connor, Sandra Day, and Alan Day. *Lazy B: Growing Up on a Cattle Ranch in the American Southwest.* New York: Random House, 2002.

OFFICE FOR CIVIL RIGHTS

The Office for Civil Rights (OCR) is an office within the U.S. Department of Education that is charged with ensuring equal access to education through the enforcement of civil rights. The OCR acts to resolve discrimination complaints, and, where it finds discrimination, initiates further action. Instead of imposing sanctions, the OCR attempts, wherever possible, to obtain voluntary compliance with civil rights laws, and it provides technical assistance to help institutions achieve such compliance.

The OCR has enforcement responsibilities under a number of pieces of legislation: Title VI of the Civil Rights Act of 1964, which prohibits discrimination in programs or activities that receive federal financial assistance from the Department of Education; Title IX of the Education Amendments of 1972 and Section 504 of the Rehabilitation Act of 1973, which prohibit discrimination on the basis of disability; the Age Discrimination Act of 1975, which bars discrimination on the basis of age; Title II of the Americans with Disabilities Act of 1990, which prohibits public entities, regardless of whether they receive federal financial assistance, from discriminating against people with disabilities. As of January 8, 2002, the OCR had responsibility for enforcing the Boy Scouts of America Equal Access Act (Section 9525 of the Elementary and Secondary Education Act of 1965, as amended by the No Child Left Behind Act of 2001). Under the act no public elementary school or state or local education agency that provides an opportunity for outside youth or community groups to meet on school premises or after school hours may deny equal access to any group officially affiliated with the Boy Scouts of America or any other youth group listed as a patriotic society in Title 36 of the United States Code.

Suggested Reading

Office for Civil Rights, www.ed.gov/offices/OCR/.

OFFICE OF FEDERAL CONTRACT COMPLIANCE PROGRAM

The Office of Federal Contract Compliance Program (OFCCP) was created primarily to implement and enforce Executive Order 11246, issued by President Lyndon B. Johnson in 1965. The order banned discrimination in federal contracting and subcontracting and established affirmative action requirements for federal contractors and subcontractors. Subsequently, the OFCCP was also given responsibility for enforcing regulations (promulgated in 1970 by President Richard M. Nixon), pursuant to the 1965 order, that created goals and timetables for eliminating discrimination and promoting affirmative action in federal contracts. Thus the OFCCP was empowered to require federal contractors, as part of the affirmative action program that they are required to develop or implement, to set goals for hiring and promoting women and minorities. However, the OFCCP is prohibited from requiring race- or gender-based hiring and promotion; nor may it set racial, ethnic, or gender-based quotas. Implementing affirmative action in the face of the prohibition against quota-based hiring has made the OFCCP's mission difficult—and often controversial.

Suggested Reading

Curry, George E., and Cornel West, eds. *The Affirmative Action Debate.* New York: Perseus, 1996.

OPEN HOUSING ACT

See Fair Housing Act.

OWENS, JESSE (1913–1980)

Born James Cleveland Owens in Oakville, Alabama, Jesse Owens excelled as a high school track-and-field athlete and was sent to the 1933 National Interscholastic Championships in Chicago, where he won three events. On May 25, 1935, competing for Ohio State University in a Western Conference track-and-field meet at the University of Michigan, Ann Arbor, Owens met the world record for the 100-yard dash (9.4 seconds) and broke the world records for the 220-yard dash (20.3 seconds), the 220-yard low hurdles (22.6 seconds), and the running broad jump (8.13 meters). This spectacular performance secured him a place on the U.S. track-and-field team sent to the 1936 Berlin Olympic Games.

Adolf Hitler, then German chancellor, was eager to demonstrate the superiority of Aryan athletes and was visibly enraged when Owens, a black man, tied the Olympic record in the 100-meter run (10.3 seconds) and broke Olympic and world records in the 200-meter run (20.7 seconds). After Owens's second win, Hitler stormed out of the stadium. Because Owens's 8.13-meter 1935 jump had not yet been officially accepted, his 8.06-meter Olympic running broad jump was recorded as an Olympic as well as a world record. Owens then ran the final segment of the

4 100-meter relay in 39.8 seconds, contributing to a world record for the U.S. relay team.

Like boxer JOE LOUIS, Owens instantly became a source of racial pride for black Americans. Well aware of his importance to his race and to his nation, Owens, after retiring from competition, worked in youth guidance and training activities and served the U.S. Department of State as a goodwill ambassador to India and the Far East. He was later appointed secretary of the Illinois State Athletic Commission, then spent the remainder of his career in the private sector as a public relations executive.

Suggested Reading

Baker, William J. *Jesse Owens: An American Life.* New York: Free Press, 1988.

PAINE, THOMAS (1737–1809)

A political pamphleteer and philosopher, Thomas Paine wrote *Common Sense* in 1776, which helped to catalyze American sentiment in favor of full independence from Britain. His "Crisis" papers, published throughout the Revolution, from 1776 to 1783, were important in maintaining the American resolve to fight.

Paine was born in England, the son of a corset maker. His family's modest means prevented him from getting more than a marginal formal education, but his natural curiosity led to a wide-ranging course of self-education. Paine tried and failed at one occupation after another until 1772 when he met Benjamin Franklin in London. Impressed with the young Paine, Franklin counseled him to sail to America, arming him with letters of introduction.

Paine arrived in Philadelphia on November 30, 1774, and found employment as an assistant editor for the *Pennsylvania Magazine.* He began to publish anonymous articles of his own in that journal, including "African Slavery in America," a condemnation of the slave trade. He also became involved with the rapidly developing colonial rebellion. After the opening battles of the American Revolution in 1775, and at the prompting of Philadelphia physician and revolutionary Benjamin Rush, Paine wrote *Common Sense,* an eloquent and passionate fifty-page pamphlet advocating that the colonists elevate their revolt against unjust taxation into a full-scale war for national independence. Published on January 10, 1776, the pamphlet became a colonial best-seller and was instrumental in creating the political climate that led in July to the signing of the DECLARATION OF INDEPENDENCE.

During the Revolution Paine served as aide-de-camp to Gen. Nathanael Greene, but his most important role in the struggle was as a propagandist rather than a soldier. Between 1776 and 1783 he published sixteen "Crisis" papers intended to keep the independence effort alive and vigorous. The most famous of these papers is the first, "The American Crisis," which was published on December 19, 1776, when the Continental Army—poorly equipped, inadequately supplied, and miserably clothed—was on the verge of dissolution. "These are the times that try men's souls," Paine began. "The summer soldier and the sunshine patriot will, in this crisis, shrink from the service of their country; but he that stands by it now, deserves the love and thanks of man and woman. Tyranny, like hell, is not easily conquered; yet we have this consolation with us, that the harder the conflict, the more glorious the triumph." GEORGE WASHINGTON, encamped at Valley Forge, Pennsylvania, ordered that the pamphlet be read to his hungry, freezing troops.

In 1777 the Continental Congress appointed Paine secretary to the Committee for Foreign Affairs, but he was forced to step down after a controversy with Silas Deane, a member of the Congress. On November 2, 1779, he was appointed clerk of the General Assembly of Pennsylvania. Although a poor man himself, Paine took $500 from his salary to start a subscription fund for the relief of Washington's long-suffering troops. In 1781 he and John Laurens sailed to France, where they made a successful appeal for cash, clothing, and ammunition for the Continental Army.

Paine also published appeals to the states for greater cooperation in the struggle for independence. His 1780 pamphlet, "Public Good," called for a convention to replace the weak ARTICLES OF CONFEDERATION with a genuinely *continental* constitution.

After the Revolution Paine, perpetually impoverished, was granted £500 by Pennsylvania and, from New York, a farm near New Rochelle. Paine spent several years pursuing invention, including a design for an iron bridge without piers and a candle that produced no smoke. In 1787, to raise money to finance a single-arch bridge over Philadelphia's Schuylkill River, Paine traveled to Europe. Once in England, however, he turned again to political pamphleteering, now focusing his efforts on the French Revolution. The result was *Rights of Man,* published on March 13, 1791. A brilliantly argued justification for the revolution, the book was enormously popular in Europe and the United States. It was followed, in 1792, by *Rights of Man, Part II.* Together the works constituted an analysis of the social and governmental evils attendant upon monarchy and offered a comprehensive plan for a republican government that would provide for the needs of all classes. Paine outlined schemes of universal public education; relief for the poor; government-funded pensions for the aged; and unemployment relief through the construction of great public works. To pay for these endeavors Paine advocated the introduction of a progressive income tax.

As a result of the two *Rights of Man* volumes, Paine was indicted in England on a charge of treason; however, he had been elected to the French National Convention and was on his way to France before an arrest could be carried out. Tried in absentia, Paine was convicted of seditious libel, and his books were suppressed. These events served only to confirm Paine in his support of the French Revolution, although he protested the subsequent Reign of Terror and even fought to have the life of Louis XVI spared.

Imprisoned for his moderation by the regime of Maximilian Robbespierre from December 28, 1793, to November 4, 1794, Paine wrote the first part of *The Age of Reason,* which was published in 1794 while behind bars. In Part II, which appeared in 1796, Paine expounded the deist point of view: he argued his belief in a supreme being, but also built a case against organized religion—especially religion sanctioned by the state. A year after Part II of *The Age of Reason* appeared, Paine published the tract "Agrarian Justice," in some ways his most politically radical work, which analyzed the inherent inequalities of private property ownership.

Paine returned to the United States at the end of 1802 only to find that the nation he had helped to create now regarded him as a dangerous, godless radical. He lived out the rest of his life in poverty and alcoholism. He died in 1809 and was buried on his New Rochelle farm. A decade later the well-meaning British political journalist William Cobbett exhumed Paine's remains, intending to rebury them in a fitting memorial in England. The remains were lost and never recovered.

Suggested Reading

Fast, Howard. *Citizen Tom Paine.* 1943. Reprint, New York: Grove, 1983.

Foner, Eric, ed. *Thomas Paine: Collected Writings.* New York: Library of America, 1995.

PALMER RAIDS

Following the end of World War I and the success of the Bolshevik Revolution in Russia, the United States was swept by what became known as the Red Scare. In April 1919, amid this climate of anxiety and outrage over what threatened to become the worldwide spread of communism, came news that a letter bomb had exploded in the hands of a maid who was opening the mail of a Georgia senator. During the next few days Manhattan postal inspectors intercepted thirty-four more mail bombs—some of which, incredibly enough, had not been delivered because of insufficient postage. The bombs had been sent to a roster of prominent businessmen and government officials, including J. P. Morgan, John D. Rockefeller, and Supreme Court Justice Oliver Wendell Holmes. In June a bomb exploded in front of the house of A. Mitchell Palmer, the U.S. attorney general, prompting Palmer to create a new division at the Department of Justice tasked with locating and arresting anarchists and Bolsheviks.

Palmer invoked the Espionage Act of 1917 and the Sedition Act of 1918, which he interpreted as giving him broad powers to cast a dragnet in search of anyone and everyone remotely suspected of subversion or terrorism. On January 2, 1920, Palmer's agents and local law enforcement personnel conducted raids in thirty-three American cities, randomly rounding up more than five thousand resident aliens. Some were later released; others were jailed for extended periods without trial. Still others were summarily deported back to the Soviet Union (among this group was the radical feminist Emma Goldman).

The wholesale violation of civil rights was too much for Assistant Secretary of Labor Louis F. Post, who used his own limited authority to cancel some 1,500 deportations. Palmer protested that Post should be immediately dismissed, and the House of Representatives began impeachment proceedings. Post, however, was so eloquent in his indictment of what the nation was calling the Palmer Raids that the impeachment failed to carry. In the meantime, the Red Scare subsided almost as quickly as it had begun, and Palmer was largely discredited. After failing to win the Democratic nomination for president in 1920, he never again held public office. (See also Federal Bureau of Investigation and Hoover, J. Edgar.)

Suggested Reading

Feuerlicht, Roberta Strauss. *America's Reign of Terror: World War I, the Red Scare, and the Palmer Raids.* New York: Random House, 1971.

PARKS, ROSA (1913–)

Rosa Parks, often called the mother of the civil rights movement, entered history when, on December 1, 1955, she refused to obey the orders of a city bus driver to relinquish her seat to a white passenger. A Montgomery, Alabama, department store seamstress, Parks was arrested for having violated the city's segregation ordinance, and the incident sparked the MONTGOMERY BUS BOYCOTT, which inaugurated the major phase of the civil rights movement.

Parks was born Rosa Louise McCauley on February 4, 1913, in Tuskegee, Alabama. She attended Alabama State College in Montgomery, married Raymond Parks, and worked as a clerk and an insurance salesperson before getting a job as a seamstress and tailor at a major Montgomery department store. She was on her way home from a day of work at this job when the episode on the bus occurred.

Although Parks had not planned the confrontation on the bus, she did have a history of activism, and she was part of Montgomery's African American activist community, which had been contemplating a boycott to achieve integration of the city's buses. Parks had supported the SCOTTSBORO BOYS in the 1930s, joined the NATIONAL ASSOCIATION FOR THE ADVANCEMENT OF COLORED PEOPLE (NAACP) in 1943, and served as secretary to E. D. Nixon, the head of the local NAACP. Parks was also involved with the Montgomery Voters Registration League, which sponsored voter registration campaigns, and in the summer of 1955 had attended a human rights workshop held at the Highlander Folk School in Tennessee. After the bus incident Parks served on the executive committee of the MONTGOMERY IMPROVEMENT ASSOCIATION, which was the driving force behind the bus boycott.

In 1957, after she lost her job at the department store, Parks and her husband moved to Detroit where Parks joined the SOUTHERN CHRISTIAN LEADERSHIP CONFERENCE and participated in many rallies and demonstrations, including the MARCH ON WASHINGTON in 1963 and the Selma-to-Montgomery march in 1965. Also in 1965 Parks became administrative assistant to Rep. John Conyers, D-Mich., a position she held until her retirement in 1988. In 1987 Parks founded the Rosa and Raymond Parks Institute for Self-Development, a Detroit-based educational organization. Her autobiography, *Rosa Parks: My Story,* was published in 1992. (See also SELMA SNCC–SCLC DEMONSTRATION.)

Suggested Reading

Brinkley, Douglas. *Rosa Parks.* New York: Penguin, 2000.
Parks, Rosa. *Rosa Parks: My Story.* New York: Dial, 1992.

PASSIVE RESISTANCE

To engage in passive resistance means to resist authority or coercion by nonviolent means. (See also CIVIL DISOBEDIENCE and NONVIOLENCE DOCTRINE.)

PENNSYLVANIA COLONY

Present-day Pennsylvania was first settled by the Swedes in 1643; other Europeans, primarily the Dutch, established trading posts in the region beginning about 1647. In 1655 Peter Stuyvesant, governor of New Netherland (later called New York) seized all of New Sweden, which included the territory that would become Pennsylvania. When the English in turn seized New Netherland in 1664, the New Sweden territory fell under English control.

In March 1681 King Charles II granted WILLIAM PENN a charter that rendered him proprietor of the lands that Penn named Pennsylvania ("Penn's Woods") in honor of his father, Adm. Sir William Penn. The new proprietor intended Pennsylvania to serve as a refuge for his fellow Quakers, as well for as others persecuted because of their religious beliefs. Penn drew up the *Frame of Government,* also known as "The Great Law of Pennsylvania," to serve as a constitution for the colony. The document guaranteed absolute freedom of worship and explicitly guaranteed that all colonists would enjoy the traditional rights of Englishmen. Moreover, in contrast to most other colonizers, Penn took pains to establish just and friendly relations with the local Indians.

Penn had hoped that his colony would become a utopia based on Christian precepts. In fact, there was much dissension in the government, which Penn resolved by granting broad governing authority to the Pennsylvania Assembly. Political revolution in England—and the ascension to the throne of William and Mary—contributed to Penn's personal difficulties and, ultimately, he was compelled to surrender the colony to the crown, ending his unique proprietorship. However, he had established a firm foundation of tolerance and constitutional government, both of which continued to shape Pennsylvania politics and culture. Of the citizens of the thirteen original colonies, those of Pennsylvania were the most diverse in national origins and religious convictions. (See also RELIGION, FREEDOM OF.)

Suggested Reading

Kelley, Joseph J. *Pennsylvania, the Colonial Years, 1681–1776.* New York: Doubleday, 1980.

PENN, WILLIAM (1644–1718)

A prominent English Quaker, William Penn was an advocate of religious tolerance and freedom and the founder of Pennsylvania—which he established, in part, as a haven for QUAKERS as well as for members of other religious minorities.

The son of Adm. Sir William Penn, Penn the younger was expelled from Oxford in 1662, after openly rejecting Anglicanism and espousing Quaker belief. Penn subsequently received a year of legal training, then in 1666 was sent by his father to manage the family estates in Ireland, where he met the well-known Quaker preacher Thomas Loe and decided to formally join the Quakers.

Penn published forty-two books and pamphlets on Quakerism and religious freedom, and his advocacy of the faith led to four imprisonments. His best-known book, *No Cross, No Crown,* written in 1669, while he was a prisoner in the Tower of London, condemned the pomp of both Roman Catholicism and Anglicanism while praising Puritan asceticism on the one hand and Quaker social reform on the other. In 1670 he wrote *The Great Case of Liberty of Conscience Once More Debated and Defended,* in which he argued, on both theological and practical grounds, in favor of religious toleration: the Dutch, he observed, were prosperous in large part because of their national policy of tolerating all religions. That same year Penn was arrested for preaching in the street after London authorities had locked the Quaker meetinghouse. The London jury that heard Penn's case refused to convict him, despite efforts to coerce jury members through fines and even imprisonment. In a decision that forever established in English law the sovereign independence of juries, the lord chief justice, Sir John Vaughan, overturned the actions against the jury.

After the death of his father in 1670, Penn inherited extensive estates in England and Ireland and became influential in the court of King Charles II. He also became involved in the colonization of America, initially as a trustee for one of the two Quaker proprietors of West New Jersey. In 1681, with eleven other prominent Quakers, Penn purchased the proprietary rights to East New Jersey, then later in the year secured a very large tract on the west bank of the Delaware River and named it Pennsylvania in tribute to his father. Shortly afterward the Duke of York (later James II) granted Penn the territory of present-day Delaware.

Penn planned to use his proprietary holdings not only to establish a haven for Quakers and others who had been persecuted for their religious beliefs, but to create a utopian Christian commonwealth. Accordingly, in 1682 he composed the *Frame of Government,* also known as "The Great Law of Pennsylvania," a constitution that guaranteed absolute freedom of worship and that specifically protected the traditional rights of Englishmen. In Pennsylvania Penn presided over the first gathering of the members of the Pennsylvania Assembly and established friendly relations with the local Lenni Lenape Indians.

In 1685, when the Duke of York ascended the throne as James II, Penn negotiated for the release of many Quakers and political prisoners, including John Locke. Four years later, however, the downfall of James II and accession of William and Mary compelled Penn to live largely in hiding to avoid arrest. During this period he wrote *An Essay Towards the Present and Future Peace of Europe* (1693), in which he proposed the creation of an international body that would conduct arbitration as an alternative to war, and *A Brief Account of the Rise and Progress of the People Called Quakers* (1694), a history of Quakerism. In 1696 Penn drew up a prescient plan for the union of the American colonies.

In 1699 Penn returned to Pennsylvania, where the government had been torn apart by various disputes. He resolved the problems of the province by renouncing some of his prerogatives as the colony's proprietor; he granted broader authority to the Pennsylvania Assembly (1701) and allowed the dissident lower counties to form their own independent government, which became the colony of Delaware. He returned to England in 1701 and lived long enough to see most of his hopes for Pennsylvania dashed when he was forced to surrender his proprietorship to the crown. (See also RELIGION, FREEDOM OF.)

Suggested Reading

Soderlund, Jean R., and Richard S. Dunn, eds. *William Penn and the Founding of Pennsylvania: 1680–1684.* Philadelphia: University of Pennsylvania Press, 1999.

PHILADELPHIA PLAN

President LYNDON B. JOHNSON advocated AFFIRMATIVE ACTION as a means of correcting the injustices of decades of racial discrimination. While the principle of affirmative action was articulated under Johnson, it was put into effect in 1969 by the federal government under President RICHARD M. NIXON when Secretary of Labor George Schultz announced the Philadelphia Plan.

In 1968 Philadelphia had received some $250 million in federal funds for various projects, including the construction of a new U.S. mint. Surveys revealed that minorities were grossly underrepresented in the construction trades generally and in contracts for these projects specifically. Under the Philadelphia Plan contractors were required, for each project on which they bid, to submit plans that set numerical goals for minority employment. Schultz was careful to point out that the Philadelphia Plan did not call for quotas but simply for the demonstration of a good faith effort to hire members of minorities. (See also "PHILADELPHIA PLAN, REMARKS ON THE".)

Suggested Reading

Beckwith, Francis J., and Todd E. Jones, eds. *Affirmative Action: Social Justice or Reverse Discrimination?* New York: Prometheus, 1997.

Edley, Christopher, Jr. *Not All Black and White: Affirmative Action and American Values.* New York: Noonday, 1998.

"PHILADELPHIA PLAN, REMARKS ON THE" (ARTHUR FLETCHER)

The PHILADELPHIA PLAN was the pilot program in AFFIRMATIVE ACTION. In a speech given in June 1969, Arthur Fletcher, assistant secretary of labor in the administration of RICHARD M. NIXON, offered an official public explanation of the plan. (See Appendix A for excerpts from "Remarks on the Philadelphia Plan.")

Suggested Reading

Beckwith, Francis J., and Todd E. Jones, eds. *Affirmative Action: Social Justice or Reverse Discrimination?* New York: Prometheus, 1997.

Edley, Christopher, Jr. *Not All Black and White: Affirmative Action and American Values.* New York: Noonday, 1998.

PLANNED PARENTHOOD FEDERATION OF AMERICA

Founded in 1942, Planned Parenthood serves as an advocate for education and personal liberties in the areas of reproductive health care, BIRTH CONTROL, and family planning. The organization is an outgrowth of the birth control movement initiated by MARGARET SANGER—who, in defiance of multiple legal sanctions, founded the first birth control clinic in the United States in 1916. She subsequently established the American Birth Control League (1921) and the Birth Control Federation of America (1939), both predecessors of Planned Parenthood.

From its founding through the early 1970s, Planned Parenthood campaigned to educate the public about birth control and lobbied federal and state legislatures for support of family planning. The organization also provided support for the research that led to the development of the birth control pill and the intrauterine device. Through many local offices throughout the United States Planned Parenthood offered counseling in family planning, and in 1971 it began an international family planning program to help developing nations gain control over their exploding populations. Planned Parenthood was in the forefront of the campaign to guarantee the right to legal ABORTION and participated in the litigation that culminated in the 1973 SUPREME COURT decision in *ROE V. WADE*.

Since the 1970s Planned Parenthood had defined its mission as providing comprehensive reproductive health care services while preserving and protecting the privacy and rights of each individual; advocating public policies that guarantee reproductive rights and ensure access to reproductive services, including birth control and abortion; providing educational programs to promote understanding of sexuality; and promoting research in reproductive health care.

In 2000 Planned Parenthood staff and volunteers numbered 23,000 and served approximately 5 million people, 75 percent of whom had incomes at or below 150 percent of the federal poverty level. Through 128 affiliates the organization operates 875 clinics in every state (and Washington, D.C.) except North Dakota and Mississippi. In 2000 the organization provided nearly 97,000 educational programs to more than 1.25 million people. The programs focused on topics such as teenage pregnancy, contraception and family planning, sexually transmitted diseases, women's health, sexual orientation, and safer sex. Planned Parenthood uses its website to provide family planning and other information; in 2000, with 650,000 hits monthly, it was the seventh most visited health website in the world.

Suggested Reading

Planned Parenthood Federation of America, www.plannedparenthood.org.

PLESSY V. FERGUSON

On June 7, 1892, Homer Plessy, a thirty-year-old shoemaker, was arrested, convicted, and jailed for sitting in the "white" car of an East Louisiana Railroad passenger train. Plessy was one-eighth black and seven-eighths white, but under Louisiana law he was considered black and therefore required to sit in the "colored" car. Plessy took his case to court and argued in *Homer Adolph Plessy v. The State of Louisiana,* that the Separate Car Act violated the THIRTEENTH and FOURTEENTH AMENDMENTS to the Constitution.

The trial judge was John Howard Ferguson, a lawyer from Massachusetts who had previously declared the Separate Car Act "unconstitutional on trains that traveled through several states." In Plessy's case, however, he ruled that Louisiana could regulate only those railroad companies that operated within its boundaries; therefore, he found Plessy guilty of refusing to leave the white car. Plessy appealed to the Supreme Court of Louisiana, which upheld Ferguson's decision. Plessy then took the case to the U.S. Supreme Court.

The majority opinion, handed down in 1886, upheld Plessy's conviction and the constitutionality of Louisiana's segregationist law. The high court held that because the Louisiana statute required "equal but separate" rail accommodations, it did not violate the Constitution. The decision reflects the racial attitudes of highly segregated late-nineteenth-century America. Even more important, the case was long used as legal justification for the "separate but equal" segregation of public facilities—including those providing public education—in the South. The 1954 Supreme Court decision in *Brown v. Board of Education of Topeka, Kansas* overturned the decision in *Plessy v. Ferguson*. (See "separate but equal" doctrine; see Appendix A for excerpts from the majority opinion and from Justice John Marshall Harlan's dissent.)

Suggested Reading

Thomas, Brook. *Plessy v. Ferguson: A Brief History with Documents.* New York: St. Martin's Press, 1996.

POLICE BRUTALITY

The Fourth Amendment's guarantee of protection against "unreasonable searches and seizures" affords constitutional protection against police brutality, which is usually defined as the use of excessive or unreasonable force by the police against civilians. Virtually every police department in the United States has explicit policies governing the use of force; these policies are designed, on the one hand, to prevent brutality, and on the other to ensure that officers are protected from harm. The use of force by police is generally guided by the Supreme Court decision in *Graham v. Connor* (1989), which held that plaintiffs who allege excessive use of police force need show only that the officer's actions were unreasonable under the standards of the Fourth Amendment. The burden of demonstrating the use of reasonable judgment and self-restraint is therefore on police agencies and individual officers.

Especially during the height of the African American civil rights movement in the 1960s, white police officers were frequently charged with brutality against demonstrators. The racial aspect of police brutality reemerged dramatically in 1991, with the case of Rodney King, a black motorist whose violent arrest—he was kicked and beaten with batons—was recorded on video by a passerby and nationally televised. The incident provoked national outrage, and the outcome of the 1992 trial of four officers touched off major rioting in Los Angeles and other cities. Similarly shocking was the 1997 beating and sexual assault of a Haitian immigrant, Abner Louima, by New York City police officers. (See also Connor, Eugene "Bull".)

Suggested Reading

Nelson, Jill, ed. *Police Brutality: An Anthology.* New York: Norton, 2001.

POLITICAL ASYLUM

The concept of political asylum dates to ancient times, when certain places—typically, temples—were designated as sacred and inviolable: not only did they afford sovereign protection to those within their precincts, but those who were thus sheltered could not be forcibly removed. In modern international law asylum is the protection, granted by a state, of a foreign citizen against the citizen's own state. The right of asylum is not the right of the individual who seeks it but of the state that grants it, and, indeed, no state is obligated to grant asylum. International law recognizes three categories of asylum:

- Territorial asylum applies within the borders of the state that offers asylum. It is, in effect, a denial of extradition. Such asylum is typically granted to people who are accused (unjustly, in the judgment of the state that is granting asylum) of treason, sedition, political dissidence, protest, or espionage.
- Extraterritorial asylum (also called diplomatic asylum) is granted within embassies, legations, consulates, ships of war, and merchant vessels which are within foreign territory (and almost always within the territory of the state from which protection is sought).
- Neutral asylum refers to special cases in which a state that is neutral in time of war claims the right to offer asylum within its boundaries to combatants of belligerent states on the condition that those granted asylum submit to internment in the host country for the duration of the war.

Suggested Reading

Plaut, W. Gunther. *Asylum: A Moral Dilemma.* New York: Praeger, 1995.

POLL TAXES

During the late nineteenth century, especially the last decade of the century, a number of southern states attempted to circumvent the Fifteenth Amendment ("The right of citizens of the United States to vote shall not be denied or abridged by the United States or by any State on account of race, color, or previous condition of servitude") by imposing a poll tax as a prerequisite to voter registration. Many poor blacks could not afford to pay the tax and so were debarred from voting. Because poll taxes would also have excluded poor whites, however, some voting registrars simply required blacks to produce poll tax receipts and requested no such documentation from white voters.

For years federal bills to abolish poll taxes repeatedly failed to gain passage. At last on August 27, 1962, during the crucial early years of the AFRICAN AMERICAN CIVIL RIGHTS MOVEMENT, the Twenty-Fourth Amendment was passed by Congress; it was ratified on January 23, 1964. The amendment was worded in such a way that it applied only to federal elections; however, in 1966 the U.S. SUPREME COURT ruled in *Harper v. Virginia Board of Elections* that requiring payment of a poll tax as a prerequisite for eligibility to vote in state elections violated the guarantee of equal protection afforded by the FOURTEENTH AMENDMENT. This decision effectively ended the use of poll taxes throughout the United States.

Suggested Reading

Arlington, Karen M., and William L. Taylor, eds. *Voting Rights in America*. Washington, D.C.: University Press of America, 1993.

Kousser, J. Morgan. *Colorblind Injustice: Minority Voting Rights and the Undoing of the Second Reconstruction*. Chapel Hill: University of North Carolina Press, 1999.

POOR PEOPLE'S CAMPAIGN

In 1968, five years after the highly successful MARCH ON WASHINGTON, MARTIN LUTHER KING JR. proposed a new march to the nation's capital, along with a "live-in" demonstration: the Poor People's Campaign. King's assassination in April of that year put leadership of the campaign into the hands of RALPH DAVID ABERNATHY, vice president of the SOUTHERN CHRISTIAN LEADERSHIP CONFERENCE—who, as King had intended, planned the campaign not as a racial protest but as an economic one, an action that made common cause among all poor people, regardless of race.

The Poor People's Campaign drew demonstrators from across the country. They traveled to Washington by bus, car, railroad train, and even a mule train. Nine "caravans" were organized: the Appalachia Trail, the Eastern Caravan, the Freedom Train, the Indian Trail, the Midwest Caravan, the Mule Train, the San Francisco Caravan, the Southern Caravan, and the Western Caravan. Each caravan, as it passed through various regions, recruited demonstrators. In all, 2,600 people came to Washington, D.C., where they lived from May 14 to June 24 in a shantytown—christened Resurrection City—erected on the National Mall. The goal of the campaign was to protest poverty, unemployment, and racial discrimination, and organizers hoped to persuade Congress to enact legislation allocating $30 billion a year to the eradication of poverty.

For the most part the Poor People's Campaign was a dismal contrast to the 1963 March on Washington. Conditions in Resurrection City ranged from uncomfortable to miserable, and were aggravated by rainy weather, which turned the mall into a quagmire. Official Washington largely ignored the demonstrators; finally, as the campaign petered out, police were dispatched to drive out those who still camped on the mall.

Suggested Reading

Abernathy, Ralph David. *And the Walls Came Tumbling Down: An Autobiography*. New York: Harper and Row, 1989.

POWELL, ADAM CLAYTON, JR. (1908–1972)

Born in New Haven, Connecticut, Adam Clayton Powell Jr. was raised in New York's Harlem, the son of the pastor of the Abyssinian Baptist Church. In 1930 he earned a B.A. from Colgate University and, two years later, an M.A. from Columbia University. In 1937 he succeeded his father as pastor. The charisma of the younger Powell was such that church membership swelled, and his ministry became a magnet in the black community. Powell then turned to activism, using his position and growing influence to create neighborhood job and housing programs. Having built a strong local following he was elected to the New York City Council in 1941, the first black to serve. Four years later, in 1945, he was elected to Congress on the Democratic ticket and became Harlem's voice in Washington.

Throughout his eleven terms in the House, Powell fought racial segregation. In 1960 he became chairman of the House Education and Labor Committee, where he was instrumental in framing and passing important legislation, including a minimum wage act, funding for job training, a host of antipoverty acts, and federal aid to education. Powell was not, however, a typical politician. He was blunt and unsparing in his opposition to RACISM—which alone would have been sufficient to earn him enemies in Washington—but Powell was also flamboyant, even extravagant, in his personal habits. He lived in high style—probably, in part, to pique those who believed that blacks should "know their place."

Early in the 1960s Powell was embroiled in a lawsuit when a woman alleged that he had wrongfully accused her of collecting police bribes. Powell lost the suit, and in 1966, when he refused to pay the damages awarded the plaintiff, he was cited for CONTEMPT of court—and his political enemies found their opening. In 1967 a House vote deprived him of his seat. Nevertheless, Powell was reelected the following year, whereupon he was stripped of his seniority and of his chairmanship of the House Education and Labor Committee. Powell was vindicated in 1969, however, by the U.S. SUPREME COURT, which ruled that the House had acted unconstitutionally. Nevertheless, the battle had taken its toll. Broken in health, Powell was defeated in the 1970 Democratic primary. In 1971 he stepped down as pastor of the Abyssinian Baptist Church and retired to his retreat on Bimini, in the Bahamas. He died the following year.

Suggested Reading

Hamilton, Charles V. *Adam Clayton Powell, Jr.: The Political Biography of an American Dilemma.* New York: Cooper Square, 2002.

Powell, Adam Clayton, Jr. *Adam by Adam: The Autobiography of Adam Clayton Powell, Jr.* Sacramento, Calif.: Citadel, 1994.

PRISONERS' RIGHTS

Before the eighteenth century, prisoners held for criminal offenses had virtually no rights. They were, in effect, the subjects of public revenge for private wrongs, and CORPORAL PUNISHMENT and CAPITAL PUNISHMENT were the prevailing penalties (long prison terms were rarely used in the case of common criminals).

During the eighteenth century, with the rise of the Enlightenment, the notion of prisoners' rights began to take shape. The French humanists Charles Montesquieu and Voltaire wrote against the use of torture and discussed the role of humane treatment in punishment. In 1764, Cesare Bonesana, the Marchese di Beccaria, published *On Crimes and Punishments,* a scathing indictment of criminal justice in eighteenth-century Italy and, by extension, throughout Europe. Beccaria condemned the use of torture (both in punishment and in interrogation), the universal corruption of officials, and, most of all, the capricious—but very common—application of severe penalties for relatively minor offenses.

Beccaria held that the basis of punishment must be the same as that for all rational social action: doing what will create the greatest good for the greatest number. Crime, he wrote, was an injury to society, and the degree of punishment must be commensurate with the extent of the social injury; however, the chief purpose of punishment was not to avenge the crime but to deter further crime. Because the length of sentences could vary widely, Beccaria argued that imprisonment was the most humane form of punishment and the form that could most readily be made commensurate with the magnitude of the crime. Moreover, as highly visible institutions, prisons could serve as effective public deterrents to crime.

Beccaria called for prisons that provided individual quarters for inmates, with further segregation of the prison population by age, sex, and degree of criminality. In this scheme, certain prisoners' rights were implied: the right to a degree of privacy and dignity, of social identity, and even of protection—insofar as minor criminals would be segregated from those who had committed the most serious crimes and who were rightly regarded as dangerous. The French Code of Criminal Procedure (1808) and the French Penal Code (1810) were the first bodies of regulation to incorporate at least some of Beccaria's ideas.

In England the leading prison reformer of the eighteenth century was John Howard, who, as sheriff of Bedfordshire (appointed in 1773), was appalled by the prevailing conditions in prisons and in prison hulks, disused ships that were anchored offshore and used to hold prisoners. Howard discovered that the prisons of most of Europe were similarly deplorable, and he pressed to improve conditions in England through the enforcement of the Penitentiary Act. In existence since 1770, the law called for secure and sanitary prison structures, systematic inspection of prisons to ensure adequate conditions, abolition of fees paid by prisoners for their accommodations, and a reformatory regime based on the idea that prison should not merely warehouse inmates but seek to rehabilitate them.

In the American colonies the founder of Pennsylvania, WILLIAM PENN, was the first to require the humane treatment of prisoners. Under Penn, Pennsylvania law prohibited such punishments as flogging, branding, and other tortures, and outlawed capital punishment (which was later reintroduced for premeditated murder only). The Pennsylvania colony established the first prison in America intended to be used as a place of punishment and reform, not a mere holding facility. Unfortunately, Penn's humane code did not outlive him. Upon his death in 1718, the English Anglican Code supplanted Penn's system and brought into the colony some of the most brutal aspects of the English penal system.

After the American Revolution the American penal system developed in an era influenced by the great new prisons of Europe, such as the Maison de Force, in Ghent, Belgium, and the Hospice of San Michele, in Rome. The Maison de Force, built in 1773, was directed by Jean-Jacques Vilain, the first to develop a formal classification system that separated women and children (when confined as indigents) from criminals, and felons from minor offenders. By modern standards, his treatment of inmates was stern, even rigid, but it was founded on a belief that most prisoners could be reformed.

The Hospice of San Michele, built in 1704 at the direction of Pope Clement XI and intended for youth under twenty, was the world's first juvenile penal institution. The focus was on reform, with religious instruction as a means toward reform. Inmates slept in separate cells but assembled during the day in a large central work hall. They were required to maintain a code of silence, and violators of prison rules were flogged.

The Maison de Force and the Hospice of San Michele served as models for the Walnut Street Prison. Built in Philadelphia in 1790, the institution provided for the correction, not the mere incarceration, of convicted felons. In addition, the Walnut Street Prison was intended to be a model for all Pennsylvania counties, each of which was required by law to provide a similar house of correction that would replace all other punishments.

Based on the European models first embodied in the Walnut Street Prison, the so-called Pennsylvania System became the basis for the American penitentiary system during the nineteenth century. As more felons were sentenced to prison terms, however, overcrowding became a persistent problem—and led, in turn, to the construction of bigger and bigger penitentiaries, many of which fell back into old patterns—indiscriminate, congregate confinement of prisoners, enforced idleness, and unsanitary living conditions. In 1819 the New York State Penitentiary at Auburn opened, introducing the congregate system, in which prisoners, under supervision, were assembled to work in large halls during the day, then locked down in individual cells at night. Although this approach avoided the evils of both the indiscriminate housing of prisoners and of unremitting solitary confinement, discipline was rigid. Silence was absolutely enforced, and movement was *en masse* and by lockstep march. The only permitted activity, besides work, was the reading of Scripture.

The stern Auburn System became a pervasive model for the American penitentiary well into the twentieth century. Although the rules are generally more relaxed in most large prisons today, the Auburn System continues to influence the organization of many penal institutions, especially maximum-security prisons.

In 1971 the Attica Prison riot shockingly dramatized the problems inherent in a penal system that was still largely rooted in the nineteenth century. Since Attica, prisoners' rights have become a minority rights issue of increasing importance. Major advocacy organizations, including the American Civil Liberties Union, work to advance the rights of prisoners and to ensure that the rights prisoners already have are respected and observed. Although the *privileges* accorded prisoners vary widely from institution to institution, certain *rights* are guaranteed by the Constitution or by federal law. (See Appendix A for a list of some of the rights guaranteed to prisoners.)

Suggested Reading

American Civil Liberties Union. *Prisoner's Rights.* New York: ACLU, 1999.

Rudovsky, David. *The Rights of Prisoners: The Basic ACLU Guide to a Prisoner's Rights.* New York: Avon, 1981.

PRIVACY RIGHTS

The U.S. Constitution does not explicitly guarantee a right to privacy, but, building on constitutional principles, courts and legislative bodies have recognized certain privacy rights.

Under civil law people may sue for damages or obtain injunctive relief for certain invasions of privacy prompted by motives of gain, curiosity, or malice. Under constitutional law the right of privacy is generally regarded as implied by the First, Fourth, and Fifth Amendments. Both the First and the Fifth Amendments define areas in which people enjoy the liberty to be autonomous; the Fourth Amendment bars unreasonable searches and seizures, which, according to the courts, include invasions of privacy.

Until 1890, with the publication in the *Harvard Law Review* of the landmark essay "The Right to Privacy," by Samuel Warren and Supreme Court Justice Louis Brandeis, the courts had generally restricted the definition of privacy rights to protection against tangible intrusions that resulted in measurable injury. Under the influence of this article, however, federal courts tended to interpret the right to privacy far more broadly. For instance, in *Griswold v. Connecticut* (1965), the Supreme Court overturned as unconstitutional a state law barring the use of contraceptives. In his *Griswold* opinion, Justice William O. Douglas defined a "zone of privacy" within what he called a "penumbra" of rights created by the First, Fourth, and Fifth Amendments. It was also largely on the grounds of the right to privacy that the right to abortion was guaranteed by the 1973 decision in *Roe v. Wade.*

The right to privacy has further resulted in legislation designed to give people a measure of control over the personal and financial information made available to government agencies, private firms, and private individuals. The Privacy Act of 1974 (5 USC 552A) gives people access to an array of government files that pertain to themselves and prohibits government agencies from disclosing certain personal information except (in most cases) in response to a court order.

The proliferation of electronically recorded and encoded credit and other personal records has posed a titanic new challenge to the right to privacy, which lawmakers and the courts have yet to address fully.

Suggested Reading

Alderman, Ellen, and Caroline Kennedy. *The Right to Privacy.* New York: Knopf, 1995.

PROBABLE CAUSE

The Fourth Amendment to the Constitution prohibits unreasonable searches and seizures and requires searches and seizures to be conducted under the authority of a search warrant issued "upon probable cause, supported by oath or affirmation, and particularly describing the place to be searched, and the persons or things to be seized." In *Smith v. United States* (1949) the U.S. Supreme Court defined "probable cause" as "the sum total of layers of information and the synthesis of what the police have heard, what they know, and what they observe as trained officers. [The court is not to] weigh . . . individual layers but the laminated total." The decision further specifies that probable cause is that which would lead a "person of reasonable caution" to believe that something connected with a crime is on the premises or person to be searched.

The definition of probable cause also permits searches without warrant in certain well-defined circumstances: if consent is given, if the search is incidental to a lawful arrest, or if an emergency exists. In *Illinois v. Rodriguez* (1989), the U.S. Supreme Court held that officers may search if given consent by a person whom they believe to have authority to give such consent—even if it is subsequently shown that the person did not have such authority.

Every lawful arrest includes a search, for the protection of officers and others, of the person who has been arrested. Weapons, dangerous substances, or evidence recovered in such a search may be lawfully seized. In *Chimel v. California* (1969), the Supreme Court ruled constitutional the seizure of a "weapon or destructible evidence" from "the area within which the arrestee might gain possession" of the weapon or destructible evidence. However, the court narrowly defined the area as that within the arrestee's "immediate control," meaning within reach. Other Supreme Court decisions following *Chimel* have further defined what may and may not be searched or seized without a warrant (*United States v. Chadwick,* 1977; *Buie v. Maryland,* 1990).

In an emergency, lawful searches are largely defined by *Terry v. Ohio* (1968), which ruled that a frisk or patdown constitutes a "protective search for weapons" and must be confined to such a search.

Evidence that is obtained illegally—either without a search warrant or that fails to meet the required conditions in the absence of a warrant—is disallowed at trial. (See Appendix A for an excerpt from the Supreme Court decision in *Terry v. Ohio.*)

Suggested Reading

Bennet, Wayne W., and Karen M. Hess. "Searches." In *Criminal Investigation.* 5th ed., ed. Wayne W. Bennet and Karen M. Hess. Belmont, Calif.: West/Wadsworth, 1998.

PROPOSITION 187

Proposition 187 was submitted to California voters in the November 8, 1994, general election and was passed by a 59 percent majority. The proposition required the staff of law enforcement, social services, health care, and other public agencies to verify the immigration status of people with whom they came in contact, to report to state and federal officials anyone who appeared to be an illegal alien, and to deny anyone who was determined to be an illegal alien access to social services, health care, and education.

After passage, Proposition 187 was challenged in five different court actions, which were subsequently consolidated as a class action suit in the U.S. District Court, Central District of California—which on December 14, 1994, issued a preliminary injunction barring execution of the law. On May 1, 1995, the League of United Latin American Citizens and another party sought a summary judgment on the unconstitutionality of Proposition 187 on the grounds that it was preempted by the federal government's exclusive constitutional and statutory authority over the regulation of immigration. A summary judgment was not forthcoming but, in 1998, Judge Mariana Pfaelzer of the U.S. District Court, Central District of California, did rule Proposition 187 unconstitutional. (See Appendix A for portions of the text of Proposition 187.)

Suggested Reading

Ono, Kent A., and John M. Sloop. *Shifting Borders: Rhetoric, Immigration, and California's Proposition 187.* Philadelphia: Temple University Press, 2002.

PROPOSITION 209

Proposition 209 was approved by California voters in November 1996 and went into effect on August 28, 1997, as Article I, Section 31, of the state constitution. The measure eliminates state and local government AFFIRMATIVE ACTION programs in the areas of public employment, public education, and public contracting to the extent that such programs entail "preferential treatment" that is based on race, sex, color, ethnicity, or national origin.

The measure was challenged in the courts, and on November 3, 1997, after a number of lower court decisions, the U.S. SUPREME COURT barred further appeal. (See Appendix A for the text of Proposition 209.)

Suggested Reading

Curry, George E., and Cornel West, eds. *The Affirmative Action Debate.* New York: Perseus, 1996.

PUBLIC AND INDIAN HOUSING PROGRAM

The Public and Indian Housing Program is actually a range of programs authorized and funded by Congress under the provisions of the Housing Act of 1937, which created the public and Indian housing program that currently provides affordable housing to more than 1.3 million households.

The program is administered by the Office of Public and Indian Housing of the DEPARTMENT OF HOUSING AND URBAN DEVELOPMENT and is intended to ensure access to safe, decent, and affordable housing; to create opportunities for residents' self-sufficiency and economic independence; and to assure the fiscal integrity of all program participants.

Suggested Reading

Office of Public and Indian Housing, www.hud.gov/offices/pih/index.cfm.

PUERTO RICAN LEGAL DEFENSE AND EDUCATION FUND

Founded in 1972 the Puerto Rican Legal Defense and Education Fund (PRLDEF) is a privately funded, nonprofit, nonpartisan organization that works through education, litigation, and policy making to serve the Puerto Rican and the wider Latino community. The organization's goal is to secure, promote, and protect civil and human rights for Puerto Ricans and Latinos and to help them attain full participation, engagement, and empowerment in civic affairs while preserving their distinctive culture. The organization also works to ensure access to the legal profession and to other professions and to help Puerto Ricans and other Latinos achieve educational excellence.

Suggested Reading

Puerto Rican Legal Defense and Education Fund, www.prldef.org.

QUAKERS

"Quaker" is the popular name for a member of the Religious Society of Friends, a religious group founded in mid-seventeenth-century England by George Fox. While Quakerism grew out of the Puritan wing of the Anglican church and is a Christian sect, it departs radically from most modern forms of Christianity by emphasizing the guidance of individual conscience and an indwelling holy spirit, and it eschews outward rites as well as an ordained ministry. From the beginning the total rejection of violence has been a hallmark of Quaker faith and practice. Quaker pacifism encompasses the refusal to participate in military service, and observant Quakers are therefore CONSCIENTIOUS OBJECTORS. In addition to rejecting violence as individuals, Quakers have a tradition of organized opposition to war, SLAVERY, and social injustice, which they consider forms of violence. In England and elsewhere, early Quakers were subjected to vigorous persecution, and religious tolerance is a foundation of Quaker belief and practice.

The Society of Friends is loosely organized. Most individual meetings (as congregations are called) are associated with at least one of three umbrella organizations: the Friends General Conference, the Friends United Meeting, or Evangelical Friends International. Under the aegis of these organizations or with the sponsorship of one or more local meetings, various antiwar, social justice, and minority rights organizations have been formed. (See Appendix A for a list of leading Quaker activist organizations in the United States. See also PENN, WILLIAM.)

Suggested Reading

Bacon, Margaret Hope. *The Quiet Rebels: The Story of the Quakers in America.* Wallingford, Penn.: Pendle Hill, 2000.

West, Jessamyn, ed. *The Quaker Reader.* Wallingford, Penn.: Pendle Hill, 1992.

QUOTAS, IMMIGRATION

At various times in U.S. history, Congress has enacted legislation fixing quotas (limits) on immigration on the basis of national origin; the quotas are designed to restrict the immigration of some groups while favoring that of others. (See also ASIATIC EXCLUSION LEAGUE; CHINESE EXCLUSION REPEAL ACT; CHINESE EXCLUSION TREATY AND ACT; ENGLISH-ONLY LEGISLATION AND MOVEMENTS; GENTLEMAN'S AGREEMENT; HISPANIC AMERICANS; HISPANIC CIVIL RIGHTS MOVEMENT; IMMIGRATION ACT OF 1917; IMMIGRATION ACT OF 1924; IMMIGRATION ACT OF 1965; IMMIGRATION AND NATURALIZATION ACT OF 1952; IMMIGRATION REFORM AND CONTROL ACT; IMMIGRATION RIGHTS, STATUTES, AND RESTRICTIONS.)

QUOTAS, RACIAL

Racial quotas are numerical targets for the inclusion of certain minorities (typically, racial and ethnic minorities) in employment and education. Quotas were once seen as an inseparable part of AFFIRMATIVE ACTION programs, but a number of SUPREME COURT decisions—beginning with *REGENTS OF THE UNIVERSITY OF CALIFORNIA V. BAKKE* (1978)—have found the use of ethnic and racial quotas unconstitutional on the grounds that it violates the FOURTEENTH AMENDMENT guarantee of equal protection. As a result, adherence to numerical quotas is no longer a part of affirmative action programs. (See also REVERSE DISCRIMINATION.)

Suggested Reading

Curry, George E., and Cornel West, eds. *The Affirmative Action Debate.* New York: Perseus, 1996.

R

RACE RIOTS

Segregation, discrimination, and general racial tension have contributed to the periodic outbreak of race riots in the United States since at least the Civil War. Some race riots, especially during the nineteenth and early twentieth centuries, chiefly involved white mobs attacking black communities. Riots later in the twentieth century, especially during the 1960s, have generally been eruptions within black communities, expressions of collective outrage in which local businesses (some white owned, some black) were looted and burned and other local property destroyed.

Major race riots—often collectively referred to as the Draft Riots—took place in Boston, Buffalo, Chicago, Cleveland, Detroit, and New York during the Civil War; the worst occurred in New York City during four days in July of 1863. Poor immigrants, most of whom were Irish, began by protesting the inequity of the conscription laws (under which wealthy young men could legally buy their way out of service), but the protests rapidly expanded into attacks on blacks, who (the immigrants feared) would usurp all available jobs once a Union victory brought an end to SLAVERY. In New York, blacks were beaten and killed, and a black orphan asylum burned to the ground.

At the turn of the century, Brownsville, Texas (1906); Atlanta, Georgia (1906); and Springfield, Illinois (1908) erupted in acts of white mob violence against blacks. These events occurred during a period in which LYNCHING was both endemic and epidemic, especially in the South.

Despite the NONVIOLENCE DOCTRINE of MARTIN LUTHER KING JR., the rise of the AFRICAN AMERICAN CIVIL RIGHTS MOVEMENT in the 1960s saw the outbreak of riots in black communities not only in southern cities but in the North as well. Chicago, Detroit, New York, Newark (New Jersey), and the Watts neighborhood of Los Angeles saw some of the worst rioting, but, during what the media referred to as "long hot summers," riots were agonizingly common throughout the nation. Some of the worst occurred in 1968 after the assassination of Martin Luther King.

The end of the 1960s brought the era of "long hot summers" to a close, but a lingering awareness remained that what the media typically characterized as a "racial incident"—a heated argument between whites and blacks, a controversial arrest of a black suspect by white officers—might touch off a community protest that could explode into a riot. As the years went by without renewed mass violence, however, a collective sense developed that the era of large-scale urban race riots had passed.

The nation's complacency was shattered in 1992, however, when massive rioting broke out in South Central Los Angeles after the acquittal of the white police officers who had been charged with beating black motorist RODNEY KING during a routine arrest. The riot, which erupted immediately after the verdicts, on April 29, 1992, and lasted three days, engulfed some fifty square miles of Los Angeles and touched off lesser civil disturbances in Atlanta, Pittsburgh, San Francisco, and Seattle. More than fifty people died in Los Angeles, hundreds were injured, and property damage exceeded $1 billion. (See also NIAGARA MOVEMENT.)

Suggested Reading

Harris, Fred R., and Lynn A. Curtis, eds. *Locked in the Poorhouse: Cities, Race, and Poverty in the United States.* New York: Rowman and Littlefield, 1999.

RACIAL PROFILING

Targeting people for investigation by law enforcement officials on the basis of their race, national origin, or ethnicity is collectively referred to as racial profiling. It is an illegal practice, which all police jurisdictions have officially banned or renounced. Racial profiling prejudges, without probable cause, the likelihood of involvement in criminal activity on the basis of discriminatory factors, and is therefore a violation of the constitutional guarantees of DUE

PROCESS, equal protection, and the presumption of innocence. The most common form of racial profiling is the practice of stopping black drivers for minor traffic violations with the express purpose of searching their cars for contraband such as illegal drugs and weapons.

Most police departments have promulgated official policies forbidding racial profiling; a typical example is the following memorandum, issued by the commander of the Florida Highway Patrol on April 26, 1999:

> Profiling by members of the Florida Highway Patrol will not be condoned. I expect that traffic stops made by members of the Patrol will be based solely on the violation observed. I also expect that the race, ethnicity, gender, or economic status of the vehicle occupants will not be considered in deciding whether to search the vehicle. Decisions to search a vehicle are to be based on evidence and the occupant's behavior patterns. Members found to be conducting profile stops will be subject to disciplinary action.

Despite such official statements of policy, many civil rights activists assert that profiling persists as a common, if now unofficial, practice among officers in the field.

Suggested Reading

Fredrickson, Darin D., and Raymond P. Siljander. *Racial Profiling: Eliminating the Confusion between Racial and Criminal Profiling.* Springfield, Ill.: Charles C. Thomas, 2002.

Harris, David A. *Profiles in Injustice: Why Police Profiling Cannot Work.* New York: New Press, 2002.

RACISM

In its most basic meaning, racism is the belief that race accounts for certain differences in human character or abilities. However, the term often has much broader implications, according to which race not only determines differences among people but accounts for the superiority of some races over others. The assumption that inherited characteristics render some races superior and others inferior has historically provided the justification for discrimination. Racist beliefs may be associated with a range of feelings and attitudes, from violent hatred to blandly "positive" assumptions (for example, the belief among some whites that all blacks are natural athletes).

Although various attempts have been made to substantiate racist beliefs through objective research, the debate over the scientific merit of such beliefs is irrelevant to the legal status of racism in the United States. The Bill of Rights, especially the Fourth Amendment and the FOURTEENTH AMENDMENT, and a formidable body of civil rights law and case law, bar the use of race in determining the status or abridging the rights of any individual in virtually any context that law and government may regulate. This does not mean that racism is no longer a powerful influence on American life; indeed, its continued pervasiveness and influence lead minority rights and human rights organizations to continue to endeavor to change individual, institutional, and collective attitudes toward race.

Suggested Reading

Fredrickson, George M. *Racism: A Short History.* Princeton: Princeton University Press, 2002.

RADICAL REPUBLICANS

Radical Republicans were members of the Republican Party who, during the Civil War, favored immediate and unconditional emancipation of the slaves and, after the war, immediate equality and full enfranchisement for freed blacks. Not all Republicans were Radical Republicans; ABRAHAM LINCOLN, for one, was not. However, following the assassination of President Lincoln, on April 14, 1865, the Radical Republicans gained control of the party and pushed through Congress the Reconstruction Acts of 1867 and 1868, which installed military governments in the states of the former Confederacy and required immediate universal manhood suffrage.

Despite many noble intentions, RECONSTRUCTION under the Radical Republicans was harshly punitive and provoked much resentment from whites, intensifying racial tensions and, ultimately, hardening southern racism and support for segregation. When Reconstruction abruptly ended in 1877, the Radical Republicans ceased to exist.

Suggested Reading

Melvin, Harold. *The Radical Republicans and Reconstruction, 1861–1870.* Indianapolis: Bobbs-Merrill, 1967.

RANDOLPH, A. PHILIP (1889–1979)

Asa Philip Randolph was an African American labor leader and civil rights activist who founded the BROTHERHOOD OF SLEEPING CAR PORTERS, the first major, nationally recognized union of black workers.

Born in Crescent City, Florida, Randolph was the son of a Methodist minister. In 1911 he left the rural South for Harlem, in New York City, and enrolled in night school at

City College. In 1912 he and black journalist Chandler Owen founded an employment agency, which they then used as the nucleus of a black labor union. When the United States entered World War I in 1917, Randolph and Chandler, both members of the Socialist Party, began publishing the *Messenger* (renamed *Black Worker* in 1929), a magazine that advocated an expanded role for blacks both in the military and in defense industries. The *Messenger* made Randolph a nationally known figure, and after the war he lectured at New York's Rand School of Social Science and also ran for political office on the Socialist Party ticket, albeit without success.

In 1925 Randolph founded, and became the first president of, the Brotherhood of Sleeping Car Porters. Despite the fact that most of the member unions of the American Federation of Labor (AFL) were segregated, Randolph worked successfully to affiliate the Brotherhood with the AFL. However, it was not until 1937 that the union concluded its first contract with the Pullman Company, which built and managed the operation of sleeper cars for all passenger railroads. A year after this victory, Randolph protested continued widespread segregation in AFL unions by pulling the Brotherhood out of the AFL and affiliating with the newly formed, and more progressive, Congress of Industrial Organizations (CIO).

With a new war looming, Randolph approached President FRANKLIN D. ROOSEVELT (FDR) with a warning that unless he brought an end to racial discrimination in federal agencies and defense industries, Randolph would lead a mass protest march on Washington, D.C. FDR responded on June 25, 1941, by issuing Executive Order 8802, which prohibited discrimination in all federal bureaus and defense plants. The order also established the Fair Employment Practices Committee to resolve grievances.

During World War II Randolph refrained from pressing the campaign to integrate the armed forces; however, when the war ended, he founded the League for Nonviolent Civil Disobedience against Military Segregation, an organization that was instrumental in President HARRY S. TRUMAN's decision to issue, on July 26, 1948, Executive Order 9981, effectively ordering the integration of the armed forces.

In 1955 the AFL merged with the CIO, and Randolph became a vice president and member of the executive council in the new, combined organization. From 1960 to 1966 he served as the first president of the Negro American Labor Council, which he and others had founded specifically to combat racial discrimination within the AFL-CIO.

Randolph was a principal organizer of the triumphal 1963 MARCH ON WASHINGTON, and in 1965 he founded the A. Philip Randolph Institute, which continues to serve as a national organization of black trade unionists building black community support for trade unions.

During the late 1960s Randolph's health declined, prompting him to resign in 1968 as president of the Brotherhood of Sleeping Car Porters and to withdraw entirely from activism and the public spotlight.

Suggested Reading

Pfeffer, Paula A. *A. Philip Randolph: Pioneer of the Civil Rights Movement.* Baton Rouge: Louisiana State University Press, 1996.

RAP MUSIC

Rap music emerged in the Bronx, New York, during the early 1970s and within a decade had become a commercially viable form of popular music. Some rap lyrics are a form of social protest; most embody vivid images and narratives of ghetto life. One genre, known as "gangsta rap," contains violent imagery and language and even exhorts listeners to engage in violence.

The rap style began when African American disc jockeys began alternating between two turntables to "mix" prerecorded music and accompanying the mix by reciting rap phrases to the crowd. The phrases themselves can be traced to jive talk, a feature of black urban speech during the 1930s and 1940s. Jive, which gained currency largely through its use by jazz musicians, is fast paced, highly metaphorical, witty, improvisational, charged with double entendres, and often laced with slyly derogatory references to whites. H. "Rap" Brown, a charismatic and militant civil rights activist of the 1960s, energized his fiery speeches with the more politically charged form of jive that became known as rap—and may, in a sense, be regarded as the first rapper.

Suggested Reading

Keyes, Cheryl L. *Rappin' to the Beat: Rap Music as Street Culture among African Americans.* Ann Arbor: University of Michigan Press, 1992.

RAY, JAMES EARL (1928–1998)

James Earl Ray confessed to assassinating MARTIN LUTHER KING JR., pleaded guilty, then, while in prison, recanted his confession and claimed that he had been the innocent fall guy in an assassination conspiracy. Ray's attempts to secure a new trial—in actuality, a first trial, since his guilty plea meant that his case had never been tried—were supported by members of the King family, including King's widow, Coretta Scott King, who stated publicly that she did not believe Ray was her husband's killer.

Ray was a career criminal who robbed gas stations and stores. He had served prison terms in Illinois and Missouri (on two separate occasions) and had received a suspended sentence in Los Angeles. On April 23, 1967, he escaped from the Missouri State Penitentiary and in Memphis on April 4, 1968, allegedly used a rifle to fire from a flophouse window, hitting King as he stood across the street on the balcony of his room at the Lorraine Motel. Ray then fled, first to Toronto, where he obtained a Canadian passport, then to London and to Lisbon, where he obtained a second Canadian passport. With this passport he returned to London, where, on June 8, he was arrested at Heathrow Airport as he was about to leave for Brussels. The Federal Bureau of Identification (FBI) had identified him as its primary suspect immediately after the assassination.

Extradited, Ray pleaded guilty in Memphis and was sentenced to ninety-nine years in prison. Just a few months later he recanted his confession. In June 1977 he briefly escaped from prison but was recaptured.

Ray claimed that a person known to him only as Raul framed him for the assassination, and his claim has given rise to various King assassination conspiracy theories that implicate the FBI, other intelligence organizations, and even the Mafia. Ray died in prison of liver disease on April 23, 1998, without ever securing a new trial.

Suggested Reading

Pepper, William F. *Orders to Kill: The Truth Behind the Murder of Martin Luther King, Jr.* New York: Warner Books, 1998.

Posner, Gerald L. *Killing the Dream: James Earl Ray and the Assassination of Martin Luther King, Jr.* New York: Random House, 1998.

REAGAN, RONALD W. (1911–)

Ronald Wilson Reagan, the fortieth president of the United States, served two terms, from 1981 to 1989, and presided over a "conservative revolution" that saw a retreat from the liberal policies of Reagan's predecessor, Jimmy Carter, and from the tradition of activist government that had been introduced during the New Deal of Franklin D. Roosevelt. Most civil rights leaders regard the Reagan years as an era of retrenchment in which minority-oriented social policy was turned back on many fronts.

Ronald Reagan was not born into politics. He was raised in small-town Illinois, the son of a shoe salesman who, because of alcoholism, had difficulty supporting his family. Despite financial problems Reagan attended Eureka College in Illinois and served as class president his senior year. He graduated in 1932 with a bachelor's degree in economics and sociology, then became a radio sportscaster in Davenport, Iowa. He excelled at the job and soon moved up to a large station in Des Moines, Iowa. From here, in 1937, Reagan went to Hollywood, secured a screen test at Warner Bros., and embarked on a comfortable career as a second-tier actor in B movies. He married actress Jane Wyman in 1940 and was divorced from her in 1948. During World War II Reagan served in a U.S. Army film unit, based in Los Angeles, that was assigned to turn out training films.

Although Reagan had been raised as a liberal Roosevelt Democrat, he gradually became conservative. While serving as president of the Screen Actors Guild (1947–1952), Reagan testified as a friendly witness before the House Un-American Activities Committee (HUAC) and freely cooperated in the HUAC's infamous blacklisting of actors, directors, and writers suspected of communist ties. In 1950 Reagan at first supported Democratic senatorial candidate Helen Douglas, but switched his allegiance to her vehemently anticommunist opponent, Richard M. Nixon, before the election. Reagan threw his support behind Republican Dwight D. Eisenhower in the presidential elections of 1952 and 1956, and during 1960 delivered numerous campaign speeches in support of Nixon's presidential run against John F. Kennedy. It was not until 1962, however, that Reagan officially changed party affiliation. Reagan's shift toward Republican conservatism was prompted in part by his marriage, in 1952, to Nancy Davis, a minor actress who was also a strong-willed and eloquent conservative.

Reagan's acting career petered out during the 1950s, and after serving as the host of the *General Electric Theater* series on television and as a spokesman for the General Electric Company, Reagan became more deeply involved in politics, campaigning for Nixon in his unsuccessful race for governor of California in 1962 and supporting the presidential candidacy of conservative Republican Barry Goldwater in 1964. It was during the Goldwater campaign that Reagan first earned a reputation as a highly effective political orator.

In 1966 Reagan ran for governor of California against incumbent Democrat Edmund G. ("Pat") Brown, who made the mistake of failing to take Reagan's candidacy seriously and lost by almost a million votes. From 1966 to 1974 Reagan served two terms in the statehouse, where he attacked a huge budget deficit by ruthlessly scaling back state welfare programs and by enacting the largest tax increase in the history of any state.

Setting his sights on the White House, Reagan anticipated running in 1976, but the resignation of Richard Nixon in 1974 put Nixon's appointed vice president Gerald R. Ford into office and into contention for election in his own right. Reagan challenged Ford at the Republican National Convention but failed to secure the nomination. Four years later, however, Reagan swept most of the primaries and easily captured the nomination on the first ballot.

Campaigning during a period of "stagflation" (combined recession and inflation) and during the ongoing Iran hostage crisis (on November 4, 1979, an Iranian mob stormed the U.S. embassy in Tehran, Iran, and took the staff hostage; the situation was stalemated for more than a year), Reagan and his running mate, George H.W. Bush, won a landslide victory.

Reagan championed supply-side economics, which called for massive tax cuts to stimulate investment and, presumably, the economy. Simultaneously, Reagan advocated extremely large increases in military spending, with concomitant cuts in spending on social-welfare programs, including low-income housing, education, the food stamps and school-lunch programs, Medicaid, and Aid to Families with Dependent Children. Congress softened the cuts mildly, but gave the president essentially what he had asked for. Reagan's economic strategy did nothing to avert a deepening of the recession, however, in which unemployment approached 11 percent; moreover, it helped to triple the national debt. In view of these alarming statistics, Reagan backed off from strict adherence to supply-side theory and supported a tax increase in 1982, which improved the economy the following year and contributed to a period of economic growth, although critics charged that it did so at the expense of the poor and the working class.

Reagan did not aim merely to reduce taxes and curtail welfare but to reduce the role of what he called "big government" in the lives of Americans. Toward this end, he slashed the budgets of numerous government departments and lowered the level of enforcement for regulations and statutes administered by the Environmental Protection Agency, the DEPARTMENT OF THE INTERIOR, the Department of Transportation, and the Civil Rights Division of the DEPARTMENT OF JUSTICE. In general, the Reagan administration rushed to deregulate American industry.

During the Reagan administration many vacancies developed in the federal courts and three in the SUPREME COURT. The president made predictably conservative appointments, including Anthony Kennedy and Antonin Scalia to the Supreme Court, but he also appointed the first woman to that court, SANDRA DAY O'CONNOR. With the retirement of WARREN BURGER as chief justice, President Reagan elevated the conservative WILLIAM REHNQUIST to that position.

In the area of foreign relations, Reagan took an unrelenting hard line against the Soviet Union, and relations with that nation deteriorated until the ascension of Mikhail Gorbachev, in 1985, a moderate leader with whom Reagan was able to work more cooperatively. Some historians believe, with former Secretary of Defense Caspar Weinberger, that Reagan's massive military spending, directed chiefly against the Soviets, forced the Soviet Union to spend far beyond its means and contributed to the collapse of that government—and, therefore, to a final American victory in the cold war that had begun at the end of World War II.

Supporters of international human rights were often critical of Reagan's foreign policies, including the invasion of the Caribbean island nation of Grenada in 1984 and U.S. support of the right-wing military governments of El Salvador and Nicaragua. U.S. involvement in Nicaragua led to the Iran-Contra Affair, an arrangement—undertaken secretly and without congressional knowledge, let alone approval—to sell arms to Iran in exchange for that country's help in securing the release of Americans held hostage by terrorist groups in Lebanon; the revenues from these arms sales were to be used to help finance the right-wing Contras in Nicaragua.

The Iran-Contra initiative ran counter to Reagan's firmly stated resolve never to negotiate with terrorists or to aid countries (such as Iran) that supported international terrorism, and at first it appeared that the revelation of the Iran-Contra Affair would become Reagan's Watergate. Nevertheless, the enormously popular president weathered the constitutional scandal and remained sufficiently respected to prove an asset in George H.W. Bush's 1988 campaign.

After leaving the White House Reagan retired to private life and wrote an autobiography, *An American Life* (1990). In 1994, in an open letter to the American people, Reagan revealed that he was suffering from Alzheimer's disease; the disease's rapid progression has kept the former president out of the public eye.

Suggested Reading

Morris, Edmund. *Dutch: A Memoir of Ronald Reagan.* New York: Random House, 1999.

Reagan, Ronald. *Reagan, In His Own Hand: The Writings of Ronald Reagan That Reveal His Revolutionary Vision for America.* New York: Simon and Schuster, 2001.

REASONABLE DOUBT

In keeping with the presumption of innocence guaranteed by the Constitution, the American judicial system puts the burden of proof in criminal matters on the state, requiring the prosecution to prove guilt beyond a reasonable doubt. In practice, this means that to secure acquittal of a criminal charge, the defense need not prove innocence, but need only create reasonable doubt as to guilt.

Suggested Reading

Zerman, Melvyn B. *Beyond a Reasonable Doubt: Understanding the American Jury System.* New York: Crowell, 1981.

RECONSTRUCTION

Reconstruction, which followed the Civil War and spanned the years 1865 to 1877, was a well-intentioned and, in many respects, noble attempt to resolve the political, social, and economic difficulties attendant on readmitting to the Union the eleven states of the former Confederacy. But Reconstruction was also deeply flawed, coercive, punitive, and politically corrupt.

The initial feature of Reconstruction was the establishment of provisional military governments for the former Confederate states. Even before the war ended such governments were installed in areas occupied by the U.S. Army. In 1863 President Abraham Lincoln, anxious to begin healing the great American wound, put forward a plan to reestablish civil governments in occupied states wherein at least 10 percent of the voting population had taken an oath of allegiance. Radical Republicans in Congress, however, resisted this approach as far too lenient and as an executive usurpation of legislative authority.

In 1864 Congress passed the Wade-Davis Bill, which called for a military government to be established in each seceded state and to be sustained until a majority of the state's white citizens swore the prescribed oath. At that point the state could call a constitutional convention, but it was obliged to frame a constitution that abolished slavery, repudiated secession, and disqualified Confederate officials from voting or holding office. Moreover, only citizens who swore that they had never voluntarily aided the Confederacy would be enfranchised. By declining to sign the bill before the end of the congressional session, President Lincoln left the issue to Andrew Johnson, who became president after Lincoln's assassination on April 14, 1865.

Johnson attempted to implement the moderate policies that he believed Lincoln would have wanted. But Johnson was a clumsy politician and lacked Lincoln's eloquence and ability to make common cause. On one hand his conciliatory stance toward the South alienated Congress, on the other the fighting language he used against those southerners who rejected the Fourteenth Amendment (which gave full citizenship rights to blacks) alienated southerners, provoking race riots and the passage of the black codes, which imposed draconian restrictions on the rights of freed slaves. Johnson's penchant for antagonizing both sides gave the Radical Republicans a large congressional majority in the 1866 election and put this uncompromising group in charge of Reconstruction.

The Radical Republican majority passed the Reconstruction Act of 1867, by which all the former Confederate states except Tennessee (which had been readmitted to the Union in 1866) were apportioned into five military districts for purposes of more efficient government. As a requirement for readmission to the Union and the privilege of creating an elected civil government, each state was obliged to accept the Fourteenth Amendment and the Fifteenth Amendment, which prohibited states from denying anyone the vote on account of race or "previous condition of servitude."

Formed under the supervision of the U.S. Army, the new state governments created between 1868 and 1870 were dominated by blacks (newly freed slaves who were hardly prepared to govern), carpetbaggers (northern opportunists who had gone into the South), and scalawags (southerners who collaborated with the blacks and carpetbaggers). The majority of southern whites regarded these governments as both repugnant and illegitimate; they also despised the Freedmen's Bureau, which Congress had created to look after the welfare and education of the newly freed slaves and to facilitate their transition to independent life.

Southern resistance to the institutions of Reconstruction prompted the formation of a shadow government, supported chiefly by the terrorism of two secret societies, the Ku Klux Klan and the Knights of the White Camelia. Together, these societies and the shadow governments worked to circumvent the authority of both the federal government and the Freedman's Bureau, and to suppress black efforts to achieve autonomy or any voice in government. At the same time a deep-seated enmity was created between the North and the South; one result was that the South was isolated from the economically more prosperous North, impeding its recovery from the ravages of war and crippling its economy. The aftereffects—both social and economic—would be felt well into the next century.

By the mid-1870s it was apparent to most observers that Reconstruction had been a failure. It ended abruptly in 1877 when Democrats and Republicans brokered a deal to resolve the contested presidential election of 1876. Although Democrat Samuel J. Tilden had received a majority of the popular vote and, until contested, a majority of the electoral vote as well, the Democratic Party resolved to give the election (which was to be decided by a special congressional commission) to Republican candidate Rutherford B. Hayes on condition that Hayes immediately end Reconstruction. Shortly after taking office Hayes did just that, leaving the South in the hands of Democrats determined (in the phrase often heard) "to keep the blacks in their place."

From the perspective of history, the negative effects of Reconstruction are highly apparent: decades of southern economic hardship and a legacy of racial prejudice, persecution, oppression, and inequality. Less readily appreciated are the positive aspects of the attempt, however flawed, to reunite the nation while protecting the rights, welfare, and safety of the freed slaves. Reconstruction did succeed in a number of areas: by reforming and reorganizing the courts and judicial procedures; by establishing many viable public school systems; and by implementing taxation on a more equitable basis. Moreover, while Reconstruction undeniably created grave political and social problems, it did not give rise to the condition that, more often than not, follows civil war: an ongoing, undeclared state of guerrilla warfare. However imperfectly, the Union—and, with it, peace—were restored.

Suggested Reading

Foner, Eric. *Reconstruction: America's Unfinished Revolution, 1863–1877.* New York: HarperCollins, 1989.

Melvin, Harold. *The Radical Republicans and Reconstruction, 1861–1870.* Indianapolis: Bobbs-Merrill, 1967.

REEB, JAMES (1927–1965)

Born in Wichita, Kansas, James Reeb was a white minister of the Unitarian Church who became active in the AFRICAN AMERICAN CIVIL RIGHTS MOVEMENT and joined the SOUTHERN CHRISTIAN LEADERSHIP CONFERENCE (SCLC). While participating in the SELMA SNCC–SCLC DEMONSTRATION in 1965, Reeb was attacked by a white mob on March 8, the day after BLOODY SUNDAY, the police assault on SCLC demonstrators. Savagely beaten and clubbed, he sustained severe head injuries and died in the hospital on March 11. The grisly death of this white minister horrified the nation, raising the consciousness of northern whites and intensifying the condemnation of southern RACISM.

Suggested Reading

Howlett, Duncan. *No Greater Love: The James Reeb Story.* Boston: Skinner House, 1993.

REGENTS OF THE UNIVERSITY OF CALIFORNIA V. BAKKE

The 1978 SUPREME COURT case of *Regents of the University of California v. Bakke* challenged the principles and assumptions of AFFIRMATIVE ACTION.

Allan Bakke was one of 2,664 applicants for a hundred openings at the medical school of the University of California at Davis. Sixteen of the available slots were reserved for African American, Latino, Asian, and Native American applicants who, under a special admissions program, were admitted with lower test scores and grade-point averages than other applicants. The university maintained a separate admissions committee for minority applicants, and during years in which some minority applicants with lower scores than Bakke's were accepted, Bakke was twice rejected for admission.

Bakke filed suit on the grounds that the university's special admissions program violated Title VI of the CIVIL RIGHTS ACT OF 1964, which barred racial or ethnic preferences in programs supported by federal funds. Bakke's suit also contended that the program violated his FOURTEENTH AMENDMENT rights, specifically the guarantee of equal protection. In effect, Bakke alleged REVERSE DISCRIMINATION. The high court held that the special admissions program did indeed violate the equal protection clause of the Fourteenth Amendment; however, while the decision invalidated the program at Davis, it did not strike down affirmative action itself; on the contrary, the ruling affirmed the right of universities to take race into account as a factor in admissions. Nevertheless, *Regents v. Bakke* has cast under legal suspicion all affirmative action programs since. (See Appendix A for an excerpt from the Court's decision, as announced by Justice Lewis Powell.)

Suggested Reading

Spann, Girardeau A. *The Law of Affirmative Action: Twenty-Five Years of Supreme Court Decisions on Race and Remedies.* New York: New York University Press, 2000.

REHNQUIST, WILLIAM H. (1924–)

Appointed by President RONALD REAGAN in 1986, William Hubbs Rehnquist, the sixteenth chief justice of the United States, brought to the high court a dominant conservative note.

Born and raised in Milwaukee, Wisconsin, Rehnquist graduated from Stanford University in 1948 and earned his law degree from Stanford Law School in 1952. After serving as law clerk to SUPREME COURT Justice Robert H. Jackson, Rehnquist practiced in Phoenix, Arizona, from 1953 to 1969. During this period he became active in conservative Republican politics.

In 1969 President RICHARD M. NIXON appointed Rehnquist assistant attorney general of the Office of Legal Counsel for the DEPARTMENT OF JUSTICE. In this post Rehnquist supported the expansion of police powers and was generally hostile to civil rights legislation. When a vacancy opened on the Supreme Court in 1971, President Nixon nominated

Rehnquist. After a long and rancorous debate in the Senate, where he was assailed by liberals, Rehnquist was confirmed and assumed his seat in January 1972.

Unlike some appointees of conservative presidents, who prove more moderate than conservative once in office, Rehnquist held no surprises. He consistently voted with the minority conservative bloc on the high court, moving President Reagan in 1986 to nominate him to replace Warren E. Burger as chief justice. The Rehnquist court has been, in the main, a conservative one.

Rehnquist dissented in *Roe v. Wade* (1973), which affirmed the right of abortion. In *Lewis v. United States* (1980), he wrote the majority opinion declaring that a person who has been convicted of a crime in a state court may also be convicted of a federal crime for possession of firearms. In *Planned Parenthood of Southeastern Pennsylvania v. Casey* (1992), Rehnquist dissented insofar as the decision reaffirmed *Roe v. Wade,* but he agreed with the majority in upholding certain restrictions on abortion under Pennsylvania law. In *Saenz v. Roe* (1999), Rehnquist dissented from the majority opinion, which held that a state may not deny benefits to new arrivals. He wrote the majority opinion in *United States v. Morrison* (2000), which held that Congress lacked authority to enact a law providing a federal civil remedy for the victims of gender-motivated violence.

Suggested Reading

Belsky, Martin H. *The Rehnquist Court: A Retrospective.* New York: Oxford University Press, 2002.

RELIGION, FREEDOM OF

The First Amendment to the Constitution bars Congress from making any "law respecting an establishment of religion, or prohibiting the free exercise thereof." In this single phrase, Americans are guaranteed a right rare in the history of civilization: freedom of religion and, equally important, freedom *from* religion.

Both Spain and England, the two principal colonizers of America, had state religions: Roman Catholicism in the case of Spain and Anglicanism in the case of England. Spanish missionaries sought to disseminate Catholicism throughout the New World. The English colonists of Virginia, however—who were, for the most part, Anglican—had little interest in missionary work. In New England the first settlers were Puritans, radical Anglicans, who had been persecuted in their mother country and had come to America in search of freedom of worship. However, Puritan government was theocratic and intolerant of other religions, including other forms of Christianity. In 1636, exiled from Massachusetts for his religious liberalism, Roger Williams founded Providence, the first settlement of the Rhode Island colony, where he offered toleration to all Christian religions. Other English colonists also established varying degrees of religious freedom, most notably William Penn, in Pennsylvania (1681), and the Calverts, proprietors of Maryland—where, in 1649, the General Assembly passed the Act Concerning Religion (later known as the Act of Religious Toleration).

Despite the Puritan heritage of *intolerance,* by the time of the American Revolution a tradition of religious tolerance had been well established, and the architects of independence readily incorporated religious freedom into the fabric of the new government. The leading principles of the Virginia Statute for Religious Freedom, drafted by Thomas Jefferson in 1777, would later guide James Madison in preparing the provision in the First Amendment relating to religion.

Constitutionally, the United States is a disestablished nation (a nation with no state religion), and its laws are founded on a strict separation of church and state. Nevertheless, the majority of Americans have historically been Christian, and Christianity informs both American culture and government—a circumstance that, through the years, has led to some clashes and crises, including alleged violations of the separation of church and state. In 1962, for example, in *Engel v. Vitale* (1962), mandatory prayer in public schools was struck down by the U.S. Supreme Court, and subsequent high court decisions have barred attempts to introduce voluntary prayer and even the legally sanctioned observance of a "moment of silence" (*Wallace v. Jaffree,* 1985). The issue of prayer in public schools is by no means dead, however, and, in many school districts, debate continues. Another heated issue concerns tax credits (known as voucher plans) for parents who choose to send their children to private schools, including schools run by religious bodies. In *Zelman v. Simmons-Harris* (2002), the Supreme Court upheld, in a 5–4 ruling, the constitutionality of a school voucher program in Cleveland, Ohio. Advocates for the separation of church and state, such as Americans United for Separation of Church and State, have condemned the decision. However, many of the same advocates have praised a 2002 ruling by the Ninth Circuit Court of Appeals (*Newdow v. U.S. Congress*), which holds that, in 1954, Congress violated the Constitution by adding the phrase "under God" to the Pledge of Allegiance recited by the children in America's public schools.

Finally, and perhaps most important, having the legal right to practice one's religion (or to adhere to no organized religion) does not guarantee acceptance of one's faith or practice. In the course of American history, Mormons, Jews, Catholics, and others have been the targets of discrimination, and in recent years, especially following the terrorist attacks on September 11, 2001, prejudice against Muslims has become an increasing concern.

Despite the continued existence of religious prejudice and despite conflict over issues such as SCHOOL PRAYER and vouchers, it is also true that Americans' religious liberty—both freedom of religion and freedom from religion—probably far exceeds that enjoyed by any nation at any time. (See also HUTCHINSON, ANNE.)

Suggested Reading

Hamburger, Philip. *Separation of Church and State.* Cambridge: Harvard University Press, 2002.

REPARATIONS ASSESSMENT GROUP

In November 2000 a group of lawyers and law professors—including Charles Ogletree of Harvard Law School and the criminal and civil rights attorney Johnnie Cochran, as well as a cadre of prominent class-action attorneys—announced that they were forming the Reparations Assessment Group (RAG), an organization whose mission is to seek, through the courts, reparation for millions of torts—including battery, false imprisonment, and conversion of chattel (the unlawful use or taking of another's property), for example—committed during the era of SLAVERY. Contending that the federal government, local governments, institutions, corporations, and individuals wrongfully benefited from these torts, RAG plans massive class actions suing for damages.

Critics of RAG's actions argue that many generations separate the slaves from their descendants, and that the descendants of slaves were not directly harmed. Moreover, critics hold that it is unfair to burden present-day taxpayers and corporate entities for acts committed by slave owners. RAG plans to counter such arguments by calling on experts in education, politics, family development, health, and economics to testify to the continuing impact of slavery.

In March 2002 RAG brought its first suit, a class action filed on behalf of some 35 million descendants of black slaves against three corporations with historical ties to the slave trade: Aetna, an insurance company; FleetBoston, a major banking firm; and CSX, a Virginia-based railroad company. The amount of damages sought was unspecified at the time of filing, but the suit asks that any award be deposited in a fund to improve social, health, and educational opportunities for African Americans.

It is expected that many more suits—against perhaps a hundred other major U.S. corporations—will be brought.

Suggested Reading

Horowitz, David. *Uncivil Wars: The Controversy over Reparations for Slavery.* San Francisco: Encounter, 2001.

RESERVATIONS, INDIAN

The federal government officially recognizes more than five hundred Indian tribes, most of which have reservations west of the Mississippi River. In all, there are about three hundred federal Indian reservations, most of which consist of land that the tribes kept when they entered into treaties with the federal government. All reservations are designated for the exclusive use of the tribes to which they have been assigned, and are governed, on a day-to-day basis, by tribal authority, including (usually) tribal court systems, departments of justice, and police forces. Reservations vary greatly in size. The largest is the Navajo Reservation, which covers approximately fourteen million acres—more than the combined areas of Connecticut, Delaware, Hawaii, Maryland, Massachusetts, New Hampshire, New Jersey, Rhode Island, and Vermont.

The first Indian reservation in North America, designated for the exclusive use of about a hundred Unami Indians, was established in 1758 at Edge Pillock, New Jersey. Not until the beginning of the nineteenth century, however, when the Louisiana Purchase made available vast new tracts of land, did the idea of creating reservations gain broad currency. President THOMAS JEFFERSON, who made the purchase, believed that by "removing" Indians from the East and sending them to the new land in the West, he could bring an end to the endemic conflict between whites and Indians east of the Mississippi. Although Indian removal was not carried out on a large scale until the INDIAN REMOVAL ACT OF 1830, the area encompassing present-day Oklahoma and parts of Kansas and Nebraska had been designated Indian Territory as early as 1817 and earmarked to receive "removed" Indians. The territory was, in effect, the first large reservation.

As white settlement moved west of the Mississippi, the size of Indian Territory was gradually reduced and, instead of being concentrated in the territory, reservations were established throughout the country, especially in the West. From the mid-nineteenth century until the massacre at Wounded Knee, South Dakota, in December 1890, the INDIAN WARS fought in the West arose almost exclusively from federal efforts to force recalcitrant tribes and portions of tribes to take up residence on designated reservations. This prospect was in itself repugnant to many Indians; even worse, however, from roughly 1870 to 1920, most Indian reservations were sternly regulated but poorly administered by federal authorities.

Throughout the nineteenth century the Department of War and the DEPARTMENT OF THE INTERIOR contended for authority over the Bureau of Indian Affairs, which administered the reservations. Under the Department of the Interior, reservation policies were generally more humane than under the Department of War. However, under both departments, administration of the reservations was incompetent at best and corrupt at worst. Between 1834 and 1907, twenty-one men served as commissioners of Indian Affairs: most were patronage appointments handed out to political hacks who stood to profit, both legally and illegally, from the position. It has been estimated that between 1834 and 1890, 85 percent of all congressional funds appropriated for Indian subsistence, education, and land payments (treaty obligations) were diverted by the Bureau of Indian affairs to cover padded administrative costs, overpriced supplies, and outright fraud (Alan Axelrod, *Chronicle of the Indian Wars,* New York: Macmillan, 1993, 158). As a result the residents of the reservations were chronically plagued by poor health—from disease to malnutrition to outright starvation—as well as by general despair.

While physical conditions on the reservations were usually deplorable, their political intent was also insidious: to replace traditional tribal authority and organization with systems that were more in keeping with white ideas of government. Attempted reform of the reservation system began with the DAWES SEVERALTY ACT of 1887—which, however, introduced its own set of injustices. The most meaningful reforms came in 1937, with the INDIAN REORGANIZATION ACT. Even this legislation proved inadequate, however, and much of the self-government and autonomy that had been introduced by the 1937 act was eroded by the reactionary federal policies of the 1950s. It was not until the NATIVE AMERICAN CIVIL RIGHTS MOVEMENT of the 1960s that more politically, economically, and culturally far-reaching changes were made in the governance of reservations and in reservation life. These changes notwithstanding, most reservations remain places of significant poverty, poor health, high unemployment, poor education, and limited opportunity.

Suggested Reading

Frantz, Klaus. *Indian Reservations in the United States: Territory, Sovereignty, and Socioeconomic Change.* Chicago: University of Chicago Press, 1999.

REVERSE DISCRIMINATION

Reverse discrimination is a phrase used by opponents of AFFIRMATIVE ACTION to describe legally mandated or sanctioned preferences for some groups (typically, ethnic or racial minorities). In the view of their opponents, such preferences constitute discrimination against *other* groups (typically, the ethnic or racial majority).

Suggested Reading

Fullinwider, Robert K. *The Reverse Discrimination Controversy: A Moral and Legal Analysis.* Lanham, Md.: Rowman and Littlefield, 1980.

RHODE ISLAND COLONY

In 1636 ROGER WILLIAMS, banished from the Massachusetts Bay Colony for his religious heterodoxy—including his belief in the spiritual liberty of the individual—founded the settlement of Providence, near the head of Narragansett Bay. Two years later more exiles, including ANNE HUTCHINSON, who were similarly convinced of the right to freedom of conscience in matters of religion, purchased the island of Aquidneck and founded Portsmouth. When this settlement split, some of the settlers founded Newport. Yet another town, Warwick, was established in 1643. In this same year Williams sailed to England, where he obtained a royal patent for what was to be the Rhode Island colony. However, it was not until 1647 that the four towns were able to hammer out even a loose confederacy among themselves.

Under the influence of Williams, colonial Rhode Island became a haven of religious toleration and of the principle of the separation of church and state. Williams believed that state religion was coerced religion and therefore intolerable both to the individual and to God. Thanks to Williams's respectful regard for the Indians, Rhode Island also enjoyed peaceful relations with the local tribes until King Philip's War, which engulfed all of New England in 1675–1676. (See also RELIGION, FREEDOM OF.)

Suggested Reading

McLoughlin, William G. *Rhode Island: A History.* New York: Norton, 1986.

RICHARDSON, GLORIA ST. CLAIR HAYES (1922–)

Gloria St. Clair Hayes Richardson, an important figure in the African American civil rights movement of the 1960s, led the Cambridge Nonviolent Action Committee (CNAC), an affiliate of the Student Nonviolent Coordinating Committee (SNCC), and was responsible for mounting some of the most militant demonstrations of the civil rights era.

Richardson was born in Baltimore on May 6, 1922, but at an early age moved with her family to Cambridge on Maryland's Eastern Shore, her mother's hometown. She graduated from Howard University in 1944, married, had two children, divorced, and returned to Cambridge. In 1962, after SNCC sponsored Freedom Rides in Cambridge, black leaders in the community created the CNAC, of which Richardson soon assumed leadership. Under her guidance the organization was unremitting in its demonstrations and protests—one of which, in the spring of 1963, ended in a riot. The National Guard restored order but had to remain in the community for a year. U.S. attorney general Robert F. Kennedy negotiated a special agreement with Richardson and local authorities to guarantee the peace.

As controversial as Richardson's militancy was, her refusal to compromise by accepting anything less than total victory made her even more notorious, both within and outside the black community. In the autumn of 1963 she persuaded blacks to boycott a vote on a town ordinance that would have integrated public facilities. Because of the boycott, the segregationists won the day, and Richardson was criticized for sacrificing civil rights progress to her own need for martyrdom.

Although she moved to New York City in 1964 after marrying Frank Dandridge, an African American photojournalist who had covered the civil rights protests in Cambridge, Richardson remained active in Cambridge throughout the rest of the decade. (When she brought the charismatic militant activist H. "Rap" Brown to Cambridge, in 1967, another riot was touched off.) Richardson was also active in New York, first in the protest movement and then in government, as head of the New York City Manpower Development Office and, later, as director of the city's department of aging.

Suggested Reading

Levy, Peter B. "Gloria St. Clair Hayes Richardson." In *The Civil Rights Movement*. Westport, Conn.: Greenwood, 1998.

RIGHT TO DIE

As medical science has made available a vast arsenal of drugs and technologies that can extend life, patients and medical ethicists alike have come to question the value of sustaining life at all costs and under all circumstances—and have asserted, under certain circumstances, a "right to die." The debate over this right generally poses two questions: first, does a patient have the right to refuse unwanted medical treatment or to have care withdrawn, even if doing so will result in death? Second, does a patient have the right to euthanasia, including physician-assisted suicide?

The right to die movement had begun to emerge by the 1970s. In the forefront of the movement were organizations such as the Hemlock Society, which asserted the right to die a natural death and to die with dignity, and that also assisted patients and their families to legally challenge the nonvoluntary use of life-sustaining technology.

Provided that the patient is competent—possesses the capacity to make life-or-death decisions—courts have consistently viewed patients' right to self-determination as encompassing decisions about life-or-death treatment. However, the Supreme Court, in *Washington v. Glucksberg* (1997) and *Vacco v. Quill* (1997), ruled that state prohibitions against assisted suicide—including physician-assisted suicide in the case of terminally ill patients—are constitutional. On November 6, 2001, U.S. attorney general John Ashcroft directed federal officials in Oregon to prosecute any physicians or other health care providers who participated in assisted suicide pursuant to the Oregon Death with Dignity Act, which went into effect in October 1997. On April 16, 2002, however, a federal judge in Oregon ruled that the U.S. Department of Justice does not have the power to overturn the Oregon statute—which, as of late 2002, was unique among the states.

Laws—and the specificity of laws—vary from state to state, but factors that may override a patient's right to die include protection of the interests of innocent third parties and maintenance of the ethical integrity of the medical profession. Even in cases where a patient is so incapacitated as to be incompetent to make a life-or-death decision, or is incapable of making his or her wishes known, written directives, such as a living will, drawn up before the incapacity, carry legal weight and can be used to determine whether or not to withdraw life-sustaining measures. "Substituted judgment"—statements made by the patient prior to becoming incompetent—may also be taken into consideration. Under limited circumstances, in cases of the patient's incapacity, family members may also make the decision to withdraw life support.

Suggested Reading

Beauchamp, Tom L., and Robert M. Veatch, eds. *Ethical Issues in Death and Dying.* 2d ed. Englewood Cliffs, N.J.: Prentice Hall, 1995.

Hillyard, Daniel, and John Dombrink. *Dying Right: The Death with Dignity Movement.* New York: Routledge, 2001.

RIGHT-TO-LIFE MOVEMENT

Following the Supreme Court's decision in *Roe v. Wade* (1973) affirming the right to abortion, a right-to-life (or prolife) movement developed in the United States. The movement's ultimate objective is to achieve passage of a constitutional amendment banning abortion; its interim objectives, among others, are to limit access to abortion and to eliminate federal funding for abortion. The movement also actively campaigns to dissuade women from choosing abortion. In the more extreme segments of the movement, such efforts have included harassment of patients entering abortion clinics and physicians who perform abortions. Violence has not been uncommon: physicians have been physically intimidated and even murdered (as in the shooting of Amherst, New York, physician Barnett Slepian in 1998), and attacks against abortion clinics have ranged from vandalism to arson and bombing.

The largest right-to-life organizations, such as the National Right to Life Committee, disavow the use of violence and intimidation and instead advocate political lobbying and public education, including the publication of graphic accounts and photographs of abortion procedures. Recently, so-called partial-birth abortions, the term used to refer to abortions performed between the twentieth and the thirty-second week of pregnancy, have become a major issue among supporters of the right-to-life movement. Although members of the right-to-life movement believe that all abortion is the taking of a human life—even during the first trimester of pregnancy, when the fetus is not viable outside the womb—they argue that partial-birth abortion, even when performed in the interests of the mother's health or survival, constitutes homicide, because babies born at twenty-three weeks or more often survive. As of late 2002 thirty states had banned partial-birth abortions, in some cases making exceptions when the mother's life is in jeopardy and in fewer cases making exceptions when her health—but not life—may be threatened. The courts frequently hear cases relating to partial-birth abortions, and, in *Stenberg v. Carhart* (2000), the U.S. Supreme Court ruled unconstitutional a Nebraska statute criminalizing the procedure, a decision that was based chiefly on the fact that the Nebraska statute failed to make an exception for the preservation of the health of the mother.

Suggested Reading

Gorney, Cynthia. *Articles of Faith: A Frontline History of the Abortion Wars.* New York: Simon and Schuster, 1998.

National Right to Life Committee, www.nrlc.org.

Operation Rescue, www.orn.org.

ROBINSON, JACKIE (1919–1972)

Jackie Robinson became the first black to cross the color line in professional baseball—signing with the Brooklyn Dodgers in 1947. The symbolism inherent in integrating America's national pastime was extraordinarily powerful, and Robinson's quiet dignity and impressive athletic performance in the face of the inevitable jeers, threats, and slurs were inspiring.

Born Jack Roosevelt Robinson in Cairo, Georgia, Jackie Robinson was raised in Pasadena, California, and showed himself to be an exceptional athlete at Pasadena Junior College and the University of California at Los Angeles (UCLA). In addition to baseball he played college football and basketball and ran track. During his third year at UCLA, Robinson withdrew to help support his family. He joined the army during World War II in 1942, was enrolled in officer candidate school, and commissioned a second lieutenant in 1943. After his discharge in 1945, Robinson played minor-league football in Hawaii, and baseball with the Kansas City Monarchs, of the segregated Negro National League.

Branch Rickey, the forward-thinking president and general manager of the Brooklyn Dodgers, saw the potential of Robinson and other black athletes and decided that the time was right for the integration of major-league baseball. In October 1945, he signed Robinson and another black player, pitcher John Wright, to play on a Dodger farm team, the Montreal Royals, of the International League. Robinson immediately proved himself as a league-leading batter, and Rickey brought him to Brooklyn for the 1947 season.

Robinson was not the first black to play in the majors. During the 1870s, in the very early days of professional ball, a few blacks played on a few teams. However, the proliferation of Jim Crow laws in the South and elsewhere soon prompted adherence to strict segregation. Barred from the white leagues, blacks formed their own teams, the best of which, during the 1920s, joined in the loosely constituted Negro National League.

Before signing Robinson, Rickey extracted from him a promise to endure, silently and without protest, any abuse he might receive from fans. This was not easy for a man who, in the army, had risked court-martial by challenging the segregation of a military bus. But Robinson did honor his pledge through his first two years, during which his magnificent play made him a hero not only among blacks but among legions of white sports fans as well. In 1949, the year he won the batting championship with a .342 average and was voted the league's most valuable player, Robinson did begin to speak out against racial discrimination, Jim Crow laws, and even the slow pace at which professional baseball had moved forward with integration.

Robinson retired from baseball in 1957 with a .311 career average and engaged in a successful business career.

Suggested Reading

Robinson, Jackie. *Never Had It Made: An Autobiography.* 1972. Reprint, New York: Ecco, 1997.

Tygiel, Jules. *Baseball's Great Experiment: Jackie Robinson and His Legacy.* New York: Oxford University Press, 1997.

ROE V. WADE (1973)

The 1973 SUPREME COURT ruling concerning ABORTION RIGHTS is among the most controversial rulings ever handed down by the high court. For advocates of a woman's right to choose, *Roe v. Wade* is a foundation; for members of the RIGHT-TO-LIFE MOVEMENT, it is a lightning rod and a target.

The facts of the case are these: Jane Roe (a pseudonym for Norma McCorvey), a single pregnant woman, joined in a suit challenging the criminal abortion law of Texas, which restricted abortion to circumstances of emergent medical necessity (that is, where the mother's life was in jeopardy). Roe demanded unrestricted legal access to abortion.

Justice HARRY A. BLACKMUN delivered the opinion of the court, which upheld the unrestricted right to abortion in the first three months of pregnancy on the basis of an inherent right to privacy. (In the second three months of pregnancy, concern for the mother's health might justify state restrictions on abortion. In the last three months, the state could intervene on behalf of the unborn child, asserting a mandate to protect the public welfare, which supercedes the rights of the pregnant woman.)

Subsequent Supreme Court rulings retreated somewhat from the blanket authorization granted in *Roe v. Wade*—but, despite intense pressure from prolife groups and politicians, the ruling has thus far stood. (See Appendix A for excerpts of the majority opinion issued in *Roe v. Wade.*)

Suggested Reading

Faux, Marian. *Roe v. Wade.* New York: Cooper Square, 2000.

Garrow, David J. *Liberty and Sexuality: The Right to Privacy and the Making of Roe v. Wade.* Berkeley: University of California Press, 1998.

Solinger, Rickie. *Wake Up, Little Susie: Single Pregnancy and Race before Roe v. Wade.* New York: Routledge, 2000.

ROOSEVELT, ELEANOR (1884–1962)

Wife and political partner of President FRANKLIN DELANO ROOSEVELT (FDR), Eleanor Roosevelt was, in her own right, an inspiring leader of social reform who served as an example of leadership and achievement for America's women. She guided and encouraged her husband in formulating the sweeping programs of social change that marked his administration, and, independently of FDR, she advocated and helped to develop initiatives promoting racial equality and WOMEN'S RIGHTS, as well as aid programs for the poor and the disadvantaged. Her support of the UNITED NATIONS (UN) was instrumental in generating popular support for that organization in the United States. As chair of the UN Commission on Human Rights, she played a major role in drafting the *UNIVERSAL DECLARATION OF HUMAN RIGHTS* (1948), which she considered the most important achievement of her career.

Born to a privileged New York City family, Anna Eleanor Roosevelt (niece of President Theodore Roosevelt), grew up a shy, plain, and awkward girl. Privately tutored at home, she was later packed off to Allenswood, an exclusive finishing school near London. There she came under the tutelage of the school's headmistress, Marie Souvestre, who succeeded in bringing the shy student out of her shell and awakening her to the world of social responsibility. Upon her return to New York in 1902, Roosevelt threw herself into charity work at a slum settlement house.

In 1905 Eleanor Roosevelt married her fifth cousin once removed, Franklin. The couple had six children, one of whom died in infancy. Throughout the marriage Eleanor had to compete for FDR's affections—not only with his domineering and imperious mother but with other women, most notably her own social secretary, Lucy Mercer. Although Eleanor and FDR reconciled after she discovered the affair with Mercer, they went on to lead somewhat independent lives, with Eleanor becoming a leader in the League of Women Voters, the Women's Trade Union League, and the women's division of the Democratic Party. However, when FDR was stricken with polio in 1921, it was Eleanor who nursed him back to physical and spiritual health—and who, against his mother's wishes, persuaded him to remain in politics. During FDR's long convalescence, Eleanor often acted as her husband's stand-in, and thus became a well-known public figure in her own right.

In 1926 Eleanor Roosevelt became one of the founders of a custom furniture factory established near the Roosevelt estate, in Hyde Park, New York, that provided training and skilled work for the unemployed. In 1927 she acquired an ownership interest in New York's progressive Todhunter School, where she served as vice principal and as an instructor in history and government.

After her husband entered the White House in 1933, Eleanor shattered the traditional image of the first lady as sedate hostess. She held weekly press conferences with women reporters and embarked on nationwide lecture tours, promoting New Deal social policies. She had her own nationally broadcast radio program and a popular syndicated newspaper column, "My Day." She felt that her role was, in part, to serve as her husband's eyes and ears, and she traveled the nation, becoming keenly attuned to the plight of a people in the grip of the Great Depression. She also lent her voice in support of legislation to aid minorities and the poor.

During World War II Eleanor frequently toured both the European and Pacific fronts, as well as military bases throughout the United States. She was a strong supporter of the Tuskegee airmen, a program that trained black pilots for service in the U.S. Army Air Force. Both during and after the war Eleanor was an advocate of racial justice and integration. Perhaps her most memorable public stand on the issue came in 1939, when she condemned the Daughters of the American Revolution and resigned from that organization after it refused to allow the famed African American contralto Marian Anderson to sing in Washington's Constitution Hall, which the organization owned. The First Lady was instrumental in arranging an alternative venue, on the steps of the Lincoln Memorial, for a concert that drew 75,000.

The death of President Roosevelt early in his fourth term, on April 12, 1945, from a cerebral hemorrhage, did not take his wife out of the public spotlight. On the contrary, she became, if anything, even more active. In December 1945 Roosevelt's successor, Harry S. Truman, appointed her a member of the U.S. delegation to the newly formed UN, and she became chair of the UN Commission on Human Rights. She resigned from this post in 1952 but was reappointed by President John F. Kennedy in 1961.

Eleanor Roosevelt also remained active in Democratic politics, campaigning on behalf of Adlai Stevenson, who unsuccessfully challenged Dwight D. Eisenhower for the White House in 1952 and 1956. She also wrote several books, including the autobiographical volumes *This Is My Story* (1937), *This I Remember* (1949), and *On My Own* (1958).

Suggested Reading

Roosevelt, Eleanor. *The Autobiography of Eleanor Roosevelt.* Compilation reprint of *This Is My Story, This I Remember,* and *On My Own.* New York: Da Capo, 2000.

ROOSEVELT, FRANKLIN DELANO (1882–1945)

Franklin Delano Roosevelt (FDR), the thirty-second president of the United States, led the United States through two of its gravest crises, the Great Depression and World War II. He was elected to an unprecedented four terms and served from 1933 to 1945.

A social progressive, Roosevelt introduced a welter of government welfare programs with the objective of relieving the effects of the depression. This legislation set the precedent for Lyndon Johnson's Great Society programs of the 1960s.

FDR was born on his family's estate at Hyde Park, New York, the son of a patrician family dominated by a loving but overbearing matriarch. Through age fourteen Roosevelt was tutored at home, then attended the Groton School in Massachusetts (1896–1900), where the headmaster, Rev. Endicott Peabody, instilled in Roosevelt and the school's other privileged charges an ethic of public service—the notion that the wealthy owed a special debt of service to society. From Groton Roosevelt went on to Harvard, graduating in 1904. The next year he married Eleanor Roosevelt, his fifth cousin once removed and the niece of Theodore Roosevelt. Like FDR, Eleanor had been born into wealth but possessed a driving force to do social good. Indeed, her influence helped to shape and reinforce FDR's own social consciousness.

Roosevelt attended Columbia University Law School until the spring of 1907, but, after passing the New York state bar examination immediately took up the practice of law rather than complete his degree. Although he joined a top Wall Street firm he did not find corporate law to his taste and instead devoted much of his time to the firm's pro bono work for indigent clients.

FDR ran for the state senate in 1910, easily winning election in a traditionally Republican district. He rapidly became known as a Progressive reformer and an opponent of machine politics. In 1912 he campaigned for Democratic presidential candidate Woodrow Wilson, then achieved reelection to the state senate. Instead of taking his seat, however, he accepted the subcabinet post of assistant secretary of the navy in the Wilson administration. In addition to elevating Roosevelt to the level of national politics, the position also provided an arena in which he was able to demonstrate both his administrative brilliance and his profound ability to deal effectively with people of all types and from every class—whether they were admirals, bureaucrats, or shipyard workers.

In 1920 Roosevelt was nominated as the vice-presidential running mate of James M. Cox, the Democratic governor of Ohio. When the Cox-Roosevelt ticket was defeated by Republican Warren G. Harding, FDR returned to the practice of law and also became vice president of a financial firm. His promising political career was threatened when, in 1921, he was stricken with polio, which left him a paraplegic. With the support of his wife, however, he resisted his mother's entreaties to retire and instead embraced politics with even greater fervor. In 1928 FDR was elected to the first of two terms as governor, where he introduced at the state level many of the kinds of social programs he would make part of the New Deal when he became president. Initiatives that FDR ushered through the legislature included state-supported old-age pensions and unemployment insurance, an important set of labor laws, and legislation promoting the public development of electric power.

As the Great Depression deepened, FDR became the first governor to create an effective state relief administration. He also introduced the "Fireside Chats," a series of radio broadcasts to explain issues and programs directly and with engaging informality to the people of the state. The technique would also become a mainstay of his presidency. When he was reelected to the statehouse in 1930 by the largest margin in New York history, Roosevelt recruited what he called a "brain trust," made up of Columbia University professors, to help him formulate social and economic programs to fight the hard times. This group was retained during FDR's presidency, where it became instrumental in building the New Deal.

FDR was elected to his first term as president in 1932, when the depression was at its worst. During the first "Hundred Days" of his administration, he introduced precedent-shattering programs of relief and public works, a plan to curb the agricultural overproduction that was depressing farm prices, and policies to conserve environmental resources, generate public power, provide old-age pensions and unemployment insurance, and regulate the stock exchange. He also promoted passage and ratification of the Twenty-first Amendment, repealing Prohibition. Roosevelt radiated confidence and possessed extraordinary charisma, proclaiming famously in his inaugural address: "The only thing we have to fear is fear itself—nameless, unreasoning, unjustified terror." When he promised that, working together, the government and the people could defeat the depression, the nation believed him.

To ease credit and provide some relief to debtors and exporters, FDR took the nation off the gold standard. He obtained from Congress $500 million for direct federal relief to states and to local agencies. The Civilian Conservation Corps, the Civil Works Administration, the Federal Emergency Relief Administration, the Home Owners Loan Corporation, and the Public Works Administration all were created to address the pressing needs of citizens of all classes. The Federal Deposit Insurance Corporation insured bank deposits, an important safeguard against disastrous banking panics and runs. The Securities and Exchange Commission inaugurated the regulation of the stock exchanges, a safeguard against the kinds of practices that had contributed to the sudden fall of the markets in 1929. The Tennessee Valley Authority built huge dams to control floods and generate cheap hydroelectric power. Two agencies of special importance were the National Recovery Administration (NRA) and the Agricultural Adjustment Administration (AAA). The NRA provided incentives to management as well as labor to establish codes of fair competition within each industry—codes that included equitable pricing and production policies, COLLECTIVE BARGAINING, minimum wages, and maximum hours. The AAA sought to raise farm prices by setting production quotas (approved by farmers in referenda) and subsidizing farmers who stayed within the quotas.

Three of FDR's most sweeping initiatives came in 1935: the Works Progress Administration, which employed millions in work relief programs; the Wagner Act, which set up the National Labor Relations Board and thereby guaranteed labor the right to bargain collectively on equal terms with management; and Social Security, which provided for federal payment of old-age pensions and for federal-state cooperation in support of unemployment compensation, relief for disabled citizens, and relief for dependent children.

In 1936, when Roosevelt was reelected by a landslide, he refused to become complacent, declaring in his second inaugural address: "I see one-third of a nation ill-housed, ill-clad, ill-nourished," and acknowledging the need to continue with reform, relief, and recovery. During his second term FDR was criticized for having fostered a growing militancy among labor, but popular confidence in the president continued to be high, and in 1940 he was reelected to an unprecedented third term.

Roosevelt guided the nation through World War II, which came to America with the Japanese attack on Pearl Harbor on December 7, 1941. In addition to taking a strong hand in directing military strategy, FDR spurred the rapid mobilization of U.S. industry at home. When black workers, led by A. PHILIP RANDOLPH, demanded an end to racial discrimination in defense industries, FDR responded by issuing Executive Order 8802, which barred discrimination in defense industries and created the Fair Employment Practices Committee to monitor and remedy any instances of discrimination in defense-related employment. Although it was motivated by the exigencies of war, the creation of the committee was nevertheless a milestone in civil rights.

With the war still raging and the United States on the offensive, Roosevelt was elected to a fourth term in 1944. Exhausted, careworn, and broken in health, FDR died early in this term, on April 12, 1945, of a cerebral hemorrhage.

Most historians—and many others—believe that Roosevelt was the greatest president of the twentieth century. Some conservatives continue to blame him for transforming the federal government into a bureaucratic monster that created a WELFARE STATE, usurped states' rights, and perhaps even compromised individual liberty. However, most social liberals praise FDR as the father of activist government—government in the service of the welfare of all Americans.

Suggested Reading

Davis, Kenneth S. *FDR: The Beckoning of Destiny, 1882–1928*. New York: G. P. Putnam's Sons, 1971.

———. *FDR: The New Deal Years, 1933–1937*. New York: Random House, 1986.

———. *FDR: The War President, 1940–1943*. New York: Random House, 2000.

Freidel, Frank. *Franklin D. Roosevelt: A Rendezvous with Destiny*. Boston: Little, Brown, 1990.

RUSTIN, BAYARD (1912–1987)

An adviser to both MARTIN LUTHER KING JR. and A. PHILIP RANDOLPH, Bayard Rustin worked behind the scenes to plan the 1963 MARCH ON WASHINGTON.

Born on March 17, 1912, in West Chester, Pennsylvania, he grew up as a Quaker in pleasant, middle-class surroundings. He moved to Harlem in the 1930s and joined the Young Communist League but broke with the communists before the end of the decade. He joined the AFRICAN AMERICAN CIVIL RIGHTS MOVEMENT early, working with A. Philip Randolph to desegregate defense-related industries during World War II. With A. J. Muste, of the radical pacifist Fellowship of Reconciliation, Rustin worked in a campaign against racial inequality. He also remained steadfast in his refusal to serve in the military and was imprisoned for more than two years. In prison he met other pacifists, some of whom would go on to found the CONGRESS OF RACIAL EQUALITY (CORE).

After the war, Rustin was one of the organizers of the JOURNEY OF RECONCILIATION, a precursor to the FREEDOM RIDES of the 1960s, which were instrumental in desegregating interstate public transportation in the South. During this period Rustin also worked for the DESEGREGATION of the armed forces, which was achieved in 1948 when President HARRY S. TRUMAN signed Executive Order 9981. Rustin also became a link between the American civil rights movement and human rights movements abroad when he traveled throughout India and Africa in the 1950s to meet with prominent anticolonial activists, including the sons of MOHANDAS GANDHI. In 1955, when the MONTGOMERY BUS BOYCOTT got under way, Rustin became an important adviser to Martin Luther King Jr. on the tactics, strategy, and general philosophy of nonviolent protest. Yet many in the early civil rights movement perceived Rustin as too radical to assume a public position in the movement, not only because of his criminal record as a World War II pacifist but because he had been a communist and was openly gay. Nevertheless, he played an important role in organizing the 1963 March on Washington.

If Rustin was seen by some as overly radical during the early 1960s, he was seen as insufficiently radical by others during the mid-1960s. The emerging black militants could not accept his uncompromising embrace of nonviolence, and such organizations as CORE and the STUDENT NONVIOLENT COORDINATING COMMITTEE objected to his willingness to work closely with white liberals and white liberal organizations. In his later years Rustin was a supporter of the emerging GAY RIGHTS movement, and from the late 1960s until his death he directed the A. Philip Randolph Institute, a New York City–based civil rights organization.

Suggested Reading

Anderson, Jervis. *Bayard Rustin: Troubles I've Seen*. Berkeley: University of California Press, 1998.

Haskins, James. *Bayard Rustin: Behind the Scenes of the Civil Rights Movement*. New York: Hyperion, 1997.

Levine, Daniel. *Bayard Rustin and the Civil Rights Movement*. New Brunswick: Rutgers University Press, 1999.

S

SACCO AND VANZETTI CASE

Spanning the years from 1920 to 1927, the Sacco and Vanzetti case—one of the great minority rights causes of the 1920s—radicalized many who came of age in that decade.

On April 15, 1920, F. A. Parmenter, paymaster of a South Braintree, Massachusetts, shoe factory, and Alessandro Berardelli, the guard accompanying him, were shot and killed in an armed robbery. Less than three weeks later, on May 5, Nicola Sacco, a shoemaker, and Bartolomeo Vanzetti, a fish peddler, were arrested and charged with the murders. Both had immigrated from Italy in 1908, and both were self-proclaimed political anarchists. Their trial, before Judge Webster Thayer of the Massachusetts Superior Court, began on May 31, 1921; both were found guilty on July 14.

Many aspects of the trial were suspect, most notably the testimony putting the pair at the scene of the crime. Moreover, the testimony of witnesses who corroborated Sacco's alibi—that he was at the Italian consulate in Boston at the time of the murders—was discounted. Not only socialists and political radicals but prominent liberals throughout the country protested the verdict, claiming that Sacco and Vanzetti had not been tried on the facts of the case but had been convicted simply because they were radicals who had the misfortune to be living in a time of xenophobia, reactionary politics, and national hysteria over Bolshevism and anarchism (see, for example, PALMER RAIDS).

Lawyers from the AMERICAN CIVIL LIBERTIES UNION (ACLU) repeatedly attempted to secure a retrial on the grounds of false identification, but all petitions for retrial were turned down. Then, on November 18, 1925, a man named Celestino Madeiros, himself under sentence for an unrelated murder, confessed that he and members of "the Joe Morelli gang" had committed the robbery and murders. Armed with this confession, the ACLU mounted a new appeal, but the Massachusetts Supreme Court refused to overturn the verdict, asserting that only the trial judge had the authority to reopen the case in light of new evidence. Thayer refused to do so, and a final sentence of death was pronounced on April 9, 1927.

Outrage, which had ebbed and flowed throughout the trial and the appeals, now swelled into a tidal wave that swept not only the nation but the world. Prominent jurists, political leaders, heads of state, writers, journalists, and even the Pope made pleas for a new trial. Mass meetings—"Save Sacco and Vanzetti" rallies—were held across the country. Responding to the overwhelming protests, Massachusetts governor Alvan T. Fuller convened an independent advisory committee consisting of A. Lawrence Lowell, president of Harvard University; Samuel W. Stratton, president of the Massachusetts Institute of Technology; and Robert Grant, a former judge. Basing his decision, in part, on the findings of the committee, the governor declared, on August 3, 1927, that he would not grant clemency. New demonstrations broke out across the United States and in major cities elsewhere in the world, and there were bombings in New York City and Philadelphia. Nevertheless, on August 23, 1927, Sacco and Vanzetti were executed in the electric chair.

Despite what was clearly an unfair trial, the innocence of Sacco and Vanzetti is by no means certain, and a number of historians have suggested that while Vanzetti was almost certainly innocent, Sacco was probably guilty. However, virtually all historians and legal scholars agree that the trial, influenced by the prevailing antiradical sentiment of the day, was improper, and that the pair deserved a retrial. In 1977 Massachusetts governor Michael S. Dukakis issued a proclamation acknowledging that Sacco and Vanzetti had not been tried fairly but did not assert their innocence; Dukakis further declared that because the pair had not properly been found guilty, they must be presumed innocent.

Suggested Reading

Avrich, Paul. *Sacco and Vanzetti*. Princeton: Princeton University Press, 1996.

SALEM WITCH TRIALS

Part of both the history and popular lore of America, the Salem witch trials are viewed by many historians and sociologists as early and highly instructive examples of intolerance supported by the weight of legal authority.

In the predominantly Puritan settlement of Salem, Massachusetts, in February 1692, two daughters of the Rev. Samuel Parris and several of their friends were diagnosed by a local physician as having been put under the spell of a witch. Under relentless questioning, the girls identified certain people as witches. When, on February 29, Salem authorities began proceedings against those accused, their action signaled the beginning of a siege of accusations that culminated in what must be described as mass hysteria.

The Salem witchcraft outbreak was hardly unique in the colonies or, for that matter, in the world. Before the 1692 outbreak more than seventy witchcraft cases had been tried in New England and had resulted in eighteen convictions. Accusations of witchcraft—some of which resulted in trial and punishment, including execution—had been common throughout Europe since medieval times.

Historians have found that the person typically accused of being a witch was a poor, elderly, propertyless woman (far less often, a man in similar circumstances), often without family, who was almost always identified as disagreeable, quarrelsome, and a social misfit—in a sense, a member of a persecuted minority. What was unique about the Salem outbreak, however was the volume of accusations—in 1692 alone more than 140 people were accused, 107 of them women—and the social circumstances of the accused. They were not all poor, propertyless outcasts but included prominent men of property and their wives. Especially vulnerable to accusation were those who protested the Reverend Parris's zeal on behalf of the prosecution. He and some seventy other Salem residents—almost all of them members of his congregation—presented themselves as witnesses to corroborate the testimony of those who had either been diagnosed as suffering from the effects of witchcraft or who claimed to be under a spell.

The Salem situation demanded the attention of the new royal governor of Massachusetts, Sir William Phipps, who established a Court of Oyer and Terminer (a special court with expeditious authority) to try the cases. The court's first session convened in June with more than seventy cases on the docket, and during that summer and into the fall fifty of the accused pleaded guilty to practicing witchcraft. Of the rest, twenty-six were tried and convicted, and nineteen were executed. The convictions were based on spectral evidence—which, by its nature, could not be corroborated or objectively demonstrated, as it was invisible, intangible, and experienced only by those witnesses who claimed to be tormented by the accused.

Alarmed by the dependence on spectral evidence and by the sheer volume of convictions, Governor Phipps dissolved the Court of Oyer and Terminer in the fall and turned over the remaining cases to the permanently established Superior Court of Judicature. From October through the end of the year this court heard fifty cases, binding over for trial twenty-one defendants, of whom only three were convicted. These convictions were overturned the following year, and defendants whose cases were still pending at the beginning of 1693 were pardoned by Phipps. He and the Superior Court further decreed that witchcraft was no longer to be regarded as a criminal offense, bringing the Salem witchcraft trials permanently to an end.

The trials persisted in exercising fascination, however; in 1953 they became the basis for Arthur Miller's *The Crucible,* a compelling allegory written in condemnation of the anticommunist "witch hunts" of the 1950s. (See also House Un-American Activities Committee and McCarthy, Joseph.)

Suggested Reading

Hill, Frances. *The Salem Witch Trials Reader.* New York: Da Capo, 2000.

SANGER, MARGARET (1879–1966)

Born Margaret Louisa Higgins in Corning, New York, Margaret Sanger is generally credited as the founder of the birth control movement in the United States and as a pioneering champion of women's rights to sex education, birth control, and abortion.

Sanger was educated at Claverack College and trained as a nurse at the White Plains (New York) Hospital and the Manhattan Eye and Ear Clinic. She married William Sanger in 1900, divorced him, then married J. Noah H. Slee in 1922. During Sanger's early career, as a teacher and then as an obstetrical nurse, she practiced in the largely immigrant community of New York City's impoverished Lower East Side—an experience that persuaded her that, in combination, poverty and high birth rates led to misery for children and parents alike. Infant mortality was high on the Lower East Side, as were maternal deaths and complications resulting from incompetent and unsanitary illegal abortions. Sanger became a committed feminist, focusing not on such issues as women's suffrage but on the right to avoid or abort unwanted pregnancy.

In 1912 Sanger left nursing and became an activist in the cause of birth control. In 1914 she began publishing the *Woman Rebel* and wrote and distributed a pamphlet, *Family Limitation,* that included information on birth control methods. Sanger was charged by federal authorities with having used the U.S. mails to distribute obscene material, but in 1916, at the outset of a highly publicized trial, the charges were dropped. Later in the year, however, after she opened the first birth control clinic in the United States (in Brooklyn), she was again arrested, this time on a misdemeanor charge of creating a public nuisance, and sentenced to thirty days in jail. While she was incarcerated in 1917 the first issue of her new journal, the *Birth Control Review,* was published.

The "public nuisance" trial was hardly the last time Sanger would undergo prosecution, but each indictment and trial only strengthened public opinion in her favor. By prosecuting her, the state became an unwilling ally in the birth control movement, because Sanger's appeals of her convictions resulted in federal court decisions holding that physicians had the right to advise patients on birth control methods. Equally significant was a U.S. Circuit Court of Appeals decision reinterpreting the Comstock Law, under which Sanger and others had been prosecuted for using the mails to deliver birth control literature and contraceptive devices. The circuit court held that physicians were permitted to import contraceptive devices, which were generally manufactured abroad, and to distribute birth control literature.

Sanger founded the American Birth Control League, a predecessor of the PLANNED PARENTHOOD FEDERATION OF AMERICA, in 1921 and served as its president until 1928. Sanger also organized the first World Population Conference in Geneva, Switzerland, in 1927. (Late in life, in 1953, she was elected the first president of the International Planned Parenthood Federation.)

Sanger's reputation was somewhat tarnished late in the 1920s when she distanced herself from radical and progressive politics, embraced eugenics, and began advocating the use of birth control by those with certain undesirable traits (such as mental retardation and various hereditary diseases) as a means of improving the overall quality of the human race. This shift in attitude notwithstanding, it is mainly as a pioneer in the area of reproductive rights that Sanger is remembered. (Also see COMSTOCK, ANTHONY.)

Suggested Reading

Kennedy, David M. *Birth Control in America: The Career of Margaret Sanger.* New Haven: Yale University Press, 1970.

The Margaret Sanger Papers Project, www.nyu.edu/projects/sanger/.

SAVIO, MARIO (1943–1996)

During the early 1960s Mario Savio was the most prominent student leader of the Free Speech Movement at the University of California at Berkeley. The movement, which encouraged the use of college campuses as centers for the free expression of liberal and radical points of view, is often cited as the prototype for the civil rights and antiwar activism that featured prominently on college and university campuses during the decade. Savio was best known for a speech he gave on December 2, 1964, in front of Berkeley's main administration building during a SIT-IN inside the building and a general campus strike protesting the university's decision to limit the activities of civil rights and political groups on the campus:

> There is a time when the operation of the machine becomes so odious, makes you so sick at heart, that you can't take part; and you've got to put your bodies upon the gears and upon the wheels, upon the levers, upon all the apparatus and you've got to make it stop. And you've got to indicate to the people who run it, to the people who own it, that unless you're free, the machine will be prevented from working at all. (Eric Pace, "Mario Savio" obituary, *New York Times,* November 8, 1996.)

Savio was born in New York City, graduated from Martin Van Buren High School in Queens, and attended Manhattan College before going to Berkeley in 1963 as a philosophy major. In 1964, before becoming a leader of the Berkeley protest, Savio had been active in the Mississippi FREEDOM SUMMER. His actions at Berkeley led to his suspension and, subsequently, to a four-month prison term.

Savio later taught mathematics as a private tutor and in public and private schools. He received bachelor's and master's degrees in physics from San Francisco State University and taught there, at Modesto Junior College, and at Sonoma State. He died of a heart attack in Sebastopol, California. (See also STUDENTS FOR A DEMOCRATIC SOCIETY.)

Suggested Reading

Cohen, Robert, and Reginald E. Zelnik, eds. *The Free Speech Movement: Reflections on Berkeley in the 1960s.* Berkeley: University of California Press, 2002.

SCHLAFLY, PHYLLIS (1924–)

Conservative political activist Phyllis Schlafly is known as one of the most highly visible and influential opponents of the women's liberation movement.

Born in Saint Louis, Schlafly attended Washington University there and earned a master's degree in political science from Harvard University (1945). She later returned to Washington University, from which she earned a law degree in 1978.

Beginning in the 1940s Schlafly was a researcher for several congressional representatives and worked on the campaign in which Republican Claude I. Bakewell was elected U.S. representative from Saint Louis. Schlafly worked in the private sector after Bakewell's victory but was a frequent delegate at Republican national conventions. In 1952 and 1970 she herself ran unsuccessfully for Congress. During the 1970s and the early 1980s Schlafly's highly vocal and abrasive opposition to the proposed EQUAL RIGHTS AMENDMENT (ERA)—which, she claimed, would require women in the military to serve in combat, negate certain legal rights of wives, harm family life, and lead, ultimately, to unisex public washroom facilities—transformed her into a media personality.

Schlafly founded Stop ERA and the Eagle Forum, two principal anti–ERA organizations. After the defeat of the ERA in 1982 Schlafly continued the Eagle Forum as a vehicle for advocacy of conservative views.

Suggested Reading

Felsenthal, Carol. *Biography of Phyllis Schlafly.* Chicago: Regnery, 1982.

The Phyllis Schlafly Report, www.eagleforum.org/psr/index.html.

SCHNEIDERMAN, ROSE (1884–1972)

A pioneering leader in the rights of American women workers, Rose Schneiderman was born in Poland and immigrated to the United States in 1890. She worked in a New York garment factory, as a lining stitcher in a millinery concern, and became a labor activist, successfully working to secure the admittance of women into the United Cloth, Hat, and Cap Makers Union. She was a leader of a highly effective 1905 strike and, in 1907, was elected vice president of the New York branch of the Women's Trade Union League. In 1918, while serving as an organizer for the league (1917–1919), she was elected president of the New York branch of the organization. In 1928 Schneiderman became president of the National Women's Trade Union League.

From 1937 to 1944 Schneiderman served as secretary of the New York State Department of Labor. Simultaneously she served as an official of the National Recovery Administration in the administration of President FRANKLIN D. ROOSEVELT and was among the economic advisers in the president's "brain trust."

Suggested Reading

Endelman, Gary E. *Solidarity Forever: Rose Schneiderman and the Women's Trade Union League.* Manchester, N.H.: Ayer, 1981.

SCHOMBURG CENTER FOR RESEARCH IN BLACK CULTURE

The Schomburg Center for Research in Black Culture is a national research library devoted to collecting, preserving, and providing access to resources that document the experiences of people of African descent throughout the world. In 1926 the personal collection of Arturo Alfonso Schomburg, a black, Puerto Rican–born scholar, became part of the Division of Negro Literature, History, and Prints of the 135th Street branch of the New York Public Library. Schomburg served as curator of this collection from 1932 until his death, in 1938, and the collection was named in his honor in 1940. Since that time, the collection has grown and, in 1972, became the Schomburg Center for Research in Black Culture and was designated as one of the research libraries of the New York Public Library.

The current holdings of the Schomburg Center consist of more than five million items relating to African American history and culture. It is the world's preeminent research facility and repository devoted to materials documenting black life.

Suggested Reading

Schomburg Center for Research in Black Culture, www.nypl.org/research/sc/sc.html.

SCHOOL PRAYER

See RELIGION, FREEDOM OF.

SCHWERNER, MICHAEL (1939–1964)

Michael Schwerner was born in New York City and graduated from Cornell University in 1961. He married Rita Levant in 1962 and, with her, joined the CONGRESS OF RACIAL EQUALITY (CORE) in 1963. Early in 1964 the

Schwerners became CORE field workers in Meridian, Mississippi, in preparation for FREEDOM SUMMER. On June 21, 1964, Schwerner, a white man, was murdered along with fellow CORE activists JAMES EARL CHANEY and ANDREW GOODMAN by members of the KU KLUX KLAN. (For the details of the crime and the subsequent trials of those accused, see CHANEY, JAMES EARL.)

Suggested Reading

Norst, Joel. *Mississippi Burning.* New York: New American Library, 1989.

SCOTTSBORO BOYS

The Scottsboro Boys were nine black youths prosecuted in Scottsboro, Alabama, in April 1931 on charges of having raped two white women. After narrowly avoiding LYNCHING, they were tried just three weeks after their arrest and were not permitted to consult an attorney until the first day of the trial, when two lawyers volunteered to defend them. Despite having been given no time to prepare a case, the attorneys called as witnesses physicians who had examined the women and who testified that no rape had occurred. Nevertheless, an all-white jury convicted all nine of the defendants, sentencing all—except the youngest, a twelve-year-old child—to death.

The verdict and sentences elicited national protest, and an appeal was mounted by northern liberal groups, most notably the AMERICAN CIVIL LIBERTIES UNION, and by radical organizations, including the Communist Party of the U.S.A. The appeals traveled rapidly up the court system to the U.S. SUPREME COURT, which, in *Powell v. Alabama* (1932) overturned the convictions on the grounds that the defendants had not been accorded adequate legal counsel in a capital case.

Alabama retried one defendant and again found him guilty. Once again, liberal and radical groups rallied, and the case was carried to the U.S. Supreme Court—which ruled, in *Norris v. Alabama* (1935)—that the conviction was invalid because the state had deliberately and systematically excluded blacks from juries. The state then tried and convicted another defendant, Haywood Patterson, who was sentenced to seventy-five years in prison. When this conviction failed to be overturned on appeal, the state retried the other defendants, and all were reconvicted by all-white juries. New appeals led some convictions to be overturned, and intense public pressure—not only from the North but now from the South as well—led to the release from prison of the four youngest defendants, each of whom had served six years. Within a short time, all the others, except Patterson, were paroled. Patterson escaped from prison in 1948 but was captured in Michigan, in 1951 and arrested for having stabbed a man. Convicted of manslaughter, Patterson died in prison.

The other Scottsboro Boys receded into obscurity, except for the last known survivor, Clarence Norris, who was formally pardoned by the governor of Alabama in 1976.

Suggested Reading

Carter, Dan T. *Scottsboro: A Tragedy of the American South.* Baton Rouge: Louisiana State University Press, 1979.

SEALE, BOBBY (1936–)

One of the leading militants of the BLACK POWER MOVEMENT of the 1960s, Bobby Seale was born in Dallas, Texas, and raised in California. He served in the U.S. Air Force, then enrolled in Merritt College in Oakland, California, where in 1962 he first heard MALCOLM X speak. This experience catalyzed Seale's militant activism, and in 1966 he and HUEY NEWTON founded the BLACK PANTHERS. As chairman of the party, Seale helped mold it not only as a militant organization but as a community organization, which sponsored day care, health care, and other programs in and for the black community.

Seale came to national attention in 1969 as one of the Chicago Seven, who were indicted and tried for conspiracy to incite riots during the 1968 Democratic national convention. When Judge Julius Hoffman denied Seale his choice of attorney, Seale vociferously protested this abrogation of his constitutional rights, and Hoffman ordered him bound and gagged. The image of Seale—tied to his chair and gagged, as depicted by a courtroom sketch artist—became one of the icons of the decade.

Convicted of sixteen counts of CONTEMPT of court and sentenced to four years in prison, Seale was tried in 1970–1971 for the 1969 murder of a Black Panther who was believed to be a police informant. The trial ended in a hung jury, and the state did not pursue a retrial.

Seale emerged from prison in 1971 not embittered but somehow at peace, publicly renouncing violence as a means of achieving civil rights and vowing to work within the political system. In 1973 he ran unsuccessfully for mayor of Oakland. By this time, the Black Panthers had all but dissolved, and Seale became a nonviolent activist in the black community.

Suggested Reading

Seale, Bobby. *A Lonely Rage: The Autobiography of Bobby Seale.* New York: Times Books, 1978.

———. *Seize the Time: The Story of the Black Panther Party and Huey P. Newton.* 1970. Reprint, Baltimore, Md.: Black Classic, 1997.

"SEGREGATION TODAY, SEGREGATION FOREVER" SPEECH (GEORGE C. WALLACE)

During the 1960s George C. Wallace, governor of Alabama, was considered by many to be the quintessential segregationist and defender of white supremacy. Wallace's most famous speech, delivered as his 1963 inaugural address upon election as Alabama's governor, pledged his allegiance to "segregation today" and "segregation forever." Warmly welcomed by most of Wallace's white constituency, it signaled to black America and to northern whites just how implacable the southern states were on the issue of racial integration. (See Appendix A for the text of Wallace's "Segregation Today, Segregation Forever" speech.)

Suggested Reading

Carter, Dan T. *The Politics of Rage: George Wallace, the Origins of the New Conservatism, and the Transformation of American Politics.* New York: Simon and Schuster, 1995.

SELECTIVE SERVICE SYSTEM

The military draft was introduced in the United States in 1862 during the Civil War and was reintroduced when the United States entered World War I in 1917. However, the first *peacetime* draft in the United States was instituted when President Franklin D. Roosevelt signed the Selective Training and Service Act of 1940, which created the Selective Service System, an independent federal agency charged with administering the induction of men to fill vacancies in the armed forces that could not be filled through voluntary enlistment.

For the most part the Selective Service System and the draft were accepted as facts of American life until the mid-1960s, when the growing unpopularity of the Vietnam War led to frequent and vehement antiwar and antidraft protests. Many young men publicly burned their draft-cards—certificates of compliance with the draft registration law—and many fled the country to avoid the draft. Most found refuge in Canada, where they were aided and supported by a network of antiwar, antidraft activists. Estimates of the number who went into exile north of the border vary wildly, from 20,000 to 200,000.

In addition to protesting against being inducted to fight a war that many considered unjust, antidraft activists argued that the draft deferments that the Selective Service System granted to white, middle-class young men were disproportionate to those granted to blacks, Hispanics, and working-class whites. The agency did not, in fact, discriminate, but the most common deferment, a II-S "student deferment," was granted to allow registrants to complete their college education before being classified I-A, which would have made them immediately eligible for service. More middle-class whites attended college than did blacks, Hispanics, and working-class whites. Nevertheless, largely in response to charges of de facto discrimination, a lottery system was introduced on December 1, 1969, under which plastic capsules, each containing one of 366 possible birth dates, were drawn randomly from a glass container. Barring deferments and other factors, the men who were among the first one hundred drawn, and who were between the ages of eighteen and twenty-six, were deemed liable for conscription. The rest were not, except in the event of a declared war or national emergency.

The peacetime draft ended in 1973, and the military was converted to an all-volunteer force. The Selective Service System continued, however, as did draft registration, until it was suspended in April 1975. On January 21, 1977, by Executive Order 11967, President Jimmy Carter proclaimed an amnesty and pardon for virtually all who had, one way or another, evaded the draft between August 4, 1964, and March 28, 1973. However, it was also President Carter who, in 1980, ordered the resumption of registration for the draft in response to the Soviet invasion of Afghanistan.

At present, registration of eighteen-year-old men continues to be required by law, and the registration process continues to be administered by the Selective Service System. (See also draft laws.)

Suggested Reading

Bernstein, Iver. *New York City Draft Riots: Their Significance for American Society and Politics in the Age of the Civil War.* New York: Oxford University Press, 1989.

Selective Service System, www.sss.gov.

SELMA (ALABAMA) SNCC–SCLC DEMONSTRATION

Campaigns run by the Student Nonviolent Coordinating Committee (SNCC) during the summer of 1964 and into early 1965 to register black voters in Alabama were met with violence, and SNCC members decided on a mass demonstration to create public support for passage of the VOTING RIGHTS ACT OF 1965, then pending in Congress. With the aid and advice of MARTIN LUTHER KING JR. and RALPH DAVID ABERNATHY of the SOUTHERN CHRISTIAN LEADERSHIP CONFERENCE (SCLC), SNCC mounted a march from Selma, Alabama, to the state capital in Montgomery. The march took place on February 1, 1965, and resulted in the arrest of 770 marchers. Subsequently, on February 18, 1965, a demonstrator named Jimmie Lee Jackson was shot and died of his wounds on February 26. A second march was led by JOHN LEWIS and Hosea Williams on March 7 to protest Jackson's murder. Participants were attacked by police and state troopers wielding tear gas and batons. The confrontation—covered by national television and newspapers—became infamous as BLOODY SUNDAY. The following day JAMES REEB, a white Unitarian minister and SCLC activist, was attacked by a white mob on a Selma sidewalk; he died of his injuries three days later.

The events of March 7 and the attack on Reeb prompted King to lead a third march on March 9. When 1,500 marchers crossed the Edmund Pettus Bridge at the Selma city limit, they were confronted by a phalanx of state troopers. King halted the marchers, led them in prayer, then turned them back. It was a move that disappointed and alienated many civil rights activists and marked the splintering of the AFRICAN AMERICAN CIVIL RIGHTS MOVEMENT into two factions: one that continued to pursue nonviolence, and one that embraced militancy and the BLACK POWER MOVEMENT.

After the third march President LYNDON B. JOHNSON (LBJ) persuaded Alabama governor GEORGE C. WALLACE to request federal aid to maintain order. LBJ authorized a contingent of troops, U.S. Marshals, and agents of the FEDERAL BUREAU OF INVESTIGATION to protect some 25,000 protesters, who marched on Thursday, March 25, to the state capitol building, where they presented Governor Wallace with a petition demanding voting rights for AFRICAN AMERICANS. Despite the federal presence, Viola Liuzzo, a young white member of the NATIONAL ASSOCIATION FOR THE ADVANCEMENT OF COLORED PEOPLE, was shot and killed by members of the KU KLUX KLAN (KKK) on the night of March 25. Allegedly, the Klansmen attacked because Liuzzo had violated a southern racial taboo by riding in a car with a black man, Leroy Moton. Liuzzo was hit in the head by two bullets. (KKK members William Orville Eaton, Eugene Thomas, and Collie Leroy Wilkins Jr. were later tried in state court for first-degree murder and found not guilty. A federal district court subsequently found all three guilty of civil rights violations and sentenced them to ten years in a federal prison. Eaton died on March 9, 1966, from natural causes before beginning his sentence.)

Despite the violence and anguish associated with the Selma demonstrations, as well as the dissension created with the civil rights movement, the actions of February and March were vital in obtaining passage of the Voting Rights Act, which was signed into law on August 6, 1965.

Suggested Reading

Boynton, Ameila Platts. *Bridge across Jordan: The Story of the Struggle for Civil Rights in Selma, Alabama.* New York: Carlton, 1979.

Leonard, Richard D. *Call to Selma: Eighteen Days of Witness.* Boston: Unitarian Universalist Association, 2001.

SENECA FALLS CONFERENCE

On July 19 and 20, 1848, 240 women and men convened at Seneca Falls, New York, for the first formal public meeting to address the rights of women. The convention produced the Seneca Falls Declaration of Sentiments, a document modeled on the U.S. DECLARATION OF INDEPENDENCE, which catalogued the acts and instances of oppression endured by American women. The government of American men, the Declaration of Sentiments held, barred women from voting, from holding property in their own right and name, and from access to the wealth of educational and employment opportunities readily available to men.

The Seneca Falls Conference was organized by feminists ELIZABETH CADY STANTON and Lucretia Mott and is generally considered the origin not only of the organized WOMEN'S SUFFRAGE MOVEMENT but also of the more general WOMEN'S CIVIL RIGHTS MOVEMENT.

Suggested Reading

Gurko, Miriam. *The Ladies of Seneca Falls: The Birth of the Woman's Rights Movement.* New York: Random House, 1996.

"SEPARATE BUT EQUAL" DOCTRINE

For many years the legal basis for racial segregation in the South, the "separate but equal" doctrine, was born of the U.S. SUPREME COURT'S decision in *PLESSY V. FERGUSON* (1896), which held that segregation of public facilities did not violate the Constitution (in particular, the equal protection clause of the FOURTEENTH AMENDMENT) as long as the separate facilities provided for whites and blacks were "equal"—equivalent in function and in the level of accommodation and services they provided.

Although *Plessy v. Ferguson* involved segregated accommodations in railroad travel, the decision was subsequently applied most forcefully to segregated schooling. Leaders and legal strategists of the NATIONAL ASSOCIATION FOR THE ADVANCEMENT OF COLORED PEOPLE understood that to end segregated education it would be necessary to overturn *Plessy*—a goal that was accomplished in the U.S. Supreme Court decision in *BROWN V. BOARD OF EDUCATION OF TOPEKA, KANSAS* (1954). (See also *SWEATT V. PAINTER*.)

Suggested Reading

Thomas, Brook. *Plessy v. Ferguson*. New York: Bedford/St. Martin's, 1996.

SETON, ELIZABETH ANN (1774–1821)

Born Elizabeth Ann Bayley in New York City, Elizabeth Ann Seton was the first native-born American to become a Roman Catholic saint. Daughter of a prominent physician, Bayley worked with Isabella M. Graham and others to found, in 1797, the first charitable institution in New York City, the Society for the Relief of Poor Widows with Small Children.

Bayley married William M. Seton in 1794, but he died soon thereafter. Shortly after her husband's death, Seton converted to Roman Catholicism, opened a school for boys, then, in 1808, opened a school for Catholic girls in Baltimore. In 1809 she took holy vows and, with others, formed the Sisters of St. Joseph, the first American-based Catholic sisterhood. The sisters moved their home and school to Emmitsburg, Maryland, where they provided free education for the poor girls of the local parish. In 1812 the Sisters of St. Joseph became the Sisters of Charity of St. Joseph and opened houses in Philadelphia in 1814 and in New York City in 1817. Devoted to charitable works, the growing order soon became a prototype of private charity for the urban poor in the United States. At the time of Seton's death in 1821 the Sisters of Charity had twenty communities. Seton was canonized in 1975.

Suggested Reading

Brown, Dorothy M., and Elizabeth McKeown. *The Poor Belong to Us: Catholic Charities and American Welfare*. Cambridge: Harvard University Press, 2000.

SEXISM

The word *sexism* refers to beliefs, attitudes, and behaviors that are founded on the notion of inherent differences between the sexes; sexist behavior, though not always overtly discriminatory, tends to perpetuate stereotypical assumptions about sex roles. Although the term is generally used to refer to how men treat women, women's behavior toward men can also be categorized as sexist.

The word *sexism* came into vogue during the mid-1960s with the rise of the WOMEN'S LIBERATION MOVEMENT; however, the attitudes and behaviors the term describes are characteristic of a predominantly patriarchal society—and, as such, have a much older social and cultural history.

Suggested Reading

Fausto-Sterling, Anne. *Myths of Gender: Biological Theories about Women and Men*. New York: Basic, 1992.

Rothenberg, Paula S., ed. *Race, Class, and Gender in the United States: An Integrated Study*. 4th ed. New York: St. Martin's Press, 1997.

SEXUAL HARASSMENT

Definitions of sexual harassment abound—and, unfortunately, the term is often employed carelessly. Legally sexual harassment is defined as a form of sex discrimination that violates Title VII of the CIVIL RIGHTS ACT OF 1964. As federal statute and case law define it, sexual harassment includes unwelcome sexual advances, requests for sexual favors, and other verbal or physical conduct of a sexual nature that explicitly or implicitly affects a person's employment; that interferes with a person's work performance; or that creates an intimidating, hostile, or offensive work environment.

Most commonly, women are victims of sexual harassment perpetrated by men employers, supervisors, or colleagues; however, the victim may be a man and the harasser a woman, or victim and harasser may be of the same sex. While the harasser is usually in a supervisory role with respect to the victim, he or she may also be a colleague, an agent of the employer, or a nonemployee. To be considered a victim, one need not be the direct target of harassment but may simply be affected by the offensive conduct. Sexual harassment may also take place outside of the workplace—in schools, colleges, religious institutions, and many other contexts. Allegations of workplace and work-related sexual harassment are investigated by the EQUAL EMPLOYMENT OPPORTUNITY COMMISSION (EEOC). (See also HOSTILE WORK ENVIRONMENT.)

Suggested Reading

Bingham, Clara, and Laura Leedy Gansler. *Class Action: The Story of Lois Jenson and the Landmark Case That Changed Sexual Harassment Law*. New York: Doubleday, 2002.

SHAW V. RENO

Shaw v. Reno (1993) is a U.S. SUPREME COURT decision that deals with racial GERRYMANDERING. The high court held that North Carolina's Twelfth District—which was redrawn, then submitted for federal approval in compliance with Section 5 of the VOTING RIGHTS ACT OF 1965—was "especially bizarre" in that it stretched "approximately 160 miles along Interstate 85 and, for much of its length, is no wider than the I-85 corridor," but that this obvious attempt to achieve racial balance through redistricting must be "examined against the backdrop of this country's long history of racial discrimination in voting"; when so examined, the high court concluded that the redistricting does not violate the FOURTEENTH AMENDMENT and, therefore, may stand. The decision affirmed the constitutionality of redistricting for the purpose of achieving racially equitable representation in government.

Suggested Reading

Burke, Christopher Matthew. *The Appearance of Equality: Racial Gerrymandering, Redistricting, and the Supreme Court.* Westport, Conn.: Greenwood, 1999.

SHELLEY V. KRAEMER

In 1911 homeowners in a residential neighborhood of St. Louis, Missouri, signed a covenant in which all agreed to exclude blacks and Asians for a period of fifty years. In 1945 a black family purchased a home in contravention of the covenant. Other property owners, claiming that the covenant was legally binding, brought suit to restrain the sellers from concluding the purchase. A state court upheld the covenant, and the case was appealed, in 1948, to the U.S. SUPREME COURT. The high court ruled that while private agreements do not violate the FOURTEENTH AMENDMENT guarantee of equal protection, state courts do violate the equal protection clause when they enforce such covenants. Exclusionary private covenants are thus legal, but unenforceable.

Suggested Reading

Nelson, William E. *The Fourteenth Amendment: From Political Principle to Judicial Doctrine.* Cambridge: Harvard University Press, 1988.

SIEGE AT WOUNDED KNEE

In 1968 a loose organization of NATIVE AMERICANS formed the American Indian Movement (AIM). Of the several protests mounted by members, the most important began on February 27, 1973. The protest, which concerned treaty violations that had deprived the Lakota (mainly Oglala Sioux) of the sacred Black Hills, lasted seventy-days—and, although it began peacefully, it became a militant occupation known as the Siege at Wounded Knee.

On that February day a large group of armed Native Americans reclaimed—in the name of the Lakota—Wounded Knee, where on December 29, 1890, the U.S. Army had massacred some three hundred Miniconjou Sioux in a one-sided battle that effectively ended four hundred years of warfare between Indians and whites on the North American continent.

During the period leading up to the 1973 occupation, two factions among the Oglala were in a state approaching civil war. The "progressive" faction favored accommodation with the federal government; among the "traditional" faction—the Lakota—the most radical sought complete independence from the federal government and wanted to ensure that the terms of the 1868 Treaty of Fort Laramie were adhered to. Under this treaty, which was still legally binding, the Black Hills of South Dakota, sacred to the Lakota, had been ceded to the Sioux people.

Meanwhile, on the Pine Ridge reservation, runoff from strip mining was polluting the land and groundwater, and was believed to be causing illness and contributing to an elevated rate of birth defects. The tribal government had supported—and continued to support—strip mining, which paid lucrative leases to the reservation, and it also favored resolving the conflict over the treaty by formally selling the Black Hills to the federal government.

Amid growing violence between the Lakota and a sometimes violent group of progressives known as the Guardians of the Oglala Nation (which had been tagged with the derisive acronym GOON), AIM brought a fresh, hopeful—and defiant—perspective. Instead of directing militancy against another tribal faction, AIM turned its energy against the federal government. The takeover of Wounded Knee was not the work of a single tribe but an effort that succeeded in drawing and uniting representatives from some seventy-five Indian nations. Supporters poured in from all over the country.

It soon became clear that the Black Hills protest had exceeded the boundaries of a mere demonstration and become a full-scale military occupation. National Guard units, members of the U.S. Marshals Service, and agents of the FEDERAL BUREAU OF INVESTIGATION (FBI) laid siege to Wounded Knee, surrounding the demonstrators and cutting off all routes in and out. Nevertheless, infiltrators managed to gain access, adding to the number of demonstrators and supplying them with food and other necessities.

Declaring that they would lay down their arms only when

their conditions were met, the Wounded Knee demonstrators demanded a thorough investigation of the misuse of tribal funds and acts of aggression and intimidation on the part of the GOONs, a Senate committee investigation of the Bureau of Indian Affairs and the Department of the Interior, and an inquiry into the status of 371 existing treaties between the Native American nations and the federal government (all of which were claimed to have been unilaterally abrogated by the United States).

At this point negotiations broke down, and the siege reached a standoff. Federal forces intensified efforts to cut off food and supplies, and, throughout the winter, the men and women who occupied Wounded Knee subsisted on the most meager of resources. Nor was the siege peaceful. The two sides frequently traded gunfire, injuring several people on both sides and killing Buddy Lamont and Frank Clearwater, two Wounded Knee occupiers. Twelve other AIM supporters, apparently intercepted by GOONs while backpacking supplies into Wounded Knee, disappeared and were never found.

The Siege of Wounded Knee ended after seventy-one days, with the government's pledge that Native American grievances would be addressed. Subsequently, Native American representatives attended a single meeting with White House representatives who promised a congressional review of their concerns and a follow-up meeting. In fact, no further investigative or remedial action was taken—and in the immediate aftermath of the Wounded Knee occupation, federal forces arrested some 1,200 Native Americans. Tribal members believe that during the three years following the siege, the government deliberately instituted a "reign of terror," during which 64 Indians died under mysterious circumstances, some 300 were harassed or beaten, and 562 were arrested—resulting in only fifteen convictions.

Suggested Reading

Lazarus, Edward. *Black Hills, White Justice: The Sioux Nation versus the United States, 1775 to the Present.* New York: HarperCollins, 1991.

SIMPSON, O. J. (1947–)

Orenthal James (O. J.) Simpson was the subject of one of the most racially divisive criminal cases in American history. On June 12, 1994, Simpson's ex-wife, Nicole Brown Simpson, and a friend, Ronald Goldman, were brutally murdered outside her Los Angeles home. Both she and Goldman were white. Simpson, an African American, had been a celebrated football star and, later, a popular television personality and film actor. He was arrested and charged with the murders on June 17, 1994. Pleading not guilty, he assembled a legal "dream team" of prominent defense attorneys for what became an epic, nationally televised trial.

Despite what prosecutors repeatedly called a "mountain of evidence" against Simpson, Johnnie Cochran, of the defense team, argued that the evidence was the result of a frame-up by allegedly racist officers of the Los Angeles Police Department. The jury, apparently in agreement, acquitted Simpson of the murder charges on October 3, 1995.

Views on the outcome of the case were strictly divided along racial lines. Most white Americans were shocked and outraged by the verdict, whereas most black Americans approved, readily accepting the defense theory that white police officers were capable of sufficient corruption and malice to frame a black man, especially a prominent black man who had been married to a white woman. In a Gallup Poll conducted during October 19–22, 1995, 36 percent of whites thought the verdict right, 53 percent believed it wrong, whereas 73 percent of blacks thought it right and only 16 percent wrong; 11 percent of whites had no opinion, whereas only 5 percent of blacks had no opinion (www.law.umkc.edu/faculty/projects/ftrials/Simpson/polls.html).

Simpson had been born in San Francisco and was a high school football star who went on to set records at the University of Southern California during 1967–1968. Named All-American, he won the coveted Heisman Trophy as the best collegiate player of the 1968 season. He was drafted by the Buffalo Bills professional team in 1969 and in 1973 set a season record for yards gained rushing. Traded in 1978 to the San Francisco 49ers, he retired after the 1979 season because of knee injuries; he was inducted into the Pro Football Hall of Fame in 1985. Simpson's football career was followed by successes as an actor and sports commentator.

Although Simpson was acquitted of criminal charges, the families of Nicole Brown Simpson and of Ronald Goldman sued Simpson for wrongful death. He was found liable on February 4, 1997, and was ordered to pay $8.5 million in damages.

Suggested Reading

Schmalleger, Frank M. *Trial of the Century: People of the State of California vs. Orenthal James Simpson.* Englewood Cliffs, N.J.: Prentice Hall College Division, 1996.

SIT-INS

A key tactic of the AFRICAN AMERICAN CIVIL RIGHTS MOVEMENT, sit-ins were acts of civil disobedience that embodied the NONVIOLENCE DOCTRINE. The GREENSBORO SIT-IN in 1960 was typical. The demonstrators seated themselves at a segregated lunch counter. Although they were not served, they remained seated and refused to leave. As this action was repeated during the next several days, business was disrupted, and both the demonstration and the underlying issues gained national attention. Using force to eject the demonstrators would only have intensified the negative national publicity; simply allowing the situation to continue would have run the Woolworth's lunch counter out of business. The tactic compelled store and city officials to take the only viable course: integrate the lunch counter.

Civil rights demonstrators in Greensboro and elsewhere derived the sit-in chiefly from the teachings of MOHANDAS GANDHI, who had used the tactic during the campaign for Indian independence from Britain. In the United States the tactic was used during a 1937 United Automobile Workers' strike against General Motors (GM), when hundreds of workers shut down a major GM plant by sitting down and refusing to leave.

Suggested Reading

Cohen, Carl. *Civil Disobedience: Conscience, Tactics, and the Law.* New York: Columbia University Press, 1971.

Fahey, Joseph J., and Richard Armstrong, eds. *A Peace Reader: Essential Readings on War, Justice, Non-Violence, and World Order.* Rev. ed. Mahwah, N.J.: Paulist, 1992.

SITTING BULL (1831–1890)

Sitting Bull was among the most influential Sioux chiefs of the late nineteenth century. To whites of this period, he was the most famous of all Indian warrior-leaders. For many involved in the NATIVE AMERICAN CIVIL RIGHTS MOVEMENT in the 1960s and the SIEGE AT WOUNDED KNEE in the 1970s, Sitting Bull represented the embodiment of dignity and courage and offered a spiritual presence that gave moral force to the cause of Native American rights.

A member of the Hunkpapa tribe, a branch of the Teton Sioux, Sitting Bull was born on the Grand River in South Dakota, the son of a celebrated chief. Renowned as a hunter and warrior from an early age, he became an important member of the Strong Heart warrior lodge and was a prominent warrior during the INDIAN WARS. Sitting Bull also represented Indian interests in the 1868 Treaty of Fort Laramie—which, in contrast to most treaties of the period, was generally favorable to the Indians.

In 1874, when gold prospectors invaded the Black Hills, which had been acknowledged by the 1868 treaty as sacred to the Sioux, Sitting Bull became chief of a combined Sioux, Cheyenne, and Arapaho war council that convened in Montana. Although Sitting Bull did not participate in combat against GEORGE ARMSTRONG CUSTER at the Battle of the Little Bighorn on June 25, 1876, he "made the medicine"—provided the spiritual guidance—that, the warriors believed, made the Indian victory possible. In May 1877, believing that reprisals for the Little Bighorn, however belated, would eventually come, Sitting Bull led most of the Hunkpapa to refuge in Canada, where the tribe experienced great hardship, including hunger and disease. Sitting Bull eventually brought the Hunkpapa back to the United States; in July 1881 at Fort Buford, North Dakota, he and 170 of his followers surrendered, submitting to life on a reservation.

Sitting Bull himself was held at Fort Randall, South Dakota, from 1881 to 1883 before he was placed at Standing Rock Reservation in North Dakota. Although he was revered on the reservation as a champion of traditional Sioux culture, he befriended one white man—William "Buffalo Bill" Cody, the famed creator of the "Wild West Show." During 1885–1886 Sitting Bull appeared in Buffalo Bill's shows.

After returning to the reservation, Sitting Bull, believing that the movement would restore some of the dignity, sense of identity, and hope that the Indians had lost, became an adherent of the Native American religious revival that whites referred to as the Ghost Dance movement. U.S. government officials, however, regarded the Ghost Dance movement as an incipient uprising, and decided to arrest Sitting Bull. Native American reservation police officers were dispatched to his home on the Grand River in South Dakota. On December 15, 1890, during the scuffle and small-scale riot that broke out during the arrest, Sitting Bull was killed along with two of his sons.

Suggested Reading

Utley, Robert M. *The Lance and the Shield: The Life and Times of Sitting Bull.* New York: Henry Holt, 1993.

SIXTH AMENDMENT

The Sixth Amendment to the U.S. Constitution is part of the BILL OF RIGHTS and is the basis of the state's obligation to ensure that all people accused of crimes receive proper legal representation even if they cannot afford to hire an attorney. The 1932 U.S. SUPREME COURT decision in *Powell v. Alabama* overturned the verdicts in the cases of the SCOTTSBORO BOYS because of the state's failure to provide adequate counsel.

Suggested Reading

Heller, Francis. *The Sixth Amendment to the Constitution of the United States: A Study in Constitutional Development.* Westport, Conn.: Greenwood, 1951.

SLAUGHTERHOUSE CASES

Formally *The Butchers' Benevolent Association of New Orleans v. The Crescent City Live-Stock Landing and Slaughter-House Company,* the Slaughterhouse cases (filed by twenty-five butchers' firms and therefore, technically, a collection of cases), which were decided by the U.S. SUPREME COURT in 1873, upheld state, rather than federal, jurisdiction over the civil rights of a state's citizens.

In 1869, on the grounds of protecting the public health, the Louisiana legislature granted a twenty-five-year monopoly to the Crescent City Live-Stock Landing and Slaughter-House Company, of New Orleans. Competing slaughterhouses brought suit, alleging that the state-sanctioned monopoly effectively deprived them of their property (by barring trade and thereby rendering their property valueless) without due process of law, a violation of the FOURTEENTH AMENDMENT. In a 5–4 decision the Supreme Court held against the slaughterhouse operators, declaring that the Fourteenth Amendment had to be interpreted strictly in light of the original purpose of its framers, which was to guarantee the liberty and rights of former black slaves. In the Court's view, the framers did not contemplate the inclusion of the rights at issue in the Slaughterhouse cases. Furthermore, the Court concluded that the Fourteenth Amendment was not intended to deprive the state of legal jurisdiction over the civil rights of its citizens, because to have done so would have rendered the state's jurisdiction inferior to that of the federal government. In effect the decision distinguished between state citizenship and federal citizenship and defined individuals as subject to both.

Despite the decision in the Slaughterhouse cases, the Fourteenth Amendment was subsequently successfully used to support important civil rights decisions overriding state law, as in, for example, *BROWN V. BOARD OF EDUCATION OF TOPEKA, KANSAS.*

SLAVERY

Slavery is, doubtless, at least as old as civilization. It figures prominently in the Old Testament and was a feature of most of the ancient civilizations for which records exist. Apart from any slave practices that may have existed among pre-Columbian Native Americans, the institution arrived in the English colonies of North America in August 1619, when Virginia tobacco farmers purchased their first consignment of twenty slaves from Dutch traders. By this time Spanish and Portuguese colonizers had long established slavery elsewhere in the Americas.

Unlike the wealthy Spanish and Portuguese planters, however, few English farmers could afford African slaves, and it was not until the close of the seventeenth century that African slaves began to supplant white indentured servants for purposes of agricultural labor. By the beginning of the eighteenth century the price of African slaves had decreased and the wealth of Anglo-American planters had increased. Moreover, hereditary slaves were a better investment than indentured servants, whose period of servitude was limited. Not only was an African slave a slave for life—unless freed by his or her master—but the children of slaves were likewise the property of the master, and on and on through the generations.

In English America, slavery took hold chiefly in the South, where plantations were large, labor-intensive operations, and where climatic conditions were disagreeable to whites. In the northern colonies, where farms were small and usually worked by the families who owned them, slavery was far less prevalent. Antislavery sentiments were also stronger in the North than in the South, and as early as 1724 northern QUAKERS began a campaign of organized opposition to slavery.

Slavery was, of course, inherently cruel and unjust. As property—chattel—slaves were accorded neither legal nor human rights. At the will of the masters, they could be worked, controlled, punished, bought, and sold—and families could be broken up. At the same time, slaves were costly and valuable property, and few slave owners or their overseers—the men they employed to manage their slaves—could afford to be gratuitously abusive. There was no profit in starving slaves, working them to death, or failing to care for them.

The slave trade, however, was relentlessly brutal. Although slaves were a renewable commodity, their rate of birth and maturation could not meet the demand for slave labor. Throughout the eighteenth century and into the early nineteenth, slaves were continually imported from Africa, chiefly the western coastal area that is now Sierra Leone. As articles of trade between white traders and African chieftains, purchased slaves were first warehoused in overcrowded and miserable conditions, in "fortresses" in West Africa, then loaded onto slave ships, where they were packed so tightly below decks that they could lie down only in a "spoon" position, front to back. Malnutrition, starvation, and disease were common on board, and mortality rates were high. Once in the New World the slaves were either sold in Caribbean markets (typically in wholesale lots that were then transported to the retail slave markets on the mainland) or delivered directly to mainland slave markets, where they were sold much like livestock at open auction.

During the eighteenth century, as the movement toward American independence from Britain grew, the incongruity of struggling for liberty while holding slaves became apparent, at least to some. In the first draft of the DECLARATION OF INDEPENDENCE, THOMAS JEFFERSON, himself a slaveholding Virginian, condemned King George III for having forced the slave trade on the colonies, but the Continental Congress suppressed the antislavery passages of the declaration before approving the document.

The ARTICLES OF CONFEDERATION, under which the American Revolution was fought, were silent on the subject of slavery. The first federal position on the subject came with the Northwest Ordinance, which barred the introduction of slavery into the territories of the Old Northwest, which had been acquired as a result of the Revolution. The U.S. Constitution, however, protected slavery, stipulating that slaves who escaped into a free state were not thereby freed and had to be "delivered up on claim of the party to whom such labor may be due" (Article IV, Section 2, Paragraph 3). However, the Constitution also mandated the cessation of the slave trade—the importation of slaves—by 1808 (Article I, Section 9).

Although insisting that slaves were property, not human beings, Southerners demanded, for purposes of apportioning representation in Congress, that slaves be counted as part of the population. Northerners protested. The dispute was settled by the THREE-FIFTHS COMPROMISE (Article I, Section 2, Clause 3), whereby each slave would be counted as three-fifths of a person for the purposes of levying taxes and apportioning congressional representation.

By the time that the Constitution was ratified, slavery was diminishing rather than growing. As European immigration increased after the American Revolution, cheap labor became more plentiful. Moreover, the markets for the chief slave-produced crops of the South—tobacco, rice, and indigo—were mature, with little potential for growth.

Although in the popular imagination slavery is most closely associated with southern cotton plantations, the fact is that during most of the eighteenth century, cotton was a crop of only secondary importance in the South. In coastal areas, black-seed, long-staple cotton was modestly cultivated. This type of cotton could be easily cleaned of its seed—an essential step before the cotton could be exported—simply by passing the cotton bolls through a pair of rollers. The drawback of black-seed cotton was that it could be grown only in a very limited coastal area. In the interior of the South, only the green-seed, short-staple variety—whose stubborn seeds had to be cleaned by hand, one boll at a time—flourished. Even if performed by slaves, this work was unprofitably labor-intensive. In 1794, however, Eli Whitney perfected the cotton gin, a machine that automated the cleaning of short-staple cotton, suddenly creating a whole new economy for the South: during the first half of the nineteenth century, cotton exports came to exceed the value of all other American exports *combined*. As the demand for cotton exploded, so did the need for slaves—who, always important to the southern economy, now seemed absolutely indispensable.

To many southern entrepreneurs, the Louisiana Territory—some 90,000 square miles of land west of the Mississippi River purchased from the French in 1803—looked like one vast cotton field, ripe for division into any number of slaveholding states. Abolitionists pointed to the Northwest Ordinance, which had (they argued) established a precedent under which *all* new territories would be free soil. Southerners responded by insisting that the Constitution protected slavery—and, moreover, that it had reserved to the states all powers and authority not specifically assigned to the federal government; since state authority obviously included the power to regulate slavery, those states that opposed the practice could abolish it within their own borders, and those that wished to retain slavery could also do so, unmolested, within their borders.

With the addition of vast new territories, the effort to maintain a balance in the Senate between free-soil and proslavery representation led to the MISSOURI COMPROMISE in 1820; the COMPROMISE OF 1850; and the KANSAS-NEBRASKA ACT in 1854—awkward makeshifts cobbled together in hopes of avoiding the cataclysmic conflict that finally came as the Civil War. President ABRAHAM LINCOLN insisted that the object of fighting with the eleven southern states that had seceded from the Union was not to abolish slavery but to restore and preserve the Union. In an era deeply marked by RACISM, many northerners would have resisted fighting a "war to free the slaves"—although others welcomed such a cause. Nevertheless, the EMANCIPATION PROCLAMATION, made final on January 1, 1863, seemed to set the abolition of slavery as the principal northern war aim. In any case, the defeat of the Confederacy brought an immediate end to slavery in the United States. (See also INDENTURED SERVITUDE.)

Suggested Reading

Fehrenbacher, Don Edward, and Ward M. McAfee. *The Slaveholding Republic: An Account of the United States Government's Relations to Slavery.* New York: Oxford University Press, 2001.

Huggins, Nathan Irving. *Black Odyssey: The African-American Ordeal in Slavery.* New York: Random House, 1990.

SOCIAL DARWINISM

Social Darwinism is a theory most closely associated with the British philosophers Herbert Spencer (1820–1903) and Walter Bagehot (1826–1877) and with the American philosopher William Graham Sumner (1840–1910). In essence, the theory holds that individuals, groups, and races are subject to the principle of natural selection—as defined, for the natural world, by Charles Darwin in *On the Origin of Species by Means of Natural Selection* (1859). According to social Darwinism, in society as well as in nature, life is a continual struggle for existence and is governed by the unalterable principle of what Herbert Spencer called "survival of the fittest." Just as the rigors and demands of nature cull organisms that are less well adapted to the environment, allowing only the better-adapted organisms to reproduce, so among humans the weaker, less able individuals, groups, and races are diminished, while those that are more able grow in power and cultural influence, ultimately dominating the weaker.

At its most popular in the late nineteenth and early twentieth centuries, social Darwinism was used to justify social conservatism, the political status quo, and laissez-faire capitalism. Since, it was argued, those who survive and prosper in society are the strongest and most capable, their survival is crucial to the evolution of the human species. As for the poor, their circumstances prove them inherently unfit for survival—and, rather than being aided, they should be allowed to perish, for they do not contribute positively to the evolution of the species and may even retard its evolution.

Social Darwinism was also used to provide a "natural" basis for social inequality and class stratification: those who owned and controlled property obviously possessed superior natural abilities, and any attempt to legislate social equality would interfere with the natural evolution of society, to its great detriment. On an international scale, social Darwinism was used to rationalize colonial imperialism. Such "races" as the Anglo-Saxons or Aryans, it was argued, were justified in taking steps to dominate inferior "black" and "yellow" races. Indeed, they were morally and biologically obligated to achieve such domination.

Two developments contributed to the decline of social Darwinism during the twentieth century. In the United States, the rise of the Progressive movement created an activist and interventionist role for government, which contravened, in spirit and practice, social Darwinist doctrine. This movement paralleled advances in scientific research, which increasingly undermined any substantive basis for drawing an analogy between biological and social processes.

Suggested Reading

Hofstadter, Richard. *Social Darwinism in American Thought*. New York: George Braziller, 1959.

SOUTHERN CHRISTIAN LEADERSHIP CONFERENCE

The Southern Christian Leadership Conference (SCLC) was founded in 1957 by MARTIN LUTHER KING JR. and others to assist and coordinate the efforts of local civil rights organizations. Its efforts were concentrated mainly in the South and in some border states and consisted of leadership-training programs, citizen-education projects, and voter registration drives. Major SCLC efforts during the height of the AFRICAN AMERICAN CIVIL RIGHTS MOVEMENT included the BIRMINGHAM SCLC PROTESTS (1963), the MARCH ON WASHINGTON (1963), and the SELMA SNCC–SCLC DEMONSTRATIONS (1965). These SCLC–led demonstrations were instrumental in promoting passage of the CIVIL RIGHTS ACT OF 1964 and the VOTING RIGHTS ACT OF 1965.

Martin Luther King served as SCLC president until his assassination in April 1968, at which time RALPH DAVID ABERNATHY assumed leadership. With the passing of King, however, the SCLC turned away from large-scale demonstration to smaller, more tightly focused campaigns. The splintering of the civil rights movement during the late 1960s was reflected in the SCLC, which was weakened by the 1972 departure of JESSE JACKSON. The SCLC still exists, however, and continues to conduct community-oriented programs, including the Campaign for Tobacco Free Kids; the Martin Luther King, Jr., Streets Partnership; the Martin Luther King, Jr., Schools Program; the National Youth Voter Registration Campaign; the Martin Luther King, Jr., Educational Enrichment Program; and anti–death penalty and racial profiling hearings.

Suggested Reading

Fairclough, Adam. *To Redeem the Soul of America: The Southern Christian Leadership Conference and Martin Luther King, Jr.* Athens: University of Georgia Press, 2001.

SOUTHERN MANIFESTO, THE

The SUPREME COURT decisions in *BROWN V. BOARD OF EDUCATION OF TOPEKA, KANSAS*, which overturned *PLESSY V. FERGUSON* and the "SEPARATE BUT EQUAL" DOCTRINE and ordered the DESEGREGATION of public schools, sparked great resistance, especially in the South. Sen. Sam Ervin, R-N.C., led southern members of the U.S. Congress in creating and endorsing a "manifesto" protesting federally enforced desegregation and calling for lawful resistance to it. (See Appendix A for the text of the Southern Manifesto.)

Suggested Reading

Kluger, Richard. *Simple Justice: The History of Brown v. Board of Education and Black America's Struggle for Equality.* New York: Random House, 1977.

Patterson, James T. *Brown v. Board of Education: A Civil Rights Milestone and Its Troubled Legacy.* New York: Oxford University Press, 2001.

SOUTHERN NEGRO YOUTH CONGRESS

The Southern Negro Youth Congress was created in 1937 by the NATIONAL NEGRO CONFERENCE. Both organizations focused primarily on creating employment opportunities for blacks and attempting to force integration by boycotting segregated businesses. Neither the Southern Negro Youth Congress nor its parent organization lasted long or exercised much influence.

Suggested Reading

Reggio, Michael H. "Human Rights in Twentieth-Century United States." In *Civil Rights in America, 1500 to the Present,* ed. Michael H. Reggio. Detroit: Gale Research, 1998.

SOVEREIGN IMMUNITY

Sovereign immunity is a legal doctrine founded in English COMMON LAW that renders a government immune from suit unless it consents to be sued. In the United States federal as well as state and local governments enjoy varying degrees of sovereign immunity.

The original justification for sovereign immunity was that the sovereign can do no wrong. Because a republican form of government has no sovereign, however, the concept was modified in America: here, the justification for exempting government from suit is that no legal right can be exercised against the authority that makes the law on which the right depends. Moreover, because the Constitution bars any disbursements from the Treasury that have not been authorized by congressional legislation, a suit against the government must not be construed as compelling Congress to enact such legislation. In instances in which the federal government waives sovereign immunity, the waiver must be so constructed as to channel litigation into the appropriate avenue of redress, to avoid drawing money from the Treasury without congressional act.

The Eleventh Amendment to the Constitution and the Foreign Sovereign Immunities Act of 1976 bestow a special form of sovereign immunity, ensuring that one sovereign entity (government) cannot be sued in the court of another sovereign entity (government).

Suggested Reading

Durchslag, Melvyn R. *State Sovereign Immunity: A Reference Guide to the United States Constitution.* Westport, Conn.: Greenwood, 2002.

SPEECH, FREEDOM OF

See FREE SPEECH.

STANTON, ELIZABETH CADY (1815–1902)

A pioneering American feminist, Elizabeth Cady Stanton founded and led the first fully organized movement for WOMEN'S SUFFRAGE in the United States.

Born in Johnstown, New York, Elizabeth Cady was tutored at home, at the Johnstown Academy, and at Emma Willard's Troy Female Seminary. She then apprenticed in the law office of her father, Congressman Daniel Cady, who later served as a justice of the New York Supreme Court. Elizabeth Cady's legal work for her father gave her a thorough acquaintance with the state laws that discriminated against and effectively subjugated women.

In 1840 she married lawyer and abolitionist Henry Brewster Stanton. That same year, as an ardent abolitionist, she attended the World's Anti-Slavery Convention in London, where she was outraged to find that the convention denied recognition to women delegates because of their sex. When she returned to the United States, Stanton became a noted lecturer on women's rights, and, using her knowledge of the law, formulated petitions to the New York state legislature to secure passage of a bill granting women property rights. The first of its kind in the nation, the bill passed in 1848 and became a model for similar legislation in other states. Also in 1848, with Lucretia Mott, Stanton organized the SENECA FALLS CONFERENCE, the first national meeting on women's suffrage and other rights. The Seneca Falls meeting was, in effect, the beginning of the American WOMEN'S RIGHTS movement.

In 1851 Stanton formed a close working partnership with SUSAN B. ANTHONY to mount a long-term campaign for suffrage and other rights. Anthony had a genius for organization, whereas the more charismatic Stanton proved to be a brilliant orator. When Stanton was invited to address the New York legislature in 1854, her speech moved the legislators to begin formulating major women's rights legislation. In 1860 the state granted married women the sole right to any wages they earned and equal guardianship of their children, thus enabling them to sue for custody in the event of divorce. As with the 1848 legislation, the New York law became a model for other states.

With the advent of the Civil War, Stanton renewed her earlier abolitionist activity, and in 1863, as cofounder with Anthony of the Women's National Loyal League, she created and sponsored a petition calling for immediate emancipation. After the war, however, Stanton was outraged by fact that the enfranchisement of black *men* was considered separate from the issue of women's suffrage. With Anthony, she conducted a suffragist speaking tour of the nation. In 1868 she cofounded, with pioneering human rights advocate Parker Pillsbury, the *Revolution,* a weekly journal of women's rights, which she edited until the journal folded in 1870.

In 1869 Stanton was a principal organizer of the National Woman Suffrage Association, and she served as its president until 1890, when the organization merged with the American Woman Suffrage Association. She was then elected president of the new organization, the NATIONAL AMERICAN WOMAN SUFFRAGE ASSOCIATION, and served for two years.

In 1876 Stanton wrote the Declaration of Rights for Women, which was presented at the Centennial Exposition in Philadelphia. Two years later she drafted a proposed federal suffrage amendment, which was introduced in every Congress until passage of the Nineteenth Amendment in 1920. She also collaborated with Anthony Gage and Matilda Joslyn Gage on a massive, six-volume *History of Woman Suffrage* and, in 1898, published an autobiography, *Eighty Years and More.*

Suggested Reading

Dubois, Ellen Carol, ed. *The Elizabeth Cady Stanton–Susan B. Anthony Reader: Correspondence, Writings, Speeches.* Boston: Northeastern University Press, 1992.

STATES' RIGHTS

States' rights (also called *state rights* and *state's rights*) refers, first and foremost, to all governing rights and powers that are not accorded to the federal government but that are retained by the states under the Tenth Amendment to the U.S. Constitution: "The powers not delegated to the United States by the Constitution, nor prohibited by it to the States, are reserved to the States respectively, or to the people."

State's rights have been invoked to support a variety of political and social positions. THOMAS JEFFERSON and JAMES MADISON invoked them in the Kentucky and Virginia Resolutions, which were in opposition to the ALIEN AND SEDITION ACTS; and JOHN C. CALHOUN and other southerners made them a rallying cry for opposition to federal tariffs on foreign imports and for calls for the federal restriction or abolition of SLAVERY. Ultimately, states' rights were used to justify secession from the Union.

Northern victory in the Civil War settled the most extreme states' rights position—the right of secession—but the doctrine resurfaced during the 1950s and 1960s as a rationale for opposing federal efforts to integrate public schools and other public facilities in the South.

Suggested Reading

Drake, Frederick D., and Lynn R. Nelson, eds. *States Rights and American Federalism: A Documentary History.* Westport, Conn.: Greenwood, 1999.

Jeffries, John Calvin, Pamela S. Karlan, Peter W. Low, and G. Rutherglen. *Civil Rights Actions: Enforcing the Constitution.* New York: Foundation, 2000.

STEREOTYPES, ETHNIC AND RACIAL

A stereotype is a conventional, simplistic, and formulaic perception (or preconception). A predilection for stereotyping individuals according to preconceived ideas of ethnic or racial characteristics is common, even in as diverse a nation as the United States. Such stereotypes are generally perpetuated informally, from parents to children, and through what might be described as the collective folklore of a given time, place, and social milieu. In an age of mass media, however, the development and dissemination of stereotypes becomes even more powerful. The minstrel shows that were first staged in the decades before the Civil War, in which white performers blackened their faces and performed "Negro" or "darky" skits, songs, and dances, are an early example of racial stereotyping in popular entertainment. Beginning in the later nineteenth century and continuing into the early twentieth, vaudeville presented stereotypes of blacks as well as of the members of various ethnic groups, especially the Irish and the Germans (who were often called "Dutch"). Novels and other forms of popular entertainment presented many racial and ethnic stereotypes (of Asians and Jews, for example), and the advent of motion pictures, early in the twentieth century, provided a venue for yet more stereotyping.

Racial and ethnic stereotypes may be well-meaning, deliberately demeaning, or downright malicious. Many representatives of minority groups argue that *any* stereotype, regardless of motivation, is inherently demeaning and destructive. Organizations such as the ANTI-DEFAMATION LEAGUE and the NATIONAL ASSOCIATION FOR THE ADVANCEMENT OF COLORED PEOPLE, among others, devote considerable energy to monitoring the media for negative stereotypes, and one of the effects of the AFRICAN AMERICAN CIVIL RIGHTS MOVEMENT of the 1960s appears to have been a generally increased sensitivity to racial and ethnic stereotyping in the media. Since at least the late 1960s, authors and broadcasters have typically taken pains to avoid the kinds of broad stereotypes that were once common.

Nevertheless, ethnic and racial stereotyping continue to influence American life. Some urban cab drivers are reluctant to pick up young African American men. Police officers may engage in illegal RACIAL PROFILING. Someone who is looking for a clever tax preparer may seek out a Jewish accountant. Voters may assume that an Italian American politician who declines to run for president has Mafia connections to hide. To a significant degree, civil rights legislation can curb the most egregious and destructive effects of stereotyping, but it is more difficult to reform beliefs and assumptions shaped by folklore, tradition, and popular culture.

Sexual stereotyping is also a common and destructive social phenomenon; see SEXISM.

Suggested Reading

Friedman, Lester. *Unspeakable Images: Ethnicity and the American Cinema*. Champaign-Urbana: University of Illinois Press, 1991.

Samuels, Frederick. *Group Images: Racial, Ethnic, and Religious Stereotyping.* New Haven, Conn.: College and University Press, 1973.

Woll, Allen. *Ethnic and Racial Images in American Film and Television: Historical Essays and Bibliography.* New York: Garland, 1987.

STONEWALL PROTEST

Like other gay bars on or near Christopher Street in New York City's Greenwich Village, the Stonewall Inn was frequently the target of police raids and harassment during the 1960s. On June 27, 1969, New York City police officers and agents of the city's Alcoholic Beverage Control Board entered the Stonewall, purportedly to ensure that the inn was not in violation of liquor ordinances. According to patrons, the officers made derogatory and homophobic comments, checked the patrons' identification, then threw them out of the bar, one by one. In the past, such harassment had met with little or no resistance. This time, however, it triggered a raucous protest and riot that continued for the next three days.

Historians of the GAY RIGHTS movement often cite the Stonewall protest not so much as the start of the movement but as a kind of rallying point that brought many previously apathetic gay men and women into the movement and catalyzed the movement's organization and assertiveness.

Suggested Reading

Clendinen, Dudley, and Adam Nagourney. *Out for Good: The Struggle to Build a Gay Rights Movement in America.* New York: Touchstone, 2001.

Gerstmann, Evan. *Constitutional Underclass: Gays, Lesbians, and the Failure of Class-Based Equal Protection.* University of Chicago Press, 1999.

STOWE, HARRIET BEECHER (1811–1896)

Harriet Beecher Stowe is best known as the author of the enormously popular novel *Uncle Tom's Cabin* (1852), a portrayal of southern SLAVERY so compelling that it significantly advanced the cause of the ABOLITION MOVEMENT and even contributed to the advent of the Civil War.

Harriet Beecher was the daughter of the nationally famous Congregationalist minister Lyman Beecher and the sister of liberal educator Catharine Beecher and of abolitionist, orator, and preacher Henry Ward Beecher. After attending her sister's school in Hartford, Connecticut, from 1824 to 1827, Harriet became a teacher there. In 1832 she moved with her sister and father to Cincinnati and became a teacher in a school Catherine founded there. In 1836 Harriet married Calvin Ellis Stowe, a professor of theology, and took up a career as a popular author.

During her eighteen years in Cincinnati, Stowe came into frequent contact with slave owners from neighboring Kentucky as well as with fugitive slaves, an experience that created a deep impression on her. In 1850, when her husband was appointed to a professorship at Bowdoin College, she settled with him in Brunswick, Maine, and began to write *Uncle Tom's Cabin,* which appeared serially in 1851–1852 and in book form in 1852. It was a publishing sensation, widely promoted by abolitionists and denounced by southerners, who acted to suppress the book throughout the South. This effort probably only stimulated sales, however, which topped 300,000 in the book's first year of publication. Moreover, *Uncle Tom's Cabin* was immediately dramatized by both amateur and professional playwrights, enabling it to reach an even wider audience. Stowe was catapulted to national and international fame.

Keenly interested in promoting *Uncle Tom's Cabin* as an abolitionist document, in 1853 Stowe published *A Key to Uncle Tom's Cabin,* which presented the original documents and testimonies that had formed the basis of her portrayal of slave life in the book. Her next novel, *Dred: A Tale of the Great Dismal Swamp,* published in 1856, focused less on the misery of slave life than on the deleterious effects of slavery on a slaveholding society.

Stowe went on to write abolitionist essays and stories for various journals and also branched out into other subjects, producing a conventional love story (*The Minister's Wooing,* 1859), a volume of religious verse, and various literary essays. Her later efforts, however, never approached *Uncle Tom's Cabin* in influence or popularity.

Suggested Reading

Hedrick, Joan D. *Harriet Beecher Stowe: A Life.* New York: Oxford University Press, 1995.

STRAUDER V. WEST VIRGINIA

Strauder v. West Virginia (1879), in which the U.S. SUPREME COURT held that a West Virginia statute prohibiting nonwhite males from sitting on juries was unconstitutional, was the first time the equal protection clause of the FOURTEENTH AMENDMENT had been cited as providing protection for the civil rights of blacks. The high court went on to hold that any classification of jurors by race or nationality is unconstitutional. Significantly, however, the decision affirmed a state's right to prescribe other qualifications for jurors, including those based on age, sex, and education.

Suggested Reading

Green, Robert P., Jr. *Equal Protection and the African American Constitutional Experience: A Documentary History.* Westport, Conn.: Greenwood, 2000.

STUDENT NONVIOLENT COORDINATING COMMITTEE

The Student Nonviolent Coordinating Committee (SNCC)—universally referred to as "Snick"—was founded during April 16–17, 1960, on the campus of Shaw University, an African American institution in Raleigh, North Carolina. Its creation was sparked by the GREENSBORO SIT-IN of February 1, 1960, which had resulted in the DESEGREGATION of a Woolworth's lunch counter and set off a series of similar demonstrations in college towns across the South. SNCC was established in an effort to coordinate and publicize the SIT-INS and to provide support to their leaders.

SNCC's first official meeting after its founding came in Atlanta, during May 13–14, 1960. Student activist (and future Washington, D.C., mayor) Marion Barry was elected chairman, and, the following month, the first issue of the organization's periodical, *Student Voice,* was published. In November Chuck McDew replaced Barry as chairman. In May 1961 SNCC organized the FREEDOM RIDES, in which SNCC members rode buses through the South to test federal legislation barring the segregation of interstate transport. In August 1962, SNCC worked with the CONGRESS OF RACIAL EQUALITY and the SOUTHERN CHRISTIAN LEADERSHIP CONFERENCE (SCLC) to mount the first of several voter registration drives (see FREEDOM SUMMER) in the South—culminating, under the leadership of SNCC's new chairman, JOHN LEWIS, in the Freedom Summer of 1963, an intensive voter registration and voter education campaign in Mississippi.

SNCC not only supported black voter registration but was a driving force behind the MISSISSIPPI FREEDOM DEMOCRATIC PARTY—which, in an attempt to gain official recognition, challenged the regular Democratic Party of Mississippi at the 1964 Democratic National Convention in Atlantic City. SNCC also helped to found the Mississippi Freedom Labor Union, an effort to organize black cotton workers.

SNCC played a major role in organizing the 1963 MARCH ON WASHINGTON, which was instrumental in securing passage of the CIVIL RIGHTS ACT OF 1964, and the SELMA SNCC–SCLC DEMONSTRATIONS, which were instrumental in securing passage of the VOTING RIGHTS ACT OF 1965.

The Selma marches also marked SNCC's growing divergence from the NONVIOLENCE DOCTRINE of MARTIN LUTHER KING JR. and the SCLC. In 1966 John Lewis was replaced as SNCC chairman by STOKELY CARMICHAEL, who increasingly aligned the group with the militant BLACK POWER MOVEMENT. Carmichael—and, to an even greater degree, his successor, H. "Rap" Brown, who assumed leadership in 1967—rejected white liberal participation in SNCC. This stance, coupled with the group's increasingly strident militancy and its declared support of the Arab position during the Arab-Israeli Six-Day War (1967), led white liberal supporters to cut off vital funding. SNCC membership rapidly declined, and the organization effectively dissolved in 1970. (See also HAMER, FANNIE LOU.)

Suggested Reading

Carson, Clayborne. *In Struggle: SNCC and the Black Awakening of the 1960s.* 1981. Reprint, Cambridge: Harvard University Press, 1995.

STUDENTS FOR A DEMOCRATIC SOCIETY

Formed in 1959 at the University of Michigan at Ann Arbor, Students for a Democratic Society (SDS) was a radical student group founded by members of the youth branch of a socialist educational organization called the League for Industrial Democracy. The first organizational meeting of SDS, held at Ann Arbor in 1960, elected activist Robert Alan Haber president. Two years later SDS member Tom Hayden, the twenty-two-year-old former editor of the University of Michigan's student newspaper, wrote the *Port Huron Statement,* which the SDS immediately adopted as its political manifesto. The *Port Huron Statement* condemned the American political system and the U.S. government for having failed to achieve international peace and for having failed to effectively address RACISM, poverty, militarism, and materialism; the statement also called for the institution of a fully participatory democracy. Armed with the *Port Huron Statement,* SDS set out to establish itself as a nonviolent youth movement whose goal was to transform American society into such a democracy.

SDS's initial activities were in keeping with the aims of the AFRICAN AMERICAN CIVIL RIGHTS MOVEMENT and included efforts to improve conditions in urban ghettos. However, after its national march on Washington in April 1965, SDS turned away from black civil rights and focused almost exclusively on opposition to the Vietnam War. While the organization did not advocate violence, neither did it employ the PASSIVE-RESISTANCE tactics of the early civil rights movement. As SDS chapters were established on college campuses throughout the country, the organization staged deliberately raucous and disruptive demonstrations, which included occupations of college administration buildings.

Beginning in 1965 SDS came to represent the radical wing of leftist campus activism, and over the next few years its influence on college campuses was pervasive. Even students who did not actually join the organization were moved by the ideal, however vague, of a genuinely just society. SDS demonstrations on campus were often focused on the university itself, including racial discrimination and segregation in sororities and fraternities, and what SDS regarded as outmoded course requirements, rigid grading systems, and restrictive dress codes. Eventually the focus broadened to include protests against university affiliations with the military-industrial complex—which came about, for example, through research that might ultimately be applied to weapons development.

Early on SDS was in the forefront of student opposition to the Vietnam War—and in 1966, when automatic student draft deferments were abolished, the Vietnam War became the leading issue for SDS. The organization's antiwar activities included draft-card burnings, disruptions of campus Reserve Officers Training Corps (ROTC) classes, the harassment of military recruiters on campus, and even vandalism and destruction of campus ROTC facilities.

SDS became most visible during 1968 when it coordinated antiwar demonstrations on approximately a hundred campuses across the country. These protests often dovetailed with protests against racism, of which the Vietnam War was seen as both an expression and a product. At Columbia University SDS instigated a massive strike, beginning on April 23, 1968, to protest the university's relationship with the Institute for Defense Analyses—a federally funded research and development strategic policy "think tank" employing academics—and the university's allegedly racist policies toward the adjacent Harlem neighborhood. The protest began with about 150 students, then quickly grew in number. Ultimately, protesters occupied the university administration building and held three school officials hostage for twenty-four hours

In August 1968 SDS was at the core of demonstrations at the Democratic National Convention in Chicago, which sparked a violent confrontation between police and some five thousand demonstrators. Throughout 1968 and 1969 demonstrations continued as an almost routine feature of campus life; then, on May 4, 1970, during a demonstration at Kent State University, in Ohio, panicky and inexperienced National Guardsmen shot and killed four students. Although this event triggered a new wave of college protests, campus unrest had clearly peaked. From the fall of 1970 on, activism subsided—and, as it did so, SDS began to splinter. The moderate faction of the group receded into inactivity, and a small, highly militant faction emerged, embracing what it considered to be the revolutionary methods of Mao Zedong and Che Guevara.

The most visible of the militant SDS factions was the Weather Underground (also called the Weathermen), a terrorist group that is unofficially credited with some five hundred violent terrorist acts between 1969 and 1981, the year in which the organization abruptly quit operations after committing a bank robbery in which two police officers and a security guard were killed (John Pynchon Holms, with Tom Burke, *Terrorism: Today's Biggest Threat to Freedom,* New York: Pinnacle, 2001, 157). (See also DALEY, RICHARD J.; SAVIO, MARIO; and VIETNAM WAR PROTEST MOVEMENT.)

Suggested Reading

Sale, Kirkpatrick. *SDS.* New York: Random House, 1973.

SUICIDE, ASSISTED

See right to die.

SUPREME COURT

The U.S. Supreme Court was created by the Constitution as the highest court of the federal system of courts. The Constitution gives the Supreme Court authority to act in all cases that arise under the Constitution, the laws, or the treaties of the United States; the Court also has jurisdiction in cases to which the United States is a party; in controversies between states or between citizens of different states; in maritime and admiralty cases; and in cases affecting ambassadors, consuls, and public ministers.

Nowhere does the Constitution explicitly assign to the Supreme Court the function that has long been most closely identified with it—namely, judicial review, the authority to determine the constitutionality of acts of Congress, of state legislatures, and of executive and administrative orders when cases bearing upon such acts and orders are brought before it. The principle of judicial review was established by Chief Justice John Marshall in *Marbury v. Madison* (1803), in which a provision of the Federal Judiciary Act of 1789 was overturned as contrary to the Constitution. Thanks to Marshall, the Supreme Court became not only the final court of appeal but the final interpreter, arbiter, and expositor of the Constitution. In this role the Supreme Court demarcates the bounds of authority between state and nation; state and state; and, most importantly, between government and citizen. Thanks also to Marshall, the place of power held by the judicial branch is, in the system of checks and balances, commensurate with that of the executive and legislative branches.

The Constitution does not establish the size of the court, which is fixed by act of Congress. Historically, it has varied from six to ten members, but it has consisted of nine since 1869: one chief justice and eight associate justices. Like appointments to the lower federal courts, appointments to the Supreme Court are made by the president, with the advice and consent of the Senate. Tenure is for life, although removal is possible upon impeachment by the House of Representatives and trial in the Senate.

The Supreme Court takes original jurisdiction of very few cases: the overwhelming majority come to the Court on appeal or by certiorari from lower courts. By statute, the Supreme Court is obligated to hear certain classes of cases on appeal; however, in most instances the Court itself decides whether or not to hear a case, granting certiorari to those it decides to hear. If the Court were obligated to hear *all* cases brought before it, the massive case overload would create judicial paralysis. Generally, the Court chooses to hear only those cases that bring into question constitutional issues of important and enduring public interest.

The Supreme Court has played a crucial role in defining and protecting—and, in some cases, limiting—minority rights. (See also Appendix B, "Civil and Minority Rights Cases.")

Suggested Reading

Finkelman, Paul, and Melvin I. Urofsky. *Landmark Decisions of the United States Supreme Court.* Washington, D.C.: CQ Press, 2002.

Howard, John R. *The Shifting Wind: The Supreme Court and Civil Rights from Reconstruction to Brown.* Albany: State University of New York Press, 1999.

Irons, Peter H. *A People's History of the Supreme Court.* New York: Viking, 1999.

SWANN V. CHARLOTTE-MECKLENBURG BOARD OF EDUCATION

The U.S. Supreme Court decision in *Swann v. Charlotte-Mecklenburg Board of Education,* handed down on April 20, 1971, held that it was constitutional for federal district courts to supervise school busing programs until the school system in question became "unitary"—that is, racially integrated.

Prompted by the decision, district courts throughout the nation enforced extensive expansions of busing routes; however, the court-mandated programs were costly, and, to escape their effects, significant numbers of whites moved to the suburbs or enrolled their children in private schools. This trend, together with waning support for busing from the minority community, contributed to what is widely regarded as the failure of busing as a means of achieving integration of public schools. (See also busing, school.)

Suggested Reading

Schwartz, Bernard. *Swann's Way: The School Busing Case and the Supreme Court.* New York: Oxford University Press, 1986.

SWEATT V. PAINTER

The U.S. Supreme Court decided *Sweatt v. Painter,* a landmark in desegregation, on June 5, 1950. In February 1946 Heman Marion Sweatt, a black man, applied for admission to the University of Texas School of Law, and, although he met all academic qualifications for admission, was barred because of his race. Sweatt sued, claiming that although he had been denied admission pursuant to Article VII, Section 7, of the Texas Constitution, which held that "Separate schools shall be provided for the white and colored children, and impartial provision shall be made for both," Texas, in fact, provided no separate law school for blacks. In the absence of a "separate but equal" black law school, Sweatt initiated proceedings to require state and university officials to enroll him at the university. The trial judge responded by granting the state a continuance to give it time to establish a separate but equal school, and a temporary law school, the School of Law of the Texas State University for Negroes, was opened in February 1947. The case was resumed, and the judge denied Sweatt's petition to be admitted to the University of Texas School of Law.

THURGOOD MARSHALL was among the attorneys from the NATIONAL ASSOCIATION FOR THE ADVANCEMENT OF COLORED PEOPLE who argued before the U.S. Supreme Court on behalf of Sweatt. The high court held that because the facility provided by the state was indeed separate from, but hardly equal to, the University of Texas facility, the equal protection clause of the FOURTEENTH AMENDMENT required Sweatt's admission to the University of Texas School of Law. The university school, the court pointed out,

> was staffed by a faculty of sixteen full-time and three part-time professors, some of whom are nationally recognized authorities in their field. Its student body numbered 850. The library contained over 65,000 volumes. Among the other facilities available to the students were a law review, moot court facilities, . . . scholarship funds, and Order of the Coif affiliation. The school's alumni occupy the most distinguished positions in the private practice of the law and in the public life of the State. It may properly be considered one of the nation's ranking law schools.

In contrast,

> The law school for Negroes which was to have opened in February, 1947, would have had no independent faculty or library. The teaching was to be carried on by four members of the University of Texas Law School faculty, who were to maintain their offices at the University of Texas while teaching at both institutions. Few of the 10,000 volumes ordered for the library had arrived; . . . nor was there any full-time librarian. The school lacked accreditation.

Sweatt was admitted to the University of Texas Law School at the beginning of the 1950–1951 school year, as were several other blacks. While it is true that *Sweatt v. Painter* did not strike down de jure segregation or *PLESSY V. FERGUSON,* it clearly foreshadowed the death of the "SEPARATE BUT EQUAL" DOCTRINE, since, in most instances of public accommodations, it was impractical or even impossible to create genuinely separate *and* equal facilities. Because of this implication, *Sweatt v. Painter* laid the groundwork for the decision in *BROWN V. BOARD OF EDUCATION OF TOPEKA, KANSAS* (1954), which did overturn *Plessy v. Ferguson* once and for all.

Suggested Reading

Kluger, Richard. *Simple Justice: The History of Brown v. Board of Education and Black America's Struggle for Equality.* New York: Knopf, 1976.

TAILHOOK SCANDAL

In September 1991 the Tailhook Association, an organization representing approximately 16,000 U.S. Navy and Marine Corps aviators, held its thirty-fifth annual convention at the Las Vegas Hilton Hotel. In the course of the convention, some eighty to ninety women—including Lt. Paula Coughlin, USN, an admiral's aide and a helicopter pilot—were sexually harassed or assaulted by male naval and marine officers attending the convention. Coughlin was forced to run a gauntlet of men who grabbed at her breasts, crotch, and buttocks and attempted to tear the clothes from her body. When she reported the incident to her commanding officer, Adm. John W. Snyder, he dismissed it. She then filed formal charges and, after the navy failed to take action, went public with the accusations, which prompted the Naval Investigative Service (NIS) and the Navy Inspector General to investigate fully.

By February 1994 the NIS and the Navy Inspector General had formally investigated 140 cases of misconduct (involving 119 naval officers and 21 marine officers) against eighty to ninety victims, including the wives of six officers. Ultimately, the careers of fourteen admirals and nearly three hundred naval and Marine Corps aviators were either ended or damaged by the Tailhook scandal. At the top, Secretary of the Navy H. Lawrence Garrett III was compelled to resign, and Chief of Naval Operations Adm. Frank Kelso took early retirement. Coughlin's superior, Admiral Snyder, was relieved of duty for having ignored his subordinate's complaints. No criminal charges were filed in any of the cases, and the Marine Corps dropped all charges against the Marine captain whom Coughlin had specifically accused of sexual molestation. The corps determined that there was insufficient evidence to proceed with a court-martial and that Coughlin had, in any case, misidentified her assailant.

Coughlin and six of the other victims subsequently sued both the Tailhook Association and the Las Vegas Hilton Hotel for failing to provide adequate security for guests. The Tailhook Association reached a pretrial settlement with the seven victims. On October 24, 1994, after a seven-week civil trial against the Hilton and its parent corporation, a jury awarded Coughlin $1.7 million in compensatory damages for emotional distress and $5 million in punitive damages. In order to conform with Nevada law, which limits punitive damages to three times the amount of compensatory damages, Judge Philip M. Pro deducted the Tailhook pretrial settlement from the $1.7 million in compensatory damages and reduced the punitive damages to $3.9 million. Despite her legal victory, Coughlin—deluged by hate mail and believing her naval career irretrievably compromised—resigned her commission in February 1995.

The worst case of sexual harassment in the history of the American military, the Tailhook scandal brought an abrupt end to official complacency regarding harassment.

Suggested Reading

McMichael, William H. *The Mother of All Hooks: The Story of the U.S. Navy's Tailhook Scandal.* Piscataway, N.J.: Transaction, 1997.

TARBELL, IDA (1857–1944)

Ida Tarbell was a crusading journalist, most famous for her *History of the Standard Oil Company* (1904), which detailed the predatory business practices by which John D. Rockefeller had transformed Standard Oil into a nearly unassailable monopoly. Tarbell was also a voice for the poor and underprivileged and for WOMEN'S RIGHTS. Many media historians identify her as the founder of modern investigative journalism.

Tarbell was born in Erie, Pennsylvania, and was educated at Allegheny College in Meadville, Pennsylvania. After a brief teaching career she became an editor for the Chautauqua Literary and Scientific Circle (1883–1891), then studied at the Sorbonne in Paris. While abroad she wrote for various American magazines and, in 1894, was hired by *McClure's Magazine,* where her work on Standard Oil was originally published serially. President Theodore Roosevelt later identified Tarbell as a "muckraker"—his term for the new breed of investigative journalists bent on social reform who were active at the turn of the century.

Tarbell was a prolific author and was sought after for participation in a variety of government conferences, committees, and commissions concerned with industry and unemployment.

Suggested Reading

Brady, Kathleen. *Ida Tarbell: Portrait of a Muckraker.* Pittsburgh: University of Pittsburgh Press, 1989.

TENEMENT HOUSE LAW OF 1867

By the mid-nineteenth century, New York City's tenement houses were a local and national disgrace—overcrowded, filthy, poorly ventilated, and generally unsafe. In 1867 the Council of Hygiene of the New York City Citizen's Association issued a report detailing some of the worst tenement conditions. This report was sufficient to motivate the New York state legislature to pass the nation's first housing law, the Tenement House Law of 1867. The minimal requirements outlined in the law included a window or ventilator in each sleeping room, a fire escape, and adequate toilets (connected to the city sewer system) for each building. Outdoor cesspools—a major health hazard in slums—were banned, although using them was a mere misdemeanor.

Beyond these few requirements, the Tenement House Act of 1867 (known as the "Old Law" to distinguish it from later legislation, such as the Tenement House Act of 1891), did nothing to improve the dismal conditions in which New York's poor lived. (See also HOUSING RIGHTS.)

Suggested Reading

Lubove, Roy. *The Progressives and the Slums: Tenement House Reform in New York City, 1890–1917.* Westport, Conn.: Greenwood, 1974.

TEST CASE

A test case is a deliberate effort to challenge a court to interpret a statutory or constitutional provision. To create a test case, activists have often purposely defied or violated a statute; in 1933, for example, Random House publisher Bennett Cerf knowingly violated federal customs and obscenity laws by importing into the United States a copy of James Joyce's *Ulysses,* which had been declared indecent and pornographic by postal and customs officials. During the 1950s, African American civil rights protesters broke the COLOR LINES in the South by attempting to use segregated public facilities. Such actions provoked test cases that led certain legal decisions and legislation to be overturned as unconstitutional.

THIRTEENTH AMENDMENT

The Thirteenth Amendment to the U.S. Constitution, passed by the Senate on April 8, 1864, by the House on January 31, 1865, and ratified by two-thirds of the states on December 6, 1865, abolished SLAVERY as a legal institution. Following the end of the Civil War, ratification of the amendment was made one of the conditions for readmission to the Union of the states of the former Confederacy.

Suggested Reading

Vorenberg, Michael. *Final Freedom: The Civil War, the Abolition of Slavery, and the Thirteenth Amendment.* New York: Cambridge University Press, 2001.

THOMAS, CLARENCE (1948–)

A conservative African American jurist appointed to the U.S. SUPREME COURT in 1991 by President George H.W. Bush, Clarence Thomas succeeded another African American, the liberal THURGOOD MARSHALL, who retired because of age and ill health. Thomas's confirmation by the U.S. Senate was clouded by charges of SEXUAL HARASSMENT brought by a former aide, Anita Hill, a law professor at the University of Oklahoma. The rancorous hearings—at which Hill testified that Thomas, in an apparent effort to elicit sexual favors, had repeatedly made sexually offensive comments to her—were nationally televised. Thomas denied the charges and was ultimately confirmed by a close (52–48) Senate vote.

Thomas was born in a small town outside of Savannah, Georgia. Abandoned by his father when he was two years old, Thomas was raised mainly by his grandfather. He was educated at an all-black Roman Catholic primary school, then at a seminary, at Immaculate Conception Abbey, and, later, at Holy Cross College in Worcester, Massachusetts. After receiving a bachelor's degree in 1971 he enrolled at Yale University Law School, where he received his law degree in 1974.

Between 1974 and 1977 Thomas served as an assistant attorney general in Missouri, then left that post to practice corporate law for the Monsanto Company. From 1979 to 1981 Thomas was legislative assistant to Missouri Republican senator John C. Danforth. In 1981 President Ronald Reagan appointed Thomas an assistant secretary in the U.S. Department of Education. He next served as chairman of the Equal Employment Opportunity Commission from 1982 to 1990, when he was appointed to the U.S. Court of Appeals for the District of Columbia. He was appointed to the Supreme Court the following year.

On the Supreme Court Thomas has consistently taken a conservative stance: in *Mitchell v. Helms* (2000), for example, Thomas held that a government-supported program that lends educational materials to private and religious schools does not violate the separation of church and state; in *Good News Club v. Milford Central School* (2001), Thomas held that a public school had violated the First Amendment by banning a religious club from meeting on campus after school hours, even though other clubs were free to meet. In *Adarand Constructors v. Pena,* 515 U.S. 200 (1995), Thomas concurred with the majority, holding that all race-based federal actions require the closest possible scrutiny; he further observed that "Government cannot make us equal; it can only recognize, respect, and protect us as equal before the law."

Suggested Reading

Thomas, Andrew Peyton. *Clarence Thomas: A Biography.* San Francisco: Encounter, 2001.

THOREAU, HENRY DAVID (1817–1862)

One of the great figures of American literature, Henry David Thoreau was a poet, essayist, naturalist, philosopher, and theorist and practitioner of civil disobedience. He is best known for his work of philosophical autobiography, *Walden* (1854), and his essay "Civil Disobedience" (1849), which influenced such twentieth-century rights activists as Mohandas Gandhi and Martin Luther King Jr.

Thoreau was born in Concord, Massachusetts, into the family of a pencil manufacturer. He was educated at the local Concord Academy and at Harvard College, from which he graduated in 1837. He tried teaching but lasted all of two weeks before going to work at his father's factory. In 1838, however, he started his own school in partnership with his brother, John. The school, founded on progressive principles, survived for three years, after which Thoreau resolved to become a full-time poet, taking nature as his subject.

By the late 1830s Thoreau had begun a friendship with the philosopher, poet, and essayist Ralph Waldo Emerson. Under Emerson's influence Thoreau became an adherent of the philosophy of transcendentalism, which holds that a divine spirit is indwelling in all beings of nature. Thoreau also found in Emerson a kindred social and political spirit, a man who believed in the supremacy of individual conscience and who was unafraid to depart from received opinion and the cherished beliefs of the masses. It was at Emerson's prompting that Thoreau began to keep a voluminous journal, from which he mined poems and essays, some of which were published in the new transcendentalist periodical the *Dial*. Thoreau also developed into a highly original writer on natural subjects, producing a series of nature essays for the *Dial*.

In 1845 Thoreau obtained permission to build a small cabin beside Walden Pond on a plot of land that Emerson owned south of Concord. There he resolved to conduct an experiment in self-sufficiency—building the cabin himself and eating only the fruits and vegetables he found nearby and the beans he planted and cultivated. He observed all that was around him, wrote his first book-length work, *A Week on the Concord and Merrimack Rivers* (1849), and continued work on his journals, which he later developed into the text of his masterpiece, *Walden*.

An account of Thoreau's experiment in authentic living (life led according to conscience and a sense of inner values), *Walden* is an extended contemplation of nature, morality, labor, and the spiritual fulfillment that life offers when it is pared down to its essentials. Published in 1854, *Walden* met with little notice. Only after the author's death was it recognized as a classic.

In July 1846, while he was living at Walden Pond, Thoreau was approached by Sam Staples, the local constable and tax collector, who requested that Thoreau render payment of the required poll tax, which he had not paid for some years. When Thoreau refused, protesting that he would not finance a government fighting an unjust war against Mexico (the United States–Mexican War of 1846–1848), Staples took him into custody and deposited him in the Concord jail. The very next morning an unidentified woman—most likely an aunt—paid the tax on his behalf, and Thoreau was released. He was, however, inspired to write an essay, "Civil Disobedience" (not published until 1849), in which he argued that human beings owe allegiance to a law higher and greater than civil law, regardless of the consequences. Imprisonment, Thoreau argued, is actually a condition of freedom under the authority of a government that imprisons anyone unjustly. In his prison cell, he wrote, he realized that he was free, while the citizens walking freely about Concord were, in fact, prisoners. Like *Walden,* "Civil Disobedience" made little impact during Thoreau's life. Only in the twentieth century did it emerge as an inspiring, provocative, influential—and, indeed, explosive—document.

After his Walden sojourn, which ended in 1847, Thoreau made ends meet by working as a surveyor. He continued to explore the nature of New England, and he continued to turn out essays and verse, almost always with nature as their subject. He also became increasingly committed to the abolition movement and was active in the Underground Railroad, assisting fugitive slaves to escape into Canada. Never in robust health, Thoreau died of tuberculosis at age forty-five.

Suggested Reading

Paul, Sherman. *The Shores of America: Thoreau's Inward Exploration.* Champaign-Urbana: University of Illinois Press, 1958.

THREE-FIFTHS COMPROMISE

During the constitutional convention of May 1787, fifty-five delegates from the states gathered to fashion a new constitution to replace the faltering Articles of Confederation. One of the thorniest issues concerned how slaves would be treated when it came to apportioning representation in the House of Representatives. Southerners insisted that slaves should be counted with the free population; northerners countered that, as property, the slaves were not citizens and could not be counted. The convention reached a compromise, which was written into Article I, Section 2, of the Constitution: "Representation and direct taxes will be apportioned among the several states according to respective numbers determined by adding to the whole number of free persons including those bound to service for a set number of years and excluding Indians not taxed three-fifths of all other persons." The phrase "all other persons" referred to the only remaining group in this enumeration: slaves. Thus, for the purposes of determining representation and apportioning taxes, a slave was counted as three-fifths of a person.

The Three-Fifths Compromise clause was canceled in 1865 by the Thirteenth Amendment, which abolished slavery.

Suggested Reading

Huggins, Nathan Irving. *Black Odyssey: The African-American Ordeal in Slavery.* New York: Random House, 1990.

THURMOND, JAMES STROM (1902–)

Strom Thurmond, who turned 100 in 2002, has the distinction of being the oldest U.S. senator in history. His long Senate record reveals him to be a champion of states' rights; an advocate of segregation; and, generally, an opponent of civil rights.

Thurmond was born in Edgefield, South Carolina, and graduated from Clemson College, in Clemson, South Carolina, in 1923. After teaching school he became a lawyer and served as a city and county attorney through much of the 1930s. He was appointed a circuit court judge in 1938 but left the bench in 1941 to serve with great distinction in the 82nd Airborne Division of the U.S. Army, where he earned eighteen battle decorations, including the Bronze Star, the Purple Heart, and the French Croix de Guerre.

Elected governor of South Carolina in 1946, Thurmond showed himself to be a liberal, instituting a slate of reforms that included a significant expansion of the state's educational system. Two years later, however, at the 1948 Democratic National Convention, it was Thurmond who led a rebellion among southern delegates against the regular party's adoption of a civil rights plank. The rebellion gave rise to the States' Rights Democratic Party, which immediately and universally became known as the Dixiecrat Party. As the new party's presidential nominee, Thurmond garnered thirty-nine electoral votes. More significant, in 1954, when he was still a renegade from the regular party and not on the ballot, Thurmond was elected to the U.S. Senate on a write-in vote—the first person ever elected to a major national office by this method. Thurmond's election was a measure of South Carolina's resistance to the federal civil rights initiatives of the period.

In the Senate Thurmond did not disappoint his Dixiecrat constituency. Steadfastly resisting civil rights legislation, he became the personification of such opposition; at the same time, he earned a reputation as an avid supporter of military spending. Reelected on the regular Democratic ticket in 1960, he left the party again in 1964 to support right-wing Republican presidential nominee Barry Goldwater, and it was as a Republican that Thurmond was reelected to the Senate in 1966, 1972, 1978, 1984, 1990, and 1996. During this long period, in what may be considered his most enduring political legacy, Thurmond led the movement of the southern conservative vote away from the Democratic Party, the traditional party of the South, to the Republican Party. Despite his appointment in 1980 as chairman of the Senate Judiciary Committee and in 1981 as president pro tempore of the Senate, Thurmond's intransigence on civil rights—which was, by the 1960s, hopelessly out of step with the legislative mainstream—made him a somewhat marginal figure in national politics. Thurmond decided not to run for reelection in 2002.

Suggested Reading

Bass, Jack, and Marilyn W. Thompson. *Ol' Strom: An Unauthorized Biography of Strom Thurmond.* Atlanta: Longstreet, 1998.

TILL, EMMETT (1941–1955)

The murder of Emmett Till in Mississippi focused national attention on the intensity of southern racial taboos and on the persistence of racially motivated LYNCHING in the South.

Born and raised in Chicago, Till was sent to Mississippi in 1955 to spend the summer with his uncle, Mose Wright. Although he had encountered discrimination and prejudice in the North, he was unfamiliar with the racial taboos of the strictly segregated South. He bragged to boys he met in Mississippi that he had a white girlfriend up north, and he showed them a picture of her. Unbelieving, they dared him to talk to Carolyn Bryant, a white woman who was the wife of a local store owner. (Till may also have been dared to ask her for a date.) Till and the other boys went into the store, purchased some candy, and, according to some accounts, Till hugged Bryant's waist, squeezed her hand, then whistled to her as he left. It is also possible that he had no physical contact but merely said "Bye, baby" to her.

A few days after this encounter, on August 28, 1955, Bryant's husband, Roy, and his half-brother, J. W. Milam, abducted Till from his uncle's house and drove off with him. On August 31, Till's body, naked, one eye gouged out, his skull badly fractured and with a bullet hole in it, was found in the Tallahatchie River near Money, Mississippi. The boy had been beaten so severely that his uncle was able to make a positive identification only because Till was wearing an initialed ring.

Bryant and Milam were arrested for the kidnapping even before the body had been found. Although locals, white and black, expressed shock and horror at the crime, local residents closed ranks as the case gained national notoriety. Till's mother had her son's body returned to Chicago. It was photographed, and the pictures were published in *Jet,* a popular African American magazine, sparking outrage among northern blacks and whites. When the northern press condemned what it called southern barbarity, local sentiment in Mississippi turned to resentment. Whereas, immediately after the crime, no white lawyers had stepped forward to defend Bryant and Milam, now, in the wake of the national condemnation, five prominent attorneys offered their services.

The trial began in a segregated courthouse in Sumner, Mississippi, on September 19, 1955. Just as no black man would dare approach a white woman in the segregated South of 1955, so no black would dare testify against a white person. But Mose Wright did step forward to identify Milam and Bryant, an act that encouraged other black witnesses to speak as well. The testimony notwithstanding, defense attorney John C. Whitten appealed to the all-white jury to return a not-guilty verdict, in defiance of the outside pressure to convict the men. The requested verdict was returned on September 23; the jury foreman later explained that the jurors believed the state had failed to prove the identity of Till's body.

Suggested Reading

Whitfield, Stephen J. *A Death in the Delta: The Story of Emmett Till.* Baltimore, Md.: Johns Hopkins University Press, 1991.

TO SECURE THESE RIGHTS

In 1946, responding to a wave of LYNCHINGS in the South, including that of a black World War II veteran, President HARRY S. TRUMAN created the President's Committee on Civil Rights and charged it with investigating U.S. race relations and making recommendations on the basis of its findings. The committee's 1947 report, *To Secure These Rights,* catalogued the ways in which blacks were systematically denied rights guaranteed by the Constitution. The first civil rights report ever commissioned by the government, *To Secure These Rights* was the strongest federal condemnation of racial inequality and discrimination since RECONSTRUCTION. In 1948, acting partially in response to the committee's recommendations, President Truman issued an executive order desegregating the armed forces. Action on other recommendations would await the emergence of the AFRICAN AMERICAN CIVIL RIGHTS MOVEMENT in the 1960s. (See Appendix A for excerpts from *To Secure These Rights.*)

Suggested Reading

Gardner, Michael R. *Harry Truman and Civil Rights: Moral Courage and Political Risks.* Carbondale: Southern Illinois University Press, 2002.

TRAIL OF TEARS

On December 29, 1835, pursuant to the INDIAN REMOVAL ACT OF 1830, federal negotiators concluded the Treaty of New Echota with representatives of a small minority of the Cherokees, who agreed, ostensibly on behalf of the tribe, to sell to the government seven million acres of tribal land in the Southeast and to relocate, within three years, to Indian Territory (which included what is now Oklahoma and parts of adjacent states). The majority Cherokee party, called the National Party, immediately repudiated the treaty. In response, President ANDREW JACKSON issued orders forbidding the National Party from meeting among themselves to discuss the treaty or alternatives to it. The president also informed the party's leader, John Ross, that the United States would recognize no Cherokee government until removal had been completed, and warned Ross that resistance to removal would be met by military force. Despite the order and the threat, Ross and the National Party campaigned throughout 1835–1838 to expose the fraud of the New Echota treaty. By the time that the 1838 deadline for removal had passed, only about two thousand Cherokee had settled in Indian Territory, and President Martin Van Buren, Jackson's successor, appointed Maj. Gen. Winfield Scott to enforce the removal of the rest by military means.

A highly capable commander and a hero of the War of 1812, Scott effectively campaigned to round up the Cherokees, who were then held in hastily constructed stockades, pending removal. During the summer of 1838, approximately 15,000 Cherokees were confined, chiefly in Georgia. Disease took a substantial toll. The 1,200-mile march to Indian Territory began in the fall of 1838, under the often brutal supervision of the U.S. Army. Hunger and disease (mostly dysentery and cholera) marked the journey, and about 4,000 Cherokees died on what the Indians soon came to call the Trail of Tears.

Among Indian rights activists during the nineteenth and twentieth centuries, and during the height of the Native American civil rights movement of the 1960s, the Trail of Tears figured as a dramatic symbol of the injustices endured by Indians at the hands of the U.S. government.

Suggested Reading

Fleishmann, Glen. *The Cherokee Removal, 1838.* New York: Random House, 1971.

TRIANGLE SHIRTWAIST FIRE

On March 25, 1911, a fire broke out at the Triangle Shirtwaist Company factory in lower Manhattan. The fire began in a rag bin on the eighth floor of the ten-story Asch Building, of which Triangle Shirtwaist occupied the top three floors, and spread very rapidly through a building that was typical of the urban sweatshops of the period—firetraps occupied, for the most part, by poor immigrant laborers, including many women.

As piles of fabric ignited all over the eighth floor, workers' efforts to control the blaze were heroic but ineffective. When employees unrolled the only fire hose on the floor, they discovered that it was rotten and useless; the only alternative was to flee—but the single, poorly maintained fire escape soon gave way under the weight of frantic workers. As for the building's internal stairways, access to one was barred by locked doors, and another was jammed with workers descending from the tenth floor, which had already filled with smoke. For eighth-floor workers, the freight elevator was the only means of escape, and several cutters risked their lives by taking turns operating the elevator to carry their coworkers to safety.

Although eighth-floor employees had phoned throughout the building to warn of the fire, the call had not reached the ninth floor. By the time the ninth-floor workers became aware of the blaze, most avenues of escape were jammed with people or otherwise inaccessible. Some climbed down the freight-elevator cables, others filled the narrow staircase, and still others fell victim to the spindly fire escape.

Some of the seventy employees who worked on the tenth floor were able to escape by way of the stairs, and others climbed onto the roof. Of these, some were rescued by students from New York University, which was located across the street. The students used ladders to bridge the gap between their roof and the roof of the Asch Building.

After it was discovered that fire department ladders reached only to the sixth floor, many workers leaped from window ledges. Firefighters set up nets to catch them, but the weight of the jumpers—especially women who, terrified, held hands and jumped together—proved too great. The nets gave way, and the sidewalk was soon strewn with broken bodies. When the fire was over, 146 of the company's 500 workers had died.

The Triangle Shirtwaist fire brought public demand for new laws to mandate safe working conditions, especially in the teeming sweatshops that offered a livelihood to so many of urban America's immigrants. The New York Factory Investigating Commission was created to examine working conditions in factories throughout the state. After two-and-a-half years the commission released a report that brought about extensive changes to existing laws and ushered in many new regulations. The response to the Triangle Shirtwaist fire may be considered the beginning of a movement to reform working conditions, especially for the nation's poorest laborers, the new immigrants. From this time forward local, state, and federal governments took an increasingly active and interventionist role in promoting worker safety and welfare.

Suggested Reading

Stein, Leon. *The Triangle Fire.* Ithaca, N.Y.: ILR, 2001.

TRUMAN, HARRY S. (1884–1972)

The thirty-third president of the United States, Harry S. Truman succeeded to the presidency in 1945 upon the death of Franklin D. Roosevelt, and, in 1948, was elected in his own right. Truman led the country through the end of World War II and into the treacherous cold war years. The first president to take a decisive stand on civil rights and racial justice, in 1946 Truman created the President's Committee on Civil Rights—which in 1947 produced the landmark report *TO SECURE THESE RIGHTS.* In 1948 Truman issued Executive Order 9981, which ordered the integration of the U.S. armed forces.

Truman was raised in rural Missouri and attended high school in Independence, graduating in 1901. He worked as a bank clerk in Kansas City, then, in 1906, moved to the family farm near Grandview. In 1914, after his father died, Truman took over management of the farm. When the United States entered World War I in 1917, Truman—thirty-three years old and well beyond draft age—enlisted in the army. His National Guard experience earned him an officer's commission, and he was sent to France as captain of a field artillery unit.

After returning to the United States in 1919 and marrying his childhood sweetheart, Elizabeth ("Bess") Wallace, Truman entered into a partnership with Edward Jacobson to open a haberdashery. Successful at first, the business collapsed during a recession in the early 1920s. After being introduced to Thomas Pendergast, the boss of Kansas City's Democratic machine, Truman was elected county judge in 1922. He failed to gain reelection in 1924 but was elected presiding judge of the county court in 1926 and served two four-year terms. Although his first elections were the products of machine politics, the politics Truman practiced was notable for its rigorous honesty and selfless efficiency. He became a very popular figure in the county—and in 1934 the Pendergast machine, somewhat reluctantly, supported his candidacy for the U.S. Senate. He won election and took office in January 1935, soon earning a national reputation as a fighter against fraud and waste in the U.S. military, which was beginning to gear up for the war many anticipated. At the same time he was recognized for his evenhandedness; he was less interested in prosecuting contractors who behaved badly than he was in coaxing them to correct their deficiencies and to deliver whatever was required. It was also while he was a senator that Truman made his first substantive stand for minority rights—sponsoring a bill in 1939 to allow black pilots to serve in the Civilian Pilot Training Program of the U.S. Army Air Corps. This program gave rise to the celebrated TUSKEGEE AIRMEN.

In 1944 President Roosevelt tapped Truman as his running mate for his fourth reelection bid. The pair sailed into office, but less than three months after taking the vice presidential oath, Truman became president within hours after Roosevelt's sudden death from a cerebral hemorrhage on April 12, 1945.

With the exception, perhaps, of Andrew Johnson in 1865, no vice president had ever succeeded to the presidency at such a critical time for the nation, which was in the closing phases of World War II. Among other things, President Truman had to manage a highly uneasy alliance with a rapacious Soviet Union and to decide how, when, and if to employ America's new secret weapon, the atomic bomb. Truman quickly proved himself more than adequate to the tasks that confronted him. His decision to drop atomic bombs on Hiroshima and Nagasaki hastened the surrender of Japan, bringing World War II to an end. During his administration the United States played a central role in founding the UNITED NATIONS to avert the possibility of yet another world war. Truman was also faced with the menace of the rapidly expanding Soviet and Communist Chinese spheres of influence, which resulted in the opening of a "cold war." In what came to be known as the Truman Doctrine, Truman announced that the United States was committed to opposing communist expansion wherever it occurred, by whatever means necessary. In 1947 Truman championed Secretary of State George Marshall's plan to combat communism by delivering vast quantities of financial aid to rebuild a devastated Europe. Together, the Truman Doctrine and the Marshall Plan proved powerful weapons in the postwar ideological struggle between democracy and communism.

Despite Truman's demonstrated competence, few thought he would win the presidency in his own right. Not only did the Republicans have a strong candidate in Thomas E. Dewey, but Truman faced opposition from his own party—most notably from liberal Democrats, who supported the left-leaning Henry A. Wallace, and from southerners, who, alienated by Truman's stance on civil rights, supported South Carolina governor STROM THURMOND, the candidate of the breakaway Dixiecrat party. Truman campaigned with great vigor in 1948 and won the election by a narrow margin.

He began his new term in office with a program of domestic reform dubbed the Fair Deal, which called for increased federal funding for public housing and aid to education, an increase in the minimum wage, a program of national health insurance, and federal enforcement of the civil rights guaranteed by the Constitution. The president was disappointed that, despite Democratic majorities in Congress, few of his Fair Deal measures were passed, and those that did gain passage were enacted in highly diluted form. Nevertheless, the Fair Deal would serve as a model for the social reforms of President JOHN F. KENNEDY and, to an even greater extent, President LYNDON B. JOHNSON.

Just as funding for Johnson's GREAT SOCIETY programs would be sapped by the growing demands for military funding during the Vietnam War, some Fair Deal programs were doubtless cut in favor of military spending during the cold war, and in response to the even greater demands for military expenditures that followed the outbreak of the Korean War in June 1950. If the Korean War had any positive result in the area of minority rights, however, it was in overcoming the reluctance of the commanders of the armed forces to carry out Truman's Executive Order 9981, which mandated racial integration of the services. The war in Korea was fought by a racially integrated army, navy, marine corps, and air force.

The Korean War was a singularly frustrating conflict; Truman saw that his task, as commander in chief, was to contain communism without touching off a thermonuclear World War III. Conservatives demanded a more aggressive policy, and they were outraged when Truman removed Douglas MacArthur, hero of the Pacific theater during World War II, from overall command of U.S. and U.N. forces. By the time Truman left the White House in January 1953, his approval rating had sunk to 31 percent. Only in retrospect did many Americans come to regard him as perhaps the greatest of the postwar presidents.

Suggested Reading

Gardner, Michael R. *Harry Truman and Civil Rights: Moral Courage and Political Risks.* Carbondale: Southern Illinois University Press, 2002.

McCullough, David. *Truman.* New York: Simon and Schuster, 1992.

TRUTH, SOJOURNER (1797–1883)

Born in Ulster County, New York, Sojourner Truth was a black religious leader and social reformer active in the ABOLITION MOVEMENT, the WOMEN'S SUFFRAGE MOVEMENT, and the early WOMEN'S CIVIL RIGHTS movement.

Truth was born to a slave family and worked as a slave until she was given refuge by Isaac Van Wagener, who was able to secure her liberty shortly before New York state legally abolished slavery in 1827. She took the Van Wagener name as her own and was known as Isabella Van Wagener. With the aid of a group of Quakers, she was able to recover her son, who had been sold into southern slavery in violation of New York law. Accompanied by two of the five children she had borne during her time as a slave, she traveled to New York City in 1829 and found employment as a housemaid.

While in New York, Van Wagener became a follower of Elijah Pierson, a charismatic missionary who presided over the Retrenchment Society, an urban evangelical mission. In 1843, after many years of working with the Retrenchment Society, she left New York City and, taking the name Sojourner Truth, obeyed what she interpreted as a divine voice commanding her to "travel up and down the land" preaching the goodness of God and the brotherhood of man. Also in 1843, Truth became active in the abolitionist movement; she soon earned a reputation as a powerful abolitionist speaker and traveled throughout New England and the Midwest. In 1850 she dictated an autobiography, *The Narrative of Sojourner Truth,* which she sold at her lectures to support her work. Early in the 1850s Truth also became active in the field of women's rights; befriended by Lucretia Mott and other prominent suffragists, Truth began traveling and speaking on behalf of women's suffrage as well as abolition.

Truth settled in Battle Creek, Michigan, in the late 1850s. During the Civil War, she worked to obtain supplies for black volunteer regiments. In 1864 she traveled to Washington, D.C., where she was instrumental in integrating the city's streetcars. She was received at the White House by President ABRAHAM LINCOLN. In 1864 she was appointed by the National Freedmen's Relief Association to work with and counsel former slaves to help them settle into free life. Truth came to believe that integration of blacks and whites would be extremely difficult, and she encouraged freedmen to establish black communities in Kansas and Missouri.

Suggested Reading

Painter, Nell Irvin. *Sojourner Truth: A Life, a Symbol.* New York: Norton, 1997.

TUBMAN, HARRIET (CA. 1820–1913)

Born in slavery as Araminta Greene in Dorchester County, Maryland, Tubman later took her mother's first name, Harriet, and, about 1844, married John Tubman, a free black. Harriet Tubman became a fugitive in 1849, fleeing to Philadelphia when she heard a rumor that she was about to be sold and therefore separated from her husband and two children. She covertly returned to Baltimore in 1850 to lead her sister and two children to freedom. This first "mission," in which Tubman risked recapture, was the first of approximately nineteen undertaken in the decade leading up to the Civil War, in which Tubman acted as "conductor" of more than three hundred fugitive slaves, delivering them to Canada via the UNDERGROUND RAILROAD.

Tubman proved herself courageous, charismatic, highly disciplined, and a natural leader. She had the gift of inspiring her "passengers" (fugitives) with something of her own courage and will to persevere. When all else failed, she was known to "encourage" faltering fugitives at the point of a gun.

Once the Civil War broke out, Tubman volunteered her services as a Union army cook and nurse, then undertook especially hazardous duty as a spy and a guide for Union forces in Maryland and Virginia. After the war she founded a home in Auburn, New York, for aged and indigent blacks.

She managed this facility until her death on March 10, 1913. Congress, which had belatedly voted a private bill authorizing a pension for Tubman during the late 1890s, granted her burial with full military honors.

Suggested Reading

Blockson, Charles L. *Hippocrene Guide to the Underground Railroad.* New York: Hippocrene, 1994.

Petry, Ann L. *Harriet Tubman: Conductor on the Underground Railroad.* 1955. Reprint, New York: Pocket, 1984.

TUSKEGEE AIRMEN

In May 1939 two pilots of the National Airman's Association, an organization of black aviators, met with Missouri senator HARRY S. TRUMAN, who agreed to sponsor a bill to allow black pilots to serve in the Civilian Pilot Training Program of the U.S. Army Air Corps (USAAC), which was then an all-white force. In December 1940, under pressure from the administration of FRANKLIN D. ROOSEVELT, the USAAC submitted a plan to the War Department for creating an "experimental" all-black fighter squadron, consisting of thirty-three pilots. The 99th Pursuit Squadron (later renamed the 99th Fighter Squadron), created on January 16, 1941, was to be trained at Tuskegee Army Air Field in Tuskegee, Alabama. On July 19, 1941, the air corps—now redesignated the U.S. Army Air Force—instituted a program to train blacks as military pilots; primary flight training would be conducted by the Division of Aeronautics of the TUSKEGEE INSTITUTE, the celebrated institution for black higher education first led by BOOKER T. WASHINGTON in 1881. After completing primary training at Moton Field on the Tuskegee campus, each pilot was to be sent to the neighboring Tuskegee Army Air Field for advanced flight training, including the transition to combat aircraft.

The first class of Tuskegee airmen graduated on March 7, 1942, and was assigned to the 99th Fighter Squadron under the command of Lt. Col. Benjamin Davis Jr.—one of a handful of black officers in the segregated U.S. Army Air Force. On April 15, 1943, the 99th was shipped out to North Africa to fly fighter escort for bombers. On July 2, 1943, a Tuskegee pilot, Capt. Charles B. Hall, became the first of the airmen to score a victory, shooting down a German FW-190 fighter.

Later in 1943 the 322nd Fighter Group—consisting of three all-black fighter squadrons—was organized, and, with the 99th Squadron, was relocated to bases in Italy as part of the Twelfth Air Force. Although initially met with prejudice from many white pilots, the Tuskegee airmen soon amassed a superb record and were so skilled at bomber escort that Twelfth Air Force bomber crews specifically requested fighter escorts to be drawn from the black units. Four Tuskegee airmen earned the Distinguished Flying Cross, the most coveted decoration in the air force.

In September 1943 the Army Air Force began a program at Tuskegee to train black bomber pilots, but the war ended before any of the pilots saw combat. By war's end, 992 pilots had graduated from Tuskegee training, of whom 450 served in combat. Some 150 Tuskegee airmen died in training or in action. The Tuskegee program also trained blacks as flight engineers, gunners, mechanics, and for other air crew and ground crew duties. At other segregated schools set up in Texas and New Mexico, the Army Air Force trained black airmen as navigators and bombardiers.

The all-black 477th Bombardment Group, created late in the war, was stationed first at Godman Field in Kentucky, then at Freeman Field in Indiana. The Tuskegee airmen of the 477th objected to the particularly stringent segregationist policies of Freeman Field commander Col. Robert Selway, and, on April 5, 1945, black pilots tried to enter the segregated officers' club. Four days later, Colonel Selway ordered all black officers to sign a document stating that they had read and accepted Regulation 85-2, which put forth the segregation policy. One hundred and one officers refused, and the refusal was noted negatively in their service records. It was not until August 12, 1995, that the U.S. Air Force officially cleared the service records of the "Freeman Field Mutineers."

Suggested Reading

Homan, Lynn M., and Thomas Reilly. *Tuskegee Airmen.* Charleston, S.C.: Arcadia Tempus, 1998.

TUSKEGEE INSTITUTE

The Tuskegee Normal and Industrial Institute was created by the Alabama legislature in 1880 to train black teachers, and in 1881 the legislature appointed BOOKER T. WASHINGTON as principal. Under his guidance the school became the nation's foremost institution of higher learning for blacks. In keeping with Washington's philosophy of black economic self-sufficiency and self-determination, the curriculum focused on training teachers and on providing practical training in the manual trades and agriculture. It was not until after Washington's death in 1915 that Tuskegee began to shift from vocational education to academic higher education. A college department was established in 1927, and the school was renamed the Tuskegee Institute ten years later, when it became a fully accredited, degree-granting institution. In 1943 Tuskegee added a program of graduate education; in 1985 the Tuskegee Institute was renamed Tuskegee University.

The university, which enrolls about 3,300 students, continues to be a primarily black institution. Its most illustrious alumnus and faculty member was George Washington Carver, the black chemist whose agricultural research transformed the lowly peanut into a versatile cash crop that diversified the southern agricultural economy and allowed southern farmers, both black and white, to avoid the soil-depleting practice of growing cotton exclusively. During World War II the Tuskegee Institute's Division of Aeronautics conducted primary flight training for the celebrated Tuskegee airmen, the all-black fighter squadrons of the segregated U.S. Army Air Force.

Suggested Reading

Thrasher, Max B. *Tuskegee: Its Story and Its Work.* New York: Negro University Press, 1969.

UNCLE TOM

As used today, "Uncle Tom" is a derogatory term for a black person who is perceived to be excessively deferential, subservient, or sycophantic toward whites. This term was first used in the modern sense in 1943.

"Uncle Tom" comes from HARRIET BEECHER STOWE's 1852 novel *Uncle Tom's Cabin.* As early as 1853, abolitionists used "Uncle Tom" to refer to any poor, patiently suffering slave; opponents of the ABOLITION MOVEMENT used "Uncle Tomism" as a derogatory term for the sanctimonious, sentimental love of blacks that was viewed as characteristic of liberal northern whites (Stuart Berg Flexner, *I Hear America Talking*, New York: Van Nostrand Reinhold, 1976, 3–4).

Suggested Reading

Flexner, Stuart Berg. *I Hear America Talking.* New York: Van Nostrand Reinhold, 1976.

UNDERGROUND RAILROAD

The Baltimore and Ohio Railroad, which began operations in 1828, was the first railroad in the United States. Just a few years later, in the 1830s, the brand-new technology of railroading seemed to many little short of miraculous—and because those in the ABOLITION MOVEMENT sought miracles to enable them to deliver fugitive slaves to safety, "Underground Railroad" was the term they used to refer to the loose network of white abolitionists and free blacks who worked covertly to assist fugitive slaves.

From the time the system began operating, sometime in the 1830s, it relied on railroad metaphors: the escape routes, a network that eventually extended through fourteen northern states and into Canada, were called "lines," and those who actively aided the fugitives were called "conductors." The safe houses along the lines were called "stations," and the fugitives themselves were referred to either as "passengers" or "freight."

Underground Railroad activists included free blacks, former slaves (the most famous of whom was HARRIET TUBMAN), and white abolitionists, clerics, and philanthropists. HARRIET BEECHER STOWE, author of *Uncle Tom's Cabin* (1852), learned much about slave life by working with the Underground Railroad in Cincinnati, which was a very active hub on the fugitive network because of its location just across the Ohio River from slave-holding Kentucky. Levi Coffin, a white Quaker abolitionist, moved from his home in North Carolina first to Indiana and then to Cincinnati, where he became a leading figure in the Underground Railroad and was even called its "president."

The Underground Railroad operated until the outbreak of the Civil War in 1861. For the most part the railroad operated in the North, although "terminals" were located in the upper South and in slaveholding border states. The network did not extend into the deep South, however, because operations in that region would have been impossibly dangerous. Nevertheless, operating the Underground Railroad even in the North was always a risky business. "Conductors" and other supporters of the railroad were subject to threats, beatings, arson, and even murder. As for the fugitives, those who were retaken were usually severely and publicly punished as an example to others.

In 1842 the SUPREME COURT ruled in *Prigg v. Pennsylvania* that states could not be required to enforce the FUGITIVE SLAVE ACT of 1793, which provided for the return of slaves who escaped to free states. This ruling gave impetus to expanded Underground Railroad operations but also increased the intensity of southern opposition to the network. The FUGITIVE SLAVE LAW of 1850, part of the COMPROMISE OF 1850, required free states to enforce the return of escaped slaves, a development that drove the Underground Railroad deeper underground.

It is not known how many slaves found freedom via the Underground Railroad. Estimates vary from 40,000 to 100,000.

Suggested Reading

Blockson, Charles L. *The Underground Railroad: Dramatic Firsthand Accounts of Daring Escapes to Freedom.* New York: Berkley, 1994.

UNITED FARM WORKERS

See NATIONAL FARM WORKERS ASSOCIATION.

UNITED NATIONS

Founded in the wake of World War II and chartered on October 24, 1945, the United Nations (UN) is an international organization whose mission is to maintain international peace and security; to develop friendly relations among nations, in keeping with the principles of equal rights and self-determination; and to encourage international cooperation in addressing a variety of worldwide economic, social, cultural, and humanitarian problems. The phrase "United Nations" was first used during World War II to describe the alliance of nations against Germany, Japan, and Italy. This alliance for the common good and in defense of democratic principles was the basis for the postwar United Nations organization, which was conceived at a 1944 conference at Dumbarton Oaks, a Washington, D.C., estate. In subsequent organizing conferences, the Allies drafted and redrafted proposals for the international body, eager to avoid the weaknesses that had doomed the LEAGUE OF NATIONS, which had been created after World War I pursuant to the Treaty of Versailles. The first UN headquarters was in San Francisco; the permanent headquarters building, in New York City, was completed in 1953.

On December 10, 1948, the UN issued the UNIVERSAL DECLARATION OF HUMAN RIGHTS, the first of many UN declarations, resolutions, and international treaties defining, guaranteeing, and safeguarding human rights, including minority rights. Many of the various UN acts relating to human rights and minority rights reflect the spirit and even the language of such documents as the DECLARATION OF INDEPENDENCE, the U.S. Constitution, and the BILL OF RIGHTS. For the most part the United States has endorsed UN human rights and minority rights initiatives; indeed, ELEANOR ROOSEVELT was one of the principal drafters of the original 1948 declaration.

The most important UN–sanctioned human rights and minority rights agreements to which the United States is a signatory are the following:

- Universal Declaration of Human Rights (1948)
- Convention for the Suppression of the Traffic in Persons and of the Exploitation of the Prostitution of Others (1950)
- Convention Relating to the Status of Refugees (1951)
- Convention on the Political Rights of Women (1953)
- Supplementary Convention on the Abolition of Slavery, the Slave Trade, and Institutions and Practices Similar to Slavery (1956)
- Convention Concerning the Abolition of Forced Labor (1957)
- International Convention on the Elimination of all Forms of Racial Discrimination (1965)
- International Covenant on Civil and Political Rights (1966)
- International Covenant on Economic, Social and Cultural Rights (1966)
- Declaration on the Rights of Mentally Retarded Persons (1971)
- Apartheid Convention (1973)
- Convention against Torture and Other Cruel, Inhuman or Degrading Treatment or Punishment (1984)
- Body of Principles for the Protection of All Persons under Any Form of Detention or Imprisonment (1988)
- Basic Principles for the Treatment of Prisoners (1990)
- Vienna Declaration of the World Conference on Human Rights (1993)
- Convention on Human Rights and Biomedicine (1997).

A number of agreements relate specifically to the rights and welfare of children, including the following:

- Convention Concerning Minimum Age for Admission to Employment (1973)
- Convention on the Civil Aspects of International Child Abduction (1980)
- United Nations Convention on the Rights of the Child (1989)
- Convention on the Protection of Children and Cooperation in Respect of Intercountry Adoption (1993)
- Convention on Parental Responsibility (1996).

Suggested Reading

Axelrod, Alan. *Congressional Quarterly's American Treaties and Alliances.* Washington, D.C.: CQ Press, 2000, 369–393.
Ziring, Lawrence et al. *The United Nations: International Organization and World Politics.* 3d ed. London: International Thomson, 1999.

UNITED STATES V. CRUIKSHANK

The SUPREME COURT decision in *United States v. Cruikshank* (1875) stands as one of the most notorious examples of the high court's dismantling of RECONSTRUCTION. In *Cruikshank,* the Court interpreted the FOURTEENTH AMENDMENT so narrowly as to deny that it applied to cases in which private citizens violate the civil rights of another.

On Easter Sunday 1873 more than one hundred black men were attacked and gunned down in Grant Parish, Louisiana, because they had assembled to assert their right to vote. When other local blacks held a meeting to organize for community protection, the meeting was invaded by about one hundred whites, including members of the KU KLUX KLAN, who seized the blacks' guns and then killed several who were present at the meeting. Under the Enforcement Act, a federal law that was intended to enforce Reconstruction, the whites were convicted of, among other offenses, conspiring to deprive their victims of their constitutional rights to assemble and to bear arms. The convictions, on a total of thirty-two counts, were appealed to the Supreme Court.

In *United States v. Cruikshank,* the Court overturned the federal convictions of the men who had violently raided the assembly in Grant Parish. The high court held that the First and Second Amendments prevented only *federal* interference—not private interference—with the guaranteed rights. Similarly, because the perpetrators of the assault on the meeting were private individuals and not agents of the government, the Court held that the Fourteenth Amendment—which prohibited federal, state, and local governments from depriving people of their rights—did not apply. The high court further held that because the Enforcement Act protected only those rights *granted* by the Constitution—and the rights to assemble and to bear arms were inalienable rights—with which the victims were (in the words of the DECLARATION OF INDEPENDENCE) "endowed by their Creator"—these rights were not protected by the Enforcement Act, under which the charges had been brought. In a final legal twist, the high court did affirm that the right to peaceable assembly was an attribute of national citizenship and, as such, under the protection of the United States; however, the guarantee of this right was interpreted to apply only to the prohibition of any federal encroachment. (See also SLAUGHTERHOUSE CASES.)

Suggested Reading

Goldman, Robert M. *Reconstruction and Black Suffrage: Losing the Vote in Reese and Cruikshank.* Lawrence: University Press of Kansas, 2001.

UNITED STATES V. KAGAMA

In *United States v. Kagama,* decided in 1886, the U.S. SUPREME COURT held that the federal courts, not tribal authorities, have jurisdiction over crimes committed by Indians against Indians on Indian reservations, a ruling that upheld the constitutionality of the INDIAN MAJOR CRIMES ACT of 1885.

The case at issue involved Kagama, an Indian, who had been indicted for the murder of another Indian, Iyouse, on the Hoopa Valley Indian Reservation in California. A third Indian, Mahawaha, was indicted as an accessory. The justices of the U.S. Circuit Court for the District of California were divided in their opinions as to the jurisdiction of the United States over what seemed to be exclusively Indian affairs and, for that reason, certified the case to the Supreme Court.

The concluding portion of the high court's decision reveals the intellectual and political context in which the decision upholding federal jurisdiction was made:

> The power of the General Government over these remnants of a race once powerful, now weak and diminished in numbers, is necessary to their protection, as well as to the safety of those among whom they dwell. It must exist in that government, because it never has existed anywhere else, because the theater of its exercise is within the geographical limits of the United States, because it has never been denied, and because it alone can enforce its laws on all the tribes.

Suggested Reading

French, Laurence. *Indians and Criminal Justice.* New York: Rowman and Littlefield, 1982.

UNITED STATES–MEXICAN WAR

On March 1, 1845, Congress resolved to admit Texas, which had won its independence from Mexico in 1836, to the Union. For years the United States had avoided annexation because it was understood that this step would almost certainly bring war with Mexico. By 1845, however, in the face of English and French overtures of alliance to the Republic of Texas (overtures obnoxious to the United States), and in a congressional climate that favored territorial expansion, the U.S. government was not only willing to risk war but was, in many quarters, eager for it, seeing an opportunity not only to secure Texas once and for all but to acquire more northern Mexican territories.

The annexation of Texas prompted the Mexican government, which had already repudiated the Treaty of Velasco (by which a defeated General Santa Anna had recognized Texas's independence in 1836), to sever diplomatic relations with the United States. President James K. Polk made a last-ditch effort to avoid war by attempting to negotiate claims to Upper California and to resolve disputes concerning the location of the Texas border (the United States held that it was at the Rio Grande, and the Mexicans insisted that the border was properly at the Nueces River). Just to be safe, however, in July 1845 Polk dispatched troops under Brig. Gen. Zachary Taylor to take up positions on or near the Rio Grande to repel any Mexican invasion.

Taylor's force and a Mexican force faced each other across the river for some months. Taylor sent several conciliatory messages to the Mexican commander, who replied to them with hostility. At last, on April 25, 1846, Gen. Mariano Arista crossed the Rio Grande with an invasion force and attacked one of Taylor's advance detachments. Taylor sent a message to President Polk that hostilities had commenced.

In the meantime, Mexican officials summarily rebuffed Polk's offer to negotiate by purchase the acquisition of California and the adjustment of the border with Texas. Largely because of Mexico's refusal to negotiate, Polk was about to ask Congress for a declaration of war. When he received word that Mexican troops had crossed the Rio Grande, however, he suddenly had a more compelling reason to offer Congress. Revising his earlier message, Polk now asked Congress to declare war on the grounds that Mexico had invaded the United States and had killed or injured sixteen U.S. soldiers. Congress approved a declaration of war on May 13, 1846.

That the declaration sailed through Congress belied the deep ambivalence with which the people of the United States actually entered the war. Democrats, especially those in the central and western regions of the South, enthusiastically favored the conflict, seeing in it not only an opportunity for territorial expansion but for the expansion of slaveholding territory. Whigs, especially those in the Northeast, regarded the war as a naked and immoral land grab. Abolitionists looked on the war strictly as an attempt by the slave states to extend SLAVERY and thereby increase their power in Congress.

Thus, from the beginning, the United States–Mexican War had a compelling moral and political dimension. In New England, protest against the war was somewhat organized and was a frequent subject in liberal newspapers and journals. The war moved essayist, philosopher, and naturalist HENRY DAVID THOREAU to a minor act of tax rebellion: arguing that the money would be used to finance an unjust and immoral war, he refused to pay a POLL TAX. His refusal occasioned the essay "Civil Disobedience," which was first published in 1849 and, during the twentieth century, was a profound influence on social activists ranging from MOHANDAS GANDHI to MARTIN LUTHER KING JR.

What was not discussed at the time of the war was its cultural dimension. A chief underlying cause of the 1836 Texas War of Independence was the conviction, on the part of the predominantly Protestant and Anglo-Saxon colonists of Texas, that they were culturally and spiritually superior to the inhabitants of the Catholic and Hispanic country of which Texas was a part. Similar prejudices were at work in the United States–Mexican War, but it was not until the twentieth century, during the height of the HISPANIC CIVIL RIGHTS MOVEMENT of the 1960s, that the war came to be viewed, at least in part, as a product of prejudice in mainstream American society.

As for the course of the war itself, despite division on the home front, every battle ended in an American victory. Taylor's force overcame the invaders, pushed them back, and then penetrated into Mexican territory. Simultaneously, a second force under Col. Stephen Watts Kearny marched to New Mexico and California, where it encountered little resistance. Although Taylor captured the important Mexican city of Monterrey and was victorious over a vastly superior Mexican force at the Battle of Buena Vista in February 1847, he failed to capitalize on these triumphs, refraining from pressing the pursuit. Dissatisfied, President Polk sent another force, under Gen. Winfield Scott, to make an amphibious landing at Veracruz, invade, then march against Mexico City. Veracruz fell in March 1847, and Scott began a stunning and brilliant advance on Mexico City, winning one engagement after another. The Mexican capital fell to him on September 14, 1847.

On February 2, 1848, under the Treaty of Guadalupe Hidalgo, Mexico ceded to the United States all the territory that it had sought—the region encompassed by what is now California, Nevada, Utah, most of New Mexico and Arizona, and part of Colorado—in exchange for $15,000,000 and government assumption of all monetary claims brought against Mexico by U.S. citizens.

As abolitionists had feared, the acquisition of a vast new territory upset the MISSOURI COMPROMISE and threw wide open the issue of extending slavery. Rep. David Wilmot, of Pennsylvania, attempted to add an antislavery amendment to the bill that appropriated the funds necessary to execute the Treaty of Guadalupe Hidalgo. Introduced on August 8, 1846, the Wilmot Proviso would have banned slavery from any territory acquired from Mexico. The proviso failed to pass, but it touched off a new debate on the extension of slavery, which was temporarily resolved by the COMPROMISE OF 1850. (See also STEREOTYPES, ETHNIC AND RACIAL.)

Suggested Reading

Del Castillo, Richard G. *The Treaty of Guadalupe Hidalgo: A Legacy of Conflict.* Norman: University of Oklahoma Press, 1990.

DeVoto, Bernard. *The Year of Decision, 1846.* Boston: Little, Brown, 1943.

Schroeder, John H. *Mr. Polk's War: American Opposition and Dissent, 1846–1848.* Madison: University of Wisconsin Press, 1973.

UNIVERSAL DECLARATION OF HUMAN RIGHTS

On December 10, 1948, in San Francisco, forty-eight of the fifty-six members of the UNITED NATIONS (UN) General Assembly voted to adopt the Universal Declaration of Human Rights (eight members abstained, but none voted against the declaration). The original signatories were Afghanistan, Argentina, Australia, Belgium, Bolivia, Brazil, Burma, Canada, Chile, China, Colombia, Costa Rica, Cuba, Denmark, the Dominican Republic, Ecuador, Egypt, El Salvador, Ethiopia, France, Greece, Guatemala, Haiti, Iceland, India, Iran, Iraq, Lebanon, Liberia, Luxembourg, Mexico, The Netherlands, New Zealand, Nicaragua, Norway, Pakistan, Panama, Paraguay, Peru, the Philippines, Siam, Sweden, Syria, Turkey, the United Kingdom, the United States, Uruguay, and Venezuela. This first UN declaration on human rights was intended to protect the "inherent dignity and . . . the equal and inalienable rights of all members of the human family [as] the foundation of freedom, justice and peace in the world."

Since the 1948 declaration the UN has produced many conventions, declarations, and other documents relating to human rights, the most recent of which is the Vienna Declaration of the World Conference on Human Rights of 1993. (See Appendix A for the text of the Universal Declaration of Human Rights.)

Suggested Reading

Morsink, Johannes. *The Universal Declaration of Human Rights: Origins, Drafting, and Intent.* Philadelphia: University of Pennsylvania Press, 1999.

UNIVERSAL NEGRO IMPROVEMENT ASSOCIATION

The Universal Negro Improvement Association (UNIA) was founded in Jamaica in 1914 by black nationalist leader MARCUS GARVEY; Garvey's goal in founding the UNIA was to inculcate racial pride, create economic self-sufficiency, and, ultimately, to form an independent black nation in Africa. The UNIA attracted only a small following in Jamaica, but when Garvey moved to the United States and established the organization in New York City's Harlem in 1916, the UNIA's membership and influence grew rapidly.

By the early 1920s, the UNIA had some seven hundred branches in thirty-eight states, the largest of which were in Chicago, Los Angeles, and New York. Garvey claimed a membership of six million, but most historians believe membership to have been between 50,000 and 200,000 at the organization's height. The center of UNIA activity was a Harlem auditorium, purchased in 1919 and christened Liberty Hall. Here Garvey addressed mass meetings, often nightly. The year before Garvey had founded *Negro World,* the UNIA newspaper, which had a circulation approaching 200,000. Through the UNIA, Garvey funded several ambitious black enterprises, including the Negro Factories Corporation, the Black Star Line (a steamship company), a chain of restaurants, several grocery stores and laundries, a hotel, and a printing firm. However, these enterprises were undermined by poor, even fraudulent business practices, and in 1922 Garvey and other top UNIA officials were indicted on federal charges of mail fraud in connection with the sale of stock for the Black Star Line. Convicted and sentenced to prison, Garvey began serving his time in 1925. Two years later President Calvin Coolidge commuted his sentence to deportation, and Garvey left for Jamaica; he later settled into obscurity in London.

Without Garvey the UNIA quickly faded; however, as the Universal Negro Improvement Association and African Communities League, the organization continues to function as a "social, friendly, humanitarian, charitable, educational, institutional, constructive and expansive society . . . founded by persons desiring to the utmost to work for the general uplift of the people of African ancestry of the world" (UNIA–ACL, www.unia-acl.org).

Suggested Reading

Cronon, Edmund David. *Black Moses: The Story of Marcus Garvey and the Universal Negro Improvement Association.* Madison: University of Wisconsin Press, 1969.

UNIVERSITY OF CALIFORNIA V. BAKKE

See *REGENTS OF THE UNIVERSITY OF CALIFORNIA V. BAKKE.*

URBAN INSTITUTE

The Urban Institute is a nonprofit, nonpartisan policy research and educational organization that examines the social, economic, and governance problems facing the United States. The institute provides information and analysis to public and private agencies and decision makers and endeavors to increase understanding of policy issues among all citizens. The institute's work is funded by government agencies, private foundations and corporations, institutions such as the World Bank, and donations from private individuals.

The Urban Institute was founded in 1968 to monitor and evaluate the GREAT SOCIETY programs enacted during the administration of President LYNDON B. JOHNSON. Its early mission was to conduct research and analysis to better inform public policy decisions made pursuant to the Great Society programs and to improve understanding of the causes of widespread urban unrest during the period. The institute's early focus was on poverty, financing education, unemployment, urban housing, public transportation, and welfare reform. Today the organization's scope has broadened to include issues such as taxation, criminal justice, governance in new democracies, advocacy, philanthropy, and health care policy.

Urban Institute research draws on data obtained from the Census Bureau and other government agencies; from the records of Medicaid, welfare offices, and other public programs; and from interviews with households, public officials, and businesses. The institute assembles specialist consultants, including economists, public policy analysts, lawyers, statisticians, urban planners, demographers, sociologists, political scientists, and communications experts, to conduct the research and analyze the results. Often the institute works collaboratively with outside researchers, other institutions, and with federal, state, and local agencies.

Suggested Reading

Urban Institute, www.urban.org.

URBAN RENEWAL

The term *urban renewal* was most prevalent in the United States during the 1960s when the programs of social reform undertaken as part of LYNDON B. JOHNSON'S GREAT SOCIETY initiative included large-scale, federally funded slum clearance, urban revitalization, and public housing projects.

The impetus for urban renewal had both ideological and practical origins. First was the principle that everyone has an inherent right to decent housing. Second, slums had long been perceived as breeding grounds for crime, and the belief was that crime could be reduced by the eradication of slums. More recent urban renewal schemes have emphasized the revitalization of business districts as well as residential areas; the assumption is that lively commerce is essential to viable neighborhoods, and that the employment opportunities that businesses provide offer yet another means of curbing crime.

Unfortunately, many urban renewal schemes of the 1950s and 1960s simply demolished entire neighborhoods and erected massive, monolithic housing projects in their place. In many cases the result was not only oppressive for residents but actually conducive to crime, and certainly difficult to police.

All too typical of the early schemes was the Robert Taylor Homes project, which opened in Chicago in November 1962. Consisting of twenty-eight buildings with sixteen stories each—almost 4,300 apartments in all—the Taylor Homes complex extended more than two miles along State Street, on the city's South Side. The world's biggest public housing project ever, it replaced an entire neighborhood. Within three years of opening, however, the housing project had acquired a reputation as an extremely dangerous place. Street gangs commandeered lobbies, stairwells, and even apartments. Rival gangs fought over control of the lucrative drug market within the project, and shoot-outs became routine. Law-abiding residents, caught in the crossfire and randomly victimized, were afraid to leave their apartments. Because police refused to enter the project except in force—to conduct periodic, large-scale raids—individual calls for aid went unanswered. By 1992 only half of the 25,000 residents of Robert Taylor Homes lived there legally. Using federal funds, the city began demolition of the Taylor Homes complex in 1997 and also planned the demolition of other high-rise housing projects, which were written off as dismal failures.

The current approach to urban renewal emphasizes the rehabilitation of existing buildings, and new construction is typically low-rise and designed on a more human scale. In the case of both rehabilitation and new construction, the views of community residents are actively solicited; when possible, residents participate in renovation or construction. (See also HOUSING RIGHTS.)

Suggested Reading

Jacobs, Jane. *The Death and Life of Great American Cities.* 1961. Reprint, New York: Vintage, 1993.

VETERANS' RIGHTS

At times throughout history the U.S. federal government has recognized military veterans as a kind of special minority meriting certain exceptional rights. After the American Revolution, for example, those who had served as officers in the Continental Army were granted tracts of public land. The veterans of World War I were promised monetary bonuses, to be distributed in 1945 (see BONUS ARMY). But the most extensive federal action to extend special rights to veterans came near the end of World War II with passage of the Servicemen's Readjustment Act, signed into law on June 22, 1944, and more familiarly known as the GI Bill of Rights. The bill provided federal aid to help veterans adjust to civilian life, including assistance with hospitalization, purchase of homes and businesses, and education. For education the GI Bill provided tuition; an academic stipend; funding for books, supplies, and equipment; and a variety of counseling services. Almost eight million veterans took advantage of the educational benefits during the first seven years after World War II, greatly enlarging the postwar pool of college-educated men and extending the benefits of higher education to many whose socioeconomic status would have otherwise prevented them from attending college.

The GI bill has been repeatedly renewed, and in addition to the 7.8 million veterans from World War II who received aid under the bill, 2.4 million from the Korean War and 8.2 million post-Korean and Vietnam-era veterans have benefited from it ("Department of Veterans Affairs Fact Sheet," www.va.gov/pressrel/vafacts.htm). In 1930 the Veterans Administration was created to administer veterans' benefits. The Department of Veterans Affairs, a cabinet-level department, replaced this agency on March 15, 1989.

The Veterans Administration and the Department of Veterans Affairs have their critics. During and immediately after the Vietnam War scores of veterans' organizations formed to advocate and lobby for improved benefits and for more efficient and equitable administration of current benefits. Of particular concern is the nation's network of Veterans Administration hospitals, some of which have become little more than dumping grounds for indigent, infirm, and aged veterans. The care in many veterans' hospitals is notoriously poor.

The preferential treatment accorded veterans, especially in civil service hiring in some states, has created controversy among nonveterans who feel discriminated against. In some states veterans also receive special grants of money or substantial tax breaks. Critics of this treatment argue that disabled veterans may deserve special rights, but the indiscriminate distribution of governmental largesse to all who have served is excessive and reduces the pool of welfare funding for the truly needy.

Suggested Reading

Stichman, Barton F., Ronald B. Abrams, and David F. Addlestone, eds. *Veterans Benefits Manual.* Dayton, Ohio: Lexis Law, 1999.

Department of Veterans Affairs, www.va.gov.

VICTIMS' RIGHTS LEGISLATION

In response to widespread concern that the U.S. Constitution, the courts, and the criminal justice system more thoroughly protect the rights of accused criminals than those of crime victims, several states have enacted victims' rights legislation; such laws are often referred to as a "crime victims' bill of rights" or "victims' bill of rights." In most cases the legislation simply gives crime victims—or their lawful representatives (including, in the case of homicide victims, the next of kin)—the right to be informed of and to be present at all crucial stages of criminal proceedings as long as these rights do not interfere with the constitutional rights of the accused. Where relevant, and subject to the same constitutional restrictions, victims are also granted the right to be heard, typically during the sentencing phase of a criminal trial.

Suggested Reading

Hyde, Margaret Oldroyd. *The Rights of the Victim.* New York: Franklin Watts, 1983.

VIETNAM WAR PROTEST MOVEMENT

The United States' deepening involvement in the Vietnam War spawned a protest movement that dovetailed with the African American civil rights movement and the Hispanic civil rights movement as the war came to be viewed as racist in origin and as drawing disproportionately on blacks and Hispanics for military service. Moreover, civil rights activists and advocates for the poor correctly recognized that funding the war was draining money from the welfare and other social programs of the Great Society.

U.S. involvement in Vietnam began as early as August 10, 1950, during the administration of Harry S. Truman. Pursuant to the "Truman Doctrine," which called for the containment of communism wherever it posed a threat of expansion, the president authorized arms shipments to the French, who were struggling to maintain their hold on what was then French Indochina. After the Viet Minh—the communist fighters for Vietnamese independence—defeated the French at Dien Bien Phu in May 1954, France withdrew from Vietnam and the nation was divided—on a supposedly temporary basis—into a communist north and a putatively democratic south. U.S. aid to South Vietnam increased during the administration of Dwight D. Eisenhower, who sent in the first U.S. "military advisers" and was stepped up more vigorously by President John F. Kennedy. Under Kennedy's successor, Lyndon B. Johnson, the war in Vietnam became the subject of a rapidly escalating commitment of troops. On August 2, 1964, two American destroyers were reportedly attacked by North Vietnamese torpedo boats in the Gulf of Tonkin. This prompted Congress to approve the Gulf of Tonkin Resolution on August 7, 1964, which gave the president virtually unlimited authority to take military action in Vietnam. Passage of the resolution marked the beginning of the major phase of the Vietnam War. By 1968 more than a half million U.S. military personnel would be engaged in the war, and total U.S. deaths would reach 58,178. (In 1971 publication of the *Pentagon Papers,* a secret government study leaked to the press, revealed that the U.S. destroyers *Maddox* and *C. Turner Joy* were operating not in international waters, as reported, but provocatively in North Vietnamese territorial waters and that there had been no attack.)

Some of the earliest antiwar protests in the United States were the most extreme. On March 16, 1965, Alice Herz, an eighty-two-year-old survivor of Nazi concentration camps, set herself on fire in Detroit to protest President Johnson's announcement of major troop increases. On November 2, 1965, Norman Morrison, a Quaker antiwar activist, set himself on fire outside the office of Secretary of Defense Robert McNamara—an event McNamara witnessed from his office window. A week later Roger LaPorte, a member of the Catholic Worker movement, set himself ablaze near the United Nations Building in New York.

During 1966 and 1967 college campuses became centers of antiwar protest (see Savio, Mario and Students for a Democratic Society). Typically, organizers of the protests were those groups and individuals already active in civil rights and other social justice movements. Social-activist religious leaders also became involved in the protest movement, most notably the Catholic priests Philip and Daniel Berrigan. On April 4, 1967, in a speech at Riverside Church in New York City, Martin Luther King Jr. announced his opposition to the Vietnam War and deliberately linked his intention to protest the war with his commitment to the cause of civil rights. Perhaps more than any other single moment, King's pronouncement cemented the connection between civil rights and the antiwar protests. While those who opposed the war welcomed King's speech, it did not please all civil rights activists, some of whom believed that King's opposition to the war would alienate the Johnson administration, which had been so friendly to the cause of civil rights, and some simply feared that King's focus on the war would interfere with his leadership of the civil rights movement, a leadership already challenged by the militant Black Power movement.

The Tet Offensive, a massive North Vietnamese multiple-front attack beginning on the Tet lunar holiday, January 30, 1968, initiated a year of intensifying antiwar protests in the United States, culminating that year in the massive protest accompanying the Democratic National Convention in Chicago in August, which ended in a violent confrontation between five thousand protesters and the Chicago Police Department. The year also saw a wave of public draft-card burnings, as young men destroyed the certificates of draft registration they were obliged by law to carry with them.

In March President Johnson announced a bombing halt in North Vietnam, and he further announced that he would not seek reelection. Nevertheless, by the end of 1968 America was badly torn. Protest against the war merged with racial protests and even race riots in a year that saw the assassination of Martin Luther King Jr. and antiwar Democratic presidential hopeful Robert F. Kennedy.

Republican Richard M. Nixon was elected president in 1968 in part on the promise of a plan to end the war—despite the fact that he refused to furnish specifics of the plan during the campaign. The early months of the Nixon administration witnessed only one major antiwar demonstration in April

1969, but on October 15, 1969, a "Vietnam moratorium" was organized nationwide, with an estimated one million people participating in peace rallies and peace vigils, among them fifty members of Congress.

Although President Nixon repeatedly contrasted what he called the "Silent Majority" of Americans who believed in the war and its aims with a vociferous minority of protestors, it became increasingly clear that protestors' ranks were swelling and were coming to include the usually complacent white middle class. January 1970 saw revelations of extensive surveillance and infiltration of the antiwar movement by some one thousand undercover U.S. Army investigators. Under congressional pressure, Secretary of Defense Melvin P. Laird ordered the illegal army spying stopped. In the spring of 1970 forces in Congress, led by Democratic "doves" (as peace advocates were called), began initiatives to introduce legislation to end the war.

Sensing that support for the war was decreasing daily, President Nixon instituted a series of troop withdrawals in a process dubbed "Vietnamization"—the transfer of responsibility for the war from U.S. ground forces to the South Vietnamese army. Simultaneously, however, Nixon stepped up bombing and also ordered an invasion of Cambodia in an effort to interdict supply and communication lines that served communist forces in South Vietnam. This illegal incursion into a neutral Buddhist country touched off new rounds of angry protest at home, including a massive protest at Kent State College in Ohio. On May 4, 1970, four Kent State students were shot to death by Ohio National Guardsmen sent to the campus to restore order. On May 9 some eighty thousand protestors, including ten members of Congress, held an antiwar rally at the Ellipse in Washington, D.C.

The Kent State killings prompted Congress to repeal the Gulf of Tonkin resolution on January 13, 1971, and to introduce new legislation to end the war. The Weather Underground, a splinter faction of the Students for a Democratic Society, set off a bomb in a washroom in the U.S. Capitol on March 1 of that year, and a contingent of Vietnam veterans opposed to the war—Vietnam Veterans Against the War—marched on Washington on April 18, 1971. On April 24 a group calling itself the Mayday Tribe invaded several federal offices in Washington, D.C., causing sporadic work stoppages, and on May 3, 1971, 5,100 police officers and some 10,000 federal troops arrested approximately 7,000 protesters in the nation's capital. On May 4 another 2,700 arrests were made, and on May 5, 1,200 more were taken into custody during a demonstration on the east steps of the Capitol.

The next month the *Pentagon Papers* were published, having been leaked to the *New York Times* by Daniel Ellsberg, one of the government consultants who had worked on the top secret project. Officially titled *The History of the U.S. Decision Making Process in Vietnam,* the *Pentagon Papers* was a study that had been commissioned by Secretary of Defense Robert P. McNamara during the Johnson administration to untangle the long process by which the United States had become mired in the war. The *Pentagon Papers* revealed an unbroken chain of errors, misconceptions, misjudgments, deceptions, and outright lies beginning in the Truman administration and extending through that of LBJ. Publication of the document fueled more antiwar protest and prompted the Mansfield Amendment to a draft extension bill passed on June 24, 1971, calling for the withdrawal of all U.S. forces from Vietnam at the "earliest practical date." Although the phrase was vague, the amendment was the first time in modern U.S. history that Congress officially sought an end to an ongoing war.

During the rest of 1971 and 1972 President Nixon's conduct of the war was a perplexing combination of progressive ground-troop withdrawals to placate the antiwar movement at home and bombing raids to pressure the North Vietnamese into negotiating an acceptable peace. Peace talks, which had been fitful and fruitless, resumed in earnest in Paris on April 27, 1972. This prompted Nixon to increase the military pressure on the North by ordering the mining of North Vietnamese harbors on May 8, 1972—a step taken without consulting Congress. At home the result of this unauthorized action was additional opposition to the war, both inside and outside Congress. However, an initiative to compel the Supreme Court to rule on the constitutionality of the war failed, as the high court voted 7-2 not to hear *Sarnoff v. Schultz* (1972), in which taxpayers challenged the use of foreign aid funds to finance military operations in Vietnam.

On January 23, 1973, President Nixon announced an agreement to end the war, and the war officially ended on January 27. It was March 29 before the last U.S. ground troops were withdrawn, but U.S. bombing continued in Laos and Cambodia in support of South Vietnamese forces, which had invaded to interdict insurgents there. In May 1973 Congress prohibited funding for any combat in Laos and Cambodia, and on November 7, 1973, Congress overrode a presidential veto of the War Powers Act, thereby severely limiting the president's authority to commit U.S. forces without congressional approval.

On August 9, 1974, President Nixon, facing impeachment for the Watergate affair, became the first U.S. president to resign from office. His successor, GERALD FORD, introduced a conditional clemency program for Vietnam-era deserters and draft evaders on September 16, 1974, and Ford's successor, JIMMY CARTER, issued Executive Order 11967 on January 21, 1977, granting virtually unconditional amnesty and pardon for those who had evaded the draft between August 4, 1964, and March 28, 1973.

The Vietnam War radicalized many Americans, and it raised the social consciousness of many others. The perception that minority groups were drafted in disproportionate numbers was not valid, however. Approximately two-thirds of those who served in Vietnam were volunteers, not draftees. Moreover, 86 percent of the men who died in Vietnam were white, 12.5 percent black, and 1.2 percent members of other races. These figures are proportional to the number of whites, blacks, and other groups in the U.S. population at the time (Michael Clodfelter, *Warfare and Armed Conflicts: A Statistical Reference to Casualty and Other Figures, 1500–2000*. 2d ed., Jefferson, N.C.: McFarland, 2002, 782, 788–791). However, the war did divert funds from domestic social programs, and many still ponder whether the United States would have intervened so vigorously in a war between white Europeans rather than Asians.

Suggested Reading

Debenedetti, Charles. *An American Ordeal: The Antiwar Movement of the Vietnam War.* Syracuse: Syracuse University Press, 1990.

Gettleman, Marvin E., Jane Franklin, Marilyn B. Young, and H. Bruce Franklin, eds. *Vietnam and America: A Documented History.* New York: Grove, 1995.

Langston, Thomas S. *Lyndon Baines Johnson.* American Presidents Reference Series. Washington, D.C.: CQ Press, 2002.

VIOLENCE AGAINST WOMEN ACT OF 1998

In 1994 Congress enacted the first Violence Against Women Act, which recognized women as a minority especially vulnerable to certain crimes. The act encompassed an omnibus group of programs to address such offenses as sexual assault and domestic violence, to make gender-motivated violence a violation of civil rights, to address gender inequalities in the criminal justice system, to enhance protection from stalkers and domestic batterers, and to provide special programs for the protection of immigrant women.

Parts of the 1994 legislation were never fully implemented because some of the programs, although authorized, were never funded. In 1998, therefore, a new bill was introduced, which called for the following:

- Extending and funding all of the programs of the 1994 legislation and adding new provisions and new emphases, including funding for constructing battered women's shelters nationwide
- Providing more protection for women who are battered or otherwise abused in the workplace
- Funding to train judges in the law regarding domestic violence
- New initiatives against sexual violence, including support for programs that provide enhanced protection from sexual predators, prohibitions against sexual misconduct in prison between corrections staff and prisoners, creation of a national commission to review standards of practice and training for sexual assault examinations, and establishment of a National Resource Center on Sexual Assault, with a national sexual assault hotline
- Funding to improve health care services for domestic violence and sexual assault survivors
- Enhanced enforcement against gun possession by domestic violence offenders; batterers must pay restitution.

As of late 2002 the bill, having been passed by the House of Representatives in 1998, remains under consideration in the Senate. In the meantime the U.S. SUPREME COURT, in *United States. v. Morrison,* 529 U.S. 598 (2000), held unconstitutional the portion of the 1994 act that provided a federal *civil* remedy for victims of gender-motivated violence. The high court ruled this a violation of the interstate commerce clause and Section 5 of the FOURTEENTH AMENDMENT.

Suggested Reading

"NOW and the Violence Against Women Act," National Organization for Women, www.now.org/issues/violence.

Renzetti, Claire M., Jeffrey L. Edleson, and Raquel Kennedy Bergen, eds. *Sourcebook on Violence Against Women.* Thousand Oaks, Calif.: Sage, 2000.

VOTER REGISTRATION DRIVES

See FREEDOM SUMMER.

VOTING RIGHTS ACT OF 1965

In the wake of demonstrations in Selma, Alabama (see SELMA SNCC–SCLC DEMONSTRATION), the U.S. Congress quickly passed a voting rights act, which prohibited literacy (see LITERACY TESTS FOR VOTING) and other educational requirements for voting in districts where less than half of the voting-age population had been registered as of November 1, 1964. More generally, it prohibited the application of any requirements aimed at "deny[ing] or abridg[ing] the right of any citizen of the United States to vote on account of race or color." The act also provided for federal registrars to oversee voting in problem areas and for federal oversight of voting procedures. The constitutionality of the act was challenged in the SUPREME COURT in 1966 and upheld. Originally, the act was limited to a ten-year term but has been repeatedly renewed and modified. (See Appendix A for the text of the Voting Rights Act of 1965.)

Suggested Reading

Davidson, Chandler. *Controversies in Minority Voting: The Voting Rights Act in Perspective.* Washington, D.C.: Brookings Institution, 1992.

Davison, Chandler, and Bernard Grofman. *Quiet Revolution in the South: The Impact of the Voting Rights Act, 1965–1990.* Princeton: Princeton University Press, 1994.

VOUCHER PLANS

Voucher plans, or school vouchers, are programs currently administered or proposed in several states that distribute monetary vouchers to parents of school-age children, primarily in designated inner-city school districts. The tax-funded vouchers, typically valued between $2,500 and $5,000, may be used by parents to finance tuition at private schools, including those affiliated with religious organizations.

Opponents of voucher plans argue that they violate the Establishment Clause of the First Amendment, which separates church and state, barring governments from supporting religious institutions. Additionally, opponents argue that some private schools eligible for voucher money discriminate on the basis of religion, gender, physical disability, language, and socioeconomic status. Additionally, some fear that funding voucher plans will divert money from public schools and thereby decrease the quality of those schools. Finally, opponents argue that voucher plans will only increase de facto segregation in public education.

Supporters of voucher plans counter that vouchers do not directly support any single religion, because parents have the choice of sending their children to nonsectarian private schools, and that, in any event, no single religion has a monopoly on parochial education. Moreover, they argue that far from diminishing the quality of public education, vouchers offer competition that will challenge public schools to improve and achieve excellence comparable to the private institutions.

Various state voucher plans have been challenged in the courts. On June 27, 2002, in *Zelman v. Simmons-Harris,* the SUPREME COURT reversed an appeals court decision that had struck down an Ohio voucher program on the ground that nearly all the families receiving vouchers attend Catholic schools in Cleveland. In a five to four ruling the Supreme Court held that the voucher program does not constitute government establishment of religion because parents have a sufficient range of choices among secular and religious schools. President George W. Bush voiced approval of the high court's decision. (See also RELIGION, FREEDOM OF.)

Suggested Reading

Jost, Kenneth. "School Vouchers Showdown," *CQ Researcher* 12 (February 15, 2002).

Moe, Terry M. *Schools, Vouchers, and the American Public.* Washington, D.C.: Brookings Institution, 2001.

WALD, LILLIAN D. (1867–1940)

A nurse and social worker, Lillian Wald founded the Henry Street Settlement in New York City in 1893. Like JANE ADDAMS's HULL HOUSE it was a pioneering project in aid and advocacy for the urban immigrant poor.

Wald was born in Cincinnati, Ohio, and moved with her family at an early age to Rochester, New York, where she received a private-school education. Her privileged background afforded the leisure to become a young socialite, but she soon abandoned this way of life and in 1889 enrolled in the New York Hospital Training School for Nurses. After graduating in 1891 Wald worked as a nurse in the New York Juvenile Asylum, then took advanced training during 1892–1893 at the Woman's Medical College. Subsequently, she was asked to teach a course in home nursing for the poor immigrants of New York's Lower East Side. This position acquainted her with the conditions of New York slum life, and in 1893, with Mary M. Brewster, Wald left the medical college to take up residence on the Lower East Side, where she set up a practice as a visiting nurse. In 1895, backed by philanthropist Jacob H. Schiff and others, Wald opened the Nurse's Settlement, which by 1929 was staffed by more than two hundred and fifty visiting nurses.

During the 1910s the Nurse's Settlement diversified as the Henry Street Settlement, offering, in addition to the visiting nurses service, training for nurses as well as educational programs for the community and recreational clubs for neighborhood youth. The Henry Street Settlement became a nationally recognized center for innovation in social work as well as the pioneering institution in the visiting nurse profession. In 1902 nursing service was initiated in a local public school. The program proved so successful that the New York City Board of Health introduced it citywide, the first school nursing program in the world. Wald also consulted with insurance companies, successfully urging the Metropolitan Life Insurance Company to institute nursing services for its industrial clients in 1909; other insurance companies followed suit.

In 1912 Wald persuaded the American Red Cross to begin a district nursing service to serve patients in rural areas and small towns; the program was called Town and Country Nursing Service. Also in 1912 Wald founded the National Organization for Public Health Nursing and served as its first president.

Wald lobbied Congress and other governmental bodies to establish educational, recreational, social, and health programs in poor neighborhoods nationwide. Thanks in large part to her work, Congress created the U.S. Children's Bureau in 1912.

Wald's reform efforts extended to many areas. She was cofounder—with Florence Kelley—of the National Child Labor Committee and the Women's Trade Union League. In 1914, with Kelley and Jane Addams, Wald founded the American Union Against Militarism and served as its first president. However, during World War I she contributed to the war effort as chair of the committee on home nursing of the Council of National Defense and, during the disastrous influenza pandemic of 1918–1919, Wald headed the Nurses' Emergency Council.

Wald wrote two memoirs, *The House on Henry Street* (1915) and *Windows on Henry Street* (1934).

Suggested Reading

Block, Irving. *Neighbor to the World: The Story of Lillian Wald.* New York: Crowell, 1969.

WALLACE, GEORGE C. (1919–1998)

Four-time governor of Alabama and a third-party presidential candidate, George Corley Wallace became an icon of southern resistance to integration in the 1960s.

The son of an Alabama farmer, Wallace put himself through the University of Alabama Law School, from which he graduated in 1942. He served in the military during World War II, then was appointed assistant state's attorney for Alabama in 1946. After two terms in the state legislature

Wallace was elected a judge of the Third Judicial Circuit of Alabama in 1953. He was defeated in his bid for the Democratic gubernatorial nomination in 1958 largely because of his moderate views on integration. His opponent, in contrast, was an outspoken segregationist who received the endorsement of the KU KLUX KLAN. This experience moved Wallace to take a firmly segregationist stand, and he earned a reputation as the "fighting judge" when he defied and attempted to block a federal probe of Alabama's ongoing efforts to disenfranchise black voters. Wallace's growing reputation as a segregationist allowed him to capture the Democratic nomination for governor in 1962, which, in the "solid South" (solidly Democratic) of that era was tantamount to election. His inaugural address pledged "segregation forever" (see "SEGREGATION TODAY, SEGREGATION FOREVER" SPEECH). True to his word, he defied federal efforts to integrate the University of Alabama and other institutions—although he was forced to back down when National Guard troops arrived to enforce the federal integration orders.

Wallace's defiance appealed to a majority of white Alabamians, but his angry rhetoric made him a symbol of all that blacks and northern moderates and liberals found hateful about racial attitudes in the South. Arguably, Wallace's intransigence was so uncompromising that it actually accelerated federal efforts to enforce integration throughout the South.

Alabama law prevented Wallace from serving a third consecutive term as governor, so his first wife, Lurleen Wallace, was elected in 1966. She succumbed to cancer while in office in 1968, the year Wallace ran for president as candidate of the American Independent Party. He captured 13 percent of the popular vote and carried five southern states.

Wallace was reelected Alabama governor in 1970. While campaigning for the Democratic presidential nomination on May 15, 1972, in Laurel, Maryland, he fell victim to an assassin's bullet, which left him a paraplegic. Despite his disability Wallace was reelected Alabama governor in 1974, and in 1976 he again campaigned for the Democratic presidential nomination.

In 1980 the man who had promised "segregation forever" suddenly renounced this ideology and publicly sought both reconciliation with and forgiveness from the black community. As remarkable as this ideological change was, even more extraordinary was the degree of black support Wallace received when he ran for governor in 1982. Thanks in part to the black vote, he was reelected. In poor health, Wallace retired from public life in 1987.

Suggested Reading

Carter, Dan T. *The Politics of Rage: George Wallace, the Origins of the New Conservatism, and the Transformation of American Politics.* 2d ed. Baton Rouge: Louisiana State University Press, 2000.

Frady, Marshall. *Wallace.* New York: Random House, 1996.

WARDS COVE PACKING CO. V. ANTONIO (1989)

On June 5, 1989, the SUPREME COURT ruled on a suit against an Alaskan salmon cannery. The suit alleged that jobs at the Wards Cove Packing Company were of two general types: unskilled "cannery jobs," which were held mainly by nonwhites, and skilled "noncannery jobs," which were held mainly by whites. A group of nonwhite cannery workers filed a class-action lawsuit in district court under Title VII of the CIVIL RIGHTS ACT OF 1964, claiming that the company's hiring and promotion practices were responsible for the racial stratification of the work force and that nonwhites were denied employment as skilled workers on the basis of race.

The district court rejected these claims, finding that nonwhite workers were overrepresented in cannery jobs because many of the jobs were filled under an agreement with a predominantly nonwhite union.

The court of appeals reversed part of this decision, holding that respondents had made a prima facie case of "disparate impact"—the use of any employment practice that has an unjustified adverse impact on members of a protected class, even if the use of that practice is without intent to discriminate. That is, the appeals court relied solely on the statistics presented, which showed a high percentage of nonwhite workers in cannery jobs and a low percentage of such workers in noncannery positions. The appeals court concluded that once a plaintiff class has shown disparate impact caused by specific, identifiable employment practices, the burden shifts to the employer to prove the business necessity of the challenged practice. In this, the appeals court followed the precedent of the Supreme Court decision in *GRIGGS V. DUKE POWER CO.*

In hearing *Wards Cove,* however, the Supreme Court imposed a tougher burden on the plaintiff, ruling that when plaintiffs allege a disparate impact violation of Title VII, they must demonstrate that specific practices—not the cumulative effect of the employer's selection practices—adversely affected a protected group. It is insufficient to rely on statistics alone. Moreover, the high court held that to defend against a charge of disparate impact an employer need only produce evidence of a business *justification* (not a business *necessity*) for the practice—in this case, the union hiring agreement—and the burden of proof of disparate impact always rests on the employee.

Suggested Reading

Anderson, Elijah, and Douglas S. Massey, eds. *Problem of the Century: Racial Stratification in the United States.* New York: Russell Sage Foundation, 2001.

Haggard, Thomas R. *Understanding Employment Discrimination.* New York: Lexis, 2001.

WAR ON POVERTY

In a special message to Congress on March 16, 1964, President LYNDON B. JOHNSON presented a "Proposal for a Nationwide War on the Sources of Poverty" in the form of an omnibus bill.

The War on Poverty was intended to be the cornerstone of Johnson's GREAT SOCIETY, and the Economic Opportunity Act of 1964 was signed into law on August 20, 1964. The Office of Economic Opportunity administered programs authorized by the law, including VISTA (Volunteers In Service To America), the Job Corps, the Neighborhood Youth Corps, Head Start, Foster Grandparents, and programs offering adult basic education, family planning, community health, congregate meal preparation, economic development, legal services, and summer youth activities. Also funded were community and senior centers, as well as other programs. The act emphasized programs that fostered community participation.

Funding for the War on Poverty, especially for the Office of Economic Opportunity, was never adequate, and the increasing demands of the Vietnam War reduced funding even more sharply. Many of the programs were discontinued before the end of the decade. (See Appendix A for excerpts from Lyndon Johnson's "War on Poverty" speech, which presents the major components of the Economic Opportunity Act.)

Suggested Reading

Quadagno, Jill. *The Color of Welfare: How Racism Undermined the War on Poverty.* New York: Oxford University Press, 1996.

Zarefsky, David. *President Johnson's War on Poverty: Rhetoric and History.* Tuscaloosa: University of Alabama Press, 1986.

WARREN, EARL (1891–1974)

Earl Warren presided as chief justice of the United States from 1953 to 1969, a period of great social ferment that encompassed the height of the AFRICAN AMERICAN CIVIL RIGHTS MOVEMENT. The "Warren Court" was marked by liberal activism, which brought important changes in constitutional law, especially as that law affects race relations and criminal procedure.

Warren came from a blue-collar Los Angeles family—his father was a railroad worker—and Warren earned his law degree from the University of California, Berkeley. He never entered private practice but served as district attorney for Alameda County, California, from 1925 to 1939, when he was appointed attorney general of California. His advocacy of the internment of American citizens of Japanese birth or ancestry at the outbreak of World War II belied his later social liberalism (see JAPANESE INTERNMENT). In 1943 Warren was elected governor of California as a Republican and served for three terms.

President DWIGHT D. EISENHOWER nominated Warren as chief justice of the United States in 1953, expecting that he was putting into the position a moderate conservative. Warren's liberal activism later prompted Eisenhower to declare that the nomination had been the biggest mistake of his administration.

The first major civil rights case heard by the Warren Court was the 1954 *BROWN V. BOARD OF EDUCATION OF TOPEKA, KANSAS,* in which the court unanimously overturned *PLESSY V. FERGUSON* and the "SEPARATE BUT EQUAL" DOCTRINE. *Brown* not only resulted in the integration of public education but opened the door to general integration and the end of all *de jure* racial discrimination. It provided the firm legal foundation on which the major phase of the civil rights movement was built.

As great an impact as the Warren Court had on race relations, its affect on the administration of criminal justice was at least as profound. In *Watkins v. United States* (1957), Warren wrote the majority opinion upholding the right of a witness to refuse to testify before a congressional committee. This was a major step toward ensuring that the abuses of the HOUSE UN-AMERICAN ACTIVITIES COMMITTEE and Senator JOSEPH MCCARTHY would not occur again so readily. Even more far-reaching was the impact of *MIRANDA V. ARIZONA* (1966), which held that the police must inform a suspect of his constitutional right to avoid self-incrimination by remaining silent during custody and interrogation and to have counsel present before any questioning takes place; further, the suspect must be informed that counsel will be provided at no charge if he or she cannot afford counsel. *Miranda* ruled that any confession or inculpatory statement obtained without having informed the suspect of his rights is inadmissible in court. No single SUPREME COURT decision has more powerfully affected the way police work than *Miranda v. Arizona.*

Warren also wrote the majority opinion in a landmark case relating to the apportionment of representation. In *Reynolds v. Sims* (1964), the Warren Court held that representation in state legislatures must be apportioned on the basis of population rather than on geographical area. The principle affirmed is that legislators represent people rather than acreage.

President LYNDON B. JOHNSON appointed Warren chairman of a special commission to investigate the November 22, 1963, assassination of JOHN F. KENNEDY, an event instantly shrouded in allegations of conspiracy. The so-called "Warren Commission" issued its findings ten months later—although the report, which identified Lee Harvey Oswald as the lone assassin of the president, hardly laid to rest all of the conspiracy theories.

Warren retired from the Supreme Court and from public life in 1969. He died on July 9, 1974.

Suggested Reading

Cray, Ed. *Chief Justice: A Biography of Earl Warren*. New York: Simon and Schuster, 1997.

WASHINGTON, BOOKER T. (1856–1915)

Booker T. Washington was born a slave in Franklin County, Virginia, and rose to become the foremost black educator and reformer of his time, developing the Tuskegee Institute into the most famous black educational institution in the country.

After emancipation Washington moved with his family to Malden, West Virginia, where at age nine he was put to work at a salt furnace and then in a coal mine. In 1872 Washington enrolled at the Hampton Normal and Agricultural Institute in Virginia, supporting himself by working as a janitor. After graduating in 1875 Washington returned to Malden and taught school during the day and adult education classes at night. In 1878 he enrolled at Wayland Seminary in Washington, D.C., and in 1879 was appointed to the faculty of Hampton Normal.

In 1881 Alabama officials chose Washington to serve as principal of a newly established state school for blacks at Tuskegee. Called Tuskegee Normal and Industrial Institute, the school had only two buildings and almost no educational equipment of any kind. Nevertheless, for the next thirty-four years Washington developed it into a multifaceted training center intended to develop economic self-sufficiency in its 1,500 students. In its early years Tuskegee was not a college but a vocational school emphasizing the manual arts and agriculture. By training blacks to be economically autonomous, Washington believed that, eventually, they would also achieve social, political, cultural, and legal equality with whites; however, until that time came, he was willing to postpone equality. This viewpoint was called "gradualism" by some and "accommodation" by others, because it accommodated white racist conceptions of blacks. Washington believed that such accommodation was necessary to obtain the immediate economic support of the white community. In fact, his approach was successful in garnering that support; Tuskegee Institute became a handsomely endowed institution.

Washington gave succinct voice to his philosophy in the "Atlanta Compromise Speech" delivered on September 18, 1895, to a racially mixed audience at the Atlanta Exposition. Holding up his hand he declared: "In all things that are purely social we can be separate as the fingers, yet one as the hand in all things essential to mutual progress." This position outraged such progressive black leaders as W. E. B. Du Bois, who participated in the founding the National Association for the Advancement of Colored People largely as a means of countering what he believed was a dangerous and degrading doctrine.

Although Washington was a controversial—even despised—figure among many black intellectuals, most blacks and many whites admired him and approved of his goal of achieving black economic self-sufficiency. He became a man of considerable influence, not only in the black community but in society generally. White philanthropists and the government sought his advice before funding black individuals and institutions seeking money. He also reached out to the public with a dozen books, including his classic autobiography, *Up from Slavery* (1901).

Suggested Reading

Harlan, Louis R. *Booker T. Washington: The Wizard of Tuskegee, 1901–1915*. New York: Oxford University Press, 1986.

Verney, Kevern. *The Art of the Possible: Booker T. Washington and Black Leadership in the United States, 1881–1925*. New York: Routledge, 2001.

WASHINGTON, D.C., VOTING RIGHTS IN

Some citizens of Washington, D.C., view themselves as a minority uniquely discriminated against. The District of Columbia is the only U.S. region or territory that lacks congressional representation but that requires payment of federal taxes and performance of such duties as registration for the military draft and service on federal juries.

The U.S. Constitution assigns to Congress special authority to administer the District of Columbia through legislation. The Constitution does not explicitly prohibit D.C. from voting representation in Congress, but because the District is not a state, it is not automatically accorded such representation. As it currently stands the District of Columbia not only lacks federal representation, its internal affairs are subject to the approval of the representatives of all the other states, who have final say over how D.C. uses the tax funds collected from residents.

The site for the District of Columbia was acquired in 1790 from land ceded by Maryland and Virginia. For a decade residents continued to vote in their former states, and some even ran for Congress. In 1800 Congress voted to assume complete control over the District of Columbia, and federal representation for D.C. residents ended. It was not until 1871 that an elected position of a nonvoting delegate to the House of Representatives was created as Congress established a territorial government for the District. Four years later Congress revoked the territorial government and abolished the position of nonvoting delegate.

In 1961 ratification of the Twenty-third Amendment granted Washington, D.C., residents the right to vote in presidential elections for the first time, and the District was apportioned members of the Electoral College as if it were a state. In 1970 the U.S. House of Representatives restored to D.C. its nonvoting delegate and, in 1978 Congress approved the D.C. Voting Rights Amendment, which granted D.C. the congressional representation (two senators and one representative) it would be entitled to if it were a state. The amendment, however, fell far short of ratification by the states within the mandated seven years.

In 1993 the U.S. House of Representatives voted to allow the delegates from the District of Columbia and the four U.S. territories to vote on the floor of the House in the Committee of the Whole; however, in any case where the vote of the delegate would be decisive, a second vote, from which the delegate is excluded, is required. Two years later the District of Columbia's delegate was stripped of voting privileges altogether.

In 2000 a federal court of appeals rejected a suit brought by D.C. residents in an effort to gain full voting representation in Congress. After the U.S. SUPREME COURT declined to hear the case on appeal, the city of Washington, D.C., adopted a new license plate motto, "taxation without representation." In 2001 D.C. delegate Eleanor Holmes Norton and Sen. Joseph Lieberman, D-Conn., introduced the "No Taxation without Representation Act" in both houses of Congress. The act would exempt D.C. residents from paying federal income taxes until they are given full voting representation. As of September 2002, the act is still pending in Congress.

As of September 2002 three lobbying organizations, DC Rabble, DC Watch, and DC Vote, continue to work toward winning representation for the citizens of the nation's capital.

Suggested Reading

Best, Judith. *National Representation for the District of Columbia*. Frederick, Md.: University Publications, 1984.

WASHINGTON, GEORGE (1732–1799)

As the first president of the United States, George Washington guided the nation through its first years under the Constitution and shaped the office of chief executive. Indeed, one of Washington's greatest contributions to democracy and, ultimately, to minority rights, was the dominant element of restraint he introduced into the office of the presidency. His popularity was such that, elected unanimously by acclamation, Washington could have styled himself a dictator; instead, he carved out a place for the office of the executive that worked collaboratively with the legislative branch, and he introduced the tradition, formalized in the twentieth century by the Twenty-second Amendment, limiting the president to two terms of service.

Washington was born in Westmoreland County, Virginia, and was raised by his eldest brother, Lawrence, after their father's death on April 12, 1743. Given scant formal education, Washington learned the surveyor's trade and from 1749 to 1751 served as surveyor for Culpepper County. The death of his brother and his brother's daughter, both in 1752, left Washington a large inheritance, including the majestic Mount Vernon plantation estate. His status as a new member of the landed gentry prompted Washington's appointment, late in 1752, as adjutant for southern Virginia with the militia rank of major. The following year he was also named adjutant of Northern Neck (the territory between the Rappahannock and the Potomac rivers) and the Eastern Shore, and he saw extensive service as a commander of Virginia forces during the French and Indian War beginning in 1753. Earning a reputation for bravery and leadership, Washington was elected to Virginia's House of Burgesses in 1758, and after marrying Martha Dandridge Custis, a wealthy, childless widow, in 1759, he also served as justice of the peace for Fairfax County—a position he held through 1774.

Early on Washington became active in the revolutionary movement, serving in the first Virginia provincial congress in August 1774 and as one of seven Virginia delegates to the First Continental Congress (September 1774) and Second Continental Congress (May 1775). When war erupted in earnest Congress appointed Washington general-in-chief of the Continental forces. Throughout the long war for independence from 1775 to 1783, Washington managed to hold the army together and to use it effectively against the most powerful military organization in the world.

Following the Peace of Paris that ended the revolution in 1783, Washington could probably have assumed virtually unlimited powers. Instead, his task completed, he took leave of his troops at Fraunces Tavern in Manhattan on December 4, 1783, then returned to what he thought would be the life of a gentleman farmer at Mount Vernon. However, he continued to bring unity to the disparate and now-independent states, and he was elected president of the Constitutional Convention in Philadelphia in 1787. In February 1789 he was unanimously elected as the first president of the United States and was inaugurated on April 30. He was reelected to a second term in December 1792 but explicitly declined a third.

The Constitution is silent on many details of the executive branch, so that Washington took it upon himself to create the key executive departments, naming THOMAS JEFFERSON as secretary of state, Henry Knox as secretary of war, Alexander Hamilton as secretary of Treasury, Samuel Osgood as head of the post office, and Edmund Randolph as attorney general. By Washington's conduct and attitude he shaped the presidency as an office characterized by the moderate exercise of power. He avoided conflict with Congress, believing it was not the chief executive's duty to propose legislation. He also opposed the formation of political parties—although, by the time of his second term, two opposing parties had been formed: the conservative Federalists, headed by John Adams and Alexander Hamilton, and the more liberal Democratic-Republicans, headed by Thomas Jefferson.

Washington did assert the authority of the federal government in his handling of the Whiskey Rebellion, a minor but consequential tax revolt among Pennsylvania farmers in 1794, and in his defense of United States sovereignty against the efforts of the French minister Citizen Edmond Charles Genêt to enlist American privateers in a French war against England.

In March 1797, having declined a third term, Washington retired to Mount Vernon, returning to public life very briefly as army commander in chief during a crisis with France, which threatened to flame into full-scale war in 1798. Washington's retirement was cut short by a bout of laryngitis, which proved fatal. He died on December 14, 1799.

Suggested Reading

Flexner, James Thomas. *George Washington and the New Nation, 1783–1793.* Boston: Little, Brown, 1970.

Rhodehamel, John, ed. *George Washington: Writings.* New York: Library of America, 1997.

WATTS (LOS ANGELES) RACE RIOT (1965)

On Friday, August 13, 1965, a white police officer patrolling the predominantly black Watts neighborhood of Los Angeles made what should have been a routine arrest for drunk driving. However, in the racially charged atmosphere of the summer of 1965, a year that had already seen police brutality in the South (see SELMA SNCC–SCLC DEMONSTRATION) and the assassination of MALCOLM X, the sight of a white officer arresting a black man was enough to set off a powder keg. A crowd accumulated at the scene of the arrest, cries of police brutality were raised, and over the next six days the neighborhood erupted into a RACE RIOT.

The National Guard was called in to assist the Los Angeles police, but before the battle was over thirty-five people had been killed, almost all of them black, and more than a thousand injured. Property damage totaled approximately $200 million.

As many observers, white and black, saw it, Watts signaled a profound shift in attitude among African Americans. For many, the NONVIOLENCE DOCTRINE of MARTIN LUTHER KING JR. had come to seem passive and ineffectual, especially after the violence of the Selma marches. Watts was the first of many major urban race riots. In 1966 riots broke out in New York and Chicago. In 1967 Newark and Detroit were hardest hit. And in 1968, after King's assassination, more than a hundred cities erupted.

Suggested Reading

Horne, Gerald. *Fire This Time: The Watts Uprising and the 1960s.* Charlottesville: University Press of Virginia, 1995.

WELFARE STATE

In a "welfare state" the government actively promotes the protection and economic and social well-being of all citizens, regardless of their socioeconomic status. A welfare state is founded on principles of equal opportunity, the equitable distribution of wealth, and public assistance to ensure that even the poorest have access to the means of subsistence. Although the principles of a welfare state may be applied in varying degrees and in a variety of government types, all welfare states provide some form of social insurance—for example, Social Security and related programs—generally financed by compulsory contributions from workers' wages.

Prior to the New Deal and other social programs introduced during the administration of FRANKLIN D. ROOSEVELT, the United States had very few hallmarks of a welfare state. The GREAT SOCIETY programs of the LYNDON B. JOHNSON administration introduced additional elements. While some conservatives bemoan the transformation of the nation into a welfare state, the United States remains far less a welfare state than the nations of western Europe, which typically offer full comprehensive health coverage and state-subsidized education through the university level.

Suggested Reading

Lin, Ann Chih, ed. *Welfare Reform*. CQ's Vital Issues Series. Washington, D.C.: CQ Press, 2002.

Trattner, Walter I. *From Poor Law to Welfare State: A History of Social Welfare in America*. New York: Free Press, 1999.

"WE SHALL OVERCOME"

By the mid 1960s "We Shall Overcome" had become the unofficial hymn and anthem of the African American civil rights movement. The song was sung at meetings, rallies, and protests. The lyrics were adapted from a gospel song of 1900, "I'll Overcome Some Day," by Charles Tindley, and the melody from a spiritual, "No More Auction Block for Me," which dates from before the Civil War.

Two musicians associated with the Highlander Research and Education Center (formerly called the Highlander Folk School, a center devoted to the culture and social well-being of the Appalachian South), Guy and Candie Carawan, are generally credited with having adapted the Tindley lyrics and the old spiritual to produce the civil rights anthem. (See Appendix A for the lyrics of "We Shall Overcome.")

Suggested Reading

Carawan, Guy, and Candie Carawan, eds. *Sing for Freedom*. Bethlehem, Penn.: Sing Out!, 1997.

WHEELER-HOWARD INDIAN REORGANIZATION ACT

Also called the Wheeler-Howard Act and the Indian Reorganization Act, the legislation became Public Law 73-576 on June 18, 1934, and was part of the "Indian New Deal" introduced during the administration of Franklin D. Roosevelt. The act was intended to undo the damage to Native American well-being and culture created by the Dawes Severalty Act of 1887 by reducing federal control of Indian affairs and increasing tribal self-government and responsibility.

Major provisions of the act greatly curtailed allotment of communal tribal lands to individuals (who typically sold the land to whites), mandated the return of "surplus" Indian lands to the tribes rather than distribution to homesteaders, promoted the creation of written tribal constitutions, empowered tribes to assume management of many of their internal affairs, and funded a revolving credit program for tribal land purchases, for education, and for creating tribal governments.

Despite federal retrenchment on many aspects of Native American affairs during the 1950s, the Wheeler-Howard Indian Reorganization Act improved life for Native Americans, and it remains today the foundation for all federal legislation relating to Indian affairs. (See Appendix A for the act. See also Native American civil rights movement and Native Americans.)

Suggested Reading

Taylor, Graham D. *The New Deal and American Indian Tribalism: The Administration of the Indian Reorganization Act, 1934–45*. Lincoln: University of Nebraska Press, 2001.

WHITE SUPREMACY MOVEMENTS

White supremacists share a belief in the supremacy of the white race above all others and a further belief that this supremacy confers on whites the right and duty to dominate and subjugate other races. Typically, white supremacists regard minorities as distinct races. Jews, for example, are not considered members of the white race but of an inherently inferior Jewish race. Indeed, most American white supremacists believe that the United States is not only properly a white nation, but a Christian (that is, Protestant, not Catholic) nation, and that the white Christian race constitutes the chosen of God. It is, therefore, a sacred duty of the white race to resist integration and the "mongrelization" of the white race by contact with other races. It is also a sacred duty to suppress, by violence if necessary, the presence and influence of nonwhites in American government, society, and all institutions.

According to the Center for Democratic Renewal, a nonprofit research clearinghouse for information on white supremacist hate groups and hate crimes in the United States, only some twenty-five thousand Americans are currently "hardcore ideological activists for the white supremacist movement." These individuals belong to about three hundred different organizations, ranging from religious organizations to tax protest groups to the larger militant bodies, including the Ku Klux Klan (KKK), the Aryan Nations, and the American Nazi Party. While membership in such groups may number no more than twenty-five thousand, an estimated one hundred and fifty thousand to two hundred thousand individuals subscribe to publications produced by some of these groups and attend marches and rallies (Loretta

J. Ross, *White Supremacy in the 1990s,* Atlanta: Center for Democratic Renewal, 1994, http://nwcitizen.com/publicgood/reports/whitesup.htm). Doubtless, Internet websites maintained by some white supremacist groups reach many more people.

Historically, in the United States the KKK has been the largest and best-known white supremacist group, having come into existence during RECONSTRUCTION following the Civil War, with two major resurgences during the 1920s and again in the 1960s—the latter corresponding to the rise of the AFRICAN AMERICAN CIVIL RIGHTS MOVEMENT. During the mid-1960s KKK membership may have topped forty thousand; however, by the 1970s the KKK receded in importance relative to the rise of neo-Nazi groups.

Fascist and Nazi organizations first formed in the United States shortly after fascism took hold of Italy under Benito Mussolini during the 1920s and National Socialism came to dominate Hitler's Germany in the 1930s. The American organizations defined themselves chiefly in opposition to left-wing politics—communism—and to Jews. The onset of World War II caused the suppression of these organizations in America. In 1958, however, a right-wing journalist and political activist, George Lincoln Rockwell (1918–1967), organized the American Nazi Party, which attracted a substantial following, maintained a fairly high profile, and remains active today.

The 1990s have seen the rise of Aryan Nations and similar groups that embrace the idea of "Christian Identity," a belief that whites are the original Lost Tribes of Israel, Jews are descended from Satan, and that people of color, including blacks, are subhuman beings created by God before the creation of Adam, who was the first white man. Inasmuch as Jews and people of color are defined as soulless and, therefore, nonhuman, it is both morally permissible and even desirable to eliminate them.

Some white supremacist groups, most notably the Church of the Creator, founded in 1973, are committed to a vast racial holy war—referred to by the acronym RAHOWA—pitting the Aryan race against the so-called mud races or mud people.

Related to the white supremacist movement are various groups that identify themselves as "skinheads," because of the extremely close "buzz" haircut they typically adopt. Skinheads are young for the most part. Of all the supremacist groups, it is the skinheads who have been most frequently implicated in hate crimes against blacks and gays. Looked at another way, young people commit the majority of hate crimes in America (National Center for Victims of Crime, "Hate Crime," www.ncvc.org/special/hatec.htm). Groups such as the ANTI-DEFAMATION LEAGUE, the NATIONAL ASSOCIATION FOR THE ADVANCEMENT OF COLORED PEOPLE, and the Center for Democratic Renewal, which monitor the white supremacist movement, have observed that active supremacists readily join multiple groups or drift from one group to another. And the supremacist groups themselves are unstable; leadership is frequently contested and in flux. What does remain constant is the belief in white supremacy and the hatred of all those who do not fall within the white race as more or less commonly defined by the groups.

Suggested Reading

Dobratz, Betty A., and Stephanie L. Shanks-Meile. *The White Separatist Movement in the United States: White Power, White Pride.* Baltimore: Johns Hopkins University Press, 2000.

Ridgeway, James. *Blood in the Face: The Ku Klux Klan, Aryan Nations, Nazi Skinheads, and the Rise of a New White Culture.* 2d ed. Berkeley, Calif.: Thunder's Mouth, 1995.

Swain, Carol M. *The New White Nationalism in America.* New York: Cambridge University Press, 2002.

WILKINS, ROY O. (1901–1981)

Roy Wilkins was the executive secretary of the NATIONAL ASSOCIATION FOR THE ADVANCEMENT OF COLORED PEOPLE (NAACP) from 1955 until shortly before his death in 1981, the years in which the organization was most active and most successful in promoting major civil rights initiatives.

Wilkins was born in St. Louis on August 30, 1901, but moved to St. Paul, Minnesota, after his mother's death in 1905. There he was raised by an aunt and uncle. He earned a B.A. from the University of Minnesota in 1923 and became a journalist in St. Paul, then settled in Kansas City where he edited the *Kansas City Call,* a black newspaper. He joined the NAACP during this period, and in 1931 NAACP director Walter White invited Wilkins to join the national staff in New York City. When W. E. B. DU BOIS resigned as editor of the NAACP magazine, *THE CRISIS,* in 1934, Wilkins took up the post and edited the magazine for the next decade and a half. Wilkins became NAACP administrator in 1950, and when White died in 1955 Wilkins was elected to replace him as leader of the organization.

Wilkins became the most prominent leader of the nation's most prominent civil rights organization, presiding over extraordinary growth in membership, finance, and influence. Tapped by the press and presidents as the voice of civil rights, Wilkins was informally and universally known as "Mr. Civil Rights." This, however, often put him at odds with many in the civil rights movement. Wilkins was perceived as too willing to work within the system, even when this meant drastic compromise. He shunned direct-action protest, which was the lifeblood of the civil rights movement during the 1960s, and he supported Lyndon B. Johnson's Vietnam policy, which earned him the condemnation of radicals and young liberals, black and white alike. Wilkins was an outspoken, even bitter critic of black nationalism and black militancy.

On balance, Wilkins guided the NAACP on a mostly effective middle course between the direct-protest wing of the civil rights movement and the cultural, economic, and political establishment. He worked well with every president from Franklin D. Roosevelt to Jimmy Carter and maintained viable, if strained, working relations with such organizations as the Southern Christian Leadership Conference (SCLC), Student Nonviolent Coordinating Committee (SNCC), and the Congress of Racial Equality (CORE). Wilkins died on September 9, 1981. His autobiography, *Standing Fast,* was published a year later.

Suggested Reading

Wilkins, Roy. *Standing Fast: The Autobiography of Roy Wilkins.* 1980. Reprint, New York: Da Capo, 1994.

WILLIAMS, ROGER (CA. 1603–1683)

Expelled from the Massachusetts Bay Colony because of his liberal religious views, Roger Williams founded Providence, the anchor of what became the Rhode Island colony, an early American haven of religious tolerance and the first government in North America founded on the principle of the separation of church and state.

Williams was born in London, the son of a tailor, and was educated in the law by no less a figure than the great English jurist Sir Edward Coke. After apprenticing with Coke, Williams enrolled at Cambridge, where he prepared for the clergy. At Cambridge, Williams became a Puritan and in 1631 left England for Boston in the Massachusetts Bay Colony. Almost immediately Williams clashed with the Anglican Puritans in Boston. He moved to the Plymouth Colony in 1632 but, falling into a political dispute there, returned to the Bay Colony in 1633 and settled in Salem. The next year he became pastor of the Salem church.

Williams was soon banished from Salem and the Massachusetts Bay Colony because of his stubborn advocacy of two principles: First, he held that patents issued by the king of England did not confer legal title to American land, which could be obtained only by purchase from the Indians, who had natural right to the land. Second, he advocated the separation of church and state, arguing that civil magistrates must not interfere in matters of religion and that religion enforced upon people by law was coercive and therefore incompatible with true conviction, conscience, and faith.

In January 1636 Williams moved to Narragansett Bay and in the spring purchased land from the Narragansett Indians, on which he founded the town of Providence. The new settlement quickly drew religious dissenters from all over New England, especially Anabaptists and Quakers, as well as those like Anne Hutchinson, whose religious convictions were even more individualist, placing personal conscience above all other authority. In 1643 Williams sailed to England to secure a charter for Rhode Island; he returned to England in 1651–1654 to ensure the confirmation of the charter. Under the charter Williams served as the first president of Rhode Island.

In addition to offering religious toleration and refusing state sanction of religion, Williams established friendly relations with local Indians on the basis of mutual respect. He learned the Narragansett language and even wrote a learned study of Indian languages, *A Key into the Language of America.*

Suggested Reading

Gaustad, Edwin S. *Liberty of Conscience: Roger Williams in America.* Valley Forge, Penn.: Judson, 1999.

Hall, Timothy L. *Separating Church and State: Roger Williams and Religious Liberty.* Champaign-Urbana: University of Illinois Press, 1998.

WOMEN'S CIVIL RIGHTS MOVEMENT

This entry treats the women's civil rights movement after passage of the Nineteenth Amendment in 1920, giving women the right to vote. The women's civil rights movement in the United States before 1920 is discussed in women's suffrage movement.

The passage of the Nineteenth Amendment was a great triumph for women's civil rights in the United States. With the issue of voting rights settled, activists sought to broaden the scope of women's rights and, ultimately, to achieve full equality with men.

Reproductive Rights and Equal Rights

In 1921 Margaret Sanger addressed women's reproductive rights by founding the American Birth Control League, which evolved into the Planned Parenthood Federation of America in 1942. In 1923, just three years after women were given the vote, the Supreme Court in *Adkins v. Children's Hospital* struck down a 1918 District of Columbia minimum-wage law for women. The high court held that enfranchisement was an acknowledgment of the full equality of women and men under the law. This ruling invalidated all state laws that set different minimum wages for men and women. Also in 1923 Alice Paul and the National Woman's Party succeeded in getting the Equal Rights Amendment introduced in Congress. This was an attempt to obtain an explicit constitutional guarantee of equality.

Politics and History

Given the vote, women did not automatically constitute themselves as a political bloc. Although many men expected that women would tip the electoral balance leftward, as a group women voted neither more nor less liberally than men. Indeed, if anything, women voters contributed to the presidential victory of status quo Republican Warren G. Harding over his more progressive Democratic opponent, James M. Cox, in the election of 1920. However, women did begin to run for office—and with some success. In 1924 Nellie Tayloe Ross of Wyoming became the nation's first woman governor, and two years later Bertha Knight Landes of Seattle was elected the first woman mayor of a large American city.

Having attained an essential measure of political power, some women organized to claim an equitable measure of historical recognition as well, convening in 1928 the Berkshire Conference on the History of Women to study women's history, a field almost entirely ignored by academic historians.

Employment Rights: The Depression and World War II

The onset of the Great Depression in 1929 brought a major setback to women's rights, as men were given top priority for employment in a shrinking job market. Even the legislation of the New Deal worked against the employment of women; the 1932 National Recovery Act barred more than one family member from holding a government job. But in 1933 President Roosevelt named as secretary of labor Frances Perkins, the first woman to serve in a presidential cabinet. In 1935 Mary McLeod Bethune organized the National Council of Negro Women as a lobbying coalition of black women's groups. Under Bethune's presidency (through 1949) the coalition emerged as a major force against employment discrimination based on race and gender.

If the depression had a negative impact on women in the workplace, the outbreak of World War II suddenly put unprecedented numbers of women to work in war industries. This experience stimulated interest in the rights of women workers, and as the war drew to a close in 1945 an Equal Pay for Equal Work bill, first introduced in Congress in 1872 and aimed at eliminating salary discrimination against women, was reintroduced. It did not pass in 1945, however, and would not pass until 1963. Moreover, although many women who had worked during the war expressed their desire to continue working, large numbers lost their jobs when the war ended, war production wound down, and men returned from the armed forces seeking civilian employment.

Two Milestones in Reproductive Rights

In terms of reproductive rights, a 1936 decision by the U.S. Second Circuit Court in *United States v. One Package of Japanese Pessaries* upheld a challenge to a U.S. Customs Service seizure of contraceptive pessaries sent to Margaret Sanger's birth control clinic, thereby effectively legalizing birth control, because the court held that the demonstrated presence of disease was no longer required for women to receive medical counseling in contraception.

In 1960 the U.S. Food and Drug Administration would approve birth control pills, which gave women an almost unlimited ability to make reproduction a matter of choice. The pills were first marketed in the United States the following year. In 1965 the Supreme Court (*Griswold v. Connecticut*) overturned one of the last state laws prohibiting the use of contraceptives by married couples.

New Awakenings: The Early 1960s

Despite advances in political and reproductive rights women still earned much less than men for the same work (about 60 cents for every dollar men earned) and were sometimes barred from certain employment as well as from some educational opportunities. In 1961 President John F. Kennedy created the President's Commission on the Status of Women, chaired by Eleanor Roosevelt. Each of the fifty states ultimately followed suit by establishing their own commissions. Thanks in large part to the Presidential Commission, the Equal Pay Act was finally passed. Excluded from coverage, however, were domestics, agricultural workers, executives, administrators, and those classified as professionals; the law applied chiefly to hourly workers and lower-level salaried workers. (The law was extended to executives and administrators in 1971.) In addition the 1963 report of the president's commission made further recommendations for sweeping reforms.

The president's commission report reawakened intense interest in women's rights. Into this new and highly receptive context, Betty Friedan published her epoch-making bestseller *The Feminine Mystique,* which exposed and analyzed women's discontent with their expected role in society. The book became the foundation for the modern feminist movement and what came to be called the Women's Liberation Movement.

The women's movement also benefited from passage of the Civil Rights Act of 1964, Title VII of which bars employment discrimination based on race, sex, and other grounds. From 1964 to 1969 the Equal Employment Opportunity Commission (EEOC), created under Title VII, received fifty thousand complaints of gender-based employment discrimination. Using Title VII, National Organization for Women (NOW) attorneys successfully argued in the Fifth Circuit Court (*Weeks v. Southern Bell* [1969]) against gender discrimination in employment without proof that all or substantially all women would be unable to do the job in question safely and efficiently. This decision marked the beginning of the end for a host of restrictive labor laws and company regulations, and it rapidly opened to women many previously male-only jobs.

The Women's Liberation Movement Begins: 1967–1971

By the later 1960s an increasingly radical faction appeared within the ranks of those working for women's civil rights. In 1967 the Chicago Women's Liberation Group organized—the first group to apply the term "liberation" to the cause of women's rights. Later in the year, New York Radical Women was founded and, in 1968, began a process of what members called "consciousness raising" by sharing life stories with one another. "Consciousness Raising Groups" soon become a national vogue among women. Also in 1968 the first national women's liberation conference was held in Chicago.

The year 1968, a time of great ferment for minority rights generally, saw the founding of the National Abortion Rights Action League (NARAL), which began an effort to overturn state antiabortion laws. In the same year the Equal Opportunity Commission ruled against sex-segregated help-wanted newspaper ads, and a host of women's liberation publications began to appear, most notably *The Voice of the Women's Liberation Movement,* edited in Chicago by Jo Freeman and others. In 1969 Chicago women's liberation activists organized Jane (for "Jane Doe"), an abortion referral service, which worked quietly to provide women with safe abortions. The year 1969 also saw publication of one of the most influential popular books for women, *Our Bodies, Ourselves: A Book by and for Women,* which provided relevant, frank, and nonjudgmental medical information based on a combination of expert advice and personal experiences.

As women gradually gained control over reproductive rights, they also gained a significant measure of control over their rights in marriage. California in 1969 became the first of many states to adopt "no fault" divorce, which allows couples to divorce by mutual consent without having to demonstrate other cause.

Sexual Politics, by Kate Millett, was published in 1970 and raised the issue of women's rights to a new intellectual level, which was reflected in the establishment later that year of the nation's first college-level women's studies program at San Diego State College, California.

While women's studies became an academic field, other women were concerned with what they believed were more urgent matters and established in 1971 the nation's first shelter for battered women in Urbana, Illinois. In New York the New York Radical Feminists held a series of "speakouts" and a conference on rape and the treatment of women by the criminal justice system. Susan Brownmiller's 1975 book about rape, *Against Our Will,* was based in large part on the program. Nationwide, rape crisis centers began to open.

The Second Wave: 1970s

What came to be called the "Second Wave" of feminism was inaugurated in 1971 by Gloria Steinem's *Ms.,* a popular magazine with a contemporary feminist viewpoint. In the same year the National Women's Political Caucus was formed to encourage and support women who run for public office.

In 1972, in *Eisenstadt v. Baird,* the Supreme Court ruled that the right to privacy encompasses an unmarried person's right to use contraceptives. In 1973 another decision, *Roe v. Wade,* used the right to privacy to establish a woman's right to abortion, thereby overturning antiabortion laws in forty-six states.

The year 1972 also saw congressional passage of the Equal Rights Amendment, which had languished in Congress since 1923. The amendment would, however, fail to receive the requisite ratification by two-thirds of the states even after Congress extended the ratification deadline to June 30, 1982.

During the early 1970s the country made considerable progress toward achieving equality in employment and education. In 1974 the Equal Credit Opportunity Act barred discrimination in all consumer credit practices on the basis of sex; this was extended to commercial credit in 1988. In 1976 the United States military academies opened admissions to women.

Conservatism and Backlash: 1977–

Opposition to *Roe v. Wade* took the form of the Hyde Amendment of 1977, which eliminated federal funding for abortion procedures. This created a trend among many states. In 1989 the Supreme Court in *Webster v. Reproductive Health Services* upheld the right of states to deny public funding for abortions and to prohibit public hospitals from performing them. However, in a victory for reproductive rights the 1978 Pregnancy Discrimination Act amended the Civil Rights Act of 1964 by banning employment discrimination against pregnant women. In 2000 in *Stenberg v. Carhart* the Supreme Court retreated somewhat from *Roe* by finding unconstitutional, as well as "deceptive" and "extreme," so-called partial-birth abortions—that is, abortions performed late in pregnancy, when the fetus is viable outside the womb. However, in this decision, the high court struck down a Nebraska statute banning partial-birth abortions because it did not provide an exception for the health of the mother. In spring 2002 legislation was introduced in Congress to ban partial-birth abortions (except when the mother's life or health is in jeopardy), and President George W. Bush indicated his intention to sign such legislation. In the 1990s President Bill Clinton had twice vetoed such bills.

The 1980s ushered in a period of comparative conservatism in all areas of minority rights. Nevertheless, in 1985 a Connecticut woman made legal history by winning a civil suit as a battered wife, and in 1986 the Supreme Court declared sexual harassment to be a form of illegal job discrimination in its decision in *Meritor Savings Bank v. Vinson.*

Originally vetoed by President George H.W. Bush, the Family and Medical Leave Act was signed into law by Bill Clinton in 1993, entitling employees to take up to twelve weeks of unpaid, job-protected leave in a twelve-month period for specified family and medical reasons, thereby enabling and encouraging more women to balance work and family life.

The omnibus Violence Against Women Act of 1994 created a wide array of services for victims of rape and domestic violence, allowed women to seek civil rights remedies for gender-related crimes, provided sensitivity training for police and court officials in the areas of rape and domestic violence, and established a national twenty-four-hour hotline for battered women. In 2000 the U.S. Supreme Court, in *United States. v. Morrison,* 529 U.S. 598 (2000), held unconstitutional the portion of the act that provided a federal *civil* remedy for victims of gender-motivated violence, ruling this a violation of the interstate commerce clause and Section 5 of the Fourteenth Amendment. The Violence against Women Act of 1998, renewing and significantly expanding the provisions of the 1994 legislation, had not cleared the Senate as of late 2002.

Assessment

There can be little doubt that women have made substantial gains in civil rights since passage of the Nineteenth Amendment. Nevertheless, women continue to be particularly vulnerable to violent crime, and, as the latest Department of Labor statistics attest, they still do not enjoy employment compensation, on average, equal to that of men. "Women who usually worked full time had median earnings of $521 per week, or 76.3 percent of the $683 median for men. The female-to-male earnings ratios were higher among blacks (88.0 percent) and Hispanics (85.7 percent) than among whites (75.5 percent)" (Bureau of Labor Statistics, "Usual Weekly Earnings of Wage and Salary Workers: Second Quarter 2002," www.bls.gov/news.release/wkyeng.nr0.htm).

Suggested Reading

Cushman, Clare, ed. *Supreme Court Decisions and Women's Rights: Milestones to Equality.* Washington, D.C.: CQ Press, 2000.

Echols, Alice. *Daring to Be Bad: Radical Feminism in America, 1967–1975.* Minneapolis: University of Minnesota Press, 1990.

Evans, Sara. *Personal Politics: The Roots of Women's Liberation in the Civil Rights Movement and the New Left.* New York: Random House, 1980.

Rosen, Ruth. *The World Split Open: How the Modern Women's Movement Changed America.* New York: Penguin USA, 2001.

WOMEN'S LAW PROJECT

A nonprofit, feminist, legal advocacy organization, the Women's Law Project (WLP) was founded in 1974 to advance the legal and economic status of women and their families through litigation, public education, and individual counseling.

The Law Project came to national attention for its ERA Project, which combined litigation under state equal rights amendments with a public education effort to generate support for the proposed federal Equal Rights Amendment. Since then the WLP has served as a counseling center for women faced with issues involving sex discrimination, employment and housing problems, divorce, domestic violence, child support, and child custody.

WLP is also active in legal opposition to restrictive abortion rights laws and in advocating for the rights of lesbian parents.

Suggested Reading

Steiner, Gilbert. *Constitutional Inequality: The Political Fortunes of the Equal Rights Amendment.* Washington, D.C.: Brookings Institution, 1985.

WOMEN'S LIBERATION MOVEMENT

See women's civil rights movement.

WOMEN'S RIGHTS

See Women's civil rights movement and women's suffrage movement.

WOMEN'S SUFFRAGE MOVEMENT

Before the ratification of the Nineteenth Amendment in 1920, American women had no federally granted right to vote. During the American Revolution New Jersey briefly permitted women's suffrage, but only because it had carelessly drafted its voting law, specifying that all "individuals" worth fifty pounds or more were eligible to vote. New Jersey women who met the fifty-pound criteria voted in 1777, but the law was reworded, changing the gender-neutral "individuals" to "men," and the loophole was closed before the next election.

The organized women's suffrage movement commenced in 1848 with the SENECA FALLS CONFERENCE, which brought together 240 women and men who drew up a list of grievances and a set of resolutions for action. Organized by ELIZABETH CADY STANTON and Lucretia Mott, both active in the ABOLITION MOVEMENT, the meeting was reconvened in upstate New York annually.

After the Civil War women suffragists became divided over whether to tie the campaign for women's rights to the campaign to ensure the enfranchisement of former slaves. Stanton and SUSAN B. ANTHONY fought strenuously for constitutional amendments that would enfranchise both blacks and women, and Mott was elected chair of an Equal Rights Association. When the FOURTEENTH AMENDMENT and FIFTEENTH AMENDMENT, extending the vote to black men, failed to address women's rights, Stanton and Anthony broke with Mott's group to form the National Woman Suffrage Association, which opposed the Fifteenth Amendment and accepted only women as members. Another splinter group, the American Woman Suffrage Association, supported the Fifteenth Amendment as a necessary first step in the broadening of voting rights. These national groups were joined in the later years of the nineteenth century by federations of women's clubs, which, since the late 1860s, had devoted much attention to women's issues. For example, members of the Woman's Christian Temperance Union also joined the crusade for women's suffrage.

In 1890 the National Woman Suffrage Association and the American Woman Suffrage Association ended their rivalry by merging under the leadership of Anna Howard Shaw and Carrie Chapman Catt to become the NATIONAL AMERICAN WOMAN SUFFRAGE ASSOCIATION. From 1900 to 1920 this organization led an ambitious propaganda campaign for suffrage and, with the exception of the Congressional Union's National Women's Party, created a unity of purpose that had earlier eluded the movement.

The Congressional Union's National Women's Party, organized by Alice Paul, was more militant in its suffrage campaign. Members picketed, staged hunger strikes, and engaged in other forms of civil disobedience in an attempt to gain a constitutional amendment that would not only give women the right to vote but would explicitly confer on women equal rights with men (see EQUAL RIGHTS AMENDMENT).

In 1890 Wyoming became the first state (discounting the eighteenth-century New Jersey aberration) to give women the vote, and a number of western states followed suit. On the national front Theodore Roosevelt's Progressive ("Bull Moose") Party endorsed women's suffrage in 1912, and during World War I President Woodrow Wilson endorsed a constitutional amendment granting women the right to vote as a vitally necessary war measure. The Nineteenth Amendment was passed by Congress on June 4, 1919, and was ratified by the states on August 18, 1920. (For a discussion of women's civil rights after 1920, see WOMEN'S CIVIL RIGHTS MOVEMENT.)

Suggested Reading

Baker, Jean H., ed. *Votes for Women: The Struggle for Suffrage Revisited.* New York: Oxford University Press, 2002.

DuBois, Ellen Carol. *Feminism and Suffrage: The Emergence of an Independent Women's Movement in America, 1848–1869.* Ithaca: Cornell University Press, 1999.

Flexner, Eleanor. *Century of Struggle: The Women's Rights Movement in the United States.* Cambridge, Mass: Belknap, 1996.

Kraditor, Aileen S. *The Ideas of the Woman Suffrage Movement, 1890–1920.* New York: Norton, 1981.

WOOLWORTH LUNCH COUNTER SIT-IN

See GREENSBORO SIT-IN.

YOUNG NEGROES COOPERATIVE LEAGUE

The Young Negroes Cooperative League was founded in New York's Harlem neighborhood by pioneering civil rights activist Ella Jo Baker. The league pooled community resources to provide goods and services to members at reasonable cost and for the profit of black-owned community businesses. League membership was open to blacks between the ages of eighteen and thirty-five, who engaged in small-scale cooperative ventures, including buying clubs, grocery stores, and bulk distribution networks. The league also promoted general consumer education in the black community.

Chapters of the Young Negroes Cooperative League were soon started in several black communities across the country. In 1931 Baker was elected the organization's first national director. The league was active throughout the 1930s.

Suggested Reading

Grant, Joanne. *Ella Jo Baker: Freedom Bound.* New York: Wiley, 1998.

YOUNG, WHITNEY MOORE, JR. (1921–1971)

Whitney Young was director of the National Urban League from 1961 until his death in 1971. In this position Young was able to form partnerships with business and government to bring economic aid to the black community.

Born on July 31, 1921, in Lincoln Ridge, Kentucky, Young was the son of a teacher at a black vocational high school, the Lincoln Institute. He earned a bachelor's degree from Kentucky State Industrial College in 1941, then served in the U.S. Army during World War II. He returned to college after the war, earned a master's degree from the University of Minnesota in 1947, then joined the National Urban League, first in Minneapolis-St. Paul and later in Omaha, Nebraska. Young was appointed dean of the School of Social Work of Atlanta University in 1954, became increasingly active in the cause of civil rights, and in 1961 was named head of the National Urban League.

Young steered the League in a course midway between its traditional role of working for the economic benefit of African Americans and a more activist role in concert with the direct protest tactics of the African American civil rights movement of the 1960s. He saw to it that the Urban League played a prominent role in the 1963 March on Washington, but it was in his work with business and government that Young became most visible and effective.

The National Urban League was instrumental in promoting and shaping Lyndon B. Johnson's War on Poverty, and the League took an especially active role in formulating a host of inner-city job and job-training programs. Young was a key link between the black community and the white establishment, serving on the board of directors of institutions ranging from the Rockefeller Foundation to the Federal Reserve Bank of New York. He was also president of the National Conference of Social Welfare and the National Association of Social Workers.

Young's life and career were tragically cut short when, on a trip to Lagos, Nigeria, he drowned while swimming with friends on March 11, 1971.

Suggested Reading

Dickerson, Dennis. *Militant Mediator: Whitney M. Young, Jr.* Lexington: University Press of Kentucky, 1998.

Young, Whitney M., Jr. *Beyond Racism: Building an Open Society.* New York: McGraw-Hill, 1961.

YOUTH LAW CENTER

Founded in 1978, the Youth Law Center (YLC) is a non-profit public-interest law office that works nationally as a legal advocate for children, with emphasis on children who live apart from their families in the child welfare and juvenile justice systems. YLC attorneys investigate reports of abuse of children in adult jails, juvenile detention facilities, state institutions, and child welfare systems, and, through the use of training, technical assistance, and negotiation, they attempt to bring about needed change. As a last resort the YLC employs litigation.

Suggested Reading

Humes, Edward. *No Matter How Loud I Shout: A Year in the Life of Juvenile Court.* New York: Simon and Schuster, 1996.

Maxson, Cheryl L., and Malcolm W. Klein. *Responding to Troubled Youth.* New York: Oxford University Press, 1997.

Rosenheim, Margaret K., Franklin E. Zimring, and David S. Tanenhaus, eds. *A Century of Juvenile Justice.* Chicago: University of Chicago Press, 2002.

Z

ZELLNER, ROBERT (1939–)

Robert Zellner was a white activist in the civil rights movement and among the first members of the Student Nonviolent Coordinating Committee (SNCC).

A native of Alabama and the son of a Methodist minister, Zellner had been brought up in the white supremacist climate conventional in the rural South. It was while he was studying at Huntington College in Montgomery, Alabama, that he began to question white supremacy and segregation. As a senior he decided to research racial problems in Montgomery and began to attend civil rights meetings as part of his work. This led him into active involvement in the movement despite resistance from college officials as well as officials of Montgomery city government.

He joined SNCC in 1961 as its first white staff member and was often attacked by angry whites, who derided him as a traitor to his race. Despite his courage and commitment to the movement he was purged, with other whites, from SNCC membership in 1966. This did not, however, drive him away from commitment to the African American civil rights movement. With his wife, Dottie Zellner, he founded GROW (Grass Roots Organizing Committee), a labor organization. Zellner was also active in the anti–Vietnam War movement.

Suggested Reading

Carson, Clayborne. *In Struggle: SNCC and the Black Awakening of the 1960s.* 1981. Reprint, Cambridge: Harvard University Press, 1995.

ZENGER CASE

The colonial case of John Peter Zenger was a landmark in the principle of freedom of the press and is often cited as a precedent for the subsequent protection of freedom of the press and free speech in the Bill of Rights.

In 1733 Lewis Morris, chief justice of the provincial court of New York, ruled against William Cosby, the colony's royal governor, in a salary dispute. Cosby summarily retaliated by suspending Morris, who then appealed to New York's only newspaper, the *New York Gazette,* to publish the story of this injustice. The *Gazette,* however, was wholly dependent on the patronage of the royal governor, so its editor declined to print anything critical of Cosby. Morris then assembled a group of colonial lawyers and merchants to finance a local printer, John Peter Zenger, in starting an independent newspaper, the *New-York Weekly Journal.*

Zenger commenced publication on November 5, 1733, and issued a series of attacks on Cosby, accusing him of attempting to destroy the provincial court system in violation not only of colonial laws but those of England as well.

By 1734 Cosby had had enough. He ordered Zenger's arrest on charges of seditious libel. The publisher was held in prison, without trial, for almost ten months while his wife, Anna, took over operation of the *New-York Weekly Journal.* Finally brought to trial in 1735, Zenger was defended by Andrew Hamilton, a prominent Philadelphia lawyer who argued that Zenger was innocent of seditious libel because all that he had printed was true. The biased court refused to admit evidence substantiating the truth of the articles Zenger had printed; despite this, the jury was persuaded, and Zenger was acquitted.

Ever since the Zenger verdict factual truth has been a sovereign defense against charges of libel, and this defense has served to foster a free press and free speech generally—although the Alien and Sedition Acts, enacted by the Federalists at the end of the eighteenth century, briefly threatened even this principle.

Suggested Reading

Putnam, William Lowell. *John Peter Zenger and the Fundamental Freedom.* Jefferson, N.C.: McFarland, 1997.

Rutherford, Livingston. *John Peter Zenger: His Press, His Trial, and a Bibliography.* New York: Arno, 1971.

REFERENCE MATERIALS

APPENDIX A
LIST OF DOCUMENTS

IV. U.S. Supreme Court Decisions

V. Rights Activism Documents

VI. U.S. Government Agencies

I. HISTORIC DOCUMENTS

MAGNA CARTA (1215)

1. In the first place we have granted to God, and by this our present charter confirmed for us and our heirs forever that the English Church shall be free, and shall have her rights entire, and her liberties inviolate; and we will that it be thus observed; which is apparent from this that the freedom of elections, which is reckoned most important and very essential to the English Church, we, of our pure and unconstrained will, did grant, and did by our charter confirm and did obtain the ratification of the same from our lord, Pope Innocent III, before the quarrel arose between us and our barons: and this we will observe, and our will is that it be observed in good faith by our heirs forever. We have also granted to all freemen of our kingdom, for us and our heirs forever, all the underwritten liberties, to be had and held by them and their heirs, of us and our heirs forever. . . .
7. A widow, after the death of her husband, shall forthwith and without difficulty have her marriage portion and inheritance; nor shall she give anything for her dower, or for her marriage portion, or for the inheritance which her husband and she held on the day of the death of that husband; and she may remain in the house of her husband for forty days after his death, within which time her dower shall be assigned to her.
8. No widow shall be compelled to marry, so long as she prefers to live without a husband . . .
9. Neither we nor our bailiffs will seize any land or rent for any debt, as long as the chattels of the debtor are sufficient to repay the debt. . . .
20. A freeman shall not be amerced for a slight offense, except in accordance with the degree of the offense; and for a grave offense he shall be amerced in accordance with the gravity of the offense, yet saving always his "contentment"; and a merchant in the same way, saving his "merchandise"; and a villein shall be amerced in the same way, saving his "wainage" if they have fallen into our mercy: and none of the aforesaid amercements shall be imposed except by the oath of honest men of the neighborhood.
21. Earls and barons shall not be amerced except through their peers, and only in accordance with the degree of the offense. . . .
24. No sheriff, constable, coroners, or others of our bailiffs, shall hold pleas of our Crown. . . .
28. No constable or other bailiff of ours shall take corn or other provisions from anyone without immediately tendering money therefor, unless he can have postponement thereof by permission of the seller. . . .
30. No sheriff or bailiff of ours, or other person, shall take the horses or carts of any freeman for transport duty, against the will of the said freeman.
31. Neither we nor our bailiffs shall take, for our castles or for any other work of ours, wood which is not ours, against the will of the owner of that wood.
32. We will not retain beyond one year and one day, the lands those who have been convicted of felony, and the lands shall thereafter be handed over to the lords of the fiefs. . . .
36. Nothing in future shall be given or taken for a writ of inquisition of life or limbs, but freely it shall be granted, and never denied. . . .
38. No bailiff for the future shall, upon his own unsupported complaint, put anyone to his "law," without credible witnesses brought for this purposes.
39. No freemen shall be taken or imprisoned or disseised or exiled or in any way destroyed, nor will we go upon him nor send upon him, except by the lawful judgment of his peers or by the law of the land.
40. To no one will we sell, to no one will we refuse or delay, right or justice. . . .
42. It shall be lawful in future for anyone (excepting always those imprisoned or outlawed in accordance with the law of the kingdom, and natives of any country at war with us, and merchants, who shall be treated as if above provided) to leave our kingdom and to return, safe and secure by land and water, except for a short period in time of war, on grounds of public policy—reserving always the allegiance due to us. . . .
45. We will appoint as justices, constables, sheriffs, or bailiffs only such as know the law of the realm and mean to observe it well. . . .
52. If anyone has been dispossessed or removed by us, without the legal judgment of his peers, from his lands, castles, franchises, or from his right, we will immediately restore them to him; and if a dispute arise over this, then let it be decided by the five and twenty barons of whom mention is made below in the clause for securing the peace. . . .
54. No one shall be arrested or imprisoned upon the appeal of a woman, for the death of any other than her husband.
55. All fines made with us unjustly and against the law of the land, and all amercements, imposed unjustly and against the law of the land, shall be entirely remitted. . . .
60. Moreover, all these aforesaid customs and liberties, the observances of which we have granted in our kingdom as far as pertains to us towards our men, shall be observed by all of our kingdom, as well clergy as laymen, as far as pertains to them towards their men. . . .

63. Wherefore we will and firmly order that the English Church be free, and that the men in our kingdom have and hold all the aforesaid liberties, rights, and concessions, well and peaceably, freely and quietly, fully and wholly, for themselves and their heirs, of us and our heirs, in all respects and in all places forever, as is aforesaid. An oath, moreover, has been taken, as well on our part as on the part of the barons, that all these conditions aforesaid shall be kept in good faith and without evil intent. Given under our hand—the above named and many others being witnesses—in the meadow which is called Runnymede, between Windsor and Staines, on the fifteenth day of June, in the seventeenth year of our reign.

Source: Albert Beebe White and Wallace Notestein, eds., *Source Problems in English History* (New York: Harper and Brothers, 1915), 38–43. For online version see "Medieval Sourcebook: Magna Carta 1215," www.fordham.edu/halsall/source/mcarta.html.

MASSACHUSETTS *BODY OF LIBERTIES* (1641)

1. No man's life shall be taken away, no man's honor or good name shall be stained, no man's person shall be arrested, restrained, banished, dismembered, nor any ways punished, no man shall be deprived of his wife or children, no man's goods or estate shall be taken away from him, nor any way indamaged under color of law or countenance of authority, unless it be by virtue or equity of some express law of the country warranting the same, established by a general court and sufficiently published, or in case of the defect of a law in any particular case by the word of God. And in capital cases, or in cases concerning dismembring or banishment, according to that word to be judged by the General Court.
2. Every person within this jurisdiction, whether inhabitant or foreigner, shall enjoy the same justice and law that is general for the plantation, which we constitute and execute one toward another without partiality or delay. . . .
7. No man shall be compelled to go out of the limits of this plantation upon any offensive wars which this Commonwealth or any of our friends or confederates shall voluntarily undertake. But only upon such vindictive and defensive wars in our own behalf or the behalf of our friends and confederates as shall be enterprised by the counsel and consent of a court general, or by authority derived from the same.
8. No man's cattle or goods of what kind soever shall be pressed or taken for any public use or service, unless it be by warrant grounded upon some act of the General Court, nor without such reasonable prices and hire as the ordinary rates of the country do afford. And if his cattle or goods shall perish or suffer damage in such service, the owner shall be sufficiently recompensed. . . .
17. Every man of, or within, this jurisdiction shall have free liberty, notwithstanding any civil power to remove both himself and his family at their pleasure out of the same, provided there be no legal impediment to the contrary.
18. No man's person shall be restrained or imprisoned by any authority whatsoever, before the law hath sentenced him thereto, if he can put in sufficient security, bail, or mainprise, for his appearance, and good behavior in the meantime, unless it be in crimes capital, and contempts in open court, and in such cases where some express act of court cloth allow it. . . .
41. Every man that is to answer for any criminal cause, whether he be in prison or under bail, his cause shall be heard and determined at the next court that hath proper cognizance thereof and may be done without prejudice of justice.
42. No man shall be twice sentenced by civil justice for one and the same crime, offense, or trespass.
43. No man shall be beaten with above forty stripes, nor shall any true gentleman, nor any man equal to a gentleman be punished with whipping, unless his crime be very shameful, and his course of life vicious and profligate.
44. No man condemned to die shall be put to death within four days next after his condemnation, unless the court see special cause to the contrary, or in case of martial law, nor shall the body of any man so put to death be unburied twelve hours, unless it be in case of anatomy.
45. No man shall be forced by torture to confess any crime against himself nor any other, unless it be in some capital case where he is first fully convicted by clear and sufficient evidence to be guilty, after which if the cause be of that nature, that it is very apparent there be other conspirators, or confederates with him, then he may be tortured, yet not with such tortures as be barbarous and inhumane.
46. For bodily punishments we allow amongst us none that are inhumane, barbarous, or cruel. . . .
58. Civil authority hath power and liberty to see the peace, ordinances, and rules of Christ observed in every church according to his Word. So it be done in a civil and not in an ecclesiastical way.
59. Civil authority hath power and liberty to deal with any church member in a way of civil justice, notwithstanding any church relation, office, or interest.
60. No church censure shall degrade or depose any man from any civil dignity, office, or authority he shall have in the Commonwealth. . . .

66. The freemen of every township shall have power to make such by-laws and constitutions as may concern the welfare of their town, provided they be not of a criminal, but only of a prudential nature, and that their penalties exceed not 20 shillings for one offense, and that they be not repugnant to the public laws and orders of the country. And if any inhabitant shall neglect or refuse to observe them, they shall have power to levy the appointed penalties by distress.
67. It is the constant liberty of the freemen of this plantation to choose yearly at the Court of Election out of the freemen all the general officers of this jurisdiction. If they please to discharge them at the day of election by way of vote, they may do it without showing cause. But if at any other general court, we hold it due justice that the reasons thereof be alleged and proved. By general officers we mean our governor, deputy governor, assistants, treasurer, general of our wars. And our admiral at sea, and such as are, or hereafter may be, of the like general nature.
68. It is the liberty of the freemen to choose such deputies for the General Court out of themselves, either in their own towns or elsewhere as they judge fittest. And because we cannot foresee what variety and weight of occasions may fall into future consideration and what counsels we may stand in need of, we decree, that the deputies (to attend the General Court in the behalf of the country) shall not any time be stated or inacted, but from court to court, or at the most but for one year, that the country may have an annual liberty to do in that case what is most behooveful for the best welfare thereof.
69. No General Court shall be dissolved or adjourned without the consent of the major party thereof.
70. All freemen called to give any advice, vote, verdict, or sentence in any court, counsel, or civil assembly shall have full freedom to do it according to their true judgments and consciences, so it be done orderly and inoffensively for the manner. . . .
80. Every married woman shall be free from bodily correction or stripes by her husband, unless it be in his own defense upon her assault. If there be any just cause of correction, complaint shall be made to authority assembled in some court, from which only she shall receive it. . . .
83. If any parents shall wilfully and unreasonably deny any child timely or convenient marriage, or shall exercise any unnatural severity toward them, such children shall have free liberty to complain to authority for redress. . . .
85. If any servants shall flee from the tyranny and cruelty of their masters to the house of any freeman of the same town, they shall be there protected and sustained till due order be taken for their relief. Provided due notice thereof be speedily given to their masters from whom they fled. And the next assistant or constable where the party flying is harbored.
86. No servant shall be put off for above a year to any other neither in the lifetime of their master nor after their death by their executors or administrators unless it be by consent of authority assembled in some court or two assistants.
87. If any man smite out the eye or tooth of his manservant, or maidservant, or otherwise maim or much disfigure him, unless it be by mere casualty, he shall let them go free from his service, and shall have such further recompense as the court shall allow him.
88. Servants that have served diligently and faithfully to the benefit of their masters seven years shall not be sent away empty. And if any have been unfaithful, negligent, or unprofitable in their service, notwithstanding the good usage of their masters, they shall not be dismissed till they have made satisfaction according to the judgment of authority.
89. If any people of other nations professing the true Christian religion shall flee to us from the tyranny or oppression of their persecutors, or from famine, wars, or the like necessary and compulsory cause, they shall be entertained and succored amongst us, according to that power and prudence God shall give us.
90. If any ships or other vessels, be it friend or enemy, shall suffer shipwreck upon our coast, there shall be no violence or wrong offered to their persons or goods. But their persons shall be harbored, and relieved, and their goods preserved in safety till authority may be certified thereof, and shall take further order therein.
91. There shall never be any bond slavery, villeinage, or captivity amongst us unless it be lawful captives taken in just wars, and such strangers as willingly sell themselves or are sold to us. And these shall have all the liberties and Christian usages which the law of God established in Israel concerning such persons doth morally require. This exempts none from servitude who shall be judged thereto by authority.
92. No man shall exercise any tyranny or cruelty toward any brute creature which are usually kept for man's use. . . .
94. CAPITAL LAWS
1. If any man after legal conviction shall have or worship any other god, but the Lord God, he shall be put to death.
2. If any man or woman be a witch (that is, hath or consulteth with a familiar spirit), they shall be put to death.
3. If any man shall blaspheme the name of God, the Father, Son, or Holy Ghost, with direct, express, presumptuous, or high-handed blasphemy, or shall curse God in the like manner, he shall be put to death.

Source: "Massachusetts Body of Liberties," Constitution Society, www.constitution.org/bcp/mabodlib.htm.

DECLARATION OF INDEPENDENCE (1776)

IN CONGRESS, July 4, 1776,

The unanimous Declaration of the thirteen united states of America,

When in the Course of human events, it becomes necessary for one people to dissolve the political bands which have connected them with another, and to assume among the powers of the earth, the separate and equal station to which the Laws of Nature and of Nature's God entitle them, a decent respect to the opinions of mankind requires that they should declare the causes which impel them to the separation.

We hold these truths to be self-evident, that all men are created equal, that they are endowed by their Creator with certain unalienable Rights, that among these are Life, Liberty and the pursuit of Happiness.—That to secure these rights, Governments are instituted among Men, deriving their just powers from the consent of the governed,—That whenever any Form of Government becomes destructive of these ends, it is the Right of the People to alter or to abolish it, and to institute new Government, laying its foundation on such principles and organizing its powers in such form, as to them shall seem most likely to effect their Safety and Happiness. Prudence, indeed, will dictate that Governments long established should not be changed for light and transient causes; and accordingly all experience hath shewn, that mankind are more disposed to suffer, while evils are sufferable, than to right themselves by abolishing the forms to which they are accustomed. But when a long train of abuses and usurpations, pursuing invariably the same Object evinces a design to reduce them under absolute Despotism, it is their right, it is their duty, to throw off such Government, and to provide new Guards for their future security.—Such has been the patient sufferance of these Colonies; and such is now the necessity which constrains them to alter their former Systems of Government. The history of the present King of Great Britain is a history of repeated injuries and usurpations, all having in direct object the establishment of an absolute Tyranny over these States. To prove this, let Facts be submitted to a candid world.

He has refused his Assent to Laws, the most wholesome and necessary for the public good.

He has forbidden his Governors to pass Laws of immediate and pressing importance, unless suspended in their operation till his Assent should be obtained; and when so suspended, he has utterly neglected to attend to them.

He has refused to pass other Laws for the accommodation of large districts of people, unless those people would relinquish the right of Representation in the Legislature, a right inestimable to them and formidable to tyrants only.

He has called together legislative bodies at places unusual, uncomfortable, and distant from the depository of their public Records, for the sole purpose of fatiguing them into compliance with his measures.

He has dissolved Representative Houses repeatedly, for opposing with manly firmness his invasions on the rights of the people.

He has refused for a long time, after such dissolutions, to cause others to be elected; whereby the Legislative powers, incapable of Annihilation, have returned to the People at large for their exercise; the State remaining in the mean time exposed to all the dangers of invasion from without, and convulsions within.

He has endeavored to prevent the population of these States; for that purpose obstructing the Laws of Naturalization of Foreigners; refusing to pass others to encourage their migration hither, and raising the conditions of new Appropriations of Lands.

He has obstructed the Administration of Justice, by refusing his Assent to Laws for establishing Judiciary Powers.

He has made Judges dependent on his Will alone, for the tenure of their offices, and the amount and payment of their salaries.

He has erected a multitude of New Offices, and sent hither swarms of Officers to harass our people, and eat out their substance.

He has kept among us, in times of peace, Standing Armies without the Consent of our legislatures.

He has affected to render the Military independent of and superior to the Civil Power.

He has combined with others to subject us to a jurisdiction foreign to our constitution, and unacknowledged by our laws; giving his Assent to their Acts of pretended Legislation:

For Quartering large bodies of armed troops among us:

For protecting them, by a mock Trial, from punishment for any Murders which they should commit on the Inhabitants of these States:

For cutting off our Trade with all parts of the world:

For imposing Taxes on us without our Consent:

For depriving us in many cases, of the benefits of Trial by Jury:

For transporting us beyond Seas to be tried for pretended offences:

For abolishing the free System of English Laws in a neighbouring Province, establishing therein an Arbitrary government, and enlarging its Boundaries so as to render it at once an example and fit instrument for introducing the same absolute rule into these Colonies:

For taking away our Charters, abolishing our most valuable Laws, and altering fundamentally the Forms of our Governments:

For suspending our own Legislatures, and declaring themselves invested with power to legislate for us in all cases whatsoever.

He has abdicated Government here, by declaring us out of his Protection and waging War against us.

He has plundered our seas, ravaged our Coasts, burnt our towns, and destroyed the lives of our people.

He is at this time transporting large Armies of foreign Mercenaries to compleat the works of death, desolation and tyranny, already begun with circumstances of Cruelty & perfidy scarcely paralleled in the most barbarous ages, and totally unworthy the Head of a civilized nation.

He has constrained our fellow Citizens taken Captive on the high Seas to bear Arms against their Country, to become the executioners of their friends and Brethren, or to fall themselves by their Hands.

He has excited domestic insurrections amongst us, and has endeavoured to bring on the inhabitants of our frontiers, the merciless Indian Savages, whose known rule of warfare, is an undistinguished destruction of all ages, sexes and conditions.

In every stage of these Oppressions We have Petitioned for Redress in the most humble terms: Our repeated Petitions have been answered only by repeated injury. A Prince whose character is thus marked by every act which may define a Tyrant, is unfit to be the ruler of a free people.

Nor have We been wanting in attention to our British brethren. We have warned them from time to time of attempts by their legislature to extend an unwarrantable jurisdiction over us. We have reminded them of the circumstances of our emigration and settlement here. We have appealed to their native justice and magnanimity, and we have conjured them by the ties of our common kindred to disavow these usurpations, which, would inevitably interrupt our connections and correspondence. They too have been deaf to the voice of justice and of consanguinity. We must, therefore, acquiesce in the necessity, which denounces our Separation, and hold them, as we hold the rest of mankind, Enemies in War, in Peace Friends.

We, therefore, the Representatives of the united States of America, in General Congress, Assembled, appealing to the Supreme Judge of the world for the rectitude of our intentions, do, in the Name, and by Authority of the good People of these Colonies, solemnly publish and declare, That these United Colonies are, and of Right ought to be Free and Independent States; that they are Absolved from all Allegiance to the British Crown, and that all political connection between them and the State of Great Britain, is and ought to be totally dissolved; and that as Free and Independent States, they have full Power to levy War, conclude Peace, contract Alliances, establish Commerce, and to do all other Acts and Things which Independent States may of right do. And for the support of this Declaration, with a firm reliance on the protection of divine Providence, we mutually pledge to each other our Lives, our Fortunes and our sacred Honor.

John Hancock.

New Hampshire:
Josiah Bartlett, William Whipple, Matthew Thornton.

Massachusetts:
Samuel Adams, John Adams, Robert Treat Paine, Elbridge Gerry.

Rhode Island:
Stephen Hopkins, William Ellery.

Connecticut:
Roger Sherman, Samuel Huntington, William Williams, Oliver Wolcott.

New York:
William Floyd, Philip Livingston, Francis Lewis, Lewis Morris.

Pennsylvania:
Robert Morris, Benjamin Harris, Benjamin Franklin, John Morton, George Clymer, James Smith, George Taylor, James Wilson, George Ross.

Delaware:
Caesar Rodney, George Read, Thomas McKean.

Georgia:
Button Gwinnett, Lyman Hall, George Walton.

Maryland:
Samuel Chase, William Paca, Thomas Stone, Charles Carroll of Carrollton.

Virginia:
George Wythe, Richard Henry Lee, Thomas Jefferson, Benjamin Harrison, Thomas Nelson Jr., Francis Lightfoot Lee, Carter Braxton.

North Carolina:
William Hooper, Joseph Hewes, John Penn.

South Carolina:
Edward Rutledge, Thomas Heyward Jr., Thomas Lynch, Jr., Arthur Middleton.

New Jersey:
Richard Stockton, John Witherspoon, Francis Hopkinson, John Hart, Abraham Clark.

Source: United States Government Manual, 2001–2002, www.access.gpo.gov/nara/browse-gm-01.html.

ARTICLES OF CONFEDERATION (1781)

Articles of Confederation and perpetual Union between the States of New Hampshire, Massachusetts-bay, Rhodeisland and Providence Plantations, Connecticut, New York, New Jersey, Pennsylvania, Delaware, Maryland, Virginia, North Carolina, South Carolina, and Georgia.

Article I. The stile of this confederacy shall be "The United States of America."

Article II. Each State retains its sovereignty, freedom, and independence, and every power, jurisdiction and right, which is not by this confederation expressly delegated to the United States in Congress assembled.

Article III. The said States hereby severally enter into a firm league of friendship with each other, for their common defence, the security of their liberties, and their mutual and general welfare, binding themselves to assist each other, against all force offered to, or attacks made upon them, or any of them, on account of religion, sovereignty, trade, or any other pretence whatever.

Article IV. The better to secure and perpetuate mutual friendship and intercourse among the people of the different States in this Union, the free inhabitants of each of these States, paupers, vagabonds, and fugitives from justice excepted, shall be entitled to all privileges and immunities of free citizens in the several States; and the people of each state shall have free ingress and regress to and from any other State, and shall enjoy therein all the privileges of trade and commerce, subject to the same duties, impositions and restrictions as the inhabitants thereof respectively, provided that such restrictions shall not extend so far as to prevent the removal of property imported into any State, to any other State of which the owner is an inhabitant; provided also that no imposition, duties, or restriction shall be laid by any State, on the property of the United States, or either of them.

If any person guilty of, or charged with treason, felony, or other high misdemeanor in any State, shall flee from justice, and be found in any of the United States, he shall upon demand of the Governor or Executive power, of the State from which he fled, be delivered up and removed to the State having jurisdiction of his offence.

Full faith and credit shall be given in each of these States to the records, acts and judicial proceedings of the courts and magistrates of every other State.

Article V. For the more convenient management of the general interests of the United States, delegates shall be annually appointed in such manner as the legislature of each State shall direct, to meet in Congress on the first Monday in November, in every year, with a power reserved to each State, to recall its delegates, or any of them, at any time within the year, and to send others in their stead, for the remainder of the year.

No State shall be represented in Congress by less than two nor by more than seven members; and no person shall be capable of being a delegate for more than three years in any term of six years; nor shall any person, being a delegate, be capable of holding any office under the United States, for which he, or another for his benefit receives any salary, fees or emolument of any kind.

Each State shall maintain its own delegates in a meeting of the States and while they act as members of the committee of the States.

In determining questions in the United States, in Congress assembled, each State shall have one vote.

Freedom of speech and debate in Congress shall not be impeached or questioned in any court, or place out of Congress, and the members of Congress shall be protected in their persons from arrests and imprisonments, during the time of their going to and from, and attendance on Congress, except for treason, felony, or breach of the peace.

Article VI. No State, without the consent of the United States in Congress assembled, shall send any embassy to, or receive any embassy from, or enter into any conferrence, agreement, alliance, or treaty with any king, prince, or state; nor shall any person holding any office of profit or trust under the United States, or any of them, accept of any present, emolument, office, or title of any kind whatever from any king, prince or foreign state; nor shall the United States in Congress assembled, or any of them, grant any title of nobility. . . .

Article VIII. All charges of war, and all other expenses that shall be incurred for the common defence or general welfare, and allowed by the United States in Congress assembled, shall be defrayed out of a common treasury, which shall be supplied by the several States, in proportion to the value of all land within each State, granted to or surveyed for any person, as such land and the buildings and improvements thereon shall be estimated according to such mode as the United States in Congress assembled, shall from time to time direct and appoint.

The taxes for paying that proportion shall be laid and levied by the authority and direction of the Legislatures of the several States within the time agreed upon by the United States in Congress assembled.

Article IX. The United States in Congress assembled, shall have the sole and exclusive right and power of determining on peace and war, except in the cases mentioned in the sixth article—of sending and receiving ambassadors—

entering into treaties and alliances, provided that no treaty of commerce shall be made whereby the legislative power of the respective States shall be restrained from imposing such imposts and duties on foreigners, as their own people are subjected to, or from prohibiting the exportation or importation of any species of goods or commodities whatsoever—of establishing rules for deciding in all cases, what captures on land or water shall be legal, and in what manner prizes taken by land or naval forces in the service of the United States shall be divided or appropriated—of granting letters of marque and reprisal in times of peace—appointing courts for the trial of piracies and felonies committed on the high seas and establishing courts for receiving and determining finally appeals in all cases of captures, provided that no member of Congress shall be appointed a judge of any of the said courts.

The United States in Congress assembled shall have authority to appoint a committee, to sit in the recess of Congress, to be denominated "a Committee of the States," and to consist of one delegate from each State; and to appoint such other committees and civil officers as may be necessary for managing the general affairs of the United States under their direction—to appoint one of their number to preside, provided that no person be allowed to serve in the office of president more than one year in any term of three years. . . .

The Congress of the United States shall have power to adjourn to any time within the year, and to any place within the United States, so that no period of adjournment be for a longer duration than the space of six months, and shall publish the journal of their proceedings monthly, except such parts thereof relating to treaties, alliances or military operations, as in their judgment require secresy; and the yeas and nays of the delegates of each State on any question shall be entered on the journal, when it is desired by any delegate; and the delegates of a State, or any of them, at his or their request shall be furnished with a transcript of the said journal, except such parts as are above excepted, to lay before the Legislatures of the several States.

Article X. The committee of the States, or any nine of them, shall be authorized to execute, in the recess of Congress, such of the powers of Congress as the United States in Congress assembled, by the consent of nine States, shall from time to time think expedient to vest them with; provided that no power be delegated to the said committee, for the exercise of which, by the articles of confederation, the voice of nine States in the Congress of the United States assembled is requisite. . . .

Article XIII. Every State shall abide by the determinations of the United States in Congress assembled, on all questions which by this confederation are submitted to them. And the articles of this confederation shall be inviolably observed by every State, and the Union shall be perpetual; nor shall any alteration at any time hereafter be made in any of them; unless such alteration be agreed to in a Congress of the United States, and be afterward confirmed by the Legislatures of every State.

And whereas it has pleased the Great Governor of the world to incline the hearts of the Legislatures we respectively represent in Congress, to approve of, and to authorize us to ratify the said articles of confederation and perpetual union. Know ye that we the undersigned delegates, by virtue of the power and authority to us given for that purpose, do by these presents, in the name and in behalf of our respective constituents, fully and entirely ratify and confirm each and every of the said articles of confederation and perpetual union, and all and singular the matters and things therein contained: and we do further solemnly plight and engage the faith of our respective constituents, that they shall abide by the determinations of the United States in Congress assembled, on all questions, which by the said confederation are submitted to them. And that the articles thereof shall be inviolably observed by the States we re[s]pectively represent, and that the Union shall be perpetual. In witness whereof we have hereunto set our hands in Congress.

U.S. CONSTITUTION (1788–1992)

Material deleted by subsequent amendments is enclosed in brackets.

[Preamble:] We the People of the United States, in Order to form a more perfect Union, establish Justice, insure domestic Tranquility, provide for the common defence, promote the general Welfare, and secure the Blessings of Liberty to ourselves and our Posterity, do ordain and establish this Constitution for the United States of America.

ARTICLE I

Section 1. All legislative Powers herein granted shall be vested in a Congress of the United States, which shall consist of a Senate and House of Representatives.

Section 2. The House of Representatives shall be composed of Members chosen every second Year by the People of the several States, and the Electors in each State shall have the Qualifications requisite for Electors of the most numerous Branch of the State Legislature.

No Person shall be a Representative who shall not have attained to the age of twenty five Years, and been seven Years a Citizen of the United States, and who shall not, when elected, be an Inhabitant of that State in which he shall be chosen.

[Representatives and direct Taxes shall be apportioned among the several States which may be included within this Union, according to their respective Numbers, which shall be determined by adding to the whole Number of free Persons, including those bound to Service for a Term of Years, and excluding Indians not taxed, three fifths of all other Persons.] The actual Enumeration shall be made within three Years after the first Meeting of the Congress of the United States, and within every subsequent Term of ten Years, in such Manner as they shall by Law direct. The Number of Representatives shall not exceed one for every thirty Thousand, but each State shall have at Least one Representative; and until such enumeration shall be made, the State of New Hampshire shall be entitled to chuse three, Massachusetts eight, Rhode-Island and Providence Plantations one, Connecticut five, New-York six, New Jersey four, Pennsylvania eight, Delaware one, Maryland six, Virginia ten, North Carolina five, South Carolina five, and Georgia three.

When vacancies happen in the Representation from any State, the Executive Authority thereof shall issue Writs of Election to fill such Vacancies.

The House of Representatives shall chuse their Speaker and other Officers; and shall have the sole Power of Impeachment.

Section 3. The Senate of the United States shall be composed of two Senators from each State, [chosen by the Legislature thereof,] for six Years; and each Senator shall have one Vote.

Immediately after they shall be assembled in Consequence of the first Election, they shall be divided as equally as may be into three Classes. The Seats of the Senators of the first Class shall be vacated at the Expiration of the second Year, of the second Class at the Expiration of the fourth Year, and of the third Class at the Expiration of the sixth Year, so that one third may be chosen every second Year; [and if Vacancies happen by Resignation, or otherwise, during the Recess of the Legislature of any State, the Executive thereof may make temporary Appointments until the next Meeting of the Legislature, which shall then fill such Vacancies.]

No Person shall be a Senator who shall not have attained to the Age of thirty Years, and been nine Years a Citizen of the United States, and who shall not, when elected, be an Inhabitant of that State for which he shall be chosen.

The Vice President of the United States shall be President of the Senate, but shall have no Vote, unless they be equally divided.

The Senate shall chuse their other Officers, and also a President pro tempore, in the Absence of the Vice President, or when he shall exercise the Office of President of the United States.

The Senate shall have the sole Power to try all Impeachments. When sitting for that Purpose, they shall be on Oath or Affirmation. When the President of the United States is tried, the Chief Justice shall preside: And no Person shall be convicted without the Concurrence of two thirds of the Members present.

Judgment in Cases of Impeachment shall not extend further than to removal from Office, and disqualification to hold and enjoy any Office of honor, Trust or Profit under the United States: but the Party convicted shall nevertheless be liable and subject to Indictment, Trial, Judgment and Punishment, according to Law.

Section 4. The Times, Places and Manner of holding Elections for Senators and Representatives, shall be prescribed in each State by the Legislature thereof; but the Congress may at any time by Law make or alter such Regulations, except as to the Places of chusing Senators.

The Congress shall assemble at least once in every Year, and such Meeting shall [be on the first Monday in December], unless they shall by Law appoint a different Day.

Section 5. Each House shall be the Judge of the Elections, Returns and Qualifications of its own Members, and a Majority of each shall constitute a Quorum to do Business; but a smaller Number may adjourn from day to day, and may be authorized to compel the Attendance of absent Members, in such Manner, and under such Penalties as each House may provide.

Each House may determine the Rules of its Proceedings, punish its Members for disorderly Behaviour, and, with the Concurrence of two thirds, expel a Member.

Each House shall keep a Journal of its Proceedings, and from time to time publish the same, excepting such Parts as may in their Judgment require Secrecy; and the Yeas and Nays of the Members of either House on any question shall, at the Desire of one fifth of those Present, be entered on the Journal.

Neither House, during the Session of Congress, shall, without the Consent of the other, adjourn for more than three days, nor to any other Place than that in which the two Houses shall be sitting.

Section 6. The Senators and Representatives shall receive a Compensation for their Services, to be ascertained by Law, and paid out of the Treasury of the United States. They shall in all Cases, except Treason, Felony and Breach of the Peace, be privileged from Arrest during their Attendance at the Session of their respective Houses, and in going to and returning from the same; and for any Speech or Debate in either House, they shall not be questioned in any other Place.

No Senator or Representative shall, during the Time for which he was elected, be appointed to any civil Office under the Authority of the United States, which shall have been created, or the Emoluments whereof shall have been encreased during such time; and no Person holding any Office under the United States, shall be a Member of either House during his Continuance in Office.

Section 7. All Bills for raising Revenue shall originate in the House of Representatives; but the Senate may propose or concur with Amendments as on other Bills.

Every Bill which shall have passed the House of Representatives and the Senate, shall, before it become a Law, be presented to the President of the United States; If he approve he shall sign it, but if not he shall return it, with his Objections to that House in which it shall have originated, who shall enter the Objections at large on their Journal, and proceed to reconsider it. If after such Reconsideration two thirds of that House shall agree to pass the Bill, it shall be sent, together with the Objections, to the other House, by which it shall likewise be reconsidered, and if approved by two thirds of that House, it shall become a Law. But in all such Cases the Votes of both Houses shall be determined by Yeas and Nays, and the Names of the Persons voting for and against the Bill shall be entered on the Journal of each House respectively. If any Bill shall not be returned by the President within ten Days (Sundays excepted) after it shall have been presented to him, the Same shall be a Law, in like Manner as if he had signed it, unless the Congress by their Adjournment prevent its Return, in which Case it shall not be a Law.

Every Order, Resolution, or Vote to which the Concurrence of the Senate and House of Representatives may be necessary (except on a question of Adjournment) shall be presented to the President of the United States; and before the Same shall take Effect, shall be approved by him, or being disapproved by him, shall be repassed by two thirds of the Senate and House of Representatives, according to the Rules and Limitations prescribed in the Case of a Bill.

Section 8. The Congress shall have Power To lay and collect Taxes, Duties, Imposts and Excises, to pay the Debts and provide for the common Defence and general Welfare of the United States; but all Duties, Imposts and Excises shall be uniform throughout the United States;

To borrow Money on the credit of the United States;

To regulate Commerce with foreign Nations, and among the several States, and with the Indian Tribes;

To establish an uniform Rule of Naturalization, and uniform Laws on the subject of Bankruptcies throughout the United States;

To coin Money, regulate the Value thereof, and of foreign Coin, and fix the Standard of Weights and Measures;

To provide for the Punishment of counterfeiting the Securities and current Coin of the United States;

To establish Post Offices and post Roads;

To promote the Progress of Science and useful Arts, by securing for limited Times to Authors and Inventors the exclusive Right to their respective Writings and Discoveries;

To constitute Tribunals inferior to the supreme Court;

To define and punish Piracies and Felonies committed on the high Seas, and Offences against the Law of Nations;

To declare War, grant Letters of Marque and Reprisal, and make Rules concerning Captures on Land and Water;

To raise and support Armies, but no Appropriation of Money to that Use shall be for a longer Term than two Years;

To provide and maintain a Navy;

To make Rules for the Government and Regulation of the land and naval Forces;

To provide for calling forth the Militia to execute the Laws of the Union, suppress Insurrections and repel Invasions;

To provide for organizing, arming, and disciplining, the Militia, and for governing such Part of them as may be employed in the Service of the United States, reserving to the States respectively, the Appointment of the Officers, and the Authority of training the Militia according to the discipline prescribed by Congress;

To exercise exclusive Legislation in all Cases whatsoever, over such District (not exceeding ten Miles square) as may, by Cession of particular States, and the Acceptance of Congress, become the Seat of the Government of the United States, and to exercise like Authority over all Places purchased by the Consent of the Legislature of the State in which the Same shall be, for the Erection of Forts, Magazines, Arsenals, dock-Yards, and other needful Buildings;—And

To make all Laws which shall be necessary and proper for carrying into Execution the foregoing Powers, and all other Powers vested by this Constitution in the Government of the United States, or in any Department or Officer thereof.

Section 9. The Migration or Importation of such Persons as any of the States now existing shall think proper to admit, shall not be prohibited by the Congress prior to the Year one thousand eight hundred and eight, but a Tax or duty may be imposed on such Importation, not exceeding ten dollars for each Person.

The Privilege of the Writ of Habeas Corpus shall not be suspended, unless when in Cases of Rebellion or Invasion the public Safety may require it.

No Bill of Attainder or ex post facto Law shall be passed.

No Capitation, or other direct, Tax shall be laid, unless in Proportion to the Census or Enumeration herein before directed to be taken.

No Tax or Duty shall be laid on Articles exported from any State.

No Preference shall be given by any Regulation of Commerce or Revenue to the Ports of one State over those of another; nor shall Vessels bound to, or from, one State, be obliged to enter, clear, or pay Duties in another.

No Money shall be drawn from the Treasury, but in Consequence of Appropriations made by Law; and a regular Statement and Account of the Receipts and Expenditures of all public Money shall be published from time to time.

No Title of Nobility shall be granted by the United States: And no Person holding any Office of Profit or Trust under them, shall, without the Consent of the Congress, accept of any present, Emolument, Office, or Title, of any kind whatever, from any King, Prince, or foreign State.

Section 10. No State shall enter into any Treaty, Alliance, or Confederation; grant Letters of Marque and Reprisal; coin Money; emit Bills of Credit; make any Thing but gold and silver Coin a Tender in Payment of Debts; pass any Bill of Attainder, ex post facto Law, or Law impairing the Obligation of Contracts, or grant any Title of Nobility.

No State shall, without the Consent of the Congress, lay any Imposts or Duties on Imports or Exports, except what may be absolutely necessary for executing it's inspection Laws: and the net Produce of all Duties and Imposts, laid by any State on Imports or Exports, shall be for the Use of the Treasury of the United States; and all such Laws shall be subject to the Revision and Controul of the Congress.

No State shall, without the Consent of Congress, lay any Duty of Tonnage, keep Troops, or Ships of War in time of Peace, enter into any Agreement or Compact with another State, or with a foreign Power, or engage in War, unless actually invaded, or in such imminent Danger as will not admit of delay.

ARTICLE II

Section 1. The executive Power shall be vested in a President of the United States of America. He shall hold his Office during the Term of four Years, and, together with the Vice President, chosen for the same Term, be elected, as follows

Each State shall appoint, in such Manner as the Legislature thereof may direct, a Number of Electors, equal to the whole Number of Senators and Representatives to which the State may be entitled in the Congress: but no Senator or Representative, or Person holding an Office of Trust or Profit under the United States, shall be appointed an Elector.

[The Electors shall meet in their respective States, and vote by Ballot for two Persons, of whom one at least shall not be an Inhabitant of the same State with themselves. And they shall make a List of all the Persons voted for, and of the Number of Votes for each; which List they shall sign and certify, and transmit sealed to the Seat of the Government of the United States, directed to the President of the Senate. The President of the Senate shall, in the Presence of the Senate and House of Representatives, open all the Certificates, and the Votes shall then be counted. The Person having the greatest Number of Votes shall be the President, if such Number be a Majority of the whole Number of Electors appointed; and if there be more than one who have such Majority, and have an equal Number of Votes, then the House of Representatives shall immediately chuse by Ballot one of them for President; and if no Person have a Majority, then from the five highest on the list the said House shall in like Manner chuse the President. But in chusing the President, the Votes shall be taken by States, the Representation from each State having one Vote; A quorum for this Purpose shall consist of a Member or Members from two thirds of the States, and a Majority of all the States shall be necessary to a Choice. In every Case, after the Choice of the President, the Person having the greatest Number of Votes of the Electors shall be the Vice President. But if there should remain two or more who have equal Votes, the Senate shall chuse from them by Ballot the Vice President.]

The Congress may determine the Time of chusing the Electors, and the Day on which they shall give their Votes; which Day shall be the same throughout the United States.

No Person except a natural born Citizen, or a Citizen of the United States, at the time of the Adoption of this Constitution, shall be eligible to the Office of President; neither shall any Person be eligible to that Office who shall not have attained to the Age of thirty five Years, and been fourteen Years a Resident within the United States.

In Case of the Removal of the President from Office, or of his Death, Resignation, or Inability to discharge the Powers and Duties of the said Office, the Same shall devolve on the Vice President, and the Congress may by Law provide for the Case of Removal, Death, Resignation or Inability, both of the President and Vice President, declaring what Officer shall then act as President, and such Officer shall act accordingly, until the Disability be removed, or a President shall be elected.

The President shall, at stated Times, receive for his Services, a Compensation, which shall neither be encreased nor diminished during the Period for which he shall have been elected, and he shall not receive within that Period any other Emolument from the United States, or any of them.

Before he enter on the Execution of his Office, he shall take the following Oath or Affirmation:—"I do solemnly swear (or affirm) that I will faithfully execute the Office of President of the United States, and will to the best of my Ability, preserve, protect and defend the Constitution of the United States."

Section 2. The President shall be Commander in Chief of the Army and Navy of the United States, and of the Militia of the several States, when called into the actual Service of the United States; he may require the Opinion, in writing, of the principal Officer in each of the executive Departments, upon any Subject relating to the Duties of their respective Offices, and he shall have Power to grant Reprieves and Pardons for Offences against the United States, except in Cases of Impeachment.

He shall have Power, by and with the Advice and Consent of the Senate, to make Treaties, provided two thirds of the Senators present concur; and he shall nominate, and by and with the Advice and Consent of the Senate, shall appoint Ambassadors, other public Ministers and Consuls, Judges of the supreme Court, and all other Officers of the United States, whose Appointments are not herein otherwise provided for, and which shall be established by Law: but the Congress may by Law vest the Appointment of such inferior Officers, as they think proper, in the President alone, in the Courts of Law, or in the Heads of Departments.

The President shall have Power to fill up all Vacancies that may happen during the Recess of the Senate, by granting Commissions which shall expire at the End of their next Session.

Section 3. He shall from time to time give to the Congress Information of the State of the Union, and recommend to their Consideration such Measures as he shall judge necessary and expedient; he may, on extraordinary Occasions, convene both Houses, or either of them, and in Case of Disagreement between them, with Respect to the Time of Adjournment, he may adjourn them to such Time as he shall think proper; he shall receive Ambassadors and other public Ministers; he shall take Care that the Laws be faithfully executed, and shall Commission all the Officers of the United States.

Section 4. The President, Vice President and all civil Officers of the United States, shall be removed from Office on Impeachment for, and Conviction of, Treason, Bribery, or other high Crimes and Misdemeanors.

ARTICLE III

Section 1. The judicial Power of the United States, shall be vested in one supreme Court, and in such inferior Courts as the Congress may from time to time ordain and establish. The Judges, both of the supreme and inferior Courts, shall hold their Offices during good Behaviour, and shall, at stated Times, receive for their Services, a Compensation, which shall not be diminished during their Continuance in Office.

Section 2. The judicial Power shall extend to all Cases, in Law and Equity, arising under this Constitution, the Laws of the United States, and Treaties made, or which shall be made, under their Authority;—to all Cases affecting Ambassadors, other public Ministers and Consuls;—to all Cases of admiralty and maritime Jurisdiction;—to Controversies to which the United States shall be a Party;—to Controversies between two or more States; —between a State and Citizens of another State; —between Citizens of different States;—between Citizens of the same State claiming Lands under Grants of different States, and between a State, or the Citizens thereof, and foreign States, Citizens or Subjects.

In all Cases affecting Ambassadors, other public Ministers and Consuls, and those in which a State shall be Party, the supreme Court shall have original Jurisdiction. In all the other Cases before mentioned, the supreme Court shall have appellate Jurisdiction, both as to Law and Fact, with such Exceptions, and under such Regulations as the Congress shall make.

The Trial of all Crimes, except in Cases of Impeachment, shall be by Jury; and such Trial shall be held in the State where the said Crimes shall have been committed; but when not committed within any State, the Trial shall be at such Place or Places as the Congress may by Law have directed.

Section 3. Treason against the United States, shall consist only in levying War against them, or in adhering to their Enemies, giving them Aid and Comfort. No Person shall be convicted of Treason unless on the Testimony of two Witnesses to the same overt Act, or on Confession in open Court.

The Congress shall have Power to declare the Punishment of Treason, but no Attainder of Treason shall work Corruption of Blood, or Forfeiture except during the Life of the Person attainted.

ARTICLE IV

Section 1. Full Faith and Credit shall be given in each State to the public Acts, Records, and judicial Proceedings of every other State. And the Congress may by general Laws prescribe the Manner in which such Acts, Records and Proceedings shall be proved, and the Effect thereof.

Section 2. The Citizens of each State shall be entitled to all Privileges and Immunities of Citizens in the several States.

A Person charged in any State with Treason, Felony, or other Crime, who shall flee from Justice, and be found in another State, shall on Demand of the executive Authority of the State from which he fled, be delivered up, to be removed to the State having Jurisdiction of the Crime.

[No Person held to Service or Labour in one State, under the Laws thereof, escaping into another, shall, in Consequence of any Law or Regulation therein, be discharged from such Service or Labour, but shall be delivered up on Claim of the Party to whom such Service or Labour may be due.]

Section 3. New States may be admitted by the Congress into this Union; but no new State shall be formed or erected within the Jurisdiction of any other State; nor any State be formed by the Junction of two or more States, or Parts of States, without the Consent of the Legislatures of the States concerned as well as of the Congress.

The Congress shall have Power to dispose of and make all needful Rules and Regulations respecting the Territory or other Property belonging to the United States; and nothing in this Constitution shall be so construed as to Prejudice any Claims of the United States, or of any particular State.

Section 4. The United States shall guarantee to every State in this Union a Republican Form of Government, and shall protect each of them against Invasion; and on Application of the Legislature, or of the Executive (when the Legislature cannot be convened) against domestic Violence.

ARTICLE V

The Congress, whenever two thirds of both Houses shall deem it necessary, shall propose Amendments to this Constitution, or, on the Application of the Legislatures of two thirds of the several States, shall call a Convention for proposing Amendments, which, in either Case, shall be valid to all Intents and Purposes, as Part of this Constitution, when ratified by the Legislatures of three fourths of the several States, or by Conventions in three fourths thereof, as the one or the other Mode of Ratification may be proposed by the Congress; Provided [that no Amendment which may be made prior to the Year One thousand eight hundred and eight shall in any Manner affect the first and fourth Clauses in the Ninth Section of the first Article; and] that no State, without its Consent, shall be deprived of its equal Suffrage in the Senate.

ARTICLE VI

All Debts contracted and Engagements entered into, before the Adoption of this Constitution, shall be as valid against the United States under this Constitution, as under the Confederation.

This Constitution, and the Laws of the United States which shall be made in Pursuance thereof; and all Treaties made, or which shall be made, under the Authority of the United States, shall be the supreme Law of the Land; and the Judges in every State shall be bound thereby, any Thing in the Constitution or Laws of any State to the Contrary notwithstanding.

The Senators and Representatives before mentioned, and the Members of the several State Legislatures, and all executive and judicial Officers, both of the United States and of the several States, shall be bound by Oath or Affirmation, to support this Constitution; but no religious Test shall ever be required as a Qualification to any Office or public Trust under the United States.

ARTICLE VII

The Ratification of the Conventions of nine States, shall be sufficient for the Establishment of this Constitution between the States so ratifying the Same. Done in Convention by the Unanimous Consent of the States present the Seventeenth Day of September in the Year of our Lord one thousand seven hundred and Eighty seven and of the Independence of the United States of America the Twelfth. IN WITNESS whereof We have hereunto subscribed our Names,

George Washington, *President and deputy from Virginia.*

New Hampshire: John Langdon,
Nicholas Gilman.

Massachusetts: Nathaniel Gorham,
Rufus King.

Connecticut: William Samuel Johnson,
Roger Sherman.

New York: Alexander Hamilton.

New Jersey: William Livingston,
David Brearley,
William Paterson,
Jonathan Dayton.

Pennsylvania: Benjamin Franklin,
Thomas Mifflin,
Robert Morris,
George Clymer,
Thomas FitzSimons,
Jared Ingersoll,
James Wilson,
Gouverneur Morris.

Delaware: George Read,
Gunning Bedford Jr.,
John Dickinson,
Richard Bassett,
Jacob Broom.

Maryland: James McHenry,
Daniel of St. Thomas Jenifer,
Daniel Carroll.

Virginia: John Blair,
James Madison Jr.

North Carolina: William Blount,
Richard Dobbs Spaight,
Hugh Williamson.

South Carolina: John Rutledge,
Charles Cotesworth Pinckney,
Charles Pinckney,
Pierce Butler.

Georgia: William Few,
Abraham Baldwin.

AMENDMENTS (First ten amendments ratified December 15, 1791.)

Amendment I

Congress shall make no law respecting an establishment of religion, or prohibiting the free exercise thereof; or abridging the freedom of speech, or of the press; or the right of the people peaceably to assemble, and to petition the Government for a redress of grievances.

Amendment II

A well regulated Militia, being necessary to the security of a free State, the right of the people to keep and bear Arms, shall not be infringed.

Amendment III

No Soldier shall, in time of peace be quartered in any house, without the consent of the Owner, nor in time of war, but in a manner to be prescribed by law.

Amendment IV

The right of the people to be secure in their persons, houses, papers, and effects, against unreasonable searches and seizures, shall not be violated, and no Warrants shall issue, but upon probable cause, supported by Oath or affirmation, and particularly describing the place to be searched, and the persons or things to be seized.

Amendment V

No person shall be held to answer for a capital, or otherwise infamous crime, unless on a presentment or indictment of a Grand Jury, except in cases arising in the land or naval forces, or in the Militia, when in actual service in time of War or public danger; nor shall any person be subject for the same offence to be twice put in jeopardy of life or limb; nor shall be compelled in any criminal case to be a witness against himself, nor be deprived of life, liberty, or property, without due process of law; nor shall private property be taken for public use, without just compensation.

Amendment VI

In all criminal prosecutions, the accused shall enjoy the right to a speedy and public trial, by an impartial jury of the State and district wherein the crime shall have been committed, which district shall have been previously ascertained by law, and to be informed of the nature and cause of the accusation; to be confronted with the witnesses against him; to have compulsory process for obtaining witnesses in his favor, and to have the Assistance of Counsel for his defence.

Amendment VII

In Suits at common law, where the value in controversy shall exceed twenty dollars, the right of trial by jury shall be preserved, and no fact tried by a jury, shall be otherwise re-examined in any Court of the United States, than according to the rules of the common law.

Amendment VIII

Excessive bail shall not be required, nor excessive fines imposed, nor cruel and unusual punishments inflicted.

Amendment IX

The enumeration in the Constitution, of certain rights, shall not be construed to deny or disparage others retained by the people.

Amendment X

The powers not delegated to the United States by the Constitution, nor prohibited by it to the States, are reserved to the States respectively, or to the people.

Amendment XI (Ratified February 7, 1795.)

The Judicial power of the United States shall not be construed to extend to any suit in law or equity, commenced or prosecuted against one of the United States by Citizens of another State, or by Citizens or Subjects of any Foreign State.

Amendment XII (Ratified June 15, 1804.)

The Electors shall meet in their respective states and vote by ballot for President and Vice-President, one of whom, at least, shall not be an inhabitant of the same state with themselves; they shall name in their ballots the person voted for as President, and in distinct ballots the person voted for as Vice-President, and they shall make distinct lists of all persons voted for as President, and of all persons voted for as Vice-President, and of the number of votes for each, which lists they shall sign and certify, and transmit sealed to the seat of the government of the United States, directed to the President of the Senate;—The President of the Senate shall, in the presence of the Senate and House of Representatives, open all the certificates and the votes shall then be counted;—The person having the greatest number of votes for President, shall be the President, if such number be a majority of the whole number of Electors appointed; and if no person have such majority, then from the persons having the highest numbers not exceeding three on the list of those voted for as President, the House of Representatives shall choose immediately, by ballot, the President. But in choosing the President, the votes shall be taken by states, the representation from each state having one vote; a quorum for this purpose shall consist of a member or members from two-thirds of the states, and a majority of all the states shall be necessary to a choice. [And if the House of Representatives shall not choose a President whenever the right of choice shall devolve upon them, before the fourth day of March next following, then the Vice-President shall act as President, as in the case of the death or other constitutional disability of the President.] The person having the greatest number of votes as Vice-President, shall be the Vice-President, if such number be a majority of the whole number of Electors appointed, and if no person have a majority, then from the two highest numbers on the list, the Senate shall choose the Vice-President; a quorum for the purpose shall consist of two-thirds of the whole number of Senators, and a majority of the whole number shall be necessary to a choice. But no person constitutionally ineligible to the office of President shall be eligible to that of Vice-President of the United States.

Amendment XIII (Ratified December 6, 1865.)

Section 1. Neither slavery nor involuntary servitude, except as a punishment for crime whereof the party shall have been duly convicted, shall exist within the United States, or any place subject to their jurisdiction.

Section 2. Congress shall have power to enforce this article by appropriate legislation.

Amendment XIV (Ratified July 9, 1868.)

Section 1. All persons born or naturalized in the United States, and subject to the jurisdiction thereof, are citizens of the United States and of the State wherein they reside. No State shall make or enforce any law which shall abridge the privileges or immunities of citizens of the United States; nor shall any State deprive any person of life, liberty, or property, without due process of law; nor deny to any person within its jurisdiction the equal protection of the laws.

Section 2. Representatives shall be apportioned among the several States according to their respective numbers, counting the whole number of persons in each State, excluding Indians not taxed. But when the right to vote at any election for the choice of electors for President and Vice President of the United States, Representatives in Congress, the Executive and Judicial officers of a State, or the members of the Legislature thereof, is denied to any of the male inhabitants of such State, being twenty-one years of age, and citizens of the United States, or in any way abridged, except for participation in rebellion, or other crime, the basis of representation therein shall be reduced in the proportion which the number of such male citizens shall bear to the whole number of male citizens twenty-one years of age in such State.

Section 3. No person shall be a Senator or Representative in Congress, or elector of President and Vice President, or hold any office, civil or military, under the United States, or under any State, who, having previously taken an oath, as a member of Congress, or as an officer of the United States, or as a member of any State legislature, or as an executive or judicial officer of any State, to support the Constitution of the United States, shall have engaged in insurrection or rebellion against the same, or given aid or comfort to the enemies thereof. But Congress may by a vote of two-thirds of each House, remove such disability.

Section 4. The validity of the public debt of the United States, authorized by law, including debts incurred for payment of pensions and bounties for services in suppressing insurrection or rebellion, shall not be questioned. But neither the United States nor any State shall assume or pay any debt or obligation incurred in aid of insurrection or rebellion against the United States, or any claim for the loss or emancipation of any slave; but all such debts, obligations and claims shall be held illegal and void.

Section 5. The Congress shall have power to enforce, by appropriate legislation, the provisions of this article.

Amendment XV (Ratified February 3, 1870.)

Section 1. The right of citizens of the United States to vote shall not be denied or abridged by the United States or by any State on account of race, color, or previous condition of servitude.

Section 2. The Congress shall have power to enforce this article by appropriate legislation.

Amendment XVI (Ratified February 3, 1913.)

The Congress shall have power to lay and collect taxes on incomes, from whatever source derived, without apportionment among the several States, and without regard to any census or enumeration.

Amendment XVII (Ratified April 8, 1913.)

The Senate of the United States shall be composed of two Senators from each State, elected by the people thereof, for six years; and each Senator shall have one vote. The electors in each State shall have the qualifications requisite for electors of the most numerous branch of the State legislatures.

When vacancies happen in the representation of any State in the Senate, the executive authority of such State shall issue writs of election to fill such vacancies: *Provided,* That the legislature of any State may empower the executive thereof to make temporary appointments until the people fill the vacancies by election as the legislature may direct.

This amendment shall not be so construed as to affect the election or term of any Senator chosen before it becomes valid as part of the Constitution.

Amendment XVIII (Ratified January 16, 1919.)

Section 1. After one year from the ratification of this article the manufacture, sale, or transportation of intoxicating liquors within, the importation thereof into, or the exportation thereof from the United States and all territory subject to the jurisdiction thereof for beverage purposes is hereby prohibited.

Section 2. The Congress and the several States shall have concurrent power to enforce this article by appropriate legislation.

[Section 3. This article shall be inoperative unless it shall have been ratified as an amendment to the Constitution by the legislatures of the several States, as provided in the Constitution, within seven years from the date of the submission hereof to the States by the Congress.]

Amendment XIX (Ratified August 18, 1920.)

The right of citizens of the United States to vote shall not be denied or abridged by the United States or by any State on account of sex.

Congress shall have power to enforce this article by appropriate legislation.

Amendment XX (Ratified January 23, 1933.)

Section 1. The terms of the President and Vice President shall end at noon on the 20th day of January, and the terms of Senators and Representatives at noon on the 3d day of January, of the years in which such terms would have ended if this article had not been ratified; and the terms of their successors shall then begin.

Section 2. The Congress shall assemble at least once in every year, and such meeting shall begin at noon on the 3d day of January, unless they shall by law appoint a different day.

Section 3. If, at the time fixed for the beginning of the term of the President, the President elect shall have died, the Vice President elect shall become President. If a President shall not have been chosen before the time fixed for the beginning of his term, or if the President elect shall have failed to qualify, then the Vice President elect shall act as President until a President shall have qualified; and the Congress may by law provide for the case wherein neither a President elect nor a Vice President elect shall have qualified, declaring who shall then act as President, or the manner in which one who is to act shall be selected, and such person shall act accordingly until a President or Vice President shall have qualified.

Section 4. The Congress may by law provide for the case of the death of any of the persons from whom the House of Representatives may choose a President whenever the right of choice shall have devolved upon them, and for the case of the death of any of the persons from whom the Senate may choose a Vice President whenever the right of choice shall have devolved upon them.

Section 5. Sections 1 and 2 shall take effect on the 15th day of October following the ratification of this article.

Section 6. This article shall be inoperative unless it shall have been ratified as an amendment to the Constitution by the legislatures of three-fourths of the several States within seven years from the date of its submission.

Amendment XXI (Ratified December 5, 1933.)

Section 1. The eighteenth article of amendment to the Constitution of the United States is hereby repealed.

Section 2. The transportation or importation into any State, Territory, or possession of the United States for delivery or use therein of intoxicating liquors, in violation of the laws thereof, is hereby prohibited.

Section 3. This article shall be inoperative unless it shall have been ratified as an amendment to the Constitution by conventions in the several States, as provided in the Constitution, within seven years from the date of the submission hereof to the States by the Congress.

Amendment XXII (Ratified February 27, 1951.)

Section 1. No person shall be elected to the office of the President more than twice, and no person who has held the office of President, or acted as President, for more than two years of a term to which some other person was elected President shall be elected to the office of the President more than once. But this Article shall not apply to any person holding the office of President when this Article was proposed by the Congress, and shall not prevent any person who may be holding the office of President, or acting as President, during the term within which this Article become operative from holding the office of President or acting as President during the remainder of such term.

Section 2. This article shall be inoperative unless it shall have been ratified as an amendment to the Constitution by the legislatures of three-fourths of the several States within seven years from the date of its submission to the States by the Congress.

Amendment XXIII (Ratified March 29, 1961.)

Section 1. The District constituting the seat of Government of the United States shall appoint in such manner as the Congress may direct:

A number of electors of President and Vice President equal to the whole number of Senators and Representatives in Congress to which the District would be entitled if it were a State, but in no event more than the least populous State; they shall be in addition to those appointed by the States, but they shall be considered, for the purposes of the election of President and Vice President, to be electors appointed by a State; and they shall meet in the District and perform such duties as provided by the twelfth article of amendment.

Section 2. The Congress shall have power to enforce this article by appropriate legislation.

Amendment XXIV (Ratified January 23, 1964.)

Section 1. The right of citizens of the United States to vote in any primary or other election for President or Vice President, for electors for President or Vice President, or for Senator or Representative in Congress, shall not be denied or abridged by the United States or any State by reason of failure to pay any poll tax or other tax.

Section 2. The Congress shall have power to enforce this article by appropriate legislation.

Amendment XXV (Ratified February 10, 1967.)

Section 1. In case of the removal of the President from office or of his death or resignation, the Vice President shall become President.

Section 2. Whenever there is a vacancy in the office of the Vice President, the President shall nominate a Vice President who shall take office upon confirmation by a majority vote of both Houses of Congress.

Section 3. Whenever the President transmits to the President pro tempore of the Senate and the Speaker of the House of Representatives his written declaration that he is unable to discharge the powers and duties of his office, and until he transmits to them a written declaration to the contrary, such powers and duties shall be discharged by the Vice President as Acting President.

Section 4. Whenever the Vice President and a majority of either the principal officers of the executive departments or of such other body as Congress may by law provide, transmit to the President pro tempore of the Senate and the Speaker of the House of Representatives their written declaration that the President is unable to discharge the powers and duties of his office, the Vice President shall immediately assume the powers and duties of the office as Acting President.

Thereafter, when the President transmits to the President pro tempore of the Senate and the Speaker of the House of Representatives his written declaration that no inability exists, he shall resume the powers and duties of his office unless the Vice President and a majority of either the principal officers of the executive department or of such other body as Congress may by law provide, transmit within four days to the President pro tempore of the Senate and the Speaker of the House of Representatives their written declaration that the President is unable to discharge the powers and duties of his office. Thereupon Congress shall decide the issue, assembling within forty-eight hours for that purpose if not in session. If the Congress, within twenty-one days after receipt of the latter written declaration, or, if Congress is not in session, within twenty-one days after Congress is required to assemble, determines by two-thirds vote of both Houses that the President is unable to discharge the powers and duties of his office, the Vice President shall continue to discharge the same as Acting President; otherwise, the President shall resume the powers and duties of his office.

Amendment XXVI (Ratified July 1, 1971.)

Section 1. The right of citizens of the United States, who are eighteen years of age or older, to vote shall not be denied or abridged by the United States or by any State on account of age.

Section 2. The Congress shall have power to enforce this article by appropriate legislation.

Amendment XXVII (Ratified May 7, 1992.)

No law varying the compensation for the services of the Senators and Representatives shall take effect, until an election of Representatives shall have intervened.

Source: United States Government Manual, 2001–2002, www.access.gpo.gov/nara/browse-gm-01.html.

EMANCIPATION PROCLAMATION (PRELIMINARY, 1862)

Secretary of State William H. Seward's additions to Lincoln's draft are enclosed in brackets; his deletions are indicated by strike-throughs.

I, Abraham Lincoln, President of the United States of American, and Commander-in-Chief of the Army and Navy thereof, do hereby proclaim and declare that hereafter, as heretofore, the war will be prosecuted for the object of practically restoring the constitutional relation between the United States, and each of the states, and the people thereof, in which states that relation is, or may be suspended or disturbed.

That it is my purpose, upon the next meeting of Congress to again recommend the adoption of a practical measure tendering pecuniary aid to the free acceptance or rejection of all slave-states, so called, the people whereof may not then be in rebellion against the United States, and which states [~~and~~] may then have voluntarily adopted, or thereafter may voluntarily adopt, immediate, or gradual abolishment of slavery within their respective limits; and that the effort to colonize persons of African descent [with the consent] upon this continent, or elsewhere, [with the previously obtained consent of the governments existing there elsewhere,] will be continued.

That on the first day of January in the year of our Lord, one thousand eight hundred and sixty-three, all persons held as slaves within any state, or designated part of a state, the people whereof thenceforward, and forever free; and the executive government of the United States [including the military and naval authority thereof] will, ~~during the continuance in office of the present incumbents~~, recognize [and maintain the freedom of] such persons, ~~as being free~~, and will do no act or acts to repress such persons, or any of them, in any efforts they may make for their actual freedom.

That the executive will, on the first day of January aforesaid, by proclamation, designate the States, and parts of states, if any, in which the people thereof respectively, shall then be in rebellion against the United States; and the fact that any state, or the people thereof shall, on that day be, in good faith represented in the Congress of the United States, by members chosen thereto, at elections wherein a majority of the qualified voters of such state shall have participated, shall, in the absence of strong countervailing testimony, be deemed conclusive evidence that such state, and the people thereof, are not then in rebellion against the United States.

That attention is hereby called to an Act of Congress entitled "An Act to make an additional Article of War" Approved March 13, 1862, and which act is in the words and figure following:

> "Be it enacted by the Senate and House of Representatives of the United States of America in Congress assembled. that hereafter the following shall be promulgated as an additional article of war for the government of the Army of the United States, and shall be obeyed and observed as such:
>
> Article-. All officers or persons in the military or naval services of the United States are prohibited from employing any of the forces under their respective commands for the purpose of returning fugitive from service or labor, who may have escaped from any persons to whom such service or labor is claimed to be due and any officer who shall be found guilty by a court martial of violating this article shall be dismissed from the service.
>
> SEC.2. And be it further enacted, that this act shall take effect from and after its passage."

Also to the ninth and tenth sections of an act entitled "An Act to suppress Insurrection, to punish Treason and Rebellion, to seize and confiscate property of rebels, and for other purposes," approved July 17, 1862, and which sections are:

> "SEC. 9. And be it further enacted, that all slaves of persons who shall hereafter be engaged in rebellion against the government of the United States, or who shall in any way give aid or comfort thereto, escaping from such persons and taking refuge within the lines of the army; and all slaves captured from such persons or deserted by them and coming under the control of the government of the United States; and all slaves of such persons found [or] being within any place occupied by rebel forces and afterwards occupied by the forces of the United States, shall be deemed captives of war, and shall be forever free of their servitude, and not again held as slaves.
>
> "SEC. 10. And be it further enacted, That no slave escaping into any State, Territory, or the District of Columbia, from any other State, shall be delivered up, or in any way impeded or hindered of his liberty, except for crime, or some offence against the laws, unless the person claiming said fugitive shall first make oath that the person to whom the labor or service of such fugitive is alleged to be due is his lawful owner, and has not borne arms against the United States in the present rebellion, nor in any way given aid and comfort thereto; and no person engaged in the military or naval service of the United States shall, under any pretence whatever, assume to decide on the validity of the claim of any person to the service or labor of any other person, or surrender up any such person to the claimant, on pain of being dismissed from the service."

And I do hereby enjoin upon and order all persons engaged in the military and naval service of the United States to observe, obey, and enforce, within their respective spheres of service, the act and sections above recited.

And the executive will [in due time] [~~at the next session of congress~~] recommend that all citizens of the United States who shall have remained loyal thereto throughout the rebellion, shall (upon the restoration of the constitutional relation between the United States, and their respective states, and people, if that relation shall have been suspended or disturbed) be compensated for all losses by acts of the United States, including the loss of slaves.

Source: Library of Congress, http://memory.loc.gov/ammem/alhtml/alrb/step/09221862/001.html.

EMANCIPATION PROCLAMATION (FINAL, 1863)

Whereas on the 22nd day of September, A.D. 1862, a proclamation was issued by the President of the United States, containing, among other things, the following, to wit:

> "That on the 1st day of January, A.D. 1863, all persons held as slaves within any State or designated part of a State the people whereof shall then be in rebellion against the United States shall be then, thenceforward, and forever free; and the executive government of the United States, including the military and naval authority thereof, will recognize and maintain the freedom of such persons and will do no act or

acts to repress such persons, or any of them, in any efforts they may make for their actual freedom.

"That the executive will on the 1st day of January aforesaid, by proclamation, designate the States and parts of States, if any, in which the people thereof, respectively, shall then be in rebellion against the United States; and the fact that any State or the people thereof shall on that day be in good faith represented in the Congress of the United States by members chosen thereto at elections wherein a majority of the qualified voters of such States shall have participated shall, in the absence of strong countervailing testimony, be deemed conclusive evidence that such State and the people thereof are not then in rebellion against the United States."

Now, therefore, I, Abraham Lincoln, President of the United States, by virtue of the power in me vested as Commander-In-Chief of the Army and Navy of the United States in time of actual armed rebellion against the authority and government of the United States, and as a fit and necessary war measure for supressing said rebellion, do, on this 1st day of January, A.D. 1863, and in accordance with my purpose so to do, publicly proclaimed for the full period of one hundred days from the first day above mentioned, order and designate as the States and parts of States wherein the people thereof, respectively, are this day in rebellion against the United States the following, to wit:

Arkansas, Texas, Louisiana (except the parishes of St. Bernard, Palquemines, Jefferson, St. John, St. Charles, St. James, Ascension, Assumption, Terrebone, Lafourche, St. Mary, St. Martin, and Orleans, including the city of New Orleans), Mississippi, Alabama, Florida, Georgia, South Carolina, North Carolina, and Virginia (except the forty-eight counties designated as West Virginia, and also the counties of Berkeley, Accomac, Northhampton, Elizabeth City, York, Princess Anne, and Norfolk, including the cities of Norfolk and Portsmouth), and which excepted parts are for the present left precisely as if this proclamation were not issued.

And by virtue of the power and for the purpose aforesaid, I do order and declare that all persons held as slaves within said designated States and parts of States are, and henceforward shall be, free; and that the Executive Government of the United States, including the military and naval authorities thereof, will recognize and maintain the freedom of said persons.

And I hereby enjoin upon the people so declared to be free to abstain from all violence, unless in necessary self-defence; and I recommend to them that, in all case when allowed, they labor faithfully for reasonable wages.

And I further declare and make known that such persons of suitable condition will be received into the armed service of the United States to garrison forts, positions, stations, and other places, and to man vessels of all sorts in said service.

And upon this act, sincerely believed to be an act of justice, warranted by the Constitution upon military necessity, I invoke the considerate judgment of mankind and the gracious favor of Almighty God.

Source: Jerome B. Agel, *We the People: Great Documents of the American Nation* (New York: Barnes and Noble, 1997), 214–215.

TO SECURE THESE RIGHTS (1947)

The Time Is Now

Twice before in American history the nation has found it necessary to review the state of its civil rights. The first time was during the 15 years between 1776 and 1791, from the drafting of the Declaration of Independence through the Articles of Confederation experiment to the writing of the Constitution and the Bill of Rights. It was then that the distinctively American heritage was finally distilled from earlier views of liberty. The second time was when the Union was temporarily sundered over the question of whether it could exist "half-slave" and "half-free."

It is our profound conviction that we have come to a time for a third reexamination of the situation, and a sustained drive ahead. Our reasons for believing this are those of conscience, of self-interest, and of survival in a threatening world. Or to put it another way, we have a moral reason, an economic reason, and an international reason for believing that the time for action is now.

The Moral Reason

We have considered the American heritage of freedom at some length. We need no further justification for a broad and immediate program than the need to reaffirm our faith in the traditional American morality. The pervasive gap between our aims and what we actually do is creating a kind of moral dry rot which eats away at the emotional and rational bases of democratic beliefs. There are times when the difference between what we preach about civil rights and what we practice is shockingly illustrated by individual outrages. There are times when the whole structure of our ideology is made ridiculous by individual instances. And there are certain continuing, quiet, omnipresent practices which do irreparable damage to our beliefs.

As examples of "moral erosion" there are the consequences of suffrage limitations in the South. The fact that Negroes and many whites have not been allowed to vote in some states has actually sapped the morality underlying universal suffrage. . . . Wartime segregation in the armed forces is another instance of how a social pattern may wreak moral havoc. . . .

It is impossible to decide who suffers the greatest moral damage from our civil rights transgressions, because all of us are hurt. . . . All of us must endure the cynicism about democratic values which our failures breed. . . .

The Economic Reason

One of the principal economic problems facing us and the rest of the world is achieving maximum production and continued prosperity. The loss of a huge, potential market for goods is a direct result of the economic discrimination which is practiced against many of our minority groups. A sort of vicious circle is produced. Discrimination depresses the wages and income of minority groups. As a result, their purchasing power is curtailed and markets are reduced. Reduced markets result in reduced production. This cuts down employment, which of course means lower wages and still fewer job opportunities. . . .

Discrimination imposes a direct cost upon our economy through the wasteful duplication and many facilities and services required by the "separate but equal" policy. . . . Many of the prominent American minorities are confined—by economic discrimination, by law, by restrictive covenants, and by social pressure—to the most dilapidated, undesirable locations. Property in these locations yields a smaller return in taxes, which is seldom sufficient to meet the inordinately high cost of public services in depressed areas. The majority pays a high price in taxes for the low status of minorities. . . .

What we have lost in money, production, invention, citizenship, and leadership as the price for damaged, thwarted personalities—these are beyond estimate. . . .

The International Reason

Our position in the postwar world is so vital to the future that our smallest actions have far-reaching effects. . . . We cannot escape the fact that our civil rights record has been an issue in world politics. The world's press and radio are full of it. . . .

Source: "To Secure These Rights: The Report of the President's Committee on Civil Rights" (Washington, D.C.: U.S. Government Printing Office, 1947).

UNIVERSAL DECLARATION OF HUMAN RIGHTS (1948)

Article 1. All human beings are born free and equal in dignity and rights. They are endowed with reason and conscience and should act towards one another in a spirit of brotherhood.

Article 2. Everyone is entitled to all the rights and freedoms set forth in this Declaration, without distinction of any kind, such as race, colour, sex, language, religion, political or other opinion, national or social origin, property, birth or other status. Furthermore, no distinction shall be made on the basis of the political, jurisdictional or international status of the country or territory to which a person belongs, whether it be independent, trust, non-self-governing or under any other limitation of sovereignty.

Article 3. Everyone has the right to life, liberty and security of person.

Article 4. No one shall be held in slavery or servitude; slavery and the slave trade shall be prohibited in all their forms.

Article 5. No one shall be subjected to torture or to cruel, inhuman or degrading treatment or punishment.

Article 6. Everyone has the right to recognition everywhere as a person before the law.

Article 7. All are equal before the law and are entitled without any discrimination to equal protection of the law. All are entitled to equal protection against any discrimination in violation of this Declaration and against any incitement to such discrimination.

Article 8. Everyone has the right to an effective remedy by the competent national tribunals for acts violating the fundamental rights granted him by the constitution or by law.

Article 9. No one shall be subjected to arbitrary arrest, detention or exile.

Article 10. Everyone is entitled in full equality to a fair and public hearing by an independent and impartial tribunal, in the determination of his rights and obligations and of any criminal charge against him.

Article 11. (1) Everyone charged with a penal offence has the right to be presumed innocent until proved guilty according to law in a public trial at which he has had all the guarantees necessary for his defence.

(2) No one shall be held guilty of any penal offence on account of any act or omission which did not constitute a penal offence, under national or international law, at the time when it was committed. Nor shall a heavier penalty be imposed than the one that was applicable at the time the penal offence was committed.

Article 12. No one shall be subjected to arbitrary interference with his privacy, family, home or correspondence, nor to attacks upon his honour and reputation. Everyone has the right to the protection of the law against such interference or attacks.

Article 13. (1) Everyone has the right to freedom of movement and residence within the borders of each state.

(2) Everyone has the right to leave any country, including his own, and to return to his country.

Article 14. (1) Everyone has the right to seek and to enjoy in other countries asylum from persecution.

(2) This right may not be invoked in the case of prosecutions genuinely arising from non-political crimes or from acts contrary to the purposes and principles of the United Nations.

Article 15. (1) Everyone has the right to a nationality.

(2) No one shall be arbitrarily deprived of his nationality nor denied the right to change his nationality.

Article 16. (1) Men and women of full age, without any limitation due to race, nationality or religion, have the right to marry and to found a family. They are entitled to equal rights as to marriage, during marriage and at its dissolution.

(2) Marriage shall be entered into only with the free and full consent of the intending spouses.

(3) The family is the natural and fundamental group unit of society and is entitled to protection by society and the State.

Article 17. (1) Everyone has the right to own property alone as well as in association with others.

(2) No one shall be arbitrarily deprived of his property.

Article 18. Everyone has the right to freedom of thought, conscience and religion; this right includes freedom to change his religion or belief, and freedom, either alone or in community with others and in public or private, to manifest his religion or belief in teaching, practice, worship and observance.

Article 19. Everyone has the right to freedom of opinion and expression; this right includes freedom to hold opinions without interference and to seek, receive and impart information and ideas through any media and regardless of frontiers.

Article 20. (1) Everyone has the right to freedom of peaceful assembly and association.

(2) No one may be compelled to belong to an association.

Article 21. (1) Everyone has the right to take part in the government of his country, directly or through freely chosen representatives.

(2) Everyone has the right of equal access to public service in his country.

(3) The will of the people shall be the basis of the authority of government; this will shall be expressed in periodic and genuine elections which shall be by universal and equal suffrage and shall be held by secret vote or by equivalent free voting procedures.

Article 22. Everyone, as a member of society, has the right to social security and is entitled to realization, through national effort and international co-operation and in accordance with the organization and resources of each State, of the economic, social and cultural rights indispensable for his dignity and the free development of his personality.

Article 23. (1) Everyone has the right to work, to free choice of employment, to just and favourable conditions of work and to protection against unemployment.

(2) Everyone, without any discrimination, has the right to equal pay for equal work.

(3) Everyone who works has the right to just and favourable remuneration ensuring for himself and his family an existence worthy of human dignity, and supplemented, if necessary, by other means of social protection.

(4) Everyone has the right to form and to join trade unions for the protection of his interests.

Article 24. Everyone has the right to rest and leisure, including reasonable limitation of working hours and periodic holidays with pay.

Article 25. (1) Everyone has the right to a standard of living adequate for the health and well-being of himself and of his family, including food, clothing, housing and medical care and necessary social services, and the right to security in the event of unemployment, sickness, disability, widowhood, old age or other lack of livelihood in circumstances beyond his control.

(2) Motherhood and childhood are entitled to special care and assistance. All children, whether born in or out of wedlock, shall enjoy the same social protection.

Article 26. (1) Everyone has the right to education. Education shall be free, at least in the elementary and fundamental stages. Elementary education shall be compulsory. Technical and professional education shall be made generally available and higher education shall be equally accessible to all on the basis of merit.

(2) Education shall be directed to the full development of the human personality and to the

strengthening of respect for human rights and fundamental freedoms. It shall promote understanding, tolerance and friendship among all nations, racial or religious groups, and shall further the activities of the United Nations for the maintenance of peace.

(3) Parents have a prior right to choose the kind of education that shall be given to their children.

Article 27. (1) Everyone has the right freely to participate in the cultural life of the community, to enjoy the arts and to share in scientific advancement and its benefits.

(2) Everyone has the right to the protection of the moral and material interests resulting from any scientific, literary or artistic production of which he is the author.

Article 28. Everyone is entitled to a social and international order in which the rights and freedoms set forth in this Declaration can be fully realized.

Article 29. (1) Everyone has duties to the community in which alone the free and full development of his personality is possible.

(2) In the exercise of his rights and freedoms, everyone shall be subject only to such limitations as are determined by law solely for the purpose of securing due recognition and respect for the rights and freedoms of others and of meeting the just requirements of morality, public order and the general welfare in a democratic society.

(3) These rights and freedoms may in no case be exercised contrary to the purposes and principles of the United Nations.

Article 30. Nothing in this Declaration may be interpreted as implying for any State, group or person any right to engage in any activity or to perform any act aimed at the destruction of any of the rights and freedoms set forth herein.

Source: Universal Declaration of Human Rights, www.un.org/Overview/rights.html.

THE SOUTHERN MANIFESTO (1956)

DECLARATION OF CONSTITUTIONAL PRINCIPLES

The unwarranted decision of the Supreme Court in the public school cases is now bearing the fruit always produced when men substitute naked power for established law.

The Founding Fathers gave us a Constitution of checks and balances because they realized the inescapable lesson of history that no man or group of men can be safely entrusted with unlimited power. They framed this Constitution with its provisions for change by amendment in order to secure the fundamentals of government against the dangers of temporary popular passion or the personal predilections of public officeholders.

We regard the decisions of the Supreme Court in the school cases as a clear abuse of judicial power. It climaxes a trend in the Federal Judiciary undertaking to legislate, in derogation of the authority of Congress, and to encroach upon the reserved rights of the States and the people.

The original Constitution does not mention education. Neither does the 14th Amendment nor any other amendment. The debates preceding the submission of the 14th Amendment clearly show that there was no intent that it should affect the system of education maintained by the States. The very Congress which proposed the amendment subsequently provided for segregated schools in the District of Columbia. When the amendment was adopted in 1868, there were 37 States of the Union. . . .

Every one of the 26 States that had any substantial racial differences among its people, either approved the operation of segregated schools already in existence or subsequently established such schools by action of the same law-making body which considered the 14th Amendment.

As admitted by the Supreme Court in the public school case (*Brown v. Board of Education*), the doctrine of separate but equal schools "apparently originated in *Roberts v. City of Boston* (1849), upholding school segregation against attack as being violative of a State constitutional guarantee of equality." This constitutional doctrine began in the North, not in the South, and it was followed not only in Massachusetts, but in Connecticut, New York, Illinois, Indiana, Michigan, Minnesota, New Jersey, Ohio, Pennsylvania and other northern states until they, exercising their rights as states through the constitutional processes of local self-government, changed their school systems.

In the case of *Plessy v. Ferguson* in 1896 the Supreme Court expressly declared that under the 14th Amendment no person was denied any of his rights if the States provided separate but equal facilities. This decision has been followed in many other cases. It is notable that the Supreme Court, speaking through Chief Justice Taft, a former President of the United States, unanimously declared in 1927 in *Lum v. Rice* that the "separate but equal" principle is "within the discretion of the State in regulating its public schools and does not conflict with the 14th Amendment."

This interpretation, restated time and again, became a part of the life of the people of many of the States and confirmed their habits, traditions, and way of life. It is founded on elemental humanity and commonsense, for parents should not be deprived by Government of the right to direct the lives and education of their own children.

Though there has been no constitutional amendment or act of Congress changing this established legal principle almost a century old, the Supreme Court of the United States, with no legal basis for such action, undertook to exercise their naked judicial power and substituted their personal political and social ideas for the established law of the land.

This unwarranted exercise of power by the Court, contrary to the Constitution, is creating chaos and confusion in the States principally affected. It is destroying the amicable relations between the white and Negro races that have been created through 90 years of patient effort by the good people of both races. It has planted hatred and suspicion where there has been heretofore friendship and understanding.

Without regard to the consent of the governed, outside mediators are threatening immediate and revolutionary changes in our public schools systems. If done, this is certain to destroy the system of public education in some of the States.

With the gravest concern for the explosive and dangerous condition created by this decision and inflamed by outside meddlers:

We reaffirm our reliance on the Constitution as the fundamental law of the land.

We decry the Supreme Court's encroachment on the rights reserved to the States and to the people, contrary to established law, and to the Constitution.

We commend the motives of those States which have declared the intention to resist forced integration by any lawful means.

We appeal to the States and people who are not directly affected by these decisions to consider the constitutional principles involved against the time when they too, on issues vital to them may be the victims of judicial encroachment.

Even though we constitute a minority in the present Congress, we have full faith that a majority of the American people believe in the dual system of government which has enabled us to achieve our greatness and will in time demand that the reserved rights of the States and of the people be made secure against judicial usurpation.

We pledge ourselves to use all lawful means to bring about a reversal of this decision which is contrary to the Constitution and to prevent the use of force in its implementation.

In this trying period, as we all seek to right this wrong, we appeal to our people not to be provoked by the agitators and troublemakers invading our States and to scrupulously refrain from disorder and lawless acts.

Signed by:

MEMBERS OF THE UNITED STATES SENATE

Walter F. George, Richard B. Russell, John Stennis, Sam J. Elvin Jr., Strom Thurmond, Harry F. Byrd, A. Willis Robertson, John L. McClellan, Allen J. Ellender, Russell B. Long, Lister Hill, James O. Eastland, W. Kerr Scott, John Sparkman, Olin D. Johnston, Price Daniel, J. W. Fulbright, George A. Smathers, Spessard L. Holland.

MEMBERS OF THE UNITED STATES HOUSE OF REPRESENTATIVES

Alabama: Frank W. Boykin, George M. Grant, George W. Andrews, Kenneth A. Roberts, Albert Rains, Armistead I. Selden Jr., Carl Elliott, Robert E. Jones, George Huddleston Jr. Arkansas: E.C. Gathings, Wilbur D. Mills, James W. Trimble, Oren Harris, Brooks Hays, W. F. Norrell. Florida: Charles E. Bennett, Robert L.F. Sikes, A.S. Herlong Jr., Paul G. Rogers, James A. Haley, D.R. Matthews. Georgia: Prince H. Preston, John L. Pilcher, E.L. Forrester, John James Flynt Jr., James C. Davis, Carl Vinson, Henderson Lanham, Iris F. Blitch, Phil M. Landrum, Paul Brown. Louisiana: F. Edward Hebert, Hale Boggs, Edwin E. Willis, Overton Brooks, Otto E. Passman, James H. Morrison, T. Ashton Thompson, George S. Long. Mississippi: Thomas G. Abernathy, Jamie L. Whitten, Frank E. Smith, John Bell Williams, Arthur Winstead, William M. Colmer. North Carolina: Herbert C. Bonner, L.H. Fountain, Graham A. Barden, Carl T. Durham, F. Ertel Carlyle, Hugh Q. Alexander, Woodrow W. Jones, George A. Shuford. South Carolina: L. Mendel Rivers, John J. Riley, W.J. Bryan Dorn, Robert T. Ashmore, James P. Richards, John L. McMillan. Tennessee: James B. Frazier Jr., Tom Murray, Jere Cooper, Clifford Davis.

Source: Congressional Record, 84th Cong., 2d sess. 1956, pt. 4, vol. 102, pp. 4515–4516.

REPORT OF THE NATIONAL ADVISORY COMMISSION ON CIVIL DISORDERS (1968)

The summer of 1967 again brought racial disorders to American cities, and with them shock, fear and bewilderment to the nation.

The worst came during a two-week period in July, first in Newark and then in Detroit. Each set off a chain reaction in neighboring communities.

On July 28, 1967, the President of the United States established this Commission and directed us to answer three basic questions: What happened? Why did it happen? What can be done to prevent it from happening again?

To respond to these questions, we have undertaken a broad range of studies and investigations. We have visited the riot cities; we have heard many witnesses; we have sought counsel of experts across the country.

This is our basic conclusion: Our nation is moving toward two societies, one black, one white—separate and unequal.

Reaction to last summer's disorders has quickened the movement and deepened the division. Discrimination and segregation have long permeated much of American life; they now threaten the future of every American. The deepening racial division is not inevitable. The movement apart can be reversed. Choice is still possible. Our principal task is to define that choice and to press for a national resolution.

To pursue the present course will involve the continuing polarization of the American community and ultimately, the destruction of basic democratic values. The alternative is not blind repression or capitulation to lawlessness. It is the realization of common opportunities for all within a single society.

This alternative will require a commitment to national action—compassionate, massive and sustained, backed by the resources of the most powerful and the richest nation on this earth. From every American it will require new attitudes, new understanding, and, above all, new will. . . .

Segregation and poverty have created in the racial ghetto a destructive environment totally unknown to most white Americans.

What white Americans have never fully understood—but what the Negro can never forget—is that the white society is deeply implicated in the ghetto. White institutions created it, white institutions maintain it, and white society condones it. . . .

It is time to make good the promises of American democracy to all citizens—urban and rural, black and white, Spanish-surname, American Indian, and every minority group.

Source: National Advisory Commission on Civil Disorders, *Report* (Washington, D.C.: U.S. Government Printing Office, 1968), 1–2.

PROPOSED EQUAL RIGHTS AMENDMENT, ALICE PAUL VERSION (1972)

Section 1. Equality of rights under the law shall not be denied or abridged by the United States or by any state on account of sex.
Section 2. The Congress shall have the power to enforce, by appropriate legislation, the provisions of this article.
Section 3. This amendment shall take effect two years after the date of ratification.

Source: National Organization for Women, www.now.org/issues/economic/eratext.html.

CONVENTION ON THE ELIMINATION OF ALL FORMS OF DISCRIMINATION AGAINST WOMEN (1979)

Article 1. For the purposes of the present Convention, the term "discrimination against women" shall mean any distinction, exclusion or restriction made on the basis of sex which has the effect or purpose of impairing or nullifying the recognition, enjoyment or exercise by women, irrespective of their marital status, on a basis of equality of men and women, of human rights and fundamental freedoms in the political, economic, social, cultural, civil or any other field.

Article 2. States Parties condemn discrimination against women in all its forms, agree to pursue by all appropriate means and without delay a policy of eliminating discrimination against women and, to this end, undertake:

(a) To embody the principle of the equality of men and women in their national constitutions or other appropriate legislation if not yet incorporated therein and to ensure, through law and other appropriate means, the practical realization of this principle;
(b) To adopt appropriate legislative and other measures, including sanctions where appropriate, prohibiting all discrimination against women;
c) To establish legal protection of the rights of women on an equal basis with men and to ensure through competent national tribunals and other public institutions the effective protection of women against any act of discrimination;

(d) To refrain from engaging in any act or practice of discrimination against women and to ensure that public authorities and institutions shall act in conformity with this obligation;

(e) To take all appropriate measures to eliminate discrimination against women by any person, organization or enterprise;

(f) To take all appropriate measures, including legislation, to modify or abolish existing laws, regulations, customs and practices which constitute discrimination against women;

(g) To repeal all national penal provisions which constitute discrimination against women. . . .

Source: United Nations, Division for the Advancement of Women, www.un.org/womenwatch/daw/cedaw/.

PROPOSED OFFICIAL ENGLISH AMENDMENT (1981)

Section 1. The English language shall be the official language of the United States.

Section 2. Neither the United States nor any State shall make or enforce any law which requires the use of any language other than English.

Section 3. This article shall apply to laws, ordinances, regulations, orders, programs, and policies.

Section 4. No order or decree shall be issued by any court of the United States or of any State requiring that any proceedings, or matters to which this article applies be in any language other than English.

Section 5. This article shall not prohibit educational instruction in a language other than English as required as a transitional method of making students who use a language other than English proficient in English. . . .

Source: S.J.R. 72, 97th Cong., 1st sess.

II. HISTORIC SPEECHES AND WRITINGS

"ATLANTA COMPROMISE" (BOOKER T. WASHINGTON, 1885)

One third of the population of the South is of the Negro race. No enterprise seeking the material, civil, or moral welfare of this section can disregard this element of our population and reach the highest success. I but convey to you . . . the sentiment of the masses of my race when I say that in no way have the value and manhood of the American Negro been more fittingly and generously recognized than by the managers of this magnificent Exposition at every stage of its progress. It is a recognition that will do more to cement the friendship of the two races than any occurrence since the dawn of our freedom. . . .

. . . in this connection it is well to bear in mind that whatever other sins the South may be called to bear, when it comes to business, pure and simple, it is in the South that the Negro is given a man's chance in the commercial world, and in nothing is this Exposition more eloquent than in emphasizing this chance. Our greatest danger is, that in the great leap from slavery to freedom we may overlook the fact that the masses of us are to live by the productions of our hands, and fail to keep in mind that we shall prosper in proportion as we learn to dignify and glorify common labor and put brains and skill into the common occupations of life; shall prosper in proportion as we learn to draw the line between the superficial and the substantial, the ornamental gewgaws of life and the useful. No race can prosper till it learns that there is as much dignity in tilling a field as in writing a poem. It is at the bottom of life we must begin, and not at the top. Nor should we permit our grievances to overshadow our opportunities.

To those of the white race who look to the incoming of those of foreign birth and strange tongue and habits for the prosperity of the South, were I permitted I would repeat what I say to my own race, "Cast down your bucket where you are." Cast it down among the 8,000,000 Negroes whose habits you know, whose fidelity and love you have tested in days when to have proved treacherous meant the ruin of your firesides. Cast down your bucket among these people who have, without strikes and labor wars, tilled your fields, cleared your forests, built your railroads and cities, and brought forth treasures from the bowels of the earth, and helped make possible this magnificent representation of the progress of the South. Casting down your bucket among my people, helping and encouraging them as you are doing on these grounds, and to education of head, hand, and heart, you will find that they will buy your surplus land, make blossom the waste places in your fields, and run your factories. While doing this, you can be sure in the future, as in the past, that you and your families will be surrounded by the most patient, faithful, law-abiding, and unresentful people that the world has seen. As we have proved our loyalty to you in the past, in nursing your children, watching by the sick bed of your mothers and fathers, and often following them with tear-dimmed eyes to their graves, so in the future, in our humble way, we shall stand by you with a devotion that no foreigner can approach, ready to lay down our lives, if need be, in defense of yours, interlacing our industrial, commercial, civil, and religious life with yours in a way that shall make the interests of both races one. In all things that are purely social we can be as separate as the fingers, yet one as the hand in all things essential to mutual progress.

There is no defense or security for any of us except in the highest intelligence and development of all. If anywhere there are efforts tending to curtail the fullest growth of the Negro, let these efforts be turned into stimulating, encouraging, and making him the most useful and intelligent citizen. Effort or means so invested will pay a thousand per cent interest. These efforts will be twice blessed—"blessing him that gives and him that takes." . . .

. . . While we take pride in what we exhibit as a result of our independent efforts, we do not for a moment forget that our part in this exhibition would fall far short of your expectations but for the constant help that has come to our educational life, not only from the Southern States, but especially from Northern philanthropists, who have made their gifts a constant stream of blessing and encouragement.

The wisest among my race understand that the agitation of questions of social equality is the extremist folly, and that progress in the enjoyment of all the privileges that will come to us must be the result of severe and constant struggle rather than of artificial forcing. No race that has anything to contribute to the markets of the world is long in any degree ostracized. It is important and right that all privileges of the law be ours, but it is vastly more important that we be prepared for the exercises of these privileges. The opportunity to earn a dollar in a factory just now is worth infinitely more than the opportunity to spend a dollar in an opera house.

. . . I pledge that in your effort to work out the great and intricate problem which God has laid at the doors of the South you shall have at all times the patient, sympathetic help of my race; only let this be constantly in mind that, while from representations in these buildings of the product of field, of forest, of mine, of factory, letters, and art, much good will come, yet far above and beyond material benefits will be that higher good, that let us pray God will come, in a blotting out of sectional differences and racial animosities and suspicions, in a determination to administer absolute justice, in a willing obedience among all classes to the mandates of law. This, this, coupled with our material prosperity, will bring into our beloved South a new heaven and a new earth.

Source: Louis R. Harlan, ed., *The Booker T. Washington Papers,* (Champaign-Urbana: University of Illinois Press, 1974), 3:583–587.

"ADDRESS ON CIVIL RIGHTS" (JOHN F. KENNEDY, 1963)

This afternoon, following a series of threats and defiant statements, the presence of Alabama National Guardsmen was required on the University of Alabama to carry out the final and unequivocal order of the United States District Court of the Northern District of Alabama. This order called for the admission of two clearly qualified young Alabama residents who happen to have been born Negro.

That they were admitted peacefully on the campus is due in good measure to the conduct of the students of the University of Alabama, who met their responsibilities in a constructive way. . . .

It ought to be possible for American consumers of any color to receive equal service in places of public accommodation, such as hotels and restaurants and theaters and retail stores, without being forced to resort to demonstration in the street. It ought to be possible for American citizens of any color to register and to vote in a free election without interference or fear of reprisal.

It ought to be possible, in short, for every American to enjoy the privileges of being American without regard to his race or his color. In short, every American ought to have the right to be treated as he would wish to be treated, as one would wish his children to be treated. But this is not the case today.

The Negro baby born in America today, regardless of the section of the nation in which he is born, has about one half as much chance of completing high school as a white baby born in the same place on the same day, one third as much chance of completing college, one third as much chance of becoming a professional man, twice as much chance of becoming unemployed, about one seventh as much chance of earning $10,000 a year or more, a life expectancy which is seven years shorter, and the prospects of earning only half as much. . . .

The heart of the question is whether all Americans are to be afforded equal rights and equal opportunities, whether we are going to treat our fellow Americans as we want to be treated. If an American, because his skin is dark, cannot eat lunch in a restaurant open to the public, if he can not send his children to the best public school available, if he cannot vote for the public officials who represent him, if, in short, he cannot enjoy the full and free life which all of us want, then who among us would be content to have the color of his skin changed and stand in his place? Who among us would be content with the counsels of patience and delay?

One hundred years have passed since President Lincoln freed the slaves, yet their heirs, their grandsons, are not fully free. They are not yet freed from the bonds of injustice. They are not yet freed from social and economic oppression. And this nation, for all its hopes and all its boasts, will not be fully free until all its citizens are free.

We preach freedom around the world, and we mean it, and we cherish our freedom here at home; but are we to say to the world, and, much more importantly, to each other, that this is a land of the free except for the Negroes; that we have no second-class citizens except Negroes; that we have no class or caste system, no ghettos, no master race, except with respect to Negroes?

Now the time has come for this nation to fulfill its promise. . . .

We face . . . a moral crisis as a country and as a people. It cannot be met by repressive police action. It cannot be left to increased demonstrations in the streets. It cannot be quieted by token moves or talk. It is a time to act in the Congress, in your state and local legislative bodies and, above all, in all of our daily lives.

I am . . . asking the Congress to enact legislation giving all Americans the right to be served in facilities which are open to the public—hotels, restaurants, theaters, retail stores, and similar establishments. . . .

I am also asking Congress to authorize the federal government to participate more fully in lawsuits designed to end segregation in public education. We have succeeded in persuading many districts to desegregate voluntarily. Dozens have admitted Negroes without violence. Today, a Negro is attending a state-supported institution in every one of our fifty states. But the pace is very slow.

Too many Negro children entering segregated grade schools at the time of the Supreme Court's decision nine years ago will enter segregated high schools this fall, having suffered a loss which can never be restored. The lack of an adequate education denied the Negro a chance to get a decent job. . . .

Other features will also be requested, including greater protection for the right to vote. But legislation, I repeat, cannot solve this problem alone. It must be solved in the homes of every American in every community across our country.

In this respect, I want to pay tribute to those citizens, North and South, who have been working in their communities to make life better for all. They are acting not out of a sense of legal duty but out of a sense of human decency. Like our soldiers and sailors in all parts of the world, they are meeting freedom's challenge on the firing line, and I salute them for their honor and courage.

My fellow Americans, this is a problem which faces us all—in every city of the North as well as the South. Today there are Negroes, unemployed—two or three times as many compared to whites—with inadequate education, moving into the large cities, unable to find work, young people particularly out of work and without hope, denied equal rights, denied the opportunity to eat at a restaurant or lunch counter or go to a movie theater, denied the right to a decent education. . . . It seems to me that these are matters which concern us all, not merely Presidents or congressmen or governors, but every citizen of the United States.

This is one country. It has become one country because all the people who came here had an equal chance to develop their talents. . . .

We have a right to expect that the Negro community will be responsible and will uphold the law; but they have a right to expect that the law will be fair, that the constitution will be color blind, as Justice Harlan said at the turn of the century.

This is what we are talking about. This is a matter which concerns this country and what it stands for, and in meeting it I ask the support of all our citizens.

Source: Peter B. Levy, *The Civil Rights Movement* (Westport, Conn.: Greenwood, 1998), 172–175.

"SEGREGATION TODAY, SEGREGATION FOREVER" (GEORGE C. WALLACE, 1963)

. . . This is the day of my Inauguration as Governor of the State of Alabama. And on this day I feel a deep obligation to renew my pledges, my covenants with you . . . the people of this great state.

General Robert E. Lee said that "duty" is the sublimest word in the English language and I have come, increasingly, to realize what he meant. I SHALL do my duty to you, God helping . . . to every man, to every woman . . . yes, to every child in this state. . . .

Today I have stood, where once Jefferson Davis stood, and took an oath to my people. It is very appropriate then that from this Cradle of the Confederacy, this very Heart of the Great Anglo-Saxon Southland, that today we sound the drum for freedom as have our generations of forebears before us done, time and time again through history. Let us rise to the call of freedom-loving blood that is in us and send our answer to the tyranny that clanks its chains upon the South. In the name of the greatest people that have ever trod this earth, I draw the line in the dust and toss the gauntlet before the feet of tyranny . . . and I say . . . segregation today . . . segregation tomorrow . . . segregation forever.

The Washington, D.C. school riot report is disgusting and revealing. We will not sacrifice our children to any such type school system—and you can write that down. The federal troops in Mississippi could be better used guarding the safety of the citizens of Washington, D.C., where it is even unsafe to walk or go to a ballgame—and that is the nation's capital. I was safer in a B-29 bomber over Japan during the war in an air raid, than the people of Washington are walking to the White House neighborhood. A closer example is Atlanta. The city officials fawn for political reasons over school integration and THEN build barricades to stop residential integration—what hypocrisy!

Let us send this message back to Washington by our representatives who are with us today . . . that from this day we are standing up, and the heel of tyranny does not fit the neck of an upright man . . . that we intend to take the offensive and carry our fight for freedom across the nation, wielding the balance of power we know we possess in the Southland . . . that WE, not the insipid bloc of voters of some sections . . . will determine in the next election who shall sit in the White House of these United States . . . That from this day, from this hour . . . from this minute . . . we give the word of a race of honor that we will tolerate their boot in our face no longer . . . and let those certain judges put *that* in their opium pipes of power and smoke it for what it is worth. . . .

It is this theory of international power politic that led a group of men on the Supreme Court for the first time in American history to issue an edict, based not on legal precedent, but upon a volume, the editor of which said our Constitution is outdated and must be changed and the writers of which, some had admittedly belonged to as many as half a hundred communist-front organizations. It is this theory that led this same group of men to briefly bare the ungodly core of that philosophy in forbidding little school children to say a prayer. And we find the evidence of that ungodliness even in the removal of the words "in God we trust" from some of our dollars, which was placed there as like evidence by our founding fathers as the faith upon which this system of government was built. It is the spirit of power thirst that caused a President in Washington to take up Caesar's pen and with one stroke of it make a law. A Law which the law making body of Congress refused to pass . . . a law that tells us that we can or cannot buy or sell our very homes, except by his conditions . . . and except at HIS discretion. It is the spirit of power thirst that led the same President to launch a full offensive of twenty-five thousand troops against a university . . . of all places . . . in his own country . . . and against his own people, when this nation maintains only six thousand troops in the beleagured city of Berlin. We have witnessed such acts of "might makes right" over the world as men yielded to the temptation to play God . . . but we have never before witnessed it in America. We reject such acts as free men. We do not defy, for there is nothing to defy . . . since as free men we do not recognize any government right to give freedom . . . or deny freedom. No government erected by man has that right. As Thomas Jefferson said, "The God who gave us life, gave us liberty at the same time; no King holds the right of liberty in his hands." Nor does any ruler in American government.

We intend, quite simply, to practice the free heritage as bequeathed to us as sons of free fathers. . . .

This nation was never meant to be a unit of one . . . but a unit of the many . . . that is the exact reason our freedom loving forefathers established the states, so as to divide the rights and powers among the states, insuring that no central power could gain master government control. . . .

And so it was meant in our racial lives . . . each race, within its own framework has the freedom to teach . . . to instruct . . . to develop . . . to ask for and receive deserved help from others of separate racial stations. This is the great freedom of our American founding fathers . . . but if we amalgamate into the one unit as advocated by the communist philosophers . . . then the enrichment of our lives . . the freedom for our development . . . is gone forever. We become, therefore, a mongrel unit of one under a single all powerful government . . . and we stand for everything . . . and for nothing.

The true brotherhood of America, of respecting the separateness of others . . . and uniting in effort . . . has been so twisted and distorted from its original concept that there is a small wonder that communism is winning the world.

We invite the negro citizens of Alabama to work with us from his separate racial station . . . as we will work with him . . . to develop, to grow in individual freedom and enrichment. We want jobs and a good future for BOTH races . . . This is the basic heritage of my religion, in which I make full practice . . . for we are all the handiwork of God.

But we warn those, of any group, who would follow the false doctrine of communistic amalgamation that we will not surrender our system of government . . . our freedom of race and religion . . . that freedom was won at a hard price and if it requires a hard price to retain it . . . we are able . . . and quite willing to pay it. . . .

Southerners played a most magnificent part in erecting this great divinely inspired system of freedom . . . and as God is our witnesses, Southerners will save it. . . .

Source: Alabama Department of Archives and History, "The 1963 Inaugural Address of Governor George C. Wallace, January 14, 1963, Montgomery, Alabama," www.archives.state.al.us/govs_list/inauguralspeech.html. Reprinted by permission of the Alabama Department of Archives and History, Montgomery, Alabama.

"ADDRESS TO A MEETING IN NEW YORK" (MALCOLM X, 1964)

. . . I'm still a Muslim, but I'm also a nationalist, meaning that my political philosophy is black nationalism, my economic philosophy is black nationalism, my social philosophy is black nationalism. And when I say that this philosophy is black nationalism, to me this means that the political philosophy for black nationalism is that which is designed to encourage our people, the black people, to gain complete control over the politics and the politicians of our own people.

Our economic philosophy is that we should gain economic control over the economy of our own community, the businesses and the other things which create employment so that we can provide jobs for our own people instead of having to picket and boycott and beg someone else for a job.

And, in short, our social philosophy means that we feel that it is time to get together among our own kind and eliminate the evils that are destroying the moral fiber of our society, like drug addiction, drunkenness, adultery that leads to an abundance of bastard children, welfare problems. We believe that we should lift the level or the standard of our own society to a higher level wherein we will be satisfied and then not inclined toward pushing ourselves into other societies where we are not wanted.

Just as we can see that all over the world one of the main problems facing the West is race, likewise here in America today, most of your Negro leaders as well as the whites agree that 1964 itself appears to be one of the most explosive years yet in the history of America on the racial front, on the racial scene. Not only is the racial explosion probably to take place in America, but all of the ingredients for this racial explosion in America to blossom into a world-wide racial explosion present themselves right here in front of us. America's racial powder keg, in short, can actually fuse or ignite a worldwide powder keg.

And whites in this country who are still complacent when they see the possibilities of racial strife getting out of hand and you are complacent simply because you think you outnumber the racial minority in this country, what you have to bear in mind is wherein you might outnumber us in this country, you don't outnumber us all over the earth.

Any kind of racial explosion that takes place in this country today, in 1964, is not a racial explosion that can be confined to the shores of America. It is a racial explosion that can ignite the racial powder keg that exists all over the planet that we call the earth. Now I think that nobody would disagree that the dark masses of Africa and Asia and Latin America are already seething with bitterness, animosity, hostility, unrest, and impatience with the racial intolerance that they themselves have experienced at the hands of the white West.

And just as they themselves have the ingredients of hostility toward the West in general, here we also have 22,000,000 African-Americans, black, brown, red, and yellow people in this country who are also seething with bitterness and impatience and hostility and animosity at the racial intolerance not only of the white West but of white America in particular.

1964 will be America's hottest year; her hottest year yet; a year of much racial violence and much racial bloodshed. But it won't be blood that's going to flow only on one side. The new generation of black people that have grown up in this country during recent years are already forming the opinion, and it's just opinion, that if there is to be bleeding, it should be reciprocal—bleeding on both sides.

So today, when the black man starts reaching out for what America says are his rights, the black man feels that he is within his rights—when he becomes the victim of brutality by those who are depriving him of his rights—to do whatever necessary to protect himself.

There are 22,000,000 African-Americans who are ready to fight for independence right here. When I say fight for independence right here, I don't mean any non-violent fight, or turn-the-other-cheek fight. Those days are gone. Those days are over. . . .

Our people are becoming more politically mature. . . . The Negro can see that he holds the balance of power in this country politically. It is he who puts in office the one who gets in office. Yet when the Negro helps that person get in office the Negro gets nothing in return. . . .

No, something is wrong. And when these black people wake up and find out for real the trickery and the treachery that has been heaped upon us you are going to have revolution. And when I say revolution I don't mean that stuff they were talking about last year about "We Shall Overcome." . . .

And the only way without bloodshed that this can be brought about is that the black man has to be given full use of the ballot in every one of the 50 states. But if the black man doesn't get the ballot, then you are going to be faced with another man who forgets the ballot and starts using the bullet.

So you have a people today who not only know what they want, but also know what they are supposed to have. And they themselves are clearing the way for another generation that is coming up that not only will know what it wants and know what it should have, but also will be ready and willing to do whatever is necessary to see what they should have materializes immediately. Thank you.

Source: Peter B. Levy, ed., *Let Freedom Ring: A Documentary History of the Modern Civil Rights Movement* (Westport, Conn.: Praeger, 1992), 174–177.

"WAR ON POVERTY" (LYNDON B. JOHNSON, 1964)

Because it is right, because it is wise, and because, for the first time in our history, it is possible to conquer poverty, I submit, for the consideration of the Congress and the country, the Economic Opportunity Act of 1964.

. . . This Act provides five basic opportunities.

It will give almost half a million underprivileged young Americans the opportunity to develop skills, continue education, and find useful work.

It will give every American community the opportunity to develop a comprehensive plan to fight its own poverty—and help them to carry out their plans.

It will give dedicated Americans the opportunity to enlist as volunteers in the war against poverty.

It will give many workers and farmers the opportunity to break through particular barriers which bar their escape from poverty.

It will give the entire nation the opportunity for a concerted attack on poverty through the establishment, under my direction, of the Office of Economic Opportunity, a national headquarters for the war against poverty.

. . . [W]e will give high priority to helping young Americans who lack skills, who have not completed their education or who cannot complete it because they are too poor. . . .

I therefore recommend the creation of a Job Corps, a Work-Training Program, and a Work Study Program.

A new national Job Corps will build toward an enlistment of 100,000 young men. They will be drawn from those whose background, health and education make them least fit for useful work. . . .

A new national Work-Training Program operated by the Department of Labor will provide work and training for 200,000 American men and women between the ages of 16 and 21. This will be developed through state and local governments and non-profit agencies. . . .

A new national Work-Study Program operated by the Department of Health, Education, and Welfare will provide federal funds for part-time jobs for 140,000 young Americans who do not go to college because they cannot afford it.

. . . Second, through a new Community Action program we intend to strike at poverty at its source—in the streets of our cities and on the farms of our countryside among the very young and the impoverished old.

This program asks men and women throughout the country to prepare long-range plans for the attack on poverty in their own local communities. . . .

Third, I ask for the authority to recruit and train skilled volunteers for the war against poverty. . . .

Fourth, we intend to create new opportunities for certain hard-hit groups to break out of the pattern of poverty.

Through a new program of loans and guarantees we can provide incentives to those who will employ the unemployed.

Through programs of work and retraining for unemployed fathers and mothers we can help them support their families in dignity while preparing themselves for new work.

Through funds to purchase needed land, organize cooperatives, and create new and adequate family farms we can help those whose life on the land has been a struggle without hope.

Fifth, I do not intend that the war against poverty become a series of uncoordinated and unrelated efforts—that it perish for lack of leadership and direction.

Therefore this bill creates, in the Executive Office of the President, a new Office of Economic Opportunity. . . .

Source: Public Papers of U.S. Presidents, Lyndon B. Johnson, 1963–1964 (Washington, D.C.: U.S. Government Printing Office, 1965), 1, 375–380.

"THE AMERICAN PROMISE" (LYNDON B. JOHNSON, 1965)

I speak tonight for the dignity of man and the destiny of democracy.

I urge every member of both parties, Americans of all religions and of all colors, from every section of this country, to join me in that cause.

At times history and fate meet at a single time in a single place to shape a turning point in man's unending search for freedom. So it was at Lexington and Concord. So it was a century ago at Appomattox. So it was last week in Selma, Alabama.

There, long-suffering men and women peacefully protested the denial of their rights as Americans. Many were brutally assaulted. One good man, a man of God, was killed.

There is no cause for pride in what has happened in Selma. There is no cause for self-satisfaction in the long denial of equal rights of millions of Americans. But there is cause for hope and for faith in our democracy in what is happening here tonight.

For the cries of pain and the hymns and protests of oppressed people have summoned into convocation all the majesty of this great Government—the Government of the greatest Nation on earth.

Our mission is at once the oldest and the most basic of this country: to right wrong, to do justice, to serve man. . . .

The issue of equal rights for American Negroes is such an issue. And should we defeat every enemy, should we double our wealth and conquer the stars, and still be unequal to this issue, then we will have failed as a people and as a nation.

For with a country as with a person, "What is a man profited, if he shall gain the whole world, and lose his own soul?"

There is no Negro problem. There is no Southern problem. There is no Northern problem. There is only an American problem. And we are met here tonight as Americans—not as Democrats or Republicans—we are met here as Americans to solve that problem. . . .

To . . . deny a man his hopes because of his color or race, his religion or the place of his birth—is not only to do injustice, it is to deny America and to dishonor the dead who gave their lives for American freedom.

The Right to Vote

Our fathers believed that if this noble view of the rights of man was to flourish, it must be rooted in democracy. The most basic right of all was the right to choose your own leaders. The history of this country, in large measure, is the history of the expansion of that right to all of our people.

Many of the issues of civil rights are very complex and most difficult. But about this there can and should be no argument. Every American citizen must have an equal right to vote. There is no reason which can excuse the denial of that right. There is no duty which weighs more heavily on us than the duty we have to ensure that right.

Yet the harsh fact is that in many places in this country men and women are kept from voting simply because they are Negroes.

Every device of which human ingenuity is capable has been used to deny this right. The Negro citizen may go to register only to be told that the day is wrong, or the hour is late, or the official in charge is absent. And if he persists, and if he manages to present himself to the registrar, he may be disqualified because he did not spell out his middle name or because he abbreviated a word on the application.

And if he manages to fill out an application he is given a test. The registrar is the sole judge of whether he passes this test. He may be asked to recite the entire Constitution, or explain the most complex provisions of State law. And even a college degree cannot be used to prove that he can read and write.

For the fact is that the only way to pass these barriers is to show a white skin.

Experience has clearly shown that the existing process of law cannot overcome systematic and ingenious discrimination. No law that we now have on the books—and I have helped to put three of them there—can ensure the right to vote when local officials are determined to deny it.

In such a case our duty must be clear to all of us. The Constitution says that no person shall be kept from voting because of his race or his color. We have all sworn an oath before God to support and to defend that Constitution. We must now act in obedience to that oath.

Guaranteeing the Right to Vote

Wednesday I will send to Congress a law designed to eliminate illegal barriers to the right to vote. . . .

This bill will strike down restrictions to voting in all elections—Federal, State, and local—which have been used to deny Negroes the right to vote.

This bill will establish a simple, uniform standard which cannot be used, however ingenious the effort, to flout our Constitution.

It will provide for citizens to be registered by officials of the United States Government if the State officials refuse to register them.

It will eliminate tedious, unnecessary lawsuits which delay the right to vote. Finally, this legislation will ensure that properly registered individuals are not prohibited from voting. . . .

The Need For Action

. . . there must be no delay, no hesitation and no compromise with our purpose.

We cannot, we must not, refuse to protect the right of every American to vote in every election that he may desire to participate in.

And we ought not and we cannot and we must not wait another 8 months before we get a bill. We have already waited a hundred years and more, and the time for waiting is gone.

So I ask you to join me in working long hours—nights and weekends, if necessary—to pass this bill. And I don't make that request lightly. For from the window where I sit with the problems of our country I recognize that outside this chamber is the outraged conscience of a nation, the grave concern of many nations, and the harsh judgment of history on our acts.

We Shall Overcome

But even if we pass this bill, the battle will not be over. What happened in Selma is part of a far larger movement which reaches into every section and State of America. It is the effort of American Negroes to secure for themselves the full blessings of American life.

Their cause must be our cause too. Because it is not just Negroes, but really it is all of us, who must overcome the crippling legacy of bigotry and injustice.

And we shall overcome.

As a man whose roots go deeply into Southern soil I know how agonizing racial feelings are. I know how difficult it is to reshape the attitudes and the structure of our society.

But a century has passed, more than a hundred years, since the Negro was freed. And he is not fully free tonight.

It was more than a hundred years ago that Abraham Lincoln, a great President of another party, signed the Emancipation Proclamation, but emancipation is a proclamation and not a fact.

A century has passed, more than a hundred years, since equality was promised. And yet the Negro is not equal.

A century has passed since the day of promise. And the promise is unkept.

The time of justice has now come. I tell you that I believe sincerely that no force can hold it back. It is right in the eyes of man and God that it should come. And when it does, I think that day will brighten the lives of every American. . . .

This great, rich, restless country can offer opportunity and education and hope to all: black and white, North and South, sharecropper and city dweller. These are the enemies: poverty, ignorance, disease. They are the enemies and not our fellow man, not our neighbor. And these enemies too, poverty, disease and ignorance, we shall overcome. . . .

Progress through the Democratic Process

The real hero of this struggle is the American Negro. His actions and protests, his courage to risk safety and even to risk his life, have awakened the conscience of this Nation. His demonstrations have been designed to call attention to injustice, designed to provoke change, designed to stir reform.

He has called upon us to make good the promise of America. . . . For at the real heart of battle for equality is a deep-seated belief in the democratic process. Equality depends not on the force of arms or tear gas but upon the force of moral right; not on recourse to violence but on respect for law and order. . . .

In Selma as elsewhere we seek and pray for peace. We seek order. We seek unity. But we will not accept the peace of stifled rights, or the order imposed by fear, or the unity that stifles protest. For peace cannot be purchased at the cost of liberty.

In Selma tonight, as in every—and we had a good day there—as in every city, we are working for just and peaceful settlement. We must all remember that after this speech I am making tonight, after the police and the FBI and the Marshals have all gone, and after you have promptly passed this bill, the people of Selma and the other cities of the Nation must still live and work together. And when the attention of the Nation has gone elsewhere they must try to heal the wounds and to build a new community. . . .

Rights Must Be Opportunities

The bill that I am presenting to you will be known as a civil rights bill. But, in a larger sense, most of the program I am recommending is a civil rights program. Its object is to open the city of hope to all people of all races.

Because all Americans just must have the right to vote. And we are going to give them that right.

All Americans must have the privileges of citizenship regardless of race. And they are going to have those privileges of citizenship regardless of race.

But I would like to caution you and remind you that to exercise these privileges takes much more than just legal right. It requires a trained mind and a healthy body. It requires a decent home, and the chance to find a job, and the opportunity to escape from the clutches of poverty.

Of course, people cannot contribute to the Nation if they are never taught to read or write, if their bodies are stunted from hunger, if their sickness goes untended, if their life is spent in hopeless poverty just drawing a welfare check.

So we want to open the gates to opportunity. But we are also going to give all our people, black and white, the help that they need to walk through those gates. . . .

Source: Peter B. Levy, *The Civil Rights Movement* (Westport, Conn.: Greenwood, 1998), 181–184.

"REMARKS ON THE PHILADELPHIA PLAN" (ARTHUR FLETCHER, 1969)

. . . . A vital freedom guaranteed by our Constitution is the right to equal participation in the economic processes of our society. This freedom has been denied to groups within our country. This denial of fundamental participation in the advantages of capitalism has even been institutionalized in our society.

The Federal Government cannot contribute to this denial of rights through blind acceptance of customs and traditions which eliminate the contributions and talents of groups of people. *The Federal Government has an obligation* to see that every citizen has an equal chance at the most basic freedom of all—*the right to succeed.*

Millions of dollars at every level of Government are being spent to correct the symptoms of the denial of this right in our society but almost no effort has been made in the past to affect this problem at its source—where Federal dollars enter the area economy.

These Federal dollars—part of which are Black, Puerto Rican, Mexican-American, and others—enter the local economy primarily through Federal contracts. Once these dollars pass the "Gateway" of contracting procedures—the Federal Government has no further control over them. Through the "multiplier" effect experienced by imported money in the regional economy and the existence of institutionalized segregation—the Federal Government can be pictured as contributing to the denial of the right to succeed for substantial groups of people. No amount of money spent by whatever level of Government to correct this situation can be justified after the fact.

The most fair, econonomical and effective point to address this problem is at the beginning—at the time of contracting. . . .

The Philadelphia Plan applies to all Federal and federally-assisted construction contracts for projects in excess of $500,000. . . . It is also anticipated that the plan will be put into effect in all the major cities across the Nation as soon as possible. . . .

Within the plan's presently established geographical boundaries, the Office of Federal Contract Compliance will, with the assistance of representatives from the Federal contracting agencies, determine definite standards for minority participation in each of the trades named and to be used on a construction project. The standard for each trade will be included in the invitation for bids or other solicitation used for every Federally-involved construction contract. The standards will specify the range of minority manpower utilization expected for each of the named trades and such standards must be maintained during the performance of the construction contract.

The standards are to be determined in each instance by applying the following major criteria:

1. The current extent of minority group participation in the trade
2. The availability of minority group persons for employment in such trade
3. The need for training programs in the area and/or the need to assure demand for those in or from existing training programs
4. The impact of the program upon the existing labor force.

When the contractor submits his bid he must include in the bid an acceptable affirmative action program. This program must contain acceptable goals for the use of minority manpower in each of the trades named within the ranges established in the invitations for bids.

. . . Failure to meet an established standard will result in the bid being rejected. . . . After the contract is awarded post-award reviews will be conducted to determine whether the goals pledged by the contractor are being met. . . .

Perhaps I should pause at this point to discuss the concept of goals or standards for percentages of minority employees contained in the Philadelphia Plan. . . .

Segregation didn't occur naturally—it was imposed. In that process quotas, limits, boundaries were set. Sometimes written—sometimes unpublished. But official or informal the effect was total, decisive, and I might add—contrary to the American sense of fair play.

Large segments of our society were oppressed by these rules and institutions until they believed it was impossible to change them. With the increasing wealth of our economic system—the gap—visible to any thinking man—between white and black—employed and unemployed—rich and poor—was growing wider and wider. . . .

Fair play and definitive agreements concerning working conditions, promotional opportunities, ratios of skilled craftsmen to trainees, recognition of bargaining groups and seniority security are now an acceptable and respected tradition in our world of commerce. . . .

The disadvantaged of this country are now asking that the opportunities achieved through this great movement be extended to include them. No more. No less.

It might be better, admittedly, if specific goals were not required—certainly the black people of America understand taboos—but it is imperative that we face facts and dedicate ourselves to ending discrimination in employment in this country.

What is at stake here is something more than equal employment opportunity in a specific industry or named trades. What is at stake is our basic system of Government itself. Persons in the minority communities must be assured that results can be obtained by working within the framework of the existing governmental system. . . .

Source: Philadelphia Plan Document, U.S. Department of Labor, No. 6, Department of Labor Library, Washington, D.C.

III. HISTORIC LEGISLATION

FUGITIVE SLAVE ACT (1793)

. . . ART. 4. For the better security of the peace and friendship now entered into by the contracting parties, against all infractions of the same, by the citizens of either party, to the prejudice of the other, neither party shall proceed to the infliction of punishments on the citizens of the other, otherwise than by securing the offender, or offenders, by imprisonment, or any other competent means, till a fair and impartial trial can be had by judges or juries of both parties, as near as can be, to the laws, customs, and usage's of the contracting parties, and natural justice: the mode of such trials to be hereafter fixed by the wise men of the United States, in congress assembled, with the assistance of such deputies of the Delaware nation, as may be appointed to act in concert with them in adjusting this matter to their mutual liking. And it is further agreed between the parties aforesaid, that neither shall entertain, or give countenance to, the enemies of the other, or protect, in their respective states, criminal fugitives, servants, or slaves, but the same to apprehend and secure, and deliver to the state or states, to which such enemies, criminals, servants, or slaves, respectively below.

Source: University of Oklahoma Law Center, www.law.ou.edu/hist/fugslave.html.

INDIAN TRADE AND INTERCOURSE ACT (1793)

An Act to Regulate Trade and Intercourse with the Indian Tribes.

SECTION 1. . . . . no person shall be permitted to carry on any trade or intercourse with the Indian tribes, without a license under the hand and seal of the superintendent of the department, or of such other person, as the President of the United States shall authorize to grant licenses for that purpose. . . .

SEC. 8. . . . no purchase or grant of lands, or of any title or claim thereto, from any Indians or nation or tribe of Indians, within the bounds of the United States, shall be of any validity in law or equity, unless the same be made by a treaty or convention entered into pursuant to the constitution . . . .

SEC. 10. . . . the superior courts of each of the said territorial districts, and the circuit courts, and other courts of the United States of similar jurisdiction in criminal causes in each district of the United States, into which any offender against this act shall be first brought, or in which he shall be apprehended, shall have, and are hereby invested with full power and authority, to hear and determine all crimes, offenses misdemeanors against this act; such courts proceeding therein, in the same manner, as if such crimes, offenses and misdemeanors had been committed within the bounds of their respective districts: And in all cases, where the punishment shall not be death, the county courts of quarter sessions in the said territorial districts, and the district courts of the United States, in their respective districts, shall have, and are hereby invested with like power to hear and determine the same.

Source: Avalon Project at Yale Law School, "An Act to Regulate Trade and Intercourse with the Indian Tribes," www.yale.edu/lawweb/avalon/statutes/native/na025.htm.

INDIAN REMOVAL ACT (1830)

Be it enacted . . . , That it shall and may be lawful for the President of the United States to cause so much of any territory belonging to the United States, west of the river Mississippi, not included in any state of organized territory, and to which the Indian title has been extinguished, as he may judge necessary, to be divided into a suitable number of districts, for the reception of such tribes or nations of Indians as may choose to exchange the lands where they now reside, and remove there . . .

SEC. 4. . . . if, upon any of the lands now occupied by the Indians, and to be exchanged for, there should be such improvements as add value to the land claimed by any individual or individuals of such tribes or nations, it shall and may be lawful for the President to cause such value to be ascertained by appraisement or otherwise, and to cause such ascertained value to be paid to the person or persons rightfully claiming such improvements. And upon the payment of such valuation, the improvements so valued and paid for, shall pass to the United States, and possession shall not afterwards be permitted to any of the same tribe.

SEC. 5. . . . upon the making of any such exchange as is contemplated by this act, it shall and may be lawful for the President to cause such aid and assistance to be furnished to the emigrants as may be necessary and proper to enable them to remove to, and settle in, the country for which they may have exchanged; and also, to give them such aid and assistance as may be necessary for their support and subsistence for the first year after their removal . . .

Source: Civics Online, www.civics-online.org/library/formatted/texts/indian_act.html.

CONFISCATION ACT OF 1861

CHAP. LX.—An Act to confiscate Property used for Insurrectionary Purposes.
... if, during the present or any future insurrection against the Government of the United States, after the President of the United States shall have declared, by proclamation, that the laws of the United States are opposed, and the execution thereof obstructed, by combinations too powerful to be suppressed by the ordinary course of judicial proceedings, or by the power vested in the marshals by law, any person or persons, his, her, or their agent, attorney, or employé, shall purchase or acquire, sell or give, any property of whatsoever kind or description, with intent to use or employ the same, or suffer the same to be used or employed, in aiding, abetting, or promoting such insurrection or resistance to the laws, or any person or persons engaged therein; or if any person or persons, being the owner or owners of any such property, shall knowingly use or employ, or consent to the use or employment of the same as aforesaid, all such property is hereby declared to be lawful subject of prize and capture wherever found; and it shall be the duty of the President of the United States to cause the same to be seized, confiscated, and condemned.
SEC. 2. . . . such prizes and capture shall be condemned in the district or circuit court of the United States having jurisdiction of the amount, or in admiralty in any district in which the same may be seized, or into which they may be taken and proceedings first instituted.
SEC. 3. . . . the Attorney-General, or any district attorney of the United States in which said property may at the time be, may institute the proceedings of condemnation, and in such case they shall be wholly for the benefit of the United States; or any person may file an information with such attorney, in which case the proceedings shall be for the use of such informer and the United States in equal parts.
SEC. 4. . . . whenever hereafter, during the present insurrection against the Government of the United States, any person claimed to be held to labor or service under the law of any State, shall be required or permitted by the person to whom such labor or service is claimed to be due, or by the lawful agent of such person, to take up arms against the United States, or shall be required or permitted by the person to whom such labor or service is claimed to be due, or his lawful agent, to work or to be employed in or upon any fort, navy yard, dock, armory, ship, entrenchment, or in any military or naval service whatsoever, against the Government and lawful authority of the United States, then, and in every such case, the person to whom such labor or service is claimed to be due shall forfeit his claim to such labor, any law of the State or of the United States to the contrary notwithstanding. And whenever thereafter the person claiming such labor or service shall seek to enforce his claim, it shall be a full and sufficient answer to such claim that the person whose service or labor is claimed had been employed in hostile service against the Government of the United States, contrary to the provisions of this act.

Source: U.S. Statutes at Large, Treaties, and Proclamations of the United States of America (Boston: Little, Brown, 1863), 12:319.

BLACK CODE (EXAMPLE FROM LOUISIANA, 1865)

AN ACT Relative to apprentices and indentured servants.
Section 1. . . . it shall be the duty . . . civil officers of this State, to report . . . on the first Monday of each month, for each and every year, all persons under the age of eighteen years, if females, and twenty-one, if males, who are orphans, or whose parent, parents, or tutor, have not the means, or who refuse to provide for and maintain said minors; and, thereupon, it shall be the duty of the Clerks of the District Courts, Mayor and President of the Police Jury . . . to examine whether the party or parties . . . come within the purview and meaning of this Act, and if so, to apprentice said minor or minors, in manner and form as prescribed by the Civil Code of the State of Louisiana . . .
Sec. 2. . . . persons who have attained the age of majority, whether in this State or any other State of the United States, or in a foreign country, may bind themselves to services to be performed in this country, for the term of five years, on such terms as they may stipulate, as domestic servants and to work on farms, plantations or in manufacturing establishments, which contracts shall be valid and binding on the parties to the same. . . .

Source: Kalamu Magazine: The Pen of African History, "The Black Codes of Louisiana, Mississippi, and Ohio," www.kalamumagazine.com/black_codes.htm.

CIVIL RIGHTS ACT OF 1866

. . . all persons born in the United States and not subject to any foreign power, excluding Indians not taxed, are hereby declared to be citizens of the United States; and such citizens, of every race and color, without regard to any previous condition of slavery or involuntary servitude, except as a punishment for crime whereof the party shall have been duly convicted, shall have the same right, in every State and Territory in the United States, to make and enforce contracts, to sue, be parties, and give evidence, to inherit, purchase, lease, sell, hold, and convey real and personal property, and to full and equal benefit of all laws and proceedings for the security of person and property, as is enjoyed by white citizens, and shall be subject to like punishment, pains, and penalties, and to none other, any law, statute, ordinance, regulation, or custom, to the contrary notwithstanding.

Sec. 9. . . . it shall be lawful for the President of the United States, or such person as he may empower for that purpose, to employ such part of the land or naval forces of the United States, or of the militia, as shall be necessary to prevent the violation and enforce the due execution of this act.

Sec. 10. . . . upon all questions of law arising in any cause under the provisions of this act a final appeal may be taken to the Supreme Court of the United States.

Source: History Central, www.multied.com/documents/civilrights-act.html.

CIVIL RIGHTS ACT OF 1875

Whereas it is essential to just government we recognize the equality of all men before the law, and hold that it is the duty of government in its dealings with the people to mete out equal and exact justice to all, of whatever nativity, race, color, or persuasion, religious or political; and it being the appropriate object of legislation to enact great fundamental principles into law: Therefore,

Be it enacted, That all persons within the jurisdiction of the United States shall be entitled to the full and equal enjoyment of the accommodations, advantages, facilities, and privileges of inns, public conveyances on land or water, theaters, and other places of public amusement; subject only to the conditions and limitations established by law, and applicable alike to citizens of every race and color, regardless of any previous condition of servitude. . . .

SEC. 4. That no citizen possessing all other qualifications which are or may be prescribed by law shall be disqualified for service as grand or petit juror in any court of the United States, or of any State, on account of race, color, or previous condition of servitude; and any officer or other person charged with any duty in the selection or summoning of jurors who shall exclude or fail to summon any citizen for the cause aforesaid shall, on conviction thereof, be deemed guilty of a misdemeanor, and be fined not more than five thousand dollars. . . .

Source: 18 Stat. 335 ff.

CHINESE EXCLUSION TREATY (1881)

ARTICLE I. Whenever in the opinion of the Government of the United States, the coming of Chinese laborers to the United States, or their residence therein, affects or threatens to affect the interests of that country, or to endanger the good order of the said country or of any locality within the territory thereof, the Government of China agrees that the Government of the United States may regulate, limit, or suspend such coming or residence, but may not absolutely prohibit it. The limitation or suspension shall be reasonable and shall apply only to Chinese who may go to the United States as laborers, other classes not being included in the limitation. . . .

ARTICLE II. Chinese subjects, whether proceeding to the United States as teachers, students, merchants or from curiosity, together with their body and household servants, and Chinese laborers who are now in the United States shall be allowed to go and come of their own free will and accord, and shall be accorded all the rights, privileges, immunities, and exemptions which are accorded to the citizens and subjects of the most favored nation. . . .

Source: William M. Malloy, *Treaties, Conventions, International Acts, Protocols, and Agreements between the United States of America and Other Powers, 1776–1909* (Holmes Beach, Fla.: Gaunt, 1996), 1:237ff.

CHINESE EXCLUSION ACT (1882)

Preamble. Whereas, in the opinion of the Government of the United States the coming of Chinese laborers to this country endangers the good order of certain localities within the territory thereof:

Therefore, Be it enacted . . . That from and after the expiration of ninety days next after the passage of this act, and until the expiration of ten years next after the passage of this act, the coming of Chinese laborers to the United States be, and the same is hereby, suspended . . .

SEC. 2. That the master of any vessel who shall knowingly bring within the United States on such vessel, and land or permit to be landed, and Chinese laborer, from any foreign port of place, shall be deemed guilty of a misdemeanor . . .

SEC. 3. That the two foregoing sections shall not apply to

Chinese laborers who were in the United States on the seventeenth day of November, eighteen hundred and eighty, or who shall have come into the same before the expiration of ninety days next after the passage of this act. . . .
SEC. 14. That hereafter no State court or court of the United States shall admit Chinese to citizenship; and all laws in conflict with this act are hereby repealed. . . .

Source: "Chinese Exclusion Act," *Ancestors in the Americas,* Center for Educational Telecommunications, www.cetel.org/1882_exclusion.html.

INDIAN MAJOR CRIMES ACT (1885)

(a) Any Indian who commits against the person or property of another Indian or other person any of the following offenses, namely, murder, manslaughter, kidnapping, maiming . . . incest, assault with intent to commit murder, assault with a dangerous weapon, assault resulting in serious bodily injury . . . an assault against an individual who has not attained the age of 16 years, arson, burglary, robbery, and a felony . . . within the Indian country, shall be subject to the same law and penalties as all other persons committing any of the above offenses, within the exclusive jurisdiction of the United States.
(b) Any offense referred to in subsection (a) of this section that is not defined and punished by Federal law in force within the exclusive jurisdiction of the United States shall be defined and punished in accordance with the laws of the State in which such offense was committed as are in force at the time of such offense.

Source: 18 USC 1153.

IMMIGRATION ACT OF 1924

- Established two quota provisions:
  1. An annual quota of any quota nationality set at 2 percent of the number of foreign-born persons of such nationality resident in the continental United States in 1890 (total quota, 164,667); this was to remain in effect until June 30, 1927.
  2. From July 1, 1927 (later postponed to July 1, 1929), established the national origins quota system, such that the annual quota for any country or nationality had the same relation to 150,000 as the number of inhabitants in the continental United States in 1920 having that national origin had to the total number of inhabitants in the continental United States in 1920.
- Established preference quota status for unmarried children under 21, for parents, for spouses of U.S. citizens aged 21 and over, and for quota immigrants aged 21 and over who are skilled in agriculture, together with their wives and dependent children under age 16.
- Established non-quota status for wives and unmarried children under 18 of U.S. citizens, natives of Western Hemisphere countries (with their families), nonimmigrants, and certain others; subsequent amendments eliminated some elements of this law's inherent discrimination against women.
- Established the "consular control system" of immigration by mandating that no alien may be permitted entrance to the United States without an unexpired immigration visa issued by a United States consular officer abroad; this effectively gave joint control of immigration to the Department of State and the Immigration and Naturalization Service.
- Introduced the provision that no alien ineligible to become a citizen shall be admitted to the United States as an immigrant; this was directed mainly against Japanese aliens.
- Imposed fines on transportation companies that landed aliens in violation of U.S. Immigration laws.
- Defined the term "immigrant" and designated all other alien entries into the United States as "nonimmigrant" (that is, temporary visitors); established classes of admission for such nonimmigrant entries.

Source: 43 Stat. 153.

INDIAN CITIZENSHIP ACT (1924)

Be it enacted That all non-citizen Indians born within the territorial limits of the United States be, and they are hereby, declared to be citizens of the United States: Provided, That the granting of such citizenship shall not in any manner impair or otherwise affect the right of any Indian to tribal or other property.

Source: 43 Stat. 253.

WHEELER-HOWARD INDIAN REORGANIZATION ACT (1934)

. . . hereafter no land of any Indian reservation, created or set apart by treaty or agreement with the Indians, Act of Congress, Executive order, purchase, or otherwise, shall be allotted in severalty to any Indian.

Sec. 2. The existing periods of trust placed upon any Indian lands and any restriction on alienation thereof are hereby extended and continued until otherwise directed by Congress.

Sec. 3. The Secretary of the Interior, if he shall find it to be in the public interest, is hereby authorized to restore to tribal ownership the remaining surplus lands of any Indian reservation heretofore opened, or authorized to be opened, to sale, or any other form of disposal by Presidential proclamation, or by any of the public land laws of the United States. . . .

Sec. 4. Except as herein provided, no sale, devise, gift, exchange or other transfer of restricted Indian lands or of shares in the assets of any Indian tribe or corporation organized hereunder, shall be made or approved. . . .

Sec. 5. The Secretary of the Interior is hereby authorized, in his discretion, to acquire . . . any interest in lands, water rights or surface rights to lands, within or without existing reservations, including trust or otherwise restricted allotments whether the allottee be living or deceased, for the purpose of providing lands for Indians. . . .

Sec. 7. The Secretary of the Interior is hereby authorized to proclaim new Indian reservations on lands acquired pursuant to any authority conferred by this Act, or to add such lands to existing reservations. . . .

Sec. 12. The Secretary of the Interior is directed to establish standards of health, age, character, experience, knowledge, and ability for Indians who maybe appointed, without regard to civil-service laws, to the various positions maintained, now or hereafter, by the Indian office, in the administrations functions or services affecting any Indian tribe. Such qualified Indians shall hereafter have the preference to appointment to vacancies in any such positions. . . .

Sec. 16. Any Indian tribe, or tribes, residing on the same reservation, shall have the right to organize for its common welfare, and may adopt an appropriate constitution and bylaws, which shall become effective when ratified by a majority vote of the adult members of the tribe, or of the adult Indians residing on such reservation, as the case may be, at a special election authorized by the Secretary of the Interior under such rules and regulations as he may prescribe. Such constitution and bylaws when ratified as aforesaid and approved by the Secretary of the Interior shall be revocable by an election open to the same voters and conducted in the same manner as hereinabove provided. Amendments to the constitution and bylaws may be ratified and approved by the Secretary in the same manner as the original constitution and bylaws.

In addition to all powers vested in any Indian tribe or tribal council by existing law, the constitution adopted by said tribe shall also vest in such tribe or its tribal council the following rights and powers: To employ legal counsel, the choice of counsel and fixing of fees to be subject to the approval of the Secretary of the Interior; to prevent the sale, disposition, lease, or encumbrance of tribal lands, interests in lands, or other tribal assets without the consent of the tribe; and to negotiate with the Federal, State, and local Governments. The Secretary of the Interior shall advise such tribe or its tribal council of all appropriation estimates or Federal projects for the benefit of the tribe prior to the submission of such estimates to the Bureau of the Budget and the Congress.

Sec. 17. The Secretary of the Interior may, upon petition by at least one-third of the adult Indians, issue a charter of incorporation to such tribe . . .

Sec. 18. This Act shall not apply to any reservation wherein a majority of the adult Indians, voting at a special election duly called by the Secretary of the Interior, shall vote against it application. . . .

Source: P.L. 73-576.

IMMIGRATION AND NATURALIZATION ACT OF 1952

- Made all races eligible for naturalization, thereby eliminating race as a bar to immigration
- Eliminated discrimination between sexes with respect to immigration
- Revised the national origins quota system of the Immigration Act of 1924 by changing the national origins quota formula, setting the annual quota for an area at one-sixth of 1 percent of the number of inhabitants in the continental United States in 1920 whose ancestry or national origin was attributable to that area; in addition, all countries were allowed a minimum quota of 100, with a ceiling of 2,000 on most natives of countries in the Asia-Pacific triangle (that is, most of the Asian countries)
- Introduced a system of selective immigration by giving a quota preference to skilled aliens whose services were

needed in the United States and to relatives of U.S. citizens and aliens

- Capped the use of the governing country's quota by natives of colonies and dependent areas
- Provided an "escape clause" that permitted the immigration of certain former voluntary members of proscribed organizations
- Broadened the grounds for exclusion and deportation of aliens
- Provided procedures for the adjustment of status of nonimmigrant aliens to that of permanent resident aliens
- Modified and added significantly to the existing classes of nonimmigrant admission
- Enhanced procedural safeguards for aliens subject to deportation
- Introduced the alien address report system, whereby all aliens in the United States (including most temporary visitors) were required annually to report their current address to the Immigration and Naturalization Service
- Established a central index of all aliens in the United States for use by security and law enforcement agencies
- Repealed a ban on contract labor, but added other qualitative exclusions

Source: 79 Stat. 911.

CIVIL RIGHTS ACT OF 1957

An Act to provide means of further securing and protecting the civil rights of persons within the jurisdiction of the United States.... .

Part I—Establishment of the Commission on Civil Rights

Sec. 101.

1. There is created in the executive branch of the Government a Commission on Civil Rights (hereinafter called the "Commission").

2. The Commission shall be composed of six members who shall be appointed by the President by and with the advice and consent of the Senate. Not more than three of the members shall at any one time be of the same political party....

Duties of the Commission

Sec. 104.

1. The Commission shall —

1.1. investigate allegations in writing under oath or affirmation that certain citizens of the United States are being deprived of their right to vote and have that vote counted by reason of their color, race, religion, or national origin; which writing, under oath or affirmation, shall set forth the facts upon which such belief or beliefs are based;

1.2. study and collect information concerning legal developments constituting a denial of equal protection of the laws under the

1.3. Constitution; and

1.4. appraise the laws and policies of the Federal Government with respect to equal protection of the laws under the Constitution.

2. The Commission shall submit interim reports to the President and to the Congress at such times as either the Commission or the President shall deem desirable, and shall submit to the President and to the Congress a final and comprehensive report of its activities, findings, and recommendations not later than two years from the date of the enactment of this Act....

Part IV—To Provide Means of Further Securing and Protecting the Right to Vote

Sec. 131.

Section 2004 of the Revised Statutes (42 U.S.C. 1971), is amended as follows:

...."(b) No person, whether acting under color of law or otherwise, shall intimidate, threaten, coerce, or attempt to intimidate, threaten, or coerce any other person for the purpose of interfering with the right of such other person to vote or to vote as he may choose, or of causing such other person to vote for, or not to vote for, any candidate for the office of President, Vice President, presidential elector, Member of the Senate, or Member of the House of Representatives, Delegates or Commissioners from the Territories or possessions, at any general, special, or primary election held solely or in part for the purpose of selecting or electing any such candidate....

Source: History Central, www.multied.com/documents/CivilRights57.html.

EQUAL PAY ACT OF 1963

... SEC. 2. (a) The Congress hereby finds that the existence in industries engaged in commerce or in the production of goods for commerce of wage differentials based on sex—

(1) depresses wages and living standards for employees necessary for their health and efficiency;

(2) prevents the maximum utilization of the available labor resources;

(3) tends to cause labor disputes, thereby burdening, affecting, and obstructing commerce;

(4) burdens commerce and the free flow of goods in commerce; and

(5) constitutes an unfair method of competition....

SEC. 3. Section 6 of the Fair Labor Standards Act of 1938 . . . is amended by adding thereto a new subsection (d) as follows: Discrimination prohibited. . . .

> (d)(1) No employer having employees subject to any provisions of this section shall discriminate, within any establishment in which such employees are employed, between employees on the basis of sex by paying wages to employees in such establishment at a rate less than the rate at which he pays wages to employees of the opposite sex in such establishment for equal work on jobs the performance of which requires equal skill, effort, and responsibility, and which are performed under similar working conditions, except where such payment is made pursuant to (i) a seniority system; (ii) a merit system; (iii) a system which measures earnings by quantity or quality of production; or (iv) a differential based on any other factor other than sex: Provided, That an employer who is paying a wage rate differential in violation of this subsection shall not, in order to comply with the provisions of this subsection, reduce the wage rate of any employee. . . .

Source: P.L. 88-38.

CIVIL RIGHTS ACT OF 1964

Title II Sec. 201.
(a) All persons shall be entitled to the full and equal enjoyment of the goods, services, facilities, privileges, advantages, and accommodations of any place of public accommodation, as defined in this section, without discrimination or segregation on the ground of race, color, religion, or national origin.
(b) Each of the following establishments which serves the public is a place of public accommodation within the meaning of this title if its operations affect commerce, or if discrimination or segregation by it is supported by State action:
(1) any inn, hotel, motel, or other establishment which provides lodging to transient guests, other than an establishment located within a building which contains not more than five rooms for rent or hire and which is actually occupied by the proprietor of such establishment as his residence;
(2) any restaurant, cafeteria, lunchroom, lunch counter, soda fountain, or other facility principally engaged in selling food for consumption on the premises, including, but not limited to, any such facility located on the premises of any retail establishment; or any gasoline station;
(3) any motion picture house, theater, concert hall, sports arena, stadium or other place of exhibition or entertainment; and
(4) any establishment (A)(i) which is physically located within the premises of any establishment otherwise covered by this subsection, or (ii) within the premises of which is physically located any such covered establishment, and (b) which holds itself out as serving patrons of such covered establishment. . . .
Sec. 202. All persons shall be entitled to be free, at any establishment or place, from discrimination or segregation of any kind on the ground of race, color, religion, or national origin, if such discrimination or segregation is or purports to be required by any law, statute, ordinance, regulation, rule, or order of a State or any agency or political subdivision thereof.
Sec. 203. No person shall (a) withhold, deny, or attempt to withhold or deny, or deprive or attempt to deprive, any person of any right or privilege secured by section 201 or 202, or (b) intimidate, threaten, or coerce, or attempt to intimidate, threaten, or coerce any person with purpose of interfering with any right or privilege secured by section 201 or 202, or (c) punish or attempt to punish any person for exercising or attempting to exercise any right or privilege secured by section 201 or 202.

Source: P.L. 88-352.

IMMIGRATION ACT OF 1965

Abolished the national origins quota system established by the IMMIGRATION ACT OF 1924 and the IMMIGRATION AND NATIONALITY ACT OF 1952, which eliminated national origin, race, and ancestry as a basis for admission into the United States.

- Established allocation of immigrant visas on a first come, first served basis, subject to a seven-category preference system for relatives of U.S. citizens and permanent resident aliens (this to facilitate the reunification of families) and for persons with special occupational skills, abilities, or training in vocations required by the United States
- Created two categories of immigrants not subject to numerical restrictions: Immediate relatives (spouses, children, parents) of U.S. citizens, and "special immigrants," including certain ministers of religion; certain former employees of the U.S. government abroad; certain persons who lost citizenship (for example, by marriage or by service in foreign armed forces); and certain foreign medical graduates
- Maintained the principle of numerical restriction, but expanded limits to world coverage by limiting Eastern Hemisphere immigration to 170,000 and (for the first time) by placing a ceiling on Western Hemisphere immigration of 120,000 (Neither the preference categories

nor the 20,000 per-country limit were applied to the Western Hemisphere.)

- Introduced as a prerequisite for visa issuance an affirmative finding by the Secretary of Labor that an alien seeking to enter as a worker will not replace a worker in the United States nor adversely affect the wages and working conditions of similarly employed individuals in the United States

Source: 79 Stat. 911.

VOTING RIGHTS ACT OF 1965

. . . SEC. 2.

No voting qualification or prerequisite to voting, or standard, practice, or procedure shall be imposed or applied by any State or political subdivision to deny or abridge the right of any citizen of the United States to vote on account of race or color. . . .

SEC. 4.

(a) To assure that the right of citizens of the United States to vote is not denied or abridged on account of race or color, no citizen shall be denied the right to vote in any Federal, State, or local election because of his failure to comply with any test or device in any State with respect to which the determinations have been made under subsection (b) or in any political subdivision with respect to which such determinations have been made as a separate unit, unless the United States District Court for the District of Columbia in an action for a declaratory judgment brought by such State or subdivision against the United States has determined that no such test or device has been used during the five years preceding the filing of the action for the purpose or with the effect of denying or abridging the right to vote on account of race or color: Provided, That no such declaratory judgment shall issue with respect to any plaintiff for a period of five years after the entry of a final judgment of any court of the United States, other than the denial of a declaratory judgment under this section, whether entered prior to or after the enactment of this Act, determining that denials or abridgments of the right to vote on account of race or color through the use of such tests or devices have occurred anywhere in the territory of such plaintiff.

An action pursuant to this subsection shall be heard and determined by a court of three judges in accordance with the provisions of section 2284 of title 28 of the United States Code and any appeal shall lie to the Supreme Court. The court shall retain jurisdiction of any action pursuant to this subsection for five years after judgment and shall reopen the action upon motion of the Attorney General alleging that a test or device has been used for the purpose or with the effect of denying or abridging the right to vote on account of race or color.

If the Attorney General determines that he has no reason to believe that any such test or device has been used during the five years preceding the filing of the action for the purpose or with the effect of denying or abridging the right to vote on account of race or color, he shall consent to the entry of such judgment . . .

A determination or certification of the Attorney General or of the Director of the Census under this section or under section 6 or section 13 shall not be reviewable in any court and shall be effective upon publication in the Federal Register. . . .

(2) No person who demonstrates that he has successfully completed the sixth primary grade in a public school in, or a private school accredited by, any State or territory, the District of Columbia, or the Commonwealth of Puerto Rico in which the predominant classroom language was other than English, shall be denied the right to vote in any Federal, State, or local election because of his inability to read, write, understand, or interpret any matter in the English language, except that, in States in which State law provides that a different level of education is presumptive of literacy, he shall demonstrate that he has successfully completed an equivalent level of education in a public school in, or a private school accredited by, any State or territory, the District of Columbia, or the Commonwealth of Puerto Rico in which the predominant classroom language was other than English. . . .

SEC. 10.

The Congress finds that the requirement of the payment of a poll tax as a precondition to voting (i) precludes persons of limited means from voting or imposes unreasonable financial hardship upon such persons as a precondition to their exercise of the franchise, (ii) does not bear a reasonable relationship to any legitimate State interest in the conduct of elections, and (iii) in some areas has the purpose or effect of denying persons the right to vote because of race or color. Upon the basis of these findings, Congress declares that the constitutional right of citizens to vote is denied or abridged in some areas by the requirement of the payment of a poll tax as a precondition to voting. . . .

SEC. 11.

(a) No person acting under color of law shall fail or refuse to permit any person to vote who is entitled to vote under any provision of this Act or is otherwise qualified to vote, or

willfully fail or refuse to tabulate, count, and report such person's vote. (b) No person, whether acting under color of law or otherwise, shall intimidate, threaten, or coerce, or attempt to intimidate, threaten, or coerce any person for voting or attempting to vote, or intimidate, threaten, or coerce, or attempt to intimidate, threaten, or coerce any person for urging or aiding any person to vote or attempt to vote, or intimidate, threaten, or coerce any person for exercising any powers or duties under section 3(a), 6, 8, 9, 10, or 12(e)....
SEC. 16.
The Attorney General and the Secretary of Defense, jointly, shall make a full and complete study to determine whether, under the laws or practices of any State or States, there are preconditions to voting, which might tend to result in discrimination against citizens serving in the Armed Forces of the United States seeking to vote....

Source: Voting Rights Act of 1965, "Prentice Hall Documents Library," hcl.chass.ncsu.edu/garson/dye/docs/votrit65.htm.

AGE DISCRIMINATION IN EMPLOYMENT ACT (1967)

This act has been amended by the Older Workers Benefit Protection Act (P.L. 101-433) and by section 115 of the Civil Rights Act of 1991 (P.L. 102-166). These amendments appear in boldface type.

An Act
To prohibit age discrimination in employment.
STATEMENT OF FINDINGS AND PURPOSE
SEC. 621.
(a) The Congress hereby finds and declares that—
(1) . . . older workers find themselves disadvantaged in their efforts to retain employment, and especially to regain employment when displaced from jobs;
(2) the setting of arbitrary age limits regardless of potential for job performance has become a common practice, and certain otherwise desirable practices may work to the disadvantage of older persons;
(3) the incidence of unemployment, especially long-term unemployment with resultant deterioration of skill, morale, and employer acceptability is, relative to the younger ages, high among older workers; their numbers are great and growing; and their employment problems grave;
(4) the existence in industries affecting commerce, of arbitrary discrimination in employment because of age, burdens commerce and the free flow of goods in commerce....

PROHIBITION OF AGE DISCRIMINATION
SEC. 623.
(a) It shall be unlawful for an employer—
(1) to fail or refuse to hire or to discharge any individual or otherwise discriminate against any individual with respect to his compensation, terms, conditions, or privileges of employment, because of such individual's age;
(2) to limit, segregate, or classify his employees in any way which would deprive or tend to deprive any individual of employment opportunities or otherwise adversely affect his status as an employee, because of such individual's age; or
(3) to reduce the wage rate of any employee in order to comply with this chapter.
(b) It shall be unlawful for an employment agency to fail or refuse to refer for employment, or otherwise to discriminate against, any individual because of such individual's age, or to classify or refer for employment any individual on the basis of such individual's age.
(c) It shall be unlawful for a labor organization—
(1) to exclude or to expel from its membership, or otherwise to discriminate against, any individual because of his age;
(2) to limit, segregate, or classify its membership, or to classify or fail or refuse to refer for employment any individual, in any way which would deprive or tend to deprive any individual of employment opportunities, or would limit such employment opportunities or otherwise adversely affect his status as an employee or as an applicant for employment, because of such individual's age;
(3) to cause or attempt to cause an employer to discriminate against an individual in violation of this section.
(d) It shall be unlawful for an employer to discriminate against any of his employees or applicants for employment, for an employment agency to discriminate against any individual, or for a labor organization to discriminate against any member thereof or applicant for membership, because such individual, member or applicant for membership has opposed any practice made unlawful by this section, or because such individual, member or applicant for membership has made a charge, testified, assisted, or participated in any manner in an investigation, proceeding, or litigation under this chapter.
(e) It shall be unlawful for an employer, labor organization, or employment agency to print or publish, or cause to be printed or published, any notice or advertisement relating to employment by such an employer or membership in or any classification or referral for employment by such a labor organization, or relating to any classification or referral for employment by such an employment agency, indicating any preference, limitation, specification, or discrimination, based on age.

(f) It shall not be unlawful for an employer, employment agency, or labor organization—
(1) to take any action otherwise prohibited under subsections (a), (b), (c), or (e) of this section where age is a bona fide occupational qualification reasonably necessary to the normal operation of the particular business, or where the differentiation is based on reasonable factors other than age, or where such practices involve an employee in a workplace in a foreign country, and compliance with such subsections would cause such employer, or a corporation controlled by such employer, to violate the laws of the country in which such workplace is located;
(2) to take any action otherwise prohibited under subsection (a), (b), (c), or (e) of this section—
(A) to observe the terms of a bona fide seniority system that is not intended to evade the purposes of this chapter, except that no such seniority system shall require or permit the involuntary retirement of any individual specified by section 631(a) of this title because of the age of such individual; or
(B) to observe the terms of a bona fide employee benefit plan—
(3) to discharge or otherwise discipline an individual for good cause . . .

Source: U.S. Equal Employment Opportunity Commission, www.eeoc.gov/laws/adea.html; includes amendments and EEOC additions.

OCCUPATIONAL SAFETY AND HEALTH ACT (1970)

The Congress declares it to be its purpose and policy, through the exercise of its powers to regulate commerce among the several States and with foreign nations and to provide for the general welfare, to assure so far as possible every working man and woman in the Nation safe and healthful working conditions and to preserve our human resources —
(1) by encouraging employers and employees in their efforts to reduce the number of occupational safety and health hazards at their places of employment, and to stimulate employers and employees to institute new and to perfect existing programs for providing safe and healthful working conditions;
(2) by providing that employers and employees have separate but dependent responsibilities and rights with respect to achieving safe and healthful working conditions;
(3) by authorizing the Secretary of Labor to set mandatory occupational safety and health standards applicable to businesses affecting interstate commerce . . . ;
(4) by building upon advances already made through employer and employee initiative for providing safe and healthful working conditions; . . .
(9) by providing for the development and promulgation of occupational safety and health standards . . .

Source: Occupational Safety and Health Administration, OSH Act of 1970, www.osha.gov/pls/oshaweb/owasrch.search_form?p_doc_type=OSHACT&p_toc_level=0&p_keyvalue=OshAct_toc_by_sect.html.

INDIAN SELF-DETERMINATION ACT (1975)

Sec. 450.
(a) The Congress, after careful review of the Federal Government's historical and special legal relationship with, and resulting responsibilities to, American Indian people, finds that—
(1) the prolonged Federal domination of Indian service programs has served to retard rather than enhance the progress of Indian people and their communities by depriving Indians of the full opportunity to develop leadership skills crucial to the realization of self-government, and has denied to the Indian people an effective voice in the planning and implementation of programs for the benefit of Indians which are responsive to the true needs of Indian communities; and
(2) the Indian people will never surrender their desire to control their relationships both among themselves and with non-Indian governments, organizations, and persons.

(b) The Congress further finds that—
(1) true self-determination in any society of people is dependent upon an educational process which will insure the development of qualified people to fulfill meaningful leadership roles;
(2) the Federal responsibility for and assistance to education of Indian children has not effected the desired level of educational achievement or created the diverse opportunities and personal satisfaction which education can and should provide; and
(3) parental and community control of the educational process is of crucial importance to the Indian people.

Sec. 450a.
(a) Recognition of obligation of United States
The Congress hereby recognizes the obligation of the United States to respond to the strong expression of the Indian people for self-determination by assuring maximum Indian participation in the direction of educational as well as

other Federal services to Indian communities so as to render such services more responsive to the needs and desires of those communities.

(b) Declaration of commitment

The Congress declares its commitment to the maintenance of the Federal Government's unique and continuing relationship with, and responsibility to, individual Indian tribes and to the Indian people as a whole through the establishment of a meaningful Indian self-determination policy which will permit an orderly transition from the Federal domination of programs for, and services to, Indians to effective and meaningful participation by the Indian people in the planning, conduct, and administration of those programs and services. In accordance with this policy, the United States is committed to supporting and assisting Indian tribes in the development of strong and stable tribal governments, capable of administering quality programs and developing the economies of their respective communities.

(c) Declaration of national goal

The Congress declares that a major national goal of the United States is to provide the quantity and quality of educational services and opportunities which will permit Indian children to compete and excel in the life areas of their choice, and to achieve the measure of self-determination essential to their social and economic well-being.

Source: P.L. 93–638.

AMERICAN INDIAN RELIGIOUS FREEDOM ACT (1978)

Whereas the freedom of religion for all people is an inherent right, fundamental to the democratic structure of the United States and is guaranteed by the First Amendment of the United States Constitution;

Whereas the United States has traditionally rejected the concept of a government denying individuals the right to practice their religion and, as a result, has benefitted from a rich variety of religious heritages in this country;

Whereas the religious practices of the American Indian (as well as Native Alaskan and Hawaiian) are an integral part of their culture, tradition and heritage, such practices forming the basis of Indian identity and value systems;

Whereas the traditional American Indian religions, as an integral part of Indian life, are indispensable and irreplaceable;

Whereas the lack of a clear, comprehensive, and consistent Federal policy has often resulted in the abridgment of religious freedom for traditional American Indians;

Whereas such religious infringements result from the lack of knowledge or the insensitive and inflexible enforcement of Federal policies and regulations premised on a variety of laws;

Whereas such laws were designed for such worthwhile purposes as conservation and preservation of natural species and resources but were never intended to relate to Indian religious practices and, therefore, were passed without consideration of their effect on traditional American Indian religions;

Whereas such laws and policies often deny American Indians access to sacred sites required in their religions, including cemeteries;

Whereas such laws at times prohibit the use and possession of sacred objects necessary to the exercise of religious rites and ceremonies;

Whereas traditional American Indian ceremonies have been intruded upon, interfered with, and in a few instances banned: Now, therefore, be it

Resolved . . . That henceforth it shall be the policy of the United States to protect and preserve for American Indians their inherent right of freedom to believe, express, and exercise the traditional religions of the American Indian, Eskimo, Aleut, and Native Hawaiians, including but not limited to access to sites, use and possession of sacred objects, and the freedom to worship through ceremonials and traditional rights.

Source: P.L. 95-341.

INDIAN CHILD WELFARE ACT (1978)

§ 1901. Congressional findings

Recognizing the special relationship between the United States and the Indian tribes and their members and the Federal responsibility to Indian people, the Congress finds—(1) that clause 3, section 8, article I of the United States Constitution provides that "The Congress shall have Power * * * To regulate Commerce * * * with Indian tribes" and, through this and other constitutional authority, Congress has plenary power over Indian affairs; (2) that Congress, through statutes, treaties, and the general course of dealing with Indian tribes, has assumed the responsibility for the protection and preservation of Indian tribes and their resources; (3) that there is no resource that is more vital to the continued existence and integrity of Indian tribes than their children and that the United States has a direct interest, as trustee, in protecting Indian children who are members of or are eligible for membership in an Indian tribe; (4) that an alarmingly high percentage of Indian families are broken up by the removal, often unwarranted, of their children from them by nontribal public and private agencies and that an alarmingly high percentage of such children are placed in non-Indian foster and adoptive homes and institutions; and (5) that the States, exercising their recognized jurisdiction over Indian child custody proceedings through administrative and judicial bodies, have often failed to recognize the essential tribal relations of Indian people and the cultural and social standards prevailing in Indian communities and families.

§ 1902. Congressional declaration of policy

The Congress hereby declares that it is the policy of this Nation to protect the best interests of Indian children and to promote the stability and security of Indian tribes and families by the establishment of minimum Federal standards for the removal of Indian children from their families and the placement of such children in foster or adoptive homes which will reflect the unique values of Indian culture, and by providing for assistance to Indian tribes in the operation of child and family service programs. . . .

§ 1911. Indian tribe jurisdiction over Indian child custody proceedings

(a) Exclusive jurisdiction

> An Indian tribe shall have jurisdiction exclusive as to any State over any child custody proceeding involving an Indian child who resides or is domiciled within the reservation of such tribe, except where such jurisdiction is otherwise vested in the State by existing Federal law. . .

(c) State court proceedings; intervention

> In any State court proceeding for the foster care placement of, or termination of parental rights to, an Indian child, the Indian custodian of the child and the Indian child's tribe shall have a right to intervene at any point in the proceeding.

(d) Full faith and credit to public acts, records, and judicial proceedings of Indian tribes

> The United States, every State, every territory or possession of the United States, and every Indian tribe shall give full faith and credit to the public acts, records, and judicial proceedings of any Indian tribe applicable to Indian child custody proceedings to the same extent that such entities give full faith and credit to the public acts, records, and judicial proceedings of any other entity.
>
> As for the adoptive placement of Indian children under state law, "a preference shall be given, in the absence of good cause to the contrary, to a placement with (1) a member of the child's extended family; (2) other members of the Indian child's tribe; or (3) other Indian families."

Source: Legal Information Institute, U.S. Code Collection, Chapter 21—Indian Child Welfare, www4.law.cornell.edu/uscode/25/ch21.html.

IMMIGRATION REFORM AND CONTROL ACT (1986)

- Legalization (that is, temporary and then permanent resident status) for aliens who had resided in the United States in an unlawful status since January 1, 1982 (entering illegally or as temporary visitors with authorized stay expiring before that date or with the government's knowledge of their unlawful status before that date) and who are not otherwise excludable
- Sanctions prohibiting employers from knowingly hiring, recruiting, or referring for a fee aliens not authorized to work in the United States
- Increased enforcement at U.S. borders
- A new classification of seasonal agricultural worker; also provided for the legalization of certain such workers
- Extension of the registry date (that is, the date from which an alien has resided illegally and continuously in the United States and thus qualifies for adjustment to permanent resident status) from June 30, 1948 to January 1, 1972
- Adjustment to permanent resident status for Cubans and Haitians who entered the United States without inspection and who had continuously resided in country since January 1, 1982
- Increase of the numerical limitation for immigrants admitted under the preference system for dependent areas from 600 to 5,000 beginning in fiscal year 1988
- A new special immigrant category for certain retired employees of international organizations and their families (along with a new nonimmigrant status for parents and children of such immigrants)
- A nonimmigrant Visa Waiver Pilot Program, allowing certain aliens to visit the United States without applying for a nonimmigrant visa
- Allocation of 5,000 nonpreference visas in each of fiscal years 1987 and 1988 for aliens born in countries from which immigration was adversely affected by the IMMIGRATION ACT OF 1965.

Source: 100 Stat. 3359.

FLAG PROTECTION ACT (1989)

Sec. 700. Desecration of the flag of the United States; penalties

(a)(1) Whoever knowingly mutilates, defaces, physically defiles, burns, maintains on the floor or ground, or tramples

upon any flag of the United States shall be fined under this title or imprisoned for not more than one year, or both.
(2) This subsection does not prohibit any conduct consisting of the disposal of a flag when it has become worn or soiled.

Source: 18 USC 700.

AMERICANS WITH DISABILITIES ACT (1990)

SEC. 2. FINDINGS AND PURPOSES.
(a) Findings. The Congress finds that

(1) some 43,000,000 Americans have one or more physical or mental disabilities, and this number is increasing as the population as a whole is growing older;

(2) historically, society has tended to isolate and segregate individuals with disabilities, and, despite some improvements, such forms of discrimination against individuals with disabilities continue to be a serious and pervasive social problem;

(3) discrimination against individuals with disabilities persists in such critical areas as employment, housing, public accommodations, education, transportation, communication, recreation, institutionalization, health services, voting, and access to public services;

(4) unlike individuals who have experienced discrimination on the basis of race, color, sex, national origin, religion, or age, individuals who have experienced discrimination on the basis of disability have often had no legal recourse to redress such discrimination;

(5) individuals with disabilities continually encounter various forms of discrimination, including outright intentional exclusion, the discriminatory effects of architectural, transportation, and communication barriers, overprotective rules and policies, failure to make modifications to existing facilities and practices, exclusionary qualification standards and criteria, segregation, and relegation to lesser services, programs, activities, benefits, jobs, or other opportunities;

(6) census data, national polls, and other studies have documented that people with disabilities, as a group, occupy an inferior status in our society, and are severely disadvantaged socially, vocationally, economically, and educationally;

(7) individuals with disabilities are a discrete and insular minority who have been faced with restrictions and limitations, subjected to a history of purposeful unequal treatment, and relegated to a position of political powerlessness in our society, based on characteristics that are beyond the control of such individuals and resulting from stereotypic assumptions not truly indicative of the individual ability of such individuals to participate in, and contribute to, society;

(8) the Nation's proper goals regarding individuals with disabilities are to assure equality of opportunity, full participation, independent living, and economic self-sufficiency for such individuals; and

(9) the continuing existence of unfair and unnecessary discrimination and prejudice denies people with disabilities the opportunity to compete on an equal basis and to pursue those opportunities for which our free society is justifiably famous, and costs the United States billions of dollars in unnecessary expenses resulting from dependency and nonproductivity.

(b) Purpose. It is the purpose of this Act

(1) to provide a clear and comprehensive national mandate for the elimination of discrimination against individuals with disabilities;

(2) to provide clear, strong, consistent, enforceable standards addressing discrimination against individuals with disabilities;

(3) to ensure that the Federal Government plays a central role in enforcing the standards established in this Act on behalf of individuals with disabilities; and

(4) to invoke the sweep of congressional authority, including the power to enforce the fourteenth amendment and to regulate commerce, in order to address the major areas of discrimination faced day-to-day by people with disabilities. . . .

SEC. 102. DISCRIMINATION.
(a) General Rule. No covered entity shall discriminate against a qualified individual with a disability because of the disability of such individual in regard to job application procedures, the hiring, advancement, or discharge of employees, employee compensation, job training, and other terms, conditions, and privileges of employment. . . .

TITLE II PUBLIC SERVICES

Subtitle A Prohibition Against Discrimination and Other Generally Applicable Provisions
SEC. 202. DISCRIMINATION.
. . . no qualified individual with a disability shall, by reason of such disability, be excluded from participation in or be denied the benefits of the services, programs, or activities of a public entity, or be subjected to discrimination by any such entity. . . .

Source: P.L. 101-336.

NATIONAL AFFORDABLE HOUSING ACT (1990)

. . . to reaffirm the long-established national commitment to decent, safe, and sanitary housing for every American by strengthening a nationwide partnership of public and private institutions able—

(1) to ensure that every resident of the United States has access to decent shelter or assistance in avoiding homelessness;

(2) to increase the Nation's supply of decent housing that is affordable to low-income and moderate-income families and accessible to job opportunities;

(3) to improve housing opportunities for all residents of the United States, particularly members of disadvantaged minorities, on a nondiscriminatory basis;

(4) to help make neighborhoods safe and livable;

(5) to expand opportunities for homeownership;

(6) to provide every American community with a reliable, readily available supply of mortgage finance at the lowest possible interest rates; and

(7) to encourage tenant empowerment and reduce generational poverty in federally assisted and public housing by improving the means by which self-sufficiency may be achieved.

Source: U.S. Department of Housing and Urban Development, "Home Laws," Title 42—The Public Health and Welfare, Chapter 130—National Affordable Housing, Subchapter II—Investment in Affordable Housing, www.hud.gov/offices/cpd/affordablehousing/lawsandregs/laws/home/index.cfm.

CIVIL RIGHTS ACT OF 1991

SEC.2. FINDINGS AND PURPOSES. . . .

(b) PURPOSES.—The purposes of this Act are to—

(1) respond to the Supreme Court's recent decisions by restoring the civil rights protections that were dramatically limited by those decisions; and

(2) strengthen existing protections and remedies available under Federal civil rights laws to provide more effective deterrence and adequate compensation for victims of discrimination. . . .

SEC. 4. RESTORING THE BURDEN OF PROOF IN DISPARATE IMPACT CASES.

Section 703 of the Civil Rights Act of 1964 . . . is amended by adding at the end thereof the following new subsection:

"(k) PROOF OF UNLAWFUL EMPLOYMENT PRACTICES IN DISPARATE IMPACT CASES.—(1) An unlawful employment practice based on disparate impact is established under this section when— "(A) a complaining party demonstrates that an employment practice results in a disparate impact on the basis of race, color, religion, sex, or national origin, and the respondent fails to demonstrate that such practice is required by business necessity; or

"(B) a complaining party demonstrates that a group of employment practices results in a disparate impact on the basis of race, color, religion, sex, or national origin, and the respondent fails to demonstrate that such group of employment practices is required by business necessity . . .

"(2) A demonstration that an employment practice is required by business necessity may be used as a defense only against a claim under this subsection.

"(3) . . . a rule barring the employment of an individual who currently and knowingly uses or possesses an illegal drug . . . other than the use or possession of a drug taken under the supervision of a licensed health care professional, or any other use or possession authorized by the Controlled Substances Act or any other provision of Federal law, shall be considered an unlawful employment practice under this title only if such rule is adopted or applied with an intent to discriminate because of the race, color, religion, sex, or national origin.

"(4) The mere existence of a statistical imbalance in an employer's workforce on account of race, color, religion, sex, or national origin is not alone sufficient to establish a prima facie case of disparate impact violation."

SEC. 5. CLARIFYING PROHIBITION AGAINST IMPERMISSIBLE CONSIDERATION OF RACE, COLOR, RELIGION, SEX OR NATIONAL ORIGIN IN EMPLOYMENT PRACTICES.

(a) . . . Section 703 of the Civil Rights Act of 1964 . . . is further amended by adding at the end thereof the following new subsection:

"(1) DISCRIMINATORY PRACTICE NEED NOT BE SOLE CONTRIBUTING FACTOR.—Except as otherwise provided in this title, an unlawful employment practice is established when the complaining party demonstrates that race, color, religion, sex, or national origin was a contributing factor for any employment practice, even though other factors also contributed to such practice." . . .

SEC. 12. RESTORING PROHIBITION AGAINST ALL RACIAL DISCRIMINATION IN THE MAKING AND ENFORCEMENT OF CONTRACTS.

Section 1977 of the Revised Statutes of the United States . . . is amended—

(1) by inserting "(a)" before "All persons within"; and (2) by adding at the end thereof the following new subsections:

"(b) For purposes of this section, the right to 'make and enforce contracts' shall include the making, performance, modification and termination of contracts, and the enjoyment of all benefits, privileges, terms and conditions of the contractual relationship. "(c) The rights protected by this section are protected against impairment by nongovernmental discrimination as well as against impairment under color of State law."

Source: P.L. 102-166.

EQUAL OPPORTUNITY CREDIT ACT (1991)

(a) It shall be unlawful for any creditor to discriminate against any applicant, with respect to any aspect of a credit transaction—
(1) on the basis of race, color, religion, national origin, sex or marital status, or age (provided the applicant has the capacity to contract);
(2) because all or part of the applicant's income derives from any public assistance program.

Source: 15 USC 41.

AN ACT CONCERNING HOMOSEXUALITY IN THE ARMED SERVICES (1993)

(A) FINDINGS.—CONGRESS MAKES THE FOLLOWING FINDINGS:

Section 8 of Article I of the Constitution of the United States commits exclusively to the Congress the powers to raise and support armies, provide and maintain a navy, and make rules for the government and regulation of the land and naval forces.

There is no constitutional right to serve in the armed forces.

Pursuant to the powers conferred by Section 8 of Article I of the Constitution of the United States, it lies within the discretion of the Congress to establish qualifications for and conditions of service in the armed forces.

The primary purpose of the armed forces is to prepare for and to prevail in combat should the need arise.

The conduct of military operations requires members of the armed forces to make extraordinary sacrifices, including the ultimate sacrifice, in order to provide for the common defense.

Success in combat requires military units that are characterized by high morale, good order and discipline, and unit cohesion.

One of the most critical elements in combat capability is unit cohesion, that is, the bonds of trust among individual service members that make the combat effectiveness of a military unit greater than the sum of the combat effectiveness of the individual unit members.

> Military life is fundamentally different from civilian life in that—
> (A) the extraordinary responsibilities of the armed forces, the unique conditions of military service, and the critical role of unit cohesion, require that the military community, while subject to civilian control, exist as a specialized society; and
> (B) the military society is characterized by its own laws, rules, customs, and traditions, including numerous restrictions on personal behavior, that would not be acceptable in civilian society.

The standards of conduct for members of the armed forces regulate a member's life for 24 hours each day beginning at the moment the member enters military status and not ending until that person is discharged or otherwise separated from the armed forces. Those standards of conduct, including the uniform code of military justice, apply to a member of the armed forces at all times that the member has a military status, whether the member is on base or off base, and whether the member is on duty or off duty.

The pervasive application of the standards of conduct is necessary because members of the armed forces must be ready at all times for worldwide deployment to a combat environment.

The worldwide deployment of United States military forces, the international responsibilities of the United States, and the potential for involvement of the armed forces in actual combat routinely make it necessary for members of the armed forces involuntarily to accept living conditions and working conditions that are often Spartan, primitive, and characterized by forced intimacy with little or no privacy.

The prohibition against homosexual conduct is a longstanding element of military law that continues to be necessary in the unique circumstances of military service.

The armed forces must maintain personnel policies that exclude persons whose presence in the armed forces would create an unacceptable risk to the armed forces' high standards of morale, good order and discipline, and unit cohesion that are the essence of military capability.

The presence in the armed forces of persons who demonstrate a propensity or intent to engage in homosexual acts would create an unacceptable risk to the high standards of morale, good order and discipline, and unit cohesion that are the essence of military capability.

(B) POLICY.

A member of the armed forces shall be separated from the armed forces under regulations prescribed by the secretary of defense if one or more of the following findings is made and approved in accordance with procedures set forth in such regulations:

That the member has engaged in, attempted to engage in, or solicited another to engage in a homosexual act or acts unless there are further findings, made and approved in accordance with procedures set forth in such regulations, that the member has demonstrated that-

(A) such conduct is a departure from the member's usual and customary behavior;
(B) such conduct, under all the circumstances, is unlikely to recur;
(C) such conduct was not accomplished by use of force, coercion, or intimidation;
(D) under the particular circumstances of the case, the member's continued presence in the armed forces is consistent with the interests of the armed forces in proper discipline, good order, and morale; and
(E) the member does not have a propensity or intent to engage in homosexual acts.

That the member has stated that he or she is a homosexual or bisexual, or words to that effect, unless there is a further finding, made and approved in accordance with procedures set forth in the regulations, that the member has demonstrated that he or she is not a person who engages in, attempts to engage in, has a propensity to engage in, or intends to engage in homosexual acts.

That the member has married or attempted to marry a person known to be of the same biological sex. . . .

Source: 10 USC 37.

PROPOSITION 187 (1994)

The People of California find and declare as follows:

That they have suffered and are suffering economic hardship caused by the presence of illegal aliens in this state.

That they have suffered and are suffering personal injury and damage caused by the criminal conduct of illegal aliens in this state.

That they have a right to the protection of their government from any person or persons entering this country unlawfully.

Therefore, the People of California declare their intention to provide for cooperation between their agencies of state and local government with the federal government, and to establish a system of required notification by and between such agencies to prevent illegal aliens in the United States from receiving benefits or public services in the State of California.

Source: "Proposition 187: Text of Proposed Law," *American Patrol,* www.americanpatrol.com/REFERENCE/prop187text.html.

DEFENSE OF MARRIAGE ACT (1996)

SEC. 2. POWERS RESERVED TO THE STATES.
(a) . . . Chapter 115 of title 28, United States Code, is amended by adding . . .
Section 1738C. Certain acts, records, and proceedings and the effect thereof
"No State, territory, or possession of the United States, or Indian tribe, shall be required to give effect to any public act, record, or judicial proceeding of any other State, territory, possession, or tribe respecting a relationship between persons of the same sex that is treated as a marriage under the laws of such other State, territory, possession, or tribe, or a right or claim arising from such relationship." . . .

SEC. 3. DEFINITION OF MARRIAGE.
(a) . . . Chapter 1 of title 1, United States Code, is amended by adding at the end the following:
"Section 7. Definition of 'marriage' and 'spouse'
"In determining the meaning of any Act of Congress, or of any ruling, regulation, or interpretation of the various administrative bureaus and agencies of the United States, the word 'marriage' means only a legal union between one man and one woman as husband and wife, and the word 'spouse' refers only to a person of the opposite sex who is a husband or a wife." . . .

Source: P.L. 104-199.

FREEDOM OF INFORMATION ACT (1996)

The amended material is indicated by boldface type and by strike-through text.

552. Public information; agency rules, opinions, orders, records, and proceedings . . .
(2) Each agency, in accordance with published rules, shall make available for public inspection and copying—

(A) final opinions, including concurring and dissenting opinions, as well as orders, made in the adjudication of cases;

(B) those statements of policy and interpretations which have been adopted by the agency and are not published in the Federal Register; ~~and~~
(C) administrative staff manuals and instructions to staff that affect a member of the public;
(D) copies of all records, regardless of form or format, which have been released to any person under paragraph (3) and which, because of the nature of their subject matter, the agency determines have become or are likely to become the subject of subsequent requests for substantially the same records; and
(E) a general index of the records referred to under subparagraph (D);

unless the materials are promptly published and copies offered for sale. . . . To the extent required to prevent a clearly unwarranted invasion of personal privacy, an agency may delete identifying details when it makes available or publishes an opinion, statement of policy, interpretation, ~~or staff manual or instruction~~, **staff manual, instruction, or copies of records referred to in subparagraph (D).** However, in each case the justification for the deletion shall be explained fully in writing, **and the extent of such deletion shall be indicated on the portion of the record which is made available or published, unless including that indication would harm an interest protected by the exemption in subsection (b) under which the deletion is made. If technically feasible, the extent of the deletion shall be indicated at the place in the record where the deletion was made.** Each agency shall also maintain and make available for public inspection and copying current indexes providing identifying information for the public as to any matter issued, adopted, or promulgated after July 4, 1967, and required by this paragraph to be made available or published. Each agency shall promptly publish, quarterly or more frequently, and distribute (by sale or otherwise) copies of each index or supplements thereto unless it determines by order published in the Federal Register that the publication would be unnecessary and impracticable, in which case the agency shall nonetheless provide copies of an index on request at a cost not to exceed the direct cost of duplication. **Each agency shall make the index referred to in subparagraph (E) available by computer telecommunications by December 31, 1999.** A final order, opinion, statement of policy, interpretation, or staff manual or instruction that affects a member of the public may be relied on, used, or cited as precedent by an agency against a party other than an agency only if—

(i) it has been indexed and either made available or published as provided by this paragraph; or
(ii) the party has actual and timely notice of the terms thereof. . . .

(5) Each agency having more than one member shall maintain and make available for public inspection a record of the final votes of each member in every agency proceeding. . . .

Source: 5 USC 552, as amended by P.L. 104-231.

COMMUNITY REINVESTMENT ACT (1997)

The Congress finds that—(1) regulated financial institutions are required by law to demonstrate that their deposit facilities serve the convenience and needs of the communities in which they are chartered to do business; (2) the convenience and needs of communities include the need for credit services as well as deposit services; and (3) regulated financial institutions have continuing and affirmative obligation to help meet the credit needs of the local communities in which they are chartered. (b) It is the purpose of this chapter to require each appropriate Federal financial supervisory agency to use its authority when examining financial institutions, to encourage such institutions to help meet the credit needs of the local communities in which they are chartered consistent with the safe and sound operation of such institutions.

Source: 12 USC 30.

INDIVIDUALS WITH DISABILITIES EDUCATION ACT (1997)

. . . (c) FINDINGS
(1) Disability is a natural part of the human experience and in no way diminishes the right of individuals to participate in or contribute to society. Improving educational results for children with disabilities is an essential element of our national policy of ensuring equality of opportunity, full participation, independent living, and economic self-sufficiency for individuals with disabilities.
(2) Before the date of the enactment of the Education for All Handicapped Children Act of 1975—

(A) the special educational needs of children with disabilities were not being fully met;

(B) more than one-half of the children with disabilities in the United States did not receive appropriate educational services that would enable such children to have full equality of opportunity;
(C) 1,000,000 of the children with disabilities in the United States were excluded entirely from the public school system and did not go through the educational process with their peers;
(D) there were many children with disabilities throughout the United States participating in regular school programs whose disabilities prevented such children from having a successful educational experience because their disabilities were undetected; and
(E) because of the lack of adequate services within the public school system, families were often forced to find services outside the public school system, often at great distance from their residence and at their own expense.

(3) Since the enactment and implementation of the Education for All Handicapped Children Act of 1975, this Act has been successful in ensuring children with disabilities and the families of such children access to a free appropriate public education and in improving educational results for children with disabilities.
(4) However, the implementation of this Act has been impeded by low expectations, and an insufficient focus on applying replicable research on proven methods of teaching and learning for children with disabilities.
(5) Over 20 years of research and experience has demonstrated that the education of children with disabilities can be made more effective by—

(A) having high expectations for such children and ensuring their access in the general curriculum to the maximum extent possible;
(B) strengthening the role of parents and ensuring that families of such children have meaningful opportunities to participate in the education of their children at school and at home;
(C) coordinating this Act with other local, educational service agency, State, and Federal school improvement efforts in order to ensure that such children benefit from such efforts and that special education can become a service for such children rather than a place where they are sent;
(D) providing appropriate special education and related services and aids and supports in the regular classroom to such children, whenever appropriate;
(E) supporting high-quality, intensive professional development for all personnel who work with such children in order to ensure that they have the skills and knowledge necessary to enable them –
(i) to meet developmental goals and, to the maximum extent possible, those challenging expectations that have been established for all children; and
(ii) to be prepared to lead productive, independent, adult lives, to the maximum extent possible;
(F) providing incentives for whole-school approaches and pre-referral intervention to reduce the need to label children as disabled in order to address their learning needs; and
(G) focusing resources on teaching and learning while reducing paperwork and requirements that do not assist in improving educational results.

(6) While States, local educational agencies, and educational service agencies are responsible for providing an education for all children with disabilities, it is in the national interest that the Federal Government have a role in assisting State and local efforts to educate children with disabilities in order to improve results for such children and to ensure equal protection of the law. . . .
(8) (A) Greater efforts are needed to prevent the intensification of problems connected with mislabeling and high dropout rates among minority children with disabilities. . . .
(9) (A) The opportunity for full participation in awards for grants and contracts; boards of organizations receiving funds under this Act; and peer review panels; and training of professionals in the area of special education by minority individuals, organizations, and historically black colleges and universities is essential if we are to obtain greater success in the education of minority children with disabilities. . . .
(d) PURPOSES—
(1) (A) to ensure that all children with disabilities have available to them a free appropriate public education that emphasizes special education and related services designed to meet their unique needs and prepare them for employment and independent living;
(B) to ensure that the rights of children with disabilities and parents of such children are protected; and
(C) to assist States, localities, educational service agencies, and Federal agencies to provide for the education of all children with disabilities;
(2) to assist States in the implementation of a statewide, comprehensive, coordinated, multidisciplinary, interagency system of early intervention services for infants and toddlers with disabilities and their families;
(3) to ensure that educators and parents have the necessary tools to improve educational results for children with disabil-

ities by supporting systemic-change activities; coordinated research and personnel preparation; coordinated technical assistance, dissemination, and support; and technology development and media services; and
(4) to assess, and ensure the effectiveness of, efforts to educate children with disabilities.

Source: IDEA '97, www.ed.gov/offices/OSERS/Policy/IDEA.

PROPOSITION 209 (1997)

SEC. 31. (a) The state shall not discriminate against, or grant preferential treatment to, any individual or group on the basis of race, sex, color, ethnicity, or national origin in the operation of public employment, public education, or public contracting. . . .
(e) Nothing in this section shall be interpreted as prohibiting action which must be taken to establish or maintain eligibility for any federal program, where ineligibility would result in a loss of federal funds to the state. . . .

Source: California Constitution, art. I, sec. 31.

IV. U.S. SUPREME COURT DECISIONS

DRED SCOTT V. SANDFORD (1857)

The question is simply this: Can a negro, whose ancestors were imported into this country, and sold as slaves, become a member of the political community formed and brought into existence by the Constitution of the United States, and as such become entitled to all the rights, and privileges, and immunities, guarantied by that instrument to the citizen? One of which rights is the privilege of suing in a court of the United States in the cases specified in the Constitution.

It will be observed, that the plea applies to that class of persons only whose ancestors were negroes of the African race, and imported into this country, and sold and held as slaves. The only matter in issue before the court, therefore, is, whether the descendants of such slaves, when they shall be emancipated, or who are born of parents who had become free before their birth, are citizens of a State, in the sense in which the word citizen is used in the Constitution of the United States. And this being the only matter in dispute on the pleadings, the court must be understood as speaking in this opinion of that class only, that is, of those persons who are the descendants of Africans who were imported into this country, and sold as slaves. . . .

The words "people of the United States" and "citizens" are synonymous terms, and mean the same thing. . . . They are what we familiarly call the "sovereign people," and every citizen is one of this people, and a constituent member of this sovereignty. The question before us is, whether the class of persons described in the plea . . . compose a portion of this people, and are constituent members of this sovereignty? We think they are not, and that they are not included, and were not intended to be included, under the word "citizens" in the Constitution, and can therefore claim none of the rights and privileges which that instrument provides for and secures to citizens of the United States. On the contrary, they were at that time considered as a subordinate and inferior class of beings, who had been subjugated by the dominant race, and, whether emancipated or not, yet remained subject to their authority, and had no rights or privileges but such as those who held the power and the Government might choose to grant them. . . .

It is very clear . . . that no State can, by any act or law of its own, passed since the adoption of the Constitution, introduce a new member into the political community created by the Constitution of the United States. It cannot make him a member of this community by making him a member of its own. And for the same reason it cannot introduce any person, or description of persons, who were not intended to be embraced in this new political family, which the Constitution brought into existence, but were intended to be excluded from it.

The question then arises, whether the provisions of the Constitution, in relation to the personal rights and privileges to which the citizen of a State should be entitled, embraced the negro African race, at that time in this country, or who might afterwards be imported, who had then or should afterwards be made free in any State; and to put it in the power of a single State to make him a citizen of the United States, and endue him with the full rights of citizenship in every other State without their consent? Does the Constitution of the United States act upon him whenever he shall be made free under the laws of a State, and raised there to the rank of a citizen, and immediately cloth him with all the privileges of a citizen in every other State, and in its own courts?

The court thinks the affirmative of these propositions cannot be maintained. . . .

The general words [of the Declaration of Independence] would seem to embrace the whole human family, and if they were used in a similar instrument at this day would be so understood. But it is too clear for dispute, that the enslaved African race were not intended to be included, and formed no part of the people who framed and adopted this declaration; for if the language, as understood in that day, would embrace them, the conduct of the distinguished men who framed the Declaration of Independence would have been utterly and flagrantly inconsistent with the principles they asserted; and instead of the sympathy of mankind, to which they so confidently appeared, they would have deserved and received universal rebuke and reprobation.

Yet the men who framed this declaration were great men—high in literary acquirements—high in their sense of honor, and incapable of asserting principles inconsistent with those on which they were acting. They perfectly understood the meaning of the language they used, and how it would be understood by others; and they knew that it would not in any part of the civilized world be supposed to embrace the negro race, which, by common consent, had been excluded from civilized Governments and the family of nations, and doomed to slavery. They spoke and acted according to the then established doctrines and principles, and in the ordinary language of the day, no one misunderstood them. The unhappy black race were separated from the white by indelible marks, and laws long before established, and were never thought of or spoken of except as property, and when the claims of the owner or the profit of the trader were supposed to need protection.

This state of public opinion had undergone no change when the Constitution was adopted, as is equally evident from its provisions and language.

... there are two clauses in the Constitution which point directly and specifically to the negro race as a separate class of persons, and show clearly that they were not regarded as a portion of the people or citizens of the Government then formed.

One of these clauses reserves to each of the thirteen States the right to import slaves until the year 1808, if it thinks proper. And the importation which it thus sanctions was unquestionably of persons of the race of which we are speaking, as the traffic in slaves in the United States had always been confined to them. And by the other provision the States pledge themselves to each other to maintain the right of property of the master, by delivering up to him any slave who may have escaped from his service, and be found within their respective territories. ...

No one of that race had ever migrated to the United States voluntarily; all of them had been brought here as articles of merchandise. The number that had been emancipated at that time were but few in comparison with those held in slavery; and they were identified in the public mind with the race to which they belonged, and regarded as a part of the slave population rather than the free. It is obvious that they were not even in the minds of the framers of the Constitution when they were conferring special rights and privileges upon the citizens of a State in every other part of the Union.

Indeed, when we look to the condition of this race in the several States at the time, it is impossible to believe that these rights and privileges were intended to be extended to them. ...

And upon a full and careful consideration of the subject, the court is of opinion, that ... Dred Scott was not a citizen of Missouri within the meaning of the Constitution of the United States, and not entitled as such to sue in its courts; and, consequently, that the Circuit Court had no jurisdiction of the case, and that the judgment on the plea in abatement is erroneous. ...

... if the removal of which he speaks did not give them their freedom, then by his own admission he is still a slave; and whatever opinions may be entertained in favor of the citizenship of a free person of the African race, no one supposes that a slave is a citizen of the State or of the United States. If, therefore, the acts done by his owner did not make them free persons, he is still a slave, and certainly incapable of suing in the character of a citizen. ...

In considering this part of the controversy, two questions arise: 1. Was he, together with his family, free in Missouri by reason of the stay in the territory of the United States hereinbefore mentioned? And 2. If they were not, is Scott himself free by reason of his removal to Rock Island, in the State of Illinois, as stated in the above admissions? ...

All we mean to say on this point is, that, as there is no express regulation in the Constitution defining the power which the General Government may exercise over the person or property of a citizen in a Territory thus acquired, the court must necessarily look to the provisions and principles of the Constitution, and its distribution of powers, for the rules and principles by which its decision must be governed. ...

But in considering the question before us, it must be borne in mind that there is no law of nations standing between the people of the United States and their Government, and interfering with their relation to each other. The powers of the Government, and the rights of the citizen under it, are positive and practical regulations plainly written down. The people of the United States have delegated to it certain enumerated powers, and forbidden it to exercise others. It has no power over the person or property of a citizen but what the citizens of the United States have granted. And no laws or usages of other nations, or reasoning of statesmen or jurists upon the relations of master and slave, can enlarge the powers of the Government, or take from the citizens the rights they have reserved. And if the Constitution recognizes the right of property of the master in a slave, and makes no distinction between that description of property and other property owned by a citizen, no tribunal, acting under the authority of the United States, whether it be legislative, executive, or judicial, has a right to draw such a distinction, or deny to it the benefit of the provisions and guarantees which have been provided for the protection of private property against the encroachments of the Government.

Now ... the right of property in a slave is distinctly and expressly affirmed in the Constitution. The right to traffic in it, like an ordinary article of merchandise and property, was guarantied to the citizens of the United States, in every State that might desire it, for twenty years. And the Government in express terms is pledged to protect it in all future time, if the slave escapes from his owner. This is done in plain words—too plain to be misunderstood. And no word can be found in the Constitution which gives Congress a greater power over slave property, or which entitles property of that kind to less protection than property of any other description. The only power conferred is the power coupled with the duty of guarding and protecting the owner in his rights. Upon these considerations, it is the opinion of the court that the act of Congress which prohibited a citizen from holding and owning property of this kind in the territory of the United States north of the line therein mentioned, is not warranted by the Constitution, and is therefore void; and that neither Dred Scott himself, nor any of his family, were made free by being carried into this territory; even if they had been carried there by the owner, with the intention of becoming a permanent resident. . . .

But there is another point in the case which depends on State power and State law. And it is contended, on the part of the plaintiff, that he is made free by being taken to Rock Island, in the State of Illinois, independently of his residence in the territory of the United States; and being so made free, he was not again reduced to a state of slavery by being brought back to Missouri.

Our notice of this part of the case will be very brief; for the principle on which it depends was decided in this court, upon much consideration, in the case of Strader v. Graham [(1851)]. . . . In that case, the slaves had been taken from Kentucky to Ohio, with the consent of the owner, and afterwards brought back to Kentucky. And this court held that their status or condition, as free or slave, depended upon the laws of Kentucky, when they were brought back into that State, and not of Ohio; and that this court had no jurisdiction to revise the judgment of a State court upon its own laws. . . . So in this case. As Scott was a slave when taken into . . . Illinois by his owner, and was there held as such, and brought back in that character, his status, as free or slave, depended on the laws of Missouri, and not of Illinois.

It has, however, been urged in the argument, that by the laws of Missouri he was free on his return, and that this case, therefore, cannot be governed by the case of Strader v. Graham, where it appeared, by the laws of Kentucky, that the plaintiffs continued to be slaves on their return from Ohio. But whatever doubts or opinions may, at one time, have been entertained upon this subject, we are satisfied, upon a careful examination of all the cases decided in the State courts of Missouri referred to, that it is now firmly settled by the decisions of the highest court in the State, that Scott and his family upon their return were not free, but were, by the laws of Missouri, the property of the defendant; and that the Circuit Court of the United States had no jurisdiction, when, by the laws of the State, the plaintiff was a slave, and not a citizen. . . .

Upon the whole, therefore, it is the judgment of this court, that it appears by the record before us that the plaintiff in error is not a citizen of Missouri, in the sense in which that word is used in the Constitution; and that the Circuit Court of the United States, for that reason, had no jurisdiction in the case, and could give no judgment in it. Its judgment for the defendant must, consequently, be reversed, and a mandate issued, directing the suit to be dismissed for want of jurisdiction.

Source: 60 U.S. 393 (19 How.).

PLESSY V. FERGUSON (1896)

This case turns upon the constitutionality of an act of the General Assembly of the State of Louisiana . . . providing for separate railway carriages for the white and colored races . . . The constitutionality of this act is attacked upon the ground that it conflicts both with the Thirteenth Amendment of the Constitution, abolishing slavery, and the Fourteenth Amendment, which prohibits certain restrictive legislation on the part of the States.

1. That it does not conflict with the Thirteenth Amendment, which abolished slavery and involuntary servitude, except as a punishment for crime, is too clear for argument . . .

The object of the [Fourteenth] amendment was undoubtedly to enforce the absolute equality of the two races before the law, but in the nature of things it could not have been intended to abolish distinctions based upon color, or to enforce social, as distinguished from political equality, or a commingling of the two races upon terms unsatisfactory to either. Laws permitting, and even requiring, their separation in places where they are liable to be brought into contact do not necessarily imply the inferiority of either race to the other, and have been generally, if not universally, recognized as within the competency of the state legislatures in the exercise of their police power. The most common instance of this is connected with the establishment of separate schools for white and colored children, which has been held to be a valid exercise of the legislative power even by courts of States where the political rights of the colored race have been longest and most earnestly enforced . . .

So far, then, as a conflict with the Fourteenth Amendment is concerned, the case reduces itself to the question whether the statute of Louisiana is a reasonable regulation, and with respect to this there must necessarily be a large discretion on the part of the legislature. In determining the question of reasonableness it is at liberty to act with reference to the established usages, customs and traditions of the people, and with a view to the promotion of their comfort, and the preservation of the public peace and good order. Gauged by this standard, we cannot say that a law which authorizes or even requires the separation of the two races in public conveyances is unreasonable, or more obnoxious to the Fourteenth Amendment than the acts of Congress requiring separate schools for colored children in the District of Columbia, the constitutionality of which does not seem to have been questioned, or the corresponding acts of state legislatures.

We consider the underlying fallacy of the plaintiff's argument to consist in the assumption that the enforced separation of the two races stamps the colored race with a badge of inferiority. If this be so, it is not by reason of anything found in the act, but solely because the colored race chooses to put that construction upon it. The argument necessarily assumes that if, as has been more than once the case, and is not unlikely to be so again, the colored race should become the dominant power in the state legislature, and should enact a law in precisely similar terms, it would thereby relegate the white race to an inferior position. We imagine that the white race, at least, would not acquiesce in this assumption. The argument also assumes that social prejudices may be overcome by legislation, and that equal rights cannot be secured to the negro except by an enforced commingling of the two races. We cannot accept this proposition. If the two races are to meet upon terms of social equality, it must be the result of natural affinities, a mutual appreciation of each other's merits and a voluntary consent of individuals . . . Legislation is powerless to eradicate racial instincts or to abolish distinctions based upon physical differences, and the attempt to do so can only result in accentuating the difficulties of the present situation. If the civil and political rights of both races be equal one cannot be inferior to the other civilly or politically. If one race be inferior to the other socially, the Constitution of the United States cannot put them upon the same plane . . .

[Justice John Marshall Harlan wrote a dissenting opinion]:

While there may be in Louisiana persons of different races who are not citizens of the United States, the words in the act, "white and colored races," necessarily include all citizens of the United States of both races residing in that State. So that we have before us a state enactment that compels, under penalties, the separation of the two races in railroad passenger coaches, and makes it a crime for a citizen of either race to enter a coach that has been assigned to citizens of the other race . . .

In respect of civil rights, common to all citizens, the Constitution of the United States does not, I think, permit any public authority to know the race of those entitled to be protected in the enjoyment of such rights. Every true man has pride of race, and under appropriate circumstances when the rights of others, his equals before the law, are not to be affected, it is his privilege to express such pride and to take such action based upon it as to him seems proper. But I deny that any legislative body or judicial tribunal may have regard to the race of citizens when the civil rights of those citizens are not involved. Indeed, such legislation, as that here in question, is inconsistent not only with that equality of rights which pertains to citizenship, National and State, but with the personal liberty enjoyed by every one within the United States . . .

The white race deems itself to be the dominant race in this country. And so it is, in prestige, in achievements, in education, in wealth and in power. So, I doubt not, it will continue to be for all time, if it remains true to its great heritage and holds fast to the principles of constitutional liberty. But in view of the Constitution, in the eye of the law, there is in this country no superior, dominant, ruling class of citizens. There is no caste here. Our Constitution is color-blind, and neither knows nor tolerates classes among citizens. In respect of civil rights, all citizens are equal before the law. The humblest is the peer of the most powerful. The law regards man as man, and takes no account of his surroundings or of his color when his civil rights as guaranteed by the supreme law of the land are involved. It is, therefore, to be regretted that this high tribunal, the final expositor of the fundamental law of the land, has reached the conclusion that it is competent for a State to regulate the enjoyment by citizens of their civil rights solely upon the basis of race.

In my opinion, the judgment this day rendered will, in time, prove to be quite as pernicious as the decision made by this tribunal in the Dred Scott case. . . . The destinies of the two races, in this country, are indissolubly linked together, and the interests of both require that the common government of all shall not permit the seeds of race hate to be planted under the sanction of law. . . .

I am of opinion that the statute of Louisiana is inconsistent with the personal liberty of citizens, white and black, in that State, and hostile to both the spirit and letter of the Constitution of the United States. If laws of like character should be enacted in the several States of the Union, the effect would be in the highest degree mischievous. . . .

Source: 163 U.S. 537 (1896).

BOLLING V. SHARPE (1954)

This case challenges the validity of segregation in the public schools of the District of Columbia. The petitioners, minors of the Negro race, allege that such segregation deprives them of due process of law under the Fifth Amendment. They were refused admission to a public school attended by white children solely because of their race. They sought the aid of the District Court for the District of Columbia in obtaining admission. That court dismissed their complaint. The Court granted a writ of certiorari before judgment in the Court of Appeals because of the importance of the constitutional question presented.

We have this day held that the Equal Protection Clause of the Fourteenth Amendment prohibits the states from maintaining racially segregated public schools. The legal problem in the District of Columbia is somewhat different, however. The Fifth Amendment, which is applicable in the District of Columbia, does not contain an equal protection clause as does the Fourteenth Amendment which applies only to the states. But the concepts of equal protection and due process, both stemming from our American ideal of fairness, are not mutually exclusive. The "equal protection of the laws" is a more explicit safeguard of prohibited unfairness than "due process of law," and, therefore, we do not imply that the two are always interchangeable phrases. But, as this Court has recognized, discrimination may be so unjustifiable as to be violative of due process.

Classifications based solely upon race must be scrutinized with particular care, since they are contrary to our traditions and hence constitutionally suspect. . . .

Although the Court has not assumed to define "liberty" with any great precision, that term is not confined to mere freedom from bodily restraint. Liberty under law extends to the full range of conduct which the individual is free to pursue, and it cannot be restricted except for a proper governmental objective. Segregation in public education is not reasonably related to any proper governmental objective, and thus it imposes on Negro children of the District of Columbia a burden that constitutes an arbitrary deprivation of their liberty in violation of the Due Process Clause.

In view of our decision that the Constitution prohibits the states from maintaining racially segregated public schools, it would be unthinkable that the same Constitution would impose a lesser duty on the Federal Government. We hold that racial segregation in the public schools of the District of Columbia is a denial of the due process of law guaranteed by the Fifth Amendment to the Constitution. . . .

Source: 347 U.S. 497 (1954).

BROWN V. BOARD OF EDUCATION OF TOPEKA, KANSAS (1954)

These cases come to us from the States of Kansas, South Carolina, Virginia, and Delaware. . . .

In each of the cases, minors of the Negro race, through their legal representatives, seek the aid of the courts in obtaining admission to the public schools of their community on a nonsegregated basis. In each instance, they had been denied admission to schools attended by white children under laws requiring or permitting segregation according to race. This segregation was alleged to deprive the plaintiffs of the equal protection of the laws under the Fourteenth Amendment. . . .

The plaintiffs contend that segregated public schools are not "equal" and cannot be made "equal," and that hence they are deprived of the equal protection of the laws. . . .

In the first cases in this Court construing the Fourteenth Amendment, decided shortly after its adoption, the Court interpreted it as proscribing all state-imposed discriminations against the Negro race. The doctrine of "separate but equal" did not make its appearance in this Court until 1896 in the case of *Plessy v. Ferguson* involving not education but transportation. American courts have since labored with the doctrine for over half a century. In this Court, there have been six cases involving the "separate but equal" doctrine in the field of public education. . . . In none of these cases was it necessary to reexamine the doctrine to grant relief to the Negro plaintiff. And in *Sweatt v. Painter* [(1950)] . . . the Court expressly reserved decision on the question whether *Plessy v. Ferguson* should be held inapplicable to public education.

In the instant cases, that question is directly presented. Here, unlike *Sweatt v. Painter,* there are findings below that the Negro and white schools involved have been equalized, or are being equalized, with respect to buildings, curricula, qualifications and salaries of teachers, and other "tangible" factors. Our decision, therefore, cannot turn on merely a comparison of these tangible factors in the Negro and white schools involved in each of the cases. We must look instead to the effect of segregation itself on public education.

In approaching this problem, we cannot turn the clock back to 1868, when the Amendment was adopted, or even to 1896, when *Plessy v. Ferguson* was written. We must consider public education in the light of its full development and its present place in American life throughout the Nation. Only in this way can it be determined if segregation in public schools deprives these plaintiffs of the equal protection of the laws.

Today, education is perhaps the most important function of state and local governments. Compulsory school attendance laws and the great expenditures for education both demonstrate our recognition of the importance of education to our democratic society. It is required in the performance of our most basic public responsibilities, even service in the armed forces. It is the very foundation of good citizenship. Today it is a principal instrument in awakening the child to cultural values, in preparing him for later professional training, and in helping him to adjust normally to his environment. In these days, it is doubtful that any child may reasonably be expected to succeed in life if he is denied the opportunity of an education. Such an opportunity, where the state has undertaken to provide it, is a right which must be made available to all on equal terms.

We come then to the question presented: Does segregation of children in public schools solely on the basis of race, even though the physical facilities and other "tangible" factors may be equal, deprive the children of the minority group of equal educational opportunities? We believe that it does. . . .

Whatever may have been the extent of psychological knowledge at the time of *Plessy v. Ferguson,* this finding is amply supported by modern authority. Any language in *Plessy v. Ferguson* contrary to this finding is rejected.

We conclude that, in the field of public education, the doctrine of "separate but equal" has no place. Separate educational facilities are inherently unequal. . . .

Source: 347 U.S. 483 (1954).

BROWN V. BOARD OF EDUCATION (1955)

These cases were decided on May 17, 1954. The opinions of that date, declaring the fundamental principle that racial discrimination in public education is unconstitutional, are incorporated herein by reference. All provisions of federal, state, or local law requiring or permitting such discrimination must yield to this principle. There remains for consideration the manner in which relief is to be accorded.

Because these cases arose under different local conditions and their disposition will involve a variety of local problems, we requested further argument on the question of relief. In view of the nationwide importance of the decision, we invited the Attorney General of the United States and the Attorneys General of all states requiring or permitting racial discrimination in public education to present their views on that question. The parties, the United States, and the States of Florida, North Carolina, Arkansas, Oklahoma, Maryland, and Texas filed briefs and participated in the oral argument.

These presentations were informative and helpful to the Court in its consideration of the complexities arising from the transition to a system of public education freed of racial discrimination. The presentations also demonstrated that substantial steps to eliminate racial discrimination in public schools have already been taken, not only in some of the communities in which these cases arose, but in some of the states appearing as amici curiae, and in other states as well. Substantial progress has been made in the District of Columbia and in the communities in Kansas and Delaware involved in this litigation. The defendants in the cases coming to us from South Carolina and Virginia are awaiting the decision of this Court concerning relief.

Full implementation of these constitutional principles may require solution of varied local school problems. School authorities have the primary responsibility for elucidating, assessing, and solving these problems; courts will have to consider whether the action of school authorities constitutes good faith implementation of the governing constitutional principles. Because of their proximity to local conditions and the possible need for further hearings, the courts which originally heard these cases can best perform this judicial appraisal. Accordingly, we believe it appropriate to remand the cases to those courts.

In fashioning and effectuating the decrees, the courts will be guided by equitable principles. Traditionally, equity has been characterized by a practical flexibility in shaping its remedies and by a facility for adjusting and reconciling public and private needs. These cases call for the exercise of these traditional attributes of equity power. At stake is the personal interest of the plaintiffs in admission to public schools as soon as practicable on a nondiscriminatory basis. To effectuate this interest may call for elimination of a variety of obstacles in making the transition to school systems operated in accordance with the constitutional principles set forth in our May 17, 1954, decision. Courts of equity may properly take into account the public interest in the elimination of such obstacles in a systematic and effective manner. But it should go without saying that the vitality of these constitutional principles cannot be allowed to yield simply because of disagreement with them.

While giving weight to these public and private considerations, the courts will require that the defendants make a prompt and reasonable start toward full compliance with our May 17, 1954, ruling. Once such a start has been made, the courts may find that additional time is necessary to carry out the ruling in an effective manner. The burden rests upon the defendants to establish that such time is necessary in the public interest and is consistent with good faith compliance at the earliest practicable date. To that end, the courts may consider problems related to administration, arising from the physical condition of the school plant, the school transportation system, personnel, revision of school districts and attendance areas into compact units to achieve a system of determining admission to the public schools on a nonracial basis, and revision of local laws and regulations which may be necessary in solving the foregoing problems. They will also consider the adequacy of any plans the defendants may propose to meet these problems and to effectuate a transition to a racially nondiscriminatory school system. During this period of transition, the courts will retain jurisdiction of these cases.

The judgments below, except that in the Delaware case, are accordingly reversed and the cases are remanded to the District Courts to take such proceedings and enter such orders and decrees consistent with this opinion as are necessary and proper to admit to public schools on a racially nondiscriminatory basis with all deliberate speed the parties to these cases. The judgment in the Delaware case—ordering the immediate admission of the plaintiffs to schools previously attended only by white children—is affirmed on the basis of the principles stated in our May 17, 1954, opinion, but the case is remanded to the Supreme Court of Delaware for such further proceedings as that Court may deem necessary in light of this opinion.

It is so ordered.

Source: 349 U.S. 294.

MIRANDA V. ARIZONA (1966)

... Our holding will be spelled out with some specificity in the pages which follow but briefly stated it is this: the prosecution may not use statements, whether exculpatory or inculpatory, stemming from custodial interrogation of the defendant unless it demonstrates the use of procedural safeguards effective to secure the privilege against self-incrimination. By custodial interrogation, we mean questioning initiated by law enforcement officers after a person has been taken into custody or otherwise deprived of his freedom of action in any significant way. As for the procedural safeguards to be employed, unless other fully effective means are devised to inform accused persons of their right of silence and to assure a continuous opportunity to exercise it, the following measures are required. Prior to any questioning, the person must be warned that he has a right to remain silent, that any statement he does make may be used as evidence against him, and that he has a right to the presence of an attorney, either retained or appointed. The defendant may waive effectuation of these rights, provided the waiver is made voluntarily, knowingly and intelligently. If, however, he indicates in any manner and at any stage of the process that he wishes to consult with an attorney before speaking there can be no questioning. Likewise, if the individual is alone and indicates in any manner that he does not wish to be interrogated, the police may not question him. The mere fact that he may have answered some questions or volunteered some statements on his own does not deprive him of the right to refrain from answering any further inquiries until he has consulted with an attorney and thereafter consents to be questioned. . . .

Source: 384 U.S. 436 (1966).

ROE V. WADE (1973)

... The Constitution does not explicitly mention any right of privacy. In a line of decisions, however, going back perhaps as far as *Union Pacific R. Co. v. Botsford* (1891), the Court has recognized that a right of personal privacy, or a guarantee of certain areas or zones of privacy, does exist under the Constitution. In varying contexts, the Court or individual Justices have, indeed, found at least the roots of that right in the First Amendment; in the Fourth and Fifth Amendments; in the penumbras of the Bill of Rights; in the Ninth Amendment; or in the concept of liberty guaranteed by the first section of the Fourteenth Amendment. These decisions make it clear that only personal rights that can be deemed "fundamental" or "implicit in the concept of ordered liberty," are included in this guarantee of personal privacy. They also make it clear that the right has some extension to activities relating to marriage; procreation; contraception; family relationships; and child rearing and education.

This right of privacy, whether it be founded in the Fourteenth Amendment's concept of personal liberty and restrictions upon state action, as we feel it is, or, as the District Court determined, in the Ninth Amendment's reservation of rights to the people, is broad enough to encompass a woman's decision whether or not to terminate her pregnancy. The detriment that the State would impose upon the pregnant woman by denying this choice altogether is apparent. Specific and direct harm medically diagnosable even in early pregnancy may be involved. Maternity, or additional offspring, may force upon the woman a distressful life and future. Psychological harm may be imminent. Mental and physical health may be taxed by child care. There is also the distress, for all concerned, associated with the unwanted child, and there is the problem of bringing a child into a family already unable, psychologically and otherwise, to care for it. In other cases, as in this one, the additional difficulties and continuing stigma of unwed motherhood may be involved. All these are factors the woman and her responsible physician necessarily will consider in consultation.

On the basis of elements such as these, appellant and some amici argue that the woman's right is absolute and that she is entitled to terminate her pregnancy at whatever time, in whatever way, and for whatever reason she alone chooses.

With this we do not agree. At some point in pregnancy, these respective interests become sufficiently compelling to sustain regulation of the factors that govern the abortion decision. The privacy right involved, therefore, cannot be said to be absolute. The Court has refused to recognize an unlimited right of this kind in the past.

We, therefore, conclude that the right of personal privacy includes the abortion decision, but that this right is not unqualified and must be considered against important state interests in regulation. . . .

. . . most . . . courts have agreed that the right of privacy, however based, is broad enough to cover the abortion decision; that the right, nonetheless, is not absolute and is subject to some limitations; and that at some point the state interests as to protection of health, medical standards, and prenatal life, become dominant. We agree with this approach.

Where certain "fundamental rights" are involved, the Court has held that regulation limiting these rights may be justified only by a "compelling state interest," and that legislative enactments must be narrowly drawn to express only the legitimate state interests at stake.

The appellee and certain amici argue that the fetus is a "person" within the language and meaning of the Fourteenth Amendment.

The Constitution does not define "person" in so many words. Section 1 of the Fourteenth Amendment contains three references to "person." The first, in defining "citizens," speaks of "persons born or naturalized in the United States." The word also appears both in the Due Process Clause and in the Equal Protection Clause. But in nearly all these instances, the use of the word is such that it has application only postnatally. None indicates, with any assurance, that it has any possible pre-natal application.

All this, together with our observation that throughout the major portion of the 19th century prevailing legal abortion practices were far freer than they are today, persuades us that the word "person," as used in the Fourteenth Amendment, does not include the unborn. . . .

The pregnant woman cannot be isolated in her privacy. She carries an embryo and, later, a fetus, if one accepts the medical definitions of the developing young in the human uterus. As we have intimated above, it is reasonable and appropriate for a State to decide that at some point in time another interest, that of health of the mother or that of potential human life, becomes significantly involved. The woman's privacy is no longer sole and any right of privacy she possesses must be measured accordingly.

Texas urges that, apart from the Fourteenth Amendment, life begins at conception and is present throughout pregnancy, and that, therefore, the State has a compelling interest in protecting that life from and after conception. . . .

In areas other than criminal abortion, the law has been reluctant to endorse any theory that life, as we recognize it, begins before live birth. . . .

. . . In short, the unborn have never been recognized in the law as persons in the whole sense.

In view of all this, we do not agree that, by adopting one theory of life, Texas may override the rights of the pregnant woman that are at stake. We repeat, however, that the State does have an important and legitimate interest in preserving and protecting the health of the pregnant woman . . . and that it has still another important and legitimate interest in protecting the potentiality of human life. These interests are separate and distinct. Each grows in substantiality as the woman approaches term and, at a point during pregnancy, each becomes "compelling."

With respect to the State's important and legitimate interest in the health of the mother, the "compelling" point, in the light of present medical knowledge, is at approximately the end of the first trimester. This is so because of the now-established medical fact, that until the end of the first trimester mortality in abortion may be less than mortality in normal childbirth. It follows that, from and after this point, a State may regulate the abortion procedure to the extent that the regulation reasonably relates to the preservation and protection of maternal health. . . .

This means, on the other hand, that, for the period of pregnancy prior to this "compelling" point, the attending physician, in consultation with his patient, is free to determine, without regulation by the State, that, in his medical judgment, the patient's pregnancy should be terminated. If that decision is reached, the judgment may be effectuated by an abortion free of interference by the State.

With respect to the State's important and legitimate interest in potential life, the "compelling" point is at viability. This is so because the fetus then presumably has the capability of meaningful life outside the mother's womb. . . .

Source: 410 U.S. 113 (1973).

TERRY V. OHIO (1968)

. . . When a police officer observes unusual conduct which leads him reasonably to conclude in light of his experience that criminal activity may be afoot and that the persons with whom he is dealing may be armed and dangerous, where in the course of investigating this behavior he identifies himself as a policeman and makes reasonable inquiries, and here nothing in the initial stages of the encounter serves to dispel his reasonable fear for his own or others' safety, he is entitled for the protection of himself and others in the area to conduct a carefully limited search of the outer clothing of such persons in an attempt to discover weapons which might be used to assault him. . . .

Source: 392 U.S. 1 (1968).

REGENTS OF THE UNIVERSITY OF CALIFORNIA V. BAKKE (1978)

This case presents a challenge to the special admissions program of the petitioner, the Medical School of the University of California at Davis [Petitioner], which is designed to assure the admission of a specified number of students from certain minority groups. The Superior Court of California sustained respondent's challenge, holding that petitioner's program violated the California Constitution, Title VI of the Civil Rights Act of 1964 and the Equal Protection Clause of the Fourteenth Amendment. The court enjoined petitioner from considering respondent's race or the race of any other applicant in making admissions decisions. It refused, however, to order respondent's admission to the Medical School, holding that he had not carried his burden of proving that he would have been admitted but for the constitutional and statutory violations. The Supreme Court of California affirmed those portions of the trial court's judgment declaring the special admissions program unlawful and enjoining petitioner from considering the race of any applicant. . . .

The State certainly has a legitimate and substantial interest in ameliorating, or eliminating where feasible, the disabling effects of identified discrimination. The line of school desegregation cases, commencing with *Brown,* attests to the importance of this state goal and the commitment of the judiciary to affirm all lawful means toward its attainment. In the school cases, the States were required by court order to redress the wrongs worked by specific instances of racial discrimination. That goal was far more focused than the remedying of the effects of "societal discrimination," an amorphous concept of injury that may be ageless in its reach into the past.

We have never approved a classification that aids persons perceived as members of relatively victimized groups at the expense of other innocent individuals in the absence of judicial, legislative, or administrative findings of constitutional or statutory violations. . . . After such findings have been made, the governmental interest in preferring members of the injured groups at the expense of others is substantial, since the legal rights of the victims must be vindicated. In such a case, the extent of the injury and the consequent remedy will have been judicially, legislatively, or administratively defined. Also, the remedial action usually remains subject to continuing oversight to assure that it will work the least harm possible to other innocent persons competing for the benefit. Without such findings of constitutional or statutory violations, it cannot be said that the government has any greater interest in helping one individual than in refraining from harming another. Thus, the government has no compelling justification for inflicting such harm. . . .

. . . the purpose of helping certain groups whom the faculty of the Davis Medical School perceived as victims of "societal discrimination" does not justify a classification that imposes disadvantages upon persons like respondent, who bear no responsibility for whatever harm the beneficiaries of the special admissions program are thought to have suffered. To hold otherwise would be to convert a remedy heretofore reserved for violations of legal rights into a privilege that all institutions throughout the Nation could grant at their pleasure to whatever groups are perceived as victims of societal discrimination. That is a step we have never approved. . . .

In summary, it is evident that the Davis special admissions program involves the use of an explicit racial classification never before countenanced by this Court. It tells applicants who are not Negro, Asian, or Chicano that they are totally excluded from a specific percentage of the seats in an entering class. No matter how strong their qualifications, quantitative and extracurricular, including their own potential for contribution to educational diversity, they are never afforded the chance to compete with applicants from the preferred groups for the special admissions seats. At the same time, the preferred applicants have the opportunity to compete for every seat in the class.

The fatal flaw in petitioner's preferential program is its disregard of individual rights as guaranteed by the Fourteenth Amendment. . . . Such rights are not absolute. But when a State's distribution of benefits or imposition of burdens hinges on ancestry or the color of a person's skin, that individual is entitled to a demonstration that the challenged classification is necessary to promote a substantial state interest. . . . For this reason, that portion of the California court's judgment holding petitioner's special admissions program invalid under the Fourteenth Amendment must be affirmed.

. . . however, the courts below failed to recognize that the State has a substantial interest that legitimately may be served by a properly devised admissions program involving the competitive consideration of race and ethnic origin. For this reason, so much of the California court's judgment as enjoins petitioner from any consideration of the race of any applicant must be reversed.

With respect to respondent's entitlement to an injunction directing his admission to the Medical School, petitioner has conceded that it could not carry its burden of proving that, but for the existence of its unlawful special admissions program, respondent still would not have been admitted. Hence, respondent is entitled to the injunction, and that portion of the judgment must be affirmed.

Source: 438 U.S. 265 (1978).

V. RIGHTS ACTIVISM DOCUMENTS

CLASS ACTION RACIAL DISCRIMINATION SUIT AGAINST COCA-COLA (1999)

. . . 2. This is a class action, brought by Plaintiffs Motisola Malikha Abdallah, Gregory Allen Clark, Linda Ingram, and Kimberly Gray Orton (collectively, "the named Plaintiffs"), on behalf of themselves and other similarly situated individuals against the Coca-Cola Company ("Coca-Cola," "the Company," or "Defendant"). Plaintiffs seek declaratory, injunctive and other equitable relief, and compensatory and punitive damages, based on Defendant's continuing deprivation of rights accorded to the named Plaintiffs and members of a class of African-American salaried employees . . . under Section 1981 of the Civil Rights Act of 1871, as amended by the Civil Rights Act of 1991. . . . Additionally, Plaintiff Clark seeks declaratory, injunctive and other equitable relief, and compensatory and punitive damages based on Defendant's discrimination against him in violation of Title VII of the Civil Rights Act of 1964, as amended by the Civil Rights Act of 1991. . . .

3. As evidence of Defendant's pattern and practice of race discrimination, Plaintiffs allege the following specific examples of disparate treatment:

a. Discrimination in Evaluations. The performance evaluation system is implemented by managers exercising undue authority to make biased and inconsistent determinations with little or no oversight. This system permits discrimination on the basis of race in evaluations, where raises, bonuses and stock options, as well as further advancement within the Company, are based on evaluation scores, pursuant to Coca-Cola's written policies on compensation. Because of the undue discretion of managers, African-Americans receive more low evaluation scores than Caucasians and fewer high scores. There is no factor (such as job grade, experience, or similar factors) that could explain this race-based difference in scores.

b. Discrimination in Compensation: A review of salaries paid by Coca-Cola to African-Americans compared with salaries paid to Caucasian employees reveals dramatic differences in pay in Coca-Cola's corporate headquarters. Upon information and belief, this pattern exists throughout the Company. For example, in 1995 in the corporate headquarters, the average African-American was paid over $19,000 less than the average Caucasian employee. In 1998 in the corporate headquarters, the average African-American was paid almost $27,000 less than the average Caucasian employee. . . .

c. Discrimination in Promotions. Coca-Cola's policies are not applied uniformly or fairly. The Company's written and unwritten policies and practices regarding promotions do not require posting of all positions, but allow "management nomination," which amounts to little more than word of mouth recommendations, and other closed procedures, including the use of a high-potential list. Even positions that are posted on the computerized job posting system may contain a notation that an internal candidate has already been identified. Jobs are filled without being posted, candidates are handpicked in advance, and supervisors who make hiring decisions disregard the results of panel interviews and manipulate scores in order to ensure that their favorites are chosen. As a result of this kind of discrimination, African-Americans are denied the opportunity to advance to the same level and at the same rate as equally qualified Caucasian employees.

d. "Glass Ceiling." At Coca Cola, African-American employees experience a "glass ceiling" or a barrier to equal opportunity advancement. Few African-Americans advance to senior levels in the Company, especially when compared to the significant representation of African-Americans among salaried employees. . . .

e. "Glass Walls." Not only do barriers exist for African-American employees seeking upward advancement within the Company, but similar barriers virtually segregate the Company into divisions where African-American leadership is acceptable, and divisions where it is not. . . .

f. Terminations. African-American employees at Coca-Cola are involuntarily terminated at a much higher rate than Caucasian employees. In 1997, there were 62 involuntary terminations in the corporate headquarters, and African-American employees accounted for about 37% of those, or 23 persons. . . .

5. Although Coca-Cola has carefully cultivated African-Americans as consumers of its product by public pronouncements, strategic alliances, and specific marketing strategies, it has failed to place the same importance on its African-American employees. Further, Defendant's efforts to target African-American consumers reflects stereotypical views of African-Americans who all live in the ghetto or perform low-skill or low pay jobs. Coca-Cola's marketing staff have also discriminated against African-American marketing

employees and advertising agencies. Defendant's outreach to consumers does nothing to address the racial disparities in compensation, promotions and evaluations that exist inside the Company.

Source: Abdallah, et al. v. The Coca-Cola Company, Essential Action, www.essentialaction.org/spotlight/coke/.

RIGHTS OF PRISONERS

- *The right to challenge disciplinary sanctions.* Although prisoners are entitled to due process under the FOURTEENTH AMENDMENT, the Supreme Court decision in *Sandlin v. Conner* (1995) requires prisoners to present factual evidence that the sanction at issue creates "atypical and significant hardships." In *Edwards v. Balisok* (1997), the high court ruled that prisoners cannot sue for monetary damages until their disciplinary conviction is set aside by a state court.
- *The right to medical care.* The Eighth Amendment requires prison authorities to provide prisoners with adequate medical care, regardless of any budgetary or other constraints the prison claims to operate under.
- *The right to mental health care.* The same constitutional standard that applies to medical care applies to mental health care.
- *The right to protection from assault.* Prison authorities have a legal responsibility to protect inmates from assault—from other inmates as well as from prison officers. However, the courts define the responsibility narrowly. Officials are liable for inmate assault only if they act with deliberate indifference or reckless disregard of prisoners' safety. That is, officials are not held responsible in a general way for the bad behavior of inmates. As for prison staff, while they are prohibited from assaulting inmates, they are permitted to use force as necessary in a good faith effort to restore or enforce discipline.
- *The right to access to legal counsel and legal materials.* Prisoners may consult with legal counsel at least during regular visiting hours, and they are to be given access to legal materials—such as law books—available in prison libraries.

Source: American Civil Liberties Union, "Prisoners' Rights," www.aclu.org/library/PrisonerRights.pdf.

RIGHTS OF THE MENTALLY ILL (SAMPLE STATUTE)

All people hospitalized or committed pursuant to this chapter have the following rights:

(A) The right to a written list of all rights enumerated in this chapter, to that person, his legal guardian, and his counsel. If the person is unable to read, the list shall be read and explained to him.

(B) The right at all times to be treated with consideration and respect for his privacy and dignity, including without limitation, the following:

(1) At the time a person is taken into custody for diagnosis, detention, or treatment . . . the person taking him into custody shall take reasonable precautions to preserve and safeguard the personal property in the possession of or on the premises occupied by that person;

(2) A person who is committed, voluntarily or involuntarily, shall be given reasonable protection from assault or battery by any other person.

(C) The right to communicate freely with and be visited at reasonable times by his private counsel or personnel of the legal rights service and, unless prior court restriction has been obtained, to communicate freely with and be visited at reasonable times by his personal physician or psychologist.

(D) The right to communicate freely with others, unless specifically restricted in the patient's treatment plan for clear treatment reasons . . .

(E) The right to have ready access to letter writing materials, including a reasonable number of stamps without cost if unable to pay for them, and to mail and receive unopened correspondence and assistance in writing if requested and needed.

(F) The right to the following personal privileges consistent with health and safety:

(1) To wear his own clothes and maintain his own personal effects;

(2) To be provided an adequate allowance for or allotment of neat, clean, and seasonable clothing if unable to provide his own;

(3) To maintain his personal appearance according to his own personal taste, including head and body hair;

(4) To keep and use personal possessions, including toilet articles;

(5) To have access to individual storage space for his private use;

(6) To keep and spend a reasonable sum of his own money for expenses and small purchases;

(7) To receive and possess reading materials without censorship, except when the materials create a clear and present danger to the safety of persons in the facility.

(G) The right to reasonable privacy, including both periods of privacy and places of privacy.

(H) The right to free exercise of religious worship within the facility, including a right to services and sacred texts that are within the reasonable capacity of the facility to supply, provided that no patient shall be coerced into engaging in any religious activities.

(I) The right to social interaction with members of either sex, subject to adequate supervision, unless such social interaction is specifically withheld under a patient's written treatment plan for clear treatment reasons.

Source: Ohio's Revised Code Section 5122.29, www.state.oh.us/olrs/MHRights.htm.

QUAKER ACTIVIST ORGANIZATIONS

- *American Friends Service Committee.* The best-known Quaker activist organization, AFSC includes people of various faiths who are committed to social justice, peace, and humanitarian service. The organization was founded in 1917 to provide a means by which conscientious objectors could aid civilian victims during World War I. Currently, programs are focused on promoting economic justice, peace-building and demilitarization, and social justice in the United States and elsewhere.
- *Friends Committee on National Legislation.* A Quaker lobby in the public interest, FCNL works at the legislative level to promote arms control and disarmament initiatives and to oppose the expansion of military alliances; to promote nonviolent dispute resolution; to shift budget priorities away from military spending and toward providing for human needs; to address economic, social, and racial inequalities through such measures as universal health care, progressive taxation, AFFIRMATIVE ACTION, increased educational opportunities, a living wage, and affordable housing; to reform the criminal justice system with an emphasis on restorative justice and crime prevention; and to eliminate the death penalty.
- *Friends for a Non-Violent World.* Based in St. Paul, Minnesota, the organization conducts educational programs aimed at creating a communal spirit of cooperation to work for peace and justice and to find alternatives to violence for the resolution of disputes.
- *Friends for Lesbian and Gay Concerns.* FLGC provides a religious community for lesbian, gay, bisexual, heterosexual, transgendered, and transsexual people.
- *Friends Committee to Abolish the Death Penalty.* An activist group that works to end the death penalty throughout the United States by lobbying and by demonstrating ("witnessing") at prisons and executions.
- *Nonviolent Peaceforce.* NP consists of trained volunteers who serve as an international civilian nonviolent peace force that works at the invitation of local groups to protect human rights and prevent death and destruction by such nonviolent means as interpositioning, accompaniment, presence, and witnessing.
- *Prison ministries.* Various meetings sponsor prison ministries, which visit prisons and seek to provide for the spiritual and physical well-being of prisoners. Many of the ministries support various legislative initiatives to promote the rights of prisoners (see PRISONERS, RIGHTS OF).

Source: Friends Committee on National Legislation, www.fcnl.org/links.htm#int.

"WE SHALL OVERCOME"

1. We shall overcome
We shall overcome
We shall overcome some day
Chorus:
Oh deep in my heart
I do believe
We shall overcome some day

2. We'll walk hand in hand
We'll walk hand in hand
We'll walk hand in hand some day
(Repeat chorus)

3. We shall all be free
We shall all be free
We shall all be free some day
(Repeat chorus)

4. We are not afraid
We are not afraid
We are not afraid some day
(Repeat chorus)

5. We are not alone
We are not alone

We are not alone some day
(Repeat chorus)

6. The whole wide world around
The whole wide world around
The whole wide world around some day
(Repeat chorus)

7. We shall overcome
We shall overcome
We shall overcome some day
(Repeat chorus)

Source: Guy Carawan, and Candie Carawan, eds. *Sing for Freedom* (Bethlehem, Penn.: Sing Out!, 1997), 153.

VI. U.S. GOVERNMENT AGENCIES

DEPARTMENT OF HEALTH AND HUMAN SERVICES

Agencies relevant to minority rights include:

- Public Health Service
- National Institutes of Health
- National Center for Complementary and Alternative Medicine
- National Library of Medicine
- Food and Drug Administration
- Centers for Disease Control and Prevention
- Indian Health Service
- Health Resources and Services Administration (providing access to essential health services for people who are poor, uninsured, or who live in rural and urban neighborhoods where health care is scarce)
- Substance Abuse and Mental Health Services Administration
- Centers for Medicare and Medicaid Services
- Administration for Children and Families (responsible for about 60 programs that promote the economic and social well-being of families, children, individuals, and communities)
- Administration on Aging (advocate agency for older persons and their concerns)
- U.S. Public Health Service Commissioned Corps (uniformed service of more than 6,000 health professionals who serve in HHS and other federal agencies; headed by the Surgeon General)

Source: Department of Health and Human Services, "HHS Agencies," www.hhs.gov/agencies/.

DEPARTMENT OF HOUSING AND URBAN DEVELOPMENT

The major permanent HUD programs include:

- Community Development Block Grants (CDBG), to aid economic development, job opportunities, and housing rehabilitation
- Subsidized housing (vouchers for low-income households)
- Subsidized public housing for low-income individuals and families
- Homeless assistance through local communities and nonprofit organizations
- HOME Investment Partnership Act block grants, to develop and support affordable housing for low-income residents
- Fair housing, public education and enforcement
- Mortgage and loan insurance through the Federal Housing Administration (FHA)

Source: Department of Housing and Urban Development, "HUD Programs," www.hud.gov/funds/index.cfm.

DEPARTMENT OF JUSTICE

The DOJ encompasses 38 major components; those that relate to minority and civil rights include:

- Office of the Attorney General (AG)
  AG supervises and directs the administration and operation of the Department of Justice, including the Federal Bureau of Investigation (FBI), Drug Enforcement Administration, Immigration and Naturalization Service, Bureau of Prisons, Office of Justice Programs, and the Offices of U.S. Attorneys and U.S. Marshals.
- Office of the Deputy Attorney General (DAG)
  DAG advises and assists AG.
- Office of the Associate Attorney General (AAG)
  In addition to advising and assisting AG and DAG, AAG oversees the work of the Civil, Civil Rights, Antitrust, Tax, and Environment and Natural Resources Divisions. AAG has oversight responsibility for the Office of Justice Programs, the Office of Tribal Justice, the Office of Dispute Resolution, the Office of Information and Privacy, the Community Relations Service, the Executive Office for United States Trustees, and the Foreign Claims Settlement Commission and for the implementation of the Violent Crime Control and Enforcement Act of 1994, including the Community Oriented Policing Services Program and the Violence Against Women Office.
- Office of the Solicitor General (OSG)
  OSG represents the interests of the United States before the Supreme Court and oversees appellate and certain other litigation on behalf of the United States in the lower federal and state courts.
- Office of the Inspector General (OIG)
  OIG promotes efficient and effective management within the DOJ and detects and deters wrongdoing in its

programs and operations by the use and coordination of investigative, inspection, and audit resources.

- Office of Intelligence Policy and Review (OIPR)
OIPR assists AG in fulfilling national security-related responsibilities; provides legal advice and guidance to various elements of the government engaged in national security-related activities; and oversees the implementation of the Foreign Intelligence Surveillance Act and other statutory, executive order, or AG–based operational authorities for national security-related activities.
- Office of Professional Responsibility (OPR)
OPR has jurisdiction to investigate allegations of misconduct by DOJ attorneys and to investigate allegations of misconduct by certain law enforcement personnel.
- Office of Information and Privacy (OIP)
OIP manages and coordinates the discharge of DOJ responsibilities under the Freedom of Information Act (FOIA) and the Privacy Act of 1974, through the coordination of compliance with the FOIA within all federal agencies and compliance with the Privacy Act within the DOJ.
- Executive Office for United States Attorneys (EOUSA)
EOUSA provides executive assistance to the 94 Offices of the United States Attorney and coordinates the relationship between the United States Attorneys and the organizational components of DOJ and other federal agencies.
- Civil Division (CIV)
CIV represents the interests of the United States in civil litigation and selected criminal cases.
- Civil Rights Division (CRT)
CRT enforces the Civil Rights Act of 1957, 1960, 1964 and 1968, as amended (see Civil Rights Act of 1957 and Civil Rights Act of 1964); the Voting Rights Act of 1965, as amended; the Equal Credit Opportunity Act, as amended; the Fair Housing Act of 1968 and the Fair Housing Amendments Act of 1988; Executive Order 12250 (inter alia, Title VI, Title IX and Section 504 of the Rehabilitation Act of 1973, as amended); and the Civil Rights of Institutionalized Persons Act.
- Criminal Division (CRM)
CRM serves the public interest through the development and enforcement of criminal statutes in a vigorous, fair and effective manner; and exercises general supervision over the enforcement of all federal criminal laws, with the exception of those statutes specifically assigned to the Antitrust, Civil Rights, Environment and Natural Resources, or Tax Divisions.
- Environment and Natural Resources Division (ENRD)
ENRD conducts litigation to safeguard and enhance the American environment; to acquire and manage public lands and natural resources; and to protect and manage Indian rights and property.
- Tax Division (TAX)
TAX represents the United States and its officers in civil and criminal litigation arising under the internal revenue laws, other than proceedings in the United States Tax Court.
- Bureau of Prisons (BOP)
The mission of BOP is to "maintain secure, safe, and humane correctional institutions for individuals placed in the custody of the U.S. Attorney General; to develop and operate correctional programs that seek a balanced application of the concepts of punishment, deterrence, incapacitation and rehabilitation; and provide, primarily through the National Institute of Corrections, assistance to state and local correctional agencies."
- Drug Enforcement Administration (DEA)
DEA enforces the controlled substance laws and regulations of the United States and brings to the criminal and civil justice system of the United States, or any other competent jurisdiction, those organizations, and principal members of organizations, involved in the growing, manufacture, or distribution of controlled substances appearing in or destined for illicit traffic in the United States; DEA also recommends and supports non-enforcement programs aimed at reducing the availability of illicit controlled substances on the domestic and international markets.
- Federal Bureau of Investigation (FBI)
"The mission of the FBI is to uphold the law through the investigation of violations of federal criminal law; to protect the United States from foreign intelligence and terrorist activities; to provide leadership and law enforcement assistance to federal, state, local and international agencies; and to perform these responsibilities in a manner that is responsive to the needs of the public and is faithful to the Constitution of the United States."
- Immigration and Naturalization Service (INS)
"The mission of the INS is to facilitate entry of those legally admissible as visitors or immigrants and to grant them benefits to which they are entitled; prevent improper entry and the granting of benefits to those not legally entitled to them; apprehend and remove those aliens who enter illegally and/or whose stay is not in the public interest; and to enforce sanctions against those who act or conspire to subvert the requirements for selective and controlled entry, including sanctions

against employers who knowingly hire aliens not authorized to work in the United States."

- United States Marshals Service (USMS)
  USMS enforces federal laws and provides for the security of federal court facilities and the safety of judges and other court personnel; USMS also apprehends criminals; exercises custody of federal prisoners and provides for their security and transportation to correctional facilities; executes federal court orders; seizes assets gained by illegal means and provides for the custody, management and disposal of forfeited assets; and protects endangered government witnesses and their families.
- U.S. National Central Bureau-INTERPOL (USNCBI)
  USNCBI facilitates international law enforcement cooperation as the U.S. representative with the International Criminal Police Organization (INTERPOL).
- Executive Office for Immigration Review (EPOIR)
  EPOIR interprets immigration laws and conducts administrative hearings and appellate reviews on a wide variety of immigration issues.
- Office of the Pardon Attorney (PA)
  PA assists the president in the exercise of his constitutional pardoning power by providing the best information available on which to base a fair and just decision in particular cases.
- United States Parole Commission (USPC)
  USPC makes parole release decisions for federal and District of Columbia prisoners.
- Community Relations Service (CRS)
  CRS provides violence prevention and conflict resolution services for community conflicts and tensions arising from differences of race, color, or national origin.
- Foreign Claims Settlement Commission (FCSC)
  FCSC adjudicates claims against foreign governments for losses and injuries sustained by United States nationals.
- Office of Justice Programs (OJP)
  OJP works with federal, state, local, and tribal agencies and national and community-based organizations to develop, operate, and evaluate a wide range of criminal and juvenile justice programs.
- Office of Community Oriented Policing Services (COPS)
  COPS awards competitive, discretionary grants directly to law enforcement agencies across the United States and its territories for the purposes of creating and administering community oriented policing.
- National Drug Intelligence Center (NDIC)
  NDIC coordinates and consolidates strategic organizational drug intelligence from national security and law enforcement agencies.

Source: Department of Justice, "About DOJ," www.usdoj.gov/02organizations/02_1.html.

DEPARTMENT OF THE INTERIOR

The department's divisions, relevant to minority and civil rights include:

- Bureau of Indian Affairs, which works with the governments of recognized Native American tribes and manages 53 million acres of land held by the United States government in trust for the tribes.
- Bureau of Land Management, which manages the 270 million acres of public land owned by the United States government.

Source: Department of the Interior, "Bureaus," www.doi.gov/bureaus.htm.

APPENDIX B
COURT CASES MENTIONED

Abrams v. United States, 250 U.S. 616 (1919)
Adams v. Williams, 407 U.S. 143 (1973)
Adarand Constructors, Inc. v. Peña, 515 U.S. 200 (1995)
Adkins v. Children's Hospital, 261 U.S. 525 (1923)
Alexander v. Holmes County Board of Education, 396 U.S. 19 (1969)
American Column and Lumber v. United States, 257 U.S. 377 (1921)
Amistad, 40 U.S. 518 (1841)
Baker v. Carr, 369 U.S. 186 (1962)
Balzac v. Porto Rico, 258 U.S. 298 (1922)
Barron v. Baltimore, 32 U.S. (7 Pet.) 243 (1833)
Barrows v. Jackson, 346 U.S. 249 (1953)
Board of Trustees of the University of Alabama v. Garrett, 531 U.S. 356 (2001)
Bolling v. Sharpe, 347 U.S. 497 (1954)
Bond v. Floyd, 385 U.S. 116 (1966)
Bowers v. Hardwick, 478 U.S. 186 (1986)
Boynton v. Virginia, 364 U.S. 454 (1960)
Bragdon v. Abbott, 524 U.S. 624 (1998)
Brown v. Board of Education of Topeka, Kansas, 347 U.S. 483 (1954)
Brown v. Board of Education of Topeka, Kansas, 349 U.S. 294 (1955)
Buchanan v. Warley, 245 U.S. 60 (1917)
Buie v. Maryland, 494 U.S. 325 (1990)
Burlington Industries, Inc. v. Ellerth, 524 U.S. 742 (1998)
Bush v. Gore, 531 U.S. 98 (2000)
Callins v. Collins, 510 U.S. 1141 (1994)
Cantwell v. Connecticut, 310 U.S. 296 (1940)
Chae Chan Ping v. United States, 130 U.S. 581 (1889)
Chaplinsky v. New Hampshire, 315 U.S. 568 (1942)
Chew Heong v. United States, 112 U.S. 536 (1884)
Chicago v. Morales, 527 U. S. 41 (1999)
Chimel v. California, 395 U.S. 752 (1969)
City of Mobile v. Bolden, 446 U.S. 55 (1980)
City of Richmond v. J. R. Croson Co., 488 U.S. 469 (1989)
Clinton v. Jones, 520 U.S. 681 (1997)
Columbus Board of Education v. Penick, 443 U.S. 449 (1979)
Cox v. New Hampshire, 312 U.S. 569 (1941)
Cummings v. Missouri, 71 U.S. (4 Wall.) 277 (1867)
Dickerson v. United States, 530 U.S. 428 (2000)
Doe v. Bolton, 410 U.S. 179 (1973)
Dorr v. United States, 195 U.S. 138 (1904)
Downes v. Bidwell, 182 U.S. 244 (1901)
Edwards v. Balisok, 520 U.S. 641 (1997)
Eisenstadt v. Baird, 405 U.S. 438 (1972)
Engel v. Vitale, 370 U.S. 421 (1962)
Ex parte Garland, 71 U.S. (4 Wall.) 333 (1866)
Ex parte Merryman, 17 Fed. Cas. 9487 (1861)
Ex parte Virginia, 100 U.S. 339 (1880)
Faragher v. City of Boca Raton, 524 U.S. 775 (1998)
Fong Yue Ting v. United States, 149 U.S. 698 (1893)
Fullilove v. Klutznick, 448 U.S. 448 (1980)
Furman v. Georgia, 408 U.S. 238 (1972)
Gideon v. Wainwright, 372 U.S. 335 (1963)
Gitlow v. New York, 268 U.S. 652 (1925)
Good News Club v. Milford Central School, 533 U.S. 98 (2001)
Graham v. Connor, 490 U.S. 386 (1989)
Gregg v. Georgia, 428 U.S. 153 (1976)
Griggs v. Duke Power Co., 401 U.S. 424 (1971)
Griswold v. Connecticut, 381 U.S. 479 (1965)
Guinn v. United States, 238 U.S. 347 (1915)
Hague v. Committee for Industrial Organization, 307 U.S. 496 (1939)
Harper v. Virginia Board of Elections, 383 U.S. 663 (1966)
Harris v. Forklift Systems, Inc. 510 U.S. 17 (1993)
Harris v. McRae, 448 U.S. 297 (1980)
Hernández v. Texas, 347 U.S. 475 (1954)
Hirabayashi v. United States, 320 U.S. 81 (1943)
Illinois v. Rodriguez, 497 U.S. 177 (1990)
In re Davis (1630)
In re Kemmler, 136 U.S. 436 (1890)
In re Sweet (1640)
Johnson v. Transportation Agency of Santa Clara County, 480 U.S. 616 (1987)
Jones v. Opelika, 316 U.S. 584 (1942)
Jones v. Opelika, 319 U.S. 103 (1943)
Korematsu v. United States, 323 U.S. 214 (1944)
Lau v. Nichols, 414 U.S. 563 (1974)
Lewis v. United States, 445 U.S. 55 (1980)
Local 93 International Association of Firefighters v. Cleveland, 478 U.S. 501 (1986)
Louisiana ex rel. Francis v. Resweber, 329 U.S. 459 (1947)
Loving v. Virginia, 388 U.S. 1 (1967)
Lynch v. Donnelly, 465 U.S. 668 (1984)
Mapp v. Ohio, 367 U.S. 643 (1961)
Marbury v. Madison, 5 U.S. (1 Cr.) 137 (1803)

McLaurin v. Oklahoma State Regents, 339 U.S. 637 (1950)
Meredith Corp. v. Federal Communications Commission, 809 F. 2d 863, 873 (DC Cir. 1987)
Meritor Savings Bank v. Vinson, 477 U.S. 57 (1986)
Mills v. Board of Education of the District of Columbia, 348 F. Supp. 866 (D. DC 1972)
Minersville School District v. Gobitis, 310 U.S. 586 (1940)
Miranda v. Arizona, 384 U.S. 436 (1966)
Missouri ex rel. Gaines v. Canada, 305 U.S. 337 (1938)
Mitchell v. Helms, 530 U.S. 793 (2000)
Moore v. East Cleveland, 431 U.S. 494 (1977)
Morgan v. Virginia, 328 U.S. 373 (1946)
Mount Laurel v. Southern Burlington County NAACP, 423 U.S. 808 (1975)
Muller v. Oregon, 208 U.S. 412 (1908)
New York Times v. United States, 403 U.S. 713 (1971)
Newdow v. United States Congress, 292 F. 3d 597 (2002)
Norris v. Alabama, 294 U.S. 587 (1935)
Olmstead v. United States, 277 U.S. 438 (1928)
Oncale v. Sundowner Offshore Services, Inc., 523 U.S. 75 (1998)
Pennsylvania Association for Retarded Children v. Commonwealth, 334 F. Supp. 1247 (E. Dist. Pa. 1971)
PGA Tour, Inc., v. Martin, 532 U.S. 661 (2001)
Pierce v. Society of the Sisters of the Holy Names of Jesus and Mary, 268 U.S. 510 (1925)
Planned Parenthood of Central Missouri v. Danforth, 428 U.S. 52 (1976)
Planned Parenthood of Southeastern Pennsylvania v. Casey, 505 U.S. 833 (1992)
Plessy v. Ferguson, 163 U.S. 537 (1896)
Powell v. Alabama, 287 U.S. 45 (1932)
Prince v. Massachusetts, 321 U.S. 158 (1944)
Red Lion Broadcasting Co., Inc. v. Federal Communications Commission, 395 U.S. 367 (1969)
Regents of the University of California v. Bakke, 438 U.S. 265 (1978)
Reno v. American Civil Liberties Union, 521 U.S. 844 (1997)
Reynolds v. Sims, 377 U.S. 533 (1964)
Reynolds v. United States, 98 U.S. 145 (1879)
Roe v. Wade, 410 U.S. 113 (1973)
Romer v. Evans, 517 U.S. 620 (1996)
Saenz v. Roe, 526 U.S. 489 (1999)
San Antonio Independent School District v. Rodriguez, 411 U.S. 1 (1973)
Sandlin v. Conner, 515 U.S. 472 (1995)
Santa Clara Pueblo v. Martinez, 436 U.S. 49 (1978)
Sarnoff v. Schultz, 409 U.S. 929 (1972)
Schenck v. United States, 249 U.S. 47 (1919)
Schnell v. Davis, 336 U.S. 933 (1949)
Shaw v. Reno, 509 U.S. 630 (1993)
Shelley v. Kraemer, 334 U.S. 1 (1948)
Slaughterhouse cases, 83 U.S. (16 Wall.) 36 (1873)
Smith v. Allwright, 321 U.S. 649 (1944)
South Burlington County NAACP v. Mount Laurel, 92 NJ 158, 456 A. 2d 390 (1983)
Standard Oil Co. of California v. United States, 337 U.S. 293 (1949)
State ex rel. Beattie v. Board of Education, 172 N.W. 153 (1919)
Stenberg v. Carhart, 530 U.S. 914 (2000)
Strauder v. West Virginia, 100 U.S. 303 (1879)
Swann v. Charlotte-Mecklenburg Board of Education, 402 U.S. 1 (1971)
Sweatt v. Painter, 339 U.S. 629 (1950)
Terry v. Adams, 345 U.S. 461 (1953)
Terry v. Ohio, 392 U.S. 1 (1968)
Texas v. Johnson, 491 U.S. 397 (1989)
Trop v. Dulles, 356 U.S. 86 (1958)
United States v. Chadwick, 433 U.S. 1 (1977)
United States v. Cruikshank, 92 U.S. 542 (1875)
United States v. Eichman, 496 U.S. 310 (1990)
United States v. Jung Ah Lung, 124 U.S. 621 (1888)
United States v. Kagama, 118 U.S. 375 (1886)
United States v. Lovett, 328 U.S. 303 (1946)
United States v. Morrison, 529 U.S. 598 (2000)
United States v. One Package of Japanese Pessaries, 13 F. Supp. 334 (E.D.N.Y. 1936), affirmed 86 F. 2d 737 (2d Cir. 1936) (1936)
United States v. Reese, 92 U.S. 214 (1876)
Vacco v. Quill, 521 U.S. 793 (1997)
Wallace v. Jaffree, 472 U.S. 38 (1985)
Wards Cove Packing Co. v. Antonio, 490 U.S. 642 (1989)
Watchtower Society v. Village of Stratton, 536 U.S. ___; 122 S.Ct. 2080 (2002)
Watkins v. United States, 354 U.S. 178 (1957)
Webster v. Reproductive Health Services, 492 U.S. 490 (1989)
Weeks v. Southern Bell, 408 F. 2d 228 (CA5 1969)
West Virginia State Board of Education v. Barnette, 319 U.S. 624 (1943)
Whitcomb v. Chavis, 403 U.S. 124 (1971)
White v. Regester, 412 U.S. 755 (1973)
Whitney v. California, 274 U.S. 357 (1927)
Wilkerson v. Utah, 99 U.S. 130 (1878)
Wisconsin v. Yoder, 406 U.S. 205 (1972)
Wolf v. Colorado, 338 U.S. 25 (1949)
Zelman v. Simmons-Harris, 536 U.S. ___; 122 S.Ct. 2460 (2002)

APPENDIX C

CONTACT INFORMATION FOR AGENCIES AND ORGANIZATIONS INVOLVED IN MINORITY RIGHTS

Algebra Project
99 Bishop Richard Allen Drive
Cambridge, MA 02139
Tel: (617) 491-0200
www.algebra.org.

American-Arab Discrimination Committee
4201 Connecticut Ave, NW, Suite 300
Washington, DC 20008
Tel: (202) 244-2990
Fax: (202) 244-3196
Email: ADC@adc.org

American Civil Liberties Union
125 Broad Street, 18th floor
New York, NY 10004
Email: infoaclu@aclu.org
www.aclu.org

American Council of the Blind
1155 15th Street, NW, Suite 1004
Washington, DC 20005
Tel: (202) 467-5081
Tel: (800) 424-8666
Fax: (202) 467-5085
www.acb.org

American Foundation for the Blind
11 Penn Plaza, Suite 300
New York, NY 10001
Tel: (212) 502-7755
www.afb.org

American GI Forum of the United States
206 San Pedro, Suite 200
San Antonio, TX 78205
Tel: (210) 223-4088

Americans for Democratic Action
1625 K Street, NW, Suite 210
Washington, DC 20006
Tel: (202) 785-5969
www.adaction.org

Americans United for the Separation of Church and State
518 C Street, NE
Washington, DC 20002
Tel: (202) 466-3234
Fax: (202) 466-2587
www.au.org

Asian-American Legal Defense and Education Fund
99 Hudson Street
New York, NY 10013
Tel: (212) 966-5932
Fax: (212) 966-4303
www.aaldef.org

Asian Law Caucus
720 Market Street, Suite 500
San Francisco, CA 94102
Tel: (415) 391-1655
Fax: (415) 391-0366
Email: alc@asianlawcaucus.org
www.asianlawcaucus.com

Association on American Indian Affairs
Box 268
Sisseton, SD 57262
Tel: (605) 698-3998
Fax: (605) 698-3316
Email: aaia@sbtc.net
www.indian-affairs.org

Association for Persons with Severe Handicaps
29 West Susquehanna Avenue, Suite 210
Baltimore, MD 21204
Tel: (410) 828-8274
Fax: (410) 828-6706
www.tash.org

Balch Institute for Ethnic Studies
18 South Seventh Street
Philadelphia, PA 19106
www.balchinstitute.org

Center for Civil and Human Rights
Notre Dame Law School
135 Law School
Notre Dame, IN 46556
Tel: (219) 631-8555
Fax: (219) 631-8702
Email: cchr@nd.edu

Center for Law and Social Policy
1015 15th Street, NW, Suite 400
Washington, DC 20036
Tel: (202) 906-8000
Fax: (202) 842-2885
Email: ahouse@clasp.org

Center for Women's Policy Studies
1211 Connecticut Avenue, NW, Suite 312
Washington, DC 20036
Tel: (202) 872-1770
Fax: (202) 296-8962
Email: cwps@centerwomenpolicy.org

Children's Defense Fund
25 E Street, NW
Washington, DC 20001
Tel: (202) 628-8787
Email: cdfinfo@childrensdefense.org

Child Welfare League of America
440 First Street, NW, Third Floor
Washington, DC 20001-2085
Tel: (202) 638-2952
Fax: (202) 638-4004

Chinese for Affirmative Action
17 Walter U. Lum Place
San Francisco, CA 94108
www.caasf.org

Citizen's Commission on Civil Rights
2000 M Street, NW, Suite 400
Washington, DC 20036
Tel: (202) 659-5565
Fax: (202) 223-5302
Email: citizens@cccr.org

Congress of Racial Equality
817 Broadway, 3rd Floor
New York, NY 10003
Tel: (212) 598-4000
Fax: (212) 598-4141
Email: core@core-online.org

Department of Health and Human Services, U.S.
Hubert H. Humphrey Building
200 Independence Avenue, SW
Washington, DC 20201
www.hhs.gov

Department of Housing and Urban Development, U.S.
451 7th Street, SW
Washington, DC 20410
Tel: (202) 708-1112
www.hud.gov

Disability Rights Education and Defense Fund
2212 Sixth Street
Berkeley, CA 94710
Tel: (510) 644-2555
Fax: (510) 841-8645
Email: dredf@dredf.org

Education Law Center
155 Washington Street, Suite 205
Newark, New Jersey 07102
Tel: (973) 624-1815
Fax: (973) 624-7339
www.edlawceter.org

First Amendment Foundation
336 East College Avenue, Suite 101
Tallahassee, FL 32301
Tel: (800) 337-3518

Freedom House
120 Wall Street, Floor 26
New York, NY 10005
Tel: (212) 514-8040
Fax: (212) 514-8055

Glass Ceiling Commission
U.S. Department of Labor
Office of Small and Minority Business Affairs
200 Constitution Avenue, NW, Room C2318
Washington, DC 20210
Tel: (202) 219-9148
Fax: (202) 219-9167

Gray Panthers
733 15th Street, NW, Suite 437
Washington, DC 20005
Tel: (800) 280-5362
Tel: (202) 737-6637

Fax: (202) 737-1160
Email: info@graypanthers.org
www.graypanthers.org

Human Rights Watch
350 Fifth Avenue, 34th floor
New York, NY 10118-3299
Tel: (212) 290-4700
Fax: (212) 736-1300
Email: hrwnyc@hrw.org

Indian Resource Law Center
602 North Ewing Street
Helena, Montana 59601
Tel: (406) 449-2006
Fax: (406) 449-2031
Email: mt@indianlaw.org
— *and* —
601 E Street, SE
Washington, DC 20003
Tel: (202) 547-2800
Fax: (202) 547-2803
Email: dc@indianlaw.org

Leadership Conference on Civil Rights
1629 K Street, NW, Suite 1010
Washington, DC 20006
Tel: (202) 628-4160
Fax: (202) 347-5323
www.civilrights.org/lccr/

League of United Latin American Citizens
2000 L Street, NW, Suite 610
Washington, DC 20036
Tel: (202) 833-6130

Legal Services for Prisoners with Children
1540 Market Street, Suite 490
San Francisco, CA 94102
Tel: (415) 255-7036
Email: info@prisonerswithchildren.org

Lewisburg Prison Project
P.O. Box 128
Lewisburg, PA 17837
Tel: (570) 523-1104
Fax: (570) 523-3944

Martin Luther King, Jr. Center for Social Change
Freedom Hall
449 Auburn Avenue, NE
Atlanta, GA 30312
www.thekingcenter.com
— *or* —
National Park Service Visitors Center
450 Auburn Avenue, NE
Atlanta, GA 30312
Phone: (404) 526-8900
Email: info@thekingcenter.org

Mexican-American Legal Defense and Education Fund
634 South Spring Street
Los Angeles, CA 90014
Tel: (213) 629-2512
www.maldef.org

Migrant Legal Action Program
2001 S Street, NW, Suite 310
Washington, DC 20009
Tel: (202) 462-7744

NAACP
4805 Mt. Hope Drive
Baltimore, MD 21215
Tel: (877) NAACP-98
www.naacp.org

National Abortion Rights Action League
1156 15th Street, NW, Suite 700
Washington, DC 20005
Tel: (202) 973-3000
Fax: (202) 973-3096

National Center for Lesbian Rights
870 Market Street, NW, Suite 570
San Francisco, CA 94102
Tel: (415) 392-6257
Fax: (415) 392-8442
Email: info@nclrights.org

National Center for Youth Law
405 14th Street, 15th Floor
Oakland, California 94612
Tel: (510) 835-8098
Fax: (510) 835-8099
Email: info@youthlaw.org

National Clearinghouse for the Defense of Battered Women
125 S. 9th Street, Suite 302
Philadelphia, PA 19107

Tel: (215) 351-0010
Fax: (215) 351-0779

National Congress of American Indians
1301 Connecticut Avenue, NW, Suite 200
Washington DC 20036
Tel: (202) 466-7767
Fax: (202) 466-7797

National Council of La Raza
1111 19th Street, NW, Suite 1000
Washington, DC 20036
Tel: (202) 785-1670

National Gay and Lesbian Task Force
1700 Kalorama Road, NW
Washington, DC 20009
Tel: (202) 332-6483
Fax: (202) 332-0207

National Housing Law Project
614 Grand Avenue, Suite 320
Oakland, CA 94610
Tel: (510) 251-9400
Fax: (510) 451-2300
Email: nhlp@nhlp.org

National Immigration Project
14 Beacon Street, Suite 602
Boston, MA 02108

National Lawyers Guild
143 Madison Ave, 4th Floor
New York, NY 10016
Tel: (212) 679-5100
Fax: (212) 679-2811
Email: nlgno@nlg.org

National Organization for Women
733 15th Street, NW, 2nd floor
Washington, DC 20005
Tel: (202) 628-8669
Fax: (202) 785-8576
Email: now@now.org

National Urban League
120 Wall Street
New York, NY 10005
Email: info@nul.org
www.nul.org

National Women's Law Center
11 Dupont Circle, NW, #800
Washington, DC 20036
Tel: (202) 588-5180
Fax: (202) 588-5185
Email: info@nwlc.org

Native American Rights Fund
1506 Broadway
Boulder, CO 80302
Tel: (303) 447-8760
Fax: 303-443-7776
Email: pereira@narf.org

New York Children's Aid Society
105 East 22nd Street
New York, NY 10010
Tel: (212) 949-4800
www.childrensaidsociety.org

NOW Legal Defense and Educational Fund
395 Hudson Street
New York, NY 10014
Tel: (212) 925-6635
Fax: (212) 226-1066

Puerto Rican Legal Defense and Education Fund
99 Hudson Street, 14th Floor
New York, NY 10013
Tel: (212) 219-3360
Fax: (212) 431-4276
Email: info@prldef.org

Schomburg Center for Research in Black Culture
515 Malcolm X Boulevard
New York, NY 10037-1801
Tel: (212) 491-2200

Southern Christian Leadership Conference
P.O. Box 89128
Atlanta, GA 30312
Tel: (404) 522.1420
Fax: (404) 527.4333
www.sclcnational.org.

Universal Negro Improvement Association and African Communities League
Woodson-Banneker-Jackson-Bey Division 330
P.O. Box 64038
Washington, DC 20029

Urban Institute
2100 M Street, NW
Washington, DC 20037
Tel: (202) 833-7200
Email: paffairs@ui.urban.org

Women's Law Project
125 South 9th Street, Suite 300
Philadelphia, PA 19107
Tel: (215) 928-9801

Youth Law Center
Children's Legal Protection Center
417 Montgomery Street, Suite 900
San Francisco, CA 94104-1121
Tel: (415) 543-3379
— *or* —
Children's Legal Protection Center
1010 Vermont Avenue, NW, Suite 310
Washington, DC 20005-4902
Tel: (202) 637-0377

BIBLIOGRAPHY

Abernathy, Ralph David. *And the Walls Came Tumbling Down: An Autobiography.* New York: Harper and Row, 1989.

Abourezk, James. *Advise and Dissent: Memoirs of South Dakota and the U.S. Senate.* Chicago: Lawrence Hill, 1989.

Addams, Jane. *The Jane Addams Reader.* New York: Basic Books, 2001.

———. *Twenty Years at Hull-House.* 1910. Reprint, New York: Signet, 1999.

Alderman, Ellen, and Caroline Kennedy. *In Our Defense: The Bill of Rights in Action.* New York: Morrow, 1991.

———. *The Right to Privacy.* New York: Knopf, 1995.

Alexander, Kern, and M. David Alexander. *The Law of Schools, Students and Teachers.* 2d ed. St. Paul, Minn.: West, 1995.

Amar, Akhil Reed. *The Bill of Rights: Creation and Reconstruction.* New Haven: Yale University Press, 2000.

American Civil Liberties Union. "Prisoner's Rights," www.aclu.org/library/PrisonerRights.pdf.

Amnesty International. *Annual Report.* London: Amnesty International, published annually.

Anderson, Elijah, and Douglas S. Massey, eds. *Problem of the Century: Racial Stratification in the United States.* New York: Russell Sage Foundation, 2001.

Anderson, Jervis. *Bayard Rustin: Troubles I've Seen.* New York: HarperCollins, 1997.

Anderson, Margo J., ed. *Encyclopedia of the U.S. Census.* Washington, D.C.: CQ Press, 2000.

Anderson, Marian. *My Lord, What a Morning: An Autobiography.* 1957. Reprint, Champaign-Urbana: University of Illinois Press, 2002.

Andrews, Arlene Bowers, and Natalie Hevener Kaufman, eds. *Implementing the UN Convention on the Rights of the Child.* New York: Praeger, 1999.

Angelou, Maya. *Even the Stars Look Lonesome.* New York: Random House, 1997.

———. *I Know Why the Caged Bird Sings.* New York: Random House, 1970.

Anti-Defamation League. *Annual Report.* New York, published annually.

Archer, Jules. *They Had a Dream: The Civil Rights Struggle from Frederick Douglass to Marcus Garvey to Martin Luther King and Malcolm X.* New York: Viking, 1993.

Arlington, Karen M., and William L. Taylor, eds. *Voting Rights in America.* Washington, D.C.: University Press of America, 1993.

Armor, David J. *Forced Justice: School Desegregation and the Law.* New York: Oxford University Press, 1995.

Ashworth, John. *Slavery, Capitalism, and Politics in the Antebellum Republic: Commerce and Compromise, 1820–1850.* New York: Cambridge University Press, 1996.

Avakian, Monique. *Atlas of Asian-American History.* New York: Facts on File, 2002.

Avrich, Paul. *The Haymarket Tragedy.* Princeton: Princeton University Press, 1984.

———. *Sacco and Vanzetti.* Princeton: Princeton University Press, 1996.

Axelrod, Alan. *Chronicle of the Indian Wars: From Colonial Times to Wounded Knee.* New York: Macmillan, 1993.

———. *Congressional Quarterly's American Treaties and Alliances.* Washington, D.C.: CQ Press, 2000.

———. *The International Encyclopedia of Secret Societies and Fraternal Orders.* New York: Facts on File, 1997.

———. *The Life and Work of Thomas Jefferson.* New York: Alpha, 2001.

Babcock, Richard F. *Exclusionary Zoning: Land Use Regulation and Housing in the 1970s.* New York: Praeger, 1974.

Bacon, Margaret Hope. *The Quiet Rebels: The Story of the Quakers in America.* Wallingford, Penn.: Pendle Hill, 2000.

Baker, Jean H., ed. *Votes for Women: The Struggle for Suffrage Revisited.* New York: Oxford University Press, 2002.

Baker, William J. *Jesse Owens: An American Life.* New York: Free Press, 1988.

Baldwin, Lewis V. *To Make the Wounded Whole: The Cultural Legacy of Martin Luther King Jr.* Minneapolis: Fortress, 1992.

Ball, Howard. *The Bakke Case: Race, Education, and Affirmative Action.* Lawrence: University Press of Kansas, 2000.

Banks, William H., Jr. *The Black Muslims.* New York: Chelsea House, 1996.

Banner, Stuart. *The Death Penalty: An American History.* Cambridge: Harvard University Press, 2002.

Banning, Lance. *The Sacred Fire of Liberty: James Madison and the Founding of the Federal Republic.* Ithaca: Cornell University Press, 1995.

Bass, Jack, and Marilyn W. Thompson. *Ol' Strom: An Unauthorized Biography of Strom Thurmond.* Atlanta: Longstreet, 1998.

Bates, Anna Louise. *Weeder in the Garden of the Lord: A Biography of Anthony Comstock.* Lanham, Md.: University Press of America, 1995.

Baugh, John. *Beyond Ebonics: Linguistic Pride and Racial Prejudice.* New York: Oxford University Press, 2000.

Beauchamp, Tom L., and Robert M. Veatch, eds. *Ethical Issues in Death and Dying.* 2d ed. Englewood Cliffs, N.J.: Prentice Hall, 1995.

Beckwith, Francis J., and Todd E. Jones, eds. *Affirmative Action: Social Justice or Reverse Discrimination?* New York: Prometheus, 1997.

Bedau, Hugo Adam, ed. *Civil Disobedience in Focus.* New York: Routledge, 1991.

Belfrage, Sally. *Freedom Summer.* Charlottesville: University Press of Virginia, 1990.

Belknap, Mical R., ed. *Administrative History of the Civil Rights Division of the Department of Justice during the Johnson Administration.* New York: Garland, 1992.

Belsky, Martin H. *The Rehnquist Court: A Retrospective.* New York: Oxford University Press, 2002.

Bennet, Wayne W., and Karen M. Hess. "Searches." In *Criminal Investigation,* 5th ed., ed. Wayne W. Bennet and Karen M. Hess. Belmont, Calif.: West/Wadsworth, 1998.

Bennett, Lerone, Jr. *Before the Mayflower: A History of Black America.* New York: Penguin, 1993.

Bentley, Eric, ed. *Thirty Years of Treason: Excerpts from Hearings before the House Committee on Un-American Activities, 1938–1968.* New York: Thunder's Mouth, 2002.

Bernstein, Carl, and Bob Woodward. *All the President's Men.* 1974. Reprint, New York: Touchstone Books, 1994.

Bernstein, Irving. *Promises Kept: John F. Kennedy's New Frontier.* New York: Oxford University Press, 1991.

Bernstein, Iver. *New York City Draft Riots: Their Significance for American Society and Politics in the Age of the Civil War.* New York: Oxford University Press, 1989.

Berry, Dawn Bradley. *Domestic Violence Sourcebook.* New York: McGraw-Hill/NTC, 2000.

Best, Judith. *National Representation for the District of Columbia.* Frederick, Md: University Publications, 1984.

Bingham, Clara, and Laura Leedy Gansler. *Class Action: The Story of Lois Jenson and the Landmark Case That Changed Sexual Harassment Law.* New York: Doubleday, 2002.

Bird, Stewart, Dan Georgakas, and Deborah Shaffer. *Solidarity Forever: An Oral History of the IWW.* Chicago: Lake View, 1985.

Blackburn, Robin. The Overthrow of Colonial Slavery, 1776–1848. New York: Verso, 1989.

Block, Irving. *Neighbor to the World: The Story of Lillian Wald.* New York: Crowell, 1969.

Blockson, Charles L. *The Underground Railroad: Dramatic Firsthand Accounts of Daring Escapes to Freedom.* New York: Berkley, 1994.

Bond, Julian. *A Time to Speak. A Time to Act.* New York: Simon and Schuster, 1972.

Boynton, Ameila Platts. *Bridge across Jordan: The Story of the Struggle for Civil Rights in Selma, Alabama.* New York: Carlton, 1979.

Brace, Charles Loring. *The Life of Charles Loring Brace.* New York: Charles Scribner's Sons, 1894.

Bradley Berry, Dawn. *Domestic Violence Sourcebook.* New York: McGraw-Hill, 2000.

Brady, Kathleen. *Ida Tarbell: Portrait of a Muckraker.* University of Pittsburgh Press, 1989.

Brandeis, Louis Dembitz. *Brandeis on Democracy,* ed. Philippa Strum. Lawrence: University Press of Kansas, 1995.

Bredeson, Carmen. *Ruth Bader Ginsburg: Supreme Court Justice.* Berkeley Heights, N.J.: Enslow, 1995.

Brennan, Timothy A. "The Fairness Doctrine as Public Policy." *Journal of Broadcasting and Electronic Media* (fall 1989).

Brinkley, Douglas. *Rosa Parks.* New York: Penguin, 2000.

———. *The Unfinished Presidency: Jimmy Carter's Journey Beyond the White House.* New York: Viking, 1998.

Brock, Clifton. *Americans for Democratic Action: Its Role in National Politics.* Westport, Conn.: Greenwood, 1985.

Brock, Peter, ed. *Liberty and Conscience: A Documentary History of Conscientious Objectors in America throughout the Civil War.* New York: Oxford University Press, 2002.

Brown, David S. *Thomas Jefferson: A Biographical Companion.* Santa Barbara, Calif.: ABC-CLIO, 1998.

Brown, Dorothy M., and Elizabeth McKeown. *The Poor Belong to Us: Catholic Charities and American Welfare.* Cambridge: Harvard University Press, 2000.

Brugger, Robert J. *Maryland: A Middle Temperament, 1634–1980.* 1988. Reprint, Baltimore: Johns Hopkins University Press, 1996.

Bullock, Paul. *CETA at the Crossroads: Employment Policy and Politics.* Los Angeles: Regents of UCLA, 1981.

Buranelli, Vincent. *The Eighth Amendment.* The American Heritage: History of the Bill of Rights Series. Upper Saddle River, N.J.: Silver Burdett, 1991.

Burke, Christopher Matthew. *The Appearance of Equality: Racial Gerrymandering, Redistricting, and the Supreme Court.* Westport, Conn.: Greenwood, 1999.

Burk, Robert Fredrick. *The Eisenhower Administration and Black Civil Rights, 1953–1961.* Knoxville: University of Tennessee Press, 1984.

Burstein, Paul. *Discrimination, Jobs, and Politics: The Struggle for Equal Employment Opportunity in the United States Since the New Deal.* Chicago: University of Chicago Press, 1985.

Business for Social Responsibility. "Migrant Labor" (White Paper), www.bsr.org/BSRResources/WhitePaperDetail.cfm?DocumentID=519.

Calhoun, John C. *The Papers of John C. Calhoun,* vols. 4–25, ed. Robert L. Meriwether and Clyde N. Wilson. Columbia: University of South Carolina Press, 1981–1990.

Carawan, Guy, and Candie Carawan, eds. *Sing for Freedom.* Bethlehem, Penn.: Sing Out!, 1997.

Carson, Clayborne, ed. *The Autobiography of Martin Luther King, Jr.* New York: Warner, 2001.

———. *Malcolm X: The FBI File.* New York: Carroll and Graf, 1991.

———. *In Struggle: SNCC and the Black Awakening of the 1960s.* 1981. Reprint, Cambridge: Harvard University Press, 1995.

Carter, Dan T. *The Politics of Rage: George Wallace, the Origins of the New Conservatism, and the Transformation of American Politics.* 2d ed. Baton Rouge: Louisiana State University Press, 2000.

———. *Scottsboro: A Tragedy of the American South.* Baton Rouge: Louisiana State University Press, 1979.

Castile, George Pierre. *To Show Heart: Native American Self-Determination and Federal Indian Policy, 1960–1975.* Tempe: University of Arizona Press, 1998.

Cathcart, David A., and American Law Institute-American Bar Association Committee on Continuing Professional Education. *The Civil Rights Act of 1991.* Philadelphia: American Law Institute, 1993.

Center for Civil and Human Rights. *Notre Dame Human Rights Advocate,* published periodically and available online, www.nd.edu/~cchr/publications/advocate/advocate.html.

Chafe, William Henry, Raymond Gavins, Robert Korstad, Jennifer Lynn Ritterhouse, Robert Gavins, and the staff of Behind the Veil Project, eds. *Remembering Jim Crow: African Americans Tell about Life in the Segregated South.* New York: New Press, 2001.

Chalmers, David Mark. *Hooded Americanism: The History of the Ku Klux Klan.* 3d ed. Durham: Duke University Press, 1987.

Chesler, Ellen. *Woman of Valor: Margaret Sanger and the Birth Control Movement in America.* New York: Summit, 1992.

Children's Defense Fund. *The State of America's Children Yearbook.* Washington, D.C.: Children's Defense Fund, published annually.

Chinese for Affirmative Action. *Annual Reports,* www.caasf.org.

Chisholm, Shirley. *Unbought and Unbossed.* Boston: Houghton Mifflin, 1970.

Cholewinski, Ryszard. *Migrant Workers in International Human Rights Law: Their Protection in Countries of Employment.* Oxford, U.K.: Clarendon, 1997.

Churchill, Ward, and Jim Vander Wall. *The COINTELPRO Papers: Documents from the FBI's Secret Wars against Dissent in the United States.* Cambridge, Mass.: South End, 1990.

Cimbala, Paul A., and Randall M. Miller, eds. *The Freedmen's Bureau and Reconstruction: Reconsiderations.* New York: Fordham University Press, 1999.

Clarke, John Henrik. *Malcolm X: The Man and His Times.* New York: Macmillan, 1969.

Clark, Robin E., Judith Freeman Clark, and Christine A. Adamec. *The Encyclopedia of Child Abuse.* 2d ed. New York: Facts on File, 2000.

Cleaver, Eldridge. *Soul on Ice.* New York: McGraw-Hill, 1967.

Clendinen, Dudley, and Adam Nagourney. *Out for Good: The Struggle to Build a Gay Rights Movement in America.* New York: Simon and Schuster, 1999.

Cogan, Neil H., ed. *The Complete Bill of Rights: The Drafts, Debates, Sources, and Origins.* New York: Oxford University Press, 1997.

Cohen, Adam, and Elizabeth Taylor. *American Pharaoh: Mayor Richard J. Daley—His Battle for Chicago and the Nation.* Boston: Little, Brown, 2000.

Cohen, Carl. *Civil Disobedience: Conscience, Tactics, and the Law.* New York: Columbia University Press, 1971.

Cohen, Robert, and Reginald E. Zelnik, eds. *The Free Speech Movement: Reflections on Berkeley in the 1960s.* Berkeley: University of California Press, 2002.

Colby, Kimberies W. *A Guide to the Equal Access Act.* Annandale, Va.: Christian Legal Society, 1988.

Coles, Robert. *Dorothy Day: A Radical Devotion.* Reading, Mass.: Addison-Wesley, 1987.

Collier-Thomas, Bettye, and V. P. Franklin, eds. *Sisters in the Struggle: African-American Women in the Civil Rights–Black Power Movement.* New York: New York University Press, 2001.

Colonial Laws of Massachusetts: Reprinted from the Edition of 1660, with the Supplements to 1672: Containing Also, the Body of Liberties of 1641. Littleton, Colo.: Fred B. Rothman, 1995.

Comstock, Anthony. *Traps for the Young.* 1884. Reprint, Campbell, Calif.: iUniverse, 1999.

Cornell, Tom, Robert Ellsberg, and Jim Forest, eds. *A Penny a Copy: Writings from the Catholic Worker.* Maryknoll, N.Y.: Orbis, 1995.

Cottrell, Robert C. *Roger Nash Baldwin and the American Civil Liberties Union.* New York: Columbia University Press, 2001.

Counts, I. Wilmer, Robert S. McCord, and Will Counts. *A Life Is More Than a Moment: The Desegregation of Little Rock's Central High.* Bloomington: Indiana University Press, 1999.

Crawford, James. *Hold Your Tongue: Bilingualism and the Politics of English Only.* New York: Addison-Wesley, 1992.

———, ed. *Language Loyalties: A Sourcebook on the Official English Controversy.* Chicago: University of Chicago Press, 1992.

Cray, Ed. *Chief Justice: A Biography of Earl Warren.* New York: Simon and Schuster, 1997.

Cronon, Edmund David. *Black Moses: The Story of Marcus Garvey and the Universal Negro Improvement Association.* Madison: University of Wisconsin Press, 1969.

Curry, George E., and Cornel West, eds. *The Affirmative Action Debate.* New York: Perseus, 1996.

Curry, Thomas J. *Farewell to Christendom: The Future of Church and State in America.* New York: Oxford University Press, 2001.

Curtis, Michael Kent. *No State Shall Abridge: The Fourteenth Amendment and the Bill of Rights.* Durham: Duke University Press, 1990.

Cushman, Clare. *The Supreme Court Justices: Illustrated Biographies, 1789–1995.* 2d ed. Washington, D.C.: CQ Press, 1996.

Daniels, Roger. *The Politics of Prejudice: The Anti-Japanese Movement in California and the Struggle for Japanese Exclusion.* Berkeley: University of California Press, 1978.

Davidson, Chandler. *Controversies in Minority Voting: The Voting Rights Act in Perspective.* Washington, D.C.: Brookings Institution, 1992.

Davidson, Chandler, and Bernard Grofman. *Quiet Revolution in the South: The Impact of the Voting Rights Act, 1965–1990.* Princeton: Princeton University Press, 1994.

Davis, Allen F. *American Heroine: The Life and Legend of Jane Addams.* New York: Oxford University Press, 1973.

Davis, Kenneth S. *FDR: The Beckoning of Destiny, 1882–1928.* New York: G. P. Putnam's Sons, 1971.

———. *FDR: The New Deal Years, 1933–1937.* New York: Random House, 1986.

———. *FDR: The War President, 1940–1943.* New York: Random House, 2000.

Davis, Lenwood. *Malcolm X: A Selected Bibliography.* Westport, Conn.: Greenwood, 1984.

Debenedetti, Charles. *An American Ordeal: The Antiwar Movement of the Vietnam War.* Syracuse: Syracuse University Press, 1990.

DeCaro, Louis. *Malcolm and the Cross: The Nation of Islam, Malcolm X, and Christianity.* New York: New York University Press, 1998.

DeLaughter, Bobby. *Never Too Late: A Prosecutor's Story of Justice in the Medgar Evers Case.* New York: Scribner, 2001.

Del Castillo, Richard G. *The Treaty of Guadalupe Hidalgo: a Legacy of Conflict.* Norman: University of Oklahoma Press, 1990.

Delgado, Richard, and Jean Stefancic. *Must We Defend Nazis? Hate Speech, Pornography, and the New First Amendment*. New York: New York University Press, 1999.

Deloria, Vine Jr. *Custer Died for Your Sins: An Indian Manifesto*. Norman: University of Oklahoma Press, 1988.

DeVoto, Bernard. *The Year of Decision, 1846*. Boston: Little, Brown, 1943.

Dickerson, Dennis. *Militant Mediator: Whitney M. Young, Jr.* Lexington: University Press of Kentucky, 1998.

Dixon, Susan B. *History of the Missouri Compromise and Slavery in American Politics*. 1903. Reprint, New York: Johnson Reprint Corporation, forthcoming.

Dobratz, Betty A., and Stephanie L. Shanks-Meile. *The White Separatist Movement in the United States: White Power, White Pride*. Baltimore: Johns Hopkins University Press, 2000.

Dobrich, Wanda, Steven Dranoff, and Gerald L. Maatman. *The Manager's Guide to Preventing a Hostile Work Environment*. New York: McGraw-Hill, 2002.

Dorinson, Joseph, and Joram Warmund, eds. *Jackie Robinson: Race, Sports, and the American Dream*. Tarrytown, N.Y.: M. E. Sharpe, 1998.

Douglas, William O. *The Court Years, 1939 to 1975*. New York: Random House, 1980.

Drake, Frederick D., and Lynn R. Nelson, eds. *States Rights and American Federalism: A Documentary History*. Westport, Conn.: Greenwood, 1999.

Dray, Philip. *At the Hands of Persons Unknown: The Lynching of Black America*. New York: Random House, 2002.

DuBois, Ellen Carol. *The Elizabeth Cady Stanton–Susan B. Anthony Reader: Correspondence, Writings, Speeches*. Boston: Northeastern University Press, 1992.

———, ed. *Feminism and Suffrage: The Emergence of an Independent Women's Movement in America, 1848–1869*. Ithaca: Cornell University Press, 1999.

Durchslag, Melvyn R. *State Sovereign Immunity: A Reference Guide to the United States Constitution*. Westport, Conn.: Greenwood, 2002.

Early, Gerald Lyn, ed. *The Muhammad Ali Reader*. New York: Ecco, 1998.

Echols, Alice. *Daring to Be Bad: Radical Feminism in America, 1967–1975*. Minneapolis: University of Minnesota Press, 1990.

Edley, Christopher, Jr. *Not All Black and White: Affirmative Action and American Values*. New York: Noonday, 1998.

Elshtain, Jean Bethke. *Jane Addams and the Dream of American Democracy*. New York: Basic, 2001.

Endelman, Gary E. *Solidarity Forever: Rose Schneiderman and the Women's Trade Union League*. Manchester, N.H.: Ayer, 1981.

Eskridge, William N., Jr. *Equality Practice: Civil Unions and the Future of Gay Rights*. New York: Routledge, 2001.

Etulain, Richard W., ed. *Cesar Chavez: A Brief Biography with Documents*. New York: Palgrave, 2002.

Evans, Sara. *Personal Politics: The Roots of Women's Liberation in the Civil Rights Movement and the New Left*. New York: Random House, 1980.

Evers, Myrlie B. *For Us, the Living*. Oxford: University of Mississippi Press, 1996.

Fahey, Joseph J., and Richard Armstrong, eds. *A Peace Reader: Essential Readings on War, Justice, Non-Violence, and World Order*. Rev. ed. Mahwah, N.J.: Paulist, 1992.

Fairclough, Adam. *To Redeem the Soul of America: The Southern Christian Leadership Conference and Martin Luther King, Jr.* Athens: University of Georgia Press, 2001.

Farmer, James. *Lay Bare the Heart: An Autobiography of the Civil Rights Movement*. New York: New American Library, 1985.

Fast, Howard. *Citizen Tom Paine*. 1943. Reprint, New York: Grove, 1983.

Fausold, Martin L. *The Presidency of Herbert C. Hoover*. Lawrence: University Press of Kansas, 1985.

Fausto-Sterling, Anne. *Myths of Gender: Biological Theories about Women and Men*. New York: Basic, 1992.

Faux, Marian. *Roe v. Wade*. New York: Cooper Square, 2000.

Fehrenbacher, Don E. *Abraham Lincoln: Speeches and Writings 1832–1858*. New York: Library of America, 1989.

———. *The Dred Scott Case: Its Significance in American Law and Politics*. New York: Oxford University Press, 2001.

———. *Slavery, Law and Politics: The Dred Scott Case in Historical Perspective*. New York: Oxford University Press, 1981.

Fehrenbacher, Don E., and Ward M. McAfee. *The Slaveholding Republic: An Account of the United States Government's Relations to Slavery*. New York: Oxford University Press, 2001.

Felsenthal, Carol. *Biography of Phyllis Schlafly*. Chicago: Regnery, 1982.

Ferguson, Ernest B. *Hard Right: The Rise of Jesse Helms*. New York: Norton, 1986.

Ferriss, Susan, and Ricardo Sandoval. *The Fight in the Fields: Cesar Chavez and the Farmworkers Movement*. New York: Harcourt Brace, 1997.

Feuerlicht, Roberta Strauss. *America's Reign of Terror: World War I, the Red Scare, and the Palmer Raids*. New York: Random House, 1971.

Fick, Barbara J. *The American Bar Association Guide to Workplace Law: Everything You Need to Know about Your Rights as an Employee or Employer*. New York: Times Books, 1997.

Finkelman, Paul, and Melvin I. Urofsky. *Landmark Decisions of the U.S. Supreme Court*. Washington, D.C.: CQ Press, 2002.

Fleishmann, Glen. *The Cherokee Removal, 1838*. New York: Random House, 1971.

Flexner, Eleanor. *Century of Struggle: The Women's Rights Movement in the United States*. Cambridge, Mass: Belknap, 1996.

Flexner, James Thomas. *George Washington and the New Nation, 1783–1793*. Boston: Little, Brown, 1970.

Flexner, Stuart Berg. *I Hear America Talking*. New York: Van Nostrand Reinhold, 1976.

Flynn, George Q. *The Draft, 1940–1973*. Lawrence: University Press of Kansas, 1993.

Foerstel, Herbert N. *Freedom of Information and the Right to Know: The Origins and Applications of the Freedom of Information Act*. Westport, Conn.: Greenwood, 1999.

Fogel, Walter A. *Equal Pay Act*. New York: Praeger, 1984.

Foner, Eric. *Reconstruction: America's Unfinished Revolution, 1863–1877.* New York: HarperCollins, 1989.

———, ed. *Thomas Paine: Collected Writings.* New York: Library of America, 1995.

Foner, Philip S., ed. *The Black Panthers Speak.* 1970. Reprint, New York: Da Capo, 1995.

———. *History of the Labor Movement in the United States: From Colonial Times to the Founding of the American Federation of Labor.* New York: International Publishers, 1979.

Formisano, Ronald P. *Boston against Busing: Race, Class, and Ethnicity in the 1960s and 1970s.* Chapel Hill: University of North Carolina Press, 1991.

Frady, Marshall. *Jesse Jackson: A Biography.* New York: Random House, 1996.

———. *Wallace.* New York: Random House, 1996.

Frankfurter, Felix. *Law and Politics.* New York: Peter Smith, 1971.

Franklin, John Hope. *The Emancipation Proclamation.* 1963. Reprint, Wheeling, Ill.: Harlan Davidson, 1995.

———. *From Slavery to Freedom: A History of African Americans.* New York: McGraw-Hill, 1994.

Frantz, Klaus. *Indian Reservations in the United States: Territory, Sovereignty, and Socioeconomic Change.* Chicago: University of Chicago Press, 1999.

Fraser, James W. *Reading, Writing and Justice: School Reform As If Democracy Mattered.* Albany: State University of New York Press, 1997.

Fredrickson, Darin D., and Raymond P. Siljander. *Racial Profiling: Eliminating the Confusion between Racial and Criminal Profiling.* Springfield, Ill.: Charles C. Thomas, 2002.

Fredrickson, George M. *Racism: A Short History.* Princeton: Princeton University Press, 2002.

Freedman, Eric M. *Habeas Corpus: Rethinking the Great Writ of Liberty.* New York: New York University Press, 2002.

Freedman, Estelle B. *No Turning Back: The History of Feminism and the Future of Women.* New York: Ballantine, 2002.

Freidel, Frank. *Franklin D. Roosevelt: A Rendezvous with Destiny.* Boston: Little, Brown, 1990.

Freidman, Joel, ed. *Law and Gender Bias.* New York: Rothman, 1994.

French, Laurence. *Indians and Criminal Justice.* New York: Rowman and Littlefield, 1982.

Frey, William H., Bill Abresch, and Jonathan Yeasting. *America by the Numbers: A Field Guide to the U.S. Population.* New York: New Press, 2001.

Friedan, Betty. *The Feminine Mystique.* 1963. Reprint, New York: Norton, 2001.

Fullinwider, Robert K. *The Reverse Discrimination Controversy: A Moral and Legal Analysis.* Lanham, Md.: Rowman and Littlefield, 1980.

Gardner, Michael R. *Harry Truman and Civil Rights: Moral Courage and Political Risks.* Carbondale: Southern Illinois University Press, 2002.

Garrow, David J. *Liberty and Sexuality: The Right to Privacy and the Making of Roe v. Wade.* Berkeley: University of California Press, 1998.

Gaskill, Stephen. *Solid Investment: Making Full Use of the Nation's Human Capital: Recommendations of the Federal Glass Ceiling Commission.* Collingdale, Penn.: DIANE, 1995.

Gaustad, Edwin S. *Church and State in America.* New York: Oxford University Press, 1999.

———. *Liberty of Conscience: Roger Williams in America.* Valley Forge, Penn.: Judson, 1999.

Gerber, Scott Douglas, ed. *Declaration of Independence: Origins and Impact.* Landmark Events in U.S. History Series. Washington, D.C.: CQ Press, 2002.

Gerstmann, Evan. *The Constitutional Underclass: Gays, Lesbians, and the Failure of Class-Based Equal Protection.* Chicago: University of Chicago Press, 1999.

Gettleman, Marvin E., Jane Franklin, Marilyn B. Young, and H. Bruce Franklin, eds. *Vietnam and America: A Documented History.* New York: Grove, 1995.

Giglio, James N. *The Presidency of John F. Kennedy.* Lawrence: University Press of Kansas, 1992.

Gilman, Charlotte Perkins. *The Living of Charlotte Perkins Gilman: An Autobiography.* 1935. Reprint, Madison: University of Wisconsin Press, 1991.

Ginger, Ann Fagan. *The National Lawyers Guild: From Roosevelt through Reagan.* Philadelphia: Temple University Press, 1988.

Glazer, Nathan, and Daniel Patrick Moynihan. *Beyond the Melting Pot.* 2d rev. ed. Cambridge: MIT Press, 1970.

Goldfarb, Ronald L. *Contempt Power.* New York: Columbia University Press, 1963.

Goldman, Raphael. *Capital Punishment,* ed. Ann Chih Lin. CQ's Vital Issues Series. Washington, D.C.: CQ Press, 2002.

Goldman, Robert M. *Reconstruction and Black Suffrage: Losing the Vote in Reese and Cruikshank* Lawrence: University Press of Kansas, 2001.

Goldstein, Robert Justin. *Flag Burning and Free Speech: The Case of Texas v. Johnson.* Lawrence: University Press of Kansas, 2000.

Gollaher, David L. *Voice for the Mad: The Life of Dorothea Dix.* New York: Free Press, 1995.

Gompers, Samuel. *The Samuel Gompers Papers.* 8 vols. Champaign-Urbana: University of Illinois Press, 1986-2000.

Gonzales, Sylvia Alicia. *Hispanic Voluntary Organizations.* Westport, Conn.: Greenwood, 1985.

Goodman, Walter. *The Committee: The Extraordinary Career of the House Committee on Un-American Activities.* New York: Farrar, Straus, and Giroux, 1968.

Goodrich, Thomas. *War to the Knife: Bleeding Kansas, 1854–1861.* Mechanicsburg, Penn.: Stackpole Books, 1998.

Goodwin, Doris Kearns. *Lyndon Johnson and the American Dream.* New York: St. Martin's Press, 1991.

Gorn, Elliott J. *Mother Jones: The Most Dangerous Woman in America.* New York: Farrar, Straus, and Giroux, 2002.

Gorney, Cynthia. *Articles of Faith: A Frontline History of the Abortion Wars.* New York: Simon and Schuster, 1998.

Gosselin, Denise Kindschi. *Heavy Hands: An Introduction to the Crimes of Domestic Violence.* Paramus, N.J.: Prentice Hall, 2000.

Graham, Hugh Davis. *The Civil Rights Era: Origins and Development of National Policy, 1960–1972.* New York: Oxford University Press, 1990.

Grant, Joanne. *Ella Jo Baker: Freedom Bound.* New York: Wiley, 1998.

Greene, John Robert. *The Presidency of Gerald R. Ford.* Lawrence: University Press of Kansas, 1995.

Greene, Julie. *Pure and Simple Politics: The American Federation of Labor and Political Activism, 1881–1917.* New York: Cambridge University Press, 1998.

Green, Robert P., Jr. *Equal Protection and the African American Constitutional Experience: A Documentary History.* Westport, Conn.: Greenwood, 2000.

Greenwald, Emily. *Reconfiguring the Reservation: The Nez Perces, Jicarilla Apaches, and the Dawes Act.* Albuquerque: University of New Mexico Press, 2002.

Gregory, Dick. *Callus on My Soul: A Memoir.* Atlanta: Longstreet, 2000.

———. *Nigger: An Autobiography.* 1964. Reprint, New York: Pocket Books, 1995.

Gregory, Raymond F. *Age Discrimination in the American Workplace: Old at a Young Age.* New Brunswick: Rutgers University Press, 2001.

Grimshaw, William J. *Bitter Fruit: Black Politics and the Chicago Machine, 1931–1991.* Chicago: University of Chicago Press, 1992.

Grinde, Donald A., Jr., ed. *Native Americans.* American Political History Series. Washington, D.C.: CQ Press, 2002.

Grofman, Bernard, ed. *Legacies of the 1964 Civil Rights Act.* Charlottesville: University Press of Virginia, 2000.

———. *Voting Rights, Voting Wrongs: The Legacy of Baker v. Carr.* Washington, D.C.: Priority Press Publications, 1990.

Gulick, Sidney L. *American Democracy and Asiatic Citizenship.* North Stratford, N.H.: Ayer, 1979.

Gurko, Miriam. *The Ladies of Seneca Falls: The Birth of the Woman's Rights Movement.* New York: Random House, 1996.

Guterson, David. *Family Matters: Why Homeschooling Makes Sense.* New York: Harvest Books, 1993.

Gyory, Andrew. *Closing the Gate: Race, Politics, and the Chinese Exclusion Act.* Chapel Hill: University of North Carolina Press, 1998.

Haggard, Thomas R. *Understanding Employment Discrimination.* New York: Lexis, 2001.

Hall, David D., ed. *The Antinomian Controversy 1636–1638: A Documentary History.* Durham: Duke University Press, 1990.

Hall, Timothy L. *Separating Church and State: Roger Williams and Religious Liberty.* Champaign-Urbana: University of Illinois Press, 1998.

Hamburger, Philip. *Separation of Church and State.* Cambridge: Harvard University Press, 2002.

Hamilton, Alexander, James Madison, and John Jay. *The Federalist Papers.* 1788. Reprint, New York: Mentor, 1999.

Hamilton, Charles V. *Adam Clayton Powell Jr.: The Political Biography of an American Dilemma.* New York: Cooper Square, 2002.

Hamm, Richard F. *Shaping the Eighteenth Amendment: Temperance Reform, Legal Culture, and the Polity, 1880–1920.* Chapel Hill: University of North Carolina Press, 1995.

Harlan, Louis R. *Booker T. Washington: The Wizard of Tuskegee, 1901–1915.* New York: Oxford University Press, 1986.

Harper, Judith E. *Susan B. Anthony: A Biographical Companion.* New York: ABC-CLIO, 1998.

Harris, David A. *Profiles in Injustice: Why Police Profiling Cannot Work.* New York: New Press, 2002.

Harris, Fred R., and Lynn A. Curtis, eds. *Locked in the Poorhouse: Cities, Race, and Poverty in the United States.* New York: Rowman and Littlefield, 1999.

Harris, William H. *Keeping the Faith: A. Philip Randolph, Milton P. Webster, and the Brotherhood of Sleeping Car Porters, 1925–1937.* Champaign-Urbana: University of Illinois Press, 1991.

Haskins, James. *Bayard Rustin: Behind the Scenes of the Civil Rights Movement.* New York: Hyperion, 1997.

———. *Louis Farrakhan and the Nation of Islam.* New York: Walker, 1996.

Hawkins, Hugh, ed. *Booker T. Washington and His Critics: Black Leadership in Crisis.* Boston: D.C. Heath, 1975.

Hazlett, Thomas W. "The Fairness Doctrine and the First Amendment." *Public Interest* (summer 1989).

Hedrick, Joan D. *Harriet Beecher Stowe: A Life.* New York: Oxford University Press, 1995.

Heller, Francis. *The Sixth Amendment to the Constitution of the United States: A Study in Constitutional Development.* Westport, Conn.: Greenwood, 1951.

Hempelman, Kathleen A. *Teen Legal Rights.* Westport, Conn.: Greenwood, 2000.

Henry, Charles P., ed. *Ralph Bunche: Model Negro or American Other?* New York: New York University Press, 1999.

Herman, Arthur. *Joseph McCarthy: Reexamining the Life and Legacy of America's Most Hated Senator.* New York: Free Press, 1999.

Herrmann, Dorothy. *Helen Keller: A Life.* New York: Knopf, 1998.

Heyck, Denis L., ed. *Barrios and Borderlands: Cultures of Latinos and Latinas in the United States.* New York: Routledge, 1994.

Hill, Frances. *The Salem Witch Trials Reader.* New York: Da Capo Press, 2000.

Hillyard, Daniel, and John Dombrink. *Dying Right: The Death with Dignity Movement.* New York: Routledge, 2001.

Hirsch, H. N. *The Enigma of Felix Frankfurter.* New York: Basic, 1981.

Hofstadter, Richard. *Social Darwinism in American Thought.* New York: George Braziller, 1959.

Hogrogian, John G. *Miranda v. Arizona: The Rights of the Accused.* San Diego: Lucent, 1999.

Homan, Lynn M., and Thomas Reilly. *Tuskegee Airmen.* Charleston, S.C.: Arcadia Tempus, 1998.

Horne, Gerald. *Fire This Time: The Watts Uprising and the 1960s.* Charlottesville: University Press of Virginia, 1995.

Horowitz, David. *Uncivil Wars: The Controversy over Reparations for Slavery.* San Francisco: Encounter, 2001.

Howard, A. E. Dick. *Magna Carta: Text and Commentary.* Charlottesville: University Press of Virginia, 1997.

Howard, John R. *The Shifting Wind: The Supreme Court and Civil Rights from Reconstruction to Brown.* Albany: State University of New York Press, 1999.

Howard, Oliver O. *Autobiography of Oliver Otis Howard.* 1907. Reprint, New York: Ayer, 1977.

Howlett, Duncan. *No Greater Love: The James Reeb Story.* Boston: Skinner House, 1993.

Hoxie, Frederick E. *A Final Promise: The Campaign to Assimilate the Indians, 1880–1920.* Lincoln: University of Nebraska Press, 1984.

Huber, Peter William. *Sandra Day O'Connor.* New York: Chelsea House, 1990.

Hudson, David. *The Fourteenth Amendment: Equal Protection under the Law.* Berkeley Heights, N.J.: Enslow, 2002.

Hudson, John. *The Formation of the English Common Law: Law and Society in England from the Norman Conquest to Magna Carta.* London and New York: Longman, 1996.

Huggins, Nathan Irving. *Black Odyssey: The African-American Ordeal in Slavery.* New York: Random House, 1990.

———, ed. *Writings of W. E. B. Du Bois: The Suppression of the African Slave-Trade; The Souls of Black Folk; Dusk of Dawn; Essays; Articles from The Crisis.* New York: Library of America, 1996.

Hughes, Langston. *The Collected Poems.* New York: Vintage, 1995.

———. *Fight for Freedom: The Story of the NAACP.* New York: W. W. Norton, 1962.

Hull, N. E. H., and Peter Charles Hoffer. *Roe v. Wade: The Abortion Rights Controversy in American History.* Lawrence: University Press of Kansas, 2000.

Human Rights Watch. *Human Rights Watch World Report 2001.* New York: Human Rights Watch, 2002.

Humes, Edward. *No Matter How Loud I Shout: A Year in the Life of Juvenile Court.* New York: Simon and Schuster, 1996.

Hutchinson, Edward Prince. *Legislative History of American Immigration Policy: 1798–1965.* Philadelphia: University of Pennsylvania Press, 1981.

Hyde, Margaret Oldroyd. *The Rights of the Victim.* New York: Franklin Watts, 1983.

Ichioka, Yuji. *The Issei: The World of the First Generation Japanese Immigrants, 1885–1924.* New York: Free Press, 1990.

Irons, Peter H. *Justice Delayed: The Record of the Japanese American Internment Cases.* Middletown: Wesleyan University Press, 1989.

———, ed. *A People's History of the Supreme Court.* New York: Viking Press, 1999.

Jacobs, Gregory S. *Getting around Brown: Desegregation, Development, and the Columbus Public Schools.* Columbus: Ohio State University Press, 1997.

Jacobs, Jane. *The Death and Life of Great American Cities.* 1961. Reprint, New York: Vintage, 1993.

Jacobs, Ronald N. *Race, Media, and the Crisis of Civil Society: From Watts to Rodney King.* New York: Cambridge University Press, 2000.

Jacoway, Elizabeth, and C. Fred Williams, eds. *Understanding the Little Rock Crisis: An Exercise in Remembrance and Reconciliation.* Little Rock: University of Arkansas Press, 1999.

Jeffries, John Calvin, et al. *Civil Rights Actions: Enforcing the Constitution.* New York: Foundation, 2000.

Jencks, Christopher. *The Homeless.* Cambridge: Harvard University Press, 1994.

Jensen, Merrill. *The Articles of Confederation: An Interpretation of the Social-Constitutional History of the American Revolution, 1774–1781.* Madison: University of Wisconsin Press, 1970.

Joel, Lewin G., III. *Every Employee's Guide to the Law: Everything You Need to Know About Your Rights in the Workplace and What to Do If They Are Violated.* New York: Pantheon, 1997.

Johnson, Timothy V. *Malcolm X: A Comprehensive Annotated Bibliography.* New York: Garland, 1986.

Jones, B. J. *The Indian Child Welfare Act Handbook: A Legal Guide to the Custody and Adoption of Native American Children.* Washington, D.C.: Section of Family Law, American Bar Association, 1978.

Jones, Howard. *Mutiny on the Amistad.* New York: Oxford University Press, 1997.

Jost, Kenneth. "Affirmative Action." *CQ Researcher,* September 11, 2001, 737–760.

———. "Rethinking the Death Penalty." *CQ Researcher,* November 16, 2001, 945–967.

Kaminski, John P., ed. *A Necessary Evil? Slavery and the Debate over the Constitution.* Madison, Wisc.: Madison House, 1995.

Kaufman, Burton I. *The Presidency of James Earl Carter, Jr.* Lawrence: University Press of Kansas, 1993.

Kaufman, Stuart B., ed. *The Samuel Gompers Papers: The Early Years of the American Federation of Labor, 1887–90.* Champaign-Urbana: University of Illinois Press, 1987.

Kelley, Joseph J. *Pennsylvania, the Colonial Years, 1681–1776.* New York: Doubleday, 1980.

Kellogg, Charles Flint. *NAACP: A History of the National Association for the Advancement of Colored People.* Baltimore: Johns Hopkins University Press, 1973.

Kennedy, David M. *Birth Control in America: The Career of Margaret Sanger.* New Haven: Yale University Press, 1970.

Kennedy, Kathleen. *Disloyal Mothers and Scurrilous Citizens: Women and Subversion during World War I.* Bloomington: Indiana University Press, 1999.

Kerr, Edward. *The Insular Cases: The Role of the Judiciary in American Expansionism.* Port Washington, N.Y.: Kennikat, 1982.

Kerr, K. Austin. *Organized for Prohibition: A New History of the Anti-Saloon League.* New Haven: Yale University Press, 1985.

Keyes, Cheryl L. *Rappin' to the Beat: Rap Music as Street Culture among African Americans.* Ann Arbor: University of Michigan Press, 1992.

Keynes, Edward. *Liberty, Property, and Privacy: Toward a Jurisprudence of Substantive Due Process.* State College: Pennsylvania State University Press, 1996.

Keyssar, Alexander. *The Right to Vote: The Contested History of Democracy in the United States.* New York: Basic, 2001.

Kirp, David L. *Our Town: Race, Housing, and the Soul of Suburbia.* New Brunswick: Rutgers University Press, 1996.

Klein, Irving J. *Principles of the Law of Arrest, Search, Seizure, and Liability Issues.* Coral Gables, Fla.: Coral Gables, 1994.

Klein, Joe. *The Natural: The Misunderstood Presidency of Bill Clinton.* New York: Doubleday, 2002.

Klingaman, William K. *Abraham Lincoln and the Road to Emancipation, 1861–1865.* New York: Viking, 2001.

Kluger, Miriam P., Gina Alexander, and Patrick A. Curtis, eds. *What Works in Child Welfare.* Washington, D.C.: Child Welfare League of America, 2001.

Kluger, Richard. *Simple Justice: The History of* Brown v. Board of Education *and Black America's Struggle for Equality.* New York: Knopf, 1976.

Knock, Thomas J. *To End All Wars.* Princeton: Princeton University Press, 1995.

Kornweibel, Theodore Jr. *"Investigate Everything": Federal Efforts to Compel Black Loyalty During World War I.* Bloomington: Indiana University Press, 2002.

Kousser, J. Morgan. *Colorblind Injustice: Minority Voting Rights and the Undoing of the Second Reconstruction.* Chapel Hill: University of North Carolina Press, 1999.

Kraditor, Aileen S. *The Ideas of the Woman Suffrage Movement, 1890–1920.* New York: Norton, 1981.

Kuklinski, Joan. *American Indian Land Claims: A Selected Bibliography.* Monticello, Ill.: Vance Bibliographies, 1982.

Kwame Ture, and Charles V. Hamilton. *Black Power: The Politics of Liberation.* 1968. Reprint, New York: Vintage, 1992.

Lamb, Charles M., and Stephen C. Halpern, eds. *The Burger Court: Political and Judicial Profiles.* Champaign-Urbana: University of Illinois Press, 1991.

Landsberg, Brian K. *Enforcing Civil Rights: Race Discrimination and the Department of Justice.* Lawrence: University Press of Kansas, 1997.

Lang, Robert, ed. *The Birth of a Nation.* New Brunswick: Rutgers University Press, 1994.

Langston, Thomas. *Lyndon Baines Johnson.* American Presidents Reference Series. Washington, D.C.: CQ Press, 2002.

Las Casas, Bartolomé de. *Short Account of the Destruction of the West Indies.* 1552. Translated by Nigel Griffin, New York: Penguin, 1999.

Lash, Joseph P. *Helen and Teacher: The Story of Helen Keller and Anne Sullivan Macy.* New York: Perseus, 1997.

Laughlin, Kathleen A. *Women's Work and Public Policy: A History of the Women's Bureau, U.S. Department of Labor, 1945–1970.* Boston: Northeastern University Press, 2000.

Lawson, Steven F. *Black Ballots: Voting Rights in the South, 1944–1969.* New York: Columbia University Press, 1976.

Layton, Sanford J. "Homestead Act of 1862." In *Encyclopedia of the American West,* ed. Charles Phillips and Alan Axelrod. New York: Macmillan Reference USA, 1996.

Lazarus, Edward. *Black Hills, White Justice: The Sioux Nation versus the United States, 1775 to the Present.* New York: HarperCollins, 1991.

Lee, Chana Kai. *For Freedom's Sake: The Life of Fannie Lou Hamer.* Champaign-Urbana: University of Illinois Press, 2000.

Lemann, Nicholas. *The Promised Land: The Great Black Migration and How It Changed America.* New York: Vintage, 1992.

Lemoncheck, Linda, and James P. Sterba, eds. *Sexual Harassment: Issues and Answers.* New York: Oxford University Press, 2001.

Lence, Ross M., ed. *Union and Liberty: The Political Philosophy of John C. Calhoun.* Indianapolis: Liberty Fund, 1992.

Leonard, Richard D. *Call to Selma: Eighteen Days of Witness.* Boston: Unitarian Universalist Association, 2001.

Lerner, Gerda. *The Grimké Sisters from South Carolina: Pioneers for Women's Rights and Abolition.* New York: Oxford University Press, 1998.

Levine, Daniel. *Bayard Rustin and the Civil Rights Movement.* New Brunswick: Rutgers University Press, 1999.

Levy, Leonard Williams. *Origins of the Bill of Rights.* New Haven: Yale University Press, 1999.

Levy, Peter B., ed. *The Civil Rights Movement.* Westport, Conn.: Greenwood, 1998.

———. "Gloria St. Clair Hayes Richardson." In *The Civil Rights Movement,* ed. Peter B. Levy. Westport, Conn.: Greenwood, 1998.

Lewis, David L., ed. *The Portable Harlem Renaissance Reader.* New York: Penguin, 1995.

Lewis, John, with Michael D'Orso. *Walking with the Wind: A Memoir of the Movement.* 1998. Reprint, New York: Harvest, 1999.

Lichtenstein, Nelson. *State of the Union: A Century of American Labor.* Princeton: Princeton University Press, 2002.

Lightner, David L., ed. *Asylum, Prison, and Poorhouse: The Writings and Reform Work of Dorothea Dix in Illinois.* Carbondale: Southern Illinois University Press, 1999.

Lin, Ann Chih, ed. *Welfare Reform.* CQ's Vital Issues Series. Washington, D.C.: CQ Press, 2002.

Lindsey, Daryl. *Gays in the Military: Don't Ask, Don't Tell, Don't Fall in Love.* New York: Salon.com, 2001.

Lively, Donald E. *The Constitution and Race.* New York: Praeger, 1992.

Loevy, Robert D., ed. *The Civil Rights Act of 1964: The Passage of the Law That Ended Racial Segregation.* Albany: State University of New York Press, 1997.

Lowance, Mason I. *Against Slavery: An Abolitionist Reader.* New York: Penguin, 2000.

Lubove, Roy. *The Progressives and the Slums: Tenement House Reform in New York City, 1890–1917.* Westport, Conn.: Greenwood, 1974.

Lunardini, Catherine A. *From Equal Suffrage to Equal Rights: Alice Paul and the National Woman's Party, 1910–1928.* Lincoln, Neb.: iUniverse.com, 2000.

Lyons, Christina L. "Adoption Controversies." *CQ Researcher,* September 10, 1999.

Mace, Nancy. *In the Company of Men: A Woman at the Citadel.* New York: Simon and Schuster, 2001.

Madhubuti, Haki R., and Maulana Karenga, eds. *Million Man March/Day of Absence: A Commemorative Anthology.* Chicago: Third World Press, 1996.

Maier, Pauline. *American Scripture: The Making of the Declaration of Independence.* New York: Knopf, 1997.

Malone, Dumas. *Jefferson and His Time.* 6 vols. Boston: Little, Brown, 1948–1981.

Maltz, Earl M. *The Chief Justiceship of Warren Burger, 1969–1986.* Columbia: University of South Carolina Press, 2000.

Mandela, Nelson. *Long Walk to Freedom: The Autobiography of Nelson Mandela.* New York: Little, Brown, 1995.

Manegold, Catherine S. *In Glory's Shadow: Shannon Faulkner, the Citadel, and a Changing America.* New York: Knopf, 2000.

Manis, Andrew Michael. *A Fire You Can't Put Out: The Civil Rights Life of Birmingham's Reverend Fred Shuttlesworth.* Tuscaloosa: University of Alabama Press, 1999.

Marcus, Eric. *Making Gay History: The Half-Century Fight for Lesbian and Gay Equal Rights.* New York: Harper Perennial, 2002.

Marmor, Theodore. *The Politics of Medicare.* 2d ed. New York: Aldine de Gruyter, 2000.

Martinez, Oscar J. *Mexican-Origin People in the United States: A Topical History.* University of Arizona Press, 2001.

Masud-Pilato, Felix Roberto. *From Welcomed Exiles to Illegal Immigrants: Cuban Migration to the U.S., 1959–1995.* New York: Rowman and Littlefield, 1996.

Mathews, John Mabry. *Legislative and Judicial History of the Fifteenth Amendment.* Johns Hopkins University Studies in Historical and Political Science, Ser. 27, No. 6-7. Union, N.J.: The Lawbook Exchange, 2001.

Maxson, Cheryl L., and Malcolm W. Klein. *Responding to Troubled Youth.* New York: Oxford University Press, 1997.

McAdam, Douglas. *Freedom Summer.* New York: Oxford University Press, 1990.

McCain, Charles. *Japanese Immigrants and American Law: The Alien Land Laws and Other Issues.* New York: Garland Publishing, 1994.

McCullough, David. *Truman.* New York: Simon and Schuster, 1992.

McDonnell, Janet. *The Dispossession of the American Indian.* Bloomington: Indiana University Press, 1991.

McElvaine, Robert S. *Franklin Delano Roosevelt.* American President Reference Series. Washington, D.C.: CQ Press, 2002.

McKenzie, V. Michael. *Domestic Violence in America.* Lawrenceville, Va.: Brunswick, 1995.

McLoughlin, William G. *Rhode Island: A History.* New York: Norton, 1986.

McMichael, William H. *The Mother of All Hooks: The Story of the U.S. Navy's Tailhook Scandal.* Piscataway, N.J.: Transaction Publishers, 1997.

McMurtry, Larry. *Crazy Horse.* New York: Viking, 1999.

McWilliams, Carey, and Douglas C. Sackman. *Factories in the Field: The Story of Migratory Farm Labor in California.* Berkeley: University of California Press, 2000.

Mead, Christopher. *Champion: Joe Louis, Black Hero in a White World.* New York: Scribner, 1985.

Meier, August, and Elliott Rudwick. *CORE: A Study in the Civil Rights Movement, 1942–1968.* Champaign-Urbana: University of Illinois Press, 1975.

Meier, Matt S., and Margo Gutierrez, eds. *Encyclopedia of the Mexican American Civil Rights Movement.* Westport, Conn.: Greenwood, 2000.

Melvin, Harold. *The Radical Republicans and Reconstruction, 1861–1870.* Indianapolis: Bobbs-Merrill, 1967.

Meredith, James. *Three Years in Mississippi.* Bloomington: Indiana University Press, 1966.

Merton, Thomas, ed. *Gandhi on Non-Violence.* New York: W. W. Norton, 1965.

Metz, Allan. *Bill Clinton: A Bibliography.* Westport, Conn.: Greenwood, 2002.

Mfume, Kweisi. *No Free Ride: From the Mean Streets to the Mainstream.* New York: Ballantine, 1996.

Michaels, Walter Benn. *Our America: Nativism, Modernism and Pluralism.* Durham: Duke University Press, 1997.

Mikva, Abner L., and Eric Lane. *Legislative Process.* 2d ed. New York: Aspen, 2002.

Miller, John Chester. *Crisis in Freedom: The Alien and Sedition Acts.* Boston: Little, Brown, 1951.

Miller, William. *Dorothy Day: A Biography.* New York: Harper and Row, 1982.

Mills, Kay. *This Little Light of Mine: The Life of Fannie Lou Hamer.* New York: Plume, 1994.

Moe, Terry M. *Schools, Vouchers, and the American Public.* Washington, D.C.: Brookings Institution, 2001.

Monmonier, Mark S. *Bushmanders and Bullwinkles: How Politicians Manipulate Electronic Maps and Census Data to Win Elections.* Chicago: University of Chicago Press, 2001.

Moore, Deborah Dash. *B'nai B'rith and the Challenge of Ethnic Leadership.* Binghamton: State University of New York Press, 1981.

Moran, Rachel R. *Interracial Intimacy: The Regulation of Race and Romance.* Chicago: University of Chicago Press, 2001.

Morris, Edmund. *Dutch: A Memoir of Ronald Reagan.* New York: Random House, 1999.

Morsink, Johannes. *The Universal Declaration of Human Rights: Origins, Drafting, and Intent.* Philadelphia: University of Pennsylvania Press, 1999.

Moses, Norton H. *Lynching and Vigilantism in the United States: An Annotated Bibliography.* Westport, Conn.: Greenwood, 1997.

Moses, Robert P., and Charles E. Cobb, Jr. *Radical Equations: Math Literacy and Civil Rights.* New York: Beacon Press, 2000.

Moskos, Charles C., and John Sibley Butler. *All That We Can Be: Black Leadership and Racial Integration the Army Way.* New York: Basic Books, 1996.

Mulkern, John R. *The Know-Nothing Party in Massachusetts: The Rise and Fall of a People's Party.* Boston: Northeastern University Press, 1990.

Murphy, Allen Bruce. *Fortas: The Rise and Ruin of a Supreme Court Justice.* New York: Morrow, 1988.

National Advisory Commission on Civil Disorders. *Report of the National Advisory Commission on Civil Disorders.* New York: New York Times Company, 1968.

National Council on Disability. *Equality of Opportunity: The Making of the Americans with Disabilities Act.* Washington, D.C.: U.S. Government Printing Office, 1999.

National Gay and Lesbian Task Force. www.ngltf.org.

National Housing Law Project. www.nhlp.org.

National Organization for Women. "NOW and the Violence Against Women Act," www.now.org/issues/violence/vawaind.html.

Navarro, Armando. *La Raza Unida Party: A Chicano Challenge to the U.S. Two-Party Dictatorship.* Philadelphia: Temple University Press, 2000.

Nelson, Jill, ed. *Police Brutality: An Anthology.* New York: Norton, 2001.

Nelson, William E. *The Fourteenth Amendment: From Political Principle to Judicial Doctrine.* Cambridge: Harvard University Press, 1988.

Newman, Roger K. *Hugo Black: A Biography.* New York: Fordham University Press, 1997.

Newton, Huey P. *To Die for the People: The Writings of Huey P. Newton.* 1972. Reprint, New York: Writers and Readers, 1995.

———. *Revolutionary Suicide.* 1973. Reprint, New York: Writers and Readers, 1995.

Neyland, James. *Crispus Attucks: Patriot.* New York: Holloway House, 1995.

Ng, Wendy L. *Japanese American Internment during World War II: A History and Reference Guide.* Westport, Conn.: Greenwood, 2002.

Niven, John. *John C. Calhoun and the Price of Union: A Biography.* Baton Rouge: Louisiana State University Press, 1993.

Nixon, Richard M. *RN: The Memoirs of Richard Nixon.* 1978. Reprint, New York: Touchstone, 1990.

Noriega, Chon A., and Eric R. Avila, eds. *The Chicano Studies Reader: An Anthology of Aztlan, 1970–2000.* Los Angeles: UCLA Chicano Studies Research Center, 2001.

Norst, Joel. *Mississippi Burning.* New York: New American Library, 1989.

Nunnelly, William A. *Bull Connor.* Tuscaloosa: University of Alabama Press, 1991.

Oates, Stephen B. *With Malice toward None: A Life of Abraham Lincoln.* New York: Harper Perennial, 1994.

———. *A Woman of Valor: Clara Barton and the Civil War.* New York: Free Press, 1994.

O'Connor, Sandra Day, and Alan Day. *Lazy B: Growing Up on a Cattle Ranch in the American Southwest.* New York: Random House, 2002.

Ono, Kent A., and John M. Sloop. *Shifting Borders: Rhetoric, Immigration, and California's Proposition 187.* Philadelphia: Temple University Press, 2002.

Orgill, Roxane. *Mahalia: A Life in Gospel Music.* Cambridge, Mass.: Candlewick Press, 2002.

Ottley, Roi. *The Lonely Warrior: The Life and Times of Robert S. Abbott.* Chicago: Regnery, 1955.

Pach, Chester J., and Elmo Richardson. *The Presidency of Dwight D. Eisenhower.* Rev. ed. Lawrence: University Press of Kansas, 1991.

Packard, Jerrold P. *American Nightmare: The History of Jim Crow.* New York: St. Martin's Press, 2002.

Painter, Nell Irvin. *Sojourner Truth: A Life, a Symbol.* New York: Norton, 1997.

Parks, Rosa. *Rosa Parks: My Story.* New York: Dial, 1992.

Parris, Guichard. *Blacks in the City: A History of the National Urban League.* Boston: Little, Brown, 1971.

Patterson, James T. *Brown v. Board of Education: A Civil Rights Milestone and Its Troubled Legacy.* New York: Oxford University Press, 2001.

Paul, Sherman. *The Shores of America: Thoreau's Inward Exploration.* Champaign-Urbana: University of Illinois Press, 1958.

Pelz, William A., ed. *Eugene V. Debs Reader: Socialism and the Class Struggle.* Chicago: Institute of Working Class History, 2000.

Pendergrast, Mark. *For God, Country, and Coca-Cola: The Definitive History of the Great American Soft Drink and the Company That Makes It.* 2d ed. New York: Basic, 2000.

Pepper, William F. *Orders to Kill: The Truth Behind the Murder of Martin Luther King, Jr.* New York: Warner, 1998.

Perry, Theresa, and Lisa Delpit, eds. *The Real Ebonics Debate: Power, Language, and the Education of African-American Children.* Boston: Beacon, 1998.

Peters, Shawn Francis. *Judging Jehovah's Witnesses: Religious Persecution and the Dawn of the Rights Revolution.* Lawrence: University Press of Kansas, 2000.

Petrocelli, William, and Barbara Kate Repa. *Sexual Harassment on the Job: What It Is and How to Stop It.* 4th ed. Berkeley: Nolo, 2000.

Pevar, Stephen L. *The Rights of Indians and Tribes: The Basic ACLU Guide to Indian Tribal Rights.* 2d ed. Carbondale: Southern Illinois University Press, 1992.

Pfeffer, Paula A. *A. Philip Randolph: Pioneer of the Civil Rights Movement.* Baton Rouge: Louisiana State University Press, 1996.

Pinsker, Matthew. *Abraham Lincoln.* Washington, D.C.: CQ Press, 2002.

Plaut, W. Gunther. *Asylum: A Moral Dilemma.* New York: Praeger, 1995.

Player, Mack A. *Federal Law of Employment Discrimination in a Nutshell.* Los Angeles: West Information, 1999.

Polenberg, Richard. *Fighting Faiths: The Abrams Case, the Supreme Court, and Free Speech.* New York: Penguin, 1989.

Poole, Bernice Anderson. *Mary McLeod Bethune.* New York: Holloway House, 1994.

Posner, Gerald L. *Killing the Dream: James Earl Ray and the Assassination of Martin Luther King, Jr.* New York: Random House, 1998.

Posner, Richard A. *Antitrust Law.* Chicago: University of Chicago Press, 2001.

———. *The Essential Holmes: Selections from the Letters, Speeches, Judicial Opinions, and Other Writings of Oliver Wendell Holmes Jr.* Chicago: University of Chicago Press, 1996.

Powell, Adam Clayton, Jr. *Adam by Adam: The Autobiography of Adam Clayton Powell, Jr.* Sacramento: Citadel, 1994.

Powell, Lawrence Alfred, Kenneth J. Branco, and John B. Williamson. *The Senior Rights Movement: Framing the Policy Debate in America.* New York: Twayne, 1996.

Powell, Philip Wayne. *Tree of Hate: Propaganda and Prejudices Affecting United States Relations with the Hispanic World.* New York: Basic, 1971.

Power, Jonathan. *Like Water on Stone: The Story of Amnesty International.* Boston: Northeastern University Press, 2001.

Powers, Richard G. *Secrecy and Power: The Life of J. Edgar Hoover.* New York: Free Press, 1986.

Pride, Armistead S., and Clint C. Wilson II. *A History of the Black Press.* Washington, D.C.: Howard University Press, 1997.

Pride, Richard A. *The Burden of Busing: The Politics of Desegregation in Nashville, Tennessee.* Knoxville: University of Tennessee Press, 1985.

Prucha, Francis Paul. *Documents of United States Indian Policy.* 2d ed. Lincoln: University of Nebraska Press, 1990.

Putnam, William Lowell. *John Peter Zenger and the Fundamental Freedom.* Jefferson, N.C.: McFarland, 1997.

Quadagno, Jill. *The Color of Welfare: How Racism Undermined the War on Poverty.* New York: Oxford University Press, 1996.

Quarles, Chester L. *The Ku Klux Klan and Related American Racialist and Antisemitic Organizations: A History and Analysis.* Jefferson, N.C.: McFarland, 1999.

Raffel, Jeffrey A. *Historical Dictionary of School Segregation and Desegregation.* Westport, Conn.: Greenwood, 1998.

Rampersad, Arnold. *The Life of Langston Hughes.* New York: Oxford University Press, 2002.

Raskin, Jamin B. *We the Students: Supreme Court Cases for and about Students.* Washington, D.C.: CQ Press, 2000.

Reagan, Leslie J. *When Abortion Was a Crime: Women, Medicine, and Law in the United States, 1867–1973.* Berkeley: University of California Press, 1998.

Reagan, Ronald. *Reagan, In His Own Hand: The Writings of Ronald Reagan That Reveal His Revolutionary Vision for America.* New York: Simon and Schuster, 2001.

Rector Press. *Mentally Ill: Their Rights.* Civil Rights Reporter Series. Leverett, Mass., 1994.

Reed, Roy. *Faubus: The Life and Times of an American Prodigal.* Little Rock: University of Arkansas Press, 1997.

Reggio, Michael H. "Human Rights in Twentieth-Century United States." In *Civil Rights in America, 1500 to the Present,* ed. Michael H. Reggio. Detroit: Gale Research, 1998.

Rhodehamel, John, ed. *George Washington: Writings.* New York: Library of America, 1997.

Ridgeway, James. *Blood in the Face: The Ku Klux Klan, Aryan Nations, Nazi Skinheads, and the Rise of a New White Culture.* 2d ed. Berkeley, Calif.: Thunder's Mouth, 1995.

Riis, Jacob A. *How the Other Half Lives: Studies among the Tenements of New York.* 1890. Reprint, New York: Penguin, 1997.

Rimmerman, Craig A., ed. *Gay Rights, Military Wrongs: Political Perspectives on Lesbians and Gays in the Military.* New York: Garland, 1996.

Robinson, Jackie. *Never Had It Made: An Autobiography.* 1972. Reprint, New York: Ecco, 1997.

Robinson, Jo Ann. *The Montgomery Bus Boycott and the Women Who Started It.* Knoxville: University of Tennessee Press, 1987.

Robinson, Lloyd. *The Stolen Election: Hayes versus Tilden, 1876.* Chicago: University of Chicago Press, 2001.

Rodriguez, Richard. *Brown: The Last Discovery of America.* New York: Viking, 2002.

Roosevelt, Eleanor. *The Autobiography of Eleanor Roosevelt.* Compilation reprint of *This Is My Story, This I Remember,* and *On My Own.* New York: Da Capo, 2000.

Rosales, Francisco A. *Chicano! The History of the Mexican American Civil Rights Movement.* Houston: Arte Publico, 1997.

Roscoe, Will, ed. *Radically Gay: Gay Liberation in the Words of Its Founder.* Boston: Beacon, 1997.

Rose, Mike. *Possible Lives: The Promise of Public Education in America.* Boston: Houghton Mifflin, 1995.

Rosenheim, Margaret K., Franklin E. Zimring, and David S. Tanenhaus, eds. *A Century of Juvenile Justice.* Chicago: University of Chicago Press, 2002.

Rosen, Ruth. *The World Split Open: How the Modern Women's Movement Changed America.* New York: Penguin USA, 2001.

Rossbach, Jeffrey S. *Ambivalent Conspirators: John Brown, the Secret Six, and a Theory of Slave Violence.* Philadelphia: University of Pennsylvania Press, 1983.

Rothenberg, Paula S., ed. *Race, Class, and Gender in the United States: An Integrated Study.* 4th ed. New York: St. Martin's Press, 1997.

Rovere, Richard H. *Senator Joe McCarthy.* 1959. Reprint, Berkeley: University of California Press, 1996.

Rubenstein, William B., Ruth Eisenberg, and Lawrence O. Gostin. *The Rights of People Who Are HIV Positive: The Authoritative ACLU Guide to the Rights of People Living with HIV Disease and AIDS.* Carbondale: Southern Illinois University Press, 1996.

Rudovsky, David. *The Rights of Prisoners: The Basic ACLU Guide to a Prisoner's Rights.* New York: Avon, 1981.

Rutherford, Livingston. *John Peter Zenger: His Press, His Trial, and a Bibliography.* New York: Arno, 1971.

Sadker, Myra. *Failing at Fairness: How Our Schools Cheat Girls.* New York: Touchstone, 1995.

Said, Edward, and Christopher Hitchens. *Blaming the Victims: Spurious Scholarship and the Palestinian Question.* New York: W. W. Norton, 2001.

Sale, Kirkpatrick. *SDS.* New York: Random House, 1973.

Salvatore, Nick. *Eugene V. Debs: Citizen and Socialist.* Champaign-Urbana: University of Illinois Press, 1984.

Samuels, Frederick. *Group Images: Racial, Ethnic, and Religious Stereotyping.* New Haven, Conn.: College and University Press, 1973.

Sandoz, Mari. *Crazy Horse: The Strange Man of the Oglalas.* 1942. Reprint, Lincoln: University of Nebraska Press, 1992.

Sanger, Margaret. *Margaret Sanger: Pioneering Advocate for Birth Control: An Autobiography.* New York: Cooper Square, 1999.

Schickel, Richard. *D. W. Griffith: An American Life.* New York: Simon and Schuster, 1984.

Schlesinger, Arthur M., Jr. *The Age of Jackson.* 1945. Reprint, Boston: Little, Brown, 1988.

———. *A Thousand Days: John F. Kennedy in the White House.* New York: Random House, 1984.

Schlosser, Jim. "Greensboro Sit-Ins: Launch of a Civil Rights Movement." *Greensboro News and Record,* www.sitins.com.

Schmalleger, Frank M. *Trial of the Century: People of the State of California vs. Orenthal James Simpson.* Englewood Cliffs, N.J.: Prentice Hall College Division, 1996.

Schroeder, John H. *Mr. Polk's War: American Opposition and Dissent, 1846–1848.* Madison: University of Wisconsin Press, 1973.

Schwantes, Carlos A. *Coxey's Army: An American Odyssey.* Lincoln: University of Nebraska Press, 1985.

Schwartz, Bernard. *Swann's Way: The School Busing Case and the Supreme Court.* New York: Oxford University Press, 1986.

Scott, George Ryley. *History of Corporal Punishment.* Detroit: Gale Group, 1974.

Seale, Bobby. *A Lonely Rage: The Autobiography of Bobby Seale.* New York: Times Books, 1978.

———. *Seize the Time: The Story of the Black Panther Party and Huey P. Newton.* 1970. Reprint, Baltimore, Md.: Black Classic, 1997.

Senechal, Roberta. *The Sociogenesis of a Race Riot: Springfield, Illinois, in 1908.* Champaign-Urbana: University of Illinois Press, 1990.

Shattuck, George C. *The Oneida Land Claims: A Legal History.* Syracuse: Syracuse University Press, 1991.

Shilts, Randy. *Conduct Unbecoming: Gays and Lesbians in the U.S. Military.* Orlando, Fla.: World, 1998.

Sifferman, Kelly Allen. *Adoption: A Legal Guide for Birth and Adoptive Parents.* New York: Chelsea House, 1997.

Sigler, Jay A. *Civil Rights in America: 1500 to the Present.* Detroit: Gale, 1998.

Sikora, Frank. *Until Justice Rolls Down: The Birmingham Church Bombing Case.* Tuscaloosa: University of Alabama Press, 1991.

Simmons, Steven J. *The Fairness Doctrine and the Media.* Berkeley: University of California Press, 1978.

Simon, Scott. *Jackie Robinson and the Integration of Baseball.* New York: Wiley, forthcoming.

Sloane, Arthur A., and Fred Witney. *Labor Relations.* 10th ed. Paramus, N.J.: Prentice Hall, 2000.

Smith, Abbot Emerson. *Colonists in Bondage: White Servitude and Convict Labor in America, 1607–1776.* Baltimore, Md.: Clearfield, 2000.

Smith, Gibbs M. *Joe Hill.* Salt Lake City: Gibbs Smith, 1984.

Smith, Huston, and Reuben Snake, eds. *One Nation under God: The Triumph of the Native American Church.* Santa Fe, N.M.: Clear Light, 1998.

Smolla, Rodney A., and Chester James Antieau. *Federal Civil Rights Acts.* 3d ed. New York: Clark Boardman Callaghan, 1994.

Soderlund, Jean R., and Richard S. Dunn, eds. *William Penn and the Founding of Pennsylvania: 1680–1684.* Philadelphia: University of Pennsylvania Press, 1999.

Solinger, Rickie, ed. *Abortion Wars: A Half Century of Struggle, 1950–2000.* Berkeley: University of California Press, 2000.

———. *Wake Up, Little Susie: Single Pregnancy and Race before Roe v. Wade.* New York: Routledge, 2000.

Sollors, Werner. *Interracialism: Black-White Intermarriage in American History, Literature, and Law.* New York: Oxford University Press, 2000.

Spada, Marcia Darvin. *Fair Housing.* Cincinnati: South-Western, 2001.

Spann, Girardeau A. *The Law of Affirmative Action: Twenty-Five Years of Supreme Court Decisions on Race and Remedies.* New York: New York University Press, 2000.

Squires, Gregory D., and Sally O'Connor. *Color and Money: Politics and Prospects for Community Reinvestment in Urban America.* Albany: State University of New York Press, 2001.

Steiner, Gilbert. *Constitutional Inequality: The Political Fortunes of the Equal Rights Amendment.* Washington, D.C.: Brookings Institution, 1985.

Stein, Leon. *The Triangle Fire.* Ithaca, N.Y.: ILR, 2001.

Stern, Mark. *Calculating Visions: Kennedy, Johnson, and Civil Rights.* New Brunswick: Rutgers University Press, 1992.

Stevens, Mitchell L. *Kingdom of Children: Culture and Controversy in the Homeschooling Movement.* Princeton: Princeton University Press, 2001.

Stewart, James Brewer. *The Holy Warriors: The Abolitionists and American Slavery.* New York: Hill and Wang, 1997.

Stichman, Barton F., Ronald B. Abrams, and David F. Addlestone, eds. *Veterans Benefits Manual.* Dayton, Ohio: Lexis Law, 1999.

Strum, Philippa. *Brandeis: Beyond Progressivism.* Lawrence: University Press of Kansas, 1995.

———. *Women in the Barracks: The VMI Case and Equal Rights.* Lawrence: University Press of Kansas, 2002.

Suarez-Orozco, Marcelo M., and Mariela Paez, eds. *Latinos: Remaking America.* Berkeley: University of California Press, 2002.

Sudbury, Julia. *Other Kinds of Dreams: Black Women's Organizations and the Politics of Transformation.* New York: Routledge, 1998.

Sullivan, Andrew, and Joseph Landau, eds. *Same-Sex Marriage: Pro and Con.* New York: Vintage, 1997.

Swain, Carol M. *The New White Nationalism in America.* New York: Cambridge University Press, 2002.

Taylor, Graham D. *The New Deal and American Indian Tribalism: The Administration of the Indian Reorganization Act, 1934–45.* Lincoln: University of Nebraska Press, 2001.

Theoharis, A. G., and J. S. Cox. *The Boss.* New York: Bantam, 1988.

Theoharis, A. G., and Tony G. Poveda, eds. *The FBI: A Comprehensive Reference Guide.* New York: Checkmark, 2000.

Thernstrom, Stephan, and Abigail M. Thernstrom. *America in Black and White: One Nation, Indivisible.* New York: Simon and Schuster, 1997.

Thomas, Andrew Peyton. *Clarence Thomas: A Biography.* San Francisco: Encounter, 2001.

Thomas, Brook. *Plessy v. Ferguson: A Brief History with Documents.* New York: St. Martin's Press, 1996.

Thomas, Evan. *Robert Kennedy: His Life.* New York: Simon and Schuster, 2000.

Thrasher, Max B. *Tuskegee: Its Story and Its Work.* New York: Negro University Press, 1969.

Tollefson, James W. *The Strength Not to Fight: Conscientious Objectors of the Vietnam War—In Their Own Words.* New York: Brasseys, 2000.

Traboulay, David M. *Columbus and Las Casas: The Conquest and Christianization of America 1492–1566.* Lanham, Md.: University Press of America, 1994.

Trattner, Walter I. *From Poor Law to Welfare State: A History of Social Welfare in America.* New York: Free Press, 1999.

Tuck, Richard. *Natural Rights Theories.* Cambridge, U.K.: Cambridge University Press, 1982.

Tulacz, Gary. *What You Need to Know about Workplace Drug Testing.* Englewood Cliffs, N.J.: Prentice Hall, 1989.

Tushnet, Mark V. *Making Civil Rights Law: Thurgood Marshall and the Supreme Court, 1936–1961.* New York: Oxford University Press, 1996.

———. *Making Constitutional Law: Thurgood Marshall and the Supreme Court, 1961–1991. New York: Oxford University Press, 1997.*

———. *The NAACP's Legal Strategy against Segregated Education, 1925–1950.* Chapel Hill: University of North Carolina Press, 1987.

Tygiel, Jules. *Baseball's Great Experiment: Jackie Robinson and His Legacy.* New York: Oxford University Press, 1997.

Tyler, Gus. *Look for the Union Label: A History of the International Ladies' Garment Workers' Union.* Armonk, N.Y.: M. E. Sharpe, 1995.

Unger, Irwin, and Debi Unger. *LBJ: A Life.* New York: Wiley, 1999.

Unger, Nancy C. *Fighting Bob La Follette: The Righteous Reformer.* Chapel Hill: University of North Carolina Press, 2000.

United Nations. "UN Fact Sheet No. 22, Discrimination against Women: The Convention and the Committee," www.unhchr.ch/html/menu6/2/fs22.htm.

Urquhart, Brian. *Ralph Bunche: An American Odyssey.* New York: Norton, 1998.

U.S. Department of Labor. "Background on the Job Corps," www.wdsc.doleta.gov/jobcorps/menupageinfo.htm.

———. "Employee/Employer Advisor," www.dol.gov/elaws/flsa.htm.

———. "Family and Medical Leave Fact Sheet," www.dol.gov/dol/esa/fmla.htm.

U.S. Senate. *The Nation's Affordable Housing Crisis: Hearing before the Subcommittee on Housing and Urban Affairs of the Committee on Banking, Housing, and Urban Affairs, March 6, 1992.* Washington, D.C.: U.S. Government Printing Office, 1992.

Utley, Robert M. *Custer: Cavalier in Buckskin.* Revised ed. Norman: University of Oklahoma Press, 2001.

———. *The Lance and the Shield: The Life and Times of Sitting Bull.* New York: Henry Holt, 1993.

Van Caenegem, R. C. *The Birth of English Common Law.* Cambridge, U.K.: Cambridge University Press, 1989.

Van Cleve, John. "American Asylum for the Education of the Deaf and Dumb." In *Gallaudet Encyclopedia of Deaf People and Deafness,* ed. John Van Cleve. New York: McGraw-Hill, 1987.

Van Deburg, William L. *New Day in Babylon: The Black Power Movement and American Culture, 1965–1975.* Chicago: University of Chicago Press, 1993.

Van Wagoner, Richard S. *Mormon Polygamy: A History.* New York: Signature, 1992.

Verney, Kevern. *The Art of the Possible: Booker T. Washington and Black Leadership in the United States, 1881–1925.* New York: Routledge, 2001.

Vieira, Norman, and Leonard Gross, eds. *Supreme Court Appointments: Judge Bork and the Politicization of Senate Confirmations.* Carbondale: Southern Illinois University Press, 1999.

Vollers, Maryanne. *Ghosts of Mississippi: The Murder of Medgar Evers, the Trials of Byron De La Beckwith, and the Haunting of the New South.* Boston: Little, Brown, 1995.

Vorenberg, Michael *Final Freedom: The Civil War, the Abolition of Slavery, and the Thirteenth Amendment.* New York: Cambridge University Press, 2001.

Walker, Samuel. *In Defense of American Liberties: A History of the ACLU.* 2d ed. Carbondale: Southern Illinois University Press, 1999.

———. *Hate Speech: The History of an American Controversy.* Lincoln: University of Nebraska Press, 1994.

Walters, Jerome. *One Aryan Nation under God: How Religious Extremists Use the Bible to Justify Their Actions.* Naperville, Ill.: Sourcebooks, 2001.

Waluchow, Wilfrid J., ed. *Free Expression: Essays in Law and Philosophy.* Oxford, U.K.: Clarendon, 1994.

Washington, Booker T. *Booker T. Washington Papers.* 14 vols. Champaign-Urbana: University of Illinois Press, 1972–1989.

Washington, James Melvin, ed. *I Have a Dream: Writings and Speeches That Changed the World.* San Francisco: Harper San Francisco, 1992.

———. *A Testament of Hope: The Essential Writings and Speeches of Martin Luther King, Jr.* San Francisco: Harper San Francisco, 1991.

Waters, Walter W. *B.E.F.: the Whole Story of the Bonus Army.* New York: AMS, 1933.

Weber, David J. *The Spanish Frontier in North America.* New Haven: Yale University Press, 1992.

Weinberg, Arthur, ed. *Attorney for the Damned: Clarence Darrow in the Courtroom.* Chicago: University of Chicago Press, 1989.

Welch, Michael. *Flag Burning: Moral Panic and the Criminalization of Protest.* Hawthorne, N.Y.: Aldine De Gruyter, 2000.

Wells, Wyatt C. *Antitrust and the Formation of the Postwar World.* New York: Columbia University Press, 2002.

West, Jessamyn, ed. *The Quaker Reader.* Wallingford, Penn.: Pendle Hill, 1992.

Wheeler, Marjorie Spruill, ed. *One Woman, One Vote: Rediscovering the Woman Suffrage Movement.* Troutdale, Ore.: Newsage Press, 1995.

White, Deborah Gray. *Too Heavy a Load: Black Women in Defense of Themselves, 1894–1994.* New York: Norton, 1998.

White, Marjorie L., and Andrew M. Manis, eds. *Birmingham's Revolutionary: The Reverend Fred Shuttlesworth and the Alabama Christian Movement for Human Rights.* Macon and Atlanta, Ga.: Mercer University Press, 2000.

White, Vibert L. *Inside the Nation of Islam: A Historical and Personal Testimony by a Black Muslim.* Gainesville: University Press of Florida, 2001.

Whitfield, Stephen J. *A Death in the Delta: The Story of Emmett Till.* Baltimore: Johns Hopkins University Press, 1991.

Wice, Paul B. *Miranda v. Arizona: "You Have the Right to Remain Silent."* New York: Franklin Watts, 1996.

Wicker, Tom. *A Time to Die.* New York: Times Books, 1975.

Wickham, Dewayne. *Bill Clinton and Black America.* New York: Ballantine, 2002.

Wilkins, Roy. *Standing Fast: The Autobiography of Roy Wilkins.* 1980. Reprint, New York: Da Capo, 1994.

Williams, Juan. *Thurgood Marshall: American Revolutionary.* New York: Times Books, 2000.

Wills, Gary. *James Madison.* New York: Henry Holt, 2002.

Wilson, John F., and Donald L. Drakeman, eds. *Church and State in American History.* 3d ed. Boston: Beacon, forthcoming.

Wilson, Karen. *When Violence Begins at Home: A Comprehensive Guide to Understanding and Ending Domestic Abuse.* Alameda, Calif.: Hunter House, 1997.

Wilson, Theodore Brantner. *The Black Codes of the South.* Tuscaloosa: University of Alabama Press, 1965.

Woll, Allen. *Ethnic and Racial Images in American Film and Television: Historical Essays and Bibliography.* New York: Garland, 1987.

Woodward, C. Vann. *Reunion and Reaction: The Compromise of 1877 and the End of Reconstruction.* New York: Oxford University Press, 1991.

———. *The Strange Career of Jim Crow.* 1965. Reprint, New York: Oxford University Press, 2001.

Worsnop, Richard L. "Age Discrimination." *CQ Researcher,* August 1, 1997.

Wunder, John R. *Native American Cultural and Religious Freedoms.* New York: Garland, 1999.

Wynn, Linda T. "Nashville Sit-Ins (1959–1961)," www.tnstate.edu/library/digital/nash.htm.

Young, Whitney M., Jr. *Beyond Racism: Building an Open Society.* New York: McGraw-Hill, 1961.

Zarefsky, David. *President Johnson's War on Poverty: Rhetoric and History.* Tuscaloosa: University of Alabama Press, 1986.

Zerman, Melvyn B. *Beyond a Reasonable Doubt: Understanding the American Jury System.* New York: Crowell, 1981.

Ziring, Lawrence, Robert E. Riggs, and Jack C. Plano. *The United Nations: International Organization and World Politics.* 3d ed. London: International Thomson, 1999.

INDEX